Dynamic Web Application
Development using
ASP.NET

Dynamic Web Application
Development using ASP.NET

Andy Gravell & David Parsons

COURSE TECHNOLOGY
CENGAGE Learning

Australia • Brazil • Japan • Korea • Mexico • Singapore • Spain • United Kingdom • United States

COURSE TECHNOLOGY
CENGAGE Learning™

**Dynamic Web Application Development
using ASP.NET**
Andy Gravell and David Parsons

Publishing Director: Linden Harris

Publisher: Stephen Wellings

Development Editor: Rebecca Hussey

Content Project Editor: Lucy Arthy

Head of Manufacturing: Jane Glendening

Senior Production Controller: Paul Herbert

Marketing Manager: Vicky Fielding

Typesetter: Pre-PressPMG, India

Cover design: Adam Renvoize

Text design: Design Deluxe

For product information and technology assistance,
contact **emea.info@cengage.com.**
For permission to use material from this text or product,
and for permission queries,
email **clsuk.permissions@cengage.com.**

British Library Cataloguing-in-Publication Data

A catalogue record for this book is available from the British Library.

ISBN: 978-1-4080-1764-7

Cengage Learning EMEA
Cheriton House, North Way, Andover, Hampshire, SP10 5BE
United Kingdom

Cengage Learning products are represented in Canada by Nelson Education Ltd.

For your lifelong learning solutions,
visit **www.cengage.co.uk** and **course.cengage.com**

Printed by C&C Offset, China
1 2 3 4 5 6 7 8 9 10 – 12 11 10

'For Isabelle, who asked first'

— Andy Gravell

'For Abbie, last but by no means least of the three, and my dad, Roy, 1923–2008'

— David Parsons

CONTENTS

Introduction

Welcome to *Dynamic Web Application Development using ASP.NET*. This book follows on from the other books in this series: *Dynamic Web Application Development using PHP and MySQL* and *Dynamic Web Application Development using XML and Java*. Unlike these other technologies, .NET is a platform of products rather than a language, and therefore this book differs from them in covering multiple languages (VB.NET and C#) and also in considering the development tool, Visual Web Developer, in some detail. However, like those other books this text is intended to be an in-depth work that supports a deep understanding of how web applications work and how they can be developed. As such it is designed to be able to provide full support for higher education courses on web application development.

What is in the book?

This book covers the basic knowledge required for you to implement dynamic web applications using .NET tools and languages. In order to do this, it covers a number of different, but related, topics. We begin by providing some background to web applications to help you put the technologies introduced later into context, and provide an overview of some of the key analysis and design activities that are used by web application developers. The next part of the book focuses on client-side technologies that can be used within web browsers like Internet Explorer, Mozilla Firefox and Opera. We begin with the creation of web pages using the eXtensible HyperText mark-up Language (XHTML) and then introduce cascading stylesheets (CSS), which can be used to format and present those pages. We also explore the JavaScript client-side scripting language which enables you to develop more interactive and powerful web applications by writing code that can execute within the browser. We show how JavaScript can be used as part of Dynamic HTML (DHTML), in conjunction with CSS and the Document Object Model (DOM). To develop these web resources, we use the specialist editor tools provided within Visual Web Developer, part of Microsoft Visual Studio.

The following chapters concentrate on building websites that connect the browser pages to the server-side of web applications, looking at .NET tools and languages that can be used to generate dynamic content for on-line applications. We introduce web forms and controls, and show how server-side event handlers written in VB.NET or C# can be used to respond to user requests sent from the browser. We explore .NET controls for XML processing, input validation and page layout, as well as looking at some of the supporting tools in Visual Web Developer, such as the ASP.NET Configuration Tool and the debugger.

As the book progresses, we move beyond individual web pages to show how web applications may consist of multiple pages, working together to create a flexible webflow, giving the user choices about how they navigate through the site. We also show how a web application can connect to persistent data stored in a database, using both Visual Web Developer controls and code-based Data Access Objects.

In the latter chapters we integrate some more specialist features of Visual Web Developer, including Web Parts and login controls. We look at how XML documents can be used to communicate between client and server in the context of web services, and also introduce and describe AJAX, which combines a number of technologies that use asynchronous server connections and partial page updates to create web applications that look and feel more like desk top applications. In the final on-line bonus chapters we look at some advanced aspects of Visual Web Developer, including some that are only available in the full version of Visual Studio, showing you how to generate web-based interfaces for mobile devices and how to localize web applications for multiple languages.

In the remainder of this preface, we explain how we have structured this text and how we think you might use it for the greatest effect. We describe the application software you will need to use in order to make use of the different technologies described above. We describe how to install the software and where you can find more information about it. We clarify some terminology which we will introduce later in the book and also describe what additional material is available for download on the book's website. Let us begin by saying who we wrote this text for.

Who is this book for?

The intended audience for this text is deliberately quite broad, but it is essentially for those individuals who wish to learn more about how to create professional dynamic web applications. We realize that individuals' knowledge, background and web development experience will differ considerably and what knowledge and skills you may want out of a book on the subject of dynamic web development may be very different from someone else. You may have some well-practiced web development skills already, which is good as we will move quickly onto more interesting and in-depth subjects. You may have some previous programming experience in which case you are likely to find the chapters concerning non-visual programming and scripting quite familiar to you. What we have tried to do is create a text which encompasses all of the different technologies with which you will need to get to grips and illustrates how these can be combined in order for you to have the basic underpinnings to begin to create more sophisticated web applications. This is not a text designed for those with many years of web development experience nor it is a reference text. Furthermore, given the limitations of space, the coverage of individual subjects and technologies is necessarily introductory. For each one of the chapters in this book you could quite easily find a book the size of a house brick dedicated to just that single aspect of web technology. Therefore you are encouraged to seek further resources if you have a particular interest in any of the topics introduced in this book.

Book structure and features

This book is essentially divided into four sections, the first of which comprises Chapters 1 and 2, which give a general background and discuss analysis and design. The second section comprises Chapters 3 to 5. These chapters cover the essential aspects of mark-up languages and browser-based processing. Topics examined include XHTML, cascading stylesheets (CSS), and JavaScript. The third section of the book, Chapters 6 to 11, introduces Visual

Web Developer web forms and controls, and covers the core features of dynamic web applications; managing a webflow, configuring control components, processing XML and interacting with the database. The remainder of the book (including the on-line bonus chapters) covers configuration aspects, including security and internationalization and server deployment, and additional features that may be important to particular types of application, such as developing mobile clients, web services and AJAX.

We have designed the book so that, depending on your background and experience and what it is that you wish to learn, you can jump directly to that chapter and begin learning from that point. So, for example, if you are already an experienced (X)HTML and CSS developer but wish to brush up on some JavaScript then you can turn directly to the appropriate chapter (Chapter 5). If you already know the core aspects of developing web applications but want to know more about how these are implemented in Visual Web Developer, you can jump to the chapters that cover the specifics of the ASP.NET web forms and controls (Chapter 6 onwards). If, on the other hand, all you want to know about is AJAX and you already know about mark-up and web forms then you can turn directly to the chapter that covers the AJAX controls (Chapter 13).

Each chapter begins by outlining the key learning objectives that the chapter is designed to meet. In other words we tell you right at the start of the chapter what it is that you will learn within that chapter. After a brief introduction to the topics covered, the main sections of the chapter begin. Each chapter is designed to be read from start to finish. We have included many figures and screen shots to complement the text and to ensure that each topic is explained as clearly as possible. In the chapters that concentrate on different languages, such as (X)HTML, CSS and JavaScript there are many small complete examples which you can either type in and run yourself, or download from the book's website. A common theme throughout the book is a home insurance example ('WebHomeCover .com'), which is progressively developed throughout the chapters.

In the text, mark-up and source code examples are shown like this:

```
This is how source code
is shown within a chapter
```

Where server-side programming is used, code examples are provided in both Visual Basic. NET (VB.NET) and C#.

Within the text, if there are any key points which need to be highlighted, these are drawn to your attention with the use of a note, like this one:

NOTE	Important facts are highlighted like this!

Throughout each chapter there are exercises for you to check your level of understanding of the chapter contents, and self-test questions at the end. The answers to many of the exercises are available for public download from the book's website. Complete sets of solutions are available to registered instructors, who can also access additional teaching resources. Each chapter concludes with some final exercises, a summary of what has been introduced and some references and further reading on the subjects covered.

Visual development

Most of this book is about visual development of web applications. Microsoft uses the word 'visual' to describe a style of development in which the program being created is displayed on screen in much the same way as it will appear during execution. That is to say, the IDE shows you more or less what the user will see when running your program. This visual aspect therefore relates primarily to the user interface, and not the detailed internal logic of your program; you will not be programming algorithms by drawing flowcharts.

The visual style of development was first popularized with Windows programming, where the target was a graphical user interface or GUI application. In ASP.NET, you create web-based user interfaces. It is a remarkable achievement, however, that Microsoft have managed to re-create a very similar experience both for you the developer and also for the user. A rich ASP.NET application, which is running over the web, can nonetheless appear almost identical to a desktop Windows application, which is running locally. This means that if you already have experience of developing Windows programs using Visual Studio, you will find much that is familiar as you study ASP.NET development. Conversely, mastering ASP.NET development will help you get started if you find yourself working on a traditional Windows application.

What software do you need?

You will need the following software to successfully implement all of the examples within this text:

- A .NET development environment
  - Microsoft Visual Web Developer Express Edition 2008 was used in writing this book, along with some additional features of Microsoft Visual Studio 2008 in the final chapter.
- A web browser which supports (X)HTML, CSS, XSLT and JavaScript
- A database
  - Microsoft SQL Server Express Edition was used in writing this book.

The good news is that this software is easily downloaded and, in most cases, free, particularly if you are working or studying in an academic institution. Our recommendations for each of these different software components follow.

.NET development environment

The .NET development environment described in this book is Microsoft Visual Web Developer. The Express Edition (2008) of this product is currently available free of charge, and this book is written assuming you are using this package.

You can download Visual Web Developer Express Edition from Microsoft's website:

http://www.microsoft.com/express/download/

This offers you a simple installation process, where you can simply accept the default options. When asked, make sure you choose to include SQL Server Express Edition, and the additional help files with your download. Detailed step by step instructions covering this download and installation process are given in the appendices. You can also download SQL Server Express Edition separately if you need to do so. Other databases such as Microsoft Access can also be used with Visual Web Developer, but using SQL Sever Express Edition makes database configuration very easy.

Alternatively you can use one of the various versions of Microsoft Visual Studio instead of Visual Web Developer. If you choose to use Visual Studio, this will not prevent you from learning ASP.NET using this book, as Visual Web Developer is just a component of Visual Studio specifically aimed at creating ASP.NET websites. All the features, commands and options of Visual Web Developer are available via Visual Studio. The only difficulty you may find with using Visual Studio is that it has more features, commands and options, which can be confusing, at least to start with. Visual Studio, for example, allows you to create not only ASP.NET websites but also Windows desktop applications. It also supports a wider range of languages, and comes with additional development tools. If you do not intend to use these extra features, it is often easier to stick with Visual Web Developer. Most of the examples in this book only require the Express edition of Visual Web Developer, which can be acquired as a separate and free download. You should note, however, that the on-line bonus Chapter 15, which covers mobile controls and localization, requires the full version of Visual Web Developer, as shipped with Visual Studio, because these features are not currently available in the Express edition of Visual Web Developer.

At the time of writing, Visual Web Developer Express Edition 2008 was the most recent version available for download. However, such applications are regularly updated, so bear in mind that downloaded versions may vary in terms of appearance and functionality from the version used in this book. At the time of writing, Visual Web Developer 2010 was in preparation to replace the 2008 edition.

If you are a student or academic, you will probably be able to access a copy of the full version of Microsoft Visual Studio through the Microsoft Developer Network Academic Alliance (MSDNAA) licensing arrangements. However, the options will depend on the territory you are in, so you are advised to discuss your requirements with your local Microsoft representative.

Web browser

The web browser is used to display page mark-up in HTML, XML or XHTML. For the examples in this book it also needs to be able to run JavaScript. Visual Web Developer comes with its own built-in browser that you can use for testing purposes. However our examples have also been tested using Microsoft Internet Explorer 7 and 8, Mozilla Firefox 2 and 3 and Opera 9. Windows Vista comes with Internet Explorer 7 pre-installed but if you are using an earlier version of the operating system you can get it from:

http://www.microsoft.com/windows/downloads/ie/getitnow.mspx

The latest version of Firefox is available from:

http://www.mozilla.com/en-US/firefox/

Opera can be downloaded from:

http://www.opera.com/download/

There are also a number of other web browsers you can use, including Apple Safari and Google Chrome, among others.

Hardware requirements

The examples in this text have all been tried and tested on PCs running both Microsoft Windows XP and Microsoft Windows Vista. The following system requirements were those specified for installing and running Visual Web developer Express Edition 2008 at the time of writing on the Microsoft web page:

Supported Architectures

- x86
- x64 (WOW)

Supported Operating Systems

- Microsoft Windows XP
- Microsoft Windows Server 2003 Service Pack 2
- Microsoft Windows Server 2008
- Windows Vista

Hardware Requirements

- Minimum: 1.6 GHz CPU, 192 MB RAM, 1024 × 768 display, 5400 RPM hard disk
- Recommended: 2.2 GHz or higher CPU, 384 MB or more RAM, 1280 × 1024 display, 7200 RPM or higher hard disk
- On Windows Vista: 2.4 GHz CPU, 768 MB RAM
- 1.3 GB of available disk space for the full installation

Hosting

In this book, the example applications are deployed on a server running on your local machine. However, when you have developed your own web applications you may wish to host them so that anyone using the Internet can see and access them. In order to do this, most people require a 'service provider' who will host your applications on their web server.

How exactly you upload your code and configure your database on your service provider's computer system differs considerably from one provider to the next and we couldn't possibly explain how to do this for all of them. However, in the most part, service providers have excellent help and support to guide you through the process of transferring your web applications from your local PC onto their web server.

Further resources available on-line

In addition to what is included in the book, we have made a number of on-line resources available to the reader or instructor using this textbook as their primary teaching aid:

- PowerPoint slides to accompany each chapter
- Complete source code for the examples
- Model solutions to the examples at the end of each chapter
- Multiple choice test questions
- Bonus materials

Summary

In this preface we have introduced this book and described who it is targeted at and what knowledge and skills it covers. We have explained the structure of the book and how best to use it in order to get the best learning experience. We have introduced the software that we will be using and explained how to install it correctly. You are now ready to begin the first chapter of the book which introduces the concept of web applications.

Acknowledgments

The authors would like to thank everyone at the publishers, Cengage Learning (EMEA), who have worked so hard to bring this book to print. In particular we would like to thank Gaynor Redvers Mutton, who initiated the project and introduced the authors to each other in 2007.

Introduction to Web Applications

LEARNING OBJECTIVES

- **To understand the main features and services of web applications**

- **To understand some of the basic technological building blocks of web applications**

- **To understand how the World Wide Web has evolved from the Internet**

- **To understand some of the key aspects of the Web 2.0**

INTRODUCTION

The World Wide Web has had a profound impact on our lives since the 1990s. Some of the most successful companies that based their business on web technologies, such as Amazon, Yahoo and Google, have become as well known as the most famous global manufacturing and service companies of previous eras. We now expect all the major organizations with which we have contact to have a web presence. Not only that, we also expect that presence to include web-based applications that let us perform tasks such as managing our money, booking travel and purchasing goods and services without having to step away from the computer. Just having a web*site* is no longer enough; that site must support web *applications*.

In this chapter we will see what a web application does, then see how it does it by looking at the fundamental technologies that make web applications work, see how they fit together and consider some important features of web application architecture. We conclude the chapter by looking at the *Web 2.0*, a set of ideas that have had an important influence on how modern web applications are built.

1.1 What a web application does

What makes any kind of programming hard is largely a question of scale. Things that are easy to program inside a single computer become much more difficult when we want to distribute those things over space (to many users) and time (to exist beyond the run time

1

of a single program). For example, let us assume that you are working as a software developer and, like many developers, have a text document stored on your computer that you use as a log of things that you find helpful to keep track of, such as references to useful resources or solutions to problems you have discovered. You can use text editors or word processors installed on your own computer to access and edit that document. Now, what if you want to be able to make that document available to others, because you feel that this information may be helpful to, for example, other developers in your team? You could, of course, distribute print or email copies, but that would get very tedious if you had to keep doing this every time you made a new document entry, and after a while there would be lots of different versions of your document floating around. What you need to do, of course, is to make the document available on a *web server* so that others can read it over the *World Wide Web*. Hey presto, your document is now a *blog*! (short for *web log*). This leads us to the first thing that a web application can do.

- *A web application enables us to distribute documents over the World Wide Web*

Before going further we should perhaps make one thing clear, which is that we are introducing things that a web application can do, but in fact we are really talking about what a web application *server* can do. A web application server is the software that hosts your web applications, and provides all of the services that we introduce in this section.

Now, maybe you are such a great writer, doing such interesting stuff, that you become a very popular blogger. Many thousands of people all over the world start reading your blog. Now, there can be many people all wanting to access your blog at the same time. Luckily, your server is able to cope with these multiple concurrent requests for your document without any problem. This brings us to another thing that web applications can do.

- *A web application manages concurrency for you, enabling access to a single web-based resource by multiple users*

After a while, you find that people reading your blog keep sending you emails for suggestions about what you should include in it. Eventually you get so fed up with this that you change your blog so that others can contribute their own entries to the on-line document. Hey presto, you have a *Wiki*! (A Wiki is a website that is open to editing by anyone.) To make this work, your server has to be able to let users not only download your document, but upload their own content as well. It then has to be able to dynamically recreate the updated document for subsequent readers. This brings us to an essential role of web applications.

- *A web application can generate dynamic content, building web pages on the fly from sources of data that may include data supplied by users*

Eventually you find that your blog/wiki is becoming too difficult to manage because too many people are able to make changes to it and they keep messing up your pages. You decide that only people who register with you will be able to access and modify your site. This is another important service that web applications can provide.

- *A web application can include declarative, role-based, security, which enables you to allow or deny access to specific resources to users based on their user role*

Over time, your original single document has become a large quantity of data, a kind of *Wikipedia* (www.wikipedia.org) of knowledge related to your own areas of interest, partly created by you but also created in large part by others. Instead of a single, simple piece of data, your Wiki now consists of many related pieces of data. Since there is now too much information to be kept in a few pages, the underlying data that has been contributed to your system requires some kind of managed data storage so that we can keep it for a long time, re-use the same content in different contexts across different parts of the overall system, and ensure that it has some kind of existence outside of our running web application. To do this we need some kind of *persistence*, some way of storing our web application content in a database or some other form of secondary storage, and we need some way of connecting our web application to the database. Fortunately, web applications can help us to do that as well.

- *A web application provides facilities to connect to a database so that its content can be kept in permanent storage, to be retrieved when required*

If the content of our web application is stored in a database, then we need to make sure that any changes made to parts of it by others are handled correctly so that, for example, changes made by one client do not clash with changes made simultaneously by another. This means we have to be able to support *transactions* in our objects. Transactions make sure that any changes made to persistent data are made in a managed and consistent way, so that if two users try to change the same component, either access is only allowed to one user at a time (pessimistic locking) or both users can try to make changes at the same time, but only the first to submit their changes (to *commit*), will be successful (optimistic locking).

- *A web application is able to utilize the transactional services of a database so that updates to its content are reliable and consistent*

After all this we might also consider performance and reliability. How long might someone have to wait before getting access to the web application if many others want to do the same thing, and what happens if the machine that the application is running on fails for some reason? It may be that we need to provide more than one copy of the application so that multiple clients can access it at the same time, and so that if one machine fails we are still able to provide the necessary services to our clients. In particular, we may find that over time we need to support more and more clients without breaking the system we already have, so we need some way of scaling our system to maintain performance and reliability.

- *A web application is able to leverage the services of its underlying hardware and software infrastructure to run the same application across multiple machines, enabling scalability*

Figure 1.1 summarizes some of the web application features we have introduced in this section.

All of the issues we have touched on in this section are common to web applications, and all are difficult, tedious and expensive to program from scratch. Therefore it is very useful if we can reuse an existing set of tools to provide all of these services, leaving us free to write the code that addresses our particular business problem. The role of web application development languages and their supporting tools is to provide just such a framework for all of these services. However, web applications cannot work in isolation because they rely on the fundamental technologies of the Internet and the World Wide Web. In the next section we explain some of the most important features of these technologies.

FIGURE 1.1 Some web application features

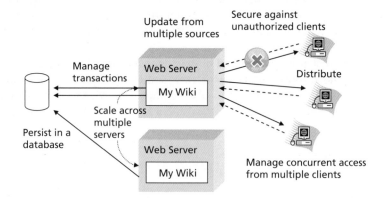

1.2 E-everything – the Internet and the World Wide Web

Web applications rely on both the Internet and the World Wide Web to work, and one important point to bear in mind is that the Internet and the World Wide Web are not the same thing, since the first version of the Internet pre-dated the World Wide Web by more than 10 years. The Internet is a network of networks that was developed from the *ARPAnet*, a project that began in the 1970s. Its name comes from its sponsor, the U.S. government Advanced Research Projects Agency (ARPA). It originally linked a small number of research sites together, but used the same core technologies that now support the much bigger Internet. In contrast, the World Wide Web (the WWW, or W3, for short) is a hypertext-based collection of multimedia information accessible via the Internet that dates from the 1990s (hypertext means that the content on the web is linked together so that we can easily navigate between web pages that can be physically located anywhere in the world.) We might say, perhaps, that the Internet is the information superhighway and the World Wide Web is the traffic that travels on it.

What has now become the World Wide Web was first developed by Tim Berners Lee at CERN (originally the acronym for the French *Conseil Européen pour la Recherche Nucléair*, more generally known in English as the European Organisation for Nuclear Research) in 1990. It was originally a distributed hypertext system for managing information at CERN (based on previous hypertext research), but quickly developed into something much bigger. From an academic tool that was intended to assist researchers, it evolved into both an important platform for leisure applications and a key element in business, not only for the exclusively web-based *dot coms* but also as part of the IT strategy of major corporations, governments and other organisations.

From an internal research tool, the web began to evolve into something much bigger and more important. Between 1991 and 1993, web servers began to come on-line outside of CERN, using the underlying technology of the Internet. CERN made the WWW technology free so it was easy for others to build on these systems. Originally, communication over the web was text-based and therefore not very user-friendly. The first graphical *web browser* (an application able to display content from the web) had been written by Tim Berners Lee in 1991, but this was internal to CERN. However other graphical browsers were soon developed and in 1993 the NCSA (National Center for Supercomputing

Applications) made their Mosaic graphical browser publicly available. This was soon followed by the first versions of the commercial browsers, Netscape Navigator and Microsoft Internet Explorer, to be joined in subsequent years by many other increasingly sophisticated browsers including Opera, Mozilla Firefox, Apple Safari and Google Chrome.

Graphical browsers, being able to display images and a range of text fonts, made access to the World Wide Web easy and attractive and expanded its potential user base from just technical specialists to the general public. The web began to get press coverage and reach a wider audience, and in 1994 the W3C (World Wide Web Consortium) was formed to create web standards and ensure that the proliferation of web technologies did not lead to incompatibility between different systems. In 1993 the first tools for writing dynamic web pages on the server had been created using the CGI (Common Gateway Interface) developed by the NCSA. These made it possible for web pages to be generated on the fly on the server. Instead of simply providing static content to users, where everyone sees the same pages, CGI made it possible to generate pages for individual users, so they could see their own search results, bank account details, flight bookings, shopping carts, etc. Other server-side technologies followed, including PHP (Originally 'Personal Home Page Tools', later renamed 'PHP: Hypertext Preprocessor'), Java and Microsoft.NET, making it possible to develop industrial strength applications that ran over the web. In 1995 HotJava, the first Java-aware browser, was launched by Sun Microsystems, and Netscape introduced the first version of JavaScript, bringing the potential for applications that could run inside a browser. As both browser and server technologies continued to develop, terms like 'web surfing', 'going on-line' and 'e-business' entered common speech and things have never been quite the same since.

1.3 Important Internet technologies

The World Wide Web depends on some important Internet technologies in order to work. These include:

- TCP/IP (Transmission Control Protocol / Internet Protocol)
- IP addresses
- Domain Names

1.3.1 TCP/IP (Transmission Control Protocol / Internet Protocol)

TCP/IP is actually a whole set of related protocols and tools that help computers to communicate with each other. Some that are used on the Internet include SMTP (Simple Mail Transfer Protocol) for sending email messages and FTP (File Transfer Protocol), which allows files to be easily copied to and from remote sites.

1.3.2 IP addresses

Computers on the Internet are initially connected to some kind of local network, either within an organization or as part of the services of an Internet Service Provider (ISP). To build all these separate systems into one, hardware devices known as *routers* are used to glue all the different networks together. For this to work, every machine on the Internet has to have a unique IP (Internet Protocol) address so that communications can be routed to the correct computer. An IP address is a large binary number giving billions of possible addresses. The current version (IPv4) uses a 32 bit binary number, where IP addresses are expressed as four sets of dotted decimal numbers using the format *nnn.nnn.nnn.nnn*. Each of these numbers falls in the range 0–255, for example 127.0.0.1. The next version (IPv6) will cater for the growth of the Internet by supporting far more addresses by using a 128 bit binary number.

 NOTE | IPv6 addresses are written as eight 4-digit hexadecimal numbers separated by colons.

Given an IP address, one machine can connect to another as if they were on the same physical network. Some machines have fixed IP addresses, while others are temporarily allocated an IP address from a pool when they connect, a technique known as DHCP (Dynamic Host Configuration Protocol.) This pooling of IP addresses is more efficient in terms of being able to reuse the same address for different machines at different times. It also reduces the administration required to ensure that each machine has an appropriate address, particularly for systems that have to give Internet access to very large numbers of computers, such as commercial ISPs.

1.3.3 Domain names

Most computers that host websites use *domain names* rather than actual IP addresses. This means that users can, for example, visit 'www.w3.org' rather than use the actual IP address of the World Wide Web consortium site. The *Domain Name System* (DNS) enables domain names to be converted into a valid IP address. *Resolver* programs query name servers for IP addresses and enable clients to be routed to the actual host machine. The DNS consists of a number of dedicated servers (a distributed database) that maintain naming information for different *zones*. A zone is a set of related domain names, e.g. '.com', '.org', etc. that appear at the same level of the DNS, which has a tree structure (Figure 1.2).

FIGURE 1.2 The DNS tree structure with some of the Internet zones and domains

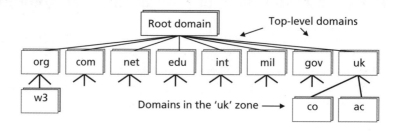

Specific domains appear in a particular zone, for example the W3C domain is within the 'org' zone ('w3.org'). The highest level zone is known as the 'root domain', and under this comes the zone that encompasses all the 'top level domains', including the country code

domains. For each country, there is a zone that contains the various types of domain within that country, using zones such as 'co' for companies and 'ac' for academic institutions. Because of this tree structure, with layers of zones each managed separately, several different name servers may be involved in resolving a single domain name request. Domain names are controlled by the Internet Assigned Numbers Authority (IANA), which is administered by the Internet Corporation for Assigned Names and Numbers (ICANN). The number of domain types made available by these organizations has increased steadily over the years as new types of website have been developed, including the '.tv' domain for television services and '.mobi' for mobile services.

Using domain names is better than just using IP addresses because domain names are easier to remember and the names usually reflect the identity of the owner (e.g. 'ibm.com', 'w3.org', 'harvard.edu', etc). It is also more flexible to use DNS names rather than IP numbers, since the mapping between a domain name and an IP address can change, so the same name can migrate between different host systems. Domain names are also important for email, since they are used in email addresses (e.g. 'web-human@w3.org').

1.4 Important World Wide Web technologies

On its own, the Internet provides the possibility for different computers across the world to connect to each other and transfer data. However the World Wide Web adds some very important technologies to the underlying platform of the Internet. These include:

- HyperText Transfer Protocol (HTTP)
- HTML
- URLs, URIs and URNs

1.4.1 HyperText Transfer Protocol (HTTP)

The World Wide Web uses the *HyperText Transfer Protocol* (HTTP) to send information. When using this protocol, the domain name (or IP address) is preceded by 'http://' (e.g. 'http://www.webhomecover.com'). Web browsers usually have 'http://' as their default protocol so this prefix is frequently left off website names. HTTP is a 'request-response' protocol. Clients (usually browser software) send a request to a web server, which is software that is able to host web-based content and serve it to clients on request. The server handles the incoming request and provides a response, usually in the form of a page written in the HyperText Mark-up Language (HTML), which browsers can interpret. HTTP requests are handled by default on port 80 of the server. A server port is a number used to identify a particular process on the server that another system can connect to. Many common services, including HTTP, are allocated standard port numbers to simplify communication.

HTTP requests are always of a specific type, one of GET, POST, HEAD, PUT, DELETE, CONNECT, OPTIONS or TRACE. All of these request types have their uses, but in most web applications the requests are usually limited to being either GET or POST. In most cases either of these can be used to achieve the same result, but in principle a GET request is intended to retrieve information *from* the server, and it often contains a search query or other parameter data. A POST request is intended to send data *to* the server, in most cases from an HTML form. A form is a part of a web page that lets a user provide data using components such as text fields, select lists and radio buttons. Forms have an 'action' which contains the web address of an application running on a server that knows how to process the contents of the form. This is where the data is sent when the user presses the 'submit' button on the web page.

What comes back from the server, following an HTTP request, is an HTTP response, which in many cases will be a web page, but can also be some kind of code number to indicate errors, problems, or actions that the browser should take such as redirecting to another website. Some examples of HTTP response codes are '200 OK' (the code that is used with a web page), '401 Unauthorized' (where security is being used) and '404 Not Found' (when the requested page cannot be found). Figure 1.3 shows the basic HTTP request-response cycle.

FIGURE 1.3 The HTTP request-response cycle

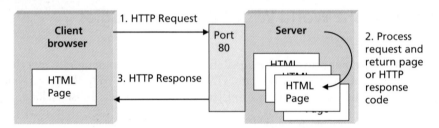

Normal HTTP traffic is not encrypted in any way, so is not secured against being read by a third party. In most cases this does not matter, but sometimes we need to send or receive information over the web that we do not want others to be able to read. Therefore HTTP also comes in a secure form that allows us to transfer sensitive data, such as credit card numbers, safely across the Internet. This version of HTTP is known as HTTPS and uses a number of technologies including *Public Key Infrastructure* (PKI), encryption and *digital certificates*. The 'S' in 'HTTPS' comes from the *Secure Sockets Layer* (SSL), a secure communication protocol originally developed by Netscape. HTTPS connections use a special server port (443) to separate secure traffic from normal HTTP connections. As well as HTTPS being necessary for securing user data, many web-based systems need to authenticate users (find out who they are, generally by asking for a user name and password) and then authorize them to have access to appropriate resources. HTTPS is also used to enable this kind of secure login by ensuring that the username and password are encrypted.

1.4.2 HTML

As we saw in the previous section, web clients use browser software to request, download and display information from web servers. That information is mainly in the form of HTML (Hypertext Mark-up Language) pages. HTML pages are text documents that contain special *tags* telling the browser what type of information they contain. These tags are surrounded by angle brackets and indicate the *mark-up* of the web page, to control the structure and presentation of the content. This, for example, is how a typical HTML page begins, specifying the text to appear in the browser's title bar:

```
<html>
 <head>
  <title>My Page</title>
 </head>
 <body>...
```

 NOTE This is a somewhat simplified view of HTML, but is perfectly acceptable to most web browsers.

Tags do not specify exactly how a page will appear. It is up to the browser to format the page and manage its content, so the same page can look different in different browsers. Users can customize their browser to make pages appear in the way that they want, so they can, for example, change the size or style of the standard text font. As well as text, these pages can contain images, sound, animations and other downloadable programs.

Using a web browser as the client for a web application is great for supporting large numbers of casual users (such as those using an on-line store, or downloading music to their mobile phones) because it would not be realistic to expect all users to install separate special client programs just to use a particular service. However, browsers do support 'plugins', which are programs that can be installed into the browser to provide additional functionality. Common examples of plugins include Flash, Real Player and Acrobat Reader. Browsers can also support programming languages such as JavaScript and Java Applets, enabling simple programs to be downloaded and run within the browser window.

1.4.3 URLs, URIs and URNs

Uniform Resource Locators (URLs) are the complete locations of an Internet resource, comprising a number of elements:

- The protocol of the request (the browser's default is usually http://)
- The IP address or domain of the server
- The port number (port 80 for HTTP, 443 for HTTPS)
- The subdirectory path from the 'document root' (if applicable)
- The name of the resource (though there is often a default page which is loaded if no name is specified)

For example, the following URL includes all of these elements:

```
http://www.webhomecover.com:80/help/callcenters.htm
```

Since the http protocol is usually the browser's default, and the port number is the default on the server, in most cases we can exclude them, so our previous example is more likely to be written as:

```
www.webhomecover.com/help/callcenters.htm
```

If we only use the domain name, many websites will be configured with a default resource, which will be loaded when no specific file is requested. If the example domain has a default resource, then the following URI should result in a page being served to the browser:

```
www.webhomecover.com
```

A URL is a specific kind of URI (*Uniform Resource Identifier*) which identifies a resource that can be downloaded from the web. Another specific type of URI is the URN, or *Uniform Resource Name*. Although these have similar formats to URLs, they do not necessarily specify a downloadable resource. The purpose of a URN is simply to provide a globally unique name for something, not necessarily to provide a name that points to a web-based resource. The term URL is very widely used, but URI is the more general (and correct) term.

1.5 Special types of web applications: intranets, extranets and portals

The web is full of public websites that provide information using web pages to anyone who can connect to the World Wide Web using a browser. There is also a very large number of Business to Customer (B2C) websites that make products and services available to anyone who has an Internet connection and a web browser. However there are some special purpose web applications that have particular characteristics. Three important examples of these are Intranets, Extranets and Portals.

1.5.1 Intranets

As well as having a public presence on the Internet, many organizations maintain a private *intranet* behind a security firewall. An intranet consists of web pages and other resources that are only available inside the organization. Intranets have a low cost of ownership because they use the standard technologies of the Internet. They increase internal communication while using less paper for things like internal phone books, software and procedure manuals, forms, etc. They get information out of central databases in a form everyone can use from, the desktop. Intranets have proved valuable for all kinds of organizations, for example credit card companies work with many banks, and an intranet can be used as a central repository for information about all those banks, while pharmaceuticals companies have used intranets to draw information from many sources worldwide on drug trials and new drug submission regulations for all countries.

1.5.2 Extranets

An extranet falls somewhere between the Internet and an organization's intranet. Only selected outsiders, such as customers, suppliers or other trading partners, are allowed access. Extranets can range from highly secure Business to Business (B2B) systems to self-registration systems like those frequently used for downloading evaluation software. Extranets can be used, for example, to allow web shopper customers to log in to check the status of their orders over a secure connection, or users of courier companies to check where their delivery is at any point in time.

1.5.3 Portals

A portal is a special kind of web application. Its role is to act as a gateway (the meaning of 'portal') into a number of other applications. The structure of a portal is typically to present a number of *portlets*, which are window-based links into other applications. They also commonly provide faculties for personalization, so that users can customize which portlets they are presented with and also change the layout and look and feel of the portal. Portals are often used by public sites that encourage user registrations, such as Yahoo. They are also often used by organizations as a route into the various applications provided on the company intranet. In the mobile context, portals are a popular way for mobile service providers to enable easy access to the mobile Internet. Mobile portals such as Vodafone Live! provide links to various applications within the 'walled garden' of services provided by the mobile network carrier, as well as more general access into the mobile Internet.

1.6 Web application architectures

To understand how a web application provides services to clients across the web, it is necessary to have some understanding of the architectures of distributed computer systems. In this section we introduce the concepts of layers and tiers.

1.6.1 Layers

The concept of a layered architecture is one where we regard different parts of a software system as having different and separate roles. This is a conceptual, rather than necessarily a physical, layering of system components. The basic three layers are the presentation layer (that deals with the user interface), the business logic layer (that handles the business processes and concepts used in the application) and the data management layer (that deals with managing and persisting the underlying data in the system).

If you think about how this model relates to, for example, the type of word processor that runs 'standalone' on a desktop computer, you can see that there are certain parts of a word processing program that deal with presentation, that is, how we see the document on the screen. This may be quite complex and allow multiple different views of the same document, for example an editing view and a print preview. Behind this layer is the business logic layer that contains all the processes that we need to perform when creating and editing documents. These include things like spell checking, formatting, paginating, editing, etc. This layer also contains the main concepts that we deal with in the application, which in the case of a word processor would be things like documents, paragraphs, words, letters, diagrams, etc. Finally, beneath this layer, is the data management layer. The job of this layer is to enable our documents to be saved and reloaded, probably in simple flat (sequential) files so that they can persist between different runs of the word processing program.

The important feature to note about our layered word processing example is that we assume that all three layers would be implemented in a single program running on one computer. In other words the layers are conceptual, not physical (Figure 1.4).

FIGURE 1.4 The conceptual layers of a word processing system

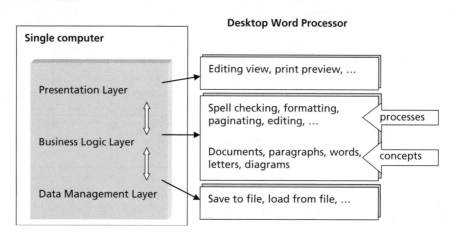

1.6.2 Tiers and distributed systems

When we talk about *tiers*, we are also talking about layers. However, the difference is that the term 'tiers' is generally used to mean physically separate devices. A multi-tier system is therefore one that is deployed on multiple different nodes (computers). Using multiple tiers is necessary when we want to make our applications distributed and scaleable. For example, in a web-based banking system the presentation layer, which would be a web browser, would be distributed across all the users' computers, but the application layer would be running on a central computer, or multiple computers, somewhere at the bank. This tier would manage the business process such as checking accounts, transferring funds, ordering cheque books, etc. Also in this layer would be the business objects such as accounts, customers, transactions and statements. To cope with large numbers of users and to assist in security, the data management layer would also be run on a separate machine (probably several). For complex large-scale data storage like this, instead of simple flat files, we would use a database management system for the four basic operations on data, namely *create*, *read*, *update* and *delete* (CRUD for short). Once we start using large numbers of computers running different parts of the system across multiple tiers, we have an *n-tier architecture* (Figure 1.5). N-tier architectures are a fundamental part of web applications because the presentation layer (running in web browsers) is always widely distributed, and the large number of users of some of these systems means that the business logic and data management layers may also have to be distributed across multiple machines.

FIGURE 1.5 The tiers of an n-tier web-based banking system

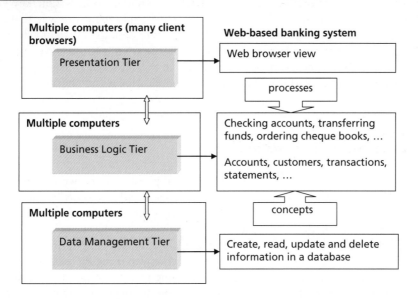

1.7 The Web 2.0 and AJAX

Since the mid-2000s it has been hard to discuss the World Wide Web without mentioning the Web 2.0 and AJAX. The Web 2.0 is a term that has become widely used since the first Web 2.0 Conference in 2004. Although it might be categorized as an umbrella marketing term rather than a specific technology or architecture, some authors (notably O'Reilly, 2005) have given it some concrete specifications through a set of published principles, practices and patterns. Many publications that discuss the Web 2.0 focus on rich user interfaces, in particular the use of AJAX (Asynchronous JavaScript and XML), but the ideas of the Web 2.0 go beyond AJAX to include a wide range of ideas about how modern web applications should be developed. The key ideas underlying the Web 2.0 may perhaps be summarized as:

- The web as a software platform
- Service oriented architectures
- User and contributor communities

In this section we briefly explore some of these ideas, which will re-emerge at various points throughout this book. Above all, the role of the *eXtensible Mark-up Language* (XML), which underlies service oriented architectures, and can be seen as an important component of many of aspects of the Web 2.0.

1.7.1 The web as a software platform

In the past, the software platform that applications were built on was a particular computer operating system, for example Microsoft Windows or Linux. In contrast, web applications are able to span multiple operating systems because web browsers can render the same content regardless of the original system from which the page was downloaded. The server may run on one operating system and its clients on many others. One key Web 2.0 pattern is *software above the level of a single device*, which is about the way that applications can span different types of device, from web servers to desk top PC to mobile phones to portable media players. For example, to download music we might use a PC to connect to a web server and also connect a mobile device to the PC, all using a single application. In this type of situation, the platform that the overall application is running on is the web, not just a single device.

1.7.2 Service oriented architectures

In the early days of the web, the focus was on the applications that were being used. For example the 'browser wars', primarily between Netscape and Microsoft in the mid-1990s, were about which application would be used to access the web. More recently, the focus has been more on the underlying content available via the web, rather than the specific applications that might be used. This content is made available using various forms of web service, which are data sources made available over the web using the eXtensible Mark-up Language (XML). Systems that are built by combining together multiple web services are known as *Service Oriented Architectures* (SOA). Examples of content that can be accessed through web services include news, weather, map data, and book information. Some authors use the term *the programmable web* to describe the ability to build applications that utilize content from multiple web-based resources, using freely available Application Programming Interfaces (APIs) to create *mashups*. A mashup, in web terms, is an application that mixes together content from different sources. Some mashups combine content from a number of different services to produce an overall application, while others use a single service but reorganize the content to suit their requirements.

One simple example of a web service is RSS (an acronym that has multiple roots, Really Simple Syndication, Rich Site Summary and RDF Site Summary), which uses XML to supply feeds of frequently updated information such as news and weather.

1.7.3 User and contributor communities

Traditional software construction is about building self-contained applications for a particular purpose, for example to process a company payroll or manage company accounts. This type of application is generally intended for 'in house' use, though it may expose certain features to customers. For example, software used by banks is primarily used internally, but may expose some web-based services enabling customers to perform certain transactions on their accounts. In many Web 2.0 applications, instead of this type of central control, applications are about a community of users who participate in the application itself. A good example of this is Wikipedia, an on-line encyclopaedia where anyone can create or edit entries. Other applications may consist largely of content provided by a single organization but allow users to make some contribution. An example of this would be music download sites that enable users to post their own reviews. Of course opening up a web application to contributions from the user community is not appropriate for every system, but certain aspects of this approach to software development can be incorporated into many different types of web application.

1.7.4 AJAX

Asynchronous JavaScript and XML (AJAX) is a term coined by Garrett (2006) in an article about current trends in web development. JavaScript is a programming language that can be run inside a browser, making it possible to run programs that connect to the server while a page is being viewed. We cover AJAX in more detail later in this book, but its relationship to the Web 2.0 is primarily in the area of providing a rich user experience in the browser environment. At its simplest, AJAX makes it possible to update parts of a web page with data read from a server without having to refresh the whole page, making the user experience more like using a traditional desktop application rather than surfing a website. There are many tools for developing AJAX applications, ranging from using a just few lines of JavaScript code to sophisticated frameworks. Later in this book we introduce some of the controls available for creating AJAX enabled applications within the.NET framework.

NOTE	In this book we refer to AJAX using upper-case letters. However, the originator of the term did not use upper-case (Garrett, 2005). In addition, since AJAX techniques can use a range of technologies, and as AJAX does not have to be asynchronous, using AJAX as a specific acronym can be unnecessarily restrictive. However, we use it here for consistency with Visual Web Developer, which uses the name AJAX.

1.8 So you want to be a web application developer?

There are many challenges for developers in building web applications. There are choices about technology that have to be made, choices about architecture, choices about design, and choices about implementation. In making decisions about how to build web applications there are always compromises and trade offs, and we have to be aware of the reasons for making certain choices and the consequences of them. Fortunately there are also many tools, techniques and reusable designs (design patterns) that can help us to meet these challenges. The purpose of this book is to explore some important issues in the development of modern web applications and provide some examples of how we might approach a solution, avoiding as best we can the hype of this week's technology while taking full advantage of the lessons we can learn from others, and getting the best from the available technologies.

Self Study Questions

1. What is the term 'blog' short for?
2. What is a wiki?
3. What is the format of an IPv4 IP address?
4. Which of the following is not a top level domain: org, int, ant, mil?
5. What type of HTTP request is normally used to send data to the server?
6. What is the usual port number of non-secure HTTP connections?
7. What is the name given to web-based resources that are not public but only available behind an organization's firewall?
8. What are the window-based application links in a portal sometimes called?
9. What is Wikipaedia?
10. What is meant by an n-tier architecture?

Exercises

1.1 In Figure 1.2 we saw some of the top level domains in the Domain Name System (DNS). Look up some of these domains by using a web search and find out what types of organization use, for example, the 'int' domain. Find some other top level domains that are not included in the diagram. For your web searches you will find the ICANN and IANA websites useful (http://www.icann.org and http://www.iana.org).

1.2 In our example of a layered architecture we referred to a word processor running on a single machine. We compared this with a layered and tiered architecture, using the example of a web-based banking system. However, web-based word processors are becoming more popular. Do an Internet search and find some examples of word processors that work on the web. From their descriptions, how do you think the layers in the word processing example would be applied to tiers in the context of a web-based word processor? You may find it helpful in answering this question to spend some time using one of these web-based word processors.

1.3 Look at the Wikipedia website (http://www.wikipedia.org). What are the processes that you have to follow in order to add or modify an entry in this on-line encyclopaedia? There have been a few controversial problems with some entries made on Wikipedia in the past. See if you can find some reference to these by doing a web search, and see what policy changes were necessary in managing the wiki website.

1.4 Find a popular blog on the web. Describe the author and content of the blog. Why do you think this blog is popular?

1.5 One of the common features of portals is that they can be personalized. Find a web-based portal that you can personalize (e.g. http://www.yahoo.com). Make a list of the things that you are able to personalize on this site.

1.6 A simple example of how AJAX can update the current page with data from the server is Google Suggest. Go to a Google Suggest web page (at the time of writing this could be found at http://www.google.com/webhp?complete=1&hl=en, or you can find it with a web search) and start typing a search term. The system will suggest possible searches as you type.

SUMMARY

In this chapter we introduced the principal features, technologies and uses of web applications. These covered aspects of both the Internet and the World Wide Web, the distributed architectures that web applications use and some special types of web application. The following table (Table 1.1) summarizes the various acronyms and shorthand terms that were introduced, along with their definitions.

TABLE 1.1

Acronym / term	Meaning
AJAX	Asynchronous JavaScript and XML
API	Application Programming Interface
ARPA	Advanced Research Projects Agency (originator of the ARPANet)
B2B	Business to Business
blog	Web log. A web-based diary intended for public access
CERN	Conseil Européen pour la Recherche Nucléair, more generally known in English as the European Organisation for Nuclear Research
CGI	Common Gateway Interface
CRUD	Create, Read, Update, Delete
DHCP	Dynamic Host Configuration Protocol
DNS	Domain Name System
FTP	File Transfer Protocol
HTML	HyperText Mark-up Language
HTTP	HyperText Transfer Protocol
IANA	Internet Assigned Numbers Authority
ICANN	Internet Corporation for Assigned Names and Numbers
IPv4	Internet Protocol Version 4
IPv6	Internet Protocol Version 6
ISP	Internet Service Provider
NCSA	National Center for Supercomputing Applications
PHP	Originally Personal Home Page Tools, later renamed PHP: Hypertext Preprocessor
PKI	Public Key Infrastructure
RSS	Really Simple Syndication / Rich Site Summary / RDF Site Summary
SMTP	Simple Mail Transfer Protocol
SOA	Service Oriented Architecture
SSL	Secure Sockets Layer
TCP/IP	Transmission Control Protocol / Internet Protocol
URI	Uniform Resource Identifier
URL	Uniform Resource Locator
URN	Uniform Resource Name
W3C	World Wide Web Consortium
Wiki	A website that is open to public contributions and editing
WWW / W3	World Wide Web
XML	eXtensible Mark-up Language

References and further reading

Berners-Lee, T. 2000. *Weaving the Web: The Original Design and Ultimate Destiny of the World Wide Web*, New York: HarperCollins.

Garrett, J.J. 2005. *Ajax: A New Approach to Web Applications*. http://www.adaptivepath.com/publications/essays/archives/000385.php.

O'Reilly, T. 2005. *What is Web 2.0: Design Patterns and Businesses Models for the Next Generation of Software*. O'Reilly Network, http://www.oreilly.com/pub/a/oreilly/tim/news/2005/09/30/what-is-web-20.html.

Shklar, L. and Rosen, R. 2009. *Web Application Architecture: Principles, Protocols, and Practices (2nd edition)*, John Wiley and Sons.

W3C, 1992, *About The World Wide Web*, http://www.w3.org/WWW/.

CHAPTER 2

Web Application Requirements Analysis and Design

LEARNING OBJECTIVES

- **To understand some of the techniques used in analyzing web application system requirements**

- **To be able to use some notation from the UML related to web applications**

- **To understand some aspects of the processes involved in the development lifecycle of web applications**

- **To be able to apply some common design patterns to the structure of web pages**

INTRODUCTION

In this chapter we look at some techniques for analyzing the requirements for a web application. Some of the notation used comes from the *Unified Modeling Language* (UML) with some special extensions that were developed to meet the particular requirements of designing for the web. There are also some informal diagrams that do not come from any specific notation. The process is based on aspects of the *Unified Process* (UP), but with a lightweight 'agile' approach. We conclude the chapter with some considerations relating to system design, and describe a number of web usability patterns.

2.1 What's different about web application requirements?

The development of a web application is similar in many ways to that of any other software system. We have to find out what the users require, choose an appropriate software architecture, design and build the overall framework and create all the necessary components, all the while testing the evolving system against its technical and user expectations and adapting to changing requirements and circumstances. In some ways, however, web applications have their own special requirements. Perhaps the most obvious is that web applications have a special kind of user interface. Their presentation may be via many different types of device, ranging from desktop computers to mobile phones, and that presentation is based on some form of web page running in a browser. Also, unlike many software systems, a web application often caters for very large numbers of anonymous users, potentially located anywhere in the world. This means that our design has to take account of the issues of data communications and multiple access to the same resources. Its underlying communications protocol is based on the request-response model, where the application is on a system that is remote from the user, and the user's device has to make requests of the application to perform activities on its behalf. This contrasts with desktop applications that may have a richer, more interactive and immediate interface. In building such systems, we also have to be constantly aware that parts of our application will be running on central servers while other parts will be running on many different client devices. All of these differences (and more) mean that we have to extend our understanding of analysis and design to cater for all the special concerns of web applications.

2.2 Software development lifecycles

Although we have said that web applications have some special requirements, any development method that we adopt needs to provide four services to support us during the project *lifecycle* (the processes and events that take place between the project's beginning and its end):

- It needs to guide us through the various activities
- It needs to specify the artefacts (such as documents, diagrams and/or software components) that should be created during the development of the system
- It should direct the tasks of the individuals and teams working on the project
- It should provide appropriate criteria for measuring and monitoring progress and production

To achieve these objectives it needs to help the system developers to know their roles, activities and workflows, and the final software products that they need to create. The way that these features are defined does not have to be excessively prescriptive, particularly for a small project. Many software development methods used from the 1990s onwards stress *agility*, which in many cases means producing the simplest possible artefacts by performing activities in the simplest possible workflows. Regardless, most current methods of software development use the concept of iteration which has gradually replaced older methods based on the *waterfall model*.

2.2.1 The waterfall model

Early approaches to developing software systems tended to follow a traditional engineering approach, whereby a system had to have all of its requirements gathered before it could be analyzed, be completely analyzed before it could be designed, fully designed before it could be implemented and only then could it be tested. This is known as the waterfall model because the development process can be seen as a sequence of separate stages that occur in a fixed order (Figure 2.1). There is the notion of some feedback between adjacent stages, so that we might revisit certain aspects of the design in the light of implementation, for example, or rewrite code if it fails a test, but no concept of being able to cope with evolving requirements, or start testing early in the project lifecycle.

FIGURE 2.1 The waterfall model

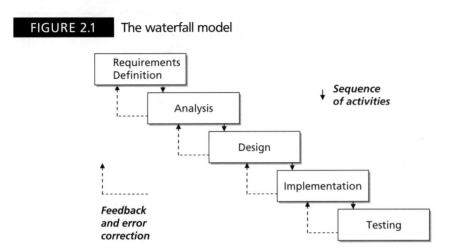

This type of approach may work well in many engineering contexts but does not work so well for most software projects. This is because the requirements for software tend to be more fluid and dynamic, changing over time to respond to changing application environments. To address this more flexible design process, *iterative* methods have been developed.

2.2.2 Iterative methods

An iterative approach is like a series of mini waterfalls, where we gather requirements, analyze, design, build and test part of a system, reflect on it, adapt our plans in the light of experience, and then repeat the process a number of times until the project is complete (Figure 2.2). Thus the feedback loop, which at any given point in the waterfall model only includes the previous stage, covers all of the activities of analysis, design, implementation and testing. As we progress through the iterations, the emphasis of our activities changes. Initially we focus mostly on requirements and analysis, and later we focus more on implementation and testing. The relative sizes of the boxes in Figure 2.2 are meant to suggest this gradual evolution though the iterations.

When using an iterative approach we still have an overall vision and plan for developing the system but we are more able to respond to new or changing requirements because we do not assume that we can identify all the requirements up front. Many iterative methods stress that each iteration should result in something concrete that provides a milestone for the project. In other words an iteration does not end just because a time period has expired but also because the required deliverable has been created. Iterative methods are also flexible in that their expected deliverables can be changed by trading off, in a managed way, new expectations against the original ones. In other words, if additional expectations are added to an iteration then an equivalent amount of effort has to be moved out of that iteration to enable the schedule to remain realistic.

FIGURE 2.2 The iterative model

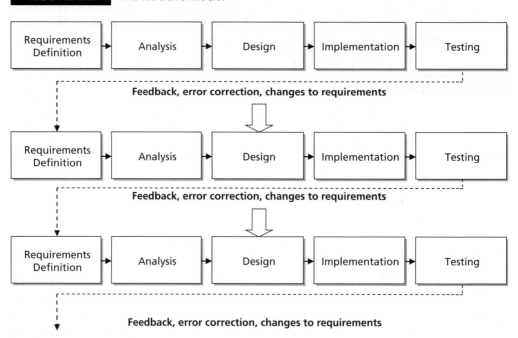

2.3 The Unified Modeling Language and The Unified Process

In the 1990s there were many notations and processes proposed for the development of object-oriented systems. So many, in fact, that the competition between the various approaches during this period became known as the 'method wars'. However, after a while it became evident that three methods in particular were gaining more traction than most of the others. These were the Object Modeling Technique (OMT) developed by a group led by James Rumbaugh at General Electric, the Booch method developed by Grady Booch at Rational Corporation, and Objectory, developed by Ivar Jacobsen at Eriksson. Largely at the instigation of Grady Booch, these three methods were fused together, along with input from other methods, when both Rumbaugh and Jacobsen joined Booch at Rational. The first result of this collaboration was the Unified Modeling Language (the UML) which was a standard analysis and design notation for object-oriented systems. This standard language was published by the Object Management Group, a non-profit industry standards organization, with the first version being finalized in 1999. Later, a design process (the Unified Process, or UP) was also published as a series of books, while a related set of tools and materials to support this process (the Rational Unified Process, or RUP) was developed by Rational, a company since acquired by IBM. Although in book form the UP is not product-related, it is not currently supported by an open standards organization.

2.3.1 The Unified Modeling Language (UML)

The UML is a very rich modeling language with many different types of diagram (18 in version 2) some of which serve very similar purposes. For example, sequence diagrams and communication diagrams can be used to represent the same information, and state diagrams and activity diagrams also have much in common. Therefore it is not necessary to use all the available diagrams of the UML, but rather to select those that are most useful for a particular type of project. State diagrams, for example, can be particularly helpful in designing hardware control systems, whilst deployment diagrams are appropriate when a system will be distributed across many different machines. Some methods that have evolved since the publication of the UML choose a specific subset of diagrams. Iconix, for example, uses only four types of diagram: the use case model, the sequence diagram, the class diagram and the (otherwise little used) robustness diagram (Rosenburg *et al.*, 2005). We adopt a similar approach in this book, selecting a small number of useful diagrams from the UML along with some extensions developed specifically for designing web applications.

2.3.2 The Unified Process (UP)

The Unified Process is, like the UML, a rich specification with many possible activities and artefacts. Once again we can tailor our use of the process to the practices most appropriate for our application type. As Jacobsen himself has written about the RUP, it *'has grown and become too complex'*, so it's OK to simplify it! (Jacobson, 2004). Perhaps the most important aspect of the UP is that as well as using an iterative approach it describes both phases and disciplines. A phase is a group of iterations that fall within a specific time period within the overall project life cycle, while the disciplines are the various types of activity that take place during each iteration. The overall approach of the UP is neatly summed up by a commonly used 'whale diagram' image that shows the relationship between iterations, phases and disciplines (Figure 2.3). The 'whales' are the curves that show the level of activity in each discipline at various stages of the development process. Although the image is just an

FIGURE 2.3   The Unified Process 'whale' diagram

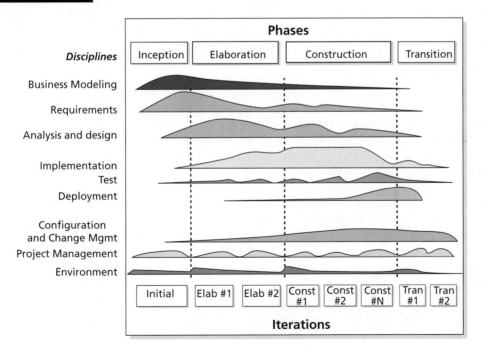

example of how the various activities in a project might move in and out of focus over time, it gives a clear idea of how an iterative process changes its emphasis as it moves through the various phases. This equates to the iterative model in Figure 2.2. To make sense of the rest of the diagram, we will look at the four phases of the UP, which appear across the top of the diagram, and the iterations that occur within them.

The inception phase

During the inception phase we explore a project to a sufficient stage to understand if it is viable. This means gathering the initial requirements, investigating relevant technical issues and building software prototypes where necessary to act as proofs of concept. During this phase, new technologies and frameworks may be investigated to evaluate whether or not they would be good choices for the project in hand. At the end of the inception phase, we should have enough information to know whether the project as a whole has a realistic chance of success, and we should also have a draft plan for the entire project, including a total budget and an overall time frame. The disciplines of the UP show that during this phase we also have to establish the development environment and processes to manage software configuration and change. For a simple project, or one that is treading familiar ground, a single iteration may be sufficient for this phase. For large projects or those that involve substantially new technology and tools, more iterations will be required. At the end of each iteration, a specific milestone should be met and a meaningful deliverable should result. For example, an iteration in the inception phase might be required to deliver a working proof of concept using a particular code framework, application server and database, along with a project plan and a budget. Experimental prototypes are sometimes known as *spikes* (Cockburn, 2005).

The elaboration phase

In many ways this is the most important phase, as it demonstrates the viability (or not) of the chosen software architecture. The most important deliverable from the elaboration phase is an 'executable architecture', which we can think of as being similar to the foundations and load bearing structure (framework) of a building. Although it may take fewer people and less time for a building's foundations to be laid and its steel skeleton to be built, when compared to the time and labor required to complete all the cladding, internal walls and fittings, it is a more crucial phase. The foundations and framework need to be able to support all the subsequent work or the building will collapse, like many a software project has in the past. In a software project the executable architecture must provide a suitable foundation and framework for all the subsequent development, so it must meet all the most important requirements of the project and also have addressed its key risk factors. For example, if a project has specific requirements in terms of performance, such as the number of concurrent users that it should be able to support, then the executable architecture should have demonstrated that it can deliver this requirement. Therefore practices such as load testing are important in the elaboration phase. Although the executable architecture can be regarded as being based on a prototype, it is an architectural prototype, which means that it is intended to be refined until it is put into production. This is different from the proof of concept prototypes that are often developed during the inception phase and then discarded once they have performed their roles of demonstrating or testing alternative approaches. Rather than a spike, it is a *walking skeleton*; the beginning of the framework what will endure throughout the rest of the system lifetime (Cockburn, 2005). Due to the importance of this phase, there may be several iterations.

The construction phase

In this phase, all the necessary components are added to the existing executable architecture. This is like adding the cladding, internal walls and fittings to a building. During this phase there may be some minor changes to the executable architecture due to new or changing requirements, but its core functionality should be stable. However, we should be able to be very flexible in terms of the components that we are developing within the framework. At the end of the construction phase we should have a complete software product that is ready for alpha testing. Unless the project is small, there will be many iterations in the construction phase.

The transition phase

In this final phase, the system moves from the development environment into its deployment environment, so at the end of the phase it should be in use. Activities from this phase can include alpha, beta and acceptance testing, installation, manufacture (in the case of shrink wrapped software), parallel running and user training. We might regard this phase as being similar to the handover of a new building to its owners. The number of iterations will depend on the type of project and its means of construction. For example an open source project that will deploy on the web could easily have a transition phase with a single iteration, while a large custom built system for a client with many sites running mission critical systems would require more. Figure 2.4 summarizes the building metaphor with the phases of the UP.

FIGURE 2.4   The phases of the Unified Process applied to a building metaphor

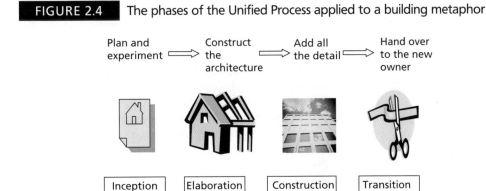

2.3.3 How long is an iteration?

In our discussion of phases we made no mention of how long an iteration should be. The general practice is to make all iterations a similar length, so that the project gets its own rhythm. How long each iteration should be is open to debate, but something around four weeks is common and anything from two to six weeks is reasonable. Anything less than two weeks is unlikely to be long enough to produce a meaningful milestone, while iterations over six weeks may lead to a lack of project rhythm and not provide the project as a whole with enough milestones to keep it on track. Within an iteration there will also be 'time boxed' activities that have their own internal deadlines based on estimations of effort and duration. The difference between effort (how much consistent effort it would take in an ideal world to produce a required artefact) and duration (how long it actually takes) is due to the realities of distractions such as meetings, holiday, illness, fire alarms and a whole host of other time-consuming events and activities. Various techniques can be used to estimate the actual time required for each task, but the best way is just to learn by experience how long a particular task will take. Definition of tasks may be done by use cases, or user stories, and with experience these can be written with a given scope in mind. Of course the number of iterations multiplied by the length of an iteration gives you how long you plan the whole project to take.

2.4 A web application inception phase

In the rest of this chapter we will look at some activities that might be appropriate during the inception phase. Taking the diagram in Figure 2.2 as a rough guide (while acknowledging that this is not meant to indicate anything other than a general impression of the process) we can see that we might expect this phase to include some initial analysis and design, as well as business modeling and requirements gathering. In fact we might regard most of this book as describing activities that are appropriate to the inception phase, in the sense that we will be exploring technologies that may be new to you and demonstrating some simple proof of concept code. As Figure 2.2 suggests, we will be doing some coding, some testing and quite a bit of exploration of a software environment. None of the application code in this book is quite sophisticated enough to be regarded as an industrial strength architectural prototype, in fact it could be regarded as a series of spikes. However it should provide enough material to enable a more extensible framework to be built. Taken together it builds into something that could be regarded as a walking skeleton for further development.

The intention of the examples that we work through in the rest of this chapter is to give some flavor of how the initial business modeling and analysis process is one of investigation and discovery, where we continually revise our initial assumptions in the light of experience and experiment. Therefore you will see that we do not present something that is seen as initially perfect, rather we present a starting point that we refine as we further explore the requirements and utilize the various analysis tools and techniques. Software development is essentially a team effort where individual skills and relationships are crucial, something that is hard to replicate in book form. Therefore you should regard the following examples as artefacts that would evolve through a process of negotiation and discussion, rather than there being one 'right answer'. Every software problem has a number of potential solutions, each with their own pros and cons. One other thing is for sure, every real-world software project is far more complex than it may at first appear!

2.5 Modeling requirements

The first step in developing any web application must be to establish the business objectives (part of the business modeling discipline of the UP). There was a time in the 'dot com' boom of the 1990s when web-based systems were developed with little realistic idea of the business objectives apart from the fact that everyone else already had a website so *'we need one too'*. Times have changed, so now there is more focus on aspects such as *return on investment* (ROI). A good focus for discussing the business objectives is to agree on a mission statement for the application, which neatly summarizes the point of the exercise.

In this book we will use a simplified case study based on a home insurance web application. This is a fictional scenario within which we will analyze and design our system.

Web Home Cover is a new enterprise set up to provide home insurance over the web. The business case is based on providing a service that is entirely on-line and therefore highly efficient in terms of the initial capital investment required by the insurance company. Since the company will only operate via the web, it must have a web application that meets the needs of all its customers and staff. It must also be written to ensure that it will work for as many web clients as possible, from desk top computers to mobile devices.

This is a possible mission statement for the project:

To bring home insurance services to every corner of the web.

This is the essence of the business case for our home insurance web application. It is short and to the point. Long buzzword bingo phrases are best left out of the mission statement.

2.5.1 Web application requirements gathering

The first step we must take on the road to actually building a web-based solution is to identify the high-level requirements (or business objectives) of the proposed system. This is rather difficult in many cases, since we may not know who our actual users will be. If the web application is intended only for a company intranet (an application that is used only internally within the organization) then it will be quite easy to find out who the potential users of the system are. If, however, we are launching an e-commerce website then we are aiming our application at a largely unknown mass of users in cyberspace. How, then, can we work out what their requirements might be? There are a number of approaches we can take. One common approach is to use focus groups, where a small number of people who are representative of our possible user base are brought together to answer questions and offer opinions in a structured and controlled context, using sample materials. Another approach is to use marketing staff to take on the role of possible users and represent their requirements, presumably on the basis that their job is to tell people what they want. In either case we need to develop a set of user profiles that will give us an idea about whose needs we are trying to meet. These user profiles can be simple demographic summaries (e.g. the age range, sex, interests, average income, etc. of our expected users) or rather more sophisticated 'personas' where fictional biographies are developed of our supposed typical users. Whoever we use to represent our actual users, at some point we need to gather a suitable set of stakeholders (those who have an interest in the system, either directly or indirectly) into a room and get them to write down an initial set of requirements in an activity known as a *joint requirements workshop*. This does not require sophisticated tools, the usual ones being flip chart pads or whiteboards and pens. Instead of the usual brainstorming approach, card storming might be used to encourage full participation. Whereas with brainstorming the participants have to take turns to call out their contributions, which can be frustrating for some and intimidating for others, in a card storming approach everyone simultaneously writes each of their contributions on a separate card. The cards are all pooled and then explored together by the group. Experience suggests that the 'magic' number of core requirements likely to emerge from such sessions is 12 (more or less), though it depends on the level of detail that you want to aim for.

We now imagine a requirements workshop for the Web Home Cover project. Who might our stakeholders be? For our purposes we might imagine a group comprising the lead software developer, the project manager, the database administrator, the marketing person who ran the focus groups (armed with a set of user profiles), the sales manager, a claims assessor and one of the insurance underwriters. By the time all the doughnuts have gone, the flip chart pads on the wall have a list of (13) requirements that looks something like this:

1. New users should be able to get an instant quote for buildings insurance
2. New users should be able to get an instant quote for contents insurance
3. If they want, new users should have the option to apply for both, or either, type of home insurance cover
4. Policy holders should be able to check their current policies and request changes using a secure login
5. New users should be able to check the status of their application using a secure login
6. Call center staff should be able to view and query all policy details using a secure login
7. Underwriters should be able to access all applications waiting for processing using a secure login
8. New users should be able to retrieve previous quotations immediately, even if they have not yet applied for a policy
9. The website should provide enough information for users to contact the company by email, telephone or in writing
10. Users should be able to access the system from both desk top and mobile devices
11. Policy holders should be able to make claims against their policies
12. The system should be available 24/7/365 and be able to cope with 10,000 concurrent users
13. The system should have a telepathic user interface

There are some things to note about this set of requirements. First, while most of them are functional requirements (what the system should do), some are non-functional (the way that the system should do what it does). For example, a functional requirement is that 'new users should be able to get an instant quote for buildings insurance'. This is something the system must do for its users. Examples of non-functional requirements are the ability to access the system from multiple devices or the system being available all the time. These are not things that the system does but characteristics of how it delivers those things. Some requirements need further exploration, for example the last two are somewhat extreme but are meant to indicate some important considerations. While it may be desirable for a system to be available all the time, we must consider how much it costs to do this versus the real need. Likewise the requirement that includes an optimistic prediction of the possible number of concurrent users. We have all heard of a few websites that were so popular that they quickly imploded under the strain of serving all their users. However, the history of the dot com era had rather more examples of systems that anticipated huge numbers of users but ended up with a trickle. Performance and availability requirements, likewise security requirements, should always be looked at carefully by applying a cost benefit analysis. For each requirement, we have to ask how much it would cost for the 'perfect' solution as opposed to an acceptable solution. The 'telepathic user interface' requirement comes from a Dilbert cartoon, but again has a serious point, which is that requirements often use arbitrary requests like 'the interface must be user-friendly' which are in fact meaningless. Requirements must be both realistic and measurable. Proposing a system that must pass certain usability or learnability metrics (measures) would be more useful.

2.5.2 Prioritizing requirements

Once we have a set of initial requirements, we need to prioritize them. This is important in an iterative development approach because we have to schedule the requirements over different iterations. Therefore if requirements will be delivered at different points in the development lifecycle then we should address the more important requirements first, particularly since new requirements may appear during the process. If any requirements get pushed to the back of the queue by this process then they should be those with a lower priority. It is not necessary to put all the requirements in order. In many cases, four levels of priority are considered acceptable, sometimes classified as:

1. Must have
2. Should have
3. Could have
4. Want to have

This prioritization method is sometimes referred to using the acronym *MoSCoW*.

One useful approach to the prioritization exercise is to have the participants vote for their requirements in two rounds from different perspectives, possibly using some multiple voting mechanism (such as the participants having 4 votes each). For example round 1 could be prioritizing requirements from a customer viewpoint, and round 2 could be prioritizing the requirements from the viewpoint of the staff.

Since it is difficult to cast a vote while in the context of a text book, we will have to assume that we have performed this exercise and come to some conclusions. Bearing in mind our mission statement, it would appear that the following requirements are 'must haves'.

1. New users should be able to get an instant quote for buildings insurance
2. New users should be able to get an instant quote for contents insurance
3. If they want, new users should have the option to apply for both, or either, type of home insurance cover
7. Underwriters should be able to access all applications waiting for processing using a secure login
10. Users should be able to access the system from both desktop and mobile devices
11. Policy holders should be able to make claims against their policies

With these requirements in place we can sell insurance over the web and reach as many people as possible

What are the 'should haves'? These are still pretty much core functions. Perhaps the following requirements fall under this category:

4. Policy holders should be able to check their current policies and request changes using a secure login
6. Call center staff should be able to view and query all policy details using a secure login
9. The website should provide enough information for users to contact the company by email, telephone or in writing

With these requirements we can help retain and support our existing customers and provide maximum opportunity to attract new business.

The following requirements are probably best categorized as 'could haves':

5. New users should be able to check the status of their application using a secure login
8. New users should be able to retrieve previous quotations immediately, even if they have not yet applied for a policy

We can live without these, but they could provide some benefit to our users. They might be regarded as 'sugar' (handy but non-essential).

These are our final two requirements:

12. The system should be available 24/7/365 and be able to cope with 10,000 concurrent users
13. The system should have a telepathic user interface

These will have to be put into the 'would like to have' category, at least for the moment. They certainly need some further work before being taken seriously as priority requirements.

What is the point of this exercise? It enables us to schedule the important requirements first when developing the system. Agile approaches would use 'story cards' for requirements, with each card representing a user story about what the system should do. By prioritizing these cards, we can put them into various iterations, with the most important in the early iterations.

2.6 Analysis tools – domain models, use cases and storyboards

In this section we introduce some basic UML notations that can help us to visualize key features of the application. Even if a development project takes an agile approach that does not worry about extensive formal documentation, using standard notations for descriptive sketches can be very useful as a common communication medium between developers and users.

2.6.1 The domain model

A useful model to build before getting into details about the system use cases is a domain model that captures the key concepts of the business domain. The domain model helps us to begin to understand how various important concepts of the domain interact in a structural way. Again, we should develop the domain model in a workshop environment. Some analysis methods suggest that the domain model should grow piecemeal out of the use case analysis, but the advantage of developing one early is that it provides a common vocabulary within which the following stages of the analysis can take place. This ensures that, for example, different threads of the analysis do not end up using two different names for the same concept because everyone can work from, and enhance, the same domain model. The model itself captures a few simple ideas:

- What are the key concepts in the domain?
- Which concepts interact with each other?
- How can we describe these interaction relationships?
- What is the *cardinality* of these interactions? (In other words, which relationships are one to one, which are one to many, and which are many to many?)

We can begin to identify the core concepts in our domain by identifying nouns in our core requirements. From our set of objectives we can find the following 27 nouns (plural nouns have been made singular) that can be our candidate list of concepts for the domain model. We might imagine them brainstormed onto a white board or card stormed onto sticky notes and then stuck on the wall (Figure 2.5).

FIGURE 2.5   Candidate list of concepts for the domain model

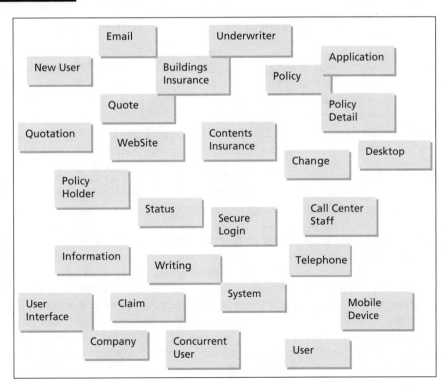

From this list we can exclude anything clearly outside the system boundary (desktop, telephone, writing), the boundary itself (user interface) or nouns that refer to the system as a whole (website, system). We should also get rid of synonyms ('user' and 'concurrent user' are other words for more specific types of user, 'quote' and 'quotation' are the same thing) and properties of other concepts (policy detail is a property of policy), though properties can be added to their matching concept if they look useful. 'Detail' is a very vague property of a policy, but 'status' might be a useful property of an application so we might choose to include it in the diagram. In this revised list (Figure 2.6), we have struck out ten of the candidate concepts, leaving seventeen (including the 'status' property).

FIGURE 2.6 Modified list of candidate concepts

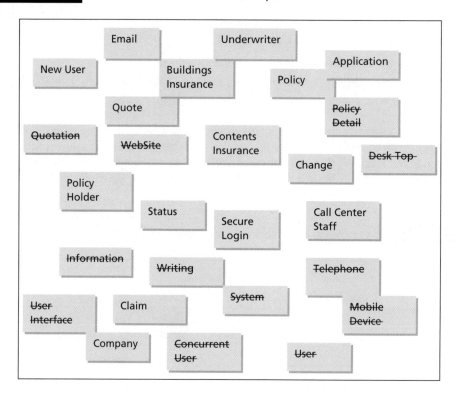

From these we draw an initial domain model (Figure 2.7). This consists of rectangles for each concept, labelled with the concept name. Any properties that are immediately evident can also be added, separated from the concept name by a horizontal line. Concepts that have some kind of relationship with one another are linked by 'association' lines, which are labelled with text that describes the association. Arrow heads by the text can be used to show the direction in which the label should be read (for example we are saying that a policy holder *lives at* an address, not that an address *lives at* a policy holder). By default, an association line implies that the cardinality of the relationship is 'one to one', for example there is one policy holder to one account. To show a 'one to many' relationship we use the asterisk (*), so for example one policy can have many claims made against it. If the asterisk appears at both ends of an association then this means a 'many to many' association. In our domain model, one call center staff member may query many policies, and a single policy may be queried by many call

FIGURE 2.7　A domain model for the home insurance system

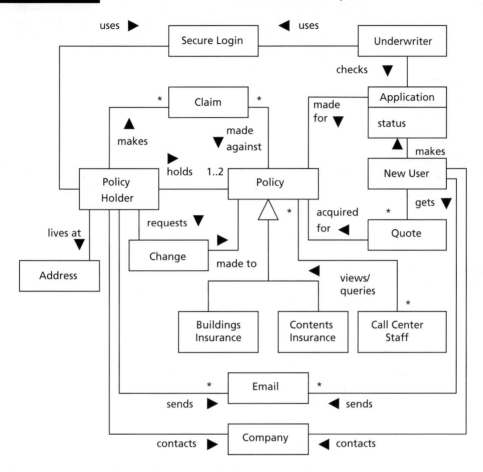

center staff members. Occasionally we can define a cardinality number or range more exactly. For example we know that a policy holder will have either exactly one policy (buildings OR contents insurance) or exactly two policies (both buildings AND contents insurance).

Sometimes we identify concepts that appear to be specializations or generalizations of one another. In our model we have policies, but we also have references to contents insurance policies and buildings insurance polices. The concept of a 'Policy' here could be seen as a generalization of the two more specific (specialized) types of policy. We indicate this in the domain model using an arrow with an open triangular head pointing from the specializations to the generalization. Initial assumptions like this in the domain model may be modified later. We may find that the 'Policy' generalization is not useful. Alternatively we may find that we need a generalization of 'New User' and 'Policy Holder', the 'User' concept that we previously discarded. These kinds of decision are made as we evolve the analysis domain model into a design class model, as the process of iterative analysis and design gives us more information about the concepts in our model. A class model shows concepts that will become software artefacts in the implementation. Some concepts will not become classes, whereas many new classes will be introduced as the need for them becomes evident.

Now that we have a domain model, we can use it as a guide in the use cases. For example, there should be no ambiguities about whether we should use the concept name 'Quote' or 'Quotation' in the use cases. We check the domain model and use 'Quote'. At this stage it is useful also to start building a glossary for the system (on a web page, of course) which defines our interpretation of what these concept names mean.

2.6.2 Use case diagrams

Use case diagrams are very simple. They help us to show the different types of users and the goals they have in using a system. Because they are an analysis tool they do not anticipate any specific type of technology and do not anticipate how the system will actually deliver its requirements. All they do is specify what those requirements are (in a very broad way). Figure 2.8 shows the notation for the main component types in a use case diagram.

FIGURE 2.8   Use case diagram notation

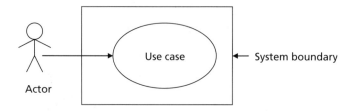

As you can see, there are only three, the actor, the use case and the system boundary. Use cases are inside the system boundary and the actors are outside. Arrows are used to indicate which actors use which use case(s). It is important to note that actors do not represent individual people, rather they represent different roles that different people can take when using the system. In some cases, the same person might take on different roles at different times. In our system for example, a person my be a member of the call center staff but may also apply for insurance as a 'new user'. Similarly, 'new users' will change into 'policy holders' if their policy applications are approved. In addition, actors are not always roles taken by people. They can equally be representative of other systems or manual processes. For this reason, we sometimes see the arrows going out from a use case to an actor representing an external system.

Actors and use cases describe *roles and goals*. Each actor should be named using a noun that describes a user role, as opposed to an individual, for example 'Policy Holder'. Each use case should describe a user's goal in using the system, so they should be named using verb phrases (e.g. 'Apply for Policy'). Although in some cases there may be a one-to-one correspondence between a use case and a requirement, a single use case may also meet more than one requirement. You will see an example of this later in this chapter.

Figure 2.9 shows a use case diagram taken from the functional requirements we listed in our workshop. Note that we have five actors taken from our requirements, 'new user',

FIGURE 2.9 A use case diagram for the home insurance web application

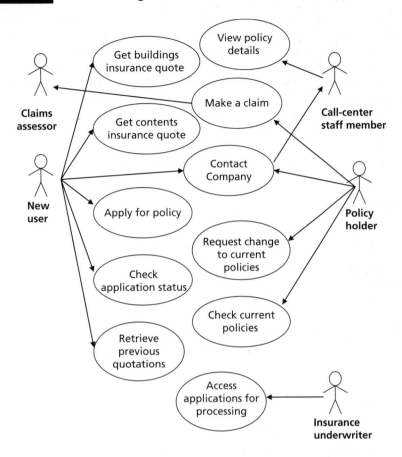

'policy holder', 'call center staff', 'claims assessor' and 'insurance underwriter'. There are ten use cases. Note how some actors have associations with more than one use case.

Use case realization

Once we have decided on what our use cases should be, we have to find some way of showing what happens inside them. This is known as a *use case realization*. There are a number of different notations that we can use to do this, ranging from simple text descriptions to various diagrams. Here, we introduce some sequence diagram notation from the UML along with some informal storyboarding. Since we are designing a web application, the realization is specific to an environment where the actors interact with page-based presentations. Sequence diagrams capture user interaction with the system, while storyboards are useful for modeling page-based systems because they provide a simple way of describing the page flow and alternate paths that are typical of web applications. They can also be used to informally describe the layout and content of web pages. To link web pages and our UML diagrams we can use the Web Application Extensions (WAE) to the UML for designing web-based systems (Conallen, 1999). These are a special set of icons that can be used in UML models to represent components that are specific to web applications, such as web pages.

Use case descriptions

Before embarking on drawing diagrams, however, we begin by writing a textual description of each use case that summarizes the sequence of interactions that the actor has with
the system. It will also capture any selections or iterations that take place. The nature of
these textual descriptions varies from project to project, and some suggested formats and
contents are much stricter and more complex than others. The approach we suggest here
is to keep things simple but to number each interaction. This makes it easier to 'plug in'
alternative sequences of events. The style of a use case description is conversational, this is,
it describes a series of actor requests and system responses, in pairs.

As an example, we will begin with the 'Get Buildings Insurance Quote' use case. In the
text description, we capture some important information:

- The name of the use case
- The actor(s) that use it
- The start page (this is specific to a web application)
- A brief description of what happens in the use case

Here is the example use case:

Use Case Name: *Get Buildings Insurance Quote*

Actors: *New user*

Start page: *Home page*

Use Case Description:

1. The actor chooses to get an insurance quote
2. The system requests the actor's personal details
3. The actor enters his/her personal details
4. The system displays a choice of available insurance quotes
5. The actor chooses to get a buildings insurance quote
6. The system requests information about the building to be insured
7. The actor enters data about the building
8. The system displays the buildings quote

2.6.3 System sequence diagrams

Now that we have a textual description of the use case, we can draw a system sequence
diagram. This shows the interactions between the actor and the system in a notation from
the UML.

The components of a system sequence diagram are the actor for the use case, the
component(s) that they interact with, labelled arrows showing the messages that pass
between the actor and the other components and a vertical time axis. In fact it is possible
to draw sequence diagrams with a horizontal time axis but this is not usually supported by
software tools. The component type that an actor interacts with is known as a boundary

object, because it exists on the boundary between the system and the actors. Therefore a boundary object is usually some kind of graphical interface component. In a web application, this will be accessed via web pages. The UML notation for a boundary object is shown in Figure 2.10.

FIGURE 2.10   UML notation for a boundary object

Here is our system sequence diagram (Figure 2.11):

FIGURE 2.11   A system sequence diagram

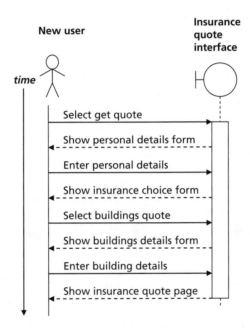

2.6.4 Designing pages and webflow with storyboards

If you have seen system sequence diagrams before, you may notice that the one in Figure 2.11 is a bit different from the norm in that it indicates the forms and pages being displayed by the system interface boundary object. In a web application the interaction is via a series of pages, so the view of the system from the actor perspective is page-based. By using the style of sequence diagram in Figure 2.11 we can begin to explore the pages and their sequences that will be used in the storyboards. The sequences of pages that appear in a use case are sometimes known as a *webflow*, which is simply a use case workflow that uses a series of web pages to achieve its goal.

Since our interactions are with a web application, via web pages, we will utilize the web page icon from the UML Web Application Extensions in some of our diagrams (Figure 2.12a). Web pages are *'architecturally significant components'* that exist both in the analysis and design models and the coded system (Conallen, 1999). The pages may be coded in static mark-up (e.g. HTML) or be dynamic pages generated by programming tools (e.g. .NET Web Forms). Using the formal symbols can be useful in documentation and artefacts created in software packages. However, when informally working through the analysis on paper or whiteboards, it is often easier just to use *stereotype* labels to indicate components like web pages (Figure 2.12b). Whether you use symbols or stereotypes is up to you, and the symbols do not have to be exact. Indeed, Conallen himself uses different version of the symbols in different published sources (see Conallen (1999) and Conallen (2001)).

FIGURE 2.12   The UML extension symbol for a web page (a) and its stereotype equivalent (b)

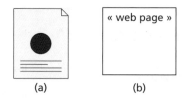

(a)   (b)

Having outlined the user interaction in the system sequence diagram, we might usefully draw a first cut of a storyboard, representing the pages that are accessed during the use case (Figure 2.13). For this initial storyboard we will describe only the page names, navigation routes and events that trigger the transitions between pages.

FIGURE 2.13   A simple storyboard

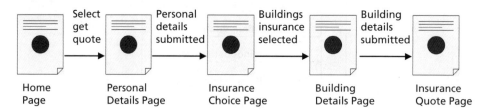

Because storyboarding is an informal design tool, there is little consensus on notation, style or even when it should be done. Some developers suggest you can create an entire website storyboard in one step. Whilst this can work for simple sites that are mostly static content, more dynamic and complex web applications require a more incremental approach. Therefore we suggest the approach of developing a storyboard for each use case. Eventually, all the storyboards can be collected together to summarize the navigation paths of the entire web application.

One option for a storyboard is to define the types of page using the UML extension symbols for client pages and forms (Figure 2.14) rather than using the generic web page icon from Figure 2.12.

Note that in this notation, we normally use the form icon as a composition component of a client page (the black diamond indicates that the page is partly composed of the form). However if we follow the *one form per page* usability pattern (Graham, 2002), also known

FIGURE 2.14   UML extension symbols for a client page (a) and a form (b)

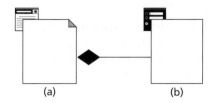

(a)   (b)

2

as *button gravity*, because it puts the emphasis on a single 'submit' button on each page, then we can dispense with the separate page icon and use the form icon to represent a complete form page.

Looking at each page in turn, we might define the home page and buildings quote page using the 'client page' icon, whereas the others use the 'form' icon. There is no requirement to use these symbols, but they can help to visualize a typical webflow, which will frequently start from a client page, then move through one or more form pages, gathering data in a 'Wizard' style, and finally arrive at a summary page that shows the user the result of the webflow (Figure 2.15).

FIGURE 2.15   Page types for the 'Get Buildings Insurance Quote' storyboard

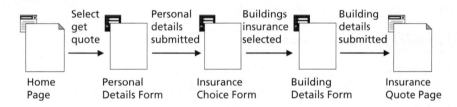

| Home Page | Personal Details Form | Insurance Choice Form | Building Details Form | Insurance Quote Page |

2.7 Building further use cases

So far, so good. We have written some use case realization for the 'Get Buildings Insurance Quote' use case and we have a simple storyboard, but as we are performing analysis activities we have made no attempt to consider data types, page layout, component types or any other aspect that would be considered a design activity. Now we move on to the 'Get Contents Insurance Quote' use case. We could, of course, start writing a separate use case description, but it would soon become obvious that we start off in exactly the same way, by gathering the user's personal details and offering a choice of insurance quotes. How do we progress? We might consider adding a use case to gather the user's personal details, which we then progress from to create the two use cases for different types of insurance. However, this implies that getting the two types of insurance quote are exclusive acts. Do we want a user to have to go through two separate use cases if they want both contents *and* buildings insurance? Once we begin to think about this, it becomes clear that we don't really want two separate use cases for the two types of insurance. In fact we want one use case ('Get Insurance Quote') that is flexible enough for the user to be able to get a buildings insurance quote, a contents insurance quote, or both. In other words we have one use case that meets two requirements. With this in mind, let's revisit our existing use case and consider the need for *alternate flows*.

An alternate flow occurs when the activities in a single use case may take different paths depending on some condition. In this example, the condition is the user's choice of insurance. Here is a modified use case description for the renamed 'Get Insurance Quote' use case.

Use Case Name: *Get Insurance Quote*

Actors: *New user*

Start page: *Home page*

Use Case Description:

1. The actor chooses to get an insurance quote
2. The system requests the actor's personal details
3. The actor enters his/her personal details
4. The system displays a choice of available insurance quotes
5. The actor chooses to get a buildings insurance quote
6. The system requests information about the building to be insured
7. The actor enters data about the building
8. The system displays the buildings quote

Alternate flow – contents insurance only

5. (a) The actor chooses to get a contents insurance quote
6. (a) The system requests information about the contents to be insured
7. (a) The actor enters data about the contents
8. (a) The system displays the contents quote

Alternate flow – both types of insurance

5. (b) The actor chooses to get both a buildings insurance quote and a contents insurance quote 6, 7, 6(a), 7(a)
8. (b) The system displays both a contents quote, a buildings quote and a total

With a modified use case, we need a modified system sequence diagram. This can be seen in Figure 2.16. There is an important addition to the notation in this diagram, which is how we should show selection between alternate flows. There has historically been a degree of confusion and lack of clarity about this in the UML, but we usually show conditional statements by using square brackets, e.g. [Select buildings quote OR select both quotes]. In our diagram we then use a larger square bracket to indicate the set of operations which are part of that conditional block. There are some more complex notations but they do not have much in the way of added value over this simple version.

As well as an updated system sequence diagram, we have a modified storyboard that shows the alternate flows. In this version we also use the two icons for client pages and forms to emphasize the 'Wizard' style webflow of a series of forms for user input (Figure 2.17).

FIGURE 2.16 The modified system sequence diagram

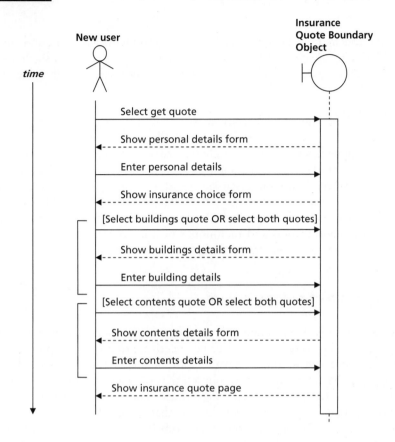

FIGURE 2.17 Updated storyboard with 'client page' and 'form (page)' icons

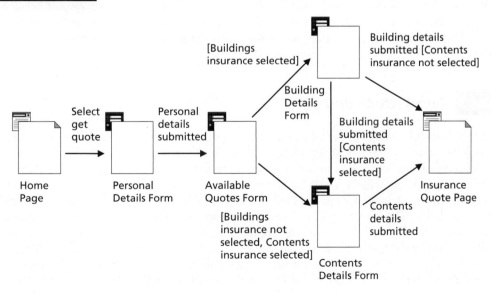

2.8 From analysis to design

So far we have touched on the key stages of the requirements gathering and analysis processes for developing a web application by exploring some aspects of a single use case. In the last part of this chapter we will introduce some concepts related to moving from analysis to design.

In an iterative process, the transfer from analysis to design can be seamless, simply a matter of continually adding more detail. However the level of documentation that we use in the analysis discipline has the important characteristic of being largely non-technical and understandable by non-developers. As such, analysis documents like use case diagrams and storyboards can be directly used in discussions with customers and potential users. As we move into design, we begin to move away from diagrams that are readily comprehended to those outside the development team and move either into more detailed diagrams that clearly reflect the chosen tools and techniques of implementation, or, if using an agile approach, simply embody the emergent design in the code itself.

2.8.1 Design is technology aware

Requirements analysis is about defining the problem domain and specifying how we anticipate the system will be used from the user perspective. From this viewpoint it is technology agnostic, meaning that we do not have to know about the technology used to solve the problem, only the characteristics of the solution that we want. In contrast, design is about how we plan the solution, so it is technology aware. This means that we cannot design a solution until we know something about the way that we will build it. If you were asked, for example, to design a can opener, you would probably be able to come up with a reasonable design, because you probably already have some idea about the way that can openers work. If, however, you were asked to design a time machine, you would probably struggle, being unfamiliar with time machine technology. You can contrast this with analyzing the requirements for a time machine, which would be perfectly possible in the absence of knowing about the design. Although our analogy suggests that there is large gulf between analysis and design, the transition from analysis to design is a gentle one in an iterative process. Unlike going over a waterfall, our design starts off at a high level, not too far removed from our analysis, and becomes more detailed.

2.8.2 Architectural design

If, to successfully design in detail, you need to understand the technology of the solution, it would be premature to talk about detailed design in the early part of this book. As we work though the chapters and the case study you will learn to use a number of ASP.NET features, and once you know these you will be able to design systems that use them in detail. However, at this stage, our approach to design will be at a higher level, often known as *architectural design*. The overall architectures of web applications reveal some common themes regardless of the actual domain of the application. These common themes can be encapsulated into design patterns, which enable us to reuse design features between different systems. The concepts of design patterns in software first became popular in the 1990s, in particular with the publication of the 'Design Patterns' book in 1995 (Gamma *et al.*, 1995).

This introduced the software community to the idea that common components of software design, developed over multiple applications, could be reused by other applications. These patterns can be expressed in a number of ways, but typically they include some sort of diagram, which may be written using UML or something more informal.

2.8.3 Static and dynamic content

An important consideration in our design will be the balance between static and dynamic content, and how we represent that content. Our design has to take into account how much of the application will be represented by pages that are static (are the same for every client) and how much will have to be dynamically generated content. In most web applications there will be a proportion of the site that consists of static content such as HTML, PDF (Portable Document Format), images, video or other types of content that are served to any client. On the other hand any useful web application will almost certainly have to include dynamic content generated on the fly for specific clients, using some type of server page technology. This is why distinguishing between different types of page is useful in design diagrams.

2.9 Webflow design

Earlier in this chapter we introduced some analysis level diagrams that used web application extension symbols to show how the dependencies between a series of form pages and a final client page might describe the structure of a user webflow. While this client-centric view of a webflow is helpful at the analysis stage, because it helps us to visualize how the client interacts with the web application, at the design stage we have to consider both the client and the server. In this section we are going to introduce a design model for webflow that describes the structural relationships between client and server that can support the generation of dynamic content. In the diagrams we introduce another WAE icon, representing a server page (Figure 2.18), which is a page that generates dynamic content.

FIGURE 2.18   The WAE server page icon

We begin with a simple model of a single HTTP request/response interaction, where an HTML form within a static web page submits its content to the server and a client page is dynamically built and sent back to the client. In this first model (Figure 2.19) we assume that the server page both manages any necessary business logic and generates the HTML response.

This model is similar to the ones we introduced at the analysis stage, but includes the server page, which builds the client page dynamically. Although this model of dependencies

FIGURE 2.19 The structure of a form on a static web page, submitted to a server
page that builds a client page

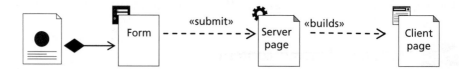

works within the context of a single request/response cycle, it has some drawbacks. The main problem is that we started with an assumption that the form was part of a static web page. This mix of static and dynamic pages does not work particularly well. For example, if the form is not dynamically generated then it cannot be repopulated with error messages and previous entries if the user makes a mistake when entering data to the form. This means that the user would have to start again from scratch if the data they entered was for some reason invalid. Another serious problem is that it may not be possible to maintain a user's 'session' over a series of interactions. HTTP is a 'stateless protocol', which means that it does not maintain connections between a client and a server. Instead, each request/ response cycle may use a new connection to the server. Because of this, the server cannot 'remember' the client using the HTTP connection, so instead we have to manage a server-side session component, which keeps track of a particular user. Each session on the server has a unique identifier for the client, and that identifier must also be available to the client. Then, when the client sends a request, the session ID can be sent along with the request and the server can locate the client session with the matching ID. The problem with this is that the preferred way to store the session ID on the client is in a browser *cookie* (a cookie is a small piece of text-based data that a browser can extract from an HTTP response and store in a file), but the user may have chosen to disable cookies in their browser. If this is the case, the server must use an alternative way of storing the session ID on the client, and this requires the use of dynamically generated web pages, because the session ID has to be written into the pages themselves.

2.9.1 Dynamic client pages

Given the problem with mixing static and dynamic content described above, our next design model uses only dynamically generated client pages (Figure 2.20). This makes it possible for the server to guarantee that it can handle the client's session. It is also possible for the server page to build, and rebuild, the form page, so that if the user makes a mistake when filling in the form, a new form page can be provided that contains the data they have already entered along with the necessary error messages, to help them to correct their entries.

FIGURE 2.20 Page structure that includes dynamic form generation

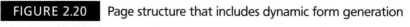

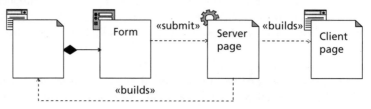

Now, the server page dynamically generates a client page with a form, which submits back to same server page until the next client page can be generated. Although this is a somewhat simple model, it provides the basic static structure that can provide the foundation for a dynamic webflow. There is a problem, however, in that the server page is now tasked with making decisions about the webflow and generating one of two possible pages, either an updated form or the next client page. To provide a better separation of concerns a common architectural approach is to include an *action object* that takes responsibility for webflow decisions. The action object can then delegate to further server pages to either regenerate the form page or build the next client page (Figure 2.21). In the .NET framework the action objects are implemented as Web Form event handlers.

FIGURE 2.21   Including an action object and specialized server pages

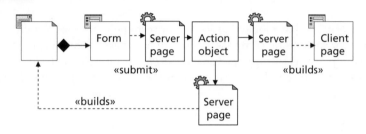

2.9.2 Modeling dynamic webflow

The diagrams we have used so far are static diagrams showing the relationships between different web components. In order to visualize the dynamic webflow that these components contribute to, it can be useful to sketch some sequence diagrams. The sequence diagram in Figure 2.22 includes some of the participating components from the static model in Figure 2.21, identifying the messages that pass between them over time. In this case we are only modeling the situation where the original form does not have to be regenerated, but this can easily be added to the diagram using a condition, as we did in Figure 2.16.

FIGURE 2.22   Modeling the dynamic webflow with a sequence diagram

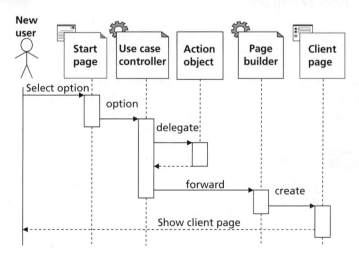

The diagram in Figure 2.22 represents the typical interactions in one request response cycle for a web application. However, before digging any deeper into our own designs we must first explore in more detail what we mean by a *server page* and an *action object*. We also need to understand what we mean by 'forward', how a server page 'delegates' to an action object, and so on. We will also need to see how we can represent the contents of our domain concepts on web pages. In the chapters that follow we will explore all of these concepts and the necessary technologies to implement them and build a complete design once we understand how all the various components can work together.

2.10 Design patterns for web page structure

The design patterns we have looked at so far address the higher level architecture of the system in terms of server-side components. In the final part of this chapter we will look at some page design patterns that are relevant to the client. Like the patterns described previously, these patterns are reusable across many different web applications. The patterns we will be looking at are:

- Site logo at top left
- Use cases and the navigation bar
- Breadcrumbs
- Three-region layout
- Home page
- Site map
- Store content in the database

The main focus of these patterns is usability, making it easy for the user to navigate our web applications. These patterns all come from 'A Pattern Language for Web Usability' (Graham, 2002).

2.10.1 Site logo at top left

The site logo at top left pattern is a very simple one, but one that you will see commonly used across the web. The site logo, as well as appearing at the top left-hand corner of the page (as the name of the pattern suggests) should also always act as a hyperlink back to the site's home page (Figure 2.23). The point of this pattern is that it enables the user at any time to have a quick and easy route back to the home page. Once you are aware of this pattern, it is very irritating to visit sites that do not use it!

FIGURE 2.23 The 'site logo at top left' pattern

2.10.2 Use cases and the navigation bar pattern

Earlier, we introduced use cases as a way of specifying our actors' high level goals for the web application. These main use cases will be starting points for user navigation. Within these high level use cases, there may be a number of more detailed use cases that relate to specific tasks. The navigation bar pattern is a way of providing the user with a simple way of navigating a website based on this combination of general tasks and related sub-tasks. The pattern suggests that the main use cases will appear in a navigation bar across the top of the page, making it easy for users to perform the most important functions easily. The left-hand side can be used for service navigation (i.e. what is inside the current use case). This would enable someone to access a high level use case for the navigation bar, for example 'Contact Us', and the service navigation bar might include use case options inside that high level use case, such as 'office locations', 'email addresses', 'departments', etc. Figure 2.24 shows the general layout of a page using the navigation bar pattern.

FIGURE 2.24   The 'navigation bar' pattern

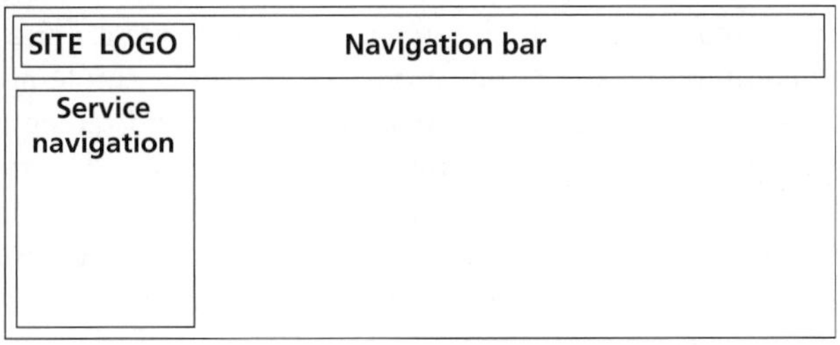

The navigation bar will include the 'site logo at top left' which as we have seen already acts as a home page link. It also typically includes links to information about the organization/company that owns the website, such as their privacy policy and contact information. More specific links will depend on the nature of the web application. For example, e-commerce sites would include things like registration and log-in, checkout, shopping cart and account information. There are a whole range of other possibilities, depending on the type of application. These may include downloadable items, site map, communities, frequently asked questions, news and press releases, jobs, etc.

In the WebHomeCover application, high level uses case for the navigation bar would include those we looked at in the previous chapter, for example 'change policy details'. For this use case the service navigation bar might include detailed use case options from inside that high level use case such as 'change address', 'change level of cover', 'add cover', etc.

2.10.3 The breadcrumbs pattern

The idea of breadcrumbs comes from fairy stories where the characters leave a trail of breadcrumbs through the woods in order to find their way home again. Unfortunately in stories these are usually eaten by birds, leading to disaster, but this is unlikely to happen on websites. The role of breadcrumbs is to tell the user where they are relative to the home page. Each time the user moves to a new page, another breadcrumb is added to the list, so it is easy for the user to see the path they have taken through the site. In addition, the components of the breadcrumb list should be hyperlinked, so clicking on any breadcrumb will take you to that page. Breadcrumbs are often a secondary part of the navigation bar, and may be used in conjunction with a search box (Figure 2.25).

FIGURE 2.25   The 'breadcrumbs' pattern

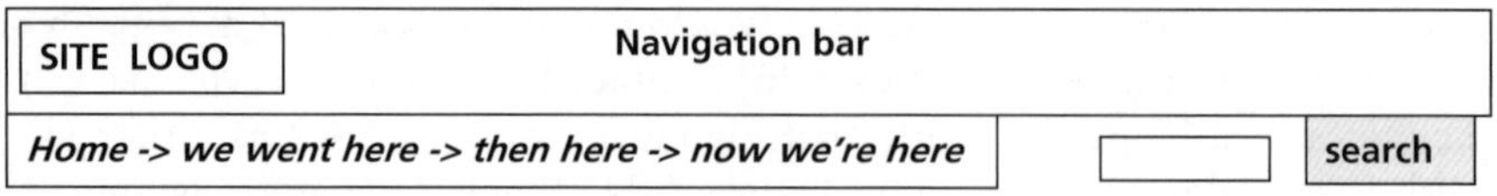

2.10.4 The three-region layout pattern

The three-region layout pattern is actually based largely on the patterns we have already introduced (site logo at top left, use cases and the navigation bar and breadcrumbs). If we use these patterns, two regions, the top and side navigation bars, are already used, and we are left with a main page area, which will contain the current content (Figure 2.26). This pattern is very common in web applications, and it can be implemented using tables, frames or stylesheets. We will favor stylesheets over tables and tables over frames, since one heuristic we should be aware of is 'no frames on public sites!' The main reason for not using frames is that browser support is not very reliable for frames, in particular when presenting pages on the mobile Internet. However we may consider not using the three-region layout at all when supporting mobile clients, and favor simpler approaches that separate out the navigation from the content. We will address these issues when we look at adaptive web applications for mobile clients in a later chapter. In terms of tables, although many sites still use them for structure, ever-increasing browser support for sophisticated stylesheets means that they are becoming the more favored approach.

FIGURE 2.26   The 'three-region layout' pattern

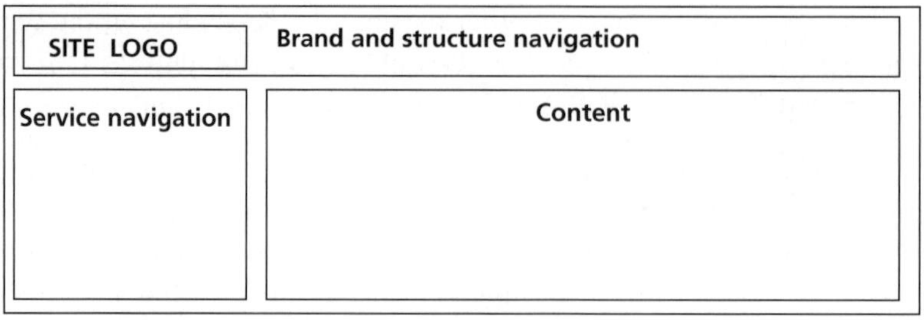

2.10.5 The home page pattern

The previous design pattern we introduced (three-region layout) is recommended as a consistent layout for all the pages on a website. The home page, however, can be an exception to the three-region layout rule, since it has a special role as the starting point for users, and can therefore have some special characteristics. It should not, however, be just a splash screen, which users may find frustrating as it may take a long time to load and run (if, for example, it includes an animation or movie, as some websites favor). Rather, it needs to include navigation to the main use cases to enable the user to quickly and easily get started on their goals. Figure 2.27 shows a suggested outline for the home page pattern. It gives the site logo more prominence than the three-region layout pattern, placing it in the center of the screen. Beneath the logo there is some brief information that should convey the main message of the website. Beneath this message, prominent links, perhaps using buttons or images, provide quick access to all the most important use cases in the system. Finally, some more information about the main features of the site may appear. Overall the intention of the home page pattern is to have a high level of impact while enabling the user to get started on their goals as quickly as possible.

FIGURE 2.27 The 'home page' pattern

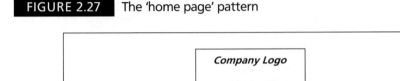

2.10.6 The site map pattern

One of the suggested links for the navigation bar is the site map. Like the home page, the site map has a special role in a web application, because it provides a bird's eye view of the whole application to the user, allowing direct access to any part of the site (or at least those parts that would sensibly allow direct access) without needing to know how to navigate through other pages. Many site maps are just lists of text. However a more interesting and useful site map would provide a workflow overview, showing not just a list of links but a visual map of the routes through the web application. Exactly how the site map might appear depends on the application, but Figure 2.28 indicates some of the features that might be included: visual components that represent hyperlinks to web pages but also some indication of the links that already exist between these pages. There are many ways of laying out a graphical site map. Doing a web search for 'graphical site map' should give you plenty of links to sites with different styles that can be used.

2.10.7 Storing content in the database

Web applications often have to provide the same content across many different pages of a website. Figure 2.29 shows a very simple example of this type of requirement. Here, we may want to add a simple footer ('© WebHomeCover.com 2000-2010') to the bottom of

FIGURE 2.28 The 'site map' pattern

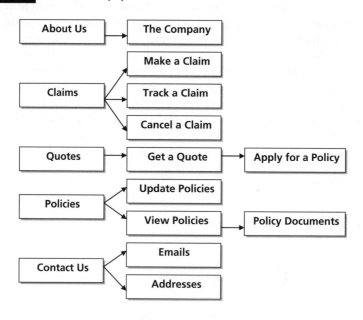

FIGURE 2.29 Reusing content across multiple pages

every page. The last thing we would want to have to do would be to add this to every single page and have to maintain each instance of this data separately. If, for example, we had 154 pages in our web application, and we wanted to update the footer to '© WebHome-Cover.com 2000-2011', we would have to do this 154 times. It should be noted that the footer example has a number of simple solutions, because it is consistent across every page, but it illustrates a concept that is very common in web applications, which is that the same underlying data may need to appear in different ways across different parts of a website. As a more complex example, consider a site where the user logs in. In applications like this, the user's login name, or perhaps some alias, often appears somewhere on the pages that they visit after the point where they have logged in.

The most important pattern that we have in dynamic web applications is simply to store content in a database. Maintaining a web application can get very complex, and we do not want to have to copy and paste large amounts of content for every update to the application. Therefore we need to store content in one place, in the database, and construct pages dynamically. To take our simple 'footer' example, the string of text used for the page footer could be stored in one place, in the database, and read from that database each time it is required in a page. If the footer needs to be updated, it only needs to be updated in one place – the database.

2.10.8 Some general design guidelines

There are many sources for general design guidelines for web applications. These are just one example, taken from Sparks (2004):

Design around existing content, not future content

A web application should be based around what you already have, not what you might have later. This is a basic principle of agile development – we get the simplest thing possible working early and then develop it over time. An over-complex application structure designed to cater for things that might come along later is unnecessary.

Avoid unnecessary images

Images take time to load and every image download is a separate HTTP connection. There are many contexts (e.g. on a mobile device) where this is a major overhead. Don't use images where text will suffice.

Exploit hyperlinks

Use hyperlinks as much as possible. This is really only directly relevant to static rather than dynamic content, since in a lot of dynamic content scenarios we have to guide the user through a restricted set of pathways. However we should make sure that the navigation around our site is well supported by hyperlinks.

Use cascading stylesheets

As well as being difficult to build and maintain, HTML that includes its own presentation can get very large. Using cascading stylesheets (covered in Chapter 4), among other advantages, reduces the size of HTML page downloads and gives us more flexibility and control over website presentation.

Make navigation flow

This is an important aspect of web applications, because the user workflow has to make sense. We need to take care with providing the right number of user pathways from particular points in time. One important aspect is making sure that the user can backtrack correctly from any point in a web application, for example being able to easily get out of the checkout in on-line purchasing situation in a controlled way.

Visit your own site regularly

You are more likely to spot problems in your web applications by approaching them as a user from the outside in, rather than just looking at them from the developer perspective, from the inside out.

Self Study Questions

1. Is the Unified Process a waterfall or an iterative process?
2. What acronym is sometimes used to refer to the four levels of priority for requirements?
3. What type of diagram shows the main concepts and relationships in a system?
4. What name is given to a user in a particular role in a use case diagram?
5. What is a storyboard?
6. In a sequence diagram, in which direction does the time axis usually go?
7. Is a server page used for static content or dynamic content?
8. Where is the site logo commonly found on web pages?
9. What is the purpose of breadcrumbs on a website?
10. What is one way of reducing the size of HTML downloads?

Exercises

2.1. Using the example of a customer login, where the user enters a user name and password into a form on a client page, draw a sequence diagram showing the various interactions. Consider the webflow for both a successful and an unsuccessful login.

2.2. Create the following artefacts for the View Policy Details use case:

- A use case description with at least one alternate flow
- A system sequence diagram
- A storyboard

Are there any updates that you feel are necessary to the domain model?

2.3. This exercise is best done in groups, so you can try out the idea of a requirements workshop. You need to identify some high level requirements for this project, a domain model and a use case diagram:

Project description:

Many research studies rely on questionnaires to gather their data. Doing this on-line can help to improve the number of returns, so your team has been asked to develop a web application to support the creation of web-based research questionnaires. The system needs to be able to gather questionnaire data, store it, allow it to be retrieved and generate simple statistical reports.

In your requirements workshop, adopt some roles that you think would be appropriate to this scenario and consider the requirements of the stakeholders in those roles.

2.4. Design a home page for the WebHomeCover application, selecting the most important use cases and messages from the analysis.

2.5. Design the web page structure for any of the high level use cases described in this chapter. Use the three-region layout, with all the high level use cases in the top level navigation bar and service level navigation on the left-hand side.

2.6. Take the basic designs of your home page and three-region layout from questions 4 and 5 and apply them to the questionnaire application.

2.7. Consider how the webflow might work for a simple questionnaire that has five questions, each appearing on a separate page. What might the breadcrumb trail look like after you had answered the final question?

SUMMARY

This chapter began by looking at how requirements might be gathered and analyzed in order to develop a web-based application, introducing some practices such as joint development workshops and use case analysis. We applied some notation from the UML, including some special extensions for web applications, to help us describe components and workflows within a web-based system. We also saw how the iterative approach and phases of the Unified Process can help us to organize a web development project. In the latter part of the chapter we focussed on architectural approaches to web application design, introducing important aspects of server-side components and webflow. We introduced some common design patterns for web pages, intended to assist in the usability of a web application. The following table (Table 2.1) summarizes the acronyms that were introduced in this chapter. In the chapters that follow, we will apply these architectural and usability patterns as we begin to build the components and interactions of a working web application.

TABLE 2.1

Acronym	Meaning
UML	Unified Modeling Language
UP	Unified Process
ROI	Return on Investment
MoSCoW	Must have, Should have, Could have, Want to have
WAE	Web Applications Extensions
PDF	Portable Document Format
CSS	Cascading StyleSheets

References and further reading

Cockburn, A. 2005. *Crystal Clear: A Human-Powered Methodology for Small Teams*. Boston: Addison-Wesley.

Conallen, J. 1999. *Building Web Applications with UML*. Reading, Mass.: Addison-Wesley.

Conallen, J. 2001. Modeling Web-Tier Components. *Dr. Dobbs Journal*. http://www.ddj.com/dept/architect/184414696.

Fowler. M. 2002. Patterns of Enterprise Application Architecture. Addison-Wesley.

Gamma, E., Helm, R., Johnson, R. and Vlissides, J. 1995. *Design Patterns: Elements of Reusable Object-Oriented Software*. Addison-Wesley.

Graham, I. 2002. *A Pattern Language for Web Usability*. London: Addison-Wesley.

Jacobson, I. 2004. What I don't like in RUP. http://www.jaczone.com/postcards/, January 7, 2004.

Rosenberg, D., Stephens, M., and Collins-Cope, M. 2005. *Agile Development with Iconix Process – People, Process and Pragmatism*. New York: Apress.

Sparks, M. 2004. *Extreme Website Design*. Exoftware Agile Solutions, http://www.exoftware.com/whitepapers.

Structure and Content in the Presentation Layer: The eXtensible HyperText Mark-up Language (XHTML)

LEARNING OBJECTIVES

- **To understand the origins of XHTML**

- **To understand the importance of separating content, structure and presentation in web applications**

- **To understand the main XHTML page authoring tools available in Visual Web Developer**

- **To understand some of the most commonly used elements in XHTML**

- **To be able to create valid XHTML pages using both source and design views**

INTRODUCTION

In this chapter, and the ones that follow, we trace the development of the mark-up languages that have been used to structure and present the pages on the World Wide Web; HTML, CSS, XML and XHTML. HTML and XHTML are covered in detail in this chapter and CSS in Chapter 4, followed later by various aspects of XML that relate to web applications. We begin by looking at some of the key features of the common root of these mark-up languages, SGML. We move on to see how XHTML can be used to build web page structure and content, including lists and tables. Throughout the chapter we see how the various tools within Visual Web Developer can help us to create valid web pages by supporting both text-based and visual XHTML editing. It should be noted that at this stage we are dealing only with static content; pages that will be presented in the same way to all clients. In Chapter 6, we will look at Web Forms, which can be used to create dynamic content. Nevertheless, many of the XHTML features we introduce in this chapter will be important for understanding how dynamic web pages are generated.

3.1 Where it all begins – SGML

In this book we use a number of different, but similar, types of mark-up syntax. Mark-up is information that comes over and above the content of a document to give us guidance about its structure and/or presentation. These mark-up indicators are generally known as 'tags'. Mark-up is a type of *metadata*, in that it enables us to provide *data about data*, for example by specifying how some data should be organized on a web page. Most of the mark-up syntax we look at has a common origin in SGML (Standard Generalized Mark-up Language). Although this language had many roots, a major thread in the story was earlier work at IBM, where Charles Goldfarb, Ed Mosher and Ray Lorie developed a mark-up language in 1969 that was named after the initial letters of their surnames: GML. This was made public (i.e. published outside IBM) in 1973. The basic principles of this language, as expressed at that time, were that it should be possible to design a generalized mark-up language so that the mark-up would be useful for more than one application or computer system. The mark-up would be defined by tags that meant information that was marked up by a particular type of tag would be processed in exactly the same way, regardless of where the tag appeared or however many times it was used. The actual processing, however, would not be defined in the mark-up, since this would depend on the context in which the document was being processed. As GML was further developed, one of the important features that was added was the possibility of *validation*, meaning that a document that used GML mark-up could be checked to ensure that it used that mark-up in an appropriate way. This meant that it was necessary to have some way of expressing the correct way(s) that a particular set of mark-up tags could be used (Goldfarb, 1996).

Later, SGML was developed from the foundations of GML and various other similar research efforts. In 1978 the American National Standards Institute (ANSI), with Goldfarb strongly involved, established the Computer Languages for the Processing of Text committee, and published the first draft of SGML in 1980. Unlike GML, SGML is not named after anyone, but stands for Standard Generalized Mark-up Language. It also differs from GML in the way that it expresses mark-up, so although it is similar in principle it is different in syntax. In 1986, with the participation of the ISO (International Organization for Standardization) the first international standard for SGML was published.

Before we look at the specific mark-up languages of interest in this chapter, in particular HTML and XHTML, we will introduce some very basic concepts that both of these languages (and others) take from SGML. These concepts are tags, elements, attributes and 'well-formedness'.

3.1.1 Tags

Although there is some flexibility about the way that tags can be expressed in SGML, the 'reference' syntax uses angle brackets to indicate a tag. The name of the tag appears between the angle brackets, like this:

```
<tag_name>
```

This is in fact a start tag, which means that it indicates the start of the content that is to be marked up using this tag. At the end of the marked up content, there is an end tag, which is similar to the start tag, except that the tag name is preceded by a forward slash, i.e.

```
</tag_name>
```

3.1.2 Elements

A pair of start and end tags, and the marked-up content in between, is known as an *element*. The general format for an element is therefore:

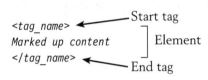

The characteristics defined by the tag are applied to the content of the element. Elements can have other elements nested inside them, to any level of nesting. A nested element is known as a 'child' element, and begins and ends inside its 'parent' element.

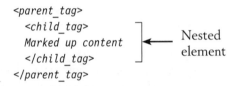

3.1.3 Attributes in tags

Some elements have *attributes*, which configure the element in some way. Attributes appear inside the opening tag, and consist of one or more name-value pairs, using the format:

```
attribute_name="attribute_value"
```

For example, if we had an element called 'document' it might have an attribute called 'language' with a value that used a standard language code, such as French (fr):

```
<document language="fr">
```

Single quotes can be used around attribute values instead of double quotes, i.e:

```
<document language='fr'>
```

It is important to make sure that the double and single quotes you use are the vertical type (Unicode character numbers 22 and 27 respectively), known as the *quotation mark* and the *apostrophe*. Be careful if you edit your XHTML documents in a word processor, because it will probably use the left and right quotation marks (numbered 91–94 in Unicode) that will cause errors in your documents. Rather than a word processor, it is therefore better to use a dedicated editor for mark-up, such as Visual Web Developer, which we use in this chapter.

Attributes are used in a different way from elements because they are about providing *metadata* (data about data) to an element. In other words, they are used to provide extra information about an element or apply some additional configuration to it. The language in which a document is written is information about the document, not part of its content, so specifying the language as an attribute makes more sense than using an element.

An element may have more than one attribute, in which case they all appear inside the opening tag. Perhaps the 'document' element, as well as having a language attribute, also has a 'type' element to indicate what type of document it is, for example the document might be an instruction manual:

```
<document language="fr" type="manual">
```

Where an opening tag contains more than one attribute, their order is unimportant. Therefore this opening tag has exactly the same meaning as the previous one.

```
<document type="manual" language="fr">
```

3.1.4 Empty elements

An empty element is one that, instead of having separate opening and closing tags, consists of a single tag, with no closing tag either required or implied. Instead, there is a forward slash before the closing bracket.

```
<tag_name />
```

Because empty elements have no body, it is often the case that they will include attributes in order to represent their content. This version of the 'document' tag for example is an empty element with attributes:

```
<document type="manual" language="fr" />
```

3.1.5 Well-formed documents

Although things can become complex in SGML, the main rules for what constitutes a well-formed document are quite simple. Here, we lay out the four most important:

- In a well-formed document, all tags must be balanced so that an element has both an opening and a closing tag:

```
<tag>...</tag>
```

- Tags must also be correctly nested so that a child tag must be closed before its parent tag is closed:

```
<parent_tag>
 <child_tag>
   ...
 </child_tag>
</parent_tag>
```

- A document must have a root element that surrounds the whole document, so that its start tag is the first tag in the document and its end tag is the last.
- All attribute values must be written in quotes. Both single and double quotes are valid, but they must be matched correctly (i.e. you cannot mix single and double quotes around the same attribute value).

```
<tag name="value"> or <tag name='value'>
```

These basic ideas from SGML apply to both the HyperText Mark-up Language (HTML) and the eXtensible Mark-up Language (XML), both of which are implementations of SGML. Since XHTML is a combination of HTML and XML, that also follows the same patterns. However, SGML has many complex rules about what syntax is valid, including a number of features that enable parts of the syntax to be minimized or omitted. This complexity helps to explain how HTML ended up as a seemingly rather inconsistent syntax, and why browsers are very tolerant of variations in the use of HTML tags. This is not, however, the case with XHTML mark-up, which must be well formed.

3.2 HTML – a language for web pages

In this section we introduce the HyperText Mark-up Language (HTML), which is a specific application of SGML-based languages for marking up web pages and for years was the mainstay of the World Wide Web. However, early versions of HTML were rather a blunt instrument for creating web application presentation, and has evolved into XHTML, which is the mark-up we will be using with Visual Web Developer. Nevertheless, some knowledge about the differences between HTML and XHTML is useful if we are to understand the way that mark-up of web pages has evolved since the beginnings of the World Wide Web, and it also helps us to understand why other technologies have begun to complement or replace aspects of HTML in web applications.

HTML began with the advent of the World Wide Web in 1991, when Tim Berners Lee at CERN (the European Organization for Nuclear Research) added the first web protocols and tools to the Internet. One of his contributions was the first version of HTML. Berners Lee's original version contained a small number of tags, many of which survive into XHTML today. The main idea behind HTML was that it would enable documents to be hypertext linked to one another, so that clicking on something in one document would take you to another, related, document. In principle, these hyperlinks were to be bidirectional, but HTML does not automatically do this, so hyperlinks in HTML pages work in one direction only. However there have been other mark-up languages that also work with hyperlinks, for example HyTime (Hypermedia/Time-based Structuring Language) and the

XML Pointer Language (XPointer). These languages, and others, provide different perspectives on the implementation of hyperlinks in web pages.

As the popularity of the web increased over subsequent years, and graphical browsers became more common, HTML evolved largely by an ad hoc process, with various features being added to different browsers and gradually becoming common practice. By 1995, with the proliferation of browsers and the increasing popularity of the World Wide Web, it was necessary to try to apply some more rigorous standards to the evolving language, so HTML version 2.0, which included the definition of HTML as the 'text/html' Internet media type, was defined by the Internet Engineering Task Force (IETF). The standard was simply a way of formalizing what was already in use, so HTML 2.0 'roughly corresponds to the capabilities of HTML in common use prior to June 1994' (Connolly, 1995).

The next version of HTML was version 3.2, in 1996. This version was recommended as a specification by the World Wide Web Consortium, and was again a formalization of common practice, this time from early 1996. Some features added in version 2.0 included tables, Java applets and text flow around images.

Version 4.0 dates from 1998, and included new multimedia options, scripting languages, stylesheets, better printing facilities, accessibility features for the disabled and internationalization support. Version 4.01 brought along some minor changes in 1999. Between 2000 and 2002, the W3C developed the specifications for XHTML, initially version 1.0, quickly followed by version 1.1. The next version of the language will be HTML 5, which will re-unify the somewhat differing approaches of HTML and XHTML. In the remainder of this chapter we will focus on XHTML as the mark-up language supported by default by Visual Web Developer.

3.3 XHTML document structural elements

XHTML documents are just plain text files with tags that mark-up the content of the page. They become web pages when they are made available over the Internet using a web server and are rendered on the client machine using a web browser. XHTML tags are enclosed in angle brackets, the same as the SGML reference syntax. Elements using XHTML tags can be used to specify both the structure and the style of the information shown in a web page. The browser uses these tags to organize the text between them, applying the specified mark-up to anything between the opening and closing tags. For example the paragraph element, defined by the p tag, is used for organizing text into paragraphs.

```
<p>some text in paragraph one...</p>
<p>some text in paragraph two...</p>
```

The use of lower-case for element names (and also for attribute names) is required for XHTML, though older HTML versions were not case sensitive, and upper-case was often used.

Paragraphs, and other similar elements, can be regarded as *structural* elements because they organize the content in some semantic way. In other words they help us to understand its meaning. A paragraph usually groups together some sentences that refer to the same topic. Similarly, a tag such as h1, for main heading elements, can be seen as structural. Organizing text into headings, subheadings, paragraphs, etc. is about providing structure in terms of how different blocks of text relate to one another. It does not, however, specify how those headings, subheadings, etc. should look. In contrast, older versions of HTML contained many tags that were to do with the presentational styles of a document, to change the font, color or other aspects of style. A simple example of this type of tag is the *bold* (b) tag:

```
<b>this text will be presented in bold face</b>
```

A tag like this is specifically used to define how part of the document looks when displayed, and has nothing to do with the structure or semantics of the text. Most presentational tags have been removed from XHTML (though the bold tag still survives into version 1.1), and the preferred way of handling the presentation of a page is to use cascading stylesheets (CSS), which we cover in the next chapter.

3

3.3.1 Creating an XHTML document

The simplest possible XHTML document contains a small set of structural and content elements. These are: *html*, *head*, *title* and *body*. The first and the last thing in an XHTML document should always be the tags that surround the root (html) element, i.e. <html>...</html>. Inside the html element, there is a nested head element, <head>...</head> (a nested element being one that appears inside another element). The head element contains the document header information, including the title of the document. The title element is nested inside the head element, using <title> and </title> tags. The content of the title element will appear at the top of the browser's title bar, in the history list and your bookmark file if you create a bookmark to the page. The body element comes after the head element and represents the page content that would be shown in a browser window. Here is an XHTML document with this minimal set of elements.

```
<html>
  <head>
    <title>Untitled Page</title>
  </head>
  <body>
  </body>
</html>
```

Although this is a well formed set of tags, it is not necessarily *valid*. As we will see in the next section, when we begin to create web pages using Visual Web Developer, there are some additional entries in an XHTML page that define the type of XHTML document that is being created and enable us to validate it.

3.4 Creating an XHTML document in Visual Web Developer

In this chapter, we will be editing our XHTML documents using Visual Web Developer. When you first launch the program, you should see a window looking something like the one in Figure 3.1.

FIGURE 3.1 Visual Web Developer start page

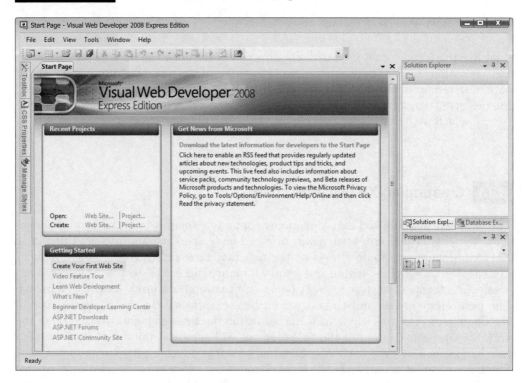

You will notice that this window has the usual familiar features such as a title bar, menu of commands, and a tool bar. The main part of the window, however, is divided further into a number of panes or sub-windows, each of which has its own name and window menu at its top right-hand corner. These controls allow you to move each sub-window around the screen, to hide or to close it. In addition, each pane can have its own scroll bar. Finally, note that the 'Start Page' is itself divided into a number of smaller boxes each of which has rounded corners. You will notice that the title of the Start Page appears in a tab. As you open new windows they will be added as new tabbed windows. You can click on a tab to bring its associated pane or sub-window to the front.

If you have used Visual Studio or a similar Integrated Development Environment (IDE) such as Eclipse you will be familiar with this rich style of user interface. If, however, you are not familiar with this type of environment, it is worth taking some time to familiarize yourself with the additional facilities it provides. Let your mouse cursor rest over each of the icons in the toolbar to see the associated tool-tip. Then, right-click in the title bar of a sub-window to see its 'Window Position' menu (also accessible by clicking on the downward arrow head in the title bar). Experiment by setting the sub-window's location to each of the possible settings on this menu: floating, dockable, tabbed, autohide and hide. If you lose one of the sub-windows, for example by hiding it, don't worry as you can easily bring it back using the 'View' menu. If you get Visual Web Developer in a real mess, you can always use the 'Window' → 'Reset Window Layout' menu command to get back to the initial layout.

Clearly, even though Visual Web Developer may have fewer features than Visual Studio, it is still a professional development environment. It is easy to see why professional developers like to use a high resolution monitor, or even better several of them. Learning to find your way around this rich user interface takes time, so we will go slowly to start with. In the next section, we will take our first web development step by using Visual Web Developer to create a website containing a simple XHTML page.

Finally note that in the 'Start Page' sub-window the 'Getting Started' box lists a number of additional community and learning resources. If you are connected to the Internet, these will bring up web pages with on-line forums and tutorials. You should also plan to spend some time in the future finding your way around these resources: if you find you have questions that are not answered in this book, it is worth checking to see if the answer is easily available on-line before resorting to more detailed references.

3.4.1 Creating a web page with Visual Web Developer

It is possible to create a standalone XHTML page in Visual Web Developer, but it is easier to test your pages if you start by creating a website and then add XHTML pages to it, because then they can then be viewed in a browser from within the development environment. In the context of Visual Web Developer, a 'Website' is synonymous with a project. As with other Integrated Development Environments (IDEs), a project is a means of grouping related resources together for a single application. For this reason, too, it makes sense for us to begin by creating a website, since we will be creating many different resources over this and the following chapters. To create a new website, click on 'File' on the main menu, then choose 'New Website . . .'. In the dialog box that appears, select 'Empty Website'. By default, Visual Web Developer will provide a directory path and file name, called something like *c:\user\Visual Studio 2008\Websites\WebSite1*. You can browse to a different folder and/or modify the default name of the website if you want to. When you click the 'OK' button, the website's name will now appear in the 'Recent Projects' box of the Start Page. If this website is selected, the details of the website project should appear in the 'Solution Explorer' window to the right of the screen (if the solution explorer is not visible, select 'View' → 'Solution Explorer' from the main menu bar.).

Now we have an empty website, we will add a new XHTML page to it. Choose 'File' from the main menu and then 'New File'. In the dialog box that appears (Figure 3.2), select 'HTML Page'. Note that although it is referred to as an HTML page, Visual Web Developer will, by default, support XHTML rather than HTML as the mark-up language. The default file name will be something like 'HTMLPage.htm'. You can change this if you wish, then press the 'Add' button.

At this point Visual Web Developer pops up a window displaying the contents of 'HTMLPage.htm' so that you can edit it, and adds the file name to project in the Solution Explorer window. As you can see in Figure 3.3, there are three ways to view and edit this

FIGURE 3.2
The dialog box that allows you to add a new file or item to an existing website

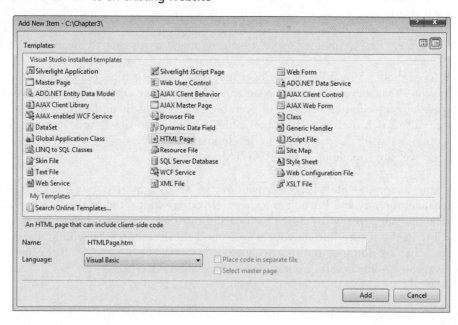

FIGURE 3.3
The Design, Split and Source view buttons at the bottom of the editing window, with Source view selected

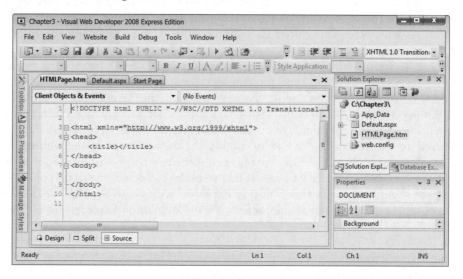

page. Source view is an editor for XHTML mark-up, whereas Design view is a WYSIWYG editor that shows you roughly how the page might appear in a browser. The third option, 'Split' is a combination of Source and Design views. To switch between these views, click on the Design, Source or Split buttons at the bottom left of the editor sub-window (somewhat oddly, it is not possible to use the View menu to do this). We will see in the next section how to use Source view to edit our page and look at using Design view later in the chapter.

3.4.2 Valid XHTML documents

It is good practice to not only write well-formed XHTML but also to validate it against the 'rules' for XHTML documents. This helps ensure that the same document can be rendered correctly by different browsers, since one type of browser may cope with poorly structured HTML but another one may not.

Since HTML 2, public *Document Type Definitions* (DTDs) have been available for validating HTML documents. XHTML 1.0 provides three of these DTDs with different sets of rules regarding valid documents; 'strict', 'transitional' and 'frameset'. The transitional and frameset versions allow a wider range of elements and more flexible structure than the 'strict' version, and allow extensive mixing of presentation with content and structure. A full discussion of validation is beyond the scope of this book, but we should ensure that our XHTML documents are valid against the XHTML 1.0 transitional document type definition, since this is the default used by Visual Web Developer. Conforming to a DTD like this means that our documents are much more likely to work consistently across different browsers and devices. If you look at the XHTML page generated by the tool, you will see that it begins with the following line:

```
<!DOCTYPE html PUBLIC "-//W3C//DTD XHTML 1.0 Transitional//EN"
"http://www.w3.org/TR/xhtml1/DTD/xhtml1-transitional.dtd">
```

This states that the document that follows should meet the requirements for XHTML 1.0 validation. The 'DOCTYPE' refers to a DTD that is publicly available for validating documents. Another feature of the code generated by the tool is the opening html tag, which contains an 'xmlns' attribute:

```
<html xmlns="http://www.w3.org/1999/xhtml">
```

This attribute relates to the *XML namespace* that defines where the 'html' element definition comes from. A complete discussion of namespaces is not appropriate here, but they are important in distinguishing between different sources of mark-up. To identify the correct namespace, an XHTML document requires this attribute in its opening html tag (though previous versions of HTML did not).

As you enter mark-up into your XHTML page in source view, it will be automatically validated to ensure that you have used the tags correctly, as we will see in a later example. However, Visual Web Developer does not use the DOCTYPE at the top of the document to do this. Rather, it uses the currently selected option from the 'HTML Source Editing' toolbar, which is available when using Source view. If this is not currently visible, select 'View' → 'Toolbars' → 'HTML Source Editing' from the main menu bar. In this toolbar, the type of validation to be used can be chosen from the drop-down list on the right (Figure 3.4). By default, validation will be based on XHTML 1.0 Transitional.

If you choose to change the validation from XHTML 1.0 Transitional, you should be aware that this does not change the DOCTYPE that is generated by the tool at the top of HTML pages, which would have to be changed manually. This is because once the page has been

FIGURE 3.4   The HTML Source Editing Toolbar

deployed somewhere outside of Visual Web Developer, other tools will attempt to validate the document using the stated DOCTYPE.

3.5 Using Source view to edit XHTML pages

In this section we take a closer look at Visual Web Developer's Source view. This is a smart code editor which you use to enter and edit code for various types of file associated with web applications. The editor supports all the languages you use for web development, not just XHTML, but also C#, VB.NET, JavaScript, XML, and CSS. We look initially at useful features such as syntax coloring and Intellisense® code completion which help you create code free of tedious spelling and grammatical errors. Some other useful features are considered such as validation, bookmarks, outlining, and split panes.

You can use Source view to directly enter and edit code, moving the insertion point using the mouse or arrow keys. For example, you can directly edit the text following the opening title tag, to change it from the default 'Untitled Page'. When you start typing, you may notice an asterisk appearing after the file name in the tab at the top of the Source view sub-window. This shows you there are unsaved changes. You can use the 'File' → 'Save' menu options, or Ctrl+S, to save your changes at any time.

As you move the cursor around the document, notice how the Tag Navigator, which appears to the bottom right of the editing window, changes to show your current location in terms of the currently selected tag, as do the line ('Ln'), column ('Col'), and character ('Ch') numbers shown just below.

3.5.1 Intellisense® Smart Code Completion

To see Intellisense® Smart Code Completion in action in Source view, we will now add a paragraph element to the body of the XHTML page. If you now move your cursor down to the empty body element, and type an opening tag character (<) you will see Intellisense® giving you context relevant assistance as shown in Figure 3.5.

A drop-down menu has appeared showing all available XHTML tags. At this point you can do one of two things: you can ignore the menu and carry on typing, or you can select the tag you want from the list. To select from the list you can use the mouse to scroll through and double click the item you want, or you can use the arrow keys to scroll through and press Enter when you have reached the item you want. At this stage, while we are learning about Source view, you could try all three ways to enter the required paragraph tag. You will notice that if you use Intellisense® to do so, it leaves the tag open, giving you <p without the closing angle bracket. This is so you can continue entering attributes into the tag. Try pressing the space bar, for example, at this stage. You should see something like the list of available attributes in Figure 3.6.

Figure 3.6 shows you being offered a drop-drop menu of valid attributes for the paragraph tag. It is unlikely, however, you will need to add any attributes to a simple paragraph, so you should instead press backspace to remove the space following the <p and type a > character to close the tag. Notice that, once again, Microsoft's smart code completion system helps out by providing you with the matching closing tag (</p>).

FIGURE 3.5	Intellisense® code completion in action

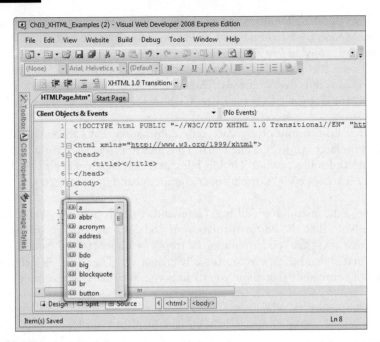

FIGURE 3.6	Intellisense® code completion also works on HTML tag attributes

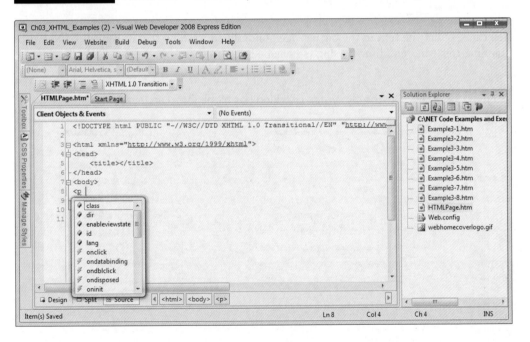

A couple of final points to remember about Intellisense®. To display the list of keywords available at any point you can type Ctrl+J. Also, to automatically complete a longer keyword you are typing, it is often quicker to press Alt+→ (Alt key + right arrow) rather than selecting from the drop-down list. If you don't want to remember these keyboard shortcuts, these features are also available via the 'Edit' → 'Intellisense' menu command.

3.5.2 Other editing facilities

All the usual text editing facilities are available to you in Source view such as using the delete and backspace keys to erase text, using the mouse or shifted arrow keys to select text, and using cut, copy and paste, which you will find on the 'Standard' toolbar, or via the Edit menu. Also on the 'Standard' toolbar (which is visible in most of the previous figures) are the usual 'Undo' and 'Redo' buttons. The usual keyboard shortcuts are also in operation such as Ctrl+C for Copy, Ctrl+V for Paste, Ctrl+X for Cut, and Ctrl+Z for Undo.

In addition, the 'Edit' menu offers you some commands that can be particularly useful when working on larger projects. The usual 'Find and Replace' sub-menu has variants that work across multiples files, called 'Find in Files' and 'Replace in Files'. The 'Find Symbol' command only searches code, skipping over comments and quoted text.

Also under the 'Edit' menu you will find commands to re-format the whole document or selected text. Note that the editor formats your code as you enter it, so you should only need to re-format text that you have imported from elsewhere (though you may not like the automatic format style and choose to manually change it). The 'Edit' → 'Advanced' option has a number of commands that allow you to add or remove tabs, white space, and indents.

Finally, note the facility to validate the whole document using the 'Edit' → 'Advanced' → 'Validate Document' menu command. By default, Visual Web Developer validates your source code as you enter it, so you should not need to trigger manual validation very often. As an example, note what happens if you enter some invalid HTML such as `<this is not a valid tag>` as shown in Figure 3.7.

You can see that the text in the tag has been underlined to show that it is invalid. (Notwithstanding this, the matching closing tag has been created automatically.) To find out more

FIGURE 3.7   On-the-fly syntax checking has highlighted an invalid tag

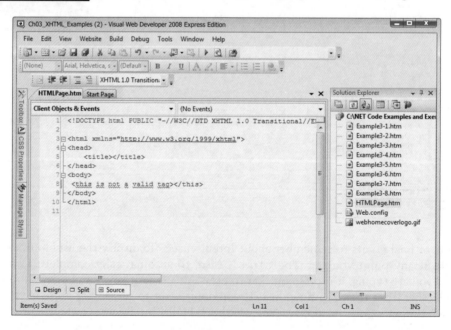

about an error such as this, you can use the 'View' → 'Error List' menu command to bring up the error window, as shown in Figure 3.8. Note that, as is often the way, the erroneous tag has generated six error messages, of which the last is the most meaningful.

The Error List tells us about the problems that have been found

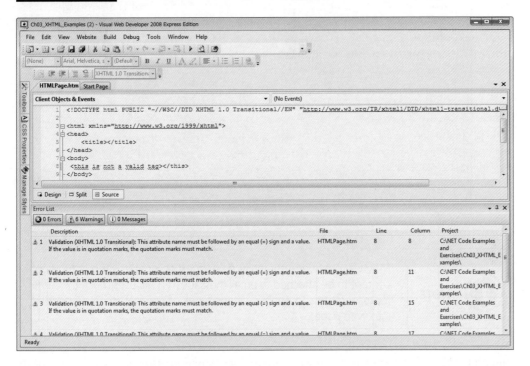

Note that some of the commands discussed above are also available via the 'HTML Source Editing' toolbar. For example, this toolbar allows you to change indentation, or to format the currently selected text.

As you can see, Source view provides a rich editing environment. If you do not like the way things work, you can personalize the system using the 'Tools' → 'Options' menu command. Here you will find a dialog for setting your preferences as shown in Figure 3.9. If you check the 'Show all settings' box on this dialog you will see even more options. For example if you decide you don't like tabbed windows, you can switch them off by checking 'Show all settings' and the first option in the list becomes 'Environment'. Within this dialog you can choose between 'Tabbed documents' or 'Multiple documents'. Selecting the latter will show you a stack of separate document windows rather than a single one with tabs.

3.6 Content types

Within the document body, the content is frequently organized into blocks of textual information, such as headings, paragraphs, lists and tables. There may also be other *media types* in the body, such as images, sound clips and movies. A media type is some kind of MIME (Multipurpose Internet Mail Extension) type that defines a particular type of file that can be used on the Internet.

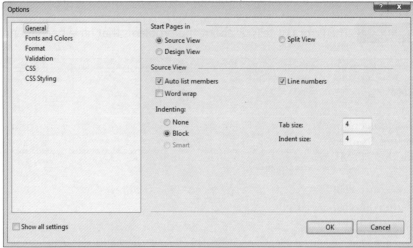

 NOTE MIME types were originally developed to enable various types of content to be attached to email messages. HTML uses much the same representations to enable various types of content to be embedded into web pages.

Since HTML 4, the preferred term is *content type*, since *media type* is more properly applied to types of output device. Regardless, the type of an XHTML document is 'text/html', but such documents may contain references to other content that is of a different type. XHTML provides a large number of tags for organizing the structure of a document's content, including all the other content types that may be included inside it. In this chapter we look at the main organizing elements: headings, paragraphs, lists and tables.

3.6.1 Text elements

Much of the content of web pages is based on the management of text. The structure of the text can be organized using headings, subheadings and paragraphs. Some other types of content can usefully be structured in terms of lists (which may be ordered in some way) or tables. There are also certain semantic aspects of text that can be included in mark-up, to provide emphasis or indicate quotations, for example. In this section we look at some of the basic structural elements that assist in organizing content in XHTML pages.

A very common way of organizing text-based content is to use headings, subheadings and paragraphs. The h1, h2, h3, h4, h5 and h6 elements can be used for various levels of heading and subheading. h1 is the largest heading and h6 the smallest. Because a heading is generally larger than the text that follows, it may not be sensible to use more than the first two or three levels of heading. In many browsers the smallest heading types will be smaller than standard paragraph text.

As we have already seen, the XHTML syntax for a paragraph element is p. You should ensure that the closing tag (</p>) is added at the end of each paragraph to make the element 'well formed' (this should be added automatically by the Visual Web Developer editor, and the validator will indicate if this is not the case). In the example that follows we use an h1 element for a main heading and h2 elements as subheadings, with the main body of the text in paragraphs, using the p element. This example also includes the comment syntax in XHTML, which looks like this:

```
<!-- this is a comment -->
```

We will use this comment syntax throughout the book to indicate the source file that is being referred to in each example. (Text can also be commented or uncommented using buttons on the 'HTML Source Editing' toolbar.)

```
<!DOCTYPE html PUBLIC "-//W3C//DTD XHTML 1.0 Transitional//EN"
"http://www.w3.org/TR/xhtml1/DTD/xhtml1-transitional.dtd">
<html xmlns="http://www.w3.org/1999/xhtml">
 <head>
  <title>Versions of HTML</title>
 </head>
 <body>
  <!-- File: Example3-1.htm -->
  <h1>Versions of HTML</H1>
  <h2>HTML 1.0</h2>
  <p>
   The first version of HTML dates from 1991, and was developed
   by Tim Berners Lee. It was very different from the HTML
   we know today...
  </p>
  <h2>HTML 2.0</h2>
  <p>
   The second version of HTML, in 1996, was an attempt
   to standardize the language, which was being widely
   implemented by different vendors' web browsers...
  </p>
 </body>
</html>
```

To see what the web page looks like in a browser, you can choose the 'View in Browser Ctrl+Shift+W' option from the 'File' menu. This has the effect of sending the '.htm' file currently being edited to your browser. If there are outstanding changes, Visual Web Developer will ask you if you wish to save the file first. Finally, you will see your work rendered using Internet Explorer, or Firefox, or whatever browser you have currently chosen as your main one. To switch between different browsers you can choose 'Browse With . . .' from the File menu and select any of the browsers that are available on your machine. If you do not have any external browsers available, Visual Web Developer can use its own internal browser which it will display in a new tabbed window.

Figure 3.10 shows what the body of the text looks like when browsed using Microsoft Internet Explorer 7. Note the different sizes of text for headings, subheadings and paragraphs.

FIGURE 3.10   Headings, subheadings and paragraphs in a web browser

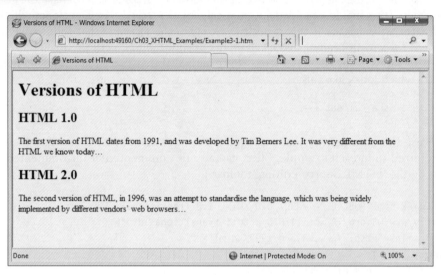

One trick your browser can do for you is to show you the raw HTML source that Visual Web Developer has sent, via the 'View Source' command (or similar, depending on the browser). To access this command, right click with your cursor on the HTML page. If you are using the internal browser, the view simply switches to the source editor. However, external browsers are also able to display the source HTML, for example Figure 3.11 shows the page source displayed in the Mozilla Firefox 3 browser.

> **NOTE**   Viewing the source in an external browser does not give you access to the original source mark-up. It simply displays the mark-up received by the browser via the web server.

FIGURE 3.11   Viewing the XHTML mark-up source in the Mozilla Firefox 3 browser

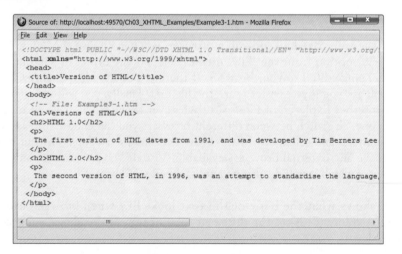

Behind the covers, when you ask Visual Web Developer to send a web page to your browser, it starts up its own internal web server. This web server is running locally on your machine, which is why the URL at the top of Figure 3.11 begins 'http://localhost:', followed by a port number, which will vary as it is decided by Visual Web Developer. This will not be the standard HTTP port number (80) but some other number selected so as not to interfere with services using other ports on your machine (as we saw in Chapter 1, ports are connections that your machine can use to communicate with the outside world). This internal web server is not as powerful as Microsoft's Internet Information Services (IIS) but it does provide sufficient features to allow you to debug all the ASP.NET code covered later in this book. Fortunately, it cannot be accessed externally, so there should be no security holes for you to worry about at this stage.

A well as structuring our pages into headings and paragraphs, there are a number of other structural elements that we can apply to XHTML documents. In the following sections we look at some of these elements.

3.6.2 Line breaks and horizontal rules

Line breaks (br) and horizontal rules (hr) are examples of *empty elements*. As previously explained, an empty element in XHTML is one that, instead of having separate start and end tags, consists of a single tag, with no closing tag either required or implied. Instead, there is a forward slash before the closing bracket. One example of an empty element in HTML is the line break:

```
<br />
```

Unlike the paragraph element, which starts a new line and leaves a space before the paragraph, a br element starts a new line but does not force a blank line to be inserted. The space between the element name and the forward slash is not an essential feature of XHTML. However, in order to ensure backward compatibility with older browsers, the W3C recommendation is that all empty elements in XHTML should have a space before the final '/>' characters.

The horizontal rule (hr) is another example of an empty element:

```
<hr />
```

A browser usually displays the horizontal rule as a graphical line. Of course one might question whether the hr element is structural or just presentational. Its definition in the various HTML specifications has evolved from 'a divider between sections of text', via 'used to indicate a change in topic' to 'a horizontal rule to be rendered by visual user agents', so one could make a case for either interpretation (Korpela, 2002).

In earlier versions of HTML, these empty elements did not contain the final forward slash, so were not well formed. For example, the line break tag was written like this:

```
<br>
```

Visual Web Developer will automatically correct these empty tags if you try to type them in without the required forward slash (go on, try to type <br> into the HTML editor and see what happens).

<table>
<tr>
<td> NOTE</td>
<td>If you need to use the old style HTML tag in a page that needs to be written using legacy mark-up such as HTML 4.01, for example because you are maintaining legacy pages from an existing website, then you will need to edit the tag after it has been written by deleting the forward slash and the extra space. However to ensure the page was still valid you would need to change the DOCTYPE at the top of the page to HTML 4.01, change the validation option to HTML 4.01 and also remove the 'xmlns' attribute from the html opening tag so that the page was valid HTML 4.01.</td>
</tr>
</table>

3.6.3 Citations and block quotes

There are many structural elements in XHTML, some more commonly used than others. Although cite and blockquote are not often required, they are useful examples of elements that have some semantics attached to them; they convey something about the meaning of the text and its relationship to other parts of the document around them rather than hierarchical structure or presentation.

It is common in documents for longer quotations and citations to be structured differently from the main body of the text. XHTML includes the blockquote element for long quotations and the cite element for citations. The next example is similar to the last one, but is modified to include cite and blockquote elements. You should note that blockquote elements should not directly contain text. Rather, they should contain structural elements such as paragraphs or headings, with the text inside those. Here, we use a paragraph element.

```
<!DOCTYPE html PUBLIC "-//W3C//DTD XHTML 1.0 Transitional//EN"
"http://www.w3.org/TR/xhtml1/DTD/xhtml1-transitional.dtd">
<html xmlns="http://www.w3.org/1999/xhtml">
 <head>
  <title>Versions of HTML</title>
 </head>
 <!-- File: Example3-2.htm -->
 <body>
  <h1>Versions of HTML</h1>
  <h2>HTML 1.0</h2>
  <p>
  The first version of HTML dates from 1991, and was developed
  by Tim Berners Lee. It was very different from the HTML
  we know today.
  <cite>Tim Berners Lee </cite>
  is quoted as saying
</p>
<blockquote>
  <p>
  If you use the original World Wide Web program, you never
  see a URL or have to deal with HTML. That was a surprise to
  me...that people were prepared to painstakingly write HTML.
```

```
  </p>
 </blockquote>
 <h2>HTML 2.0</h2>
  <p>
  The second version of HTML, in 1996, was an attempt to
  standardize the language, which was being widely implemented
  by different vendors' web browsers...
  </p>
 </body>
</html>
```

Figure 3.12 shows how the complete page looks in Internet Explorer 7.

FIGURE 3.12   Using the cite and blockquote elements

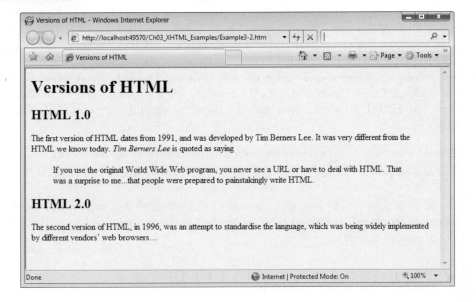

In this browser the citation appears in italics and the block quote is separated from the previous text and indented. It is important to note however that we are not using elements here for the purposes of indenting paragraphs or applying an italic text style. The cite and blockquote elements are about the structure and meaning of the text, not for controlling its appearance. We are letting the browser decide how a citation or a block quote should actually appear, so the fact that the quote is indented and the citation text is italic is not something explicitly defined. This is an important point, since we should be aware of the difference between structural and presentational tags and how to use them. The use of blockquote simply to indent a paragraph is *deprecated*, which means that although the tag may be displayed that way in a particular browser it should not be used simply to get that presentational effect. The blockquote element is an indication that the body of the element should be given some special handling to recognize that it is a long quotation. It should not be used as a convenient way of achieving a specific format, regardless of the actual content of the element. Perhaps even more obviously, using the cite element should not be seen simply as a way of making text italic.

3.6.4 Idiomatic (phrase) elements

The cite element is one of the *idiomatic* or *phrase* elements. These elements relate to common types of usage in terms of how we express ourselves in writing. For example, we look for ways to emphasize specific parts of text. To support these idioms, XHTML includes elements such as em for emphasis, and strong for stronger emphasis. Browsers will usually render emphasized text in italics and strong text in bold face, but as with the cite element, the actual way that the browser chooses to render these elements is independent of our use of the tags. We use them to indicate a type of expression, not to select a particular appearance for the text.

3.6.5 Subscripts and superscripts

The sub (subscript) element uses a small font aligned towards the bottom of the regular character height, while the sup (superscript) element uses a small font aligned towards the top of the regular character height. These elements might appear to occupy a grey area between the structural and the presentational. However there are important accepted uses for these aspects of content, for example in scientific notation or in rendering some languages. Superscript is commonly used to indicate references, footnotes or trademarks, and in mathematical formulae, while subscript is used in chemical formulae. The HTML 4 specification includes these two useful examples of superscript and subscript:

`H<sub>2</sub>0`	to represent H_2O (the chemical symbol for water)
`E = mc<sup>2</sup>`	to represent $E = mc^2$ (Einstein's equation for relativity)

Because of these specific applications, the use of the subscript and superscript elements can be seen as structural, as long as they are applied in these generally accepted contexts rather than just for effect.

3.6.6 XHTML character references

Because XHTML pages use a mark-up syntax, there are certain symbols, in particular '<' and '>' that have special meaning to the applications (like browsers) that process

TABLE 3.1 XHTML character references

HTML character reference	Equivalent character	Meaning
&lt;	<	Less than
&gt;	>	Greater than
&quot;	"	Quotation mark
&amp;	&	Ampersand
	(a space)	Non-breaking space
&reg;	®	Registered trademark
&copy;	©	Copyright

them. XHTML character references are numeric or symbolic names that can be used instead of literal characters in an XHTML document. They are useful for referring to special characters outside the normal number and letter ranges in character sets, or those that have other meanings in the mark-up language and could therefore cause processing problems for browsers. All of the XHTML character references begin with a '&' sign and end with a semicolon. Some examples of XHTML character references are shown in Table 3.1. If you use these in an XHTML document, Visual Web Developer will highlight them in red.

Section summary and quick exercises

In this section we introduced the Visual Web Developer source view for creating XHTML documents, and saw how to build an XHTML document using a number of structural elements to organize the document and the text within it. We also introduced the comment syntax for XHTML and how to represent special XHTML characters using character references. The elements we have introduced so far are summarized in Table 3.2.

EXERCISE 3.1

Figure 3.13 shows an XHTML page displayed in a browser. Using Visual Web Developer, create a page that looks similar to this one. It uses three levels of heading, paragraph text, a horizontal rule, superscript and some XHTML special characters.

TABLE 3.2   XHTML elements introduced in this section

Element	Meaning
html	The root element that surrounds the whole document
head	Document header information
title	The text that appears in the browser's title bar
body	The body content of the page displayed in the browser
p	Paragraph
h1, h2, h3, h4, h5 and h6	Different levels of heading
br	Line break
hr	Horizontal rule
cite	Citation
blockquote	Block quotations
em	Emphasis
strong	Strong emphasis
sub	Subscript
sup	Superscript
& ;	Character reference (start and end characters)
<!-- -->	Comment text (start and end characters)

FIGURE 3.13   An XHTML document using a range of structural elements

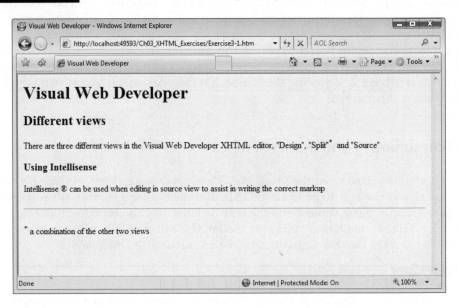

EXERCISE 3.2

Create your own XHTML page that contains headings and paragraph text. Include a referenced quotation related to web application development. Apply XHTML elements from Table 3.2 as you see fit.

3.7 Attributes in XHTML tags

So far we have seen a number of XHTML elements but none of these have used attributes. Nevertheless most XHTML tags can have a number of attributes. Many of these attributes could be categorized as presentational, and in fact the use of attributes for presentation in XHTML gives us a good indication of how the usage of elements and attributes differs. Elements are intended for the content of a document, whereas attributes tend to provide additional configuration of these elements. If we regard presentation of an element as part of its *metadata* (data about data), then we can see that attributes are a good way of applying metadata to XHTML elements. However attributes are not confined solely to defining presentation. They can also be used for some structural aspects, as we will see in the coming examples.

3.7.1 Images

Having said that we are currently dealing with content and structure rather than presentation, it may at first glance seem a little strange to be introducing images. However, an image in a web page is an instance of a *content type*, which means that it is part of the content of the page, not its presentation. It just happens to be content that has visual characteristics. Images can be added to a web page using the img empty element, but unlike the previous empty elements we have seen (br and hr), img elements cannot be used without any attributes. The essential attribute is src, which indicates the URL (Uniform Resource Locator) of the image file to be included in the page. The most common image file types used on the web are GIF (Graphics Interchange Format), JPEG (Joint Photographic Experts Group) and PNG (Portable Network Graphics), since these are relatively small in terms of file size and can therefore be downloaded reasonable quickly. GIF and PNG files are typically used for drawings, while JPEGs are used for photographs as they can manage more colors than GIFs and have a more flexible compression algorithm than PNGs. The PNG format was developed when Unisys held a patent on the GIF compression algorithm, but is also better than GIF files for rendering more than 256 colors, though the equivalent files tend to be larger than GIFs. Another feature of JPEG files is that they use 'lossy' compression, meaning that, depending on the level of compression being applied, some features of the original image may be lost. In contrast, GIF and PNG files use lossless compression.

As well as defining the source for the image, we must also provide an alternative text value using the alt attribute. This is useful both for providing a text alternative if the image cannot be loaded (e.g. if the user has disabled image loading in the browser for speed) and for providing text to be read out for those users who are unable to see images. Here is an img element that uses a GIF file as its source. Note that since this is an empty element, the forward slash must appear before the closing bracket:

```
<img src="logo.gif" alt="WebHomeCover Logo" />
```

The other attributes that can be used with images are height and width, which can be used to scale the image on the page from its original size, but are more often used to specify the actual dimensions of the image (in pixels) to enable the browser to load the page faster, since it is able to anticipate the display space required before downloading the file:

```
<img src="logo.gif" alt="WebHomeCover Logo" height="115" width="102" />
```

Note that in a valid XHTML document an image tag cannot appear directly within the 'body' element but should appear inside a structural element such as a paragraph.

As we have seen before, Visual Web Developer Source view will give you support when adding attributes to an element. For example, if you add the first part of the img element (<img without the closing angle bracket) then press the space bar, a list of valid attributes for that tag will appear, from which you can select the attribute(s) you wish to include (Figure 3.14).

3.7.2 Using the Toolbox

One of the features of the editor is the Toolbox, which by default appears as a small tab on the left-hand side of the screen. The Toolbox can be used to add some of the more complex elements to a page. If this isn't currently visible, use the 'View' → 'Toolbox' menu command to open up this sub-window. If you hover over this tab with the mouse, the full Toolbox should appear (Figure 3.15). In this chapter we will only cover a few of the element types in the toolbox, but you should already recognize the 'Image' and 'Horizontal Rule' elements. The Toolbox has an 'Autohide' pin which you can toggle so that the toolbox either stays visible or only appears when you hover over the tab.

FIGURE 3.14 Intellisense® code completion with the image tag

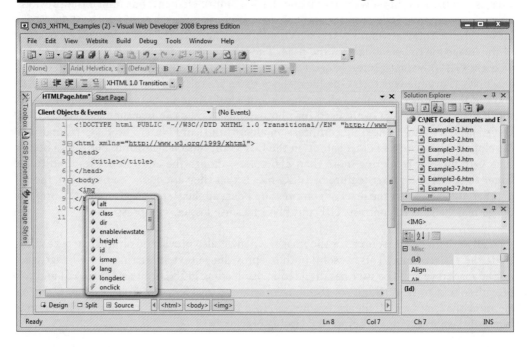

FIGURE 3.15 The Toolbox when editing an HTML page

The Toolbox contains groups of controls under various headings such as 'Standard', 'Data', 'Validation', 'Navigation', 'Login', 'WebParts', 'HTML', and 'General'. These headings will vary depending on the type of document you are editing, so when you are working with an XHTML page, only the 'HTML' and 'General' headings appear. You can open up a group by clicking on the little plus sign next to its heading, and close it again afterwards by clicking on the minus sign that appears in the same place.

You can use the Toolbox to add HTML elements to a page without having to type the tags manually. There are three ways to add a control from the Toolbox into the Design View of your current web page:

- Drag the control from the Toolbox onto the page
- Position the insertion point (text cursor) where you want the control to appear, and double click your chosen control in the Toolbox
- Copy the control out of the Toolbox (using Ctrl+C, or right click Copy) and paste it into Design View (using Ctrl+V, or right click Paste)

If you make a mistake, don't worry, as you can use the 'Edit' → 'Undo' menu command to go back a step. Two other ways to undo are via the keyboard shortcut Ctrl+Z, or the 'Undo' button included in the Standard Toolbar. Alternatively, you can simply highlight and delete any unwanted elements you may have added by mistake.

As you use the Toolbox, you may be wondering what the Pointer control is for. This is the first one listed in each Toolbox group, but is in fact just a dummy entry. You can select it to de-select any other Toolbox item, but that is all it is good for.

Figure 3.16 shows an XHTML page after an image element has been added using the Toolbox. Note that the complete element has been created, but of course the values of the attributes will need to be added manually. You can use Intellisense to add any additional attributes that you require (e.g. height and width for an image element).

FIGURE 3.16   An image element added using the Toolbar

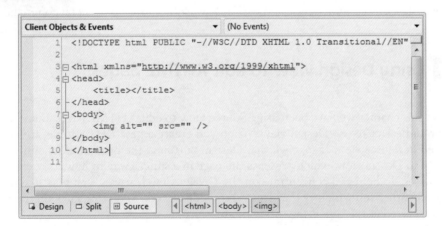

3.7.3 Document navigation

The Edit menu includes a number of commands which help you navigate around the file you are editing. For example, the 'Edit' → 'Go To...' command allows you to jump to a specific line number. The 'Edit' → 'Bookmarks' sub-menu allows you to set or reset a book mark flag against the current line. You can jump to the next or previous bookmark. You might find this helpful, for example, when making a major change to a large file or set of files. You could flag all the lines that need changing before you make the actual edits.

Another feature which can be useful with larger documents is outlining. The structure of a document is indicated using a tree structure that is drawn in the left margin between the text and the line numbers. Major elements such as the head and body tags have small buttons with a – sign that you can click. The element will then collapse and be shown only in outline with a + sign next to it (Figure 3.17). To display the full text again, click the sign again.

FIGURE 3.17   Using outlining to collapse the body element of an HTML page

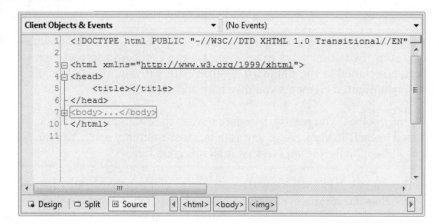

Another feature that can be useful with large files is the ability to see two parts of the same file at once. To do this, you can use the 'Window' → 'Split' menu command. The Source view splits the editing window into two separate views. You can navigate around each view independently. Any changes you make to the file in one view are automatically displayed in the other. To cancel a split view, use the 'Window' → 'Remove Split' menu command.

3.8 Using Design view to edit XHTML pages

So far in this chapter we have been using Source view to edit XHTML pages, but it is often quicker and easier to use Design view. When you create a new XHTML file, it is usually displayed in Source view. If so, click the 'Design' button at the bottom of its edit window to switch to Design view, which presents the page in a similar way to how it would appear in a browser. To help you concentrate on the Design view features, you may like to close or hide any other sub-windows that are currently displayed. To do this, click on the little × that is displayed at the top of the sub-window.

Figure 3.18 shows part of the Formatting Toolbar, which can be used in the Design view. If this toolbar is not currently visible, user the 'View' → 'Toolbars' menu command and make sure that the box next to 'Formatting' is checked (note that this toolbar is grayed out if you are in Source view as it only applies to Design view). The first drop-down list box contains many (though not all) of the structural elements that we have previously been working with in the source view. This drop-down list is called 'block format'. If you select a block of text, you can use this list box to apply a range of tags such as h1, h2, blockquote, etc. You can check the effect of this by looking at the 'tag navigator' which is displayed to the right of the 'Source' button at the bottom of the sub-window. If you have applied an HTML tag

FIGURE 3.18   The Formatting Toolbar, available in Design View

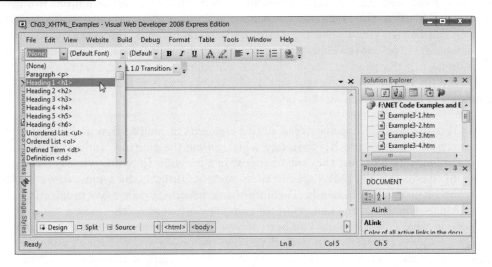

such as blockquote to a block of text, for example, this will be shown in the tag navigator, which should then display something like <html><body><p><blockquote>. You can also use the items displayed in the tag navigator list to select either the tag or its contents.

There are some other tools in the Formatting Toolbar that control presentational features such as fonts and colors, but these are associated with stylesheets, which we will look at in the next chapter. For the moment, we will only use Design view to manage structural elements.

If you click in the blank area of the design view page and start typing text, you will see that by default that text will be put inside a paragraph element (as well as seeing this in the tag navigator, you can check this by switching between Design and Source views).

Figure 3.19 shows a simple page created using Design view. There is the phrase 'Hello World' which has been put into a level one heading (h1) element. There is a

FIGURE 3.19   Some text created with Design view

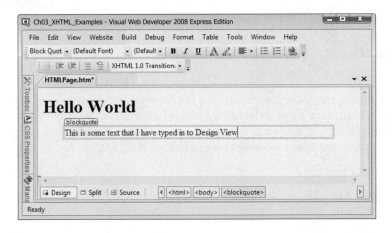

paragraph starting 'This is some text that I have typed...' which has been put into a `blockquote` element. There is also a horizontal rule. This has been added not from the Formatting Toolbar but from the Toolbox. The Toolbox works the same way in both Source and Design views. The tag navigator at the bottom of the screen shot shows `<html><body><blockquote>` showing the actual tags being applied. In addition, if you click on part of the page in Design view, the element type for that part of the page is displayed. In Figure 3.19, the text in the `blockquote` has been selected, and a tab has appeared to display the element type.

There is really no difference between adding elements in Source view and Design view. In Source view we see the XHTML tags which define the controls, and in Design view we see an indication of how they might appear in a browser. In Source view we have the freedom to edit the XHTML tags and their contents directly, by typing, or indirectly, using mouse or menu commands. This impressive feature is called synchronization. All your changes happen 'at the same time' in each view or window. This means you are free to work in whatever way suits you best. If you like the immediate visual feedback of Design view, you can stick with that. If you like the power and control of using Source view, you can use that instead. If you want to work with both at the same time, you can choose Split view.

NOTE	Note that if you try typing XHTML tags directly into Design View, Visual Web Developer treats the characters as text content, not mark-up, by converting the angle brackets into their corresponding character references. For example, if you type an opening paragraph tag (<p>) into design view, what you will see in source view will be <p> Therefore, tags can only be manually entered into Source view.

By now, you should be able to see how Visual Web Developer's Design view can be used in a WYSIWYG fashion to create text and XHTML elements, just as you might do with Microsoft Word, or a similar word processor. Unfortunately, although Design view may *look* like a word processor, it's really still only an IDE. You can tell this because, for example, there is no built-in spell-checker. This is unfortunate, as it would be really useful to be able to check our web pages for spelling errors before publishing them.

3.9 Lists

Lists can be appropriate ways of structuring certain types of content in an XHTML document. A list can present short, related items of information in an easy-to-read layout, and may be nested (i.e. a list inside a list) to produce structures like tables of contents, indexes or document outlines. There are three types of list in XHTML:

- Unordered lists
- Ordered lists
- Definition lists

3.9.1 Unordered lists

An unordered list is one that is given a list structure but there is no numbering or lettering to suggest a meaningful sequence. In other contexts this type of list is known as a *bulleted list*, and the browser will probably display each item in the list with a bullet symbol prefix. The tag name for an unordered list element is ul, which can contain any number of nested li (list item) elements, e.g.:

```
<ul>
 <li> a list item </li>
 <li> another list item </li>
 ...
</ul>
```

3.9.2 Ordered lists

In an ordered list, the list items are numbered or lettered. This is useful for lists that have a meaningful order, such as instructions, chapters, recipes or league tables. The tag name for an ordered list is ol, with li again used for nested list item elements, e.g.:

```
<ol>
  <li> the first list item </li>
  <li> the second list item </li>
  ...
</ol>
```

3.9.3 Lists in Design view

You can use the Formatting Toolbar in Design view to create lists from text on your page. All you need to do is to add the items to appear in the list on separate lines in Design view (by default each item will be in a separate paragraph). Then highlight all the items you want to appear in the list and select either 'Unordered List or 'Ordered List' from the Formatting Toolbar. There are also buttons on the toolbar to do this; the 'Bullets' button creates an unordered list and the 'Numbering' button creates an ordered list. Figure 3.20 shows the Formatting Toolbar being used to create an unordered list.

FIGURE 3.20   Creating an unordered list with the Formatting Toolbar

3.9.4 Nested lists

Lists can be nested and combined together as appropriate for the content. However there is an important thing to bear in mind when doing this, which is that any list that is nested inside another one must be in its own list item (li) element, using this kind of structure:

```
<ul>
 <li> an item in the main list</li>
 <li> Here comes a nested list...
```

```
    <ol>
     <li> an item in the nested list</li>
     <li> another item in the nested list</li>
     ...
    </ol>
   </li>
   <li> another item in the main list</li>
   ...
  </ul>
```

In this example from the home insurance system domain we use both ordered and unordered lists.

```
<!DOCTYPE html PUBLIC "-//W3C//DTD XHTML 1.0 Transitional//EN"
"http://www.w3.org/TR/xhtml1/DTD/xhtml11-transitional.dtd">

<html xmlns="http://www.w3.org/1999/xhtml">
 <head>
  <title>Making a Claim</title>
 </head>
 <body>
 <!-- File: Example3-3.htm -->
  <h1>Useful Tips</h1>
  <ul>
   <li>Making a Claim
    <ol>
     <li>
      Find as much documentation as you can (photos, receipts etc.)
     </li>
     <li>
      Fill in the on-line claim form
     </li>
     <li>
      Don't do anything until an assessor has contacted you
     </li>
    </ol>
   </li>
   <li>Changing your policy
    <ol>
     <li>
      Log in to your user account
     </li>
     <li>
      Select 'update policy details' from the list of options
     </li>
     <li>
      Follow the on-screen instructions to make the required changes
     </li>
    </ol>
   </li>
```

```
    </ul>
  </body>
</html>
```

Figure 3.21 shows how the list looks in Internet Explorer 7. You will notice that the main unordered list has round bullets and the nested ordered lists are labeled with Arabic numbers. This is the behavior of the browser, not specified by our list elements.

Note that you cannot create nested lists in Design view, so this has to be done using Source view.

FIGURE 3.21   How nested ordered and unordered lists appear in a browser

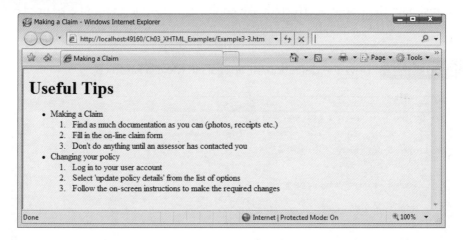

3.9.5 Definition lists

Definition lists are a bit different from the other types of list because they are structured like a glossary of terms. The outer element of a definition list uses the <dl>...</dl> (definition list) tags. Inside this element appear one or more pairs of terms and definitions. In each pair, the term is defined by a dt (Defined Term) element and the definition appears in a dd (Definition) element. Here is an example of an XHTML document containing a definition list:

```
<!DOCTYPE html PUBLIC "-//W3C//DTD XHTML 1.0 Transitional//EN"
"http://www.w3.org/TR/xhtml1/DTD/xhtml1-transitional.dtd">

<html xmlns="http://www.w3.org/1999/xhtml">
 <head>
  <title>Mark-up Languages</title>
 </head>
 <!-- File: Example3-4.htm -->
 <body>
  <dl>
   <dt>SGML</dt>
   <dd>Standard Generalised Mark-up Language</dd>
   <dt>HTML</dt>
   <dd>HyperText Mark-up Language</dd>
```

```
    <dt>XML</dt>
    <dd>eXtensible Mark-up Language</dd>
  </dl>
 </body>
</html>
```

You can create a definition list in Design view, but there is no entry in the Formatting Toolbar to create the list itself. Instead, you highlight your list items and then select either Defined Term (dt) or Definition (dd) from the Formatting Toolbar. This will create a definition list in which all the items are terms or definitions, depending on which option you have used. You can then select individual items to switch them between term and definition as required. Figure 3.22 shows how the definition list looks in Mozilla Firefox 3. In this browser there is no difference in the font size or style between the definitions and the terms, only the layout is affected. We could, however, add tags like em or strong to provide some further semantic differentiation between definitions and terms.

FIGURE 3.22   How the definition list appears in Mozilla Firefox 3

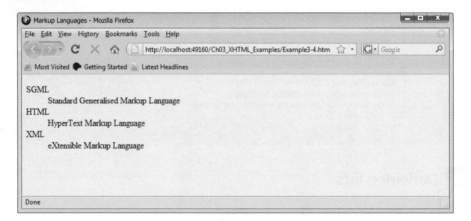

Section summary and quick exercises

In this section we introduced the Visual Web Developer Toolbox and Design view, which can help us to become more productive when creating and editing XHTML documents. We also looked at the img element and some of its attributes, which is used to include and configure images on a web page. We saw how XHTML also includes a number of elements for creating various types of lists; ordered, unordered and definition. The new elements we have introduced in this section are summarized in Table 3.3.

EXERCISE 3.3

Using the table of contents at the front of this book, Create nested ordered lists that show the contents of the first two chapters. The main ordered list will contain the chapter titles. The nested lists within these chapters will be the main subheadings. For example, the list would begin something like this:

   1. Introduction to web applications

      1. What a web application does

      2. E-everything – the Internet and the World Wide Web . . . etc.

Create a definition list that contains images of logos from the various web browsers currently available. For each definition, the definition term will be the name of the browser, and the definition will be an image of that browser's logo.

TABLE 3.3 XHTML elements used with images and tables

Element	Meaning
img	Image
ul	Unordered list
li	List item
ol	Ordered list
dl	Definition list
dt	Definition list term
dd	Definition list definition

3.10 Tables

Tables can be a useful structural element in a web page. Information can often be displayed effectively using a table-based format, particularly if the data being presented has been read from a relational database, since these databases store data in tables. A table consists of rows and columns, with optional column headings and a caption. Each part of table (where a row and column meet) is known as a cell (Figure 3.23).

FIGURE 3.23 The components of a table

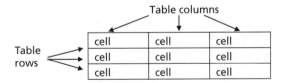

3.10.1 Table tags

In XHTML, the table is quite a complex element, with a number of nested elements used to represent the 'table model' which is the underlying table structure. This can be divided into the header, body and footer, and columns can be grouped together. However in this overview we will only cover the basics of tables.

A table element in HTML is defined by `<table>`...`</table>` tags. The table element contains all the other table-related tags that specify, for example, captions, headings and data cells. Each row in the table is defined by a table row (tr) element:

```
<tr>...</tr>
```

There are two types of table cell, those that contain column headings and those that contain data. th (table heading) tags can optionally be used to define heading elements that are used in the top row of the table columns. Other cells are defined using td (table data) tags. There is also an optional caption element that can be used to describe the table, e.g:

```
<caption>Our Call Centers</caption>
```

3.10.2 Creating tables in Design view

Design view provides some support for creating and editing tables in a visual or WYSI-WYG fashion. However, in terms of structural elements it only controls the table, tr and td tags. Other elements used to structure tables have to be edited manually in Source view.

To work with a table element, you can use the 'Table' entry in the Toolbox, but this always creates a 3 × 3 table, which you then have to modify if you want a different structure. A better option is to use the 'Table' → 'Insert Table' menu item, available on the main menu bar only when you are in Design view, which opens the dialog shown in Figure 3.24. In this dialog you can choose the number of rows and columns that you need (the other settings are related to stylesheets, which we introduce in the next chapter).

FIGURE 3.24   The 'Insert Table' dialog box can be used to control the layout of a new table

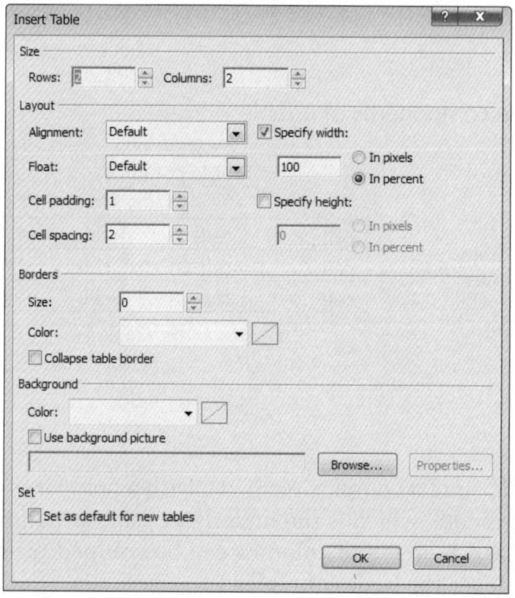

After the table is created, you can use the other options under the 'Table' menu to add or remove columns, rows or individual cells. Note that these commands are only available if you have the table, or a part of the table, selected. You can select individual cells, columns or rows in the table by clicking on the cell, the top or bottom of the column, or either end of the row. You will find this easier once you have typed some text into the table, which will then increase automatically in size.

3.10.3 Table example

As we work through the various aspects of tables, we will develop a simple example of a table that shows the locations and contact numbers of call centers. For the purposes of this example we assume that WebHomeCover has call centers in various territories, and this information will be presented on a web page in the form of a table. Figure 3.25 shows some information typed into a table created in Design view that has four columns and five rows.

FIGURE 3.25 A table created in Design view

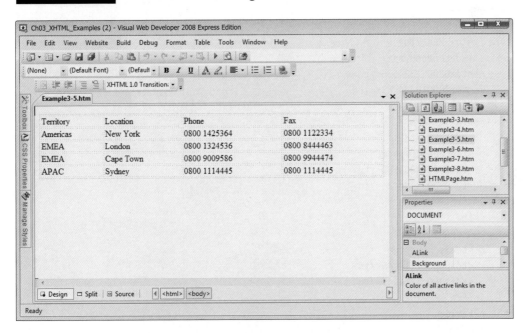

Switching to Source view for this page will show the table, tr and td tags that have been created. The source also contains a generated style element that controls the width of the table, linked to the table by the class attribute that appears in the opening table tag. However do not worry about this part of the mark-up for now, as we talk about styles in the next chapter. In the following examples we are going to focus on the structural table tags and make some changes in Source view.

```
<!DOCTYPE HTML PUBLIC "-//W3C//DTD HTML 4.01//EN"
"http://www.w3.org/TR/html4/strict.dtd">
<html>
 <head>
```

```
      <title>Our Call Centers</title>
      <style type="text/css">
       .style1 { width: 100%; }
      </style>
     </head>
     <body>
      <!-- File: Example3-5.htm -->
      <table class="style1">
       <tr>
        <td>Territory</td>
        <td>Location</td>
        <td>Phone</td>
        <td>Fax</td>
       </tr>
       <tr>
        <td>Americas</td>
        <td>New York</td>
        <td>0800 1425364</td>
        <td>0800 1122334</td>
       </tr>
       <tr>
        <td>EMEA</td>
        <td>London</td>
        <td>0800 1324536</td>
        <td>0800 8444463</td>
       </tr>
       <tr>
        <td>EMEA</td>
        <td>Cape Town</td>
        <td>0800 9009586</td>
        <td>0800 9944474</td>
       </tr>
       <tr>
        <td>APAC</td>
        <td>Sydney</td>
        <td>0800 1114445</td>
        <td>0800 1114445</td>
       </tr>
      </table>
     </body>
    </html>
```

Figure 3.26 shows what the table looks like displayed in a browser.

In the current example there is text in all of the cells, but we can choose to leave cells blank if there is no data available for them. A blank cell in Design view will contain a non-breaking space character ( ). Just for the sake of this example, we might assume that the Cape Town office does not have a fax number, so if we delete the text in Design view the tag will look like this in source view:

```
<td> </td>
```

FIGURE 3.26 A table displayed in a browser

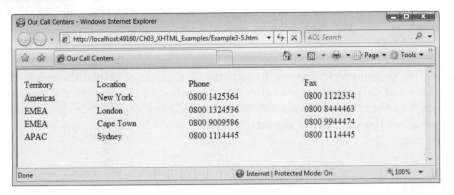

3.10.4 Spanning with attributes

Tables include a useful example of how attributes can be used to change the configuration of an element in HTML. As well as leaving data out of cells we can also make data span more than one cell. In Design view we can do this by selecting two or more adjacent cells and using the 'Table' → 'Modify' → 'Merge Cells' option.

In our example, there are a couple of places where the same data appears in adjacent cells. 'EMEA' appears twice in the 'Territory' column and the phone and fax numbers for the APAC office are the same. We might choose to restructure the table so that the same data can span across multiple cells to avoid repeating the data unnecessarily. Figure 3.27 shows what the table looks like in Design view if these two pairs of cells have been merged (when

FIGURE 3.27 The table after cells have been merged

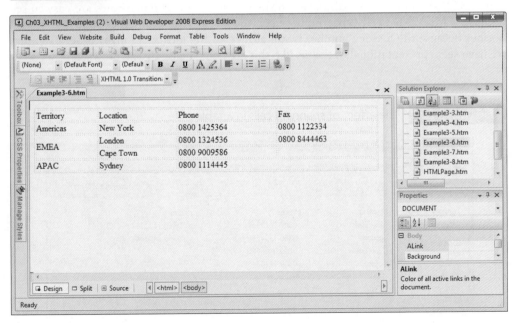

you merge cells the data is also merged, so you will need to manually delete the unnecessary duplications). Note that Design view indicates the outlines of the cells, making it possible to see the difference between the EMEA fax cell, which is empty, and the APAC phone and fax cells, which have been merged (the source for this example can be found in Example3-6.htm).

If you switch to Source view, you will see that this merging of cells is the result of using the rowspan and colspan attributes that can be applied to the td tags. e.g. colspan="2" means span 2 columns and rowspan="2" means span 2 rows. Figure 3.28 shows how these attributes affect the structure of the table.

FIGURE 3.28   Spanned rows and columns in the table

<th>...</th>	<th>...</th>	<th>...</th>	<th>...</th>
<td>...</td>	<td>...</td>	<td>...</td>	<td>...</td>
<td rowspan="2">... </td>	<td>...</td>	<td>...</td>	<td>...</td>
	<td>...</td>	<td>...</td>	<td>...</td>
<td>...</td>	<td>...</td>	<td colspan="2">...</td>	

In the modified source for the table, you should be able to see that the rowspan attribute has been used in the territory column and the colspan attribute in the APAC row:

```
<td rowspan="2">EMEA</td>
...
<td colspan="2">0800 1114445</td>
```

Figure 3.29 shows the table displayed in the browser. The spanned rows are easy to see because 'EMEA' has been centered between the rows. The spanned columns are not so obvious because the Sydney number is still aligned to the left. As in many other examples we have seen, presentational decisions like this are being made by the browser.

FIGURE 3.29   The effect of spanning cells in a table

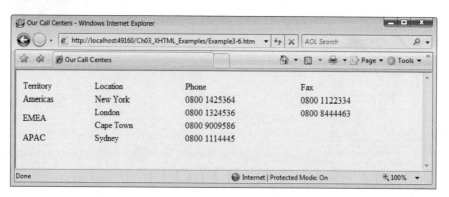

3.10.5 Modifying tables in Source view

Design view provides the tools to manage most of the structural aspects of tables. However we can also make some useful edits in Source view. For example the td tags used for the cell in the top row can be changed into th (table heading) tags, and a caption could also be added. Here is the first part of the table with these changes made in Source view (the full source can be found in Example3-7.htm.):

```
<table class="style1">
 <caption>Our Call Centers</caption>
 <tr>
  <th>Territory</th>
  <th>Location</th>
  <th>Phone</th>
  <th>Fax</th>
 </tr>
```

Figure 3.30 shows the modified table in Design view, with the caption at the top of the table and the table headings rendered differently.

FIGURE 3.30   The table with table header cells and a caption

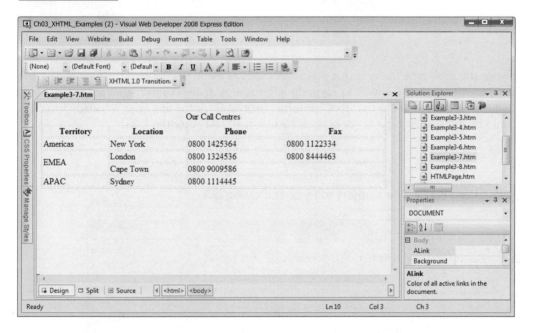

3.11 Links

One of the most important aspects of the World Wide Web is the *link*, also known as a *hyperlink* or a *web link*, which enables us to go from one web-based resource to another, regardless of where on the web the other resource may be. A link has two ends known as *anchors*, with the source anchor being in the current document and the destination anchor being the web resource (document, image, sound file, etc.) that is being linked to. Clicking on a link in a web page lets us retrieve the linked web resource. The full detail of links in HTML is quite complex, so we will only cover the basics here.

The element name used for anchors in HTML documents is a, and the most important attribute is href (Hypertext REFerence), which contains the URI of the linked resource. Here, for example is an anchor that would link to the URI of the WebHomeCover site.

```
Click <a href="http://www.webhomecover.com">here</a> for a great
insurance deal...
```

The text in the body of the anchor element ('here') is the actual hyperlink that will appear in the browser.

You can easily convert some text into a hyperlink in Design view using the 'Convert to Hyperlink' button on the formatting toolbar (Figure 3.31).

FIGURE 3.31 The 'Convert to Hyperlink' button in the Formatting Toolbar

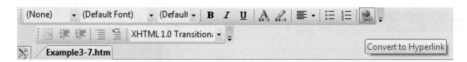

To use this tool, type the text that you want to act as the hyperlink into the page, select the text, then press the 'Convert to Hyperlink' button. A dialog box will appear (Figure 3.32) that allows you to choose the 'Type' (internet protocol) for the link (this is usually http: but could be some other type of connection such as ftp:) and enter the URL.

FIGURE 3.32 The 'Convert to Hyperlink' dialog box

The example in Figure 3.31 shows a full URL being entered, but not all URLs in anchor elements need to include a full web address. Many anchors used in web applications link to other pages in the same application, so the URL can be just a filename using a local path. The 'Browse...' button lets you select another page from the same web application. Here, for example, the anchor refers to a file in the local directory, selected using the 'Browse...' button. The generated anchor element seen in source view contains only the file name, not the full URL:

```
<a href="aboutus.html">About Us</a>
```

Relative paths can also be used. Here, we assume that there is a file stored in a 'pages' folder:

```
<a href="pages/map.htm">Find Us</a>
```

As well as linking to other files, anchors in an HTML page can link to specific parts of a document. If the target anchor is not a complete URL but within a document, then the anchor element can be used at the destination end of the link. For example, we might want to link to a part of a document that contains some terms and conditions about our insurance policies. To link to part of the same document, the URL used in the source anchor is the ID of the destination anchor, preceded by a hash, e.g.:

```
<a href="#terms">terms and conditions</a>
```

In this example we assume that there is a destination anchor in the same document called 'terms'. This will be defined somewhere else in the document using the id attribute of the anchor element, e.g.:

```
<a id="terms">Terms and Conditions</a>
```

Clicking on the hyperlink of the source anchor will take the user to the part of the document containing the destination anchor. The following mark-up shows how the source and destination anchors might appear in the same document.

```
Our insurance is offered according to our standard
<a href="#terms">terms and conditions</a>

which you should read carefully before making a claim ...

blah blah blah...

<h2><a id="terms">Terms and Conditions</a></h2>
WebHomeCover reserve the right to...
```

The same approach can be used when the destination anchor is in part of another document. The only difference is that the anchor name is preceded by the URL of the containing page, for example:

```
<a href="legal.html#terms">terms and conditions</a>
```

In this case we assume that the 'terms' anchor is in another document called 'legal.html'. A full address can also be used:

```
<a href="http://www.webhomecover.com/legal.html#terms">
 terms and conditions
</a>
```

Images, as well as text, can be used as link anchors by nesting image elements inside anchor elements, for example.

```
<a href="home.html">
 <img src="logo.gif" alt="WebHomeCover Logo" />
</a>
```

This is a useful technique for implementing the 'home page at top left' pattern we saw in Chapter 2, where clicking on the company logo always takes you to the home page. You can do this in Design view by selecting an image and then clicking the 'Convert to Hyperlink' button.

3.11.1 Email links

Anchors can also be used for email links. To do this you simply use a 'mailto' value in the `href` attribute, which takes this format:

```
<a href="mailto:help@webhomecover.com">Email the help desk</a>
```

When 'Email the help desk' is clicked, the web browser *may* open your email client to compose a message, though this does depend on the browser configuration so its behavior cannot be guaranteed.

The following example shows an XHTML page that includes both links and images:

```
<!DOCTYPE html PUBLIC "-//W3C//DTD XHTML 1.0 Transitional//EN"
"http://www.w3.org/TR/xhtml1/DTD/xhtml1-transitional.dtd">
<html xmlns="http://www.w3.org/1999/xhtml">
 <head>
  <title>Our Insurance</title>
 </head>
 <body>
  <!-- File: Example3-8.htm -->
  <p>
   <a href="home.htm">
    <img src="webhomecoverlogo.gif" alt="WebHomeCover Logo"
    height="67" width="294" />
   </a>
  </p>
  <h1>Our Insurance</h1>
  <p>
   Our insurance is offered according to our standard
   <a href="#terms">terms and conditions</a>
   which you should read carefully before making a claim...blah blah blah...
  </p>
  <p>
   If you have any enquiries, please
   <a href="mailto:help@webhomecover.com">Email the help desk</a>
  </p>
  <h2><a id="terms">Terms and Conditions</a></h2>
```

```
  <p>
    WebHomeCover reserve the right to...blah blah blah...
  </p>
 </body>
</html>
```

Figure 3.33 shows the page displayed in Internet Explorer 7. To see the effect of the internal link, you need to resize the window so that the 'Terms and Conditions' section is not visible before clicking the 'terms and conditions' link.

FIGURE 3.33 Links and images in an XHTML page displayed in Internet Explorer 7

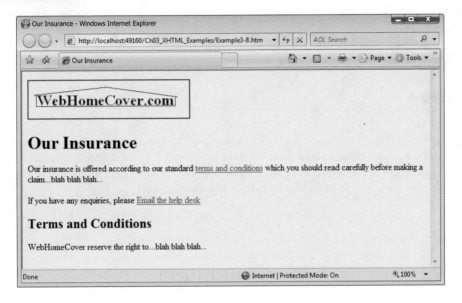

Self Study Questions

1. What is the difference between a tag and an element?
2. What characters are used around an attribute name?
3. Is XHTML case sensitive?
4. What is the <hr /> element for?
5. What do the terms 'strict', 'transitional' and 'frameset' refer to?
6. What is the special character for the copyright symbol?
7. What are the two required attributes for the image (img) element?
8. What kind of XHTML list will display in the browser as a bullet list?
9. What attributes are used to make part of a table spread over multiple rows or columns?
10. What is the name of the element that is used to create hyperlinks?

Exercises

3.5 Create a table containing hyperlinks to useful web resources related to the content of this book. Your table should look something like the following (add extra rows/topics if you like). You will need to identify suitable web links for each of the entries in the table and for each topic, include at least one link, possibly several.

Topic	Useful link(s)
Evolution of the World Wide Web	www ... www ...
Microsoft Visual Web Developer	www ...
The World Wide Web Consortium	www ...
XHTML	www ... www ...
Designing Web Applications	www ... www ...

3.6 In this and the following exercises we will develop some pages for the home insurance website. At this stage we are only looking at static pages that might be used to introduce and explain the site, not the web application processes like making claims or buying insurance.

Using XHTML, implement the content and structure of the home page from the design you created at the end of the last chapter.

3.7 Using XHTML, implement an 'about us' page for the website that uses the three region layout you designed at the end of the last chapter. Use a table to implement this layout (we will see how to do this layout with a stylesheet in the next chapter). You will need a reasonable amount of content on this page, which should include different types of information such as 'our history', 'our mission', 'our people', etc.

3.8 Create a company logo using a suitable software package and use it in your three-region layout (you may also wish to include images from other sources).

SUMMARY

We began this chapter by introducing SGML, the mark-up language from which HTML, and many other mark-up languages, have evolved. We then followed the evolution of HTML through to XHTML, and then looked at some of the most important elements used for structuring XHTML documents, including headings, lists, tables and links. We also saw how XHTML files can be validated. We introduced Visual Web Developer as a tool for creating and editing XHTML documents, and explored its various editing views, the Toolbox and parts of the Formatting Toolbar, among other features.

Table 3.4 provides a summary of all the XHTML elements introduced in this chapter, while Table 3.5 lists the new acronyms that were also introduced.

TABLE 3.4   Summary of XHTML elements introduced in this chapter

Element	Meaning
html	The root element that surrounds the whole document
head	Document header information
title	The text that appears in the browser's title bar
body	The body content of the page displayed in the browser
p	Paragraph
h1, h2 h3, h4, h5 and h6	Different levels of heading
br	Line break
hr	Horizontal rule
cite	Citation
blockquote	Block quotations
em	Emphasis
strong	Strong emphasis
sub	Subscript
sup	Superscript
ul	Unordered List
li	List item
ol	Ordered list
dl	Definition list
dt	Definition list term
dd	Definition list definition

img	Image
a	Anchor
table	Table
caption	Table caption
tr	Table row
th	Table heading
td	Table data
& ;	Character reference (start and end characters)
<!-- -->	Comment text (start and end characters)

TABLE 3.5   Summary of new acronyms introduced in this chapter

Acronym	Meaning
SGML	Standard Generalized Mark-up Language
GML	Goldfarb, Mosher, Lorie
ANSI	American National Standard Institute
ISO	International Standards Organization
MIME	Multipurpose Internet Mail Extension

References and further reading

Connolly, D. 1995. *HTML 2.0 Materials.* W3C, http://www.w3.org/MarkUp/html-spec/.

Goldfarb, C. 1996. *The Roots of SGML – A Personal recollection.* http://www.sgmlsource.com/history/roots.htm.

Korpela, J. 2002. *Empty elements in SGML, HTML, XML, and XHTML.* http://www.cs.tut.fi/~jkorpela/html/empty.html.

Raggett, D., Le Hors, A. and Jacobs, I. 1999. *HTML 4.01 specification.* http://www.w3.org/TR/html401/.

Styling in the Presentation Layer: Cascading Stylesheets (CSS)

LEARNING OBJECTIVES

- **To be able to create external stylesheets in Visual Web Developer and link them to multiple XHTML pages**

- **To be able to use Visual Web Developer to fine tune page styles using style elements and attributes**

- **To be able to build hierarchical stylesheets**

- **To be able to use stylesheets to control the layout of a web page**

- **To be able to validate CSS files**

INTRODUCTION

In the previous chapter we concentrated on looking at some of the important structural elements in XHTML. Prior to XHTML, some versions of HTML also provided a range of elements and attributes that supported the presentation of a document, including text styles and fonts, foreground and background colors, content alignment, and list and table formatting. Using this type of mark-up, however, mixes presentation together with structure and content, making it hard to separately develop and maintain the presentation layer of a web application. Therefore XHTML does not allow these presentational elements and attributes to be used, but rather takes a more flexible and maintainable approach, using cascading stylesheets (CSS) to apply presentational formatting independent of the XHTML mark-up. In this chapter we explore the syntax and use of cascading stylesheets and see how they can be applied to XHTML pages.

4.1 Separating out presentation

HTML 4.0 was the first version of HTML that explicitly attempted to separate out structure from presentation. Although the 'link' element, used for attaching a separate stylesheet to an HTML document, had been available since early versions of HTML, it was rarely used. In this section, we see how HTML developed into a mark-up language that included presentational tags, explore the development of separate stylesheets and see how CSS can be used to separate out the presentation of an XHTML document from its content and structure.

In the previous chapter we looked at XHTML syntax and saw how XHTML is used to specify the content and structure of a web page. Structural elements of XHTML pages include elements such as paragraphs, headings and tables. Although many previous versions of HTML also had presentational elements and attributes, it is preferable that any specification of style (colors, font sizes, etc.) is done separately by using a stylesheet language. Why, then, did HTML have presentational tags if stylesheets are better? This is in fact a consequence of the way that web technologies have evolved, through a combination of influential individuals, browser vendors and standards bodies. These various influences meant that the separation of structure and content for presentation using stylesheets was an approach that developed rather erratically. In the early days of HTML, there was some debate about how HTML should be styled, and whether it should be based on browser configuration or some other mechanism. Although it was always recognized that it would be good practice to separate the content of a page from the specification of its presentation, there was no common agreement on how this should be done. There was also some debate as to who should have control over the appearance of a document, the author, the viewer, or a combination of both. Various early browsers had their own ways of applying stylesheets to manage the appearance of HTML documents, but this was from the perspective of controlling the way that documents were configured in a given browser. It did not enable the author of an HTML page to specify how it should be presented. To address this issue, HTML tags that related to presentational aspects began to be supported by browsers, for example the first version of Netscape Navigator in 1994 supported the 'center' element. Since the early HTML specifications were simply a drawing together of syntax that was already being used by the leading browsers, the introduction of such tags led to their subsequent inclusion in the standard HTML specification. However, around the same time that Netscape Navigator was introducing the first presentational HTML tags, Häkon Lie at CERN published the first proposal for what he called 'cascading HTML stylesheets' (Lie and Bos, 2005). The concept of the cascade was that an HTML document could be presented using an ordered list of stylesheets, so that there might be a number of different stylesheets applied one after the other to a given HTML document, each providing more specialized formatting. Lie's proposal contained the idea of the LINK element in an HTML document that provides the URL of a separate stylesheet. The original version of this proposal looked like this:

```
<LINK REL="style" HREF="http://NYT.com/style">
```

As the idea of stylesheets was debated by the web technology community it became clear that they need not only be applicable to HTML but to other types of document as well. Therefore the reference to HTML was dropped, and they were renamed simply cascading stylesheets (CSS). Although there were alternative proposals for stylesheet technologies made around that time, CSS became the clear leader after the formation of the World Wide Web Consortium in 1995, which held an international workshop on CSS. This was followed in 1996 by the first W3C recommendation, CSS level 1, with support from the leading browsers of the time, Microsoft Internet Explorer and Netscape Navigator, though the implementations in both at that stage were limited, neither of them fully implementing the level 1 specification. The next version, CSS level 2 was published in 1998, and CSS level 3 is an ongoing recommendation.

We have talked about the need to separate structure and content from presentation, but why is this so important? Specifying the appearance of the pages in a website is not only an issue for graphic designers, but is also a management problem. It is important to maintain a uniform appearance across the pages of a website, while indicating the differences between the various concerns of the site in an organized way. For example different color schemes might be used in different parts of a website. An associated issue is that it should be possible to change the appearance of a website consistently across all pages without having to undertake a major maintenance exercise.

How, then, does CSS help us to manage the presentation of a web application in a way that enables us to apply a consistent look and feel, with customization for different parts of our website, and make it easy to change? CSS does this by providing the ability to specify style information in-line, internal to a document or externally. This means that styles can be applied at different levels of granularity: across the whole website, to a specific page, or to a specific element. CSS also provides the ability to cascade a series of stylesheets to apply to a single document, enabling a combination of styles to be blended together.

4.2 CSS syntax

CSS syntax can vary slightly, depending on where it is being used. In-line styles, internal stylesheets and external stylesheets each involve a particular type of syntax, though all are similar. The most flexible and reusable way of applying styles is to use an external stylesheet, so in this chapter we focus mainly on this approach. In-line styles and internal stylesheets can also be useful for fine tuning the presentation of particular pages, so we will cover these at the end of the chapter (parts of the Formatting Toolbar can be used for in-line and internal styles).

Although styles can be applied to individual elements or individual documents, the styles we define in this way cannot be used across multiple web pages. It is likely, however, that we would want to apply the same styles right across our web application, so that all of our pages have a consistent look and feel. If, for example we want all our major headings on all pages to be blue and center-aligned, we do not want to have to repeat this style information for every single page. Also, if we decided to change the look and feel so that all major headings were, for example, to be made left-aligned, we would want to able to make this change globally, not on individual pages. Fortunately, Visual Web Developer makes it easy to specify and maintain an external stylesheet in a separate CSS file and apply it to multiple pages.

4.2.1 Creating an external stylesheet

An external stylesheet is a file with a '.css' extension. To create a stylesheet file using Visual Web Developer, choose 'File' → 'New File' from the main menu, then select 'StyleSheet' from the list of available file types. Visual Web Developer will give the stylesheet a default name, similar to 'Stylesheet.css'. You can of course change this default name before you press the 'Open' button to save the file. As with other files, you can also rename this file after it has been created using the Solution Explorer window (right click on the name of the file and select 'Rename'). For the purposes of this example we will name the stylesheet 'webhomecover.css'.

Initially, when the new file has been created, the Visual Web Developer stylesheet editor will contain only the following CSS code, which refers to the 'body' element of an XHTML page but at this point contains no style information:

```
body {
}
```

Each component of a stylesheet is made up of three parts:

1. The name of an element type
2. The name of a presentational property of that element
3. The value of the property that is to be applied

Properties and their values appear inside braces after the element name to which they relate. Each pair of properties and values is separated by a colon, and if there is more than one pair of values then these are separated by semicolons (spaces and line feeds are not important but can aid readability):

```
element
{
  property: value;
  property: value;
  etc..
}
```

 NOTE The way that Visual Web Developer formats CSS syntax can be controlled by selecting the 'Options' dialog ('Tools → Options' from the main menu bar), checking the 'Show all settings' box, then navigating through the menus to 'Text Editor → CSS → Format'.

Going back to our new stylesheet file, you can see that Visual Web Developer has generated a stylesheet that refers to the 'body' element type, but has not applied any specific styles to it. For the moment we will not add styles to the body of the document but will begin by applying styles to different types of heading element. To apply styles to other element types, the first step is to position the cursor on the editor pane of the stylesheet and select 'Style → Add Style Rule' from the main menu (you can also right click in the editor pane and choose 'Add Style Rule'). This brings up the dialog shown in Figure 4.1. In this dialog, you can choose which XHTML element you want to create styles for using the 'Element' select box (Figure 4.1 shows that we have selected the 'h1' element in this example). Then simply click the OK button (we will look at other aspects of the dialog later).

FIGURE 4.1   Selecting an element to be styled in the 'Add Style Rule' dialog box

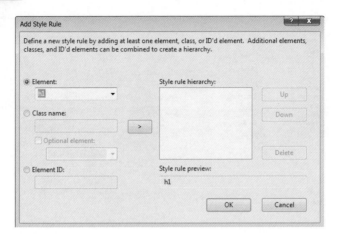

After you have added a style rule for h1 elements, the text in the stylesheet file should now look something like the following:

```
body {
}

h1
{
}
```

You can see that the 'Add Style Rule' dialog has simply added the h1 element to the list of elements that may be styled, but no styles have yet been applied (you could of course have typed this in manually without using the dialog).

   NOTE   The difference in the initial positions of the braces for the two elements is not important, and is just an inconsistent behavior by Visual Web Developer.

To apply a style to h1 elements, position the cursor between the two braces following the 'h1' element name, then select 'Build Style' from the 'Styles' menu (or right click to choose 'Build Style'). Note that this menu option is grayed out if the cursor is not positioned between a set of braces. When 'Build Style' is selected, the 'Modify Style' dialog will appear (Figure 4.2). In this example we will create a new style for h1 elements that will make them all blue and center aligned (the foreground text color can be set using the 'color' property under the 'Font' category, which will display a color palette from which the color can be selected, and the alignment using the 'text-align' property under the 'Block' category). The 'Preview' window shows the effect of the various styles chosen and the 'Description' window shows the CSS code that will be generated for the style elements. Figure 4.2 shows the dialog after both styles have been applied. Note that a category that has had styles applied for this element will appear in bold type in the 'Category' list.

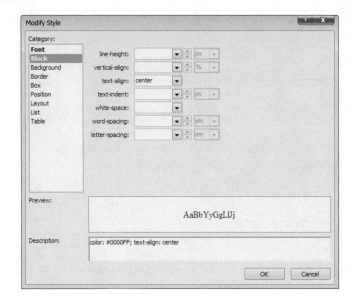

If you apply the styles selected in Figure 4.2 using the 'Modify Style' dialog and then click 'OK', you should see that the h1 style has been modified to include two style entries:

```
body {
}

h1
{
    color: #0000FF;
    text-align: center;
}
```

The color style has been applied by specifying red, green and blue values as hexadecimal numbers using the following syntax:

```
color: #rrggbb
```

Each 2 digit value can be in the range O–FF (FF being the hexadecimal equivalent of 255). In our example we have chosen a simple blue color, which has zeros for the red and green values and FF for the blue value.

 NOTE   There is a 'StyleSheet' toolbar in Visual Web Developer that contains 'Add Style Rule' and 'Build Style' buttons to invoke the two dialogs we have been using.

Throughout this chapter we will be showing examples of generating CSS code using the 'Add Style Rule' and 'Modify Style' dialog boxes, but equally you can manually write the style code directly into the CSS file. Visual Web Developer will assist you to add styles for various elements. For example if you position the cursor inside the braces of a style rule and press

CTRL+spacebar, a full list of possible style properties will appear in a list. If you select a property and then type in the following colon, pressing CTRL+spacebar again will give a list of possible values for that property. To assist you in understanding the underlying CSS code, for each example we will list the generated CSS as well as explaining the dialog boxes.

4.2.2 Selecting colors

When you select foreground and background colors using the 'Modify Style' dialog, the color palette initially shows the 16 colors specified in the W3C HTML 4.0 standard (Figure 4.3). These have the names: *aqua, black, blue, fuchsia, gray, green, lime, maroon, navy, olive, purple, red, silver, teal, white* and *yellow*, though a large number of other color names are also recognized by many browsers. By selecting 'More Colors . . .' you have access to a much greater palette.

FIGURE 4.3 The 16 colors from the W3C HTML 4.0 standard displayed in the 'Modify Style' dialog

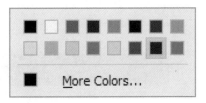

Knowing the color names is useful if you want to manually edit your stylesheets, as they can be more readable than the hexadecimal number format generated by Visual Web Developer. For example we could write 'color: blue' instead of 'color: #0000FF'. These color names are available from the list provided by pressing CTRL-spacebar if you are manually editing the source of your stylesheet.

Again, if you are manually editing CSS, there is another syntax that you may also find useful as an alternative to specifying red, green and blue value using hexadecimal numbers, which is to use decimal number values for the three colors instead, in this property format:

```
color: rgb(r,g,b)
```

In this format, each of the three color values is specified by an integer in the range 0 to 255. This is useful, when manually editing, if you want colors other than the 16 named colors in the drop-down list. However choosing these colors is probably easier to achieve using the dialogs.

 NOTE In the early days of web page design, a 216 color 'browser safe palette' was proposed that indicated which combinations of colors would work best across multiple browsers in a world where many computers only supported 8 bit color (256 colors). The 'safe' palette eliminated the 40 colors that were most likely to vary on different displays. However in the vast majority of cases this limitation no longer applies so the safe palette is largely redundant (Weinman, 2007).

Having applied a style to h1 elements, we will now also style h2 elements, so we will need to add 'h2' to the list of style rules. For this type of element, we will select white as the foreground color and italic as the font style (under the 'Font' category) and black as the background color (under the 'Background' category). Figure 4.4 shows the 'Modify Style' dialog after these styles have been selected.

FIGURE 4.4 The 'Modify Style' dialog box being used to style elements with white italic text on a black background

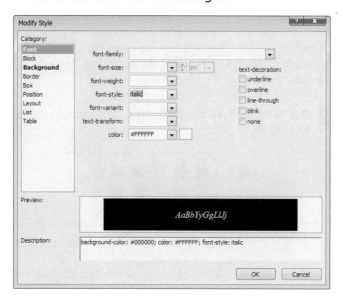

Now our stylesheet looks like this, with the body element still unstyled, but style rules applied for h1 and h2 elements.

```
body {
}

h1
{
    color: #0000FF;
    text-align: center;
}

h2
{
    background-color: #000000;
    color: #FFFFFF;
    font-style: italic;
}
```

In order to see this stylesheet in action, we need to have an XHTML document that includes h1 and h2 elements. Here is a simple example that contains both types of heading:

```
<!DOCTYPE html PUBLIC "-//W3C//DTD XHTML 1.0 Transitional//EN"
"http://www.w3.org/TR/xhtml1/DTD/xhtml1-transitional.dtd">
<html xmlns="http://www.w3.org/1999/xhtml">
 <head>
  <title>Our Insurance Cover</title>
 </head>
 <body>
  <!-- File: Example4-1.htm -->
  <h1>We provide the following types of insurance</h1>
  <h2>Buildings Cover</h2>
  <p>
   Insuring the fabric of the building you live in
  </p>
  <h2>Contents Cover</h2>
  <p>
   Insuring your possessions from theft and damage
  </p>
 </body>
</html>
```

4.3 Linking stylesheets in Visual Web Developer

If you load this file into Visual Web Developer and look at it in Design view, you will see that it has no heading styles applied yet. How, then, do we apply our stylesheet to this document? In terms of XHTML syntax, a stylesheet can be applied to a document by using the 'link' element (in the XHTML document's head element). This can be added very easily in Design view by simply dragging the stylesheet from the Solution Explorer window onto the Design view window by holding down the left mouse button over the stylesheet file and dragging it onto the page. If you release the left mouse button while the icon is over the Design view page, a 'link' element will be automatically added to the XHTML source. If you do this and then switch from Design view to Source view, you should see that the 'link' element has been added to the head element.

```
<head>
    <title>Our Insurance Cover</title>
    <link href="webhomecover.css" rel="stylesheet" type="text/css" />
</head>
```

This example assumes that the CSS file is in the same folder (either locally or on the web server) as the XHTML file. Otherwise the value of the 'href' attribute could be written to include a directory pathway or a full URL, depending on the circumstances.

 NOTE You can also add a stylesheet 'link' element by dragging the stylesheet into the head element in Source view or by selecting 'Format → Attach StyleSheet' from the main menu bar.

Within the link element, the name and location of the stylesheet is specified by the 'href' attribute, and the relationship between the XHTML page and the stylesheet by the 'rel' attribute. The value of the 'rel' attribute is set to 'stylesheet'. There is also a 'type' attribute that indicates the type of the linked document, which for a stylesheet is 'text/css'. There are some other attributes that may be used in the link element but we do not need to be concerned with them here.

 NOTE Another possible value for the 'rel' attribute is 'alternate stylesheet', where the browser may enable switching between different stylesheets, provided more than one stylesheet link element is included in the head element. However this option is poorly supported by current browsers.

Figure 4.5 shows what the XHTML page looks like in a browser after the stylesheet has been applied.

FIGURE 4.5 A web page displayed in a browser with styles applied using a stylesheet

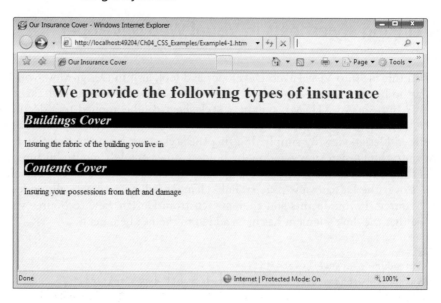

Once we have a stylesheet, we can apply it to multiple pages (just drag and drop the stylesheet file onto the surface of Design view for each page). Here, we apply the same stylesheet to a different page:

```
<!DOCTYPE html PUBLIC "-//W3C//DTD XHTML 1.0 Transitional//EN"
"http://www.w3.org/TR/xhtml1/DTD/xhtml1-transitional.dtd">
<html xmlns="http://www.w3.org/1999/xhtml">
 <head>
 <link href="webhomecover.css" rel="stylesheet" type="text/css">
 <title>Our Promise to You</title>
 </head>
```

```
<body>
<!-- File: Example4-2.htm -->
<h1>Our Promise to You</h1>
<h2>No Unreasonable Exclusions</h2>
<p>
   Many insurance companies include exclusions in their policies,
   making it difficult to claim for events such as 'acts of God',
   terrorism or subsidence. We have the smallest set of exclusions
   of any fictional insurance company.
</p>
<h2>Rapid Response</h2>
<p>
   If you make a claim, we promise to respond to you with 24 hours,
   either by settling immediately or putting you in contact with
   one of our insurance assessors.
</p>
<h2>Low, Low, Rates</h2>
<p>
   We constantly monitor our prices against our competitors, and
   guarantee that we provide the best value insurance that you can't
   actually buy.
</p>
</body>
</html>
```

4

Figure 4.6 shows that the same heading styles have been applied as appear in Figure 4.4.

Of course once we have a stylesheet being used for multiple pages, new styles or changes to existing ones can be applied consistently across all pages. For example, we might modify

FIGURE 4.6   Reusing the same stylesheet in another page

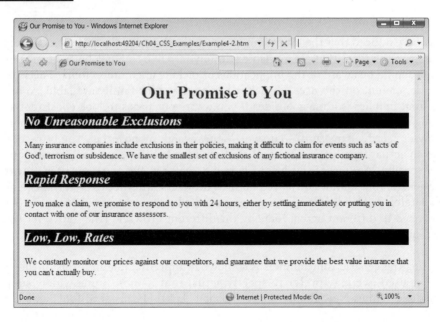

the stylesheet to apply a consistent font across all parts of every document. We might choose to do this by applying a style to the (currently unstyled) 'body' element in the stylesheet. In the following example we have used the 'Modify Style' dialog to apply a 'font-family' setting to the body element in the stylesheet (this setting can be found under the 'Font' category in the dialog). Here we have chosen the first option in the 'font-family' drop-down list, 'Ariel, Helvetica, sans-serif':

```
body
{
    font-family: Arial, Helvetica, sans-serif;
}
```

If you make this change to the stylesheet, you should see that any web pages that link to the stylesheet now appear with a consistent Ariel font across the entire body of the page. Figure 4.7 shows Example4-1.htm after the stylesheet has been modified with this body style (compare this with Figure 4.5).

(i) NOTE

If you want to add comments to your stylesheet source file, you can use the following syntax. Anything between the start characters (/*) and the end characters (*/) will be treated as a comment, which can span multiple lines:

```
/*
    Comments and /or css style(s) that you want
    to temporarily hide
*/
```

You can also use the comment syntax to temporarily remove styles while you are developing your stylesheet. This means that you don't need to use the dialogs to keep adding and removing the same styles if you are experimenting with various combinations.

You may have noticed that the list of font names in the 'font-family' dialog can be very long, depending on the fonts that are available within your environment, but when styling web pages you should be aware of the implications of picking uncommon fonts. This is because you are dependent on the user's browser having that font family available, so selecting unusual font families is not a good idea if you want your pages to look consistent across a wide range of browsers. There are five generic font families that should be supported by any browser; 'serif', 'sans-serif', 'cursive', 'fantasy' and 'monospace'. The browser should provide an actual font mapping for all of these font families, but the actual mapping is browser specific. We can see this from Figure 4.8, which shows the same page of text using the five generic font families displayed in three browsers, Internet Explorer 7, Opera 9 and Mozilla Firefox 3. The differences in appearance are because the generic font families have been mapped to different actual fonts by the different browsers (the source for this page can be found in the file 'genericfonts.htm').

Since using the generic font families is somewhat unpredictable in terms of the specific font being used, we may prefer to specify actual font names. Some widely supported fonts include 'Times New Roman' (a serif font), 'Arial' (a sans-serif font) and 'Courier'

FIGURE 4.7 A web page displayed in a browser with an Arial font applied to the body of the page

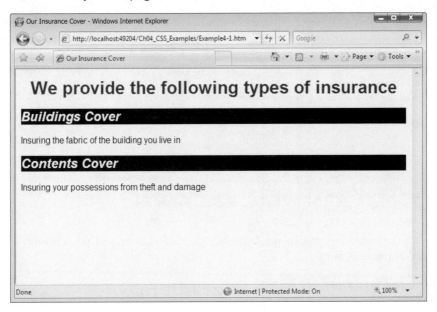

FIGURE 4.8 The five generic font families displayed by Internet Explorer 7 (left), Opera 9 (middle) and Mozilla Firefox 3 (right)

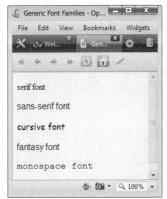

(a monospace font). Figure 4.9 shows some text using these three fonts in the three browsers. Note how they all look very similar (the source for this page can be found in the file 'commonfonts.htm').

Because of this widespread browser support, Visual Web Developer puts these three font types at the top of the drop-down as common (and wise) choices. It also applies another useful technique which is to provide a comma separated list of fonts, which becomes more general as the list progresses. With this approach, the browser will try to match the first font in the list, but if it is not able to support it then it will try to match the next one in the list and so on. Since the last entry in each of the three lists is a generic font family, it is virtually guaranteed that the browser will find some kind of usable font. If the name of a font family contains spaces then it needs to appear inside quotes or apostrophes in the

FIGURE 4.9 The Times New Roman, Arial and Courier fonts displayed by Internet Explorer 7 (left), Opera 9 (middle) and Mozilla Firefox 3 (right)

 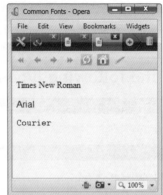 

CSS source code, as you can see from the stylesheet source if you choose 'Times New Roman' as the font family:

```
font-family: 'Times New Roman', Times, serif;
```

4.3.1 Setting the font size

There are many different ways of setting the size of the font using CSS, but as with choosing fonts there are some approaches that are more reliable than others. Figure 4.10 shows the 'font-size' drop-down list under the 'Format' category in the 'Modify Style' dialog. Most of the entries in this drop-down list provide generic descriptions of text size, including 'large', 'small', 'x-large' (extra large) and 'xx-small' (extra-extra small), etc. These are followed by relative sizes ('larger' and 'smaller') and 'inherit' which means the size will be taken from the size specified in the enclosing element.

Further down this list (not visible in Figure 4.10) is the '(value)' option (Figure 4.11) that enables you to specify a value to be used for the font size based on a selected form of measurement.

FIGURE 4.10 Options in the 'font-size' drop-down list

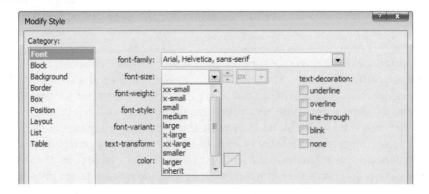

FIGURE 4.11 Setting the font size using a value in a given measurement

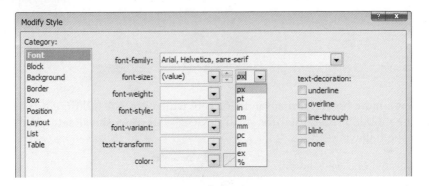

Using this option, the size of the font can be set using a number of different measures, including absolute sizes in points (pt), inches (in), centimeters (cm), millimeters (mm), or picas (pc). However, setting sizes to specific measurements is not very flexible across different browser contexts, and should only be used in specialized applications where the target client device is known. This is not the case for most web applications, so the better approach is to use a relative method of sizing text. Even here, there is more than one option; either we can use a pixel measure (px), the 'x height' of the font (ex), 'em' which relates to both the width and height of the font or a percentage measure (%). Apart from pixels, which are display dependent, all of these work in a way that is relative to the context within which an element is used. For example, if we apply a relative size to an element of a specific type (for example a paragraph element), then the actual size is based on the one that would normally be applied. In other words, setting a paragraph to be 1.5em would make it half as big again as the normal size of that paragraph. In general, then, if you want to specify text size, it is best to avoid extremes (such as xx-small) as they are likely to be unreadable on some browsers, and also to avoid the exact measures such as inches and centimeters. You should also be aware that different element types will respond differently to size settings. For example if you set the size of headings you will override their default size settings in the browser. This may mean, for example, that making a heading 'larger' in fact makes it appear smaller! Whichever approach you use, be consistent; do not switch between different types of measure in the same web application.

In this example we have used just one of the possible font size options, making paragraph text 'larger':

```
p
{
    font-size: larger;
}
```

4.3.2 Validating CSS

Visual Web Developer validates your CSS files automatically. This is useful if you are manually editing a stylesheet as it will pick up syntax errors. For example, in Figure 4.12 we can see that the 'color' property has been entered using British spelling, which is invalid in CSS. The validation level here is CSS 2.1. This may be set using the StyleSheet toolbar, which includes a drop-down list of CSS versions for validation.

FIGURE 4.12   Automatic CSS validation in Visual Web Developer

```
 5
 6   h1
 7   {
 8       colour: #0000FF;|
 9   }   Validation (CSS 2.1): 'colour' is not a known CSS property name.
10
```

If you want a more broad ranging validation tool which can assess different types of CSS such as the mobile profile used for small devices, you can also validate your CSS files on-line at the following URL:

http://jigsaw.w3.org/css-validator/

4.3.3 Style rule hierarchies

As well as applying multiple styles to a single element type, we might want to apply the same style(s) to more than one type of element. We can do this by creating style rule hierarchies. For example we might wish to apply the same formatting to both level 2 and level 3 headings (h2 and h3). This is simply done by putting them together in a list before the style definition, as in this example:

```
h2 h3
{
    background-color: #000000;
    color: #FFFFFF;
    font-style: italic;
}
```

The 'Add Style Rule' dialog supports this syntax by providing the 'Style rule hierarchy' list (Figure 4.13).

To add an element name to this list, you first select it from the 'Element' list, then press the right-hand arrow head button to make the element name appear in the hierarchy box.

FIGURE 4.13   Adding elements to the 'Style rule hierarchy' list

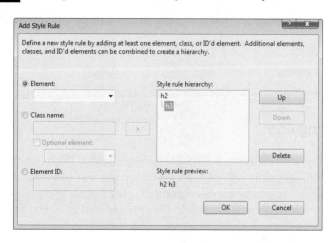

Then you can add as many other element types as you like, creating a tree structure of element names. The dialog also provides 'Up', 'Down' and 'Delete' buttons for you to manipulate this list until you are happy with it. When you press the OK button it will add the list of element names to the CSS file. However in most cases it is easier just to type the element names into the file manually.

Section summary and quick exercises

In this section we covered how to create an external stylesheet and link it to multiple web pages. We saw how to apply style rules to specific XHTML elements, and how to add different styles to those elements. In our examples we styled headings, paragraphs and the document body, and looked at setting the foreground and background colors, changing text alignment, and setting the font style and size.

In Visual Web Developer we saw how the 'Add Style Rule' dialog can be used to add an entry for an XHTML element to the stylesheet, and how the 'Modify Style' dialog can be used to add a style to these elements. In that dialog, we have seen examples of styles under the 'Font' (color, size, style and family), 'Block' (alignment) and 'Background' (color) categories. We also saw that Visual Web Developer automatically validates CSS files but that these can also be validated on-line.

4

EXERCISE 4.1

Create your own stylesheet that applies styles to h1, h2, body and p elements. Replace the stylesheet used with Example4-1.htm with your own.

EXERCISE 4.2

Experiment with different font sizes and families and browse your page in different browsers. It is important to test your web pages in multiple browsers before using them in a real website, as the same page can appear differently, as we saw with the font family example.

EXERCISE 4.3

Validate your stylesheets using the on-line validator.

4.4 Applying styles with 'class' and 'id' attributes

So far we have looked at how to apply styles to specific elements, such as h1, h2 and body. In many cases this is useful, but there are occasions when we want to:

- Apply the same style to more than one type of XHTML element
- Apply a style to some, but not all, instances of a particular XHTML element
- Apply a style to one specific instance of an element

To do this we need some way of labeling parts of our XHTML so that we can apply styles to elements that are identified by these labels. We can do this in two ways.

- We can use the 'class' attribute. This enables us to group a number of elements together as belonging to a single class. Then we can apply a style to all members of the class.

- We can use the 'id' attribute. This can be used to give an element a unique ID. This ID can be used to apply a style that is not used anywhere else in the document.

4.4.1 Using the 'class' attribute

The class attribute can be applied to many elements. In addition, a given element can belong to more than one class. The class attribute is very useful as a way of applying styles across a range of different elements. For example, let us assume that we want both major headings (h1) and subheadings (h2) to be centered, but want other aspects of their styles to be different. We could, of course, apply the same style separately to both h1 and h2 elements in the stylesheet. However a more flexible and maintainable approach is to use a class attribute. The first step is to identify both h1 and h2 elements as belonging to the same class. The name of a class is decided by the author of the page. In the next example we apply the class name 'heading' to all instances of both h1 and h2 elements.

```
<!DOCTYPE html PUBLIC "-//W3C//DTD XHTML 1.0 Transitional//EN"
"http://www.w3.org/TR/xhtml1/DTD/xhtml1-transitional.dtd">
<html xmlns="http://www.w3.org/1999/xhtml">
 <head>
  <title>Our Insurance Cover</title>
  <link href="webhomecover.css" rel="stylesheet" type="text/css" />
 </head>
 <body>
  <!-- File: Example4-3.htm -->
  <h1 class="heading">We provide the following types of insurance</h1>
  <h2 class="heading">Buildings Cover</h2>
  <p>
    Insuring the fabric of the building you live in
  </p>
  <h2 class="heading">Contents Cover</h2>
  <p>
    Insuring your possessions from theft and damage
  </p>
 </body>
</html>
```

We also need to apply a style to 'heading' elements in the stylesheet. To do this using the 'Add Style Rule' dialog box, select the radio button next to the 'Class name' option and type in the name that you want to use for the class, which in our example here would be 'heading' (Figure 4.14). You can see from the 'Style rule preview' box that in the generated CSS syntax the class name is preceded by a period.

FIGURE 4.14 Adding a class name to a stylesheet using the 'Add Style Rule' dialog box

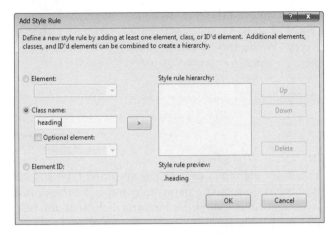

In the CSS file, the following entry should be created when you click the 'OK' button:

```
.heading
{
}
```

The 'Modify Style' dialog can then be used to apply styles to members of the 'heading' class. In this example, we center align all members of the class:

```
.heading
{
    text-align: center;
}
```

Now, any elements that belong to the 'heading' class will be center aligned, regardless of which XHTML elements the class is applied to. Figure 4.15 shows 'Example4-3.htm' rendered in a browser (Internet Explorer), with all headings centered.

FIGURE 4.15 Class styles applied to center different heading elements

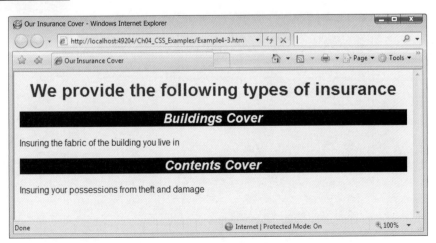

4.4.2 Applying class styles to a subset of elements

In the previous example, we used the class attribute to apply a style to multiple different elements. Another way of using the class attribute is to apply a style to a subset of elements of a specific type. We do this by putting an XHTML element name in front of the class name, like this:

```
elementname.classname
{
    style
}
```

This will specify a style for elements of both the specified type and class. For example, we could apply a special style to some paragraphs but not others. In this example, we could change the stylesheet to include styles for paragraphs that also belong to an 'emphasis' class. This makes it possible for us to create documents where some paragraphs are emphasized while others are not. To style 'emphasis' paragraphs, we add a 'p.emphasis' entry to the stylesheet. Here, we have set the 'font-weight' property to be 'bold' (in the 'Modify Style' dialog this can be set under the 'Font' category):

```
p.emphasis
{
    font-weight: bold;
}
```

To do this using the 'Add Style Rule' dialog box, as well as selecting the radio button next to the 'Class name' option and typing in the name that you want to use for the class (as we did to specify a class style) you also need to select the 'Optional element' check box. Then, from the drop-down list, select the element type that this class may be applied to, which in our example here would be 'p' (Figure 4.16). You can see from the 'Style rule preview' box that in the generated CSS syntax the element name is followed by a period and then the class name.

FIGURE 4.16 Applying class styles to specific element types

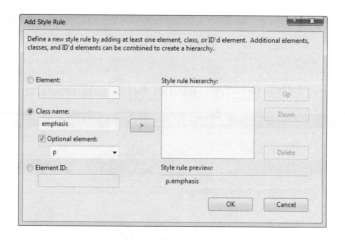

In the following example we make two of the paragraphs belong to the 'emphasis' class.

```
<!DOCTYPE html PUBLIC "-//W3C//DTD XHTML 1.0 Transitional//EN"
"http://www.w3.org/TR/xhtml1/DTD/xhtml1-transitional.dtd">
<html xmlns="http://www.w3.org/1999/xhtml">
 <head>
  <link href="webhomecover.css" rel="stylesheet" type="text/css" />
  <title>Our Insurance Cover</title>
 </head>
 <body>
  <!- File: Example4-4.htm -->
  <h1 class="heading">We provide the following types of insurance</h1>
  <h2 class="heading">Buildings Cover</h2>
  <p>
You may think you're "safe as houses" but you'd be surprised how many
things can damage the building you live in. Fires, earthquakes,
subsidence, runaway trucks,cricket balls through windows or the
occasional meteor.
  </p>
  <p class="emphasis">Best to be covered!</p>
  <h2 class="heading">Contents Cover</h2>
  <p>
You may not realize just how much the stuff you have would cost to
replace. If the burglars move in while you're on holiday, could you
afford to replace the TV, the stereo, the chairs, the cupboards, the
crockery etc?
  </p>
  <p class="emphasis">
Not only that, our contents cover means that if you have your bike
stolen, drop the vase your mother in law gave you as a wedding present,
lose your camera, leave your glasses on the train or have your mobile
phone stolen, you'll be fully compensated.
  </p>
 </body>
</html>
```

Figure 4.17 shows the page displayed in Internet Explorer. Note the second and fourth paragraphs, which belong to the 'emphasis' class, are in bold font.

4.4.3 Element 'id' attributes

Sometimes we may want to apply a style to one specific element, and no other. In this case the element needs a unique identifier that will make it different from every other element in the document. Since the 'class' attribute can be applied to multiple elements, it cannot be used to uniquely identify a specific element. Instead, we use the 'id' attribute to identify a unique instance of an element within the document, such as a particular paragraph or heading. Here, we apply a unique id ('footer') to a single paragraph:

```
<p id="footer">&copy;WebHomeCover.com 2010</p>
```

FIGURE 4.17   Applying styles to paragraphs using 'class' attributes

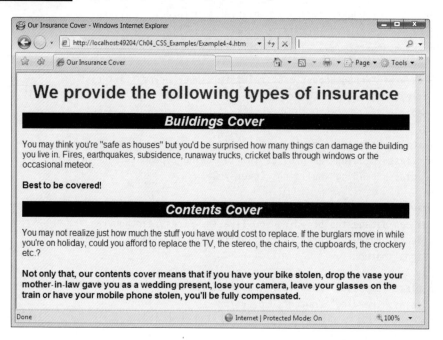

Only a single element on any one page can have the id of 'footer' (though this id can be used on multiple pages). To style 'id' elements in a stylesheet we use the following syntax:

```
#idvalue{style}
```

To create an ID style using the 'Add Style Rule' dialog box, select the radio button next to the 'Element ID' option and type in the unique ID that you want to use, which in our example here would be 'footer' (Figure 4.18). You can see from the 'Style rule preview' box that in the generated CSS syntax the ID name is preceded by a hash sign.

FIGURE 4.18   Adding styles to element IDs in the 'Add Style Rule' dialog

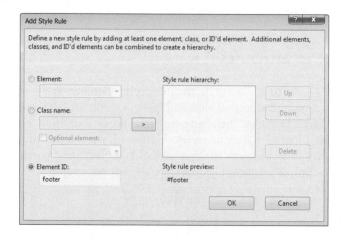

Once again, the actual styles can be applied using the 'Modify Style' dialog. Here, we apply some special styles to the 'footer' paragraph using various options that we have seen before (the colors in this example are blue on silver).

```
#footer
{
    font-weight: bold;
    font-style: italic;
    color: #000080;
    background-color: #C0C0C0;
    text-align: center;
    font-size: smaller;
}
```

Figure 4.19 shows how the footer appears in the browser using our special footer style, if it is added to the previous example XHTML page (the full source file is in 'Example4-5.htm').

FIGURE 4.19   Applying styles to a 'footer' element using an 'id' attribute

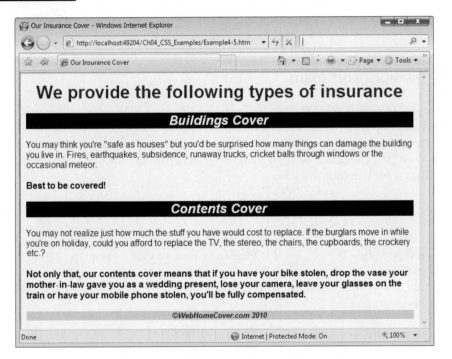

4.5 Block and inline elements

So far we have been applying styles to some of the XHTML elements that we introduced in the previous chapter. One issue with many XHTML elements is that they already have some presentational implications, for example the relative size of headings or the way that 'strong' elements are rendered, even before stylesheets are applied. Sometimes it is useful to be able to apply styles to elements that specify only the very basics of structure, with no presentational implications. In general terms, XHTML elements can be either *block-level* or *inline*. A block level element implies a block of content that is separated in some way from other blocks of content, usually by beginning on a new line, while inline content is part of a block and not separated from it in any way. Blocks can appear inside other blocks, and inline elements can appear inside other inline elements. Figure 4.20 shows the general relationships between block and inline elements.

FIGURE 4.20   Block and inline elements

block		
in-line	in-line	
block		
in-line	in-line	
	in-line	

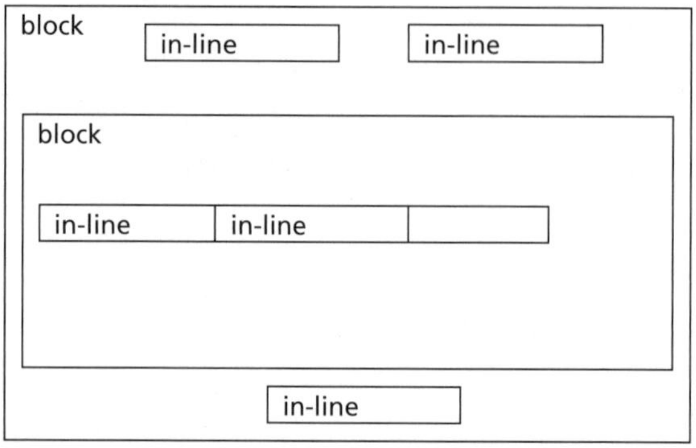

4.5.1 Divisions and spans

Block level elements in XHTML are indicated by the div (division) element, while inline elements are indicated by the span element. Their main value is in being able to provide generic structure for documents that will have stylesheets applied for presentation. Both 'id' and 'class' attributes can be used with these elements to indicate where styles can be applied to add presentational features.

The next example shows how the div and span elements can be used to structure the block and inline components of an XHTML document. Within these elements, we can apply more specific XHTML structures, such as paragraphs. In this example, paragraph elements have been used within the blocks. It is important to note that a paragraph element should not be a parent of a div element, but should be nested inside it. This makes sense, since div and span are the generic organizational elements, within which the more detailed structures and presentation can be managed.

Because these element types are generic, we are unlikely to apply styles directly to them, since the number of styles would be limited to two. Instead, we use attributes to specify IDs or classes for div and span elements so that we can apply styles to them later. In this example we apply 'heading', 'bigger' and 'text' class attributes to various elements, and 'id' attributes called 'risk' and 'items'.

NOTE	This example also shows how more than one class can be applied to a single element, by listing multiple class names separated by spaces, e.g. class="heading bigger">.

```
<!DOCTYPE html PUBLIC "-//W3C//DTD XHTML 1.0 Transitional//EN"
"http://www.w3.org/TR/xhtml1/DTD/xhtml1-transitional.dtd">
<html xmlns="http://www.w3.org/1999/xhtml">
 <head>
  <link href="divspanstyles.css" rel="stylesheet" type="text/css" />
  <title>Making a Claim</title>
 </head>
 <body>
  <!-- File: Example4-6.htm -->
  <div class="heading bigger">Buildings Insurance</div>
  <div class="text">
   <p>
You need this type of insurance to cover you in case of
<span id="risk">severe damage to your home</span> (for example fire,
flood, vehicle or tree crashing into it) as well as more everyday risks
like accidentally breaking a window
   </p>
  </div>
  <div class="heading bigger">Contents Insurance</div>
  <div class="text">
   <p>
You need this type of insurance to cover the <span id="items">things in
your house</span>, such as furniture, electrical goods, carpets and
curtains, against risks such as fire, theft, water damage (due to burst
pipes, etc) or accidental breakage
   </p>
  </div>
 </body>
</html>
```

On their own, the only effect of these elements is that div forces a new line. To overlay presentational styles on top of a document written using these tags the 'class' and 'id' attributes can be linked to a cascading stylesheet. The following stylesheet ('divspanstyles .css') applies styles to the classes and IDs used in the example above. Note that there are no styles applied here to XHTML element types, only to the classes and IDs that we have defined ourselves. When creating this kind of stylesheet using the 'Add Style Rule' dialog, we would only use the 'Class name' and 'Element ID' boxes to specify our own identifiers, and not use the drop-down lists of XHTML element names.

```
.heading
{
    text-align: center;
    color: #0000FF;
}
.text
{
    text-align: left;
    font-family: Arial, Helvetica, sans-serif;
}
.bigger
{
    font-size: 2em;
```

```
}
#items
{
    font-weight: bold;
}
#risk
{
    font-weight: bold;
    font-style: italic;
    color: #FF0000;
}
```

Figure 4.21 shows the XHTML page displayed in a browser, with all styles applied using only div and span elements.

FIGURE 4.21   Styles applied using div and span elements

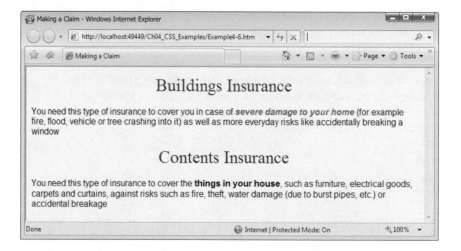

Section summary and quick exercises

In this section we saw how styles may be applied in flexible ways. We saw how style rule hierarchies enable us to apply the same style to more than one type of element. We also saw how 'class' and 'id' attributes can be used to apply styles independently of XHTML elements. Finally these class and 'id' attributes were used to style generic div and span elements that are independent of any predetermined presentation, enabling us to control page presentation very specifically.

In Visual Web Developer we saw how the 'Add Style Rule' dialog can be used to create style rule hierarchies and also apply style rules for classes and IDs. In the 'Modify Style' dialog we set the 'font-weight' property, in addition to the styles we had applied in the previous section.

EXERCISE 4.4

Create a web page that contains three paragraphs of text. Apply a 'class' attribute to two of these paragraphs so they belong to the same class. Give the third paragraph a unique 'id' attribute. Create an external stylesheet to apply styles to the paragraphs using the class and ID names.

Create a web page that contains div and span elements that belong to classes. Apply styles to these classes using an external stylesheet.

4.6 Applying styles to lists and tables

The 'Modify Style' dialog provides support for various aspects of list styles. To explore these, we will use the following example document containing our ordered and unordered lists, which we saw previously in Chapter 3 (though in this case a stylesheet link element has been added):

```
<!DOCTYPE html PUBLIC "-//W3C//DTD XHTML 1.0 Transitional//EN"
"http://www.w3.org/TR/xhtml1/DTD/xhtml1-transitional.dtd">
<html xmlns="http://www.w3.org/1999/xhtml">
 <head>
  <link href="webhomecover.css" rel="stylesheet" type="text/css" />
  <title>Making a Claim</title>
 </head>
 <body>
  <!-- File: example4-7.htm -->
  <h1>Useful Tips</h1>
   <ul>
    <li>Making a Claim
     <ol>
      <li>
      Find as much documentation as you can (photos, receipts etc).
      </li>
      <li>Fill in the on-line claim form</li>
      <li>Don't do anything until an assessor has contacted you</li>
     </ol>
    </li>
    <li>Changing your policy
     <ol>
      <li>Log in to your user account</li>
      <li>Select 'update policy details' from the list of options</li>
      <li>
      Follow the on-screen instructions to make the required changes
      </li>
     </ol>
    </li>
   </ul>
 </body>
</html>
```

The styles that can be applied to lists depend on the type of list. For example, the symbol used can be specified using the 'list-style-type' property. Unordered list bullets can be styled as 'disc', 'circle' or 'square'. These can be used to override the browser's default use of bullet symbols. The number format of an ordered list can also be specified using the 'type' attribute to select a number or letter format (Table 4.1). Alternatively we can set the value to 'none' to remove any symbols or numbers. For ordered lists, Visual Web Developer also lets you select from a number of other list-style-types from the CSS specification, based on various international numbering schemes, but these are not widely supported so should be avoided unless you know the target browser is able to render these styles.

To add list styles using Visual Web Developer, you can add style rules for the appropriate list element types (e.g. 'ol', 'ul', etc.) and then in the 'Modify Style' dialog you can choose styles under the 'List' category. The main settings are in the 'list-style-type' drop-down list, but you can also select an image to use as a bullet (Figure 4.22). The 'list-style-position' setting, which can be 'inside' or 'outside', specifies if the list character should be rendered inside or outside the rectangular area of the text in the list. In other words, 'outside' applies a hanging indent if the list text goes over more than one line.

TABLE 4.1   The styles that can be (reliably) applied to ordered lists

list-style-type attribute	Numbering style
decimal	(1,2,3…) – the default
upper-alpha	(A,B,C…)
lower-alpha	(a,b,c…)
upper-roman	(I,II,III,IV…)
lower-roman	(i,ii,iii,iv…)

FIGURE 4.22   Adding styles using the 'List' category

In this example, we have applied styles to the 'ol' and 'ul' element types, changing the unordered list bullets to the 'square' style and using lower-case Roman numerals for the ordered list:

```
ol
{
    list-style-type: lower-roman;
}
ul
{
    list-style-type: square;
}
```

Figure 4.23 shows how the page looks when rendered in Internet Explorer, with the list styles applied.

FIGURE 4.23   Formatting lists using styles

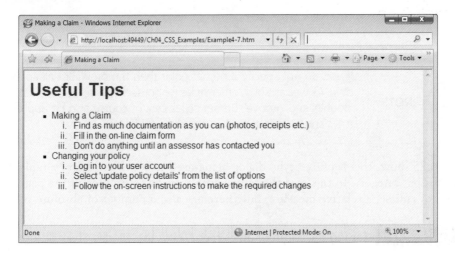

4.6.1 Table presentation

There are many styles that we can apply to the presentation of a table. Some of these are specific to table elements, such as management of table borders and the position of the caption. We can also apply more generic styles that work well with tables, such as aligning the table and its contents and setting its width.

Styles can be applied to the whole table, to parts of the table (e.g. a table row) or be applied to elements using class or 'id' attributes. For our first example we will apply some styles to a table element using some generic styles to set the position and width of the table and apply a border style. The first step is to add a style rule to the stylesheet file for the table element so we can build a style that will apply to the whole table. Figure 4.24 shows the 'Modify Style' dialog box being used to apply a border style, in this example using a solid, thin black border. You can see from the dialog that in this case the same style is being applied to all parts of the border, but it is possible to style different parts of the border in different ways.

FIGURE 4.24 Setting border properties in the 'Modify Style' dialog

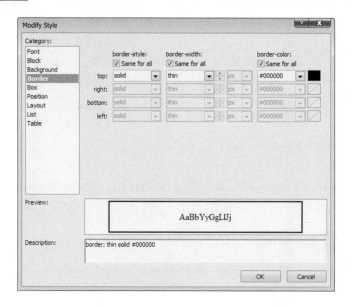

 NOTE If you do not specify a border color then the browser will apply its own. As well as 'solid', other styles for borders include 'dotted', 'dashed', 'double' and 'groove'. Border styles can, of course also be applied to rows and/or cells as well as round the table itself.

Figure 4.25 shows the 'Modify Style' dialog being used to set the width of a table, under the 'Position' category. In this case the table width is being set to 50% of the page width. This is, of course, a relative measure, but there are also a number of absolute measures

FIGURE 4.25 Setting the width of an element using the 'Modify Style' dialog

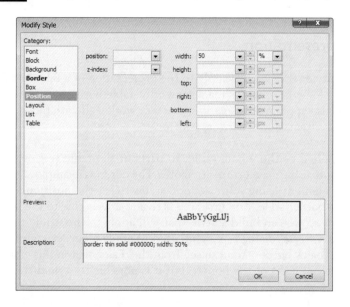

available within the dialog should you require a fixed width for your tables to prevent them from distorting if the browser window is resized.

To align the table on the page we can use the generic 'margin' property, under the 'Box' category, which can be used to set all four margins round an element. If we set the value of this property to 'auto' (Figure 4.26), the table will automatically center.

FIGURE 4.26 Aligning the table by setting automatic margins

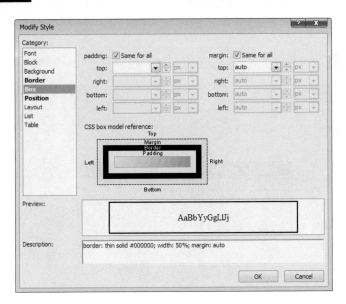

The options shown in the previous figures will generate the following CSS styles:

```
table
{
    margin: auto;
    border: thin solid #000000;
    width: 50%;
}
```

As well as applying styles to the main table element, we can apply them to any of the other elements that appear inside tables. Here, we apply some styles to the table header cells, setting the text color to white on a black background:

```
th
{
    background-color: #000000;
    color: #FFFFFF;
}
```

Here, a solid border of 1 pixel is added around each table data cell:

```
td
{
    border: 1px solid #000000;
}
```

Figure 4.27 shows the effect of these styles on the presentation of the table of call centers from the previous chapter. The only change to the XHTML page is the inclusion of the link element that applies the stylesheet (the modified XHTML is in the file 'Example4-8.htm').

Whereas the styles we have applied so far to the table could be applied to many different XHTML elements, there are some styles that apply only to tables. To access these, there is a 'Table' category in the 'Modify Style' dialog (Figure 4.28). In this example we have set the 'border-collapse' property to 'collapse', which removes the separation of the borders

FIGURE 4.27 The effect of setting styles for elements within a table

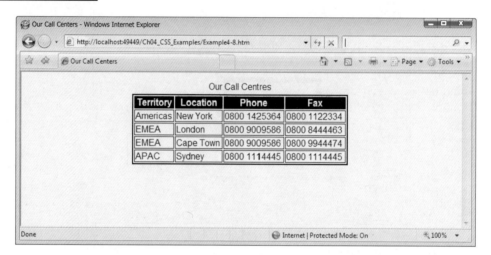

FIGURE 4.28 The 'Table' category in the 'Modify Style' dialog

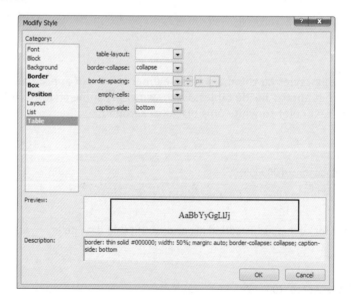

between table cells. The 'caption-side' property specifies where the caption (if one is present) will appear relative to the table.

With these additional styles, the 'table' style in 'webhomecover.css' will now contain the following properties and values:

```
table
{
    margin: auto;
    border: thin solid #000000;
    width: 50%;
    border-collapse: collapse;
    caption-side: bottom;
}
```

The effect of these various styles is shown in Figure 4.29, with the table displayed in Mozilla Firefox.

It should be noted that the way that styles affect the table will depend on the browser. For example, Mozilla Firefox 3 will reposition the caption but Internet Explorer 7 will not. Some other style settings may also have no effect on the presentation, depending on the browser you are using.

The styles we have applied to our table are just a brief introduction to what is possible. We have glossed over much of the underlying XHTML table model and the complex ways that stylesheets can be used with it. If you wish to explore this further, the 'Tables' chapter of the CSS specification provides much more detail (Bos *et al.*, 1998).

Section summary and quick exercises

In this section we applied styles to lists and borders. Some of these styles, such as adding a border or setting margins, were generic, and could also be applied to other types of element, but some were specific to the type of element being styled, for example changing list bullets or collapsing table borders.

FIGURE 4.29 The effect of adding some table-specific styles, collapsing table borders together and positioning the caption (rendered by Mozilla Firefox 3)

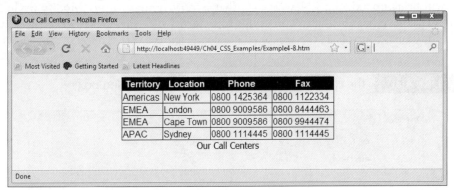

EXERCISE 4.6

Create a definition list and apply styles to it. Remember that you can apply separate styles to the list itself ('dl' elements), the terms ('dt' elements) and the definitions ('dd' elements).

EXERCISE 4.7

Some of the styles that we applied to tables in this section may be applied to other elements too. Using a paragraph with an 'id' attribute, apply the following styles to that paragraph: add a thick grooved border, cover 75% of the page width and apply automatic margins.

4.7 Applying styles within pages

So far, we have been creating generic stylesheets that may be used across multiple pages. However we sometimes want to apply styles only within a specific page, rather than more generally across a web application. For example, we may want to change the heading style on a particular page but not want to affect all the other headings in pages that use the same external stylesheet. To make this type of change, we can use internal stylesheets, which can be included in the head element of an XHTML document using the 'style' element. This element has a 'type' attribute, which should be set to 'text/css', the same as it is when used in the 'link' element for external stylesheets.

```
<style type="text/css">
...styles defined here
</style>
```

Style elements like this can be generated within Visual Web Developer by using the 'Format → New Style' option from the main menu bar.

 NOTE You must be editing a web page for the 'Format' option to appear on the menu as it is not visible if you are editing an external stylesheet. If it does not appear in Source view, switch to Design view.

This will bring up a dialog ('New Style') that is very similar to the 'Modify Style' dialog that we have been using to add styles to external stylesheets. However it includes some additional controls at the top of the dialog (Figure 4.30). The first drop-down list

FIGURE 4.30   The controls at the top of the 'New Style' dialog box

('Selector') contains all the usual XHTML elements, enabling us to apply internal styles to any of these. In addition, we can define our own names to be used to apply styles within the current page. By default, the style name will be something like '.newStyle1' but this can be changed to something more descriptive. The second drop-down list ('Define in') allows us to create styles within the current page. Note that you can also add styles to a new or existing external stylesheet, but in this section we are focusing on creating styles with an internal stylesheet, so the default selection ('Current page') should be used.

In the following example, the 'New Style' dialog has been used to create a style for h2 elements that will apply only to this page. Note that the external stylesheet is still linked to the page. However, one important aspect of cascading stylesheets is that multiple stylesheets can be used on a single page. Any styles that are defined locally inside style elements will override styles specified in external stylesheets. In this case, the new background color (gray) will override the black background that is still specified in the external stylesheet. However other external styles for h2 elements will be retained. After the dialog is closed, the new style element will be written to the document head element:

```
<head>
 <title>Our Insurance Cover</title>
 <link href="webhomecover.css" rel="stylesheet" type="text/css" />
<style type="text/css">
h2
{
 background-color: #808080;
}
</style>
</head>
```

The dialog can, of course, also be used to specify named styles. In this example, we have created a style called 'standout' (this would appear inside the same 'style' element as other internal styles):

```
.standout
{
 font-weight: lighter;
 font-size: x-large;
 font-family: "Courier New", Courier, monospace;
}
```

Since this style is applied using a style name rather than an element name, it can be applied within the current document to any element, using the 'class' attribute (this needs to be done manually in Source view). Here for example, we apply the 'standout' style to a paragraph:

```
<p class="standout">
We constantly monitor our prices against our competitors, and guarantee that we
provide the best value insurance that you can't actually buy.
</p>
```

4.7.1 Inline styles

Sometimes we might want to fine tune styles right down to the level of an individual element on a single page. CSS supports 'inline styles' for this purpose, which is where styles are added directly to XHTML elements using the 'style' attribute (as opposed to the `style` element which we use for internal stylesheets). The value of this attribute would be a style property and value using CSS syntax. For example, we could use an inline style to set the color of a single paragraph element:

```
<p style="color: #FF0000">I'm a red paragraph</p>
```

To add inline styles in Visual Web Developer you first need to position the cursor inside the element that you wish to add the style to, since inline styles apply only to a single element. Then open the 'New Style' dialog as we did to create internal stylesheets, by selecting 'Format' → 'New Style' from the main menu bar. However, this time, we need to select '(inline style)' from the 'Selector' drop-down list. The box below will then display which element is currently selected (Figure 4.31). Any styles we choose in the dialog will now be applied only to that element. In this example, we are applying the 'small-caps' font variant to an h1 element, which will style the heading using small capital letters.

The generated CSS code will look like this, adding the style using the 'style' attribute:

```
<h1 style="font-variant: small-caps">Our Promise to You</h1>
```

FIGURE 4.31   Defining an inline style in the 'New Style' dialog

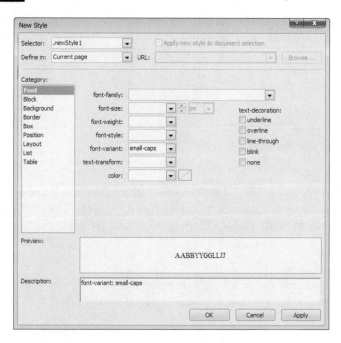

If we use inline styles in an XHTML document, we should indicate to the browser which stylesheet language we are using, since this is not specified in the 'style' attribute. We do this by adding the following 'meta' element to the head element, declaring 'text/css' as the style type, as we have done in the 'link' and 'style' elements previously (note that 'meta' is an empty element):

```
<meta http-equiv="Content-Style-Type" content="text/css" />
```

> **NOTE** There are many possible attributes that can be used with the meta element, which provides various types of information about the document that includes it. A single head element can contain multiple meta elements.

The following XHTML page, which is based on Example4-2.htm but with additional styles, includes two internal styles defined in style elements, an inline style and the meta element required when using inline styles:

```
<!DOCTYPE html PUBLIC "-//W3C//DTD XHTML 1.0 Transitional//EN"
"http://www.w3.org/TR/xhtml1/DTD/xhtml1-transitional.dtd">
<html xmlns="http://www.w3.org/1999/xhtml">
 <head>
  <meta http-equiv="Content-Style-Type" content="text/css" />
  <link href="webhomecover.css" rel="stylesheet" type="text/css">
  <style type="text/css">
  h2
  {
  background-color: #808080;
  }
  .standout
  {
   font-weight: lighter;
   font-size: x-large;
   font-family: "Courier New", Courier, monospace;
  }
  </style>
 <title>Our Promise to You</title>
 </head>
<body>
 <!-- File: Example4-9.htm -->
  <h1 style="font-variant: small-caps">Our Promise to You</h1>
  <h2>No Unreasonable Exclusions</h2>
  <p>
  Many insurance companies include exclusions in their policies,
  making it difficult to claim for events such as 'acts of God',
  terrorism or subsidence. We have the smallest set of exclusions
  of any fictional insurance company.
  </p>
  <h2>Rapid Response</h2>
  <p>
```

```
    If you make a claim, we promise to respond to you with 24 hours, either
    by settling immediately or putting you in contact with one of our
    insurance assessors.
    </p>
    <h2>Low, Low, Rates</h2>
    <p class="standout">
We constantly monitor our prices against our competitors, and guarantee
that we provide the best value insurance that you can't actually buy.
    </p>
  </body>
</html>
```

Figure 4.32 shows the page displayed in a browser, with the main heading in small capitals, a grey background to the second level headings and the final paragraph in 'standout' style.

FIGURE 4.32 Inline and internal styles applied to a web page

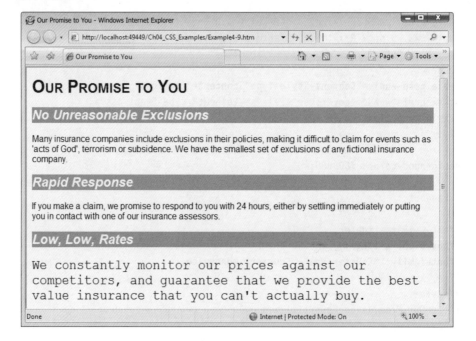

4.8 Stylesheet cascades

At the beginning of this chapter we said that Cascading StyleSheets provide an ordered list of stylesheets to be 'cascaded' in the same document, each one adding more specific styles. In this way, style information from several sources can be combined together. The following example uses two external stylesheets and one internal stylesheet:

```
<link href="webhomecover.css" rel="stylesheet" type="text/css" />
<link href="informationpage.css" rel="stylesheet" type="text/css" />
<style type="text/css">
```

```
p.important
{
  color: #FF0000;
  font-size: 1.2em;
}
</style>
```

For the purposes of this example, 'informationpage.css' contains the following styles: left aligning members of the 'heading' class and applying the 'Courier New' font to second level headings:

```
.heading
{
    text-align: left;
}
h2
{
    font-family: 'Courier New', Courier, monospace;
}
```

4.8.1 Cascading styles

When we have a series of cascading styles applied to the same document, styles are aggregated together so that the final style is a combination of multiple stylesheets. In case of conflicts, where different styles are applied to the same types of element, styles that appear later will override those that appear earlier. In our example, any styles defined in 'informationpage.css' would override styles for the same elements defined in 'webhomecover .css'. Specifically, the 'heading' style in 'informationpage.css' would override the 'center' alignment of members of the 'heading' class defined in 'webhomecover.css'. Other styles defined in 'webhomecover.css' would continue to be applied.

As we have already seen, any styles defined in a 'style' element in the header will override external styles, though in our example the only style applied (to 'important' paragraphs) is a new style so does not override anything in the external stylesheets. Any inline styles will override all the rest, as in our example where we apply the 'normal' font style to both second level headings:

```
style="font-style: normal"
```

This overrides the italic style applied by 'webhomecover.css'. Here is the complete XHTML page:

```
<!DOCTYPE html PUBLIC "-//W3C//DTD XHTML 1.0 Transitional//EN"
"http://www.w3.org/TR/xhtml1/DTD/xhtml1-transitional.dtd">
<html xmlns="http://www.w3.org/1999/xhtml">
 <head>
  <meta http-equiv="Content-Style-Type" content="text/css" />
  <link href="webhomecover.css" rel="stylesheet" type="text/css" />
  <link href="informationpage.css" rel="stylesheet" type="text/css" />
  <style type="text/css">
```

4

```
      p.important
      {
       color: #FF0000;
       font-size: 1.2em;
      }
   </style>
   <title>Information About Our Insurance Cover</title>
   </head>
   <body>
   <!-- File: Example4-10.htm -->
   <h1 class="heading">Important Information</h1>
   <h2 class="heading" style="font-style: normal">Buildings Cover</h2>
   <p>
    Buildings cover is subject to an inspection by a structural
    engineer prior to insurance being approved should WebHomeCover
    require this inspection.
   </p>
   <h2 class="heading" style="font-style: normal">Contents Cover</h2>
   <p>
    You will be required to provide documentary and/or photographic
    evidence of items to be covered on your policy where an
    individual item may be classified as a valuable antique.
   </p>
   <p class="important">
    Failure to meet these terms and conditions may invalidate
    your insurance cover.
   </p>
    <hr />
    <p id="footer">&copy;WebHomeCover.com 2010</p>
   </body>
   </html>
```

Figure 4.33 shows the effect of the cascading stylesheets on the page in Internet Explorer. Note the change in style of all the headings from the second external stylesheet, the large font of the 'important' paragraph style from the internal stylesheet, and the non-italic second level headings, specified by inline styles. Other styles, such as those applied to the footer, are unaffected.

4.8.2 Importing stylesheets

An alternative syntax to using the link element for linking external stylesheets is to use the 'import' expression, which is perhaps a little simpler. This expression appears inside a 'style' element. Here is how we would import the 'webhomecover.css' stylesheet, instead of using a link element:

```
<style type="text/css">
@import url("webhomecover.css");
</style>
```

Importing stylesheets has exactly the same effect as linking them, so from that point of view there is nothing to choose between them. However it is important to note that older

FIGURE 4.33 The effect of cascading multiple stylesheets

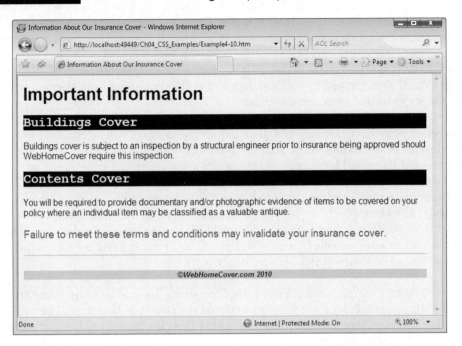

browsers will not recognize the import expression. The two types of syntax can also be used together. For example one option would be to apply the main stylesheet using the 'link' element, but if any additional cascading styles are required these could be added using imports, as in this example, which is an alternative to the two link elements in Example4-10.htm (the full source can be found in Example4-11.htm):

```
<link href="webhomecover.css" rel="stylesheet" type="text/css" />
 <style type="text/css">
  @import url("informationpage.css");
  p.important
  {
   color: #FF0000;
   font-size: 1.2em;
  }
</style>
```

4.8.3 Applying styles using the Formatting Toolbar

A subset of styles can be applied within Visual Web Developer by using the Formatting Toolbar. This toolbar contains both 'Foreground Color' and 'Background Color' buttons, 'Bold', 'Italic' and 'Underline' text style buttons, and can be also be used to align elements. The possible alignment settings are 'Justify Left', 'Justify Right', 'Justify Center' and 'Justify'. However, if you choose to use any of these buttons to add styles, you need to be aware that the way in which the styles are applied will vary depending on the context in which the toolbar is used. Depending on the circumstances, the Formatting Toolbar may create styles in an external stylesheet, an internal stylesheet or an inline style.

For Visual Web Developer to apply inline styles, you must select the whole element (including the start and end tags) in source view, then switch to design view to actually apply the style. The Formatting Toolbar is grayed out in Source view, and trying to select the element in Design view will not generate an inline style, so you have to switch between the two views. There are exceptions to this behavior, however, for example if you select part of the text in a paragraph in design view, and then apply styles using the formatting toolbar, Visual Web Developer will generate a span element around the selected text and apply the styles to that span element inline.

If you select elements in Design view, then in most cases styles will be applied using internal stylesheets rather than inline styles. Class attributes will be added to the selected elements, and these will be assigned to the styles using generated style names something like 'style1, 'style2', etc. However there are occasions when using the Formatting Toolbar can change an external stylesheet. If you select an element in Design view which has no local styles already applied, but has styles applied by an external stylesheet, then making changes using the Formatting Toolbar will actually change the external stylesheet. This may not be what you want, as this change will affect all other pages using the same stylesheet, so you just need be aware of this possible behavior.

In the following example we have used the Formatting Toolbar to apply inline styles to an XHTML page that does not have an external stylesheet linked to it. The necessary 'meta' tag has been included, and inline styles have been applied to heading and paragraph elements. The main heading has been aligned to the center and is underlined (using the 'text-decoration' property). The h2 elements both have a silver background color and are in italic style, with the first subheading in a red foreground color and the second in blue. The final paragraph has been given bold format using the 'font-weight' style (note that the toolbar has set this to '700' rather than 'bold', but this has much the same effect).

```
<!DOCTYPE html PUBLIC "-//W3C//DTD XHTML 1.0 Transitional//EN"
"http://www.w3.org/TR/xhtml1/DTD/xhtml1-transitional.dtd">
<html xmlns="http://www.w3.org/1999/xhtml">
 <head>
  <meta http-equiv="Content-Style-Type" content="text/css" />
  <title>Our Insurance Cover</title>
 </head>
 <body>
 <!-- File: Example4-12.htm -->
  <h1 style="text-align: center; text-decoration: underline;">
  We provide the following types of insurance</h1>
  <h2 style="color: #FF0000; font-style: italic;
     background-color: #COCOCO">Buildings Cover</h2>
  <p>
   You may think you're "safe as houses" but you'd be surprised
   how many things can damage the building you live in. Fires,
   earthquakes, subsidence, runaway trucks, cricket balls through
   windows or the occasional meteor. Best to be covered!
  </p>
  <h2 style="color: #0033CC; font-style: italic;
     background-color: #COCOCO">Contents Cover</h2>
  <p>
```

```
    You may not realize just how much the stuff you have would
    cost to replace. If the burglars move in while you're on
    holiday, could you afford to replace the TV, the stereo,
    the chairs, the cupboards, the crockery etc?
  </p>
  <p style="font-weight: 700">
    Not only that, our contents cover means that if you have
    your bike stolen, drop the vase your mother in law gave
    you as a wedding present, lose your camera, leave your
    glasses on the train or have your mobile phone stolen,
    you'll be fully compensated.
  </p>
  </body>
</html>
```

Figure 4.34 shows how the styled page appears in Internet Explorer 7.

FIGURE 4.34   Inline styles applied to an XHTML document using the Formatting Toolbar

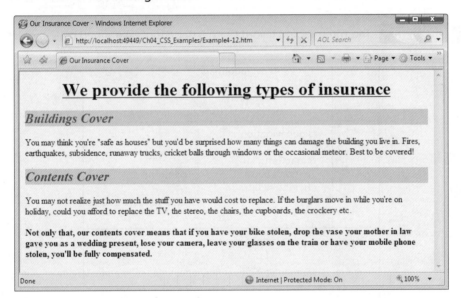

4.9 Using CSS for page layout

So far we have been looking at ways of changing the appearance of parts of a document using CSS. However we can also use it to manage the layout of a document. This is quite a complex topic, and not one we can do justice to here, but this section serves as an introduction to the general concept of page layout with CSS.

In Chapter 2 we introduced some design patterns related to generic page layout, such as the navigation bar, a site logo in the top left corner and the three region layout. In the final example in this chapter we will see how CSS can be used to implement a three-region layout.

In a previous exercise (at the end of Chapter 3) you were asked to implement a three-region layout using a table, but many authors claim that it is better to use stylesheets for this type of layout. There are many ways to approach this problem, but here we will introduce a very simple solution using the 'float' and 'clear' style properties. We can set the value of the 'float' property to 'left' or 'right' to make the associated element appear on the right or left of the page, with other elements wrapped around it. This can be useful for setting up the left-hand navigation bar of the three-region layout. To set up other elements that do not wrap around floating elements we can use the 'clear' property. The values of this property can be 'left', (do not wrap around floating elements on the left), 'right' (do not wrap around floating elements on the right) or 'both' (do not wrap around any floating elements). Figure 4.35 shows the general layout of a page with a three-region layout and also a page footer. Note that the side navigation bar uses the 'float' property to float to the left-hand side of the page and allow the main content to wrap to the right. To maintain the column layout where the content area may be longer than the side navigation bar, we set the width of the navigation bar and also the left margin of the content to the same value. This stops the content from wrapping underneath the navigation bar. We do not use 'clear' because we want the content to appear next to the side navigation bar, not above or below it. However, to keep the top navigation bar above the side navigation bar, and the page footer below it, we use the 'clear' property on both. Figure 4.35 shows how the various styles apply to the three-region layout.

FIGURE 4.35   The three-region layout (with a page footer) defined by CSS styles

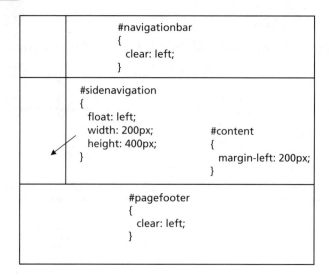

4.9.1 Using CSS with anchors

In our three region layout we are going to have links along both the top and side navigation bars. To style anchors with CSS we have to use a slightly different approach from styling simple text, because an anchor can be in one of four possible states, and each one can have a different style applied to it. The four states are:

1. **link:** a link that has not been clicked on, and the mouse pointer is not hovering over it
2. **visited:** a link that has previously been visited, and the mouse pointer is not hovering over it

3. **hover:** a link with the mouse pointer hovering over it
4. **active:** a link that is being clicked on by the mouse

To apply styles to these states we use a CSS *pseudo-class*, which appears after the element name, separated from it by a colon. For example, to set the color of an anchor that has not been clicked on using the 'link' pseudo-class, we would use the following style:

```
a:link
{
    color: #FFFFFF;
}
```

When applying styles to these pseudo classes they must appear in the correct order in the stylesheet (the order used in the list above). Here are some styles we might apply to these four anchor states:

```
a:link
{
    color: #FFFFFF;
}
a:visited
{
    color: #FFFFCC;
}
a:hover
{
    font-weight: bold;
}
a:active
{
    font-style: italic;
}
```

4.9.2 Applying the layout styles

Here are the styles that would be added to the stylesheet to enable the three-region layout. So that the layout can be applied separately from other style information, we will save it in a separate file ('threeregion.css'). In addition to the layout styles, we also apply some styles to the hyperlink anchors that will appear in the two navigation bars. Notice too the reference to 'margin-left'. In the table example we introduced the 'margin' property, which applied the same value to all four margins of an element; left, right, top and bottom. To control the margins individually, there are 'margin-left', 'margin-right', 'margin-top' and 'margin-bottom' properties. Here, we use the 'margin-left' property:

```
#navigationbar
{
    color: #FFFFFF;
    background-color: #000066;
}
```

```
#sidenavigation
{
    float: left;
    width: 200px;
    height: 400px;
    color: #FFFFFF;
    background-color: #000066;
}
#content
{
    margin-left: 200px;
}
#pagefooter
{
    clear: left;
}
.topnavigationlink
{
    clear: left;
    font-size: 1.1em;
    margin-left: 1em;
}
.sidenavigationlink
{
    font-size: 1em;
    line-height: 2em;
}
```

Here is a simple page that uses the three region style. The content here is just mocked up, with some fictional names of hyperlinked pages:

```
<!DOCTYPE html PUBLIC "-//W3C//DTD XHTML 1.0 Transitional//EN"
"http://www.w3.org/TR/xhtml1/DTD/xhtml1-transitional.dtd">
<html xmlns="http://www.w3.org/1999/xhtml">
 <head>
  <link href="webhomecover.css" rel="stylesheet" type="text/css" />
  <link href="threeregion.css" rel="stylesheet" type="text/css" />
  <title>WebHomeCover.com</title>
 </head>
 <body>
  <!-- File: Example4-13.htm -->
  <div id="navigationbar">
   <a href="home.htm">
    <img src="webhomecoverlogo.gif" alt="WebHomeCover logo" width="200">
   </a>
  <span class="topnavigationlink">
   <a href="quote.htm">Get a quote</a>
  </span>
  <span class="topnavigationlink">
```

```html
  <a href="claim.htm">Make a claim</a>
 </span>
 <span class="topnavigationlink">
  <a href="policies.htm">See my policies</a>
   </span>
 </div>
  <div id="sidenavigation">
  <div class="sidenavigationlink">
   <a href="build.htm">buildings cover</a>
  </div>
  <div class="sidenavigationlink">
   <a href="content.htm">contents cover</a>
  </div>
  <div class="sidenavigationlink">
   <a href="deal.htm">special deals</a>
  </div>
  <div class="sidenavigationlink">
   <a href="more.htm">more info</a>
  </div>
 </div>
  <div id="content">
  <h1 class="heading">We provide the following types of insurance</h1>
  <h2 class="heading">Buildings Cover</h2>
  <p>
   You may think you're "safe as houses" but you'd be surprised
   how many things can damage the building you live in. Fires,
   earthquakes, subsidence, runaway trucks, cricket balls
   through windows or the occasional meteor. Best to be covered!
  </p>
  <h2 class="heading">Contents Cover</h2>
  <p>
   You may not realize just how much the stuff you have would
   cost to replace. If the burglars move in while you're on
   holiday, could you afford to replace the TV, the stereo,
   the chairs, the cupboards, the crockery etc?
  </p>
  <p>
   Not only that, our contents cover means that if you have
   your bike stolen, drop the vase your mother in law gave
   you as a wedding present, lose your camera, leave your
   glasses on the train or have your mobile phone stole,
   you'll be fully compensated.
  </p>
  </div>
  <div id="pagefooter">
   <hr />
   <p id="footer">&copy;WebHomeCover.com 2009</p>
  </div>
 </body>
</html>
```

4

Figure 4.36 shows how the page looks in the Opera 9 browser.

FIGURE 4.36 The three-region layout using stylesheets, as displayed in the Opera 9 browser

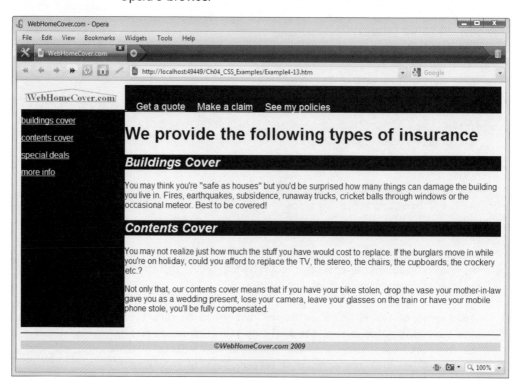

Self Study Questions

1. What file extension is used for an external cascading stylesheet?
2. When specifying styles, what character is used between the name of a style property and its value?
3. What browser foreground or background color does 'color:rgb(0, 255, 0)' refer to?
4. How many color names are specified by the W3C HTML 4.0 standard? Name three of them.
5. Which element is used to apply a stylesheet to an XHTML page? Which element must it be nested inside?
6. What is the problem that may arise if we only use the generic font family names in a 'font-family' stylesheet entry?
7. When setting font sizes in a stylesheet, is it better to use absolute or relative measures?
8. Why might we choose to add a 'class' attribute to a 'div' element?
9. How many styles can be applied to unordered list bullets?
10. What is the effect of applying the 'margin: auto' style to a table?

Exercises

4.8 Add some images of houses (provided with the example code) to the bottom of the left-hand region of the three region layout example for the home insurance system.

4.9 Create a CSS file called 'basic.css' that will provide the presentation for the pages of the research questionnaire website. At this stage we are only looking at static pages that might be used to introduce and explain the site, not the questionnaires themselves. In the first version, provide formats only for XHTML elements.

4.10 Look at your 'About Us' page to identify parts of the content that might be usefully categorized using the 'class' attribute. Having identified one or more classes of content, modify your CSS to apply styles as appropriate.

4.11 Create a CSS file called 'infopage.css'. Add at least one style that is not in 'basic.css' that can be applied to your 'About Us' page.

4.12 Use CSS to manage the layout of your pages, applying the three-region layout.

4.13 Experiment with using CSS to manage the layout of your home page.

SUMMARY

In this chapter we saw how CSS can be used to provide the presentation for XHTML files. We began by applying external stylesheets that could be used across multiple web pages. Using Visual Web Developer's tools and dialogs we applied styles to XHTML element types, as well as elements identified by class and 'id' attributes. We saw how 'div' and 'span' elements can be used in conjunction with class and 'id' attributes to gain complete control over page presentation. We then looked at fine tuning the presentation of individual pages, initially by including stylesheets in the document header using a 'style' element, so that styles could be reused for elements of the same type within a single document. Finally we saw how to add styles to individual elements using the 'style' attribute. We combined these various approaches to applying styles by exploring how cascading stylesheets enable multiple external stylesheets to be used in combination with internal styles. We saw how CSS files are validated by Visual Web Developer, but can also be validated on-line, using the W3C validator. We concluded the chapter by using CSS to manage the layout of a page. There are many aspects to CSS, far too many to cover in this chapter. The following table (Table 4.2) summarizes the CSS properties and some of their possible values that we have introduced in this chapter. This is of course just a small subset of the full available CSS syntax, but there are many books on CSS and on-line resources available if you want to explore stylesheets further. Of course you can experiment with the various styling tools in Visual Web Developer to explore those aspects of CSS that we have not been able to cover in this chapter.

TABLE 4.2   Summary of some CSS properties and possible values covered in this chapter

Property	Meaning	Some possible values	Examples
color	Foreground (text) color	Any of the 16 color names defined in HTML 4.0: aqua, black, blue, fuchsia, gray, green, lime, maroon, navy, olive, purple, red, silver, teal, white, yellow.	color: blue
		RGB color values: color: #rrggbb color: rgb(R,G,B)	color: #FFFFFF color: rgb(0,0,0)
background-color	Background color	Same values as color	background-color: black
text-align	Text alignment	left, right, center, justify	text-align: center
font-style	Font style	normal, italic, oblique	font-style: italic
font-weight	Font weight	normal, lighter, bold, bolder	font-weight: bold
font-size	Font size	A measurement in pixels (px) or em or a percentage.	font-size: 110% font-size: .8em font-size: 20px
		large, small, x-small, x-large	font-size: x-large

`font-family`	Font family	`serif, sans-serif, cursive,`
		`fantasy, monospace, Arial,`
		`Courier, 'Times New Roman'`
			`font-family:`
			`sans-serif`
			`font-family:`
			`'Times New`
			`Roman'`

`list-style-`
`type`
	Styles for list numbers or bullets	`circle, disc, square`
		
		`decimal, upper-alpha, lower-`
		`alpha, upper-roman, lower-`
		`roman`
			`list-style-`
			`type: square`
			`list-style-`
			`type: lower-`
			`roman`

`width`	Width of element (e.g. table width)	Percentage of page width	`width: 50%`

`border`	Table border	`Number of pixels, line style`
		`solid, dotted, dashed,`
		`double, groove`
			`border: 3px`
			`solid`

`margin`	All element margins	`auto`	`margin: auto`
`margin-left`	Left element margin	`A measurement in em`	`margin-left:` `1em`
`margin-` `right`	Right element margin	`A measurement in em`	`margin-right:` `3em`
`margin-top`	Top element margin	`A measurement in em`	`margin-top:` `5em`
`margin-` `bottom`	Bottom element margins	`A measurement in em`	`margin-bottom:` `2em`
`border-` `collapse`	Table border style	`collapse`	`border-collapse:` `collapse`

`link`
`visited`
`hover`
`active`
	Pseudo-classes for anchor elements	`a:link`
		`a:visited`
		`a:hover`
		`a:active`
			`a:link`
			`{`
			`color: black`
			`}`

`Float`	Relative alignment within the page	`left, right`	`float: left;`
`Clear`	Stop content wrapping around elements on the right and/ or left	`left, right, both`	`clear: both`

4

References and further reading

Bos, B., Lie, H., Lilley, C. and Jacobs, I. 1998. *Cascading StyleSheets, level 2 CSS2 Specification, W3C Recommendation 12-May-1998, Chapter 17*, http://www.w3.org/TR/REC-CSS2/tables.html.

Lie, H. and Bos, B. 2005. *Cascading StyleSheets, designing for the Web (3rd edition)*. Chapter 18, 'The CSS saga', Addison Wesley.

Raggett, D., Le Hors, A. and Jacobs, I. 1999. *HTML 4.01 Specification Section 14, StyleSheets*. http://www.w3.org/TR/html4/present/styles.html.

Weinman, L. 2007. *The Browser-Safe Web Palette*. http://www.lynda.com/hex.asp.

4

JavaScript and Dynamic HTML (DHTML)

LEARNING OBJECTIVES

- **To understand the role of client-side scripting languages in supporting application processes within the browser**

- **To understand the key features of the JavaScript language**

- **To be able to use the objects, properties and methods of the JavaScript DOM to interact with browsers and XHTML documents**

- **To be able to write simple scripts that manipulate JavaScript variables**

- **To understand how to write JavaScript functions and to put them into separate files that can be called from scripts in web pages**

- **To know the various components of Dynamic HTML (DHTML) and how they work together**

- **To be able to use events to trigger JavaScript functions**

INTRODUCTION

In this chapter we introduce the JavaScript language, which can be used to write code that runs inside the browser. We will apply some of the most important concepts in JavaScript, including the Document Object Model (DOM) and the built-in JavaScript objects. Examples in this chapter show how to use the properties and methods of JavaScript objects, how to work with simple data types including numbers, strings, dates and arrays, and how to use the arithmetic operators. We will explore the control structures of JavaScript programming and see how to write code in script elements, functions and external files. We will also see how JavaScript, along with the DOM and stylesheets, can be used to create Dynamic HTML (DHTML) pages that provide a more interactive experience for the user by responding to events in the browser and dynamically modifying the page or browser presentation.

In this book we assume that you are already familiar with either C+ or Visual Basic, and you will find JavaScript syntax in many ways similar to C++, and also sharing many characteristics with Visual Basic. However there are also some important differences, so we have attempted to highlight these (as well as the similarities) in our examples.

5.1 JavaScript and the Document Object Model (DOM)

Scripting languages are lightweight programming languages that are usually interpreted rather than compiled and run inside a particular environment.

'A client-side script *is a program that may accompany an HTML document or be embedded directly in it.'* (Raggett *et al.*, 1999)

JavaScript is the most commonly used of a number of scripting languages that can run inside web browsers. JavaScript code can be embedded in, or called from, HTML documents, and these scripts can generate page content dynamically. In general, JavaScript is used for three main purposes:

1. To improve the visual look and feel of the user's experience using a browser-based application. For example, JavaScript can be used to create pop up windows and interactive menus, and enable parts of the page, such as images, to respond to mouse events, such as the mouse pointer passing over them. JavaScript, combined with the Document Object Model (DOM) and Cascading StyleSheets (CSS), is the basis for Dynamic HTML (DHTML), which enables browser-based applications to become more interactive.
2. To offload some of the web application processing from the server to the client. A good example of this is the ability to perform client-side form validation, checking the contents of an HTML form before it is submitted to the server for further processing. Not all validation can be done on the client, but simple things like checking that required fields are not empty can still be very useful.
3. To enable AJAX (Asynchronous JavaScript and XML) implementations to provide a more seamless interaction between client and server.

JavaScript is used extensively by some Visual Web Developer controls in order to support their client-side functionality. In future chapters we will be using special controls for a number of features including menus, navigation controls, client-side validation and AJAX, all of which depend on JavaScript code that is automatically generated by Visual Web Developer. In most cases it is not necessary to understand JavaScript in order to use these controls. However it is sometimes useful to be able to write your own JavaScript code independent of these controls, so in this chapter we will focus on some basic uses of JavaScript that can improve the functionality or look and feel of your web pages.

JavaScript was originally developed in 1995 by Netscape and introduced into Netscape Navigator 2.0. It was originally called 'LiveScript' but later became 'JavaScript', and is therefore often confused with the Java programming language, though there are many differences between them. Although the term 'JavaScript' is widely used, strictly speaking the name only applies to the Netscape version. The version that runs in Microsoft browsers is called 'JScript', and there is also a standard version of the language known as 'ECMAScript'. The ECMA is a European standards consortium that began as the European Computer Manufacturers Association, hence the acronym.

5.1.1 Characteristics of JavaScript

The language constructs in JavaScript are similar to the 'C' family of languages, which includes C, C++, C# and Java, but there are some important differences. Perhaps the most obvious difference is that JavaScript is *loosely typed*, meaning that when we declare a variable we only have to declare its name, not its type. We can also use the same variable to reference different types of data at different times. This is not possible in strongly typed languages like C#.

JavaScript is not a fully object-oriented language, and does not allow the creation of new object types (though more recent versions of ECMAScript have begun to move in this direction). Rather is it an object-based, or *prototype* language, where there are a number of built-in objects and object types that can be used in programs. For example the top level object in the JavaScript DOM is the *window*, which represents the browser window (or frame).

 NOTE The JavaScript DOM we refer to in this chapter is the one that is specific to the web, in that it includes objects related to a document hosted in a web browser. JavaScript may also be used in other contexts using a DOM that is not web-specific.

5.1.2 The Document Object Model (DOM)

The Document Object Model (DOM) is a W3C specification that enables scripting languages, like JavaScript, to access and update the content, structure and style of documents, regardless of the platform or scripting language being used. The first DOM specification (level 1) was published in 1998, the second (level 2) in 2000 and the third (level 3) in 2004. The DOM consists of a set of core interfaces that apply to any structured document, with additional interfaces that are specifically intended for use with eXtensible Mark-up Language (XML) or HTML documents. As HTML has grown closer to XML with the XHTML specification, this distinction between XML and HTML has become less important (though XML has its own important features, some of which we address in Chapter 7). The term 'DOM level 0' is sometimes used to refer to the de facto object model that was used in browsers (such as Internet Explorer 3 and Netscape Navigator 3) prior to the first formal DOM specification. Some parts of the DOM API that relate specifically to HTML were included to ensure backward compatibility with these earlier document models.

The DOM represents a document as a hierarchy of nodes, some of which can have child nodes and some that are leaf nodes. The *document* node can only have one child of type *element*, which is the *root element* of the document. Other element nodes, however, can have multiple child nodes, and these may also be elements. A *text* node is a leaf, meaning that it cannot have any child nodes. As we look at JavaScript, you will find that it has its own way of modeling the document object, some of which comes directly from the standard W3C DOM and some of which is specific to JavaScript.

5.1.3 Setting the default scripting language for a web page

Since JavaScript is only one of a number of scripting languages that may be supported by browsers (others include VBScript and Tcl), it is necessary to specify that JavaScript is the language being used in a particular page. The 'meta' element should be used inside the 'head' element to set the default scripting language, like this:

```
<meta http-equiv="Content-Script-Type" content="text/javascript" />
```

It is important to set the default scripting language for scripts that are linked to *intrinsic events*, which include things like mouse buttons being pressed, keys on the keyboard being pressed and XHTML documents being loaded.

 NOTE | 'text/javascript' is likely to be replaced by 'application/javascript' in forthcoming standards but is not yet widely supported by browsers.

5.1.4 Adding scripts to web pages

Scripts can be added to a web page by using <script> ... </script> elements. These can be added either to the head or the body elements of the XHTML, or even as a separate element outside of the page definition. Scripts can also be written as reusable functions in separate files (described later). Script elements that are *not* part of JavaScript functions will be run when the page is loaded, whereas functions can be invoked at other times, for example by using an event like clicking on a button. In addition to setting the default scripting language in the document's *meta* tag, each script element should also define the scripting language being used for that particular element by setting the *type* attribute to 'text/javascript'. All script elements that use JavaScript, regardless of where they appear in the document, should therefore appear like this:

```
<script type="text/javascript">
 ... JavaScript source code goes here
</script>
```

5.2 JavaScript objects

Now we know what sort of element to use to include JavaScript in our web pages, what type of code goes into these elements? One important aspect of JavaScript is its ability to interact with objects of various types. Some of these relate to the DOM components of the browser environment, such as *window*, *document*, *location* and *navigator*. Some relate to common data types such as *Array*, *String* and *Date*, while others, like *Math*, provide some standard utility functions. The objects that relate to the browser environment have parent–child relationships, where one object contains another. Figure 5.1 shows the relationships between just a few of the browser-related JavaScript objects. The window object contains the document (that is currently loaded in the browser

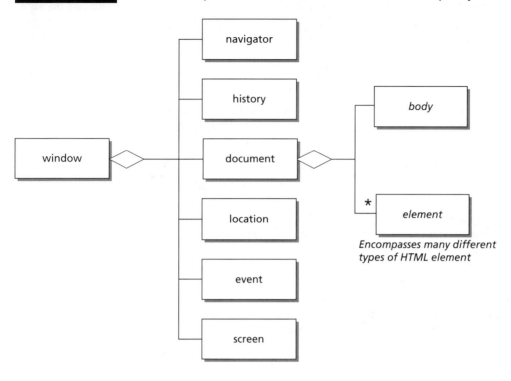

window) and other objects including the location and navigator objects, and the document will contain a body and number of XHTML elements that may in turn contain other XHTML elements.

NOTE	In this chapter we will be working with XHTML pages, and using JavaScript to interact with parts of these pages. In later chapters we will also be working with Visual Web Developer Web Forms that include special controls using JavaScript.

5.2.1 Object properties

JavaScript objects have *properties*, *methods* and *event handlers*. Properties are values that reflect the state of an object, methods are operations that it can perform and event handlers enable state changes or methods to be invoked when an event, such as a button being pressed, a component losing or gaining focus, or a document being loaded, occurs. Like Visual Basic and C#, an object's properties can be accessed using 'dot' notation, where the name of the object is followed by the name of the property, separated by a dot, i.e:

```
object.property
```

The value of the property can be set using the '=' operator. One of the properties of the document object for example is the *title*. This is the text that can appear in the title bar at the top of the browser window. This example shows the title property of the document being set:

```
document.title="JavaScript document title"
```

Here is the source of an XHTML page that sets the document title property using a script element in the body of the page. Note that the XHTML head element needs to contain a title element, even if it is empty, in order to be valid XHTML and, of course, for JavaScript to locate the element in order to populate it.

```
<!DOCTYPE html PUBLIC "-//W3C//DTD XHTML 1.0 Transitional//EN"
"http://www.w3.org/TR/xhtml1/DTD/xhtml1-transitional.dtd">
<html xmlns="http://www.w3.org/1999/xhtml">
 <head>
  <meta http-equiv="Content-Script-Type" content="text/javascript"/>
  <title></title>
 </head>
 <body>
  <!-- File: Example5-1.htm -->
  <script type="text/javascript">
    document.title="JavaScript document title"
  </script>
 </body>
</html>
```

Since scripts included in the body are executed when the document is loaded, the title bar will appear as shown in Figure 5.2 when the document is loaded into a browser (this example uses Internet Explorer 7, where the title also appears in the page tab).

FIGURE 5.2   The Internet Explorer 7 title bar set using the 'document.title' property

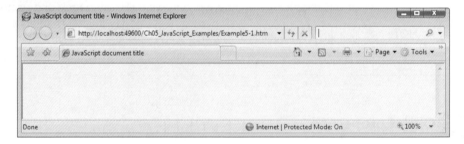

5.2.2 Comments in JavaScript source code

There are two ways that comment syntax can be useful in JavaScript. First, we can use the JavaScript comment syntax simply to add comments to our code to help others to understand it, and second, we sometimes need to 'hide' JavaScript code from the browser, for reasons we will explain shortly.

There are two types of comment syntax in JavaScript, for single line or multiple line comments (if you work with C# you will already be familiar with these). Single line comments, similar to C++ comment syntax, are preceded by a double forward slash:

```
// this is a single line comment
```

Multiple line comments use C (and CSS) style syntax, beginning with a forward slash and an asterisk, and ending with an asterisk and a forward slash:

```
/*
This is a
multiple line comment
*/
```

These types of comment are useful to help other JavaScript developers understand the scripts you have written. The second use of comment syntax is to wrap an XHTML comment, combined with a JavaScript single line comment, around the code in your script elements. There are two reasons to do this:

1. If the client's browser does not support JavaScript, or if JavaScript is disabled, the code can be hidden from the browser.
2. If you want the rest of your page to be valid XHTML, JavaScript syntax needs to be hidden from the validator, because some characters commonly used in JavaScript (e.g. '<' and '>') will cause problems in validation.

The way that we wrap comments around our scripts is to precede them with the XHTML comment opening sequence, <!--, which JavaScript treats as if it were a single line comment. Then at the end of the script, use the XHTML comment closing sequence but precede it with the JavaScript single line comment, i.e. // --> The effect of this is that JavaScript will ignore the closing XHTML comment character but the browser will recognize it as the end of the XHTML comment. Here is a modified version of the script that changes the document's title property but with the comment syntax added. Using this approach means that your scripts will not cause problems in browsers where JavaScript is not supported and your documents can still be valid XHTML.

```
<script type="text/javascript">
 <!--
   document.title="JavaScript document title"
 // -->
</script>
```

5.2.3 Objects as properties

Some properties of objects are also objects. For example the 'location' property of the window is actually a 'location' object, with its own properties and methods. We can navigate through the object hierarchy using dot notation, access the 'location' property of the 'window' object and then access its own properties. In this example, the 'protocol' property of the 'location' is accessed:

```
window.location.protocol
```

NOTE 'Location' is not a DOM object, but a JavaScript object, based on the 'location' property of the window in the DOM hierarchy.

Here is an XHTML page with a script that sets the document's title property using the value of the location's protocol:

```
<!DOCTYPE html PUBLIC "-//W3C//DTD XHTML 1.0 Transitional//EN"
"http://www.w3.org/TR/xhtml1/DTD/xhtml1-transitional.dtd">
<html xmlns="http://www.w3.org/1999/xhtml">
 <head>
  <meta http-equiv="Content-Script-Type" content="text/javascript"/>
  <title></title>
 </head>
 <body>
  <!-- File: Example5-2.htm -->
  <script type="text/javascript">
   <!--
    document.title=window.location.protocol
   // -->
  </script>
 </body>
</html>
```

Figure 5.3 shows the title bar of Internet Explorer 7, displaying the protocol when a file has been viewed in the browser via Visual Web Developer. Because Visual Web Developer always displays pages via its internal web server, the protocol here is 'http:'. Depending on what the browser is being used to display, other possible values of the 'protocol' property would include 'file:' and 'ftp:'.

FIGURE 5.3 The browser title bar set using the 'protocol' property

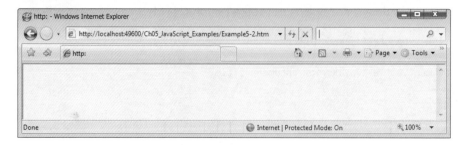

5.2.4 Object methods

As in C# and VB, methods are things that an object can do. Simple examples of JavaScript object methods are the 'write' and 'writeln' methods of the 'document' object, which allow us to write page contents to the current document. The only difference between them is that 'writeln' adds a carriage return and new line to the generated XHTML after writing the contents, but this does not insert a line break element into the actual XHTML document. To invoke a method, we use the same dot notation as when accessing properties. However, methods can have parameter arguments passed to them, in parentheses. In this example a 'write' method is passed some string data (which may include mark-up) as a parameter. A literal String in JavaScript can be enclosed by either single or double quote marks (this example uses double quote marks):

```
document.write("<h2>Subheading</h2>")
```

5.2.5 Positioning scripts in the document

Where scripts are positioned in an XHML document is important. In the next example we use the 'document.write' method to illustrate the difference between putting a script in the body of the document as opposed to the head. If we put a script in the document body, we can position it within the rest of the document in a specific place. In contrast, scripts in the head element will be run before the body content is rendered. The following example shows a script element that writes out a subheading being placed between XHTML tags that write out a main heading and some paragraph text:

```
<!DOCTYPE html PUBLIC "-//W3C//DTD XHTML 1.0 Transitional//EN"
"http://www.w3.org/TR/xhtml1/DTD/xhtml1-transitional.dtd">
<html xmlns="http://www.w3.org/1999/xhtml">
 <head>
  <meta http-equiv="Content-Script-Type" content="text/javascript"/>
  <title>Example5-3</title>
 </head>
 <body>
  <!-- File: Example5-3.htm -->
  <h1>Main Heading</h1>
  <script type="text/javascript">
   <!--
   document.write("<h2>Subheading</h2>")
   // -->
  </script>
  <p>paragraph text</p>
 </body>
</html>
```

The page displayed in a browser (Figure 5.4) shows that the script has been executed in the position where it appears in the body, between the main heading and the paragraph.

In contrast, this version of the page has the script in the 'head' element:

```
<!DOCTYPE html PUBLIC "-//W3C//DTD XHTML 1.0 Transitional//EN"
"http://www.w3.org/TR/xhtml1/DTD/xhtml1-transitional.dtd">
<html xmlns="http://www.w3.org/1999/xhtml">
 <head>
  <meta http-equiv="Content-Script-Type" content="text/javascript"/>
  <title>Example5-4</title>
  <script type="text/javascript">
```

5

```
<!--
document.write("<h2>Subheading</h2>")
// -->
</script>
</head>
<body>
 <!-- File: Example5-4.htm -->
 <h1>Main Heading</h1>
 <p>paragraph text</p>
</body>
</html>
```

Figure 5.5 shows the resulting document in the browser. Note how the script has been run before the body, meaning that the subheading now comes first.

In summary, you should put your scripts in the body element if the order of their execution in terms of other body elements is important. Otherwise they can be put into the head element.

FIGURE 5.4   The web page with the script in the body displayed in sequence in a browser

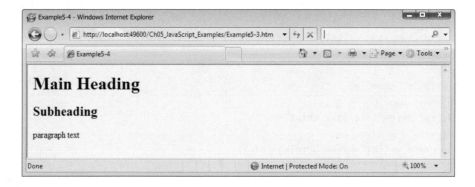

FIGURE 5.5   The page as it appears if the script that writes the subheading is in the head element

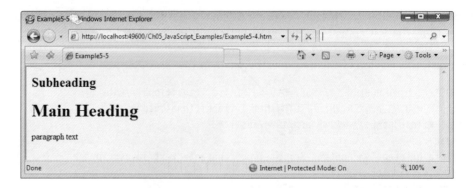

5.2.6 Debugging JavaScript

Before long, you will no doubt be having problems with errors in your JavaScript code, but how can you see what is wrong? In many cases, faulty JavaScript will mean the browser just displays a blank page. When you are developing your pages in Visual Web Developer, one option is to debug your JavaScript using the built in debugger, which we will cover in Chapter 6. However it is useful to know that browsers also provide various tools for debugging JavaScript. To debug JavaScript in Internet Explorer, make sure that the 'display a notification about every script error' box is checked in the 'Advanced' tab of the 'Internet Options' dialog. This can be accessed from the 'Tools' menu. If something goes wrong with a page containing JavaScript, a yellow triangle with an exclamation mark will appear in the bottom left hand corner of the browser frame. If you double click this you will get a pop up dialog that will show you any error messages. Internet Explorer 8 has a built in script debugger, but the debugging services in Internet Explorer prior to Version 8 are not always very helpful, and it can be easier to debug your scripts in other browsers. Mozilla Firefox, for example, has a very good error console that shows a lot of information about JavaScript errors. To access this console, just select 'Error Console' from the 'Tools' menu (this was called the 'JavaScript Console' in earlier version of the browser). Similarly, Opera 9 has an error console that can be accessed from its 'Tools' menu; select 'Advanced' from this menu and then 'Error console'.

 NOTE The browser may not indicate any error to you but the page display may not be what you expected if there is an error in your JavaScript code. You will have to open the error console to actually see the error information.

Figure 5.6 shows the Firefox error console if the line:

```
document.write("<h2>Subheading</h2>")
```

from Example5-4.htm is mistyped as:

```
document.writ("<h2>Subheading</h2>")
```

FIGURE 5.6 The JavaScript error console in Firefox indicating an error in a script element

Section summary and quick exercises

In this section we introduced some features of the way that JavaScript is able to interact with built-in objects such as the window and the document, using the properties and methods associated with them. Using these properties and methods it is possible to change the way that both the browser window and the document appear. We saw that JavaScript code appears in 'script' elements, and that the positioning of these elements in the document is important, for example a script in the 'head' element will be run before the body of the document. We saw that script elements, and a meta tag, need to specify the scripting language being used. We also saw that JavaScript can be debugged using the facilities of various browsers.

EXERCISE 5.1

One of the properties of the 'window' object that can be set is its 'status'. Add a line to Example5-1.htm to set the window status text to 'this is the status bar'.

NOTE	Note that some browsers, such as Mozilla Firefox, will not let scripts change this property until you enable this in your browser preferences. In fact Firefox has a number of JavaScript settings that you may need to configure. To do this, select Tools → Options → Content, then click the 'Advanced' button next to the 'Enable JavaScript' check box. The dialog in Figure 5.7 will appear.

EXERCISE 5.2

Use 'document.write' statements to add a heading and a paragraph of text to the body of the document.

EXERCISE 5.3

Using a web search, find the properties and methods of the 'navigator' object. Write a script that demonstrates one of these properties or methods.

FIGURE 5.7 The Advanced JavaScript Settings dialog in Mozilla Firefox

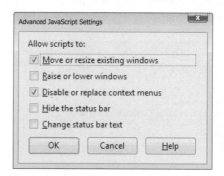

EXERCISE 5.4

The following XHTML document ('Exercise5.4.htm') contains a script with some JavaScript errors in it. Using a browser error console, correct the errors so that the script runs correctly.

```
<!DOCTYPE html PUBLIC "-//W3C//DTD XHTML 1.0 Transitional//EN"
"http://www.w3.org/TR/xhtml1/DTD/xhtml1-transitional.dtd">
<html xmlns="http://www.w3.org/1999/xhtml">
 <head>
  <meta http-equiv="Content-Script-Type" content="text/javascript"/>
  <title>Exercise5.4</title>
 </head>
 <body>
  <script type="text/javascript">
   <!--
   document.wrong("<h1>Hooray!</h1>")
   document.title()="Title"
   // -->
  </script>
 </body>
</html>
```

5.3 JavaScript types, variables and operators

Earlier in this chapter we looked at some aspects of JavaScript objects that relate to the JavaScript DOM; the 'window' and 'document' objects and some of their properties. In this section we look at data types in JavaScript, some of which are very simple types (numbers, strings, Booleans) and others that represent more complex types (Date, Math, Array). We also see how variables can be declared, and how their values may be manipulated, for example by using arithmetic expressions. If you already code with C#, you will find that a number of aspects of JavaScript syntax are familiar to you. However there are subtle and important differences between them that you need to be aware of.

5.3.1 Declaring and using variables

In the examples we have seen so far, JavaScript objects have been used to either modify the browser window or provide values that have been written directly to the document object. Sometimes, however, we need to store a value, which may be the result of calling an object's method, in a variable. In JavaScript, a variable is just a name used to refer to a particular value. It is not declared to be of any specific type, but is simply declared using the reserved word 'var', e.g:

var myVariable

Although variables need not necessarily be declared using the 'var' reserved word, it is important to understand that declaring a variable without preceding it with 'var' will make it a *global* variable. Global variables are visible to all scripts in the current page. Therefore, unless you really need to declare a global variable, always use the 'var' keyword. There are a few simple rules for JavaScript variable names:

- The first character must be a letter (upper or lower case) or an underscore
- The rest of the name can include upper or lower case letters, numbers and underscores
- Names should not begin with two underscores because names in this format are used by JavaScript for internal purposes
- Names cannot include spaces
- Names cannot be JavaScript reserved words
- Variable names are case sensitive

Although variables do not have a specific type, the values that they refer to *will* have a type. These types include simple numbers, strings (of characters) and Booleans. It can be useful to name variables in such as way that their type is indicated by their name. For example, we can prefix each variable name by a three-letter indicator of their types, e.g. 'int' for integers, 'boo' for Booleans, 'str' for strings and so on. This fragment of JavaScript shows some literal values of these three types being assigned to three variables. In each case, the variable declaration is the same, since no data typing is used:

```
var intSomeNumber = 4
var strSomeCharacters = "characters"
var booSomeIndicator = true
```

In the example above, the three variables are declared on separate lines. A new line acts as a separator between different statements in JavaScript. However, statements can also be separated by semicolons, like this:

```
var intSomeNumber = 4;
var strSomeCharacters = "characters";
var booSomeIndicator = true;
```

Which style of coding you use is up to you. If you usually code in VB then you may prefer to use line feeds as separators, but if you use C# then you may prefer to use semicolons (the examples in this book use semicolons as line separators).

5.3.2 Arithmetic on numeric variables

We can perform arithmetic with JavaScript numeric variables using these five operators:

add	+
subtract	−
multiply	*
divide	/
modulus (remainder)	%

(All of these are also present in C#. However the modulus operator, which gives the remainder from a division, is not part of VB.)

All arithmetic statements have the same format, namely that a variable on the left of an assignment (=) operator is made to equal the result of an arithmetic expression on the right:

```
variable = expression;
```

This is the same in principle as VB or C#, but the loose typing means that the variable declared on the left of the expression will not have a specified data type. Some examples (where the 'flt' prefix is being used to indicate a floating point number) might be:

```
var intTotalBananas = intMyBananas + intYourBananas;
var fltNetPay = fltGrossPay – fltDeductions;
var fltArea = fltHeight * fltWidth;
var fltDistanceInKm = fltDistanceInMiles / 0.62137;
var intParentsBiscuits = intNumberOfBiscuits % intNumberOfChildren;
```

Order of precedence (i.e., which part of the expression will be evaluated first) in JavaScript follows the standard rules used by most programming languages, so multiplication, division and modulus have a higher precedence than addition and subtraction. Parentheses can be used to change the order of precedence, as in C# and VB.

5.3.3 Increment and decrement operators

There are also some simple operators to increment and decrement the value of a variable by one (you will be familiar with these if you use C#, but these operators are not in VB). The most commonly used is probably the '++' operator that adds one to a variable, like this:

```
var intCounter = 1;
intCounter++;
```

In this example, the variable 'intCounter' would be incremented to hold the value 2. We can see that the increment operator is simply shorthand for:

```
intCounter = intCounter + 1;
```

There is also a decrement operator, which logically enough is '--' and subtracts one from the value of a variable:

```
intCounter--;
```

This would subtract 1 from the current value of 'intCounter', and is shorthand for:

```
intCounter = intCounter - 1;
```

JavaScript also supports other shorthand arithmetic expressions that are supported to some extent by both C# and VB. Table 5.1 shows examples of shorthand expressions for all five arithmetic operators.

5

Usual Expression	Shorthand Expression
fltVariable = fltVariable + 5;	fltVariable += 5;
fltVariable = fltVariable - 4;	fltVariable -= 4;
fltVariable = fltVariable * 2;	fltVariable *= 2;
fltVariable = fltVariable / 3;	fltVariable /= 3;
fltVariable = fltVariable % 4;	fltVariable %= 4;

5.4 Creating and using objects and arrays

In an earlier section we introduced some of the JavaScript objects that relate to the Document Object Model (DOM), such as 'document' and 'window'. There are a number of other types of object available to us in JavaScript. Some of these are classes that can be used directly, such as the 'Math' class, while others are types that we can create on the fly, such as Strings and Dates. In this section we will introduce some of these object types and see how they can be created and used.

5.4.1 The Math class

The arithmetic operators are fine for simple calculations, but sometimes we need the services of something that can do more complex mathematics. In these situations, the 'Math' class provides support for a number of mathematical operations, including methods for geometry, raising a number to a power, rounding and random number generation. Note that the Math class is similar in concept to the Math class in C# and VB, but with some variations in the methods available. Like them, we do not need to create an instance of 'Math' but use the class methods directly. The script in the following page uses the 'random' method to generate a pseudo-random number between zero and one:

```
<!DOCTYPE html PUBLIC "-//W3C//DTD XHTML 1.0 Transitional//EN"
"http://www.w3.org/TR/xhtml1/DTD/xhtml1-transitional.dtd">

<html xmlns="http://www.w3.org/1999/xhtml">
 <head>
  <meta http-equiv="Content-Script-Type" content="text/javascript"/>
  <title>Random number</title>
 </head>
 <body>
  <!-- File: Example5-5.htm -->
  <script type="text/javascript">
   <!--
    document.write("Here is a random number between zero and one: ");
    document.write(Math.random());
```

```
      // -->
     </script>
    </body>
   </html>
```

Figure 5.8 shows one possible output from this script. Since the number generated by the random method is always between zero and one, deriving random numbers in other ranges, or random integers, requires some further work.

FIGURE 5.8 A pseudo-random number generated by the 'Math.random()' method

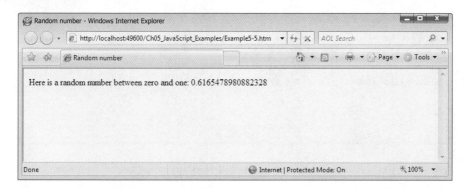

Since the various methods of the Math class return the values of mathematical operations, these returned values may be assigned to (untyped) variables, for example:

```
var fltRandomNumber = Math.random();
```

The Math class also has some properties representing common mathematical values. One of these is 'PI'. The following script element uses 'Math.PI', and the 'Math.pow' method, which raises the first parameter to the power of the second, to calculate the area of a circle. Though this is a simple example, it shows both properties and methods of the Math class, assigning results to variables, and using parentheses to ensure that parts of the calculation take place in the correct order (that is, we square the radius before multiplying by 'PI'). This example also uses string concatenation in the 'document.write' method, which works much the same as in C# and VB, concatenating string and other data using the '+' operator:

```
<!DOCTYPE html PUBLIC "-//W3C//DTD XHTML 1.0 Transitional//EN"
"http://www.w3.org/TR/xhtml1/DTD/xhtml1-transitional.dtd">
<html xmlns="http://www.w3.org/1999/xhtml">
 <head>
  <meta http-equiv="Content-Script-Type" content="text/javascript"/>
  <title>Area of a Circle</title>
 </head>
 <body>
  <!-- File: Example5-6.htm -->
   <script type="text/javascript">
    <!--
     var intRadius = 10;
     var fltArea = Math.PI * (Math.pow(intRadius, 2));
```

```
    document.write("The area of a circle of radius 10 is " + fltArea);
    // -->
  </script>
 </body>
</html>
```

Figure 5.9 shows the result of the calculation displayed in the browser.

FIGURE 5.9   The area of the circle resulting from the calculation using
              the Math object

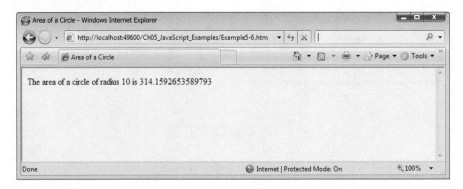

5.4.2 Strings

Unlike C# and VB, literal strings in JavaScript can be enclosed by either single or
double quotes. It does not matter which of these you use, but having the choice does
enable you to enclose one type of quote within another, which can be particularly
useful when combining JavaScript and XHTML. For example, this 'document.write'
method includes a valid JavaScript string, containing XHTML that includes quoted
attributes:

```
document.write('<img src="logo.gif" alt="logo"/>')
```

Or, of course, we could switch the quote characters around, since XHTML attributes can
also be written using either single or double quotes:

```
document.write("<img src='logo.gif' alt='logo'/>")
```

Strings also have a number of properties and methods. The 'length' property, for example,
returns the number of characters in a string, while the 'substring' method returns part of
the string between two specified character positions. The following script uses both the
'length' property and the 'substring' method to display the last character of a string. Note
that the substring returned by the method starts at the character position specified by the
first parameter, since character positions start at zero.

```
<!DOCTYPE html PUBLIC "-//W3C//DTD XHTML 1.0 Transitional//EN"
"http://www.w3.org/TR/xhtml1/DTD/xhtml1-transitional.dtd">
<html xmlns="http://www.w3.org/1999/xhtml">
 <head>
```

```
  <title>String Methods</title>
  </head>
  <body>
   <!--File: Example5-7.htm -->
   <script type="text/javascript">
    <!--
      var strFullString = "a string";
      var intLength = strFullString.length;
      var strSubString = strFullString.substring(intLength-1, intLength);
      document.write("Last character is " + strSubString);
    // -->
   </script>
  </body>
 </html>
```

Figure 5.10 shows the result of the script in a browser.

FIGURE 5.10   A substring displayed in a browser window

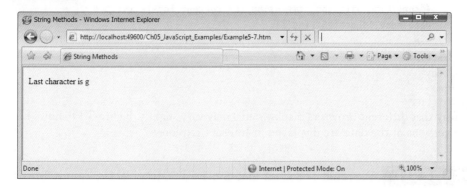

5.4.3 Date objects

Unlike objects that exist as part of the browser environment, and the 'Math' object which is built into JavaScript, 'Date' objects, which represent both a date and a time, need to be created when required. Being able to create 'Date' objects on the fly also means that we can create and manipulate as many of them as we like. Creating objects in JavaScript is done in a similar way to C#, using the reserved word 'new' and the constructor method, which has the same name as the object type and, like other methods, is followed by parentheses. The newly created 'Date' object can be assigned to a variable. Unlike C# or VB, the type of the variable that references the object is not specified, e.g.:

```
var dateToday = new Date();
```

What can we do with a date? Basically we can either use the default settings, which include the date and time of its creation, or specifically set its values. If you simply write the date object to the document, you will get the current date and time of the locale being used by your machine, relative to Universal Time Coordinated (UTC), which is based on Greenwich Mean Time. You can also display the current date and time in UTC, using the 'toUTCString' method, or display the time in the current locale with reference to UTC, using the 'toLocaleString' method. In the following script, we display the same date object in these three different ways:

```
<!DOCTYPE html PUBLIC "-//W3C//DTD XHTML 1.0 Transitional//EN"
"http://www.w3.org/TR/xhtml1/DTD/xhtml1-transitional.dtd">
<html xmlns="http://www.w3.org/1999/xhtml">
 <head>
  <title>JavaScript Date</title>
 </head>
 <body>
  <!-- File:Example5-8.htm -->
  <script type="text/javascript">
   <!--
    var dateToday = new Date();
    document.write("The current date and time is: " + dateToday);
    document.write
      ("<br />The date and time in Universal Time Coordinated is: "
      + dateToday.toUTCString());
    document.write
      ("<br />The date and time using the current locale is: " +
      dateToday.toLocaleString());
   // -->
  </script>
 </body>
</html>
```

The way that different browsers display dates may vary slightly. Figure 5.11 shows how the three versions of the date are displayed in Internet Explorer 7.

FIGURE 5.11   The result of a script that displays a 'Date' object in various formats

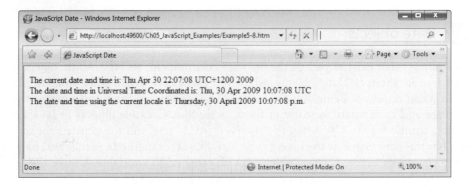

Table 5.2 shows some of the other methods of the Date class.

5.4.4 Arrays

As in C# and VB, an array is a collection of values that have the same name but are identified by an index value. The syntax for creating an array in JavaScript is, however, a little

TABLE 5.2   Some methods of the Date class

Method	Purpose
getDate / setDate	Returns / sets the day of the month (a number between 1 and 31)
getDay	Returns the day of the week as a number between 0 (Sunday) and 6 (Saturday)
getHours / setHours	Returns / sets the hour value as an integer between 0 (midnight) and 23 (11 pm)
getMinutes / setMinutes	Returns / sets the minute value as an integer between 0 and 59
getSeconds / setSeconds	Returns / sets the second value as an integer between 0 and 59
getFullYear / setFullYear	Returns / sets the year value as a four digit integer
getTime / setTime	Returns / sets the date as the number of milliseconds since the beginning of January 1st 1970

different from both of those languages. JavaScript arrays are created using the reserved word 'new', followed by the 'Array' type name, with the array size in parentheses.

```
var arrMyArray = new Array(size);
```

The 'size' parameter would be a number specifying the number of elements in the array. We can set or retrieve the values in the array using square brackets containing an index number. The array index starts at zero, so to set a value in the first element of the array, we use zero in the bracket:

```
arrMyArray[0]="a string";
```

Since the array has no specified type, the elements of the array can contain values of different JavaScript types. For example the next element of the array could contain a number:

```
arrMyArray[1]=10;
```

Here is a simple script that uses an array to write the name of the current day to the document. It uses a JavaScript Date object to get the number of the day of the week (using the 'getDay' method), then uses an array of strings to return the actual name of the day. Note that the 'getDay' method uses a zero to represent Sunday and then counts up from there through the days of the week, with six representing Saturday. This fits in quite neatly with an array, which also starts its index at zero.

```
<!DOCTYPE html PUBLIC "-//W3C//DTD XHTML 1.0 Transitional//EN"
"http://www.w3.org/TR/xhtml1/DTD/xhtml1-transitional.dtd">
<html xmlns="http://www.w3.org/1999/xhtml">
 <head>
  <title>Day Names</title>
```

```
      </head>
      <body>
       <!-- File: Example5-9.htm -->
       <script type="text/javascript">
        <!--
         var date=new Date();
         var arrDayNames=new Array(7);
         arrDayNames[0]="Sunday";
         arrDayNames[1]="Monday";
         arrDayNames[2]="Tuesday";
         arrDayNames[3]="Wednesday";
         arrDayNames[4]="Thursday";
         arrDayNames[5]="Friday";
         arrDayNames[6]="Saturday";
         var strToday = arrDayNames[date.getDay()];
         document.write("Today is " + strToday);
        // -->
       </script>
      </body>
     </html>
```

Figure 5.12 shows the result of running this script on a particular day of the week.

FIGURE 5.12   Using an array of day names to display the current day

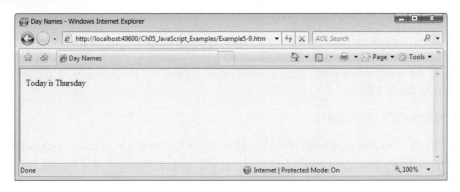

5.4.5 Initializing arrays with an initialization list

Rather than assigning the elements of an array one at a time, an alternative approach is to use an initialization list, where instead of creating an empty array and then adding data to elements using the index numbers, we simply provide the actual data in a comma separated list. For example we can both create and populate the 'arrDayNames' array like this (the complete page source can be found in Example5-10.htm):

```
var arrDayNames =
    ["Sunday","Monday","Tuesday","Wednesday",
    "Thursday","Friday","Saturday"];
```

5.5 Control structures

JavaScript has control structures for looping and decision making similar to those in many other languages. In fact C# programmers will find much of the next section very familiar indeed. The 'if' and 'if…else' structures can be used to evaluate a conditional statement and respond accordingly. There are also two types of loop, the 'while' loop and the 'for' loop.

5.5.1 'if . . . else' statements

An 'if' statement consists of two (and only two) different courses of action and a condition. A condition in JavaScript will always return a Boolean value, and which of the two courses of action is taken depends on whether that value is true or false. One course of action may be, in fact, to do nothing. 'if' statements look like this:

```
if(condition)
{
// do this
}
else
{
// do this instead
}
```

The 'else' part is optional. If the condition is false and there is no 'else' part then the script will carry on executing after the 'if' statement.

5.5.2 Relational operators

When writing any kind of conditional statement, including both 'if' statements and the loops covered in the next section, we need to express conditions that compare variables using relational operators. The operators used in JavaScript are shown in Table 5.3.

TABLE 5.3 JavaScript relational operators

Condition	Relational Operator	Example
equal to	==	if(temperature == 100)
identical to	===	if(1 === true)
not equal to	!=	if(grade != 'F')
not identical to	!==	if(1 !== false)
less than	<	if(sales < target)
less than or equal to	<=	if(engine_size <= 2000)
greater than	>	if(hours_worked > 40)
greater than or equal to	>=	if(age >= 18)

The only operators that might cause confusion here are the very similar 'identical to' and 'not identical to' operators. They differ from the 'equal to' and 'not equal to' operators only in that some type conversions are allowed for equality that do not apply with identity. The example shown in the table should illustrate this. If we test the expression:

```
1 == true
```

then this will return true, because 1 can be converted to the Boolean value 'true'. However, this expression:

```
1 === true
```

will return 'false', since the identity operator does not allow type conversions when making comparisons.

To evaluate more complex conditions we need to use logical operators to combine the simple relational operators shown in Table 5.3. The three logical JavaScript operators are shown in Table 5.4.

TABLE 5.4   Logical operators

Operator	Meaning	Example
&&	AND	if(intAge > 4 && intAge < 16)
||	OR	if(intTimeElapsed > 60 || booStopped == true)
!	NOT	if(!booFormValidated)

5.5.3 Using selection: simulating throwing a coin

The next script example makes a selection using an 'if' statement. This selection is based on using a randomly generated number to simulate throwing a coin, which may land on either heads or tails. In order to represent the flipping of the coin, we need to randomly generate a value, which of course we can do with the 'Math.random' method, which returns a random value between 0.0 and 1.0. According to the ECMA specification, the function may return zero but should never return one.

```
var fltRandomNumber = Math.random();
```

Having got this value from the 'random' method, the script then uses an 'if' statement to choose whether the coin is showing heads or tails. If the random number is less than 0.5 then the coin is set to heads, otherwise it is set to tails. Of course, from the point of view of the program it makes no difference whether we use 'less than' or 'greater than', since either way we get a 50/50 chance (more or less).

```
<!DOCTYPE html PUBLIC "-//W3C//DTD XHTML 1.0 Transitional//EN"
"http://www.w3.org/TR/xhtml1/DTD/xhtml1-transitional.dtd">
<html xmlns="http://www.w3.org/1999/xhtml">
  <head>
   <title>Coin</title>
  </head>
```

```
<body>
 <!-- File: Example5-11.htm -->
 <script type="text/javascript">
  <!--
    document.write("The coin has landed on ");
    var fltRandomNumber = Math.random();
    if(fltRandomNumber < 0.5)
    {
     document.write(" Heads!");
    }
    else
    {
     document.write(" Tails!");
    }
  // -->
 </script>
 </body>
</html>
```

Figure 5.13 shows one of the two possible outcomes from running this script.

5

FIGURE 5.13 One of the two possible outcomes from the script that simulates the tossing of a coin

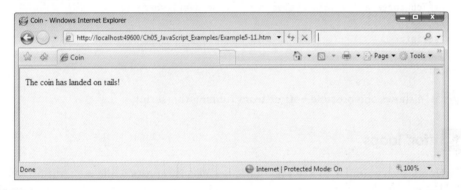

5.5.4 'while' loops

A 'while' loop can be used to write code that repeats while a given condition is true. The condition is shown in parentheses after the 'while' reserved word:

```
while(intNum <= 10)
{
// code here
}
```

In the next example a while loop is used to simulate the throwing of a die, again using the Math.random method to generate a pseudo-random floating point number. To get a random integer in the range 1 to 6, we first multiply the result of the Math.random method by 6, which will give us a floating point number in the range 0 to 6 (but not including exactly 6). To turn that floating point number into an integer, the 'floor' method is used, which simply truncates the number by removing any values after the decimal point, giving us an integer. The predictable behavior of 'floor' gives us a more 'random' number than using 'round'. Finally, this is then incremented by 1 to give an integer number in the range 1 to 6. The 'while' loop repeats until the simulated die 'throws' a 6.

```
<!DOCTYPE html PUBLIC "-//W3C//DTD XHTML 1.0 Transitional//EN"
"http://www.w3.org/TR/xhtml1/DTD/xhtml1-transitional.dtd">
<html xmlns="http://www.w3.org/1999/xhtml">
 <head>
  <title>Throw a Die</title>
 </head>
 <body>
  <!-- File: Example5-12.htm -->
  <script type="text/javascript">
   <!--
   var intDieValue=Math.floor(Math.random()*6);
   intDieValue++;
   while(intDieValue != 6)
   {
     document.write("You threw a " + intDieValue + "<br/>");
     intDieValue=Math.floor(Math.random()*6);
     intDieValue++;
   }
   document.write
     ("You threw a " + intDieValue + " - game over! <br/>");
   // -->
  </script>
 </body>
</html>
```

Figure 5.14 shows one possible output from running this script.

5.5.5 'for' loops

A 'for' loop is very similar to a 'while' loop, because it repeats while a condition remains true. However it also has two other elements, an initialization section that can be used to set the initial value of variables used in the loop, and a section that can be used at the end

FIGURE 5.14 One example of output from the script that simulates the throwing of a die using a 'while' loop

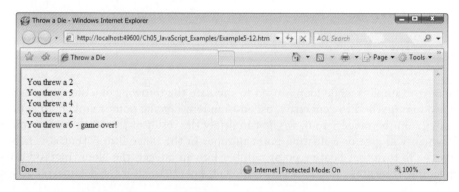

of each loop to change the value of a variable. A typical 'for' loop will initialize a variable at the beginning, use that variable as its conditional value, and increment (or decrement) the value of the variable at the end of each iteration:

```
for(initialize; condition; increment)
{
// code here
}
```

In the next script we generate a random times table. The 'for' loop is used to initialize the multiplier for the times table (at 1), provide the 'while' condition (while the multiplier is less than or equal to twelve) and the increment (incrementing the multiplier by 1). The value for the times table is generated by a random number in the range 1 to 12.

```
<!DOCTYPE html PUBLIC "-//W3C//DTD XHTML 1.0 Transitional//EN"
"http://www.w3.org/TR/xhtml1/DTD/xhtml1-transitional.dtd">
<html xmlns="http://www.w3.org/1999/xhtml">
 <head>
  <title>Times table</title>
 </head>
 <body>
   <!-- File: Example5-13.htm -->
   <script type="text/javascript">
    <!--
     var intRandomInteger=Math.floor(Math.random()*12);
     intRandomInteger++;
     document.write(intRandomInteger + " times table <br/>");
     for(var intMultiplier = 1; intMultiplier <= 12; intMultiplier++)
     {
       document.writeln(intMultiplier + " x " + intRandomInteger +
         " = " + intMultiplier * intRandomInteger);
       document.writeln("<br/>");
     }
    // -->
   </script>
 </body>
</html>
```

Figure 5.15 shows one of the twelve possible outcomes from this script, generating a twelve times table.

5.6 Writing functions

So far all our JavaScript code has been written in scripts in the body or head elements, which execute when the document is loaded. However you can also write your JavaScript code inside functions, and then call these functions from a script element somewhere else in your page. The same function can also be called from more than one place in the same page if necessary. Functions can be written inside script elements in the head or body of an XHTML document, as we have already done with our previous scripts, but may also be

FIGURE 5.15 One possible output from the script that generates random times tables

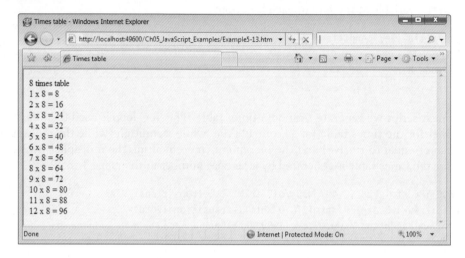

written in a separate file. The main advantage of writing functions in separate files is that they can be re-used by scripts in different web pages. Files that contain JavaScript functions are normally given a '.js' file extension.

Regardless of where they are written, functions are not invoked automatically, even if they appear in the body of the document, so they have to be called by some other script or triggered by some kind of event.

A JavaScript function is declared by simply using the key word 'function', followed by the name of the function and any parameters, in parentheses. The body of the function is surrounded by braces:

```
<script type="text/javascript">
function functionname(parameters)
{
}
</script>
```

A function may return a value, representing the end result of the function, using the reserved word 'return' followed by the variable or value that is being returned:

```
<script type="text/javascript">
function functionname(parameters) {
...
    return value
}
</script>
```

If it is included, the line that returns the value is normally the last line in the function. This is because nothing after a return statement gets executed; the function terminates at that point. This behavior can also be used to deliberately 'short circuit' a function in cases where we want to exit from the function before executing all the code, perhaps because of some error condition or because we already have the result we need.

The following script shows a simple function that uses the same array of day names that we saw in an earlier script example. The difference is that instead of writing the day name out to the document, the function returns the name of the day.

```
<script type="text/javascript">
 <!--
 function getDayName()
 {
  var date=new Date();
  var arrDayNames = ["Sunday","Monday","Tuesday","Wednesday",
     "Thursday","Friday", "Saturday"];
  return arrDayNames[date.getDay()]
 }
 // -->
</script>
```

5.6.1 Defining functions outside the body element

So far, we have been embedding our scripts into the body of the document, which means that the JavaScript will run as soon as the page is loaded. However, once we start using functions, we can put these into the head element of the document, or outside of the document altogether, and invoke them from another script or an event.

In the following example, we will see how a function (in this case added to the head of the document) can be invoked from a script in the body of the document. Because the script in the body gets invoked when the document is loaded, the function will be called at the same time. A JavaScript function is called simply by using its name, and passing any required parameters. Unlike an object method, there is nothing that needs to precede the name of the function. If the function returns a value, it can be used by the code that invokes the function. In this XHTML page, a script invokes the 'getDayName' function. There are no parameter values to be passed, but the string that gets returned from the function is written out to the document.

```
<!DOCTYPE html PUBLIC "-//W3C//DTD XHTML 1.0 Transitional//EN" "http://www.w3.org/
TR/xhtml1/DTD/xhtml1-transitional.dtd">
<html xmlns="http://www.w3.org/1999/xhtml">
 <head>
  <meta http-equiv="Content-Script-Type" content="text/javascript"/>
  <title>JavaScript day name function</title>
  <script type="text/javascript">
   <!--
    function getDayName()
    {
     var date=new Date();
     var arrDayNames =
       ["Sunday","Monday","Tuesday","Wednesday",
        "Thursday","Friday", "Saturday"];
    return arrDayNames[date.getDay()]
```

5

```
    }
    // -->
  </script>
</head>
<body>
<!-- File: Example5-14.htm -->
  <script type="text/javascript">
  <!--
    document.write("Today is " + getDayName());
    // -->
  </script>
 </body>
</html>
```

Figure 5.16 shows the result of loading the page on a particular day.

5.6.2 Using external JavaScript files

In all of the examples we have seen so far, the JavaScript has appeared in the XHTML source file. However, if we want to reuse any of our JavaScript functions then they need to be stored separately from XHTML pages. In the previous example, we used a function called 'getDayName'. Simple as it is, this function might be reusable in multiple pages, so instead of putting it into the XHTML document's header, we could put it into a separate file. You can create a JavaScript source file from Visual Web Developer's Add New Item dialog by selecting 'JScript File' from the list of templates (Figure 5.17). JavaScript source files have a '.js' extension. In this example we are creating a file called 'dayname.js'.

The file created by Visual Web Developer will be completely empty initially. Note that when JavaScript is stored separately from the XHTML source file, there is no 'script' element, just the JavaScript source code. The script element remains in the web page to specify the file that contains the JavaScript function. Here is the code that needs to be entered into the 'dayname.js' file; just the definition of the 'getDayName' function:

FIGURE 5.16   A web page displaying the current day using the 'getDayName' function

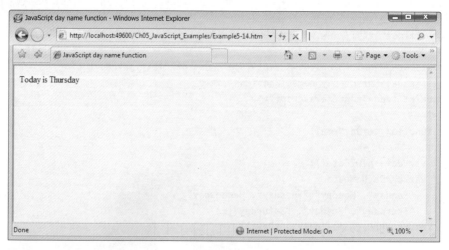

FIGURE 5.17 Creating a new JScript (JavaScript) source file

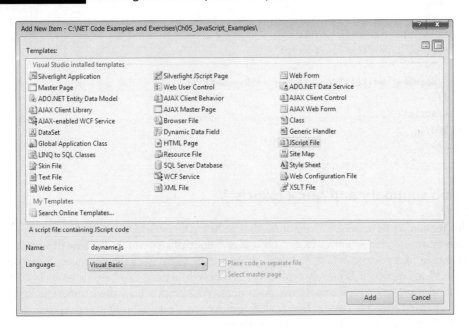

```
// File: dayname.js
function getDayName()
{
 var date=new Date();
 var arrDayNames =
   ["Sunday","Monday","Tuesday","Wednesday",
    "Thursday","Friday","Saturday"];
 return arrDayNames[date.getDay()]
}
```

To use functions defined in external files, the `script` element needs to include the 'src' attribute, which specifies the path and filename of the JavaScript source file:

```
<script type="text/javascript" src="path/filename.js"></script>
```

It is important to note that the `script` element is never an empty element. In other words, it always has separate opening and closing tags, even though nothing appears between them. This is necessary because some browsers cannot process the script element unless it has both start and end tags.

Here is an XHTML page that uses the 'getDayName' function by referencing the external JavaScript file using the script element's 'src' attribute:

```
<!DOCTYPE html PUBLIC "-//W3C//DTD XHTML 1.0 Transitional//EN"
"http://www.w3.org/TR/xhtml1/DTD/xhtml1-transitional.dtd">
<html xmlns="http://www.w3.org/1999/xhtml">
 <head>
  <meta http-equiv="Content-Script-Type" content="text/javascript"/>
  <title>JavaScript day name function</title>
  <script type="text/javascript" src="dayname.js">
```

```
      </script>
    </head>
    <body>
      <!-- File: Example5-15.htm -->
      <script type="text/javascript">
       <!--
         document.write("Today is " + getDayName());
       // -->
      </script>
    </body>
  </html>
```

Section summary and quick exercises

In this section we have been looking at JavaScript from the perspective of its basic components as a programming language; variables, objects and control structures. We saw how its syntax is similar in many ways to C#, but that there are also important differences, in particular the fact that JavaScript is loosely typed. We saw how functions can be written in JavaScript, and called from script elements in the document. We also saw how these functions could be placed in an external file (using the 'JScript' template in Visual Web Developer) that can then potentially be used by multiple scripts in different XHTML pages.

EXERCISE 5.5

Using a script in the body of an XHTML document, use the Math.random() method to display an integer value between 1 and 10.

EXERCISE 5.6

Create an external JavaScript file (using the Visual Web Developer 'JScript File' template) called 'randominteger.js'. Put your code that generates a random integer between 1 and 10 into a function called 'randomInt', defined in this file. Call the function from a script in an XHTML page.

EXERCISE 5.7

Create another JavaScript file (call it 'randomrange.js') that contains a modified version of your 'randomInt' function that takes two parameters, representing the upper and lower bounds of a range of random numbers. Change the way the function works so that it will generate a number in the specified range. Call the function from a script in an XHTML page.

EXERCISE 5.8

Write a script that uses either a 'for' or a 'while' loop to create a table showing the numbers from 1 to 10 and their squares. You will need to put all of the code that creates the table inside the script, because if you put some of the table tags outside the script the page will not be valid XHTML. Use a stylesheet to display the table and cell borders (see Figure 5.18).

FIGURE 5.18   A table of the numbers from 1 to 10 and their squares

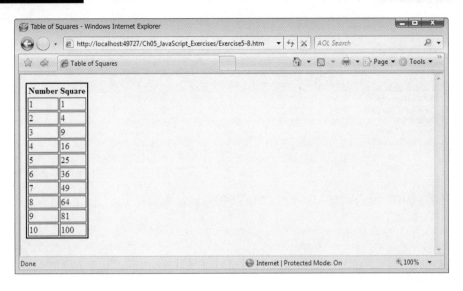

Write script that generates and displays a 'hand' of five cards from a potential pack of 52 (this script could be used as part of a larger card game application). JavaScript's loose typing is quite useful here, because we can create an array that contains both the names and numbers of playing cards. In your script, first create an array that contains these names and numbers:

'Ace','2','3','4','5','6','7','8','9','10','Jack','Queen','King'

Then create a second array containing the four suites:

'Hearts','Diamonds','Clubs','Spades'

Use a 'for' loop that iterates 5 times (for five cards). In each iteration, use the Math. Random() method to get a name or number and a suite from the arrays and display the resulting card on the screen. The final output might look something like Figure 5.19.

5.7   Navigating the DOM

Our scripts so far have been largely independent of the rest of the web page, but sometimes we want to interact more directly with the content of the document in the browser. To do this we need to be able to navigate through the DOM to find specific element, attribute or text nodes. We saw some aspects of this earlier in the chapter, when we used the 'window' and 'document' objects. The tree of nodes in the DOM that represent the

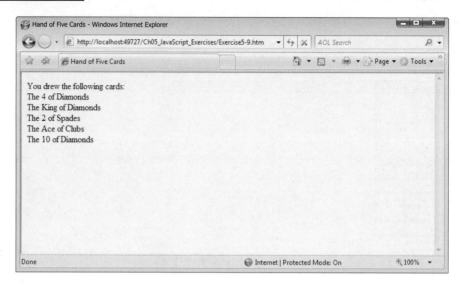

FIGURE 5.19 One possible output from the hand of cards script

elements of the XHTML document in the browser begins with the document object, from which we can navigate to other nodes, either by using unique IDs (if the 'id' attribute has been used on element nodes) or by traversing parts of the document tree, accessing the 'child' nodes (nested elements) of the current element. Two ways of doing this are to use the 'firstChild' property, which simply identifies the first child of the current node (element), or the 'childNodes' property, which represents all the children of the current node, and is accessed like an array using an index number. However, attempting to use these methods of navigation through the DOM can be very problematic due to browser incompatibilities. A more reliable approach is to use 'id' attributes on the nodes that you wish to access in your JavaScript code, and navigate to them using the 'getElementById' method. There is also a 'getElementsByTagName' method that will locate all the occurrences of a particular HTML tag. To explain how these methods work we will refer to the following XHTML document, which has several elements with 'id' attributes:

```
<!DOCTYPE html PUBLIC "-//W3C//DTD XHTML 1.0 Transitional//EN"
"http://www.w3.org/TR/xhtml1/DTD/xhtml1-transitional.dtd">
<html xmlns="http://www.w3.org/1999/xhtml">
 <head>
  <meta http-equiv="Content-Script-Type" content="text/javascript"/>
  <title>Our Insurance</title>
 </head>
 <body>
  <!-- File: Example5-16.htm -->
  <div id="heading1">Buildings Insurance</div>
  <p id="para1">
  You need this type of insurance to cover you in case of
  <span id="risk">severe damage to your home</span>
   (for example fire, flood, vehicle or tree crashing into it)
   as well as more everyday risks like accidentally breaking
   a window
  </p>
```

```
<div id="heading2">Contents Insurance</div>
<p id="para2">
You need this type of insurance to cover
<span id="items">things in your house</span>,
such as furniture, electrical goods, carpets and curtains,
against risks such as fire, theft, water damage
(due to burst pipes, etc) or accidental breakage
</p>
</body>
</html>
```

In order to navigate to the second paragraph of this document, which has the ID 'para2', we can use the following expression:

```
document.getElementById("para2");
```

Another way of achieving the same result would be to use the appropriate tag name (in this case 'p') with the getElementsByTagName method, which takes the name of an HTML tag as a parameter (the tag name parameter is not case sensitive). This is a useful alternative for elements that do not have 'id' attributes. Since the 'getElementsByTagName' method will locate all instances of the specified tag, the results are indexed like an array, starting at zero. The second paragraph therefore would have the index '1' in the collection of paragraph tags, and would be accessed like this:

```
document.getElementsByTagName("p")[1];
```

5.7.1 Interacting with nodes

Once we know how to navigate to a node using the DOM, we can interact with that node to access its properties. Properties of nodes include the 'nodeName' and 'nodeType'. These expressions, for example, would get the 'nodeName' and 'nodeType' of the first paragraph:

```
document.getElementById("para1").nodeName;
document.getElementById("para1").nodeType;
```

In this case the node name would be 'p' and the type would be '1'.

NOTE	Elements are type 1, attributes are type 2, and text nodes (the text inside the element) are type 3 (knowing this can occasionally be useful for debugging purposes – sometimes the node you are accessing is not the one you think it is!).

We can access the contents of a text node using the 'nodeValue' property. Since a paragraph is an element node and not a text node, we need to navigate to its child node to get to the text inside it. We can access the first child node of an element by using the 'firstChild' property, and then get its node value, like this:

```
document.getElementById("para1").firstChild.nodeValue;
```

This will return the text from the opening paragraph tag to the following span tag.

As well as accessing the properties of nodes we can access attributes using the 'getAttribute' method, which takes an attribute name as a parameter. To access the 'id' attribute for the first 'div' element, for example, we could use the following expression:

```
document.getElementById("heading1").getAttribute("id");
```

If you add the following script to the body of the XHTML page previously described, you can test out some of the expressions we have introduced in this section:

```
<script type="text/javascript">
  <!--
  document.write("Paragraph 1 is node name " +
    document.getElementById("para1").nodeName);
  document.write("<br />Paragraph 1 is node type " +
    document.getElementById("para1").nodeType);
  document.write("<br />The text node inside paragraph 1 is " +
    document.getElementById("para1").firstChild.nodeValue);
  document.write("<br />The attribute value of the first div is " +
    document.getElementById("heading1").getAttribute("id"));
  // -->
</script>
```

You should be aware that if you want to navigate the DOM in your script you cannot put the script in the head element, because it will execute before the body has loaded and the DOM will not yet be built! Therefore this particular script needs to be in the body.

 NOTE In fact you should never put scripts in the head element that write content to the document, unless they are in functions, because they will write their output before the document body has been loaded.

The output from the script should include the information shown in Figure 5.20.

5.7.2 Changing values in the DOM

As well as reading node properties, JavaScript and the DOM can be used to change the content of parts of a document. In the next example, we are going to use an XHTML 'input' element to create a text field (you will find this element in the Toolbox, labelled 'Input (Text)') to display the time by setting its value inside a script. The text field has been given a unique ID of 'clock' so that we can access it easily using the 'getElementById' method. It is also set to be read only (using the 'readonly' attribute), since it is only intended for display purposes and not for user input:

```
<input type="text" size="6" id="clock" readonly="readonly"/>
```

The 'id' and 'readonly' properties can be set using the Properties window, or entered manually in Source View. The following JavaScript function ('showClock') uses a newly

FIGURE 5.20 Displaying node types, names and values using the DOM

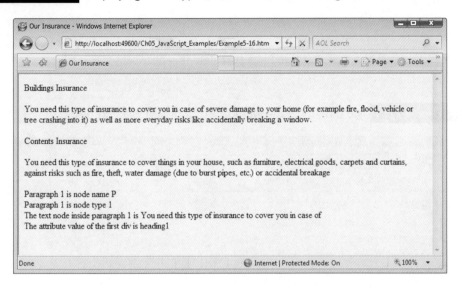

created Date object to show the time that the page was loaded. It uses 'getElementById' to locate the text field within the document, using its 'id' attribute. It then sets the 'value' property of the text field (this is from the HTML part of the DOM) to a string comprising the hours and minutes from the Date object:

```
// File: showclock.js
function showClock()
{
  var date = new Date();
  document.getElementById("clock").value=
    date.getHours() + ":" + date.getMinutes();
}
```

The following XHTML page invokes the 'showClock' function using a script in the body:

```
<!DOCTYPE html PUBLIC "-//W3C//DTD XHTML 1.0 Transitional//EN"
"http://www.w3.org/TR/xhtml1/DTD/xhtml1-transitional.dtd">
<html xmlns="http://www.w3.org/1999/xhtml">
 <head>
  <meta http-equiv="Content-Script-Type" content="text/javascript"/>
  <title>JavaScript clock</title>
  <script type="text/javascript" src="showclock.js">
  </script>
 </head>
 <body>
  <!-- File: Example5-17.htm -->
  <div>
   <input type="text" size="6" id="clock" readonly="readonly"/>
  </div>
  <script type="text/javascript">
   showClock();
```

```
    </script>
  </body>
</html>
```

Figure 5.21 shows the time displayed in a text field in a browser.

FIGURE 5.21 The time the page was loaded displayed in a text field

5.8 JavaScript events

So far, all our JavaScript code has been run as part of the XHTML page being loaded, triggered by script elements in the document body. However we do not always want JavaScript, particularly functions, to be run only when the document loads. To give us more control over the running of our scripts, and make our browser-based applications more interactive, we can use various types of event to trigger the running of JavaScript code. These events include things like the document being loaded in the browser (the 'onload' event), the mouse moving over a component of the page ('onmouseover') or a button being pressed ('onclick'). Event handlers enable JavaScript objects and functions to respond to these events.

5.8.1 The 'onload' Event

In our next example, instead of adding a script element to the body of the document, we will invoke the 'showClock' function from the 'onload' event, which is triggered when the document body is loaded:

```
<body onload="showClock()">
```

This approach means that we can have a JavaScript function run as soon as the document is loaded without using a script element in the document body.

 NOTE The 'onload' attribute here is all in lower case. You will see examples from other sources of this event referred to as 'onLoad'. However, because the event appears as an attribute of the body tag, using any upper-case letters will mean your pages will not be valid XHTML.

This script shows an XHTML page that invokes the 'showClock' function using the 'onload' event:

```
<!DOCTYPE html PUBLIC "-//W3C//DTD XHTML 1.0 Transitional//EN"
"http://www.w3.org/TR/xhtml1/DTD/xhtml1-transitional.dtd">
<html xmlns="http://www.w3.org/1999/xhtml">
 <head>
  <meta http-equiv="Content-Script-Type" content="text/javascript"/>
  <title>JavaScript clock</title>
  <script type="text/javascript" src="showclock.js">
  </script>
 </head>
 <body onload="showClock()">
  <!-- File: Example5-18.htm -->
  <div>
   <input type="text" size="6" id="clock" readonly="readonly"/>
  </div>
 </body>
</html>
```

5.8.2 Timer events

As we saw in the previous example, using the 'onload' event has the same effect as triggering a JavaScript function from a script in the document body. In the case of our clock, this is not really very helpful, since the time will soon (in no more than a minute) be wrong. We can, however, solve this problem using a JavaScript timer event. The 'setTimeOut' method can be used to set a timer that will call a function after a given interval, specified in milliseconds. In this modified version of the original 'showClock' function (called 'showTimer'), we add a 'setTimeOut' event to recursively call the 'showTime' function approximately every 1000 milliseconds (every second). To see this working more easily, the seconds, as well as the minutes and hours, are written to the text field:

```
// File: showtimer.js
function showTimer()
{
 var date = new Date();
 document.getElementById("clock").value=date.getHours() + ":" +
    date.getMinutes() + ":" + date.getSeconds();
 setTimeout("showTimer()", 1000);
}
```

The page to call this function only needs to be modified in two places, first to call the new function in the header, and second to call the new function with the 'onload' event. Therefore the only changes are to the name of the '.js' file being used and the name of the function being called:

```
<!DOCTYPE html PUBLIC "-//W3C//DTD XHTML 1.0 Transitional//EN"
"http://www.w3.org/TR/xhtml1/DTD/xhtml1-transitional.dtd">
<html xmlns="http://www.w3.org/1999/xhtml">
```

```
<head>
 <meta http-equiv="Content-Script-Type" content="text/javascript"/>
 <title>JavaScript clock</title>
 <script type="text/javascript"src="showtimer.js">
 </script>
</head>
<body onLoad="showTimer()">
 <!-- File: Example5-19.htm -->
 <div>
  <input type="text" size="6" id="clock" readonly="readonly"/>
 </div>
</body>
</html>
```

Figure 5.22 shows the modified text field, with the function showing the time in hours, minutes ands seconds.

FIGURE 5.22 The text field showing the time in hours, minutes and seconds

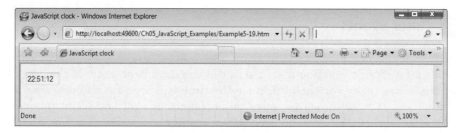

5.8.3 innerHTML and the DOM

In the previous examples, we used a text field to display the current time. An alternative approach to displaying content in a specific part of the browser is to write to a node of the document. One way of doing this is to use the interfaces of the DOM, but this can be quite complex and different browsers can react in different ways to the same scripts. Another way is to use the 'innerHTML' property of HTML elements. This enables us to access text nodes directly and update their contents.

The 'innerHTML' property is not part of the formal HTML DOM specification, and was introduced by Microsoft in Internet explorer 4 in 1997. However due to its popularity it has been incorporated into other browsers, despite not being included in any public standard, and is therefore quite reliable in terms of cross-browser support. There has been much debate about whether using 'innerHTML' is wise or not. However, it is simple to use and has been used in many AJAX implementations. One of the objections to the use of 'innerHTML' is that it can be used to include structural elements (i.e. mark-up) inside the processes of client-side scripts, which is a poor separation of concerns. It is therefore preferable to restrict the use of 'innerHTML' to the manipulation of content rather than using it to dynamically generate mark-up.

In the next example, we modify the 'showTimer' function to use the 'innerHTML' property. The changes are relatively simple. First, we replace the text input field with a suitable document node, in this case a simple 'div' element that contains no text:

```
<div id="clock"></div>
```

Then all we have to do in the JavaScript function is modify the 'div' element, accessed using the 'getElementById' method, by setting the value of its 'innerHTML' property:

```
// File: showinnertimer.js
function showTimer()
{
 var date = new Date();
 document.getElementById("clock").innerHTML= date.getHours() + ":" +
    date.getMinutes() + ":" + date.getSeconds();
 setTimeout("showTimer()", 1000);
}
```

Otherwise everything looks, and works, pretty much the same as before, except that the time appears in the browser simply as text, and not in a text field component. Here is the full XHTML page, with the 'div' element used by the function:

```
<!DOCTYPE html PUBLIC "-//W3C//DTD XHTML 1.0 Transitional//EN"
"http://www.w3.org/TR/xhtml1/DTD/xhtml1-transitional.dtd">
<html xmlns="http://www.w3.org/1999/xhtml">
 <head>
  <meta http-equiv="Content-Script-Type" content="text/javascript"/>
  <title>JavaScript clock</title>
 <script type="text/javascript" src="showinnertimer.js">
 </script>
 </head>
 <body onLoad="showTimer()">
  <!-- File: Example5-20.htm -->
  <div id="clock"></div>
 </body>
</html>
```

Figure 5.23 shows the output in the browser. The time is no longer in a text field but simply a text node of the document.

FIGURE 5.23   The current time displayed in a browser using the 'innerHTML' property

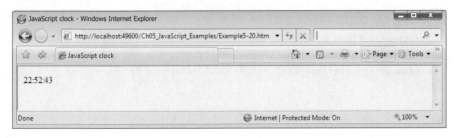

5.8.4 Responding to button events

The events we have used so far, the 'onload' event and timer events, are not related to user activity. However, if we want to make web pages more dynamic we need to be able to respond to the user's actions in the page. One way of doing this is to trigger JavaScript functions with user instigated events like buttons being pressed. XHTML button components can be linked to JavaScript functions by using their 'onclick' event. In our next example we will use button events to call the window object's 'resizeTo' method, which sets the browser window to a specified width and height. The values for the width and height appear in parentheses after the method name, separated by a comma. This example would set the window size to 400 pixels wide and 200 pixels high:

```
window.resizeTo(400,200);
```

Our next script example shows button events being used to resize the window. It also shows how a JavaScript function can be called from more than one place in a script. The function we will use is called 'resizeWindow', takes two parameters for the width and the height, and sets the size of the window accordingly:

```
// File: resize.js
function resizeWindow(width, height)
{
 window.resizeTo(width, height);
}
```

In the body of the document, there are two buttons, both of which use the 'onclick' event to call the 'resizeWindow' function. The first button (labelled 'shrink window') sets the window to be 400 by 300 pixels. The second uses two properties of the screen ('availWidth' and 'availHeight') to set the window size to the maximum available. The 'screen' object is a property of the window object:

```
<!DOCTYPE html PUBLIC "-//W3C//DTD XHTML 1.0 Transitional//EN"
"http://www.w3.org/TR/xhtml1/DTD/xhtml1-transitional.dtd">
<html xmlns="http://www.w3.org/1999/xhtml">
 <head>
  <meta http-equiv="Content-Script-Type" content="text/javascript"/>
  <title>JavaScript window resize</title>
  <script type="text/javascript" src="resize.js">
  </script>
 </head>
 <body>
  <!-- File: Example5-21.htm -->
  <div>
  <input type="button" onclick="resizeWindow(400,300)"
  value="shrink window"/>
  <input type="button"
   onclick="resizeWindow(window.screen.availWidth,
     window.screen.availHeight)" value="restore window"/>
  </div>
 </body>
</html>
```

FIGURE 5.24   The browser window after resizing using a button 'onclick' event

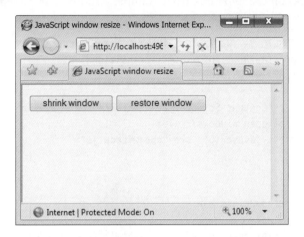

Figure 5.24 shows the browser window after the 'shrink window' button has been pressed.

 NOTE Different browsers may give you slightly different behaviors using this function. For example Opera 9 will only resize the window if it is detached, not if it is part of a tabbed window.

5.8.5 JavaScript URLs

In the previous example we saw how button events can be used to invoke JavaScript functions. Another approach to triggering JavaScript code from user actions is to use JavaScript URLs, which are preceded by a 'javascript:' prefix. This special protocol type can be used anywhere that a regular URL can be used, for example in hypertext anchors or form actions. We can follow this protocol with any JavaScript code, including function calls. This approach works well if we want to use an anchor to trigger a script or function. For example, this fragment of code shows an XHTML anchor element where the URL is a JavaScript function called 'openWindow' that takes the name of an XHTML page as a parameter:

```
<a href="javascript:openWindow('AboutUs.htm')">open window</a>
```

When the anchor is clicked in the browser, the 'openWindow' function will be invoked. Here is the 'openWindow' function implementation, which uses the 'open' method of the same name from the window object:

```
// File: openwindow.js
function openWindow(url)
{
 window.open(url);
}
```

Here is an XHTML page that includes the JavaScript URL, which will invoke the function when the user clicks on the hyperlink (this example assumes a file called 'AboutUs.htm' is available within the website):

```
<!DOCTYPE html PUBLIC "-//W3C//DTD XHTML 1.0 Transitional//EN"
"http://www.w3.org/TR/xhtml1/DTD/xhtml1-transitional.dtd">
<html xmlns="http://www.w3.org/1999/xhtml">
 <head>
  <meta http-equiv="Content-Script-Type" content="text/javascript"/>
  <title>JavaScript open window</title>
  <script type="text/javascript" src="openwindow.js">
  </script>
 </head>
 <body>
  <!-- File: Example5-22.htm -->
  <div>
   <a href="javascript:openWindow('AboutUs.htm')">open window</a>
  </div>
 </body>
</html>
```

The effect of clicking the hyperlink in the page will vary from browser to browser. In some cases a new window will be created and in others a new tab will appear. Figure 5.25 shows how Internet Explorer 7 responds to the function, opening a new window.

FIGURE 5.25   The effect of the 'openWindow' function in Internet Explorer 7, triggered by a JavaScript URL

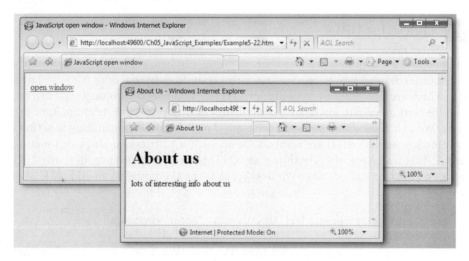

5.9 DHTML (Dynamic HTML)

DHTML (Dynamic HTML) is not a specific technology but refers to using a combination of JavaScript, the DOM and Cascading StyleSheets (CSS) to make web pages more dynamic and interactive. JavaScript code can be used to locate nodes of the DOM and interact with their contents, while styles can be used to enhance the dynamic aspects of presentation, such as showing or hiding parts of a page. The credit for inventing DHTML is generally given to Scott Isaacs at Microsoft, though DHTML is not so much a technology as a collection of existing techniques (a similar thing happened with the development of AJAX, which we look at in Chapter 13). DHTML relies on aspects of HTML that were introduced with version 4.0, along with elements of CSS, so will not work on older browsers (e.g. before version 4 of Internet Explorer or Netscape Navigator).

An important feature of DHTML is the use of stylesheets to dynamically change the presentation of the document. A commonly used example of this technique is to apply JavaScript and stylesheets to show or hide parts of a page. This technique can be used, for example, to add expandable menus to web pages. To interact with styles inside our scripts, we can use the 'style' property of the elements in the DOM to dynamically apply styles to parts of the document. The CSS style property that we can use to show or hide parts of the page is 'display', which can have the value 'block' to make the content visible, or 'none' to make it invisible. The following function uses an 'if' statement to switch the display style of an element between 'none' and 'block'. In this example, 'element' is a variable that references an element node from the current document, identified by its 'id' attribute:

```
// File: changedisplay.js
function changeDisplay(id)
{
 var element = document.getElementById(id);
 if(element.style.display == 'none')
   {
     element.style.display = 'block';
   }
   else
   {
     element.style.display = 'none';
   }
 }
```

5.9.1 Using DHTML to show and hide content

So far in this chapter we have looked at how we can use JavaScript to navigate to nodes in the DOM and to access the properties of these nodes, including the 'style' property. We have also looked at the use of events to trigger JavaScript functions. In the next example we draw all of these techniques together into a DHTML page that shows and hides parts of a page when a JavaScript URL is clicked. The page consists of two sections with the titles 'JavaScript' and 'DHTML (Dynamic HTML)' that are in anchors that use JavaScript URLs. When either of these titles is clicked, the detail text (enclosed in div tags with unique IDs) will switch between shown and hidden. The IDs of the div elements are passed to the 'changeDisplay' function in order to switch their state.

We need to be able to invoke this function in two ways. First, we need to invoke it when the page is loaded, to set the initial state of the page, using the 'onload' event. To call more than one function from the 'onload' event or, as in this case, to call the same function more than once, the function calls can be put into a comma separated list, like this:

```
<body onload="changeDisplay('jsdetail'), changeDisplay('dhtmldetail')">
```

Since the display state of the two 'div' elements has not been set initially, the first time it is called for a particular element the function will execute the 'else' block and set the display state to 'none'. From that point onwards, the JavaScript URLs will invoke the function when either one of them is clicked and switch the display state. Here is one example of these two URLs:

```
<a href="javascript:changeDisplay('jsdetail')">JavaScript</a>
```

Note how it passes the ID of one of the 'div' elements to the function. Here is the complete XHTML page:

```
<!DOCTYPE html PUBLIC "-//W3C//DTD XHTML 1.0 Transitional//EN"
"http://www.w3.org/TR/xhtml1/DTD/xhtml1-transitional.dtd">
<html xmlns="http://www.w3.org/1999/xhtml">
 <head>
  <meta http-equiv="Content-Script-Type" content="text/javascript"/>
  <title>DHTML show and hide</title>
  <script type="text/javascript" src="changedisplay.js">
  </script>
 </head>
<body onload="changeDisplay('jsdetail'), changeDisplay('dhtmldetail')">
<!-- File: Example5-23.htm -->
   <div>
    <a href="javascript:changeDisplay('jsdetail')">JavaScript</a>
   </div>
   <div id="jsdetail">
    JavaScript is a scripting language that can be run inside
    the browser to enable client-side processes.
   </div>
   <div>
    <a href="javascript:changeDisplay('dhtmldetail')">
    DHTML (Dynamic HTML)</a>
   </div>
   <div id="dhtmldetail">
    DHTML is a label given to techniques that use JavaScript,
    CSS and the DOM to make web pages more dynamic and interactive
   </div>
  </body>
 </html>
```

Figure 5.26 shows the state of the page once it has been initially loaded into the browser, with both 'div' element styles in the 'none' display state.

Figure 5.27 shows how the page looks if both the 'div' element styles are in the 'block' state (i.e. visible).

FIGURE 5.26 The div elements hidden by setting the display property of the style to 'none'

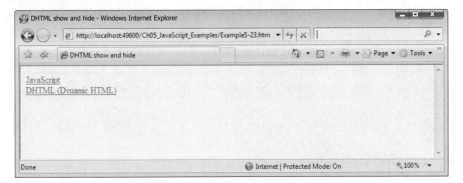

FIGURE 5.27 The div elements made visible by setting the display property of the style to 'block'

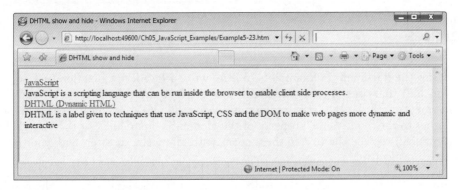

Self Study Questions

1. What does it mean when we say that JavaScript is 'loosely typed'?
2. In the JavaScript DOM, which object is the parent of the 'document'?
3. If a script element is added to the body of an XHTML document, when is it executed?
4. What is the range of possible values that may be generated by the Math.random() method?
5. What is the difference between the 'equal to' (==) and the 'identical to' (===) operators?
6. What does DHTML refer to?
7. Which DOM method can be used to access an individual element with an 'id' attribute?
8. What does the 'innerHTML' property of XHTML element enable us to do?
9. What is the purpose of a JavaScript URL?
10. Which properties of an element can be used to access or set the current CSS style?

Exercises

5.10 Using the document in Example5-15.htm, write a JavaScript function (in a separate '.js' file) that uses appropriate DOM properties and methods to locate the 'span' elements with the IDs 'risk' and 'items', Using the DOM, (you can assign the values either to the 'nodeValue' property of the element's 'firstChild', or the 'innerHTML' property) replace the text in these spans with 'domestic disaster' and 'your possessions' respectively.

Invoke the function using the 'onload' event of the document body. The resulting page should appear as Figure 5.28.

FIGURE 5.28 The expected result from Exercise 5.10

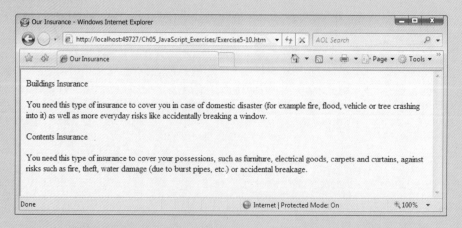

5.11 In an external file called 'mouseover.js', write two JavaScript functions to animate the WebHomeCover logo by using two different versions of the logo and switching between them when the mouse passes over the logo position. Here is an XHTML page that includes an anchor that uses the 'onmouseover' and 'onmouseout' events to trigger JavaScript functions:

```
<!DOCTYPE html PUBLIC "-//W3C//DTD XHTML 1.0 Transitional//EN"
"http://www.w3.org/TR/xhtml1/DTD/xhtml1-transitional.dtd">
<html xmlns="http://www.w3.org/1999/xhtml">
 <head>
  <meta http-equiv="Content-Script-Type" content="text/javascript"/>
  <title>Mouse over logo</title>
  <script type="text/javascript" src="mouseover.js"></script>
 </head>
 <body>
  <!-- File: Exercise5-11.htm -->
  <h2>WebHomeCover Logo</h2>
  <div>
   <a href="http://www.webhomecover.com" onmouseover="mouseOver()"
      onmouseout="mouseNotOver()">
    <img src="webhomecoverlogo.gif" alt="WebHomeCover logo" id="logo"/>
   </a>
  </div>
 </body>
</html>
```

You will need to implement the 'mouseOver' and 'mouseNotOver' functions. In these functions, use the getElementByID method to navigate to the 'logo' (the 'img' element) and set the name of the 'src' attribute to one of the two image file names (one in each function).

5.12 This exercise is quite complex and involves many steps, but provides practice with the arithmetic operators and should give you a deeper understanding of Date objects.

Write a script that creates a table of the current time in different parts of the world. You can do this by creating a Date object to get the current time, converting that to UTC, and then adding or subtracting the time differences for different places (we will not, however, concern ourselves with daylight saving, so the results may not be completely accurate). Table 5.5 shows some example time zones with their difference from UTC in hours. A more complete table can be found at http://setiathome.berkeley.edu/utc.php.

The names of the time zones can be stored in an array, and the current times in each zone generated by simple arithmetic on the millisecond value of the Date. Here is an XHTML page you can use to call your function. Note that the page assumes the function is called 'showTimeZones' and is in a file called 'timezones.js':

```
<?xml version="1.0"?>
<!DOCTYPE html PUBLIC "-//W3C//DTD XHTML 1.1//EN"
 "http://www.w3.org/TR/xhtml11/DTD/xhtml11.dtd">
<html xmlns="http://www.w3.org/1999/xhtml" xml:lang="en">
```

```
          <head>
           <meta http-equiv="Content-Script-Type" content="text/javascript"/>
           <title>International Time Zones</title>
           <script type="text/javascript" src="timezones.js">
           </script>
          </head>
          <body>
           <!-- File: Exercise5-12.htm -->
           <script type="text/javascript">
            showTimeZones();
           </script>
          </body>
      </html>
```

TABLE 5.5	Some examples of time zones and their differences from UTC in hours

Time Zone	Difference from UTC in Hours
Eastern Standard	−5
Pacific standard	−8
UTC	0
Central European	+1
Baghdad	+3
Japan Standard	+9
West Australian Standard	+10
New Zealand Standard	+12

Here are the steps your function should go through in writing your function:

1. Create an array of the names of the time zones.
2. Create an array of the time offsets of these zones from UTC.
3. Create a new Date object. This will contain the date and time in the current locale (which may not be UTC).
4. Use the 'getTime' method to get the current date and time as a value in milliseconds to make it easy to change by arithmetic.
5. Find out the difference between the current locale and UTC in minutes by using the 'getTimezoneOffset' method.
6. Convert the time in the current locale (in milliseconds) to UTC by adding the offset between them. There are 60,000 milliseconds in a minute, so you need to multiply the offset value by 60,000 before adding it to the millisecond value of the current time.
7. Write out the necessary tags to begin a table, something like this:

```
document.write("<table><tr><th>Time Zone</th><th>Offsets from UTC</th>
<th>Current Date and Time</th></tr>");
```

8. Start a 'for' loop to go through each zone in turn (use the 'length' property of the time zone array to control the loop).

9. For each time zone, work out the difference from UTC in milliseconds. There are 3,600,000 milliseconds in each hour, so multiply that by the number of hours in the offset (stored in the array) for the current zone.

10. Work out the time for the current zone (in milliseconds) by adding the offset to the UTC time.

11. Create a new Date object using the adjusted millisecond value (you can create a new Date by passing the millisecond value as a parameter to the constructor).

12. Write the next row of the table (you need to include the XHTML tags for the table row and cells). The code might look something like this:

```
document.write("<tr><td>" + arrTimeZones[i] + "</td><td>" +
arrOffsets[i] + "<td>" + zoneDate.toLocaleString() + "</td></tr>");
```

13. After the 'for' loop has finished executing, close the 'table' element.

SUMMARY

In this chapter we introduced the main features of JavaScript syntax, including interacting with parts of the Document Object Model (DOM), declaring variables, arrays and objects, performing arithmetic, concatenating strings, expressing conditions and controlling loops. We saw how it is possible to use the language to create client-side processes that can integrate small programs into the browser environment. We used a number of JavaScript object methods to, for example, generate random numbers or access date and time information. We looked at various ways of adding JavaScript code to a web page, including the body or the head of a document, or in a separate '.js' file, which makes it possible to reuse the same code, encapsulated in JavaScript functions, in different pages. This means that JavaScript code does not have to be in scripts that execute automatically, but can be in functions that can be triggered by events. In the final section of the chapter we introduced DHTML, and saw how JavaScript can be used in conjunction with the Document Object Model (DOM) and stylesheets to make the web client more interactive and dynamic, letting us navigate to parts of an XHTML document using the DOM and dynamically change their state.

The examples in this chapter show that JavaScript is able to animate and enliven our web pages, but does not, on its own, provide the dynamic content that is required in a modern web application. To create true dynamic content, we have to interact with the server to generate the page content on the fly. In the next chapter we will introduce Web Forms, which enable us to create dynamic web pages. It should be noted, however, that even when using Web Forms, JavaScript is being used behind the scenes to help create the controls that are used on the dynamically generated web pages.

Table 5.6 provides a summary of the JavaScript keywords, JavaScript object types, DOM objects and events that were introduced in this chapter. This is, of course, just a small subset of what is actually available in JavaScript.

TABLE 5.6	JavaScript keywords, types, objects and events introduced in this chapter			

Keywords	Object Types	DOM Objects	Events
new	Date	document	onload
var	String	window	onmouseover
function	Math	navigator	onmouseout
if	Array	location	onclick
else		screen	
while			
for			
return			
true			
false			

References and further reading

Flanagan, D. 2006. *JavaScript: The Definitive Guide (5th Edition)*, O'Reilly.
Kent, P. and Kent, J. 1996. *Official NetScape JavaScript Book 1.2 (11th edition)*, Ventana.
Raggett, D., Le Hors, A. and Jacobs, I. *1999. HTML 4.01 specification*, Section 18: Scripts. http://www.w3.org/TR/html4/interact/scripts.html.

5

Web Forms

LEARNING OBJECTIVES

- **To be able to create web forms in Visual Web Developer**

- **To be able to add controls to web forms and manipulate their properties**

- **To be able to create event handlers for web form controls**

- **To be able to use the configuration, debugging and tracing tools in Visual Web Developer**

- **To understand the process that web forms go through when generating dynamic content**

INTRODUCTION

The work we have done so far with Visual Web Developer has mostly been to create static XHTML pages and style them using cascading stylesheets. When these pages are displayed in a browser, they are rendered directly, so the page source in the browser is exactly the same as it is in the original editor. Even where we have applied JavaScript and DHTML, the page rendering is only dynamic in limited ways. We have manipulated the page display a little, but we have not enabled the user to interact with a server-side web application. In contrast, web forms are not static XHTML pages, or client-side scripts. Rather, they are dynamic pages that are processed on the server. The result of this process is ultimately an XHTML page sent to the client browser, but the process itself may involve complex interaction with the components on the server. In this chapter we look at how to create web forms in Visual Web Developer, how to add and configure the control components that are provided by the Toolbox, and how to add event handlers that can process form data on the server.

In the second part of this chapter we take a look at some of the project management features of Visual Web Developer that help us to organize the various components of our web applications. We begin with the Solution Explorer, which displays the various resources contained in your project. You can use the Solution Explorer to navigate to, view, and manage these items. We also introduce the ASP.NET administration tool, which includes a number of options to enable you to configure your website. We also cover techniques you can use to debug and trace your code, and consider how your website is built and run. Finally, the *page life-cycle* is explained, including postbacks and event handlers.

6.1 Web forms

Forms are a very important part of any web application, because they allow the user to send information to an application running on the server. Much of the user interaction on the web is based on HTTP 'get' requests, which enable a client to request content, such as web pages, from a server. In contrast, forms tend to use HTTP 'post' requests, which can be used to send larger amounts of data than just a page request from a client to a server and send this data in the body of the request. It is possible to use 'get' requests to send form data to the server, but the data is appended to the URL itself, which is less secure than using a 'post' request. Very simple forms that do not send confidential data, such as search engines, often use 'get' requests, but most forms will use 'post' requests.

In ASP.NET, we do not code forms in static XHTML. Instead we build dynamic pages by creating *web forms*. A web form is a server page that, when invoked, generates a client page that contains an XHTML form (Figure 6.1). By default, this form will submit its data back to the same web form that created it.

FIGURE 6.1   Web forms are server pages that generate client pages containing XHTML forms. By default, the generated form submits its data back to the same web form server page

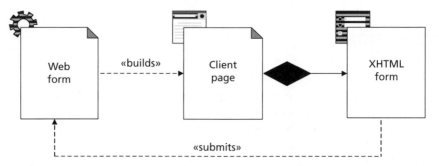

6.1.1 Creating an ASP.NET web form

Creating a web form is similar to creating an XHTML page or a stylesheet. The first step is to create a new file using the 'File' → 'New File' menu command. Select 'Web Form' as the type of item to add, select your programming language from the 'Language' drop-down list box (this can be either 'Visual Basic' or 'C#'), and tick the box that says 'Place code in separate file', making sure the 'Select master page' box is not ticked, since we do not cover master pages until Chapter 7 (Figure 6.2). For the moment, the language choice is not important. However it will have some effect on the generated source of the page.

FIGURE 6.2 Creating a new web form in the 'Add New Item' dialog (In this example Visual Basic has been selected as the programming language)

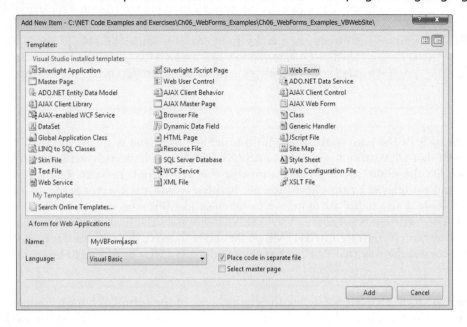

FIGURE 6.3 A newly created web form displayed using Source view (this one uses VB.NET rather than C#)

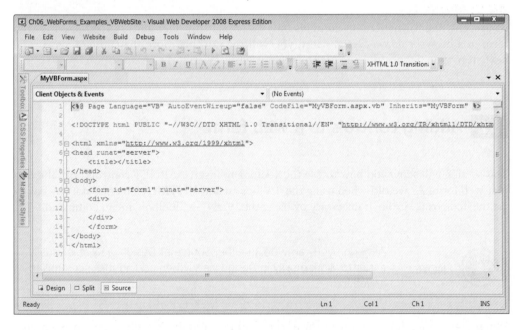

This gives you a new source file as shown in Figure 6.3. You can see that this is similar to an XHTML source file, but there are some important differences. In particular, the web form begins with an @Page directive which defines aspects of the page such as its programming language. This is not XHTML but is an ASP.NET tag (surrounded by '<%...%>' characters). These tags are not for display by a browser, they are used by the server to process the page.

NOTE

The directive at the top of the page in Figure 6.3 is the result of selecting Visual Basic as the language and placing code in a separate file. A slightly different directive will appear if you select C# and/or choose to place code in the same file. You should be able to see in the Solution Explorer window that the web form '.aspx' file has an associated code file with an '.aspx.vb' extension (for VB.NET) or an '.aspx.cs' extension (for C#).

In the body of the page itself, a web form is defined using the standard XHTML 'form' element, but with attributes specific to ASP.NET. The most important attribute is 'runat', which has the value 'server'. This means that the web form is processed on the server, not simply displayed by the client browser. In other words it is a server page, not a client page. There is also an 'id' attribute, which uniquely identifies the form component on the page. These attributes govern the way ASP.NET processes the form, and will be removed when the form is converted to XHTML on the server. Indeed, the additional tags and attributes control the way that ASP.NET generates the XHTML client page to be sent to the browser.

Inside the form element we define the components of the form. Web form components are known as *controls*. In Visual Web Developer, these controls are available in the Toolbox. Controls enable the user to provide data to be sent to the server, either by text input, using controls like text fields and text areas, or by selecting from predefined options using controls such as lists, radio buttons and check boxes.

At present, the form element contains only an empty 'div' element. If you view the web form in a browser or via Design view, you will see nothing more than a blank page. The next step, then, is to add some controls to our empty web form.

6.2 Adding controls to a web form

This section will show you how to use the Toolbox to insert ASP.NET controls onto the current web form. As we did when using the Toolbox to add XHTML elements, start by ensuring the Toolbox is visible, if necessary by using the 'View' → 'Toolbox' menu command.

 NOTE

Although you can work in either Source or Design view, it is usually easier to work mostly in Design view when adding these controls to a web form.

When you are working on a web form, the Toolbox contains a wider range of elements and controls than it does when you are editing static XHTML. Unlike the Toolbox that appears with the XHTML editor, each of the groups now has entries in it, as you will find if you open and close each of them, which you can do by clicking on the name of a group, or the plus or minus symbol beside it. This chapter will start to look at the Standard group of controls. Towards the end of the list is the HTML group of elements that we saw in Chapter 3. Later chapters will cover the other groups, including the Data, Validation, Navigation and Login controls. You should be aware that the Standard group of controls we are working with in this chapter are not the same as the elements that can be used to create forms using pure XHTML. These are specifically a set of controls used with ASP.NET development.

6.2.1 Controls and properties

As before, in the XHTML editor, the first entry in the Standard group is the dummy entry called 'Pointer'. Below this you will see the 'Label' control. A Label is simply a string of text that can be used to label other, more interesting controls. Add one of these to your web form by dragging it across and dropping it on the page. Alternatively you can use cut and paste ('Edit' → 'Cut' or Ctrl+C, and 'Edit' → 'Paste' or Ctrl+V) if you prefer.

Each control will have its own set of properties, which can be viewed and edited using the 'Properties' window. If you select any of the controls on a form, their current properties will appear in this window. If the window is not currently visible, it can be made to appear by either selecting 'View' → 'Properties Window' from the main menu, or by right clicking on the control whose properties you wish to inspect, and selecting 'Properties' from the pop-up menu. Figure 6.4 shows the Properties window being displayed for a Label control. You will notice that properties are grouped under headings such as Accessibility, Appearance, Behavior, Data, Layout and Misc(ellaneous).

FIGURE 6.4 The Properties window, showing the properties associated with an ASP.NET Label control

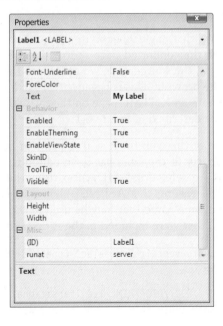

NOTE Depending on how your windows are organized, only part of the properties window may actually be visible, in which case it will have a scroll bar attached.

The most important property of a Label is called 'Text' which is the string that will be displayed when the Label is viewed in a browser. By default this property is given the rather uninteresting value 'Label', but you can click on this and type in a new value.

The second most important property of a Label is its 'ID'. All ASP.NET controls have such a property, which is the name by which this control will be known to any other controls on the web form. You will recall that the 'id' attribute in XHTML can be used to uniquely identify an element in a web page. Although the 'ID' here is in upper-case, it serves exactly the same purpose. Therefore the ID value of each control on a page must be unique. By default the value of this property is set to an automatically generated value such as 'Label1' or 'Label2', but again you can click on this and change it if you wish. Later in this chapter we will see how these IDs are used by server-side code to retrieve the data submitted in a web form.

Many of the properties here will be fairly familiar to you if you have previously done any GUI programming. To learn more about a property you can click on its name and read the description which appears in the bottom of the properties pane. By doing this you can learn, for example, that the 'AccessKey' is the 'Keyboard shortcut used by the control', and that the 'ToolTip' is 'The tooltip displayed when the mouse is over the control'.

As you click on each property, you will see that you can either type or use a drop-down list to select a new value for it. However, you will note that many of these properties are presentational, and should therefore not be set individually on elements but should be managed by a stylesheet. One of the available properties is 'CSSClass'. You can type in a class name here so that the control can be styled by a stylesheet using its class name. Any previous class names you have added for this page will appear in a drop-down list so you can reuse them if necessary. Of course all controls will already have a unique ID that can also be used to apply styles.

Having created a web form with a single label on it, it is quite informative to view the page in a browser and then view the generated page source. Unlike the static XHTML pages we have looked at previously, the source code we enter into the editor is not the same as the source of the page in the browser. This is because ASP.NET pages are processed on the server to dynamically generate an XHTML page on the fly, which is then sent back to the client browser, as previously described in Figure 6.1.

Here is the original source of the web form as it appears in Source view in Visual Web Developer (the 'Text' property of the label has been edited to read 'My Label'). We can see that ASP.NET controls are defined in XML syntax using the 'asp' namespace; they are each preceded by 'asp:'. This ensures that ASP.NET elements are distinct from any standard XHTML elements of the same name that may be used in the page. The same important attributes ('ID' and 'runat') that were included in the form tag also appear here:

```
<%@ Page Language="VB" AutoEventWireup="false" CodeFile="Example6-1.aspx.vb"
Inherits="Example6_1" %>

<!DOCTYPE html PUBLIC "-//W3C//DTD XHTML 1.0 Transitional//EN"
"http://www.w3.org/TR/xhtml1/DTD/xhtml1-transitional.dtd">
```

```
<html xmlns="http://www.w3.org/1999/xhtml">
  <head runat="server">
   <title>Untitled Page</title>
  </head>
  <body>
   <!-- File: Example6-1.aspx -->
   <form id="form1" runat="server">
    <div>
      <asp:Label ID="Label1" runat="server" Text="My Label">
      </asp:Label>
    </div>
   </form>
  </body>
</html>
```

If you use Visual Web Developer to view this page in a browser, and then view the page source from the browser menu, you will see something similar to this:

```
<!DOCTYPE html PUBLIC "-//W3C//DTD XHTML 1.0 Transitional//EN"
"http://www.w3.org/TR/xhtml1/DTD/xhtml1-transitional.dtd">
<html xmlns="http://www.w3.org/1999/xhtml">
  <head>
   <title>Example6-1</title>
  </head>
  <body>
  <!-- File: Example6-1.aspx -->
   <form name="form1" method="post" action="Example6-1.aspx" id="form1">
    <div>
      <input type="hidden" name="__VIEWSTATE" id="__VIEWSTATE"
      value="/wEPDwUJODExMDE5NzY5ZGSJ/1KqrTXbNx7U8OXOVHL/XG41kA==" />
    </div>
    <div>
      <span id="Label1">My Label</span>
    </div>
   </form>
  </body>
</html>
```

While the original source has ASP.NET controls in it, the generated page only contains standard XHTML generated by the server. You may also have noticed that the 'form' element has changed. The XHTML form tag in the generated page has different attributes to those in the original web form. One of these is the 'method' attribute, which defines the type of HTTP request that is to be used (usually 'post' for a form) and the 'action' attribute, which specifies a URI to identify which server-side component is to receive the data from the form. You can see that this form, by default, submits back to the same web form that generated it ('Example6-1.aspx' in this case).

You can see from the generated XHTML page that the Label control is just a way of adding some text in a 'span' element to your web form. You may wonder why we do not just add the span element directly onto the original form, rather than using the ASP.NET

NOTE	Do not try to apply styles to the ASP.NET control elements, since these will not appear in the XHTML client page that is generated on the server. Therefore your stylesheets should target the generated XHTML elements and/or the class and ID names, which will not change.

control. The key difference between these two approaches is that an ASP.NET control has associated properties and, as we shall see later, events. Properties in one control can depend on properties in another control, and can be set, or given new values, by event handlers. This means, for example, that even a simple text element can be dynamically transformed on the server, as we will demonstrate towards the end of this chapter. Getting and setting properties, and handling events, are the fundamental building blocks of ASP.NET programming.

The body of the generated form also contains a hidden input field called '__VIEWSTATE'. This is used by a web application to keep track of client state over the different pages of a webflow.

NOTE	As well as the 'Label' control, there is also a 'Literal' control in Visual Web Developer, which simply adds plain text to the page, without a default value. In the generated XHTML, it does not have any XHTML elements associated with it so does not have an ID, and also cannot have a class associated with it. Therefore this way of adding text is best avoided.

6.2.2 Other standard controls

If you review the controls listed in the Standard group, and compare them with the elements available in the HTML group, you will see a number of overlaps. Both groups contain items corresponding to the standard XHTML input elements such as buttons, check boxes, radio buttons, and text boxes. As noted above, the difference in such cases is that the ASP.NET control provides properties, events and event-handlers to support the ASP.NET programming model. Therefore it is better to use the ASP.NET controls on a web form as this will give you more flexibility in terms of dynamic content.

6.2.3 Editing form controls in Source view

As with XHTML pages, the Toolbar can be used to add controls in Source view, as well as in Design view. For example we might add a TextBox to the page (a TextBox will allow the user to type text into this part of the form). When you add the control to the form, make sure that you add it inside the 'div' element that is inside the form element. Source view should now show the following element:

```
<asp:TextBox ID="TextBox1" runat="server"></asp:TextBox>
```

If you want multiple controls of the same type you can use copy and paste in Source view. For example, if you select the asp:TextBox element as it appears above, then copy and paste it to the immediately following line, you now should see:

```
<asp:TextBox ID="TextBox1" runat="server"></asp:TextBox>
<asp:TextBox ID="TextBox2" runat="server"></asp:TextBox>
```

Note that the editor has automatically changed the ID to ensure uniqueness. You can add further controls to your form by using the Toolbox in any of the standard ways (drag and drop, cut and paste, or double clicking).

If you switch back to Design view you should now see the TextBoxes as they would appear on the form page. If you view the Properties window for the TextBoxes you will see that they all have identical properties, except that their IDs are different as noted above.

 NOTE   Intellisense® works for ASP.NET controls the same as it does for XHTML elements, giving drop-down lists of available elements and attributes when editing in Source view.

6.2.4 Text areas and password input

In the previous section we introduced the TextBox control, which by default is used for the input of single lines of text. However sometimes we want to have a control that will allow the entry of multiple lines of text, or to enable the safe entry of passwords so that the characters typed in are not echoed back literally to the screen. To create these types of control, we can configure the 'TextMode' property of a TextBox. This property is managed by a drop-down list that specifies the TextBox as being either 'SingleLine' (the default), 'MultiLine' or 'Password'. If we set the TextMode to 'MultiLine' we can also choose to set the 'Rows' and/or 'Columns' properties to specify the size of the textbox in terms of characters. The text typed into a multi-line TextBox will automatically wrap at the end of a line (the value of the 'Wrap' property is 'True' by default). Some default text can also be added using the 'Text' property.

Figure 6.5 shows three controls added to a page in Design view, a standard TextBox ('SingleLine' by default), a TextBox configured to be 'MultiLine', and another configured to be 'Password'.

FIGURE 6.5   Textbox components configured for single line, multiline and password inputs

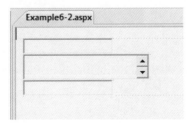

In this figure, the MultiLine TextBox is displayed differently but the password TextBox appears unchanged. However we can see in Source view that its 'TextMode' property has been set to 'Password'.

```
<%@ Page Language="VB" AutoEventWireup="false"
  CodeFile="Example6-2.aspx.vb" Inherits="Example6_2" %>
<!DOCTYPE html PUBLIC "-//W3C//DTD XHTML 1.0 Transitional//EN"
"http://www.w3.org/TR/xhtml1/DTD/xhtml1-transitional.dtd">
<html xmlns="http://www.w3.org/1999/xhtml">
  <head runat="server">
    <title>Example6-2</title>
  </head>
  <body>
    <!-- File: Example6-2.aspx -->
    <form id="form1" runat="server">
      <div>
        <asp:TextBox ID="TextBox1" runat="server"></asp:TextBox>
        <br />
        <asp:TextBox ID="TextBox2" runat="server" TextMode="MultiLine">
        </asp:TextBox>
        <br />
        <asp:TextBox ID="TextBox3" runat="server" TextMode="Password">
        </asp:TextBox>
      </div>
    </form>
  </body>
</html>
```

Figure 6.6 shows the three types of text input as they appear in a browser. Note that text typed into the password text box is obscured. If you look at the generated XHTML, you will see that a TextBox configured to use 'MultiLine' mode will generate a 'textarea' element in the resulting XHTML page:

```
<textarea name="TextBox2" rows="2" cols="20" id="TextBox2"></textarea>
```

FIGURE 6.6   Different configurations of TextBox components displayed in a browser

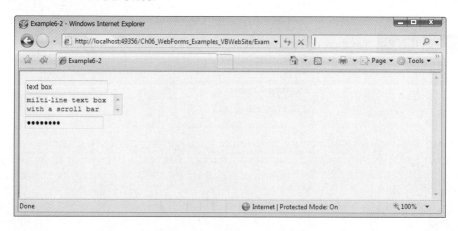

In contrast, if we set the mode to 'password' then an 'input' element will be generated, with 'password' as the type attribute:

```
<input name="TextBox3" type="password" id="TextBox3" />
```

Section summary and quick exercises

In this section we covered how to create a web form and add some simple controls to it using both Design and Source views. We saw that a web form is a server page that generates an XHTML client page to be rendered in the browser. On the server, the ASP.NET controls are processed dynamically to create a page that contains standard XHTML. Importantly, each ASP.NET control has a unique ID generated by Visual Web Developer. The properties window can be used to configure these controls, for example by assigning a CSS class name to them. We also saw how the properties of a TextBox control can be used to configure different types of text input element.

EXERCISE 6.1

Create a new web form and add two Label controls and two TextBox controls to it. Use the Properties window to change the text properties of the two labels so that the label of the first TextBox is 'Username' and the label of the second is 'Password'. Configure the second text box so that it can be used for password input. View the resulting XHTML page in a browser and compare the original ASP.NET source with the generated XHTML.

EXERCISE 6.2

Using the CSSClass property in the Properties window, give your two labels the same class name. Do the same for the text boxes but put these into a different class. Create a stylesheet that applies styles to these two classes and link it to your ASP.NET page. View the page in a browser and check that your styles have been correctly applied.

6.3 Controls with data items

The controls that we have introduced so far are either predefined text (Labels) or text input controls (single line, multi line and password). However in many case we do not want users to have to type in all the data. This can be both tedious and prone to error. Therefore there are a number of controls that enable the user to choose from predefined lists of data items. These controls include ListBoxes, DropDownLists, CheckBoxes and RadioButtons. Both CheckBoxes and RadioButtons can be grouped together in lists.

6.3.1 ListBoxes and DropDownLists

ListBoxes and DropDownLists are very similar, and in fact they both generate XHTML that uses the 'select' element. However a ListBox will show a number of items in a list, possibly with a scroll bar if there are more items than will fit into the visible list area. In contrast, a DropDownList will show only a single list item at any one time, with an arrowhead button that allows the remainder of the list to drop-down.

FIGURE 6.7   The smart tag and pop-up window in a list control

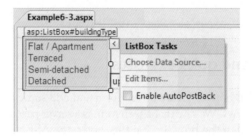

If you add either a ListBox or DropDownList control to your web form in Design view, you will notice that a pop-up window appears, giving you the chance to 'Choose Data Source...', 'Edit Items...', or 'Enable AutoPostBack'. You can dismiss this pop-up by pressing the Escape key, or by clicking elsewhere on the form. You can bring back this pop-up window later by clicking on the control's *smart tag*, which is the little right pointing arrow displayed at the top right-hand corner of the control when you select it in Design view. This pop-up shows you the 'Task List' associated with a smart control such as a ListBox (Figure 6.7). In Source view, the same configuration options that appear in this pop-up are accessible via the Properties window. For example the dialog reached via the 'Edit Items...' option in the pop-up can also be accessed by clicking on the button in the 'Items' entry in the Properties window (under the 'Misc' heading).

The Data Source property of these controls gives you a way of selecting the items in the list from a database. For now, however, we will take the more pedestrian approach of entering these manually. If you select the 'Edit Items...' task from the task list, you will see a 'ListItem Collection Editor' dialog box similar to that in Figure 6.8. This allows you to add members to the list one at a time, by pressing the 'Add' button. You can edit the four properties of each member, most importantly the text it is displayed with, and the value associated with it, which will be posted back to the server if it is selected. The list members can be re-ordered using the up and down pointing arrows in the middle of this dialog box. By default, the 'Value' entry will be the same as what you put into the 'Text' entry, but if the content of the 'Text' is complex it is better to provide a simpler version for the 'Value' as this makes it easier to process this value on the server. For example in Figure 6.8, which is about information from the home insurance domain, the text of the first item in the list is 'Flat/Apartment', but the value has been changed to the simpler 'apartment'.

Here is the resulting code in Source view for the ListBox shown in Figures 6.7 and 6.8:

```
<asp:ListBox ID="buildingType" runat="server">
 <asp:ListItem Value="apartment">Flat / Apartment</asp:ListItem>
 <asp:ListItem Value="terraced">Terraced</asp:ListItem>
 <asp:ListItem Value="semi">Semi-detached</asp:ListItem>
 <asp:ListItem Value="detached">Detached</asp:ListItem>
</asp:ListBox>
```

Here is the code generated for another list created using the DropDownList control. You will note that it is very similar:

```
<asp:DropDownList ID="marketValue" runat="server">
 <asp:ListItem Value="30000">up to 30,000</asp:ListItem>
```

```
<asp:ListItem Value="60000">30,000 - 60,000</asp:ListItem>
<asp:ListItem Value="100000">60,000 - 100,000</asp:ListItem>
<asp:ListItem Value="200000">100,000 - 200,000</asp:ListItem>
<asp:ListItem Value="500000">200,000 - 500,000</asp:ListItem>
<asp:ListItem Value="1000000">above 500,000</asp:ListItem>
</asp:DropDownList>
```

FIGURE 6.8   Defining items in a list control

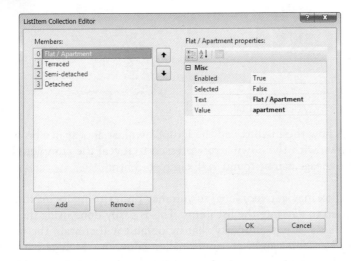

This similarity is no coincidence. In fact ASP ListBoxes and DropDownLists are both rendered in a browser by the XHTML 'select' element. A 'select' element has one or more nested 'option' elements that relate to 'asp:ListItem' tags. The difference between list boxes and drop-down lists in XHTML is the 'size' attribute, as we can see from the XHTML source that will be generated if we view the web form containing the Drop-DownList and the ListBox in a browser. The ListBox sets the size value to '4', the number of entries in the ListItemCollection Editor, which will create a list with four visible rows:

```
<select size="4" name="buildingType" id="buildingType">
 <option value="apartment">Flat / Apartment</option>
 <option value="terraced">Terraced</option>
 <option value="semi">Semi-detached</option>
 <option value="detached">Detached</option>
</select>
```

In contrast, if there is no size attribute, which will be the case for our DropDownList, the size will default to '1':

```
<select name="marketValue" id="marketValue">
 <option value="30000">up to 30,000</option>
 <option value="60000">30,000 - 60,000</option>
 <option value="100000">60,000 - 100,000</option>
 <option value="200000">100,000 - 200,000</option>
 <option value="500000">200,000 - 500,000</option>
 <option value="1000000">above 500,000</option>
</select>
```

FIGURE 6.9   The ListBox and the DropDownList as they appear in a browser

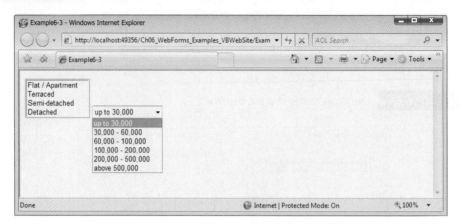

Figure 6.9 shows how the ListBox and the DropDownList appear in a browser (the Drop-DownList is shown with the down arrow pressed to reveal the complete list). The complete source of the page can be found in 'Example6-3.htm'.

Of course a ListBox may get very long, so you may prefer to fix its maximum size so that scroll bars are used to navigate the list items. This is easily done using the Properties window. A ListBox has a 'Rows' property that by default will contain the number of items in the list. However, this can be set to a smaller value, in which case only that number of rows will be visible and a scroll bar will be added to the ListBox. A DropDownList, of course, does not have this property as it always has one row.

6.3.2 Check boxes and radio buttons

Two similar types of control are check boxes and radio buttons. The important difference between them is that check boxes are always independent of any other component, whereas radio buttons can be grouped together so that only one radio button in a given group can be selected at any one time. Browsers usually show check boxes as squares that may contain a tick if they have been selected, while radio buttons usually appear as circles that may contain a disc if they have been selected. By default, radio buttons that are added to a form will not be grouped together. Here is the source of a simple web form created by adding two CheckBox controls and two RadioButton controls from the Toolbox:

```
<%@ Page Language="VB" AutoEventWireup="false" CodeFile="Example6-4.aspx.vb"
Inherits="Example6_4" %>

<!DOCTYPE html PUBLIC "-//W3C//DTD XHTML 1.0 Transitional//EN"
"http://www.w3.org/TR/xhtml1/DTD/xhtml1-transitional.dtd">
<html xmlns="http://www.w3.org/1999/xhtml">
  <head id="Head1" runat="server">
   <title>Example6-4</title>
  </head>
  <body>
  <!-- File: Example6-4.aspx -->
```

```
<form id="form1" runat="server">
 <div>
 <asp:Label ID="Label1" runat="server" Text="First check box">
 </asp:Label><asp:CheckBox ID="CheckBox1" runat="server" />
 <br />
 <asp:Label ID="Label2" runat="server" Text="Second check box">
 </asp:Label><asp:CheckBox ID="CheckBox2" runat="server" />
 <br />
 <asp:Label ID="Label3" runat="server" Text="First radio button">
 </asp:Label><asp:RadioButton ID="RadioButton1" runat="server" />
 <br />
 <asp:Label ID="Label4" runat="server" Text="Second radio button">
 </asp:Label><asp:RadioButton ID="RadioButton2" runat="server" />
 </div>
 </form>
 </body>
</html>
```

If you view this page in a browser, you will see that the check boxes are square, and can be checked or unchecked. The radio buttons, however, are round, and although they can be checked, they cannot be unchecked. They can also both be checked at the same time. Clearly, then, we need to do something further to get our radio buttons to behave as a group so that only one radio button can be checked at any one time. The solution to this problem is to use a RadioButtonList control. This is very similar to the ListBox and Drop-DownList controls that we have already seen. Once again, it has a Tasks list that lets you add items to the list. However, with this control, each item in the list will be displayed as a radio button when it appears in the browser. Here is the source for a RadioButtonList control that has been added to the form using the Toolbar and has two list items added using the ListItem Collection Editor:

```
<asp:RadioButtonList ID="RadioButtonList1" runat="server">
 <asp:ListItem>First radio button</asp:ListItem>
 <asp:ListItem>Second radio button</asp:ListItem>
</asp:RadioButtonList>
```

The full source of the page is available in 'Example6-5.aspx'. When this page is viewed in the browser, the generated XHTML will look like the following example. The radio button elements appear in a table, and each has a 'name' attribute with an identical value. This is how the different radio buttons can be treated as a single control. Text labels are added using the XHTML 'label' element, which links a text label to a specific control (clicking on a label element in a browser will move focus to the associated control). Bear in mind that this 'label' element in the generated page is not the same type as an ASP.NET 'Label' control in a web form:

```
<table id="RadioButtonList1" border="0">
 <tr>
  <td>
   <input id="RadioButtonList1_0" type="radio"
          name="RadioButtonList1" value="First radio button" />
   <label for="RadioButtonList1_0">First radio button</label>
  </td>
```

```
      </tr>
      <tr>
       <td>
        <input id="RadioButtonList1_1" type="radio"
               name="RadioButtonList1" value="Second radio button" />
        <label for="RadioButtonList1_1">Second radio button</label>
       </td>
      </tr>
    </table>
```

By default, none of the radio buttons will be selected. However it is often useful to have one of the radio buttons selected as a default choice. In Design view, this can be done in the ListItem Collection Editor (by setting the 'Selected' property as can be seen in Figure 6.8). Alternatively we can set this in Source view by selecting one of the radio button elements and then setting the 'Selected' property in the Properties window to 'True' (this appears under the 'Misc' group as a drop-down list).

Check boxes can also be grouped by creating a CheckBoxList. This is not necessary in terms of controlling which boxes are checked, since multiple check boxes can be checked at the same time. However it is useful in terms of grouping a number of related check boxes together, as the control will manage the layout of the check boxes in a single table, similar to the RadioButtonList. Like radio buttons, check boxes are unchecked by default. Again, we can change this if the check box is in a list by setting the value of the 'Selected' property attribute to 'True' using either Design or Source views. Slightly confusingly, perhaps, if the checkbox is not part of a CheckBoxList then the property is called 'Checked' rather than 'Selected'.

In the next example web form, we use radio buttons to ask the user if they want to use our website as a guest, set up a new account or log in using an existing account. These options need to be in a RadioButtonGroup so that only one of these can be selected at any one time. By default, the 'login' radio button will be selected because its 'Selected' property has been set to 'True'. There is also a check box that asks users if they wish to be added to a mailing list. This CheckBox does not appear in a CheckBoxList, so its state has been set using the 'Checked' property. Here is the page as it appears in Source view:

```
<%@ Page Language="VB" AutoEventWireup="false" CodeFile="Example6-6.aspx.vb"
Inherits="Example6_6" %>
<!DOCTYPE html PUBLIC "-//W3C//DTD XHTML 1.0 Transitional//EN"
"http://www.w3.org/TR/xhtml1/DTD/xhtml11-transitional.dtd">
<html xmlns="http://www.w3.org/1999/xhtml">
  <head id="Head1" runat="server">
   <title>Example6-6</title>
  </head>
  <body>
   <!-- File: Example6-6.aspx -->
   <form id="form1" runat="server">
    <div>
      <asp:Label ID="Label1" runat="server"
       Text="Welcome to our site. How would you like to continue? ">
      </asp:Label>
```

```
      <asp:RadioButtonList ID="RadioButtonList1" runat="server">
        <asp:ListItem Value="new">Set up a new user account</asp:ListItem>
        <asp:ListItem Value="login" Selected="True">
          Login using an existing account
        </asp:ListItem>
        <asp:ListItem Value="guest">
          Access the site as a guest
        </asp:ListItem>
      </asp:RadioButtonList>
      <asp:Label ID="Label2" runat="server"
        Text="Please check this box if you would like to be added to our
        mailing list">
      </asp:Label>
      <asp:CheckBox ID="mailinglist" runat="server" Checked="True" />
    </div>
  </form>
 </body>
</html>
```

Figure 6.10 shows the page with radio buttons and a check box displayed in Internet Explorer 7.

FIGURE 6.10　A form with radio buttons and a check box

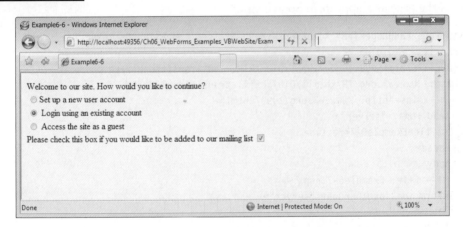

6.4 Grouping controls with panels

One control that is often useful when designing web forms is the 'Panel' control. When you drag this onto your web form you see just an empty box. In fact a panel allows you to group together a number of other controls. The Panel's properties include the 'Grouping Text' which is a heading that will appear at the top of the panel. To create the panel contents, you can drag other controls onto the panel. You can even include one panel inside another one. Figure 6.11 shows a web form with two separate panels, each containing CheckBoxList controls. The Text labels ('Mark-up Languages' and 'Programming Languages') have been set using the 'Grouping Text' property.

FIGURE 6.11 Creating a multi-panel web form

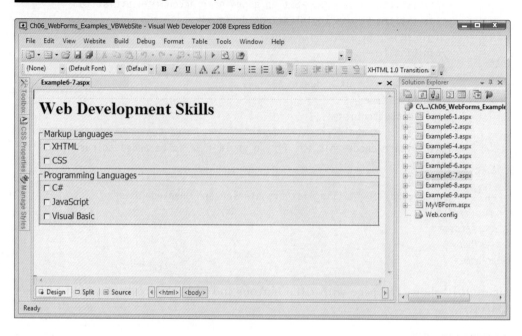

Here is the page as it appears in Source view:

```
<%@ Page Language="VB" AutoEventWireup="false" CodeFile="Example6-7.aspx.vb"
Inherits="Example6_7" %>
<!DOCTYPE html PUBLIC "-//W3C//DTD XHTML 1.0 Transitional//EN"
"http://www.w3.org/TR/xhtml1/DTD/xhtml1-transitional.dtd">
<html xmlns="http://www.w3.org/1999/xhtml">
 <head runat="server">
  <title>Example6-7</title>
 </head>
 <body>
  <!-- File: Example6-7.aspx -->
  <form id="form1" runat="server">
   <div>
    <h1>
     <asp:Label ID="Label1" runat="server"
     Text="Web Development Skills">
    </asp:Label>
    </h1>
    <asp:Panel ID="Panel1" runat="server"
     GroupingText="Mark-up Languages">
     <asp:CheckBoxList ID="CheckBoxList1" runat="server">
      <asp:ListItem>XHTML</asp:ListItem>
      <asp:ListItem>CSS</asp:ListItem>
     </asp:CheckBoxList>
    </asp:Panel>
    <asp:Panel ID="Panel2" runat="server"
     GroupingText="Programming Languages">
```

```
    <asp:CheckBoxList ID="CheckBoxList2" runat="server">
      <asp:ListItem>C#</asp:ListItem>
      <asp:ListItem>JavaScript</asp:ListItem>
      <asp:ListItem>Visual Basic</asp:ListItem>
    </asp:CheckBoxList>
   </asp:Panel>
  </div>
 </form>
</body>
</html>
```

If you view the source of this web form after it has been displayed in a browser, you will see that the XHTML element generated by a panel control is a 'fieldset'. The text label appears inside a 'legend' element:

```
<fieldset>
 <legend>Mark-up Languages</legend>
...panel content here
</fieldset>
```

You can of course apply styles to fieldset and legend elements using a stylesheet, or alternatively apply styles by setting the CSSClass properties of the panels and applying styles to those classes.

NOTE	A Panel control is only rendered with a fieldset if you set its 'GroupingText' property. If you do not set this property, a 'div' element is generated instead, so there will be no visible border around the controls when viewed in a browser.

Figure 6.12 shows the web form as it appears when displayed in the browser, in this case Internet Explorer 7. You can see that the appearance of the panels in a web page can vary quite a lot from how the controls appear in Design view of Visual Web Developer.

FIGURE 6.12   A multi-panel web form displayed in the Internet Explorer 7 browser

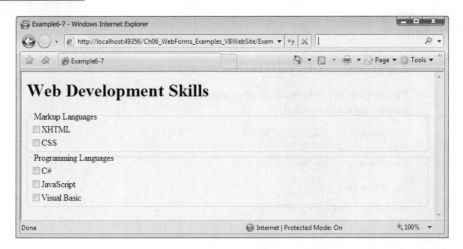

Section summary and quick exercises

In this section we covered a number of controls that enable the user to select data from a set of predefined options. These controls were ListBoxes, DropDownLists, CheckBoxes, RadioButtons, CheckBoxLists and RadioButtonLists. We saw how items can be added to these lists in design view using the ListItem Collection Editor, and how this editor can also be used to select a default item from the list. We concluded the section by introducing the Panel control.

EXERCISE 6.3

Create a web form containing a ListBox that has four items and two visible rows. Use the Toolbox to add a BulletedList control to the form. What type of XHTML element is generated by a BulletedList control?

EXERCISE 6.4

Create a web form that contains a Panel control with two other panels nested inside it. Do not set the GroupingText properties of any of these panels. In one of the nested panels add a Radio-ButtonList with three radio buttons. In the second nested panel add a CheckBoxList with two check boxes. View the page in a browser and look at the generated XHTML. Now add a value for the GroupingText properties of all three panels. View the page again in a browser, and note the changes in the generated XHTML.

EXERCISE 6.5

Create a 'Buildings Policy Details' web form from the home insurance domain that looks like Figure 6.13. The various controls are in a table, the outline of which can be seen in Design view in Figure 6.13. The form includes a 'Submit' button. In this exercise this button will have no functionality, but in the following section we will see how to attach event handlers to buttons so they can be used to submit form data to the server.

FIGURE 6.13   Buildings policy details web form in Design view

6.5 Processing form data on the server using event handlers

So far in this chapter we have been looking at web forms simply from the perspective of adding controls in Visual Web Developer. However we have not yet addressed the question of how we actually send the data in the form to a server-side process. In this section, we look at how to add and edit ASP.NET event handlers that can receive client data from web forms and process it on the server.

In the next example, we will add some interactive behavior to an ASP.NET web form. This gives us a chance to look at some .NET source code written in both C# and VB.NET. Event handlers are frequently implemented using buttons on forms, which invoke the event handler when pressed.

For our example web form event handler we will create a web form that contains two TextBoxes, some labels and button. Figure 6.14 shows the form in Design view (as well as the components, a couple of line break elements have also been added). The form acts as a simple calculator. You can enter two numbers, one in each of the TextBoxes, press the 'Calculate Total' button, and the result of adding the two numbers together appears in the label called 'result'.

FIGURE 6.14   The web form displayed using Design View

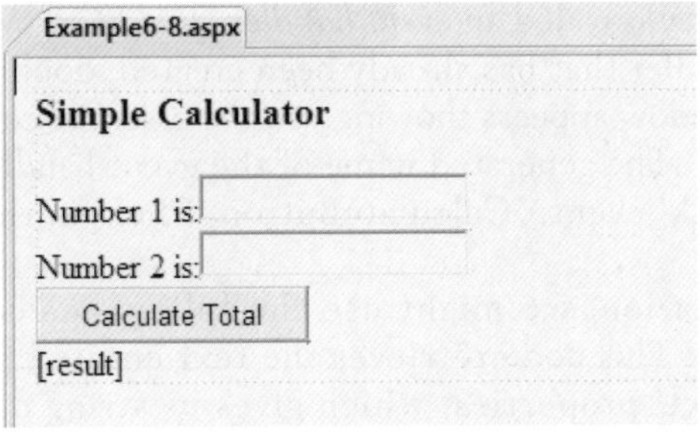

In this example, the ID properties of the two TextBoxes have been set to 'Number1' and 'Number2', and the ID of the button to 'CalculateButton', with the button text being changed to 'Calculate Total'. The 'result' label has been configured by changing the ID attribute to 'result' and deleting the default text label. Since it has no text content, Design view then shows the name of the label in square braces on the page. Source view will contain the following code:

```
<%@ Page Language="VB" AutoEventWireup="false" CodeFile="Example6-8.aspx.vb"
Inherits="Example6_8" %>
<!DOCTYPE html PUBLIC "-//W3C//DTD XHTML 1.0 Transitional//EN"
"http://www.w3.org/TR/xhtml1/DTD/xhtml1-transitional.dtd">
<html xmlns="http://www.w3.org/1999/xhtml">
  <head runat="server">
    <title>Simple Calculator</title>
  </head>
  <body>
```

6

```
<!-- File: Example 6-8.aspx -->
<form id="form1" runat="server">
  <div>
    <h3>Simple Calculator</h3>
    <asp:Label ID="Label1" runat="server" Text="Number 1 is:">
    </asp:Label>
    <asp:TextBox ID="Number1" runat="server"></asp:TextBox>
    <br />
    <asp:Label ID="Label2" runat="server" Text="Number 2 is:">
    </asp:Label>
    <asp:TextBox ID="Number2" runat="server"></asp:TextBox>
    <br />
    <asp:Button ID="CalculateButton" runat="server"
      Text="Calculate Total" />
    <br />
    <asp:Label ID="result" runat="server" Text="">
    </asp:Label>
  </div>
</form>
</body>
</html>
```

To implement the process behind the form, we will need to do some programming. Specifically, we will put the code to perform the calculation into a Visual Basic or C# method that will be invoked when the user clicks the 'Calculate Total' button. A method that is invoked in this way is called an *event handler*. To add an event handler to a button, or to view an event handler that has already been created, double click on the button in Design View. A new window appears showing you the essential code for the event handler as shown in Figure 6.15. The generated name of the event handler is based on the ID of the button and the 'Click' event, 'CalculateButton_Click' in this example.

To perform the calculation, we might use the following code for the 'Calculate-Button_Click' method. This code retrieves the text entered into the two TextBoxes by accessing their 'Text' properties, which gives us string data, and then converts these strings to their numeric equivalents using the Parse method. The result of adding these two values together is then used to populate the 'Text' property of the 'result' label. The exception handling code is useful because it means that the page will not generate an error if the user enters something that is not a number into either of the boxes and causes the Parse method to throw an exception. Instead, a message appears in the 'result' label:

VB Code

```
Protected Sub CalculateButton_Click(ByVal sender As Object, ByVal e As
System.EventArgs) Handles CalculateButton.Click
 Dim total As Integer
 Try
   total = Integer.Parse(Number1.Text) + Integer.Parse(Number2.Text)
   result.Text = "Total is " + total.ToString()
 Catch myEx As Exception
```

```
      result.Text = "Please enter two numbers to add together"
   End Try
End Sub
```

C# Code

```
protected void CalculateButton_Click(object sender, EventArgs e)
{
  try
  {
   Int32 total = Int32.Parse(Number1.Text) + Int32.Parse(Number2.Text);
   result.Text = "Total is " + total.ToString();
  }
  catch(Exception e)
  {
   result.Text = "Please enter two numbers to add together";
  }
}
```

FIGURE 6.15   The event handler for the CalculateButton has just been created and is ready to be coded. This example is in Visual Basic (the C# code looks somewhat different)

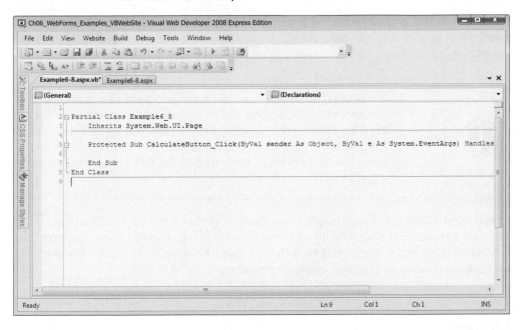

You can now test your web form is working correctly using the 'File' → 'View in Browser' menu command. (Note that this command is not available when viewing your VB.NET or C# source code, as only the '.aspx' file offers this.) If all has gone well, you will see your web form in action, and you can use it to add two numbers (see Figure 6.16). If you have made a mistake in the event handler code, your browser will instead show you a page with the compiler error message. You can use this to help you correct your code, if necessary.

FIGURE 6.16 The web form and event handler in action

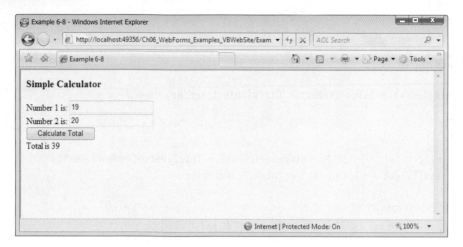

6.5.1 Adding another event handler

With the web form we currently have, you have to click the button (which has the event handler) to trigger the calculation. Only then are the TextBoxes checked for invalid data. We can improve matters a little by adding more event handlers, this time for the individual TextBoxes. If you double click on a TextBox in Design view, a new 'Text_Changed' event handler will be added to the code. Here, we can respond to the entry of data into an individual text box.

NOTE	If you select a TextBox in either Design or Source view and view its properties window, you will see an additional button at the top looking like a lightning bolt. Selecting this will show you the events that are available for this type of control. We can also select the 'Text_Changed' event handler from the 'Action' group of this list by double clicking on it (Figure 6.17).

In the 'Text_Changed' event handler, we can test if the data that has been entered is numeric as soon as this control loses focus. If we can successfully parse the text (the TextBox is the 'sender' parameter) then the message label is set to be blank. However if an exception is thrown we display a message immediately.

VB Code

```
Protected Sub Number1_TextChanged(ByVal sender As Object, ByVal e As
System.EventArgs) Handles Number1.TextChanged, Number2.TextChanged
  Try
    Integer.Parse(sender.Text)
    result.Text = ""
  Catch myEx As Exception
```

```
        result.Text = "You must enter a number"
    End Try
End Sub
```

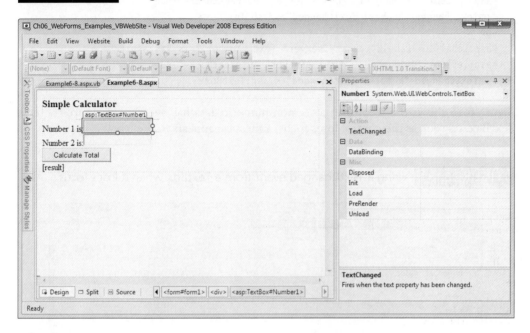

C# Code

(Note that we have to cast the 'sender' parameter down to TextBox from Object.)

```csharp
protected void Number1_TextChanged(object sender, EventArgs e)
{
  try
  {
    Int32.Parse(((TextBox)sender).Text);
    result.Text = "";
  }
  catch (Exception)
  {
    result.Text = "You must enter a number";
  }
}
```

In order for this event to be fired, the TextBox must have its 'AutoPostBack' property set to 'True'. Otherwise the TextChanged event cannot update the page.

This example applied an event handler to TextBox 'Number1' but we can reuse the same event handler for the 'Number2' TextBox as well. Simply select the second TextBox, then choose the 'Number1_TextChanged' event from the event list in the Properties window to also apply to this textbox (and also set its 'AutoPostBack' property to 'True). Then the same event handler will be applied to both controls. If we are using C# we can actually see this from Source view, though in Visual Basic this event attribute does not appear in the page source. (The full source can be found in 'Example6-9.aspx'.)

```
<asp:Label ID="Label1" runat="server" Text="Number 1 is:"></asp:Label>
<asp:TextBox ID="Number1" runat="server" AutoPostBack="True"
  ontextchanged="Number1_TextChanged"></asp:TextBox>
<br />
<asp:Label ID="Label2" runat="server" Text="Number 2 is:"></asp:Label>
<asp:TextBox ID="Number2" runat="server" AutoPostBack="True"
  ontextchanged="Number1_TextChanged"></asp:TextBox>
```

Figure 6.18 shows the web form after non-numeric data has been entered into the first TextBox. As soon as the control loses focus, a message appears in the label.

FIGURE 6.18   Firing a TextChanged event from a TextBox when it loses focus

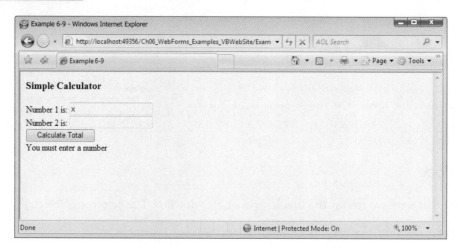

Section summary and quick exercises

In this section we introduced our first interaction with event handlers running on the server. We saw how double clicking on a control in design view automatically takes us to a section of code that will be triggered by that control, for example a button being pressed (the language of the event handlers will be determined by the language selected when creating the web form). In this code, we can interact with client-side controls to change the display of the current page. We also saw that multiple event handlers could be used on a form, and that the same event handler could be reused by multiple controls.

EXERCISE 6.6

Figure 6.19 shows a form from the home insurance domain, to gather data about contents insurance. Create a web form similar to this one (the controls here have been put into a table but no styles have been applied). The options in the drop-down list should be 10,000, 20,000, 30,000,

FIGURE 6.19   A web form from the home insurance domain

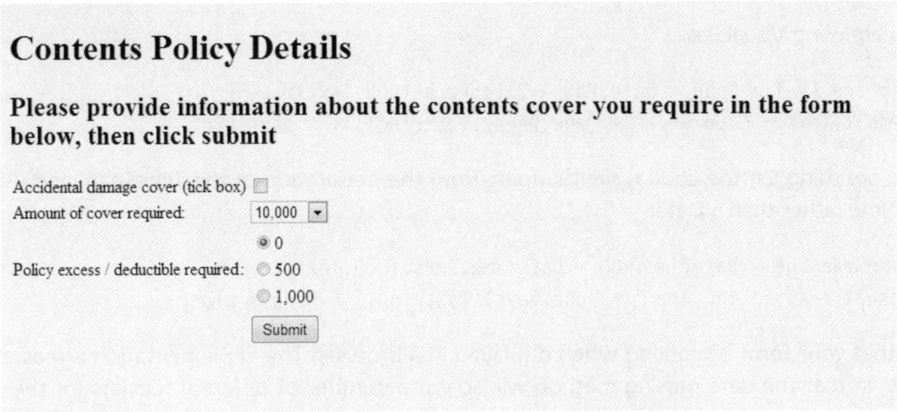

50,000 and 100,000. Add an event handler for the 'Submit' button that displays a message (using an empty label on the page) acknowledging receipt of the information.

EXERCISE 6.7

Here is the source of a web form that contains a TextBox into which you can type your date of birth, a 'Calculate Age' button, and a 'result' label:

```
<%@ Page Language="VB" AutoEventWireup="false" CodeFile="Exercise6.7.aspx.vb"
Inherits="Exercise6_7" %>
<!DOCTYPE html PUBLIC "-//W3C//DTD XHTML 1.0 Transitional//EN"
"http://www.w3.org/TR/xhtml1/DTD/xhtml1-transitional.dtd">
<html xmlns="http://www.w3.org/1999/xhtml">
  <head runat="server">
    <title>Exercise6.7</title>
  </head>
  <body>
    <!-- File: Exercise6.7.aspx -->
    <form id="form1" runat="server">
      <div>
        <asp:Label ID="Label1" runat="server" Text="Your date of birth">
        </asp:Label>
        <asp:TextBox ID="DoB" runat="server"></asp:TextBox>
        <br />
        <asp:Button ID="CalculateButton" runat="server"
          Text="Calculate Age" />
        <br />
        <asp:Label ID="result" runat="server"></asp:Label>
      </div>
    </form>
  </body>
</html>
```

6

Create the button click event handler for this form. Here is the code for the body of the 'Calculate-Button_Click' method:

If you are using Visual Basic:

```
Dim age As TimeSpan = Date.Now - Date.Parse(DoB.Text)
result.Text = "You are " + (age.Days).ToString() + " days old"
```

If you are using C# the code is similar, apart from the declaration of the TimeSpan, and using a DateTime rather than a Date:

```
TimeSpan age = DateTime.Now - DateTime.Parse(DoB.Text);
result.Text = "You are " + (age.Days).ToString() + " days old";
```

Test that your form is working when displayed in a browser. The implementation is reasonably robust in that the date parsing method will accept a number of different formats for the date, with several valid separator characters and the year accepted using either 2 or 4 digits (though the century that gets used will vary!). For example we could enter any of the following:

```
2001-12-21
31/1/1999
26.05.96
```

As the examples indicate, both American (year first) and European (year last) date formats are acceptable. However if you enter data that cannot be successfully parsed as a date then you will get a run time exception being thrown. Add the necessary exception handling code to prevent this happening.

EXERCISE 6.8

Figure 6.20 shows a simple web form in Design view that uses labels and text and password input fields to create a login page, similar to exercise 6.1. However in this case it also has a 'Login' button and a label ('message') with no text.

Create this web form and add an event handler for the 'Login' button. This event handler should check that the username could be a valid email address by checking for the presence of the '@' character and at least one period. The event handler should populate the 'message' label with a suitable response regarding the acceptability or otherwise of the username.

FIGURE 6.20 A web form displayed in Design view containing input fields for a username and password

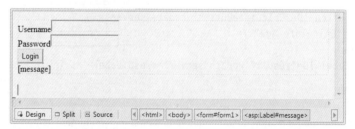

6.6 The Solution Explorer

So far, we have not considered what we mean by a website or project, except to note in Chapter 3 that these terms are synonymous when using Visual Web Developer. A large website typically consists of multiple files: web forms, source code (written in C#, VB, JavaScript, etc.), CSS files, XHTML pages and a number of other resources, such as image files. Visual Web Developer's Solution Explorer is provided to help you navigate around and manage these multiple files. In our examples so far we have already seen that there are an increasing number of files to be organized in a single website, so it will be useful to review some features of the Solution Explorer before we move onto the creation of larger and more complex examples.

You can view the Solution Explorer at any time using the 'View' → 'Solution Explorer' menu command. If you have a project open, the Solution Explorer will display its contents as a tree structure (Figure 6.21). If you don't have a project open, the Solution Explorer window will be empty. If you create, open or switch to a new project, the Solution Explorer window will update itself to show the contents of the new project.

Just as in the regular Windows File Explorer, you can use the mouse or keyboard to perform actions on a file or folder such as selecting it, opening, cutting, copying, deleting, or renaming it. You can drag files around with the mouse and drop them elsewhere. If you double click on a file displayed in Solution Explorer it will be opened for you to edit using the appropriate Visual Web Developer editor.

When adding an externally created file such as an image to your project, the easiest way is to drag it directly into the Solution Explorer window from the external File Explorer.

FIGURE 6.21   Browsing two websites using Solution Explorer. The one on the left has just been created. In the one on the right, a number of files of various types have been added

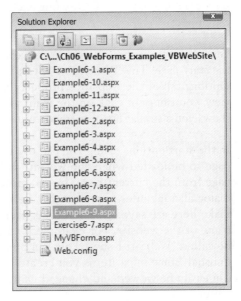

NOTE	If you rename a web form in the Solution Explorer, the associated code file will also be renamed accordingly. However the name of the 'inherits' class used in the page directive at the top of the web form and also in the code file will not change. It can be updated manually (in both files) if required. Do not update this name in only one of the files or you will get compiler errors. You should also note that hyphens in file names are converted to underscores in class names.

Alternatively, you can select 'WebSite' → 'Add Existing Item' (or right click on the website folder in Solution Explorer, and choose 'Add Existing Item'), then select the file from the file system. A further option is to copy the file directly into your project directory using the external file system. To tell Visual Web Developer to include it in the Solution Explorer window, just press the refresh button (the one with the two green arrows) at the top of the Solution Explorer window (or right click on the website folder and select 'Refresh Folder').

Solution Explorer also offers you additional features, depending on the type of file. If you look closely you will see that different types of file are displayed using different icons. If you right click on a file, or a folder, a menu of applicable commands is displayed. If you right click on an '.aspx' web form, for example, you will see a menu of commands you can apply to it. As well as the standard commands such as 'Open', 'Open With. . .', 'Cut', 'Copy', 'Delete', and 'Rename', you will notice others that are specific to web forms: 'View Code', 'View Design', 'View Mark-up', 'View in Browser', 'Browse With. . .', 'Set as Start Page', 'Build Page' and 'Exclude from Project'. The first five of these give you quick access to facilities we have already covered such as Design and Source views.

The final three commands allow you to set this web form as the start page (the one which users will see if they point their web browser at the directory containing your website), to build the page by compiling all its code, and to remove it from the project, which preserves the file in the directory but excludes it from activities such as building or copying the project.

You may wonder how Visual Web Developer records which web form has been set as the start page. The 'Website' → 'Start Options. . .' menu command shows you the Start Options tab of the website's property pages (Figure 6.22). Alternatively, to get to this view, you can right click on the main website folder in the Solution Explorer, which also shows you a similar list of menu commands, including 'Start Options. . . .'

In the start options dialog you can use the 'Start action' radio buttons to set the specific page to be loaded when the website is first started, if you want this to be a different page from the current page, for example. As you can see, the website's property pages dialog also includes pages for the 'References' and 'Build' options. The selections you make here are saved in a solutions user options ('.suo') file with a name based on the name of the website. For example if the website is called 'WebSite1' then the file will be called 'WebSite1.suo'. This is a binary file, which you cannot edit directly (this is unusual, since most items you create using Visual Web Developer are text files which can easily be viewed and changed using Visual Web Developer's editors, or an external editor).

When you right click on the top level website folder itself, or select the 'Website' option from Visual Web Developer's main menu bar, you are given additional commands which enable you to manage your website. These include 'Add ASP.NET Folder →', 'Add Reference. . .', 'Add Web Reference. . . .', 'Build WebSite', 'Copy WebSite. . .' and the 'Start Options. . .' command we just looked at.

Each website can contain any number of folders, listed in Table 6.1. Some of these have specific roles in ASP.NET.

These folders are not all created automatically, but only as you need them. For simple websites, therefore, most of these folders will not in fact be present.

FIGURE 6.22 Viewing your website's start options

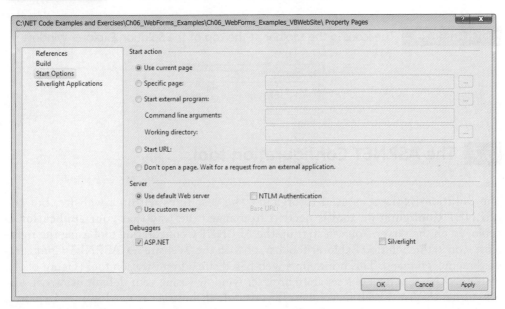

TABLE 6.1 Folders in the Solution Explorer window

Folder name	Contains
App_Code	Source code components such as business objects
App_Data	Database, XML and other data files stored locally
App_Browsers	Files used to customize ASP.NET controls for different browsers
App_LocalResources	Resource files that help with localization of international websites
App_GlobalResources	
App_WebReferences	References to external web components and services
App_Themes	Skin and theme files that affect how web pages appear
Bin	Pre-compiled code components

The 'Build WebSite' command will compile all changed source code files for you. As ASP.NET compiles each web page automatically when you view it, you do not actually need to build these files manually at all, but when we start adding code that is separate from the web forms, these will need to be built independently, so this is a useful feature.

The 'Copy WebSite. . .' command will be covered in Chapter 12, where we consider how to deploy a completed website to a production web server.

Finally, returning to the Solution Explorer, you will notice that along the top of its window are a number of icons, as illustrated in Figure 6.23. These icons allow you to (from left to right) switch to the 'Properties' window, refresh the Solution Explorer window, show related files (such as 'Default.aspx' and 'Default.aspx.cs') nested together, switch to Source view or Design view of a web form, copy a website or display and manage its configuration (as explained in the following section). That is to say, these icons mainly provide fast access to facilities that are also available through standard menu commands.

FIGURE 6.23   The icons in the toolbar at the top of the Solution Explorer window

6.7 The ASP.NET Configuration tool

The Solution Explorer is used to organize the resources within a website, but the ASP.NET Configuration tool is needed to manage the way that your application is deployed on the server. You can start up the ASP.NET Configuration tool using the rightmost icon in the Solution Explorer tool bar, or with the 'Website' → 'ASP.NET Configuration' menu command. This brings up a web-based site administration tool (Figure 6.24). Note that this tool runs in a separate browser window (using your default browser), and is external to Visual Web Developer. If your default browser is not Internet Explorer, the ASP.NET Configuration tool will most likely appear somewhat differently. It is also possible that certain actions may not function correctly in other browsers, in which case you will need to set Internet Explorer as your default browser before using the ASP.NET Configuration tool.

As you can see, this tool allows you to administer aspects of your website such as its security, application configuration and database provider. To access them, you can click on the tabs toward the top of the browser window, or follow the links on the left. The 'Security' tab allows you to set up users, roles and access rules. The 'Application' tab allows you to create and edit application settings, including those used for sending SMTP email, and to start, stop, trace or debug your application.

As an example of using the ASP.NET Configuration tool, click on Application tab, then follow the Configure Debugging and Tracing link, to reach the page shown in Figure 6.25. On this page, check the 'Enable debugging' check box to enable debugging (which we will look at next). As you do so, the tool automatically saves your selection in a website configuration file called 'web.config'. If this file does not already exist, it will be created. Refreshing

FIGURE 6.24 Visual Web Developer's web-based site administration tool

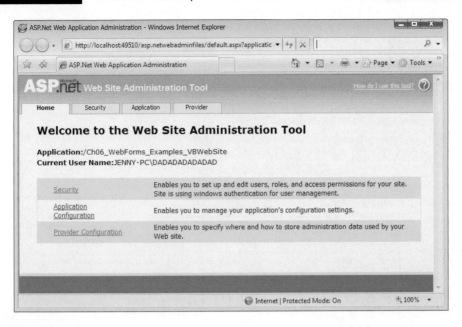

FIGURE 6.25 Using the ASP.NET configuration tool to configure debugging and tracing

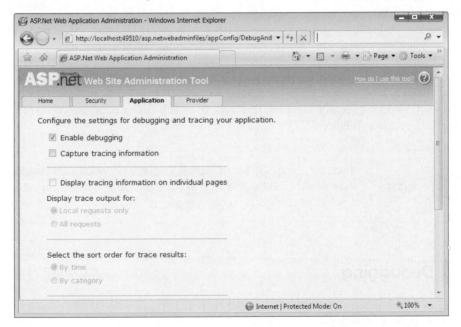

your Solution Explorer window should show you that a new 'web.config' file has appeared in your main website folder.

Most settings that you select via the ASP.NET Configuration tool are written to the web. config file. The web.config file is stored in XML format, and can be edited directly (which

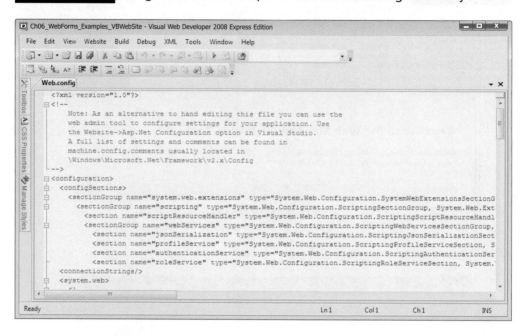

is sometimes useful) as shown in Figure 6.26. The quickest way to do this is to double click web.config in the Solution Explorer window.

The 'Provider' tab allows you to choose which database provider or providers your site will use when accessing site management data such as membership or user information. It is important to set up the database provider, because some controls, such as the SqlDataSource, will not work property unless you have done so. Select the 'Provider' tab and then click on 'Select a single provider for all site management data'. Next, select 'AspNetSqlProvider'. Finally, use the 'Test' link to check that a database connection can successfully be made (Figure 6.27).

NOTE   If you are using SQL Server Express Edition with Visual Web Developer then you should be able to make the database connection without any further configuration being required.

6.8 Debugging

Another feature of Visual Web Developer which you will find useful as your website grows is its support for debugging your code. Access to the debugging facilities is via the 'Debug' menu. This offers you the ability to start debugging, to step into or over method calls, and to set or clear breakpoints in your code. Moving the insertion point to the first line of an event handler, for example, and using the 'Debug' → 'Toggle Breakpoint' command, results in a breakpoint being added to the code, as illustrated in Figure 6.28 using the event handler code from 'Example6-9.aspx'. (You can also use the F9 shortcut key to toggle a breakpoint.) The bullet in the margin, and the colored text, indicate that a breakpoint has been set.

| FIGURE 6.27 | Configuring the data provider in the ASP.NET Website Administration tool |

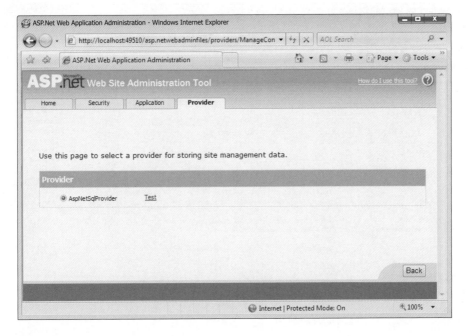

| FIGURE 6.28 | A breakpoint set for the debugger |

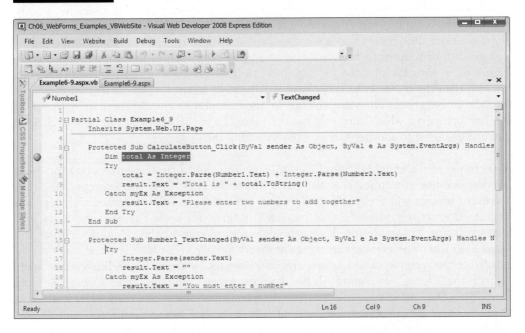

To debug your code, use the Debug → Start Debugging menu command, or press F5. The web page will appear as normal, but if a breakpoint has been set, when you trigger the event handler (for example by pressing a button on the form) the debugger window will pop-up again. That is because execution has halted at the breakpoint, which will now be displayed in yellow. If you look at the Visual Web Developer screen, you will see that

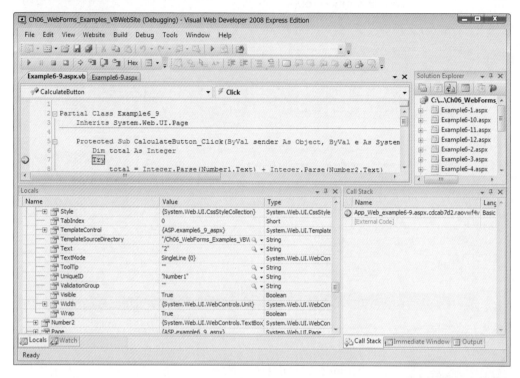

FIGURE 6.29 The 'Locals' window shows the values of local variables

some new windows have appeared. Beneath the code editor you should see the 'Locals' window, which displays the values of local variables. Note that where objects are shown in the 'Locals' window, their value is not displayed, only their type. To see useful information, you need to drill down to find variables of a value type such as Booleans or integers. In Figure 6.29, for example, the '+' sign next to 'this' (in C#) or 'Me' (in VB) has been clicked, then the one next to the 'Number1' TextBox control, enabling us to drill deeper into the current page. The values of the TextBox properties are displayed here, including its 'Text' property, which currently has the value '2'. If you like, you can double click on this and change it to another value on the fly within the debugger.

You can use the 'Debug' → 'Step Over' menu command to continue executing the event handler one line at a time. This also has a shortcut key, F10. If you keep pressing this, the event handler will eventually complete its execution, and the refreshed web page will appear. Alternatively, just select 'Debug' → 'Continue' (or press F5) to continue the current execution to completion. Using the debugger to inspect the value of variables will often help you to determine the causes of errors in your event handlers and other methods. Note that you can clear a breakpoint you have set by using 'Toggle Breakpoint' again, or with the 'Debug' → 'Delete All Breakpoints' menu command. The 'Debug' → 'Step Into'/'Step Out' commands will continue debugging into or out of a method by your event handler. There are other useful features of debugging such as the 'Call Stack' and 'Watch' windows. If you are familiar with developing software using an IDE you will no doubt have used similar facilities before. There is also a debugging toolbar, visible above the editor windows in Figures 6.28 and 6.29, which includes the main debugging actions.

The first time you debug a website, a dialog box may appear asking if you wish to enable debugging in your web.config file, if you have not already done so (Figure 6.30). If you see

6

242 CHAPTER 6 WEB FORMS

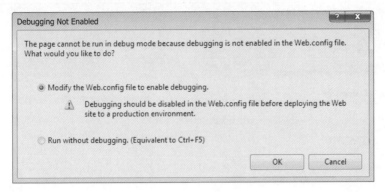

this dialog box, simply click 'Yes'. From then on, when you view your work in the browser, Visual Web Developer will start its built-in web server with debugging enabled.

 NOTE   As well as debugging code in your event handlers, the debugger will also be able to debug your JavaScript, if script debugging has been enabled in the browser.

6.8.1 Other ways to debug your code

There are, of course, other ways to debug your code. The classic solution to programming problems is to add extra lines to your code to display information about the flow of control and the state of its variables. With web development, however, this is not so easy. The web page is sent as an XHTML page to the browser, and console output produced with, for example, the Console.Write method will not appear. To insert some extra text into the web page being sent to the user you should use the Response.Write method instead. For example, if you add a line such as:

```
Response.Write("TextChanged event called in Example6-10")
```

to an event handler, you should see output similar to that in Figure 6.31 in your browser.

As you can see, however, this is not particularly well formatted or structured. ASP.NET therefore provides a more professional alternative, via its tracing facilities. To use these, edit the page directive at the top of the web form to include the Trace="true" attribute. The effect of this is to add ASP.NET tracing information to the bottom of each page that is output, as shown in Figure 6.32.

The tracing information is presented in a more professional fashion. It is, however, all generated automatically by ASP.NET and does not contain much information that is specific to our application. Fortunately, however, it is possible to augment the ASP.NET trace with additional information of our own using the Trace.Write() method. For example, adding this line to our event handler:

```
Trace.Write("Number1_TextChanged", "Event handler fired")
```

FIGURE 6.31 Simple tracing output using Response.Write()

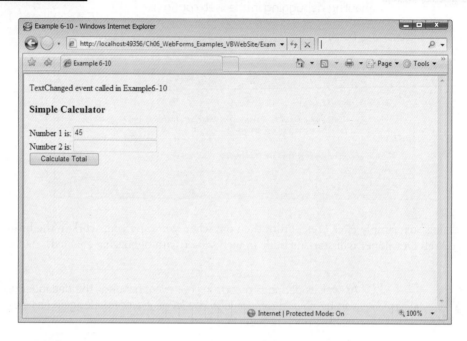

FIGURE 6.32 ASP.NET tracing output

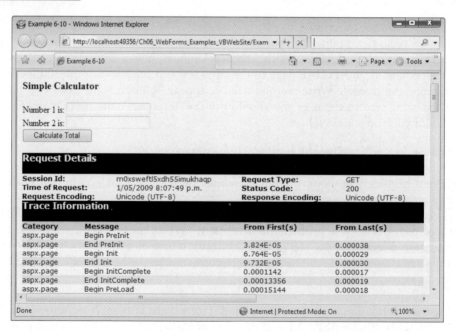

gives the trace output shown in Figure 6.33 (you will need to scroll down through the trace output to find this additional line). The first parameter to the method appears in the 'Category' column of the trace information, and the second appears in the 'message' column (all the tracing examples appear in 'Example6-10.aspx').

FIGURE 6.33 ASP.NET tracing output

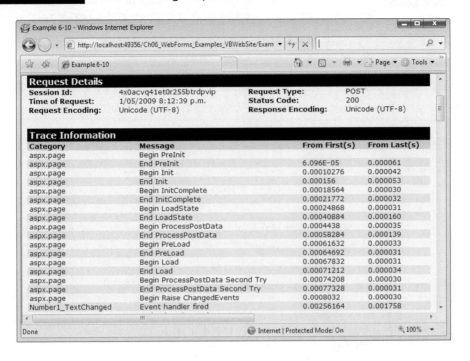

Finally, note that in many cases there may be no need for debugging or tracing. In fact, as you can see from the screen shot in Figure 6.34, ASP.NET provides as much information as it can about programming errors such as exceptions. Here the user has typed in some invalid characters into a TextBox. This has caused an exception to be raised, which ASP.NET has attempted to explain. Often, this kind of exception message gives you enough information to resolve the problem without requiring the use of the debugger.

In this case, you should add exception handling code to the event handler to allow for erroneous input, as of course we have done previously. Alternatively, as we will cover in the next chapter, you could use ASP.NET input validation facilities to prevent the problem occurring in the first place.

6.9 How web forms are built and run

At this stage, before we start creating many more ASP.NET web forms, it is probably a good time to consider in a little more depth the process whereby these forms are built and run. In particular, we will cover the ASP.NET page life cycle, which will help you when developing event handlers. Consider for example a simple web form (Example6-11.aspx) with a level 1 heading, a TextBox and a Button, as shown in Split view in Figure 6.35.

The ASP.NET mark-up for this form here has four elements whose XHTML tags have been marked runat="server", including the head and form tag. In addition, the two ASP.NET web controls (which are identified by their <asp:xxx> tags) are also tagged runat="server". Finally, note that there are a number of standard XHTML elements with tags such as <title> <div> and <br />.

FIGURE 6.34 Error information displayed when an exception occurs (for example, an invalid string of characters being entered into a TextBox)

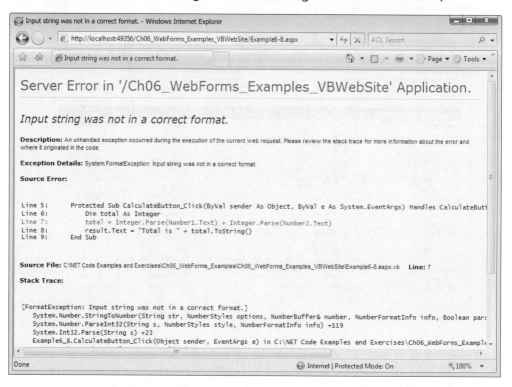

Before this web form can be run, it is turned into executable code by a compilation process. The ASP.NET mark-up in our example will be translated into executable code belonging to a class called ASP.example6_11_aspx, a name which as you can see is derived from the name of the web form. If there are any event handlers associated with the form, they will also belong to this same class when the event handler code is compiled. Thanks to a .NET feature called *partial classes*, the code derived from the form and the event handlers end up in separate source code files. The next stage of compilation is the traditional process of translating all source code files into executable code. As well as the code derived from the web form, additional source code files belonging to the project, which are typically stored in its App_Code directory, are also compiled. In the case of .NET, compilation involves translating the source code twice. It is first compiled into code for a virtual machine, in this case Microsoft Intermediate Language (MSIL), and then that code is translated again into machine code specific to the actual processor or CPU which is being used to run the web form.

The web form is therefore translated into executable .NET code. This is somewhat surprising, as you might have expected it to be translated into standard XHTML mark-up. After all, what is sent to the browser is XHTML, so you are probably wondering where this comes from. This is explained below, and is an important part of how ASP.NET provides a rich and flexible environment for web development.

As explained above, the web form is (first) translated into a VB or C# class. To understand a class, you need to know what variables and methods it possesses. In this case, the

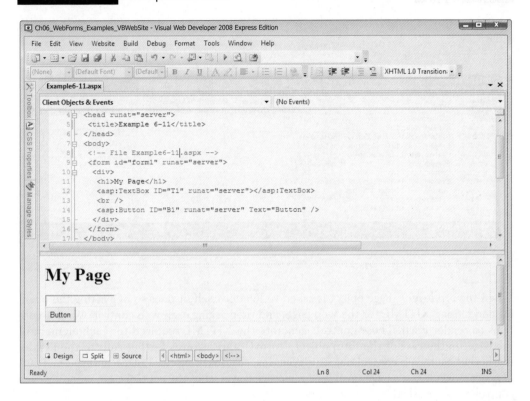

FIGURE 6.35   Example web form

most important method of the generated class is called 'Render'. This method is called by the ASP.NET run-time environment to create the XHTML mark-up which is sent back in response to an HTTP request to the browser (or other HTTP agent). The Render method is implemented by each ASP.NET web form and control, and creates the XHTML required to display the form or control as expected, which depends on its current state (the values of its member variables). This method is part of the System.Web.UI.Control class which each web form or control is based on. Typically, each web form or control will define its own implementation of Render, as each form or control has a different appearance.

Our example web form will be translated into a number of web control objects. The web form itself becomes an object of type ASP.example6_11_aspx as noted previously. This object has a member variable for each web control on the page, for example the TextBox. In addition, the other elements it contains, for example the ASP.NET form and the fragments of literal XHTML, are all converted to web control objects.

We can understand this better if we switch on tracing in our web form, for example by adding the attribute Trace="true" to the top-level page tag in our ASP.NET form. As we have seen, with tracing turned on, extra output is generated at the bottom of the form when it is viewed with a browser. This extra output contains, among other information, the form's control tree (Figure 6.36).

We can see here that the web form object contains a number of objects such as literals, as well as the XHTML 'head' and 'form' objects. In turn, the XHTML form object contains other web control objects such as the text box and button, but also more XHTML literals.

FIGURE 6.36   The web form's control tree

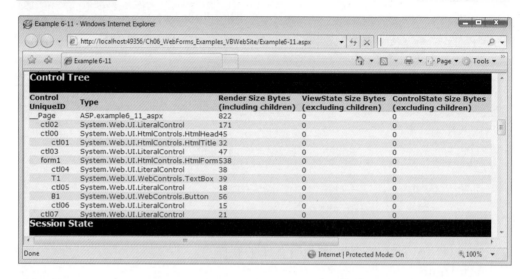

When the top level __Page object is asked to Render itself, it does so by writing the opening and closing XHTML for the web page, and then asking each web control object it contains to render itself. These controls generate the XHTML required for each element of the page. In the case of the form object, 'form1', this involves further calls to the Render method of each web control object it contains, the TextBox, the Button and so on. Thus, in general, rendering a page involves a recursive traversal of the control tree, whereby each control object is asked in turn to render itself.

In summary, an ASP.NET web form is translated first into executable objects and code, then the XHTML mark-up is generated by calling a method on each object (of course, the mark-up is then turned into a visual display on the client by the web browser, but that's another story). We can see the translation process illustrated in Table 6.2.

In this case, the XHTML produced is fairly similar to the original ASP.NET mark-up, as you can see if you view the web source using your browser, but this is not always the case. A dynamic web control such as a Calendar typically generates XHTML which is different, and more extensive, than the original ASP.NET mark-up. In addition, such objects also typically generate some client-side script code using JavaScript.

6.9.1 PostBacks and event handlers

The mark-up shown in Table 6.2 is somewhat simplified. If you look at the full <form ... > tag in the XHTML output, for example, you will see that it says something like:

```
<form name="F1" method="post" action="Example6-11.aspx" id="F1">
```

The 'action' attribute here gives the URL of the web page which receives the post request when the form is submitted. You will note that this is the same URL as that of the original web form. That is to say, when this ASP.NET web form is submitted, the post request will go back to the same web form. This is a distinctive feature of the ASP.NET web framework.

TABLE 6.2	A simplified example showing the full translation process whereby ASP.NET web forms are translated into .NET objects then rendered into XHTML for the browser. Note that the closing </form> tag is generated by F1's Render method, and the final two tags by Example6_11__aspx.

ASP.NET Web Form	.NET Objects	XHTML Output
`<%@ Page...%>`	Example6_11_aspx *(a Web. UI.Page) which has member variables*	
`<html...><body...>`		`<html...><body>`
`<form id="F1" runat="server">`	F1 *an HTMLform with members*	`<form id="F1" method=...>`
`<h1>My Page</h1>`	*literal control* `<h1>...</h1>`	`<h1>My Page</h1>`
`<asp:TextBox ID="T1" runat="server" />`	T1 *(a WebControls.TextBox)*	`<input id="T1" type="text" />`
` `	*literal control* ` `	` `
`<asp:Button ID="B1" Text="Submit" runat="server" />`	B1 *(a WebControls.Button) which has a member variable* `Text="Submit"`	`<input type="submit" id="B1" value="Submit" />`
`</form></body></html>`		`</form></body></html>`
This is translated into executable code when the page is first viewed	*A literal object is generated for each fragment of raw XHTML, as well as one for each ASP. NET web control*	*Produced by calling the Render method for each web control object in the page's control tree in turn*

Websites written using PHP or Java are less likely to feature web pages which post back to themselves.

To keep track of previous interactions, ASP.NET web forms use hidden fields such as the VIEWSTATE. As this is a hidden field, you cannot see it in the web page, but if you use your browser to view the generated XHTML output there should be a line such as:

```
<input type="hidden" name="__VIEWSTATE" value="wEPD..." />
```

This field records (encoded in a binary format which we cannot easily interpret) the value of the textbox as sent to the user. If this value has changed when the form is submitted back to the web server, the ASP.NET run-time environment will therefore detect this. When such a change occurs, ASP.NET invokes the TextChanged event handler. This allows the page to respond to the request, for example by inserting the data into a database, or by altering the appearance of the page, or both. For example, if web page includes a label called L1, we could code the following response via the event handler:

VB Code

```
Protected Sub T1_TextChanged(ByVal sender As Object, ByVal e As System.EventArgs)
Handles T1.TextChanged
  If Not (T1.Text = "") Then
    L1.Text = "Hello " + T1.Text
  End If
End Sub
```

C# Code

```
protected void T1_TextChanged(object sender, EventArgs e)
{
  if(T1.Text.Length > 0)
  {
    L1.Text = "Hello " + T1.Text;
  }
}
```

This would display a greeting in the L1 Label using the text that had been entered by the user into textbox T1.

As we have seen, there are a number of events which ASP.NET raises, each of which has an associated event handler you can program in order to add dynamic behavior to your web pages. The most common event handler is the one associated with the Page_Load event. The Page_Load event is raised, and the handler invoked, each time the page is loaded. This event handler usually tests the IsPostBack variable to check the state of the interaction with the user. If IsPostBack is false, that means this user is visiting the page for the first time, so this is a sensible opportunity to execute any page specific initialization code. If IsPostBack is true, the user has just viewed and interacted with the page, and re-submitted it, or posted it back, to the web server. For example, suppose we want label L1 to display a message when the page is first displayed, but have this message removed on subsequent visits. We could code our Page_Load event handler as follows:

VB Code

```
Protected Sub Page_Load(ByVal sender As Object, ByVal e As System.EventArgs)
Handles Me.Load
  If (IsPostBack = False) Then
    REM first visit to the page
    L1.Text = "Please enter your name"
  Else
    REM page is being re-displayed
    L1.Text = ""
  End If
End Sub
```

C# Code

```
protected void Page_Load(object sender, EventArgs e)
{
 if(!IsPostBack)
 {
  // first visit to the page
  L1.Text = "Please enter your name";
 }
 else
 {
  // page is being re-displayed
  L1.Text = "";
 }
}
```

The user would be prompted to enter their name when the page was first displayed, but not thereafter.

Note that the Page_Load event is raised before TextChanged. Thus, even though the Page_ Load handler has set the Text in L1 to be an empty string, if the text in the TextBox has changed the TextChanged event handler will still be able to ensure that the label L1 contains the new text before the page is rendered and displayed. That is to say, these events handlers are invoked in the order Page_Load, TextChanged then Render. You can confirm the order in which ASP.NET events occur by examining the page trace again (Figure 6.37).

FIGURE 6.37   Trace of events raised by ASP.NET

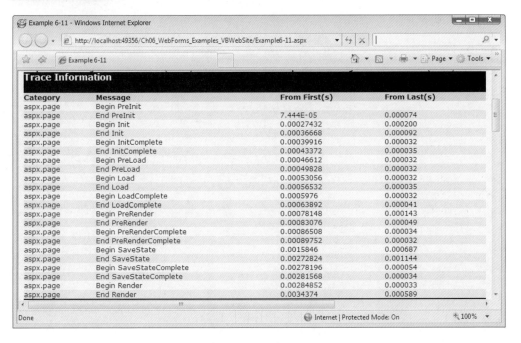

Category	Message	From First(s)	From Last(s)
aspx.page	Begin PreInit		
aspx.page	End PreInit	7.444E-05	0.000074
aspx.page	Begin Init	0.00027432	0.000200
aspx.page	End Init	0.00036668	0.000092
aspx.page	Begin InitComplete	0.00039916	0.000032
aspx.page	End InitComplete	0.00043372	0.000035
aspx.page	Begin PreLoad	0.00046612	0.000032
aspx.page	End PreLoad	0.00049828	0.000032
aspx.page	Begin Load	0.00053056	0.000032
aspx.page	End Load	0.00056532	0.000035
aspx.page	Begin LoadComplete	0.0005976	0.000032
aspx.page	End LoadComplete	0.00063892	0.000041
aspx.page	Begin PreRender	0.00078148	0.000143
aspx.page	End PreRender	0.00083076	0.000049
aspx.page	Begin PreRenderComplete	0.00086508	0.000034
aspx.page	End PreRenderComplete	0.00089752	0.000032
aspx.page	Begin SaveState	0.0015846	0.000687
aspx.page	End SaveState	0.00272824	0.001144
aspx.page	Begin SaveStateComplete	0.00278196	0.000054
aspx.page	End SaveStateComplete	0.00281568	0.000034
aspx.page	Begin Render	0.00284852	0.000033
aspx.page	End Render	0.0034374	0.000589

As you can see, there are several events here, more than discussed above. For example, loading the page is actually marked by three events, PreLoad, Load and LoadComplete, and similarly for rendering. The numbers following the names of the events are timings, given in seconds. The first number gives the time which has elapsed since the page request was received. The second number gives the time taken to execute the event handler, which is typically rather small, demonstrating how efficient ASP.NET is.

Note that there is no TextChanged event in the trace in Figure 6.36. That is because the user did not, on this occasion, change the string in the text box before submitting the web form back to the server.

To find more about how ASP.NET web pages are built and run, and the events that are raised when they run, you can read the description in books such as Esposito (2008). Alternatively, you can find descriptions of the so-called 'ASP.NET Page Life Cycle' by searching for this phrase using a search engine. At the time of writing, for example, the first result this search returns is a link to a page on MSDN (the Microsoft Developer Network) with a more detailed description of the events discussed above, as well as several additional events not covered here. Understanding these events, and the order they are raised, is sometimes required to achieve certain advanced effects in ASP.NET web development.

6

Self Study Questions

1. Which two languages are available to choose from when creating a new web form in Visual Web Developer?
2. Which property of a control can be used to set the class of that control so that styles may be applied?
3. What types of text input element can be created by setting the 'TextMode' property of a TextBox control?
4. How can we get multiple radio buttons to behave as a group, so that only one can be checked at any one time?
5. In an event handler, which property of a TextBox control can be used to set its current text value?
6. How can you add an existing file to an existing project?
7. Where are the start options for a website stored?
8. Where are your ASP.NET website configuration options stored?
9. Which menu command can be used for setting and clearing a breakpoint? What is the alternative shortcut key to do the same thing?
10. What is the name of the window which the debugger uses to display the values of variables?

Exercises

6.9 Locate an external image file and add it to your website, then use it in a web form.

6.10 Insert a syntactic error (such as a missing quote or bracket) into one of the event handlers from the previous chapter. Build the website and see how the compiler reports the error.

6.11 Insert a logical error (such as dividing by 0) into an event handler (or even better, ask a friend to do this for you). Use the debugger to step to the erroneous line of code.

6

SUMMARY

In this chapter we focused on web forms and the standard controls that can be used on them. We looked at how a web form is not a static client page but a dynamic server page; web form control mark-up is processed on the server to generate XHTML pages. In addition, we can add event handlers to these controls so that they trigger server-side processes that can be used to generate dynamic content for the client. Table 6.3 provides a summary of the web form controls that were introduced in this chapter, along with the related XHTML elements that are generated from them and what they are used for.

Web Form Controls	XHTML Element	Used for
TextBox (SingleLine),	`input type="text"`	Text input field
TextBox (MultiLine)	`textarea`	Multi line text entry box
TextBox (Password)	`input type="password"`	Password input field
CheckBox	`input type="checkbox"`	Check box
RadioButtonList	`input type="Radio"` (within a table element)	List of related radio buttons
ListBox	`select size="n"`	Select list
DropDownList	`select size="1"`	Drop-down list
Panel	A `fieldset` with a `legend`	A way of grouping controls together in a frame with a label

References and further reading

Esposito, D. 2008. *Programming ASP.NET 3.5*, Microsoft Press.

Homer, A. 2004. *Pro ASP.NET Web Forms Techniques* (Second Edition), Apress.

Reilly, D. 2006. *Programming Microsoft® Web Forms*, Microsoft Press.

Sussman, D. and Homer, A. 2006. *Wrox's ASP.NET 2.0 Visual Web Developer 2005 Express Edition Starter Kit*.

CHAPTER 7

Controls and Master Pages

LEARNING OBJECTIVES

- **To be able to use standard controls from the Toolbox**

- **To be able to use validation controls**

- **To be able to implement design patterns for page layout**

- **To be able to apply master pages to web forms**

- **To be able to create customized page components using Web User Controls**

INTRODUCTION

In this chapter we begin by further exploring the Toolbox of ASP.NET server controls, which we first introduced in Chapter 3, when we looked at some of the controls in the HTML group in the context of creating XHTML pages. In the previous chapter (Chapter 6) we went on to introduce some of the controls in the Standard group, which we used in conjunction with web forms. In this chapter we provide a brief introduction to some further controls from the Standard group, before looking at the controls available in the Validation group. In the final part of the chapter we turn our attention to one of the design patterns we introduced in Chapter 2, the three-region layout, and see how it can be implemented in Visual Web Developer by using master pages. This pattern also incorporates the site logo at top left and navigation bar patterns. As we add more and more pages to a website it is important to support site navigation in a consistent and easy to use way. Providing a common page structure that incorporates navigation bars can help to achieve this. In the context of navigation bars, we also introduce Web User Controls, which provide another way of efficiently managing website resources by allowing developer created content to be reused in multiple pages.

7.1 ASP.NET server controls

In the Toolbox, the ASP.NET server controls are organized into groups. The most commonly used ones occur in the Standard group, which we continue to explore in this chapter, as well as controls from the Validation group. This book's coverage of the various control groups is shown in Table 7.1.

TABLE 7.1	Control groups and the chapters in which they are covered in this book

Control Group	Type of Control	Chapter(s)
HTML	Some standard HTML elements are found here	3
Standard	The most commonly used controls	6, 7 and 8
Validation	Controls used to check data the user has entered	7
Navigation	Menu and breadcrumb controls based on a site map file	8
Data	Access to data stored in an XML file or relational database	10
Login	Controls to allow login and user management	12
AJAX	Interactive controls using JavaScript on the client	13
Web Parts	A set of controls used to create a web portal or intranet site	14 (on-line)
General	Initially blank, may be used for controls you add yourself	Not covered

In addition to the so called 'server' controls, there are also Web User Controls, which are ones you can create yourself, introduced briefly towards the end of this chapter.

7.1.1 Standard controls

In the previous chapter we introduced some of the controls available from the Standard group in the Toolbox. In this chapter we will introduce a number of other controls, and write some simple event handlers to demonstrate their properties and events. Some of the most commonly used controls, properties and events are shown in Table 7.2.

You will already be familiar with some of the controls in Table 7.2 from the examples given in the previous chapter. Mostly these controls represent a single XHTML element as an ASP.NET server control (with the runat="server" property). By now, you should be comfortable with the way ASP.NET controls work, and how you can customize their appearance and behavior using their properties and events. These controls all inherit from the same base class, System.Web.UI.WebControls. This means they share a large number of common properties. As well as the properties controlling their appearance and style such as BackColor, BorderWidth, CssClass (introduced in Chapter 4, for linking to external stylesheets), ForeColor, Height and Width, there are inherited properties which affect behavior in a standard way across all controls, listed in Table 7.3.

When you use more advanced controls, you will note that there are certain commands that frequently appear on their tasks menu. These are summarized in Table 7.4 (later in this chapter you will see an example of an Auto Format being used).

The rest of this section covers some controls which are somewhat more specialized than those listed in Table 7.2, but nonetheless may be useful to you in certain situations. Each of them provides complex behavior, which means they can save you quite a bit of coding.

TABLE 7.2　Commonly used controls, properties and events in the Standard group of the Toolbox

Control	Commonly Used Properties ...	... and Events
Button	CommandName, CommandArgument: *provided to the Command event handler* Text: *string to display inside the button*	OnClick Command
Hyperlink	NavigateURL: *the URL of the target page* Text: *string used as the anchor text*	
Image	ImageURL: *the URL of the image or picture file*	
Label	Text: *string to display*	
LinkButton	CommandName, CommandArgument: *provided to the Command event handler* Text: *string to display as the link/button text*	OnClick Command
TextBox	Text: *string used to initialize the display* TextMode: *SingleLine, MultiLine or Password*	TextChanged

TABLE 7.3　Standard properties for ASP.NET controls

Property	Use / Effect
Enabled	*If this property is set to false, the control appears grayed out, and does not allow interaction with the user*
ID	*The control's XHTML ID is also the name used by event handlers to access its properties and methods*
runat	*All ASP.NET server controls automatically have the runat="server" attribute. This indicates that they are compiled to an ASP.NET object as described in the section in Chapter 6 on the ASP.NET page lifecycle. It should be noted, however, that some controls render JavaScript as well as XHTML. This means that some of their behavior is also controlled on the client-side.*
ToolTip	*Can be used to provide a short description which pops up when the user hovers their mouse over the control*
Visible	*Determines whether the control is appears at all. If set to false, the control does not render any XHTML to be sent to the browser*

7

7.1.2　BulletedList

This control displays a bulleted list of items. This provides an alternative to creating bulleted lists using the HTML 'ul' and 'li' elements, either manually or from the formatting toolbar. You can set the BulletStyle property to values such as Numbered, Circle, Square, or CustomImage to control the appearance of the bullets, much as you can with the standard HTML element. Of course as a control, the BulletedList provides much more functionality

TABLE 7.4   Task menu commands for some advanced controls

Task Menu Commands	Application
Auto Format …	Allows you to select the layout and appearance from a menu of pre-defined professionally designed layouts
convert to template	Some controls combine a number of other controls in a specific organization. Converting a compound control to a template allows you to change the way the child controls are organized
edit template	Allows you to edit the contents of a control template to change its contents or their appearance and layout

than a simple HTML list. Figure 7.1 shows a BulletedList control being created. The items in the list can be entered directly, if they are known in advance, or can be read dynamically from an XML file or relational database (in the next chapter we will cover XML Data Sources, and database access will be covered in Chapter 10). The control has a Tasks menu with two commands; 'Choose Data Source' allows you to select an XML file or relational database where the items are stored, and 'Edit Items' brings up the 'ListItem Collection Editor' dialog which allows you to enter the values directly. Since we have not yet shown you how to set up a data source, the list items in Figure 7.1 have been entered directly into the ListItem Collection Editor. Each item has two flags which determine whether it is enabled or selected, and two strings, the first of which is the text displayed to the user, and the second the value passed to an event handler or a link to another web page.

FIGURE 7.1   A BulletedList control in Design view, with the ListItem Collection Editor

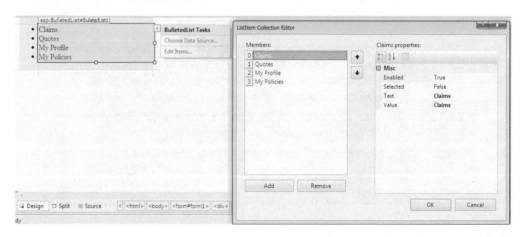

Figure 7.2 shows the BulletedList as it appears when viewed in the browser. (The source of this web form can be found in Example7-1.aspx.)

The BulletedList also has a property called 'DisplayMode'. This can have one of three values; 'Text' (as shown in Figure 7.2), 'Hyperlink' (in which case each item's value should be the URL of a target page to link to), or 'LinkButton'. If the 'LinkButton' DisplayMode

FIGURE 7.2	A BulletedList being viewed in a web browser

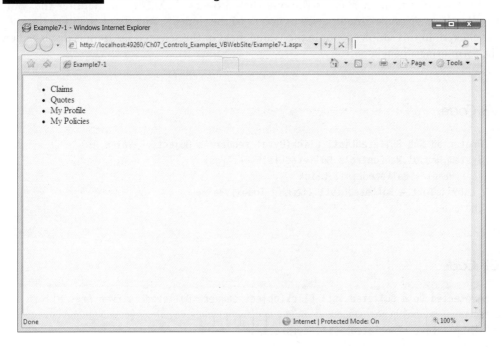

is used, you will need to code an event handler for the click event triggered by clicking on one of the list items. Here is the source for a web form containing a BulletedList configured to use LinkButtons (note the value of the 'DisplayMode' property).

```
<%@ Page Language="VB" AutoEventWireup="false"
CodeFile="Example7-2.aspx.vb" Inherits="_Default" %>
<!DOCTYPE html PUBLIC "-//W3C//DTD XHTML 1.0 Transitional//EN"
"http://www.w3.org/TR/xhtml1/DTD/xhtml1-transitional.dtd">
<html xmlns="http://www.w3.org/1999/xhtml">
  <head runat="server">
   <title>Example7-2</title>
  </head>
  <body>
    <form id="form1" runat="server">
     <div°
      <asp:BulletedList ID="BulletedList1" runat="server"
        DisplayMode="LinkButton">
      <asp:ListItem>Claims</asp:ListItem>
      <asp:ListItem>Quotes</asp:ListItem>
      <asp:ListItem>My Profile</asp:ListItem>
      <asp:ListItem>My Policies</asp:ListItem>
      </asp:BulletedList>
      <asp:Label ID="Label1" runat="server" Text="Label"></asp:Label>
     </div>
    </form>
  </body>
</html>
```

7

To respond to click events triggered by selecting an item in the list, we need to provide a suitable event handler such as the one shown below. In this event handler the 'BulletedListEventArgs' parameter gives us access to the 'Index' property of the item the user has clicked. In this simple example the 'Value' field of the selected list item is displayed on the form using a Label control:

VB Code

```
Protected Sub BulletedList1_Click(ByVal sender As Object, ByVal e As
System.Web.UI.WebControls.BulletedListEventArgs)
    Handles BulletedList1.Click
  Label1.Text = BulletedList1.Items(e.Index).Value
End Sub
```

C# Code

```
protected void BulletedList1_Click(object sender, BulletedListEventArgs e)
{
  Label1.Text = BulletedList1.Items[e.Index].Value;
}
```

Figure 7.3 shows the web form running in a browser after the third item in the list has been selected. The text from the list item now also appears in the Label.

FIGURE 7.3   A BulletedList configured with LinkButtons being viewed in a web browser

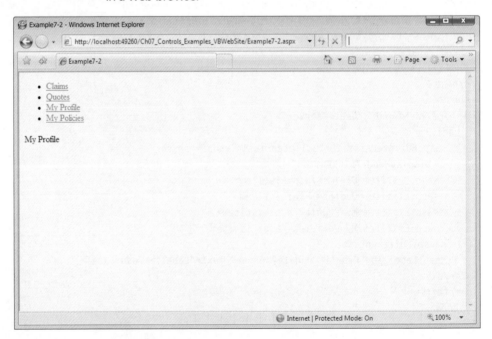

7.1.3 Calendar

The Calendar control allows the user to select a date using their mouse, rather than having to type a date into a textbox. An automatically generated format can be selected from the list provided via the control's smart tasks menu. Figure 7.4 shows a Calendar control in Design view, with the 'Simple' Auto Format chosen, while Figure 7.5 shows the same control viewed via the browser. In this example, the date the user selects by clicking is displayed via the Label control added beneath the Calendar. Here is the source of the web form prior to selecting an Auto Format, with the Calendar and Label controls:

```
<!DOCTYPE html PUBLIC "-//W3C//DTD XHTML 1.0 Transitional//EN"
"http://www.w3.org/TR/xhtml1/DTD/xhtml1-transitional.dtd">
<html xmlns="http://www.w3.org/1999/xhtml">
  <head runat="server">
   <title>Example7-3</title>
  </head>
  <body>
    <form id="form1" runat="server">
      <div>
        <asp:Calendar ID="Calendar1" runat="server"></asp:Calendar>
        <asp:Label ID="Label1" runat="server" Text="Label"></asp:Label>
      </div>
    </form>
  </body>
</html>
```

You may find it informative to apply an Auto Format to the Calendar control in this web form and see what changes are made to its properties in Source view.

The code which responds to the user's selection and populates the Label is in the Calendar's 'SelectionChanged' event handler. To create this handler, double click on the Calendar control in Design view and the stub of a 'SelectionChanged' event handler will be created for you. The following implementation uses the 'SelectedDate' property of the Calendar control, and populates the Label text using this date:

C# Code

```
protected void Calendar1_SelectionChanged(object sender, EventArgs e)
{
  Label1.Text = Calendar1.SelectedDate.ToString();
}
```

VB Code

```
Protected Sub Calendar1_SelectionChanged(ByVal sender As Object,
ByVal e As System.EventArgs)
  Handles Calendar1.SelectionChanged
 Label1.Text = Calendar1.SelectedDate.ToString()
End Sub
```

FIGURE 7.4   A Calendar control in Design view

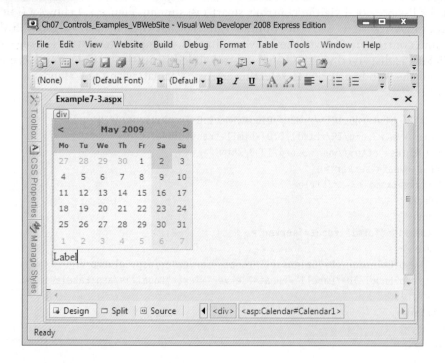

FIGURE 7.5   The Calendar control from Figure 7.4 viewed in a browser, with the selected date displayed in the Label control below the Calendar

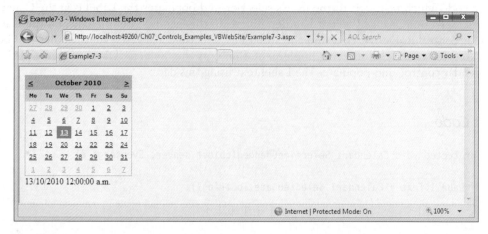

The FileUpload control provides a relatively easy way to upload files to the web server. Figure 7.6 shows one of these controls added to a web form in Design view, with a Button control also added so that we can trigger the upload after browsing for the file, and a Label so that we can display a message to the user to indicate the success or failure of the upload (the source of the web form can be found in Example7-4.apsx).

The 'Browse' button that is part of the FileUpload control enables the user to select a file from the file system. We will also need an event handler that will actually upload the selected file. The first thing we need to specify is where the uploaded file will be placed in the web application. For this example we will assume that we have created a subfolder in our website folder called 'Uploads'. In the event handler, this folder is used as the path that specifies where to store the uploaded file. We then use the 'PostedFile' property of the FileUpload control to save the file using the specified path. If this process does not throw an exception then we display a success message.

Here is the event handler:

VB Code

```
Protected Sub Button1_Click(ByVal sender As Object, ByVal e As
System.EventArgs) Handles Button1.Click
  If FileUpload1.HasFile() Then
    Dim path As String = Server.MapPath("~/Uploads/")
    Try
      FileUpload1.PostedFile.SaveAs(path + FileUpload1.FileName)
      Label1.Text = "Upload successful"
    Catch
      Label1.Text = "Upload failed"
    End Try
  End If
End Sub
```

FIGURE 7.6   A FileUpload control in Design view

After you view the web form in a browser, and upload a file, you will need to refresh the Solution Explorer view in order to see that the file has been added to the 'Uploads' folder (assuming the upload has been successful). Figure 7.7 shows the web form viewed in a browser.

FIGURE 7.7   A FileUpload control viewed via the browser

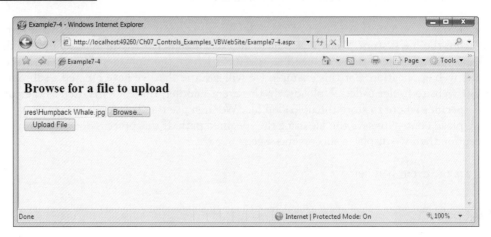

In our home insurance domain, a FileUpload control might be used by employees, for example, to upload images to be used for advertisements, or it could be used by customers to provide digital photographs giving evidence in support of their insurance claims. However, whenever a website provides a file upload facility, the security implications must be considered seriously. Obviously, the web server must have write access to the directory where the files are to be stored. Should new files be allowed to overwrite existing ones? Are there privacy or copyright issues? Will malicious users be able to learn how your site is structured internally, and exploit this in some way? These are all issues you should consider before adding file upload functionality to your web applications.

7.1.5   ImageMap

The ImageMap control provides a way to add an image to a web form, and to determine what happens when the user clicks on the image (or part of it). The image associated with the control is determined by setting the 'ImageUrl' property. In addition, an ImageMap has a 'HotSpot' property, which is a collection of HotSpots, defined using the 'HotSpot Collection Editor'. Each HotSpot can be circular, rectangular, or some other polygon in shape. Each hotspot has properties which define which part of the image it relates to.

To provide a simple example of how an ImageMap works, we will use the image shown inside an ImageMap in Design view in Figure 7.8.

The image used in this example is 220 pixels wide and 100 pixels high and comprises two areas (meant to represent buildings policies on the left or contents policies on the right.) It can be easily divided into two rectangular HotSpots, both 100 pixels high and 110 pixels wide. To apply these HotSpots, we need to press the small button next to the 'HotSpot (Collection)' property of the ImageMap. This will open the HotSpot Collection

FIGURE 7.8 An ImageMap control in Design view, with its image set by the 'ImageURL' property

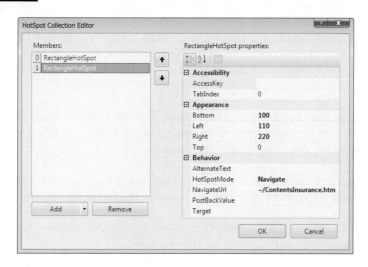

```
asp:ImageMap#ImageMap1
```

Design | Split | Source   ◄ | <div> | <asp:ImageMap#ImageMap1> | ►

FIGURE 7.9   Creating RectangleHotSpots in the HotSpot Collection editor

HotSpot Collection Editor

Members:

0	RectangleHotSpot
1	RectangleHotSpot

RectangleHotSpot properties:

Accessibility	
AccessKey	
TabIndex	0
Appearance	
Bottom	100
Left	110
Right	220
Top	0
Behavior	
AlternateText	
HotSpotMode	**Navigate**
NavigateUrl	**~/ContentsInsurance.htm**
PostBackValue	
Target	

Add ▼   Remove

OK   Cancel

editor (Figure 7.9). In this editor we can add multiple HotSpots using the 'Add' Button. Note that this button contains a drop-down list. The default HotSpot shape is actually a CircleHotSpot because the HotSpot names are in alphabetical order. To create a RectangleHotSpot you will need to click on the small arrow head on the button to access the drop-down list.

For each HotSpot there are 'Bottom', 'Top', 'Right' and 'Left' properties in the 'Appearance' group. These values are measured in pixels from the top left corner of the image. In Figure 7.9 you can see, from the values that have been entered, that the right-hand area of the image is being defined as a RectangleHotSpot, starting 110 pixels from the left of the image.

7

FIGURE 7.10 An ImageMap control viewed via the browser, with the 'NavigateTo' URL indicated at the bottom of the screen

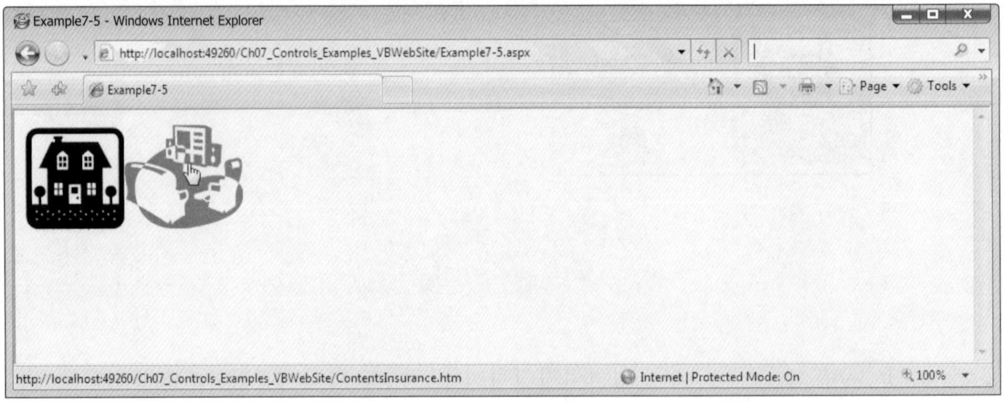

The behavior of the ImageMap when it is clicked is determined using the 'HotSpotMode' property, which can be set to 'Navigate' or 'PostBack', depending on what type of response we want from the ImageMap when we click on it. If the ImageMap or HotSpot's mode is set to 'Navigate', clicking on that part of the image will navigate to the target page defined via the 'NavigateUrl' property. Otherwise, clicking will cause a 'PostBack' event which you can handle via the ImageMap control's click event. Where hot spots overlap, the one with the lowest order number is chosen, which is why the 'HotSpot Collection Editor' provides the facility to re-order them using the arrows in the middle of its dialog box. In our example, we have chosen to navigate to different XHTML pages from the two parts of the image map.

Figure 7.10 shows the example ImageMap being displayed in a browser. In this case, the second hot spot is set to Navigate to 'ContentsInsurance.htm', as can be seen in the figure as the mouse is moved over that area of the image.

An image map can provide an attractive and compact menu structure. In recent years, however, graphical menus have fallen out of favor for the following reasons:

- They are not particularly accessible
- They may not scale well to small and large screens
- They may prevent search engines from being able to crawl and index the site

You may, therefore, feel that ImageMaps are inappropriate for your site. If so, an alternative approach is to provide a conventional text-based menu, for example by using the ASP.NET navigation controls which we will look at in the next chapter.

7.2 Compound controls

Compound controls are those that group together other controls. In this section we look at the MultiView, which groups together view controls, and Wizards, which group controls together into a simple webflow.

7.2.1 MultiView

The MultiView is a compound control which can contain any number of view controls but no more that one view may be visible at a time, as determined by the MultiView's 'Index' property. It can be a good way of switching the view in part of a web page without affecting the rest of the content, and/or revealing content that is initially hidden.

Figure 7.11 shows a MultiView control containing two views displayed in Design view. In this context, all of the view controls are visible at the same time, but at run time only one of the views will be visible. In this example, each of the views is quite simple, containing some text and an image, but a view can contain as much mark-up and as many controls as you like. Note that a view may only be added to a MultiView control, and not placed anywhere else on a web form.

The web form in this example also includes a DropDownList control with three items, which have the text 'Select a type of insurance . . .', 'Contents Insurance' and 'Second view' respectively. The DropDownList controls which view is displayed, an effect which is triggered by the list's 'SelectedIndexChanged' event handler.

FIGURE 7.11   A MultiView control in Design view, containing two views

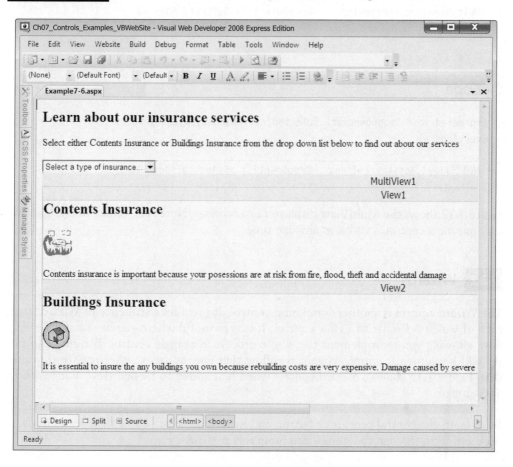

NOTE	To trigger the event handler it is important that you check the 'Enable Auto Postback' check box in the DropDownList's tasks menu, since this forces a postback to the page each time an item is selected from the list (you can also set this property to 'True' in the Properties window). If you want to show one of the views when the page is first loaded, set the 'ActiveViewIndex' property of the MultiView to the appropriate value (the default is −1, which signals that no view should be displayed).

In the following event handler for the DropDownList, the MultiView's 'Index' property is set to be one less the DropDownLists's 'SelectedIndex' property. This is because both the views and the list selections are numbered from zero upwards. When we choose the second item in the list (number 1) we want to show the first view (number zero).

VB Code

```
Protected Sub DropDownList1_SelectedIndexChanged(ByVal sender As
Object, ByVal e As System.EventArgs)
     Handles DropDownList1.SelectedIndexChanged
  MultiView1.ActiveViewIndex = DropDownList1.SelectedIndex -1
End Sub
```

C# Code

```
protected void DropDownList1_SelectedIndexChanged(object sender,
EventArgs e)
{
  MultiView1.ActiveViewIndex = DropDownList1.SelectedIndex -1;
}
```

Figure 7.12 shows the MultiView displayed in a browser. Note that, unlike in Design view, only one view control is visible at any one time.

7.2.2 Wizards

The Wizard control is another compound control. It provides a sequence of WizardSteps, each of which is similar to a view control. It is very useful where you have a simple webflow, allowing you to implement the whole process in a single control. For our example, we will implement a simple Wizard webflow that encapsulates a user registration process. Figure 7.13 shows a Wizard control when first added to Design view, along with its Tasks menu.

By default, the control provides a button and hyperlinks which allow the user to navigate back and forth through the steps, or to jump to a particular step.

FIGURE 7.12 A MultiView control displayed in a browser, with one of the views selected

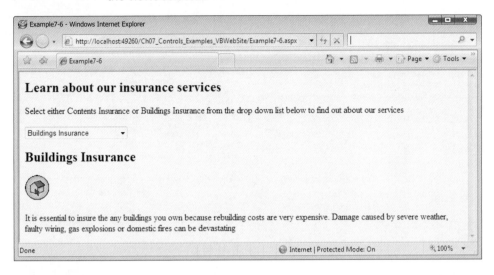

FIGURE 7.13 A Wizard control in Design view and its Tasks menu

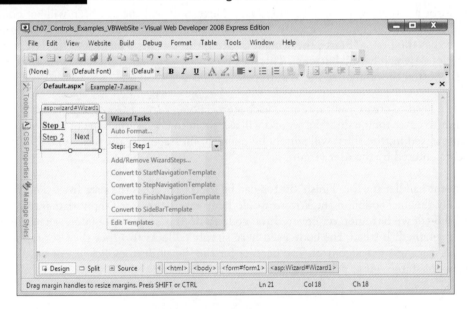

We are going to create a simple Wizard process with four steps; 'Contact Details', 'Preferences', 'Confirmation' and 'Completed'. To do this, we select 'Add/Remove Wizard-Steps…' from the menu to display the 'WizardStep Collection Editor', where we can add or remove steps and set their properties (Figure 7.14). In this example we have added all the four steps, and edited the 'Title' properties of the steps.

Note that the 'StepType' property of each step is set to 'Auto' by default. This means that the first step will be treated as a 'Start' step (which has a 'Next' button), any middle step

FIGURE 7.14 The WizardSteps Collection Editor which is used to add, remove, and re-order steps, as well as set their properties

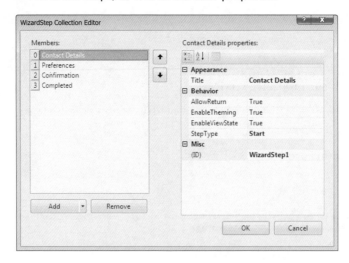

will just be a 'Step' (which has 'Previous' and 'Next' buttons) the last Step will be 'Finish' (with 'Previous' and 'Finish' buttons). However we will explicitly set the 'StepType' property so that the first is 'Start', the second is 'Step' the third is 'Finish' and the last step is 'Complete' (which has no buttons). This means we can write an event handler for the final 'Finish' button to summarize the Wizard process in the 'Complete' step.

Now we need to create the content of each step. The first step ('Contact Details') will ask the user to enter their name, the second will ask them to choose the type of insurance they are interested in, the third will simply be a 'finish' message and the last step will display the data entered by the user (Figure 7.15).

The event handler for the 'Finish' button can be used to process the data from the Wizard. Typically the final action of the Wizard would be to insert the user's input data into a database, though we have not yet covered the code to do this so the data in our example will not be retained. Instead, the code used here simply collects together the user input and displays it using a Label control. The handler for the 'FinishButtonClick' event has a single assignment statement to achieve this effect:

VB Code

```
Protected Sub Wizard1_FinishButtonClick(ByVal sender As Object,
  ByVal e As System.Web.UI.WebControls.WizardNavigationEventArgs)
     Handles Wizard1.FinishButtonClick
  Message.Text = "Thank you " + Name.Text +
     " for registering your interest in " +
        InsuranceChoice.SelectedItem.Text
End Sub
```

FIGURE 7.15   The four WizardSteps in Design view

(a)

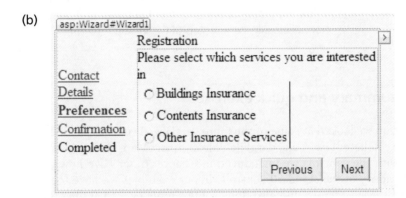

(b)

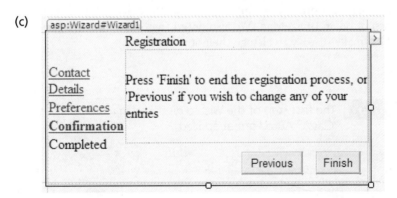

(c)

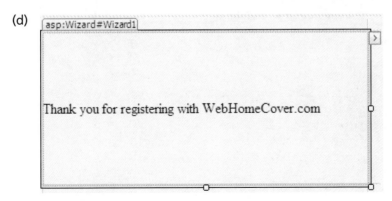

(d)

7

C# Code

```
protected void Wizard1_FinishButtonClick(object sender, WizardNavigationEventArgs e)
{
  Message.Text = "Thank you" + Name.Text + " for registering your interest in " +
    InsuranceChoice.SelectedItem.Text;
}
```

Like a number of other controls, the Wizard has an 'Auto Format' option. Figure 7.16 shows the first step of the Wizard with the 'Classic' Auto Format applied, displayed in a browser.

 NOTE The step displayed initially in the browser when viewed from within Visual Web Developer will be the one currently shown in Design view, not necessarily the first step of the Wizard.

Section summary and quick exercises

In this section we looked at some of the more specialized controls in the Standard group of the toolbox; BulletedList, Calendar, FileUpload, ImageMap, view, MultiView and Wizard. Together with the controls we introduced in Chapter 6, we have now given some coverage to a majority of the standard controls. In our examples we have focused on the main features of these controls, and also done some simple event handing that enabled us to retrieve information from these controls, such as the selected date on a Calendar, or the current hotspot on an ImageMap. We also noted that some controls have an Auto Format option, which makes it easy to change their appearance.

FIGURE 7.16 The first step of the Wizard displayed in a browser with the 'Classic' Auto Format applied

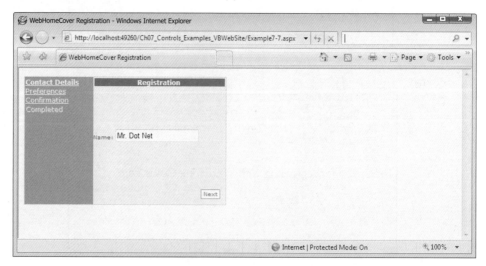

Create a web form containing a BulletedList control that has its 'DisplayMode' property set to 'Hyperlink'. Add several list items and ensure that each one links to a valid URL.

Create a web form that contains an ImageMap using a 'target' image with three rings. Use CircleHotSpots so that each ring of the target will lead to a different URL.

Create a Wizard control that has three steps, leaving the 'StepType' property of each step set to 'Auto'. Observe the default behavior of the steps in terms of the buttons that are shown for each step.

7.3 Validation controls

One of the most important things that we need to do with web forms is to validate the data that is entered by the user before we try to process it. For example if a user makes an insurance claim but provides an invalid policy number, then we will be unable to process that claim. Therefore if the user enters incorrect or inconsistent data then we need to deal with that immediately, and inform the user about what they have done wrong and how to fix it. The validation controls provided in Visual Web Developer enable us to apply various rules to the data entry components on our web forms so that data can be quickly and efficiently validated. These controls provide client-side validation using code automatically generated in JavaScript. By default, validation takes place on both the client (i.e. in the browser) and the server when using validation controls. Validating on the server as well as the client is essential, since not all browsers will support JavaScript, so we cannot rely on client-side validation taking place in all situations.

We can only provide *surface validation* when validating form data on the client. For example we can check that a credit card number matches the correct format for credit card numbers, or check that a particular type of card, such as a Visa card, starts with the correct numbers for that type, but we could not actually check the validity of the credit card itself in the browser. That would have to be done by a server-side process. Surface validation includes things like checking for empty fields, checking that selections have been made (for example from radio buttons or drop-down lists) rather than leaving empty defaults, checking that numeric, date, email or credit card fields contain the right types of characters and so on. Because the Visual Web Developer controls are intended to perform the same validation processes on both client and server, they can only perform surface validations.

 NOTE It is possible to configure the validation controls so that validation happens only on the server. However, even if we do this, the controls can still only perform surface validation. Further validation of the data may also be required once these initial tests have been passed.

Figure 7.17 shows the Validation section of the Toolbox, containing the seven controls that can be used for form validation. Table 7.5 explains briefly what these controls can do.

FIGURE 7.17   The validation controls in the Toolbox

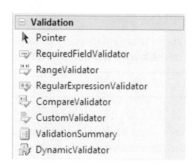

TABLE 7.5   Validation controls and their uses

Validation Control	Purpose
RequiredFieldValidator	Checks if a required field has been left empty
RangeValidator	Checks if a value entered by the user is within a valid range
Regular-Validator	Checks if a value entered by the user matches a set of rules about valid characters and their sequences. Some built-in expressions are supplied by the control
CompareValidator	Compares what is entered by the user with some other value, which may come from another control on the form, for example you might check if an end date comes after a start date. Can also be used for simple data type checks
CustomValidator	Allows you to write your own validation code in JavaScript
ValidationSummary	Groups all the various validation messages together in one place on the form so they are easy to present to the user
DynamicValidator	Specialist validator for use with the LINQ to SQL classes used for database access (these are introduced in Chapter 10)

7.3.1 Processing forms on the client

With the web forms we have created so far, triggering an event related to a control (for example by pressing a button) invokes a server-side process than handles the event. For example this simple web form contains TextBox fields for an insured item's description and value, along with a button that will invoke a button clicked event on the server:

```
<%@ Page Language="VB" AutoEventWireup="false" CodeFile="Example7-8.aspx.vb"
Inherits="_Default" %>
<!DOCTYPE html PUBLIC "-//W3C//DTD XHTML 1.0 Transitional//EN"
"http://www.w3.org/TR/xhtml1/DTD/xhtml1-transitional.dtd">
```

```
<html xmlns="http://www.w3.org/1999/xhtml">
  <head>
   <title>Example7-8</title>
  </head>
  <body>
  <!-- File Example7-8.aspx -->
   <h1>Claim Detail Form - large item</h1>
   <p>
    Please fill in the form below when making claims for large items
   </p>
  <form id="form1" runat="server">
    <div>
      <asp:Label ID="Label1" runat="server" Text="Item description">
      </asp:Label>
      <asp:TextBox ID="description" runat="server"></asp:TextBox>
      <br />
      <asp:Label ID="Label2" runat="server" Text="Approximate value">
      </asp:Label>
      <asp:TextBox ID="value" runat="server"></asp:TextBox>
      <br />
      <asp:Button ID="SubmitButton" runat="server" Text="Submit" />
    </div>
  </form>
  </body>
</html>
```

Once the form data is submitted to the server by the button being pressed, it is too late to validate any of the form data in the browser. However, validation controls can be added to intercept the button click event and enable validation processing routines to take place in the browser before the form data is processed by event handlers on the server. These routines can check whether the contents of the form are valid or not. If the form data is valid then it will be submitted to the server-side application. If not, then the submission is cancelled, and we can give the user the opportunity to correct the data they have entered.

 NOTE The web form used in these examples is deliberately simple so that we can focus on the validation controls, so the page layout is very basic.

7

The simplest and perhaps most commonly used type of form validation is to check if required fields have some content in them. If a required field is empty then there is no point submitting the form data to the server, so this is a useful check to perform. Visual Web Developer includes a RequiredFieldValidator for this purpose, which is very simple to use. For each required field, we add a separate RequiredFieldValidator control to the web form. The position of the validator control defines where its error message will appear on the page. Figure 7.18 shows the web form in Design view with two RequiredFieldValidator controls added. The default error message ('RequiredFieldValidator') is shown in Design view at the control position (the source of this web form can be found in 'Example7-9.aspx').

Claim Detail Form - large item

Please fill in the form below when making claims for large items

Item description   RequiredFieldValidator

Approximate value   RequiredFieldValidator

Submit

FIGURE 7.19   Setting the 'ErrorMessage' and 'ControlToValidate' properties
of a RequiredFieldValidator control

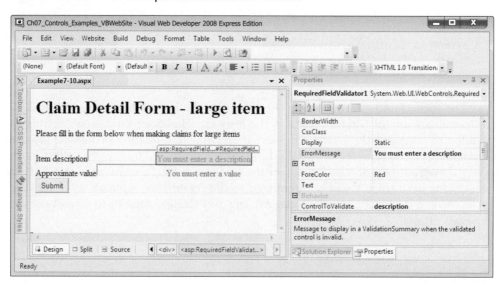

To configure the validators to work correctly, we need to edit their error messages and associate them with specific controls. This is done using the Properties tab, while a validator control is selected. Figure 7.19 shows the two properties being edited for the first validation control. The 'ErrorMessage' property has been set to 'You must enter a description', and the 'ControlToValidate' property has been selected from a drop-down list to be 'description'. Similar changes need to be made to the other control, providing a suitable error message and associating it with the 'value' TextBox.

Once the validators have been added to the page and configured, when the web form is viewed in the browser the validation process will be triggered as soon as the button is pressed. If either or both of the fields fail validation because they are empty, the error messages will be displayed and the server-side button click event will not be invoked. Figure 7.20

FIGURE 7.20 Error messages displayed by RequiredFieldValidator controls

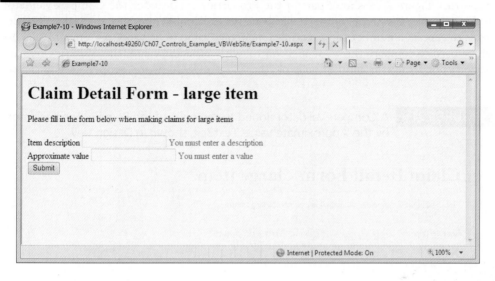

shows what the web form looks like if the button is pressed when both of the text boxes are left empty. (The source of this web form can be found in 'Example7-10.aspx'.)

7.3.2 Using the CompareValidator

In addition to checking if text fields are empty, a common process for mandatory fields, we can do other more specific types of check. For example we can check if a field that is supposed to contain a number actually has numeric data in it. To do this type of check, we can use the 'CompareValidator'. A CompareValidator is able to compare a value entered by the user with either another value (which may be the value entered into another control on the form) or a specific data type. In this example we will use a data type check so that the value entered into the 'value' TextBox will only be valid if it matches the 'Double' (floating point number) data type. To add this validation to the web form, we need to add a second validator for the 'value' TextBox.

 NOTE For our example we still need the RequiredFieldValidator, because the CompareValidator will only be applied if there is some data entered into the textbox. If you wanted to validate a numeric field that was not mandatory you would only need to use the CompareValidator, but in this case we still want to force the user to enter something into the 'value' TextBox.

Figure 7.21 shows the web form ('Example7-11.aspx') in Design view with a Compare-Validator added to the right of the existing RequiredFieldValidator. The 'ErrorMesage' property for this validator has been set to 'You must enter a number in this field', and the 'ControlToValidate' property has been set to 'value'.

Other properties that need to be set for a CompareValidator are the 'Operator' and 'Type' properties. Figure 7.22 shows part of the Properties window for the CompareValidator. In this example, the 'Type' property has been set to 'Double', because the 'value' TextBox needs to contain a number representing a monetary value to be valid. A CompareValidator can be used to compare the value in a control with a specific value (the 'ValueToCompare' property) or a value in another control (the 'ControlToCompare' property). You can see

FIGURE 7.21   A CompareValidator added to the right of the RequiredFieldValidator by the 'Approximate value' TextBox, shown in Design view

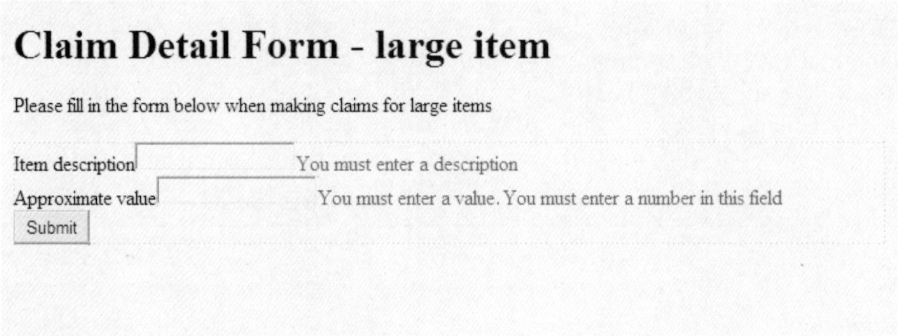

Claim Detail Form - large item

Please fill in the form below when making claims for large items

Item description| You must enter a description
Approximate value| You must enter a value. You must enter a number in this field
Submit

FIGURE 7.22   Setting the properties of a CompareValidator to check for a particular data type

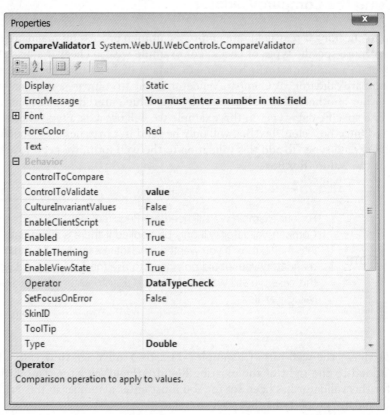

from Figure 7.22 that in this example, both of these properties are blank. This is because we are simply going to check the data type of the value entered, not compare it with a specific value. To do this, we have selected 'DataTypeCheck' from the drop-down list for the 'Operator' property. This means the validator will simply check if the data in the control is of type 'Double', rather than comparing it with any other value.

There is one other property that is useful to be aware of in this example. In Design view, the two validators next to the 'value' TextBox appear one after the other. If the error message for the CompareValidator is displayed, it will appear in the position it occupies in design view, which will look rather odd, since there will be a large space, occupied by the other validator control, between the TextBox and the message. To overcome this problem, we can set the 'display' properties of the validators to 'Dynamic' (the default is 'Static'). A dynamic validator only takes up space on the page when it is displayed. This means that if the message from the CompareValidator needs to be displayed, it will display immediately to the right of the 'value' TextBox. Figure 7.23 shows the CompareValidator in action, checking the data type of the value entered into the control.

Sometimes, checking the type of data entered into a control is sufficient. However, we may want to do more with a CompareValidator, such as check for a minimum or maximum value. For example we could modify our validator so that instead of simply checking that a Double value is entered into the control, we could check that the value for a large item should be above a certain threshold. To do this, all we need to do is to change the 'Operator' property to 'GreaterThanEqual', and enter a value for the 'ValueToCompare' property. These changes have been made in Figure 7.24 (the value to compare has been set to '250') along with a change to the error message to make it more appropriate.

Figure 7.25 shows the web form with the modified validator ('Example7-12.aspx'). A value has been entered into the 'value' TextBox that is below the minimum value for a large item claim.

FIGURE 7.23   A CompareValidator being used to check the data type of a control

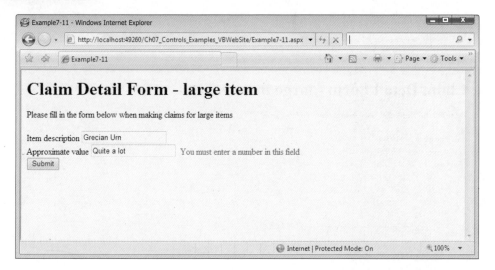

FIGURE 7.24
Configuring the CompareValidator to check a control for a value greater than a specified minimum

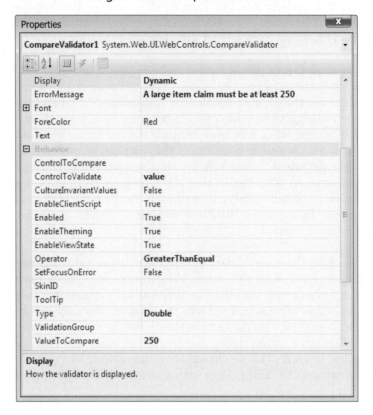

FIGURE 7.25
A CompareValidator being used to check if the value entered is greater than a specified minimum

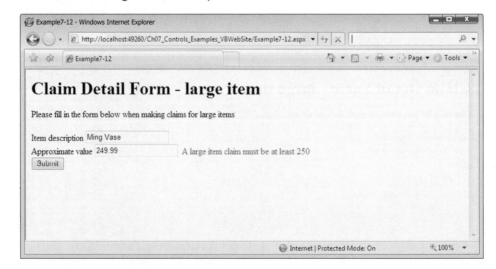

7.3.3 Using the RangeValidator

Although the CompareValidator allows us to compare a value with a minimum or maximum value, it does not support checking against a range of valid values. For this requirement, we need to use a RangeValidator. A RangeValidator is quite simple. We just need to specify the 'MinimumValue' and 'MaximumValue' properties. Figure 7.26 shows the properties of a RangeValidator applied to the 'value' TextBox in our web form (this can replace the previous CompareValidator, since a RangeValidator will also check the data type). In this example, we assume that a claim for a large item must fall in the range 250 to 10,000.

Figure 7.27 shows the RangeValidator in action ('Example7-13.aspx'). A value has been entered that is outside the valid range and the error message has been displayed.

7.3.4 Using the RegularExpressionValidator

So far we have been concentrating on validating numeric data, but there are many different types of data that need to be validated, not just numbers. Some types of data can be checked against a regular expression, enabling us to apply structural rules to the characters entered into a TextBox. The RegularExpressionValidator uses an expression language to compare the data entered into a control with a pattern of valid characters. These patterns

FIGURE 7.26 Configuring a RangeValidator

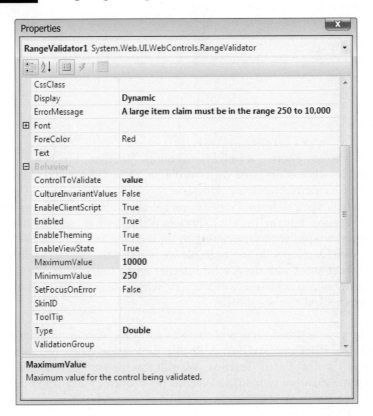

FIGURE 7.27 A RangeValidator being used to check that data fall within a valid range

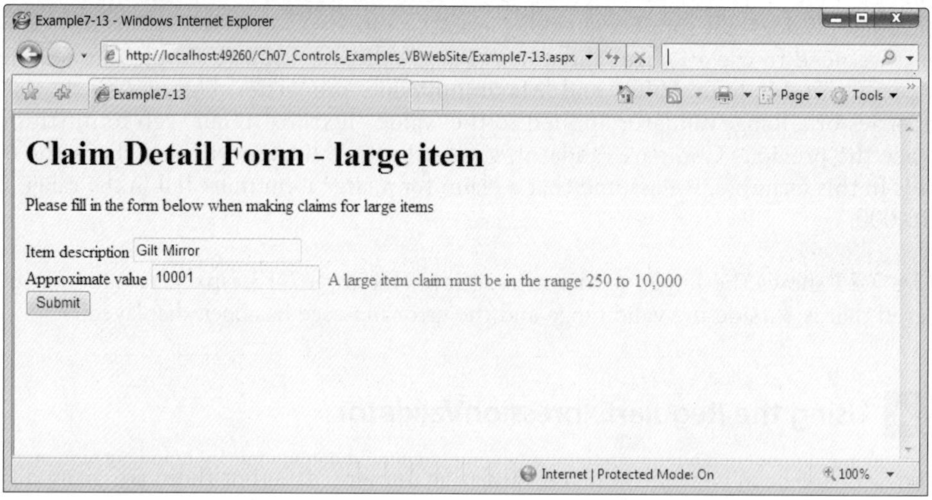

FIGURE 7.28 A RegularExpressionValidator added to the web form

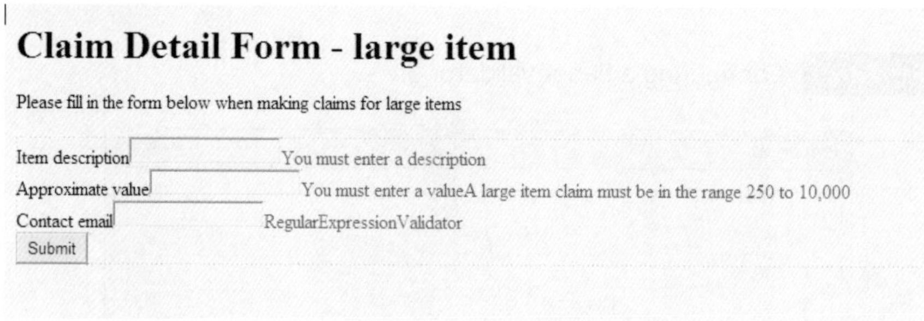

can get quite complex. There is a well known quote (attributed to Jamie Zawinski) that says 'Some people, when confronted with a problem, think "I know, I'll use regular expressions." Now they have two problems!'. However regular expressions can be extremely useful, if initially challenging to learn. Proper coverage of regular expression syntax is beyond the scope of this book, but the RegularExpressionValidator has some built-in expressions that can be reliably used without needing to understand the expression language used within Visual Web Developer. In our example we will use the built-in expression that can validate an Internet email address. A valid Internet email address consists of some characters, the '@' symbol and some more characters, with at least one period between them. These rules are checked by the validator.

Figure 7.28 shows a modified version of the web form we used in the previous examples, with an additional label and TextBox. A RegularExpressionValidator has been added to the right of the 'Contact Email' TextBox. We will assume for this example that the contact email is not a mandatory field, so there is no RequiredFieldValidator used for this TextBox.

As with previous validators, we configure the validator in the Properties window. Figure 7.29 shows the properties of the RegularExpressionValidator. The 'ErrorMessage' property has been set to 'The email address is invalid', and the 'ControlToValidate' property has been set to 'email' (the ID that has been used for the third TextBox). The other property to be set is the 'ValidationExpression'. To the right of this property is a button that will invoke the Regular Expression Editor dialog, which can be seen in Figure 7.30.

In the Regular Expression Editor we can either create our own expression or select one from the list of built-in expressions. One of these is the 'Internet email address' expression. If

FIGURE 7.29 Setting the properties of a RegularExpressionValidator

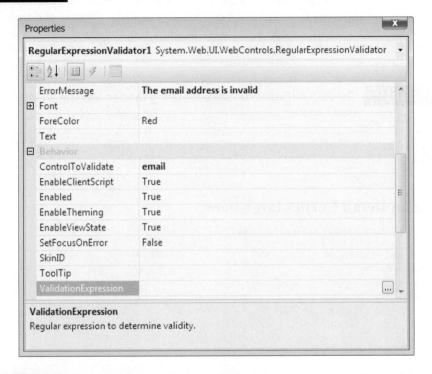

FIGURE 7.30 Selecting 'Internet email address' from the list of built-in validation expressions in the Regular Expression Editor

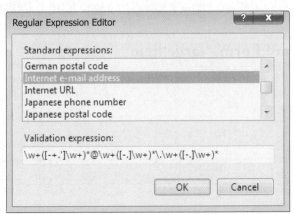

you select this, you will see that the expression is quite complex (see Figure 7.30), but you do not need to be concerned with this if you are only using the built-in expressions.

Figure 7.31 shows the RegularExpressionValidator in action in the web form ('Example7-16.aspx'). An email address has been entered that does not meet the rules of the expression because there is no period in the text that follows the '@' symbol. Therefore it cannot be a valid Internet email address.

7.3.5 Adding a ValidationSummary

If you have a number of validators on a single form, there may be several error messages all being displayed at the same time. A ValidationSummary provides a means of drawing all of these messages together into a single position on the page. It optionally allows you to pop-up an alert box if there are any error messages. Figure 7.32 shows a ValidationSummary being

FIGURE 7.31 The RegularExpressionValidator being used to validate an Internet email address

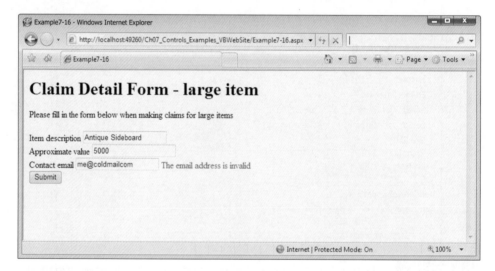

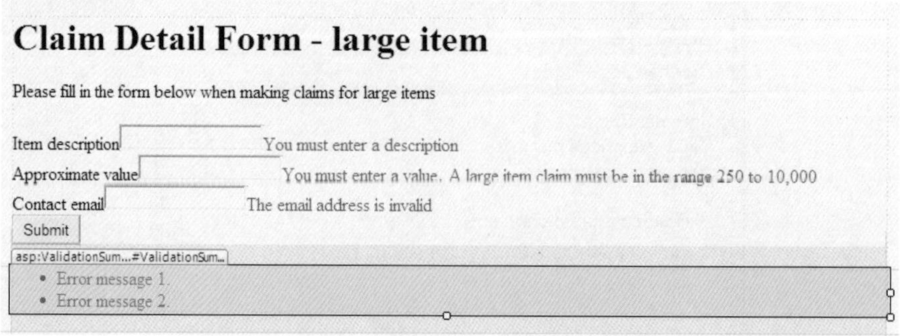

FIGURE 7.32 A ValidationSummary added to a web form in Design view

added to our web form in Design view. Wherever the ValidationSummary is positioned on the web form, that is where the combined error messages will appear on the page at run time.

The ValidationSummary will display all the error messages from the validators on the form. Figure 7.33 shows the ValidationSummary added to our previous web form, redisplaying all the error messages from the rest of the page ('Example7-17.aspx').

Using a ValidationSummary for a web form as small as the one in Figure 7.33 is probably not all that useful, but in a large form it can assist the user to see all the validation errors without having to scan through the whole page.

If you prefer, you can configure the ValidationSummary to display the error messages in a small pop-up 'alert' box. This is simple to configure. Simply change the ValidationSummary's 'ShowMessageBox' property from 'false' to 'true'. If you do not want both an alert and a list, you can also set the 'ShowSummary' property to false so that only the alert is shown. Figure 7.34 shows how the ValidationSummary appears if an alert is used.

Another useful refinement is that you can have different messages appearing in the ValidationSummary than appear at the validator positions. This means we can use longer explanations in the validation summary with just brief messages appearing in the form itself. This is done by providing values for the 'Text' properties of the validators. In our previous examples, the Text property has been empty, so the 'ErrorMessage' property has been used when a validator indicates an error. However, if we enter a message into the 'Text' property, then that text will be used as the error message that appears at the validator position. The text in the 'ErrorMessage' property will then be used only by the ValidationSummary. Figure 7.35 shows the web form after short messages have been added to the 'Text' properties of the validators (see 'Example7-17.aspx').

FIGURE 7.33   The ValidationSummary in action in a web form

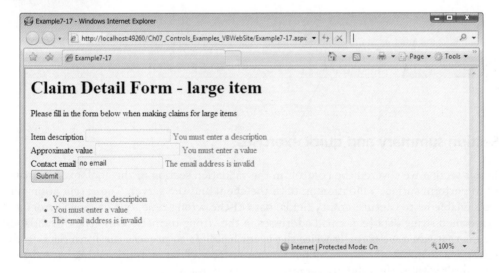

FIGURE 7.34   An alert being used to display validation error messages

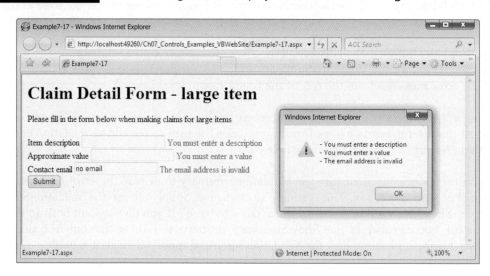

FIGURE 7.35   Using short error messages in the validators

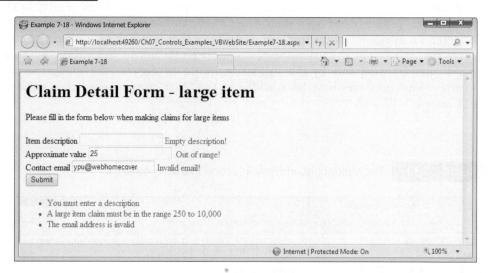

Section summary and quick exercises

In this section we covered the controls in the validation section of the Toolbox that enable us to perform surface validation on both the client and the server. These validation controls enable us to capture empty fields, data of the wrong type, out of range errors and malformed string data (e.g. email addresses in the wrong format). This type of validation means that when we actually write the event handlers to process the form data on the server, we do not need to worry about writing surface validation routines that have already been dealt with by the validation controls in the web form.

EXERCISE 7.4

Create a web form that has a Label, a TextBox and a Button. Set the label to have the text 'Internet URL'. Add a RequiredFieldValidator to validate the TextBox and set both its 'Text' (short error message) and 'ErrorMessage' (long error message) properties. Test that the validator is working correctly when the page is viewed in a browser.

EXERCISE 7.5

Add a RegularExpressionValidator to your web form and use it to validate the TextBox (in addition to the existing RequiredFieldValidator). Use the provided 'Internet email address' validation from the Regular Expression Editor. Set the 'Display' property of the RequiredFieldValidator to 'Dynamic' to improve the message layout at runtime. Remember that this validator can only check the format of the URL. It will not check if that URL actually exists on the web.

EXERCISE 7.6

Write a web form that might be appropriate for a vendor in an on-line auction. It should contain two TextBoxes, one for the reserve price of the item to be auctioned, and one for the 'buy now' price. Use a CompareValidator to ensure that the 'buy now' price is higher than the reserve.

EXERCISE 7.7

One validation control that we have not demonstrated so far is the CustomValidator, which can be used to apply your own JavaScript functions to the data being validated. In this exercise we will use a pre-written JavaScript function, 'isCreditCard', that can check if a credit card number is in a valid format (this function can be found in the file 'ccvalidation.js').

Create a web form that contains a TextBox and a Button. Add a Label that says 'Enter credit card number' and add a CustomValidator control that will validate the text box. Set the 'ClientValidationFunction' property to 'isCreditCard'. Test the web form in a browser with both made up and valid credit card numbers.

7.4 Page layout with master pages

In Chapter 2 we introduced the three region layout page design pattern and in Chapter 4 we implemented this pattern in an XHTML page using Cascading StyleSheets. However in that example we simply created a single page that demonstrated one approach to how the three region layout could be created. The idea of the three region layout is that it creates a common page layout throughout a web application, providing a consistent set of navigation tools (site logo at top left, and side and top navigation bars) that are available from any page.

Master Pages in Visual Web Developer are a way of providing a common template for multiple web pages. A master page contains mark-up that can be reused, with special content placeholders for the mark-up that will be specific to individual pages. You may recall that the concept of the three-region layout is that the top navigation bar is often consistent across all pages, whereas the side navigation bar may be context-specific. If we follow this pattern, then a master page is an ideal way of applying the navigation bar pattern. The top navigation can be part of the master page and the side navigation can be added to a content placeholder.

7.4.1 Creating a master page

In this section we will show you how to integrate the navigation bars from the three-region layout example into a master page. The look and feel will be similar to the previous static XHTML version, which contained a footer in addition to the header and sidebar information and the site logo at top left. In the master page we will integrate the complete mark-up for the top navigation bar and the footer, which will both be consistent across every page of the web application. Initially, we will leave the side navigation bar empty, because this will not be the same for every page (later in this chapter we will populate the side navigation bar with a Web User Control).

The first step is to create a new master page. To do this, select, 'File' → 'New File . . .' from the main menu. In the dialog, select the 'Master Page' template and save it using a suitable file name. (In this example the file has been named 'WebHomeCover.master', Figure 7.36.)

When the master page opens, it will contain mark-up similar to the following (this example is a VB page). The most important parts of the page are the two 'asp:ContentPlaceholder' elements, highlighted in bold below. It is in these placeholders that individual web pages will add their own content to the page. The first placeholder ('head') allows page-specific content

FIGURE 7.36   Creating a new master page in the Add New Item dialog

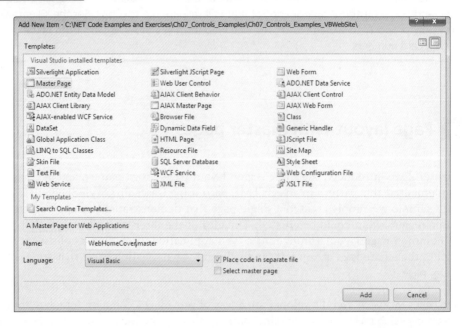

to be added to the head element. The second ('ContentPlaceHolder1') allows content to be added to the main body of each page. Any other mark-up that appears in the master page will be replicated across all pages that use this master:

```
<%@ Master Language="VB" CodeFile="WebHomeCover.master.vb"
Inherits="WebHomeCover" %>

<!DOCTYPE html PUBLIC "-//W3C//DTD XHTML 1.0 Transitional//EN"
"http://www.w3.org/TR/xhtml1/DTD/xhtml1-transitional.dtd">

<html xmlns="http://www.w3.org/1999/xhtml">
  <head runat="server">
   <title>Untitled Page</title>
   <asp:ContentPlaceHolder id="head" runat="server">
   </asp:ContentPlaceHolder>
  </head>
  <body>
   <form id="form1" runat="server">
    <div>
     <asp:ContentPlaceHolder id="ContentPlaceHolder1" runat="server">
     </asp:ContentPlaceHolder>
    </div>
   </form>
  </body>
</html>
```

Before using this master page for our own application, we will need to modify it to include the necessary common content. The first step is in fact to remove some elements that we do not want. First, we will remove the default 'title' element from the head of the document. Otherwise we will not be able to add our own titles to the individual pages. We will also remove the 'form' element, as we do not want to use the same form across all of our web pages. The core of the master page will therefore be reduced to this:

```
<%@ Master Language="VB" CodeFile="WebHomeCover.master.vb"
Inherits="WebHomeCover" %>

<!DOCTYPE html PUBLIC "-//W3C//DTD XHTML 1.0 Transitional//EN"
"http://www.w3.org/TR/xhtml1/DTD/xhtml1-transitional.dtd">

<html xmlns="http://www.w3.org/1999/xhtml">
  <head runat="server">
   <asp:ContentPlaceHolder id="head" runat="server">
   </asp:ContentPlaceHolder>
  </head>
  <body>
   <div>
    <asp:ContentPlaceHolder id="ContentPlaceHolder1" runat="server">
    </asp:ContentPlaceHolder>
   </div>
  </body>
</html>
```

At this stage there is a placeholder for the header and another for the main body of the page. However, to implement a three region layout we need another placeholder so that context-relevant sidebar information can be applied at the page level. The easiest thing to do is to copy the complete 'div' element from the page body and paste it immediately below (so that both content placeholders appear within their own 'div' elements within the body). Visual Web Developer will automatically provide a different ID for the new element. The master page should now look like this:

```
<%@ Master Language="VB" CodeFile="MasterPage.master.vb"
Inherits="MasterPage" %>

<!DOCTYPE html PUBLIC "-//W3C//DTD XHTML 1.0 Transitional//EN"
"http://www.w3.org/TR/xhtml1/DTD/xhtml1-transitional.dtd">

<html xmlns="http://www.w3.org/1999/xhtml">
  <head runat="server">
    <asp:ContentPlaceHolder id="head" runat="server">
    </asp:ContentPlaceHolder>
  </head>
  <body>
    <div>
      <asp:ContentPlaceHolder id="ContentPlaceHolder1" runat="server">
      </asp:ContentPlaceHolder>
    </div>
    <div>
      <asp:ContentPlaceHolder id="ContentPlaceHolder2" runat="server">
      </asp:ContentPlaceHolder>
    </div>
  </body>
</html>
```

To make it easier to work with the master page later, it would be helpful to use 'id' values that relate to the parts of the page that the content placeholders relate to. In this version, we rename the first content placeholder 'SideNavigation' and the second content placeholder 'Content':

```
<%@ Master Language="VB" CodeFile="MasterPage.master.vb"
Inherits="MasterPage" %>

<!DOCTYPE html PUBLIC "-//W3C//DTD XHTML 1.0 Transitional//EN"
"http://www.w3.org/TR/xhtml1/DTD/xhtml1-transitional.dtd">

<html xmlns="http://www.w3.org/1999/xhtml">
  <head runat="server">
    <asp:ContentPlaceHolder id="head" runat="server">

    </asp:ContentPlaceHolder>
  </head>
  <body>
    <div>
      <asp:ContentPlaceHolder id="SideNavigation" runat="server">

      </asp:ContentPlaceHolder>
    </div>
```

```
    <div>
      <asp:ContentPlaceHolder id="Content" runat="server">

      </asp:ContentPlaceHolder>
    </div>
  </body>
</html>
```

Now we can look at adding our own content to the head and body of the master page. In the head, we will add a link element to apply a CSS file called 'master.css'. Note that this does not appear inside the 'asp:ContentPlaceHolder' element, since it applies to all pages that will use this master. Of course it will still be possible for individual pages to add further stylesheets, as well as adding a title element, using the content placeholder.

```
<head runat="server">
  <link href="master.css" rel="stylesheet" type="text/css" />
  <asp:ContentPlaceHolder id="head" runat="server">
  </asp:ContentPlaceHolder>
</head>
```

Here is the 'master.css' stylesheet that we will use as the example for our master page. It combines together a number of styles that we have previously introduced in the 'web-homecover.css' and 'threeregion.css' stylesheets used in Chapter 4.

```
h1
{
  color: rgb(0,0,150)
}
h2
{
  color: rgb(150,0,0);
  font-style: italic
}
body
{
  font-family: sans-serif;
  background-color:rgb(200,200,255)
}
a:link
{
  color: white
}
a:visited
{
  color: red
}
a:hover
{
  color: black;
  background-color: white
}
```

```
a:active
{
  font-style: italic
}
#navigationbar
{
  color: white;
  background-color: rgb(0,0,150)
}
.topnavigationlink
{
  clear: left; margin-left: 1em; font-size: 1.1em
}
#sidenavigation
{
  float: left;
  height: 400px;
  width: 15%;
  color: white;
  background-color: rgb(0,0,150)
}
#content
{
  margin-left: 10em
}
#pagefooter
{
  clear: left; font-weight: bold;
  font-style: italic; font-size: .7em;
  color: white; background-color: rgb(0,0,150); text-align: center
}
```

We now need to add the necessary mark-up to the body of the master page to add the top navigation bar. The first div element in the body contains the mark-up for this navigation bar. This needs to appear before the 'SideNavigation' content placeholder element. Its 'id' has been set to 'navigationbar' so that CSS styles can be applied. The content is a series of anchors to other pages. For the purpose of this example, we will assume pages called 'Home.aspx', 'RegisterWizard.aspx' and 'Services.aspx' (we can use two of the web forms included earlier in this chapter to provide these last two pages). The div element that contains the 'SideNavigation' placeholder has been given the id 'sidenavigation', again so that CSS styles can be applied. There is no mark-up in the side navigation bar of the master page, since this will not be common across all pages. There is some mark-up for the footer in a separate div with the ID 'pagefooter'. This appears after the content place holder elements so the side navigation bar and the main page content appears between the header and the footer. Here is the master page with the mark-up added:

```
<%@ Master Language="VB" CodeFile="WebHomeCover.master.vb"
Inherits="WebHomeCover" %>

<!DOCTYPE html PUBLIC "-//W3C//DTD XHTML 1.0 Transitional//EN"

"http://www.w3.org/TR/xhtml1/DTD/xhtml1-transitional.dtd">
<html xmlns="http://www.w3.org/1999/xhtml">
```

```
<head runat="server">
  <link href="master.css" rel="stylesheet" type="text/css" />
  <asp:ContentPlaceHolder ID="head" runat="server">
  </asp:ContentPlaceHolder>
</head>
<body>
  <div id="navigationbar">
    <a href="Home.aspx">
      <img src="webhomecoverlogo.gif" alt="WebHomeCover logo" />
    </a>
    <span class="topnavigationlink">
      <a href="Home.aspx">Home</a>
    </span>
    <span class="topnavigationlink">
      <a href="RegisterWizard.aspx">Register</a>
    </span>
    <span class="topnavigationlink">
      <a href="Services.aspx">Services</a>
    </span>
  </div>
  <div id="sidenavigation">
    <asp:ContentPlaceHolder ID="SideNavigation" runat="server">
    </asp:ContentPlaceHolder>
  </div>
  <div id="content">
    <asp:ContentPlaceHolder ID="Content" runat="server">
    </asp:ContentPlaceHolder>
  </div>
  <div id="pagefooter">
    <hr />
    &copy;WebHomeCover.com 2000-2010
    <hr />
  </div>
</body>
</html>
```

Now that the master page is complete, we will be able to use it in our web application.

7.5 Using master pages with content pages

It is not possible to view a master page directly in a browser, so in order to see the master page in action we will have to create a new content page that uses it. At the moment, the top navigation bar refers to a web form called 'Home.aspx'. This page does not yet exist so we will create it using the master page. There are two ways to create a new page using an existing master. One option is to right click in the editor pane when viewing the master page and then select 'Add Content Page' (Figure 7.37). This will immediately create a new content page using a default filename (something like 'Default.aspx'). You can then rename the file to something more specific in the Solution Explorer.

Another option is to use the 'Add New Item' dialog from the 'File' → 'New File . . .' menu option. This means that you can choose the filename of the web form before it is created. When you create a new web form, you can check the 'Select master page' check box to apply a master page (Figure 7.38). When you click the 'Add' button you will be shown a second dialog that lets you select an existing master page. In this case, we select the 'WebHomeCover.master' page (Figure 7.39).

FIGURE 7.37 Adding a content page using the pop-up menu in the master page editing pane

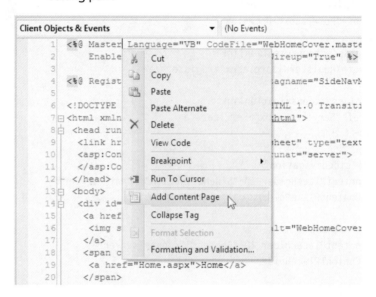

FIGURE 7.38 Choosing to select a master page for a new web form

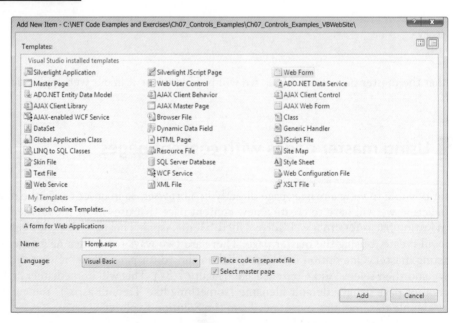

FIGURE 7.39   Selecting a master page to apply to a new web form

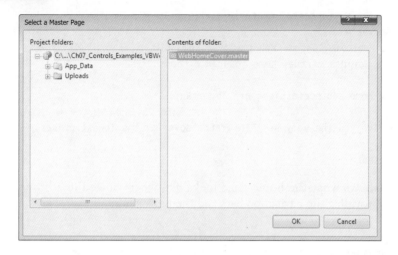

Here is what the 'Home.aspx' page looks like when it is first created. You will see that the ASP element at the top of the page includes the name of the master file (MasterPage-File="~/WebHomeCover.master"), and that the body of the page consists only of three 'asp:Content' elements. The first of these is for the head element, the other two are for the side navigation bar and the main body content of the page.

```
<%@ Page Language="VB" MasterPageFile="~/WebHomeCover.master"
AutoEventWireup="false" CodeFile="Home.aspx.vb" Inherits="Home"
title="Untitled Page" %>

<asp:Content ID="Content1" ContentPlaceHolderID="head"
Runat="Server">
</asp:Content>
<asp:Content ID="Content2" ContentPlaceHolderID="SideNavigation"
Runat="Server">
</asp:Content>
<asp:Content ID="Content3" ContentPlaceHolderID="Content"
Runat="Server">
</asp:Content>
```

Here is the 'Home.aspx' page with a title element added to the first 'asp:Content' element, and XHTML mark-up for the main body of the page added to the third 'asp:Content' element (for the moment we will be leaving the side navigation bar blank).

```
<%@ Page Language="VB" MasterPageFile="~/WebHomeCover.master"
AutoEventWireup="false" CodeFile="Home.aspx.vb" Inherits="Home"
title="Untitled Page" %>

<asp:Content ID="Content1" ContentPlaceHolderID="head"
Runat="Server">
<title>Welcome to WebHomeCover</title>
</asp:Content>
<asp:Content ID="Content2" ContentPlaceHolderID="SideNavigation"
```

7

```
Runat="Server">
</asp:Content>
<asp:Content ID="Content3" ContentPlaceHolderID="Content"
Runat="Server">
   <h1><em>Welcome to</em> WebHomeCover.com</h1>
   <h2>The world's virtual home insurance company</h2>
   <p>
      Your home and possessions are important.
      <br/>
      We give you the very best insurance cover at the lowest prices.
   </p>
</asp:Content>
```

Figure 7.40 shows what the home page looks like when viewed in a browser, with the master page providing the navigation bars and the page footer.

7.5.1 Applying a master page to existing web forms

When the 'Home.aspx' page is viewed in a browser, clicking the 'Home' link or the site logo (at top left) simply reloads the home page. Clicking on either of the other two links in the navigation bar ('Register' and 'Services') will give us a 'page not found' error. To implement these links, we will use a copy of 'Exercise 7.6.aspx' and rename it 'Services.aspx' and use

FIGURE 7.40   The home page using the master page

a copy of 'Exercise7.7.aspx' to implement 'RegisterWizard.aspx'. With these pages, the links in the navigation bar will take us to those web forms. However as soon as we do this, the navigation bars and footer disappear, because these forms are not currently using the master page. So far in this chapter we have seen how a new web form can be created that uses an existing master page, but sometimes we also want to be able to apply master pages to web forms that already exist. This is quite simple, but has to be done manually.

As an example, we will take the 'Services' web form, 'Services.aspx', which contains the MultiView control. The first step is to apply the master page file. This can be done by manually adding the necessary attribute to the ASP element at the top of the source file. However it can also be done by placing the cursor inside this element, then navigating to the 'MasterPageFile' entry in the Properties window. If you press the button on the right of this property you can select the name of the master page file from the 'Select master page' dialog (as previously seen in Figure 7.41).

FIGURE 7.41   Selecting the MasterPageFile using the Properties window

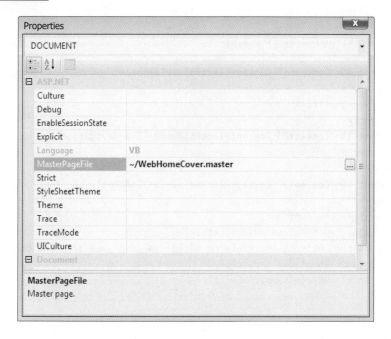

Selecting the MasterPageFile property will update the Page element with the name of the master page file (the attribute added is shown in bold print):

```
<%@ Page Language="VB" AutoEventWireup="false"
CodeFile="Services.aspx.vb" Inherits="Services"
MasterPageFile="WebHomeCover.master" %>
```

Once you have added the master page, you will not be able to view the page in a browser until it has been modified to include the necessary 'asp:Content' elements. You can copy these from another content page, since they are always the same for a given master page:

```
<asp:Content ID="Content1" ContentPlaceHolderID="head"
Runat="Server">
```

```
</asp:Content>
<asp:Content ID="Content2" ContentPlaceHolderID="SideNavigation"
Runat="Server">
</asp:Content>
<asp:Content ID="Content3" ContentPlaceHolderID="Content"
Runat="Server">
</asp:Content>
```

You will need to remove the tags from the page that already appear in the master file, which in this case will be those from the 'html', 'head' and 'body' elements. We will also need to remove the DOCTYPE entry. After that, the remaining content needs to be moved into the bodies of the 'asp:Content' elements for the head and main content. The title element should be moved into the first of these, and all the rest into the third ('Content3') element. Here is the modified version of 'Services.aspx', using the master page (not all of the mark-up seen previously is repeated here). The asp:Content element tags have been highlighted in bold. Note that there is no mark-up in a content page that falls outside of these elements.

```
<%@ Page Language="VB" AutoEventWireup="false"
CodeFile="Services.aspx.vb" Inherits="Services"
MasterPageFile="WebHomeCover.master" %>

<asp:Content ID="Content1" ContentPlaceHolderID="head"
Runat="Server">
<title>Services</title>
</asp:Content>
<asp:Content ID="Content2" ContentPlaceHolderID="SideNavigation"
Runat="Server">
</asp:Content>
<asp:Content ID="Content3" ContentPlaceHolderID="Content"
Runat="Server">
<!-- File: Services.aspx -->
<h2>Learn about our insurance services</h2>
<p>Select either Contents Insurance or Buildings Insurance from the drop-down list
below to find out about our services</p>
<form id="form1" runat="server">
  <div>
...etc..
  </div>
</form>
</asp:Content>
```

Figure 7.42 shows the 'Services' web form integrated into the master page.

7.6 Web User Controls

A Web User Control is a way of reusing page fragments in multiple web forms. The three-region layout is a good example of where a simple Web User Control might be used, because the same sidebar content might be used across multiple pages. However, because the sidebar content is also context sensitive, it cannot be placed directly into the master

FIGURE 7.42 The 'Services' web form integrated into the master page

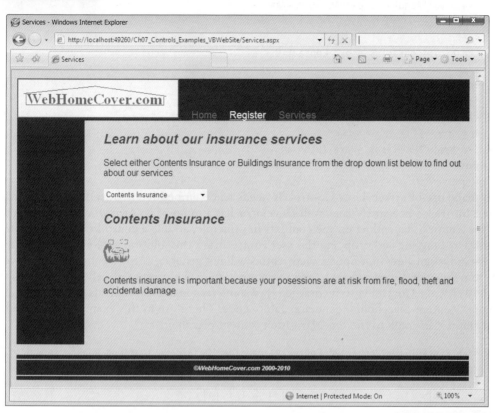

page, because master page content is the same for every page. In the following example, we will create a simple Web User Control to populate the side navigation bar of a page using the three-region layout master page.

To create a new Web User Control, open the Add New Item dialog (with 'File' → 'New File') and select the 'Web User Control' option. This will create a file with an 'ascx' extension. For our first example we will create a Web User Control called 'SideNavMain.ascx' (Figure 7.43).

When first created, a Web User Control source file contains only an ASP tag:

```
<%@ Control Language="VB" AutoEventWireup="false"
CodeFile="SideNavMain.ascx.vb" Inherits="SideNavMain" %>
```

We now need to add the mark-up that will give the control some content. For our example this will just be some simple XHTML that will provide a menu that can be added to the side navigation bar of the three region layout. This just consists of some anchors, inside paragraphs, to pages that we will create later. Note that there are no 'div' elements used here because the enclosing 'div' element in the master page has a CSS class applied. If we added more divs here we would have to apply the appropriate class to avoid problems with the styling of the page:

```
<%@ Control Language="VB" AutoEventWireup="false"
CodeFile="SideNavMain.ascx.vb" Inherits="SideNavMain" %>
```

```
<p>
 <a href="AboutUs.aspx">About Us</a>
</p>
<p>
 <a href="ContactUs.aspx">Contact Us</a>
</p>
<p>
 <a href="Deals.aspx">Special Deals</a>
</p>
<p>
 <a href="More.aspx">More Info</a>
</p>
```

To make use of a Web User Control, it needs to be embedded in a web form. This can be a bit tricky, because Visual Web Developer has a mind of its own when adding a Web User Control, depending on the context. In principle, adding a control can be done very easily by dragging and dropping the user control from the solution explorer into the host page in Design view (not Source view, as this will not generate the correct code). However before doing so it is necessary to add some mark-up to the content placeholder into which the Web User Control is to be dragged. For some reason adding controls to a completely empty content placeholder generates faulty code. Therefore in this example we first add an empty paragraph to the SideNavigation content placeholder:

```
<asp:Content ID="Content2" ContentPlaceHolderID="SideNavigation" Runat="Server">
<p></p>
</asp:Content>
```

FIGURE 7.43   Creating a new Web User Control

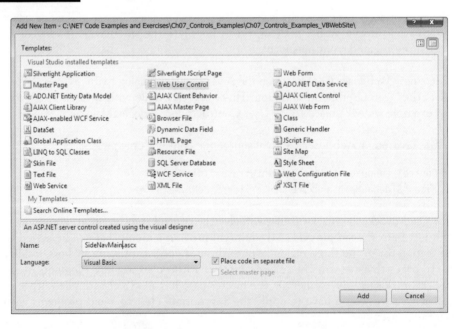

Now it will be possible to successfully add a control to the 'SideNavigation' content placeholder in Design view, and generate the correct code. Figure 7.44 shows the user control dragged and dropped into the side navigation bar of the home page.

FIGURE 7.44   A Web User Control added to the side navigation bar of a web form in Design view

If you look at Source view for the home page, you should see the following tag added near the top of the page, which registers the tag name 'SideNavMain' to be an instance of our Web User Control.

```
<%@ Register src="SideNavMain.ascx" tagname="SideNavMain" tagprefix="uc1" %>
```

Further down in the content placeholder for the side navigation bar, you should see that a user control tag has been added. If there is not already a form tag in the page, Visual Web Developer will also add a form tag around the control. This can be deleted if you need to have another form on the same page (it is not possible to have more than one form tag in a single web form as this causes a run time error):

```
<form id="form1" runat="server">
 <p> </p>
 <uc1:SideNavMain ID="SideNavMain1" runat="server" />
</form>
```

Figure 7.45 shows the home page viewed in a browser after the Web User Control has been added to the side navigation bar.

Of course the reason for populating the side navigation bar with a Web User Control, rather than simply adding that content to the master page, is that we would expect to use different Web User Controls in different page contexts. To illustrate this, we will create a second Web User Control called 'SideNavContact.ascx'. Here is the source for this Web User Control:

```
<%@ Control Language="VB" AutoEventWireup="false"
CodeFile="SideNavContact.ascx.vb" Inherits="SideNavContact" %>
```

```
<p>
  <a href="Mail.aspx">Contact us by snail mail</a>
</p>
<p>
  <a href="Email.aspx">Contact us by email</a>
</p>
<p>
  <a href="Phone.aspx">Contact us by phone or fax</a>
</p>
```

FIGURE 7.45 The side navigation bar populated with a Web User Control

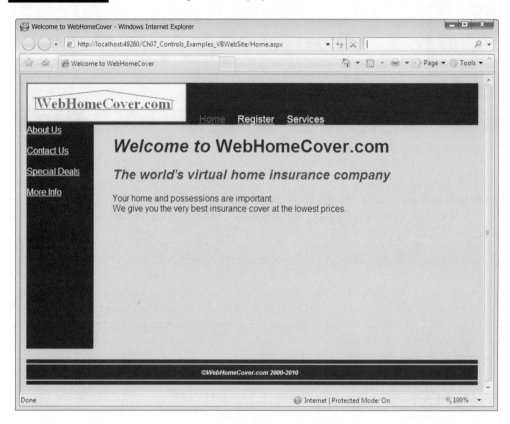

Like our first Web User Control, this example also contains just a few anchors to pages that do not yet exist, separated by paragraph tags. As before, this control can be added to the 'SideNavigation' content placeholder of any suitable pages, by dragging and dropping the control in Design view. Here is an (almost empty) 'ContactUs.aspx' page that includes the 'SideNavContact' Web User Control in its side navigation bar:

```
<%@ Page Language="VB" MasterPageFile="~/WebHomeCover.master"
AutoEventWireup="false" CodeFile="ContactUs.aspx.vb"
Inherits="ContactUs" title="Untitled Page" %>
<%@ Register src="SideNavContact.ascx" tagname="SideNavContact"
tagprefix="ucl" %>
```

```
<asp:Content ID="Content1" ContentPlaceHolderID="head"
Runat="Server">
 <title>Contact Us</title>
</asp:Content>

<asp:Content ID="Content2" ContentPlaceHolderID="SideNavigation"
runat="server">
 <uc1:SideNavContact ID="SideNavContact1" runat="server" />
</asp:Content>

<asp:Content ID="Content3" ContentPlaceHolderID="Content"
Runat="Server">
<h1>Contact Us</h1>
 <p>
Use the links on the left to contact us by mail, email, phone or fax
 </p>
</asp:Content>
```

Figure 7.46 shows the page viewed in a browser, with the Web User Control in the side
navigation bar. You should be able to see the side navigation bars working if you start at the
home page, and then click on 'Contact Us' in the side navigation bar. As soon as this page is
loaded, the side navigation bar changes.

FIGURE 7.46 The Web User Control for contact links added to the side navigation
bar of the three-region layout

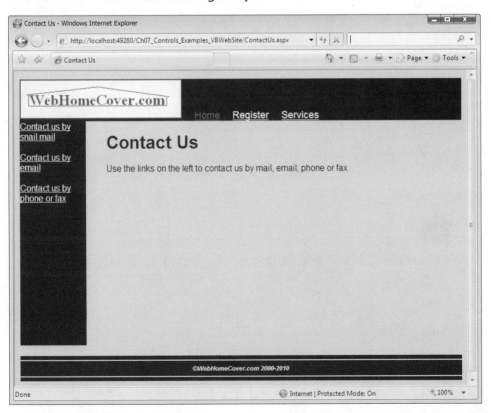

Now you should be able to continue to add pages to your website that can all use the same master page, but can have context sensitive side navigation bars. Because each page specifies which side navigation user control is to be applied, each of these pages must include the appropriate 'Register' tag and the correct user control identifier in the side navigation content placeholder. These parts of the page can easily be copied and pasted from one page source to another.

Self Study Questions

1. What are the three types of HotSpot that can be added to an ImageMap?

2. What type of control can a view be added to?

3. What are the four types of step in a Wizard control?

4. Where does validation always take place, and where can it additionally take place?

5. What kind of validation control would you use if you wanted to check if one date selected from a Calendar control occurred after another date selected from another Calendar?

6. Is it possible to check that a credit card number is valid in a validation control?

7. What kind of validator would you use if you wanted to check that a TextBox contained a valid U.S. Social Security Number?

8. Can the master page being used with a page be changed?

9. How many content place holders can you specify in a master page?

10. What must you do to an empty ContentPlaceHolder before attempting to drag a Web User Control into it in Design view?

Exercises

7.8 Modify 'RegisterWizard.aspx' so that it uses the master page and the 'SideNavMain' Web User Control for its side navigation bar.

7.9 Create the 'AboutUs.aspx' page using the master page. This page should also use the 'SideNavMain' Web User Control for its side navigation bar.

7.10 Create three new web forms, 'Mail.aspx', 'Email.aspx' and 'Phone.aspx'. Make sure that each of these is created using the master page, and that they all use the 'Side-NavContact' Web User Control. You can use the table of phone and fax numbers from Chapter 3 to provide the content for the 'Phone.aspx' page.

SUMMARY

In this chapter we introduced some more controls from the Standard group of the Toolbox, and then looked at the controls available for surface validation, in the Validation group of the Toolbox. In the latter part of the chapter we integrated some of the page design patterns introduced in Chapter 2 into our web application. We began by creating a master page that would incorporate the navigation bar and site logo at top left patterns. We concluded the chapter by adding a side navigation bar with some context relevant links to apply the three region layout pattern to our example application. This was achieved by creating Web User Controls that could be reused across different content pages whilst being independent of the master page.

For further assistance in learning to use controls in web forms, you can use the Visual Web Developer help facility or a broader web search. In addition to the copious amounts of help, tutorials and reference information provided by Microsoft, a number of third parties also provide their own advice, information and help on using these controls. There are also forums where you can post questions. Finally, you should be aware that it is possible to purchase and download third party controls which provide additional functions or features not provided by the ones provided (free) with Visual Web Developer.

References and further reading

Giffs, N. and Howard, R. 2003. *Microsoft ASP.NET Coding Strategies with Microsoft ASP.NET TEAM*, REDMOND: Microsoft Press.

Sussman, D. and Homer, A. 2006. *Wrox's ASP.NET 2.0 Visual Web Developer 2005 Express Edition Starter Kit*.

7

CHAPTER 8

XML Data Sources and Navigation Controls

LEARNING OBJECTIVES

- **To understand how XML documents are structured**

- **To be able to construct well-formed XML documents for use in Visual Web Developer controls**

- **To be able to apply XPath expressions to an XML document**

- **To be able to apply a simple XSL transformation to an XML document**

- **To be able to use a browser to test XSL transformations**

- **To be able to implement design patterns for page navigation**

- **To be able to use XML Site Map documents to configure Visual Web Developer navigation controls**

INTRODUCTION

In this chapter we introduce the key features of the eXtensible Mark-up Language (XML) and then explore how XML can be used to represent data in a .NET web application. We introduce the XmlDataSource control and see how it can be used to take data from an XML document and populate other controls such as the GridView. We also see how the XMLDataSource control can apply XPath and XSL transformations to an XML document in order to filter XML data or make its structure compatible with other controls in Visual Web Developer. In the final section of the chapter we use an XML site map file to implement the Site Map and Breadcrumbs page design patterns we introduced in Chapter 2.

8.1 Semi-structured data

The eXtensible Mark-up Language (XML) is designed to support semi-structured data, so before we look at XML specifically we will explain what is meant by this type of data. Semi-structured data contains no type information, is self-describing, and can have variations in its structure. It is self-describing because it contains labels; each piece of data contains a metadata label that tells us about that data element. This means that a document of semi-structured data can support interoperability between systems, because when it is serialized (sent as a stream of data) between different applications it carries its own labels with it, helping the receiving system to process its content. This is the basis upon which XML web services work.

Perhaps the best way to explain semi-structured data is to start with an example of some structured data:

```
02 03 1959 15 08 1977 08 04 1994
```

If you look at this data you can see that it follows a repeating and consistent structure. There are three groups of numbers, and in each group there are two numbers of two digits followed by a third number of four digits. The different numbers are separated by spaces. The important feature of structured data is that it follows a consistent and predictable format. In this case you can probably see that the data represents a series of dates in European format, though there is nothing in the data to tell you that, other than the knowledge you already have about dates (that they have a day number, a month number and, particularly since the 'millennium bug' panic in the late 1990s, a four digit year). If you look a bit more closely you might assume that the day number comes before the month number in each group, because '15' could not be a month number. However with just the structured data to go on this is just supposition. The data may not represent dates at all. Maybe it is a single part number from a catalogue, or some sports results. Without a bit of metadata to help us we do not really know.

Assuming that the data is, in fact, a series of dates, any application that processes this data needs to know that each data item is separated by its neighbors by spaces and that it occurs in groups of three, each group representing the day, month and year of the date in that order. That information is not carried with the data itself, so we have to 'just know' it. In contrast, semi-structured data is human readable and self-describing. This example shows the same data with some text labels applied:

```
dates
    date
        day=03
        month=02
        year=1959
    date
        day=15
        month=08
        year=1977
    date
        day=08
        month=04
        year=1994
```

In this version, the data is both human readable and self-describing because the data describes itself using recognizable names. Thanks to the labels, we can clearly see that the data represents a series of dates, and that each date consists of the day, the month and the year.

8.1.1 Variations in structure

One of the key features of semi-structured data is that it allows for variations in the structure of the data so that the order and number of elements can be varied. In this version of the data, we add a 'day-name' to the first date but not to the other dates:

```
dates
      date
              day-name=Tuesday
              day=03
              month=02
              year=1959
      date
              day=15
              month=08
              year=1977
      date
              day=08
              month=04
```

This type of structure would be very difficult, if not impossible, to process without the metadata provided by the labels. An application would have to check for the type of data at the beginning of every date to see if it was text (the day name) or a number (the day). Imagine, however, if we made the structure more complex, with many optional parts to the data. Eventually, it would be impossible to process this information without the identifying labels. The point about semi-structured data is that the self-descriptiveness makes it possible for the data to vary in structure, because it provides the context for applications to identify the nature of a piece of data by the label that is attached to it. As a side effect, making these labels human readable can be very useful as well.

Our examples so far have used simple lists of labels and data. However to handle semi–structured data effectively we need a more formal and powerful syntax. This is what XML provides.

8.2 What is XML?

XML is the eXtensible Mark-up Language, an official recommendation of the W3C. It has no presentational components, though CSS can be used to present an XML document in a similar way to how it is used with XHTML. The XHTML specification is based upon XML, as are many other special purpose XML-based specifications. Some of the design goals for XML were that it should be simple to use over the Internet, make documents easy to create, be human-legible and reasonably clear, support a wide variety of applications and make it easy to write programs that process XML documents (Bray *et al.*, 2005).

XML is not so much a language but rather a *metalanguage*. The term 'meta' means (approximately) 'about', so a metalanguage can provide information about a specific language. In the case of XML, it is a metalanguage used to describe other specific mark-up languages, specifying the syntax of the language being defined. XML is designed to be semi-structured, enabling exact, yet flexible, rules to be applied about how data can be organized. Importantly, it is also designed to be extensible in the sense that many different XML-based languages can be built from it, which is what makes it a metalanguage. XML has no predefined tags so you can define your own terms and mark-up. In contrast, a language like XHTML is not a metalanguage because it consists of a set of predefined tags that can be used in a document. You cannot invent new tags for XHTML because they are already specified as part of its syntax.

An XML document consists of a series of elements that can be traversed in a specific order based on the sequence and nesting of those elements inside each other, known as the *document order*. When we use XML data in Visual Web Developer controls, this document order is used to organize the presentation of XML data.

8.2.1 What is XML used for?

Among many other uses, XML can be used to create web pages, with XHTML mark-up. XHTML is, however, just one example of how XML can be applied. XML is a data description (mark-up) language that manages content. It provides a definition of data structures and syntax, but not semantics (it does not specify what the data actually means). It can be applied in many contexts, for example to exchange data between different applications (e.g. web services). Using XML as a communication mechanism between different systems avoids having to use many different file formats. Various industries have standardized on special XML-based languages, enabling them to exchange data using a common format. Examples of this type of format include the B2B (business to business) XML document specifications defined by the RosettaNet organization, principally for the electronic component industry and HL7 (Health Level 7) for clinical and administrative data in health care. XML can be (and has been) used to represent a huge range of different types of information. The following example contains some fragments from a much larger document from the universal protein knowledge base (UniProt, 2008), that describes the DNA of tuberculosis. Here, XML is being used to represent non-textual data:

```
<?xml version="1.0" encoding="UTF-8" ?>
<UniRef xmlns="http://uniprot.org/uniref">
 <entry id="UniRef100_P71715" updated="2008-07-22">
  <name>Cluster: Endonuclease PI-MtuHIP</name>
  <property type="member count" value="2" />
  <property type="common taxon" value="Mycobacterium tuberculosis" />
  <property type="common taxon ID" value="1773" />
  <representativeMember>
  <!-- some content removed here -->
   <sequence length="874" checksum="894155A86DCB9D70">
MAVVDDLAPGMDSSPPSEDYGRQPPQDLAAEQSVLGGMLLSKDAIADVLERLRPGDFYRPAHQNVYDAILD
LYGRGEPADAVTVAAELDRRGLLRRIGGAPYLHTLISTVPTAANAGYYASIVAEKALLRRLVEAGTRVVQY
GYAGAEGADVAEVVDRAQAEIYDVADRRLSEDFVALEDLLQPTMDEIDAIASSGGLARGVATGFTELDEVT
NGLHPGQMVIVAARPGVGKSTLGLDFMRSCSIRHRMASVIFSLEMSKSEIVMRLLSAEAKIKLSDMRSGRM
```

```
SDDDWTRLARRMSEISEAPLFIDDSPNLTMMEIRAKARRLRQKANLKLIVVDYLQLMTSGKKYESRQVEVS
EFSRHLKLLAKELEVPVVAISQLNRGPEQRTDKKPMLADLRESGCLTASTRILRADTGAEVAFGELMRSGE
RPMVWSLDERLRMVARPMINVFPSGRKEVFRLRLASGREVEATGSHPFMKFEGWTPLAQLKVGDRIAAPRR
VPEPIDTQRMPESELISLARMIGDGSCLKNQPIRYEPVDEANLAAVTVSAAHSDRAAIRDDYLAARVPSLR
PARQRLPRGRCTPIAAWLAGLGLFTKRSHEKCVPEAVFRAPNDQVALFLRHLWSAGGSVRWDPTNGQGRVY
YGSTSRRLIDDVAQLLLRVGIFSWITHAPKLGGHDSWRLHIHGAKDQVRFLRHVGVHGAEAVAAQEMLRQL
KGPVRNPNLDSAPKKVWAQVRNRLSAKQMMDIQLHEPTMWKHSPSRSRPHRAEARIEDRAIHELARGDAYW
DTVVEITSIGDQHVFDGTVSGTHNFVANGISLHNSLEQDADVVILLHRPDAFDRDDPRGGEADFILAKHRN
GPTKTVTVAHQLHLSRFANMAR</sequence>
   </representativeMember>
   <!-- some content removed here -->
  </entry>
 </UniRef>
```

The next example also uses XML, but is very different. This is again a tiny fragment of a much larger XML document, but this time contains TV listings, in XMLTV format (Eden, 2005), from the UK *Radio Times* (BBC, 2005). Here, the content is primarily text-based:

```
<?xml version="1.0" encoding="ISO-8859-1"?>
<!DOCTYPE tv SYSTEM "xmltv.dtd">
<tv source-info-name="Radio Times"
 generator-info-name="XMLTV"
 generator-info-url="http://membled.com/work/apps/xmltv/">
 <channel id="channel4.com">
  <display-name>Channel 4</display-name>
  <display-name>4</display-name>
 </channel>
 <programme start="20050102010500 UTC" stop="20050102024000 UTC"
channel="channel4.com">
  <title>The Rachel Papers</title>
  <desc lang="en">A 19-year-old studying to go to Oxford enters all the
information about his love life into his computer in a determined
effort to find the perfect seduction technique. But his system
collapses when he meets and falls in love with the beautiful Rachel, an
American living in London. The couple spend a passionate weekend
together, but then the dream begins to fall apart.</desc>
  <credits>
   <director>Damian Harris</director>
   <actor>Dexter Fletcher</actor>
   <actor>Ione Skye</actor>
   <actor>Jonathan Pryce</actor>
   <actor>James Spader</actor>
   <actor>Bill Paterson</actor>
   <actor>Shirley Anne Field</actor>
  </credits>
  <date>1989</date>
  <category lang="en">film</category>
  <category lang="en">Film</category>
  <video>
   <aspect>15:9</aspect>
```

```
      </video>
      <subtitles type="teletext" />
      </programme>
    </tv>
```

8.3 Components of XML

An XML document consists of a series of tags surrounded by angle brackets, and start tags may include attributes. There are, however, one or two additional aspects to XML, including what is known as the *prolog*. There are a number of possible parts to the prolog, but here we introduce two of them, the *XML declaration* and *processing instructions*.

8.3.1 The XML declaration

An XML document should begin with the XML declaration. This identifies it as an XML document and also declares its version number. Note the question marks that come inside the angle brackets.

```
    <?xml version="1.0"?>
```

 NOTE The 'xml' should be in lower-case. Though some XML processors may well accept other combinations of case, it would be wise to stick to lower-case to avoid potential problems.

The most commonly used version of XML is version 1.0. There is a version 1.1 specification (Bray *et al.*, 2004) but this is largely to enable wider character sets in names than are specified by XML version 1.0, to be able to adapt to the continued development of the Unicode character set.

 NOTE The XML version 1.1 specification states that any XML document that does not explicitly have an XML declaration with a version value of 1.1 will be assumed to be using version 1.0.

The character encoding used in the document may also be specified, though it will default to utf-8 (Unicode Transformation Format 8). This is an encoding scheme that is backward compatible with ASCII (American Standard Code for Information Interchange, an older standard 8 bit character encoding) and uses from 1 to 4 bytes to represent each character. You can choose to explicitly specify utf-8 as the encoding like this:

```
    <?xml version="1.0" encoding="utf-8"?>
```

Other common encodings that you may see used include ISO-8859-1, which is for the Latin character set on the Internet, and utf-16, which uses at least two bytes per character (i.e. is at least 16 bits). Either of these, or indeed any of a number of other character encodings, can appear in the 'encoding' attribute, e.g.:

```
<?xml version="1.0" encoding="ISO-8859-1"?>
```

or

```
<?xml version="1.0" encoding="utf-16"?>
```

The implication of these differences in encoding is that you should make sure that whatever editor you may be using to create and edit XML documents is saving those documents in the same encoding that you have specified. If not, software tools, including browsers, will not be able to process the XML properly. For all of our examples we will be using the default encoding of utf-8.

8.3.2 Processing instructions

The XML declaration can be followed by *processing instructions* that are intended to provide information to applications that need to process the document, such as software that transforms the XML into another type of document. Browsers and other tools can understand this type of processing instruction and handle the XML document accordingly. A processing instruction is identified by special tags that include question marks, similar to the XML declaration.

```
<? processing instruction ?>
```

An example of a processing instruction is one that applies a CSS stylesheet to an XML document. Such an instruction looks something like this:

```
<?xml version="1.0"?>
<?xml-stylesheet href="styles.css" type="text/css"?>
```

8.3.3 Elements and parsed character data

Regardless of the content of the prolog, at a minimum an XML document must contain a root element, which could be the only element in the document, for example:

```
<weather-forecast>rain</weather-forecast>
```

In XML version 1.0, everything except the declaration of the root element can be omitted. Nevertheless we will be including the XML declaration at the top of all our XML files from now on (the XML version 1.0 specification states that XML documents 'should' begin with this declaration, even though it is not compulsory).

The content in the body of an XML element ('rain', in our example) is *parsed character data*. This means that it is data that will be parsed (processed) by any program that handles the XML document. Parsed character data has no type defined by XML, it is just characters.

An XML Document will generally consist of the root element, parsed character data and sub-elements (elements nested inside other elements). For example, we might extend our 'weather-forecast' example to include nested elements to describe the weather forecast for today and tomorrow:

```
<?xml version="1.0" encoding="utf-8"?>
<!-- File: Example8-1.xml -->
<weather-forecast>
 <today>
  rain
 </today>
 <tomorrow>
  showers
 </tomorrow>
 <long-range>
  unsettled
 </long-range>
</weather-forecast>
```

Although our example so far only nests elements to a depth of one, elements can be nested to any depth. XML itself allows any combination of elements to be used, but we should group related elements together give them some meaningful structure. For example, we might provide some temperature information that relates to either today or tomorrow, and group this information into nested elements, as in the next example. Note how this XML document has now acquired a more flexible structure (i.e. is evidently semi-structured). The 'today' and 'tomorrow' elements now have different structures from the 'long-range' element.

```
<?xml version="1.0"?>
<!-- File: Example8-2.xml -->
<weather-forecast>
 <today>
  <general>Rain</general>
  <temperature>
   <maximum>15</maximum>
   <minimum>11</minimum>
  </temperature>
 </today>
 <tomorrow>
  <general>Showers</general>
  <temperature>
   <maximum>20</maximum>
   <minimum>15</minimum>
  </temperature>
 </tomorrow>
 <long-range>Unsettled</long-range>
</weather-forecast>
```

It is perhaps worth emphasizing at this point that an XML document says nothing about the presentation of data, it is primarily about the representation of data. The weather forecast document is only about the underlying structure of its data content, not about how it might, for example, be presented on a web page. It is also not comprised of predefined elements, as an XHTML document would be. The elements 'weather-forecast', 'today', 'temperature', etc. have been created specifically as mark-up for this document.

8.3.4 Editing XML documents in Visual Web Developer

Visual Web Developer provides a special editor for XML files that will automatically check if files are well formed. To create a new XML file select 'File' → 'New File…' from the main menu and then select 'XML File' from the 'Add New Item' dialog (Figure 8.1).

FIGURE 8.1   Creating a new XML document in Visual Web Developer

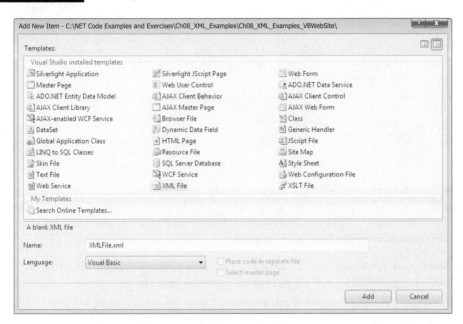

As you enter XML mark-up into the editor, the syntax will be automatically color coded. In addition, if your XML is not well formed, the green bar on the left will turn yellow where there are errors, and the errors will be underlined in red. If you hover with the mouse pointer over an underlined error, a message will pop-up. Figure 8.2 shows an XML file in the editor with an error in the closing 'tomorrow' tag, which means the document is not well formed. The XML editor has indicated the error by underlining parts of the document related to the error, changing the bar on the left-hand side from green to yellow by the incorrect tag and showing an error message when the mouse hovers over the tag. Of course this is similar to the way that the XHTML editor indicates errors but in this case the editor cannot check for the correctness of the tags themselves since these are up to the writer. Therefore the editor can only check that the document is well formed. Once the document is well formed the whole bar should be green with no red underlines.

8.3.5 Attributes versus elements in XML

As in XHTML, XML opening tags may contain attributes to define properties that are related directly to this element rather than being defined by other elements. Of course when you use attributes in XHTML you are constrained by XHTML syntax. In contrast, if you are creating an XML document structure then you will have to decide what data should be represented by elements and what should be represented by attributes. Being more tightly coupled to their host element than nested tags, attributes are less flexible but

```
<?xml version="1.0" encoding="utf-8" ?>
<!-- Example8-2.xml -->
<weather-forecast>
    <today>
        <general>Rain</general>
        <temperature>
            <maximum>15</maximum>
            <minimum>11</minimum>
        </temperature>
    </today>
    <tomorrow>
        <general>Showers</general>
        <temperature>
            <maximum>20</maximum>
            <minimum>15</minimum>
        </temperature>
    </tomorrow>
    <l Expecting end tag </tomorrow>.ong-range>
</weather-forecast>
```

have some special properties. How do you decide, then, whether a particular piece of data should be modelled as an element or an attribute? The general rule of thumb is that you should use elements unless you have a particular need to use attributes. This is because there are many advantages to using elements:

- You cannot have multiple attributes of the same name in a single element, but you can have multiple nested elements that have the same name.
- Attributes are less flexible if you want to change the structure of a document later.
- Attributes cannot be used to describe hierarchical structures, but elements can be nested into these hierarchies.
- Attributes are more difficult to manipulate by software programs that process XML.
- You cannot specify a meaningful order of attributes, but a series of elements at the same level of nesting do have a meaningful order (they are part of the document order).

The overall message is that if you use attributes simply as a way of holding the data in your XML document, then you may end up with documents that are difficult to read and maintain. Why, then, would we ever want to use attributes instead of elements? In fact attributes are very useful in special circumstances. These include:

- Representing metadata. Elements should be used to contain data, but attributes are good for providing further information about that data, for example the language in which it is presented, or perhaps the version number of the content if it relates to some product documentation.
- You want to provide unique IDs for elements that can be used to cross reference data. There are special types of attribute to do this, and these enable an XML tree to also act like a graph (i.e. elements that are not nested inside each other can still be associated together).
- You want to reference external entities (like other files) in your XML document. Attributes have special types that do this.

A more technical concern is that attributes are often better where processing speed is important. The way that some programs process XML means that you can get better performance from these programs using attributes (Eckstein, 2002). This explains why XML data that is being used to configure parts of a web application often uses attributes in preference to elements. You will see later that the XML documents we use with Visual Web Developer controls favor the use of attributes over elements, so it is important that you understand how they are used in an XML document.

The following example shows an XML document that includes attributes. In this case we have some 'date' elements with 'calendar' attributes added. We could, of course, use an element to contain the information about the type of calendar being used (the Gregorian calendar in this example), but this could reasonably be regarded as metadata, and therefore may be better represented as an attribute.

```
<?xml version="1.0" encoding="utf-8" ?>
<!-- File: Example8-3.xml -->
<dates>
 <date calendar="gregorian">
  <day>1</day>
  <month>3</month>
  <year>2005</year>
 </date>
 <date calendar="gregorian">
  <day>2</day>
  <month>3</month>
  <year>2005</year>
 </date>
</dates>
```

8.3.6 Viewing XML pages in a browser

Like XHTML pages and web forms, XML documents can be viewed in a browser using Visual Web Developer' 'View In Browser' menu option. Figure 8.3 shows how our 'dates' XML document appears in the Internet Explorer browser. The behavior of this browser (though not all) is to show an XML document as a tree structure, and enable elements to be expanded or collapsed. As you can see from this figure, the second 'date' element has been collapsed, and is preceded by a '+' symbol to indicate this, but the first 'date' element is expanded (all expanded elements are preceded by a '−' symbol). Clicking on these symbols will expand or contract the element they are associated with.

The ability to display an XML document in a browser is not, on its own, very useful. However it does demonstrate that browsers are able to handle XML documents as well as XHTML, and can also perform a number of other processes using XML data. Which processes are available on a particular browser depends not only on the basic features of the browser but also the special browser plug-ins that might be available. Later in this chapter we will look at a simple plug-in for Internet Explorer that can help us to test XSL Transformations on XML documents.

FIGURE 8.3   An XML document displayed in the Internet Explorer browser

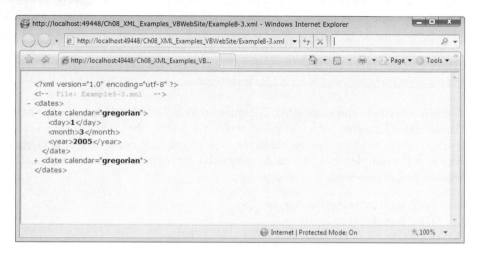

8.4   Using an XmlDataSource in Visual Web Developer

Now that we have covered the basics of XML, we will see how we can use some XML data in a web form. The first step is to create an XML document that represents its data in a format suitable for use within Visual Web Developer. The XmlDataSource control, which appears under the 'Data' section of the Toolbox, can be used to link an XML document with various display controls on a web form. To use an XML document directly with this control, it is necessary for the XML to have a very simple element structure and represent all its data using attributes. The XML document must only have elements nested to one level below the root element. Any elements that are nested more than this will be ignored by the control. To see an example of what this means, take a look at the following document:

```
<?xml version="1.0" encoding="utf-8"?>
<!-- File: Example8-4.xml -->
<dates>
    <date calendar="gregorian">
        <day name="Saturday" number="20" month="9" year="2008" />
    </date>
    <date calendar="gregorian">
        <day name="Sunday" number="21" month="9" year="2008" />
    </date>
</dates>
```

In this example, only the attributes of the 'date' elements would be processed by an Xml-DataSource control, because these elements are nested immediately under the 'dates' root element. The 'day' elements and their attributes will be ignored, since they are nested further inside 'date' elements. If we wanted to use this XML data in a Visual Web Developer control we would therefore need to represent all of the data using attributes. We would have to rewrite the XML document like this:

```
<?xml version="1.0" encoding="utf-8" ?>
<!-- File: Example8-5.xml -->
```

```
<dates>
    <date calendar="gregorian" name="Saturday" day="1"
        month="3" year="2005" />
    <date calendar="gregorian" name="Sunday" day="2"
        month="3" year="2005" />
</dates>
```

You might be wondering what you can do if you have an XML document that uses elements rather than attributes but you want to use its data in a Visual Web Developer control without changing the original document. Later in this chapter we will see how an XML document can be transformed from one structure to another, in order to achieve this. In the meantime, however, we will work with documents that already have the necessary structure. Given the constraints of having to represent all of our XML data using attributes, the following XML document, 'policies.xml', which lists some insurance policy information, has an appropriate structure for use with an XmlDataSource control:

```
<?xml version="1.0" encoding="utf-8"?>
<!-- File: policies.xml -->
<policies>
  <policy policy-number="1625344" policy-type="buildings"
      start-date="2007-12-12" annual-premium="45.50"
      number-of-claims="5" paid-up="true"/>
  <policy policy-number="0352342" policy-type="contents"
      start-date="2004-11-23" annual-premium="30.00"
      number-of-claims="0" paid-up="true"/>
  <policy policy-number="0353424" policy-type="buildings"
      start-date="2008-04-01" annual-premium="75.00"
      number-of-claims="0" paid-up="false"/>
  <policy policy-number="2231425" policy-type="contents"
      start-date="1998-01-11" annual-premium="25.00"
      number-of-claims="2" paid-up="true"/>
  <policy policy-number="2837362" policy-type="contents"
      start-date="2000-10-15" annual-premium="39.50"
      number-of-claims="1" paid-up="true"/>
  <policy policy-number="1827322" policy-type="buildings"
      start-date="2003-06-28" annual-premium="58.50"
      number-of-claims="0" paid-up="true"/>
</policies>
```

You will need to have this document available within the folders of a Visual Web Developer website project to use it as the data source for an XmlDataSource component. To use this document in a web form, we will first need to add a new XmlDataSource control (from the Toolbox) to the form. Figure 8.4 shows the XmlDataSource control listed in the Data section of the Toolbox, and one of these controls added to a form ('Example8-6.aspx') in Design view. Like a number of the other controls we have seen before, this control has a 'Tasks' menu that can be invoked by clicking on the arrow head that appears when the control is selected.

The XmlDataSource Tasks menu contains an option called 'Configure Data Source. . .' If you click on this option, the dialog shown in Figure 8.5 will appear, enabling you to associate a specific XML file with the data source. If you click the 'Browse. . .' button next to the 'Data file:' text field, you will be able to select from a list of available XML files within the web application. In Figure 8.5, the 'policies.xml' file has been selected. For the first example we will be leaving the 'Transform file:' and 'XPath expression:' text boxes blank.

Once the XML file has been selected, click the 'OK' button. The appearance of the data source control in Design View will be unchanged, but if you switch to Source view

FIGURE 8.4   Adding an XmlDataSource control to a web form

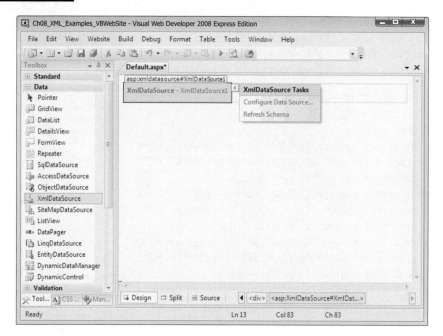

FIGURE 8.5   Selecting an XML source file in the Configure Data Source dialog

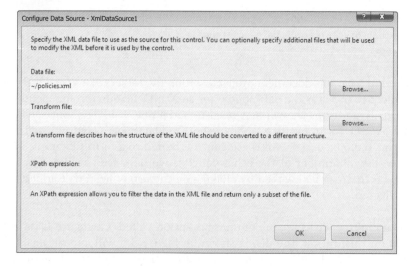

you will see that the name of the XML file has been added to the 'asp:XmlDataSource' element:

```
<div>
  <asp:XmlDataSource ID="XmlDataSource1" runat="server"
     DataFile="~/policies.xml">
  </asp:XmlDataSource>
</div>
```

At this stage, viewing the web form in a browser will simply give us an empty page. This is because we need to use one of the view controls in the Data section of the Toolbox to actually display the data from the XmlDataSource. For this example, we will be using the GridView control, which will display the data from the XML document using a table.

You will need to add a GridView control to your web form. Initially, this GridView will not be associated with any data source, so if you look at it in Design view, it shows some default data. To associate this view with an XmlDataSource, you need to select the name of the data source from the 'Choose Data Source:' drop-down list, which appears on the 'GridView Tasks' menu (Figure 8.6).

Once you choose the data source (in our example 'XmlDataSource1', which is the default name given by Visual Web Developer), Design view will immediately update to show the actual data from the XML document associated with the control (Figure 8.7).

FIGURE 8.6   A GridView added to a web form, displaying some default data. The GridView Tasks menu is displayed, which includes the 'Choose Data Source' option

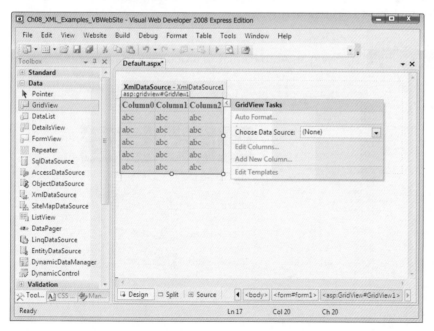

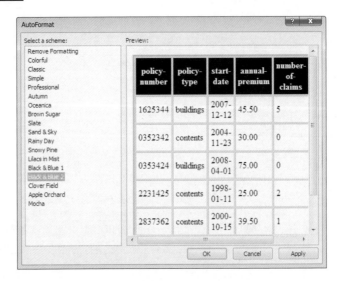

8.4.1 Formatting a GridView

The GridView as it stands does not look all that great. Fortunately the GridView Tasks menu includes an 'Auto Format...' option that lets you format the GridView by selecting from a number of different styles. This example ('Example8-7.aspx') uses the 'Black & Blue 2' auto format (Figure 8.8).

FIGURE 8.8   Applying an Auto Format to a GridView component

Another aspect of the GridView is that the column headings are by default taken directly from the attribute names in the XML document being used as the data source. Since these attribute names do not necessarily make good column headings we can change them using the 'Edit Columns' options of the GridView Tasks menu. Figure 8.9 shows the 'Fields' dialog. A field selected from the lower left list window can be edited in the 'BoundField properties' window on the right of the dialog. In Figure 8.9 we can see the 'Header Text' property being edited for the first column of the table.

FIGURE 8.9 Editing the column headings of a GridView in the Fields dialog

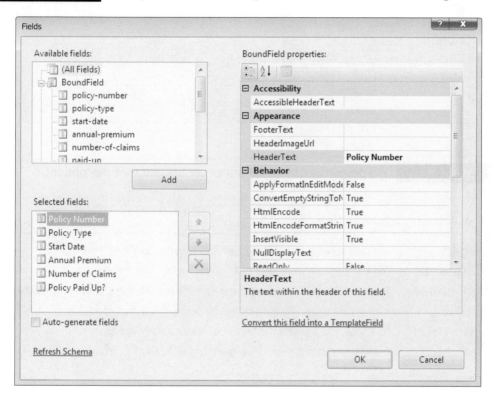

Figure 8.10 shows the GridView displayed in a browser after the format and column headings have been modified (see 'Example8-8.aspx'). You should note, however, that changes made to the column headings will be undone if we change the underlying data source in any way and then refresh the schema.

8.4.2 Using an XML data source with an AdRotator control

The GridView is not the only control that can be configured using an XmlDataSource. In fact there are several, one of which is the AdRotator, which can be found in the 'Standard' group of the Toolbox. The AdRotator control is used to display an image, selected at random from a number of available advertisements. The next image is selected and displayed each time the page is viewed or refreshed. In a context like the WebHomeCover site, an AdRotator control might be used to include advertisements for complementary partner products (perhaps integrated using Web Services). The information that can be associated with each advertisement is specified by the properties shown in Table 8.1.

FIGURE 8.10 A GridView with an AutoFormat applied and modified column headings

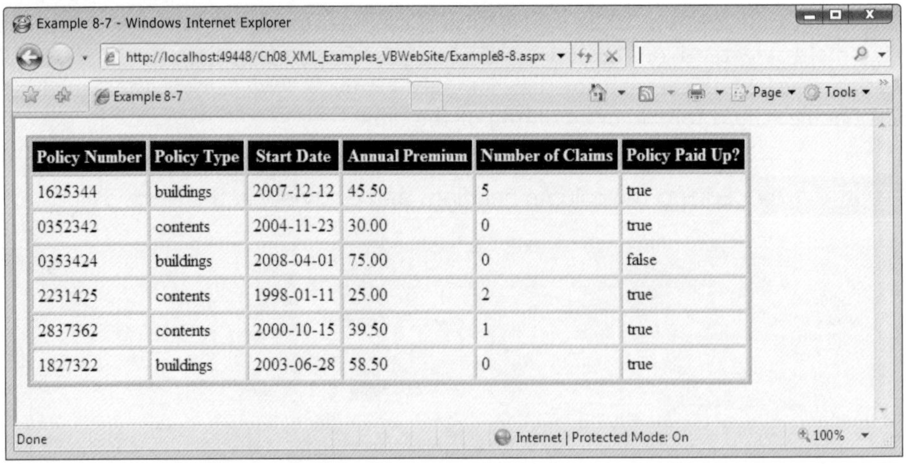

Policy Number	Policy Type	Start Date	Annual Premium	Number of Claims	Policy Paid Up?
1625344	buildings	2007-12-12	45.50	5	true
0352342	contents	2004-11-23	30.00	0	true
0353424	buildings	2008-04-01	75.00	0	false
2231425	contents	1998-01-11	25.00	2	true
2837362	contents	2000-10-15	39.50	1	true
1827322	buildings	2003-06-28	58.50	0	true

TABLE 8.1   The properties of the AdRotator control and their descriptions

Property	Description
ImageURL	The web address of the image file containing the advert
NavigateURL	The link to follow when user clicks on the image
AlternativeText	The text to be displayed if an image cannot be viewed, to improve accessibility
Keyword	A keyword that can be used by the control to filter a class of adverts
Impressions	An integer that weights the frequency with which the ad appears
Width, Height	Override the default dimensions given by the AdRotator control

The AdRotator control can be configured to use an XmlDataSource to provide this information. The XML file associated with the data source must have the correct structure to provide the necessary information to the AdRotator. This is an example of a correctly structured XML file defining a set of advertisement images. It has an 'Advertisements' root element, within which are a series of one or more 'Ad' elements. Within each 'Ad' element you need to provide at least the first three subelements for each 'Ad' entry in the Advertisements file (i.e. 'ImageUrl', 'NavigateUrl' and 'AlternateText' are required, but 'Impressions' and 'Keyword' are optional). You will note that the rules for creating an advertisements file for an AdRotator are very different from those that apply when you are creating your own XML data for other types of control. In the previous example, we had to provide all of our data as attributes. However for an AdRotator the required structure is specified by the control, and is based on nested elements.

```
<?xml version="1.0" encoding="utf-8" ?>
<!-- File: adverts.xml -->
```

```
<Advertisements>
 <Ad>
  <ImageUrl>insurepet.jpg</ImageUrl>
  <NavigateUrl>PetInsurancePartner.htm</NavigateUrl>
  <AlternateText>Link to pet insurance</AlternateText>
  <Impressions>1</Impressions>
  <Keyword>animal</Keyword>
 </Ad>
 <Ad>
  <ImageUrl>carinsure.jpg</ImageUrl>
  <NavigateUrl>CarInsurancePartner.htm</NavigateUrl>
  <AlternateText>Link to car insurance</AlternateText>
  <Impressions>2</Impressions>
  <Keyword>vehicle</Keyword>
 </Ad>
</Advertisements>
```

In this example, the second image would appear twice as frequently as the first, because of the value of the 'Impressions' element. Also, if the AdRotator's 'KeywordFilter' property is set to 'vehicle' the first advert will not appear, only the second one, and any others tagged with the same keyword.

Figure 8.11 shows an example of a web form ('Example8-9.aspx') that uses the AdRotator control in Design view. The XmlDataSource needs to be associated with the 'adverts.xml' file using its tasks menu (as we did in the previous example). Then the XmlDataSource needs to be applied to the AdRotator.

FIGURE 8.11 An XmlDataSource and an AdRotator control in Design view, with the AdRotator's Tasks menu and Properties window

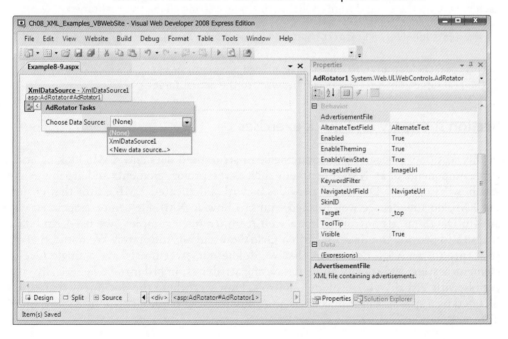

The images will not be visible in Design view, only when the page is viewed in a browser. Figure 8.12 shows one of the advert images being displayed by the AdRotator.

FIGURE 8.12   An image displayed by an AdRotator viewed in a browser

With an AdRotator, the XML file can also be specified using its 'AdvertisementFile' property, instead of using an XmlDataSource. You should note, however, that using this option means that you would not be able to apply XPath expressions or XSL transformations (covered in the next section) to the XML file. It is also possible to configure an AdRotator to retrieve its image data from other data sources such as a database, or directly from a handler for the control's 'AdCreated' event.

It is possible to gather statistics on the popularity of the different advertisements by routing each advert via the same dummy URL with a query string giving the real target.

```
<NavigateUrl>dummyURL.aspx?target=advertTwo.html</NavigateUrl>
```

In this case, the dummyURL must have a 'Page_Load' event handler which counts accesses to the real target, then redirects the browser to the actual target.

Section summary and quick exercises

In this section we began by introducing semi-structured data and XML, looking at the core components of an XML document such as the prolog, elements and attributes. We saw how Visual Web Developer provides us with a dedicated XML editor that ensures our XML documents are well formed, and saw how an XML file can be associated with an XmlDataSource control within a web form. In our examples, we used XmlData-Sources to provide the data for both a GridView and an AdRotator. We noted that the structure for an XML document that we define ourselves must have a single level of element nesting, and specify all its data using attributes, in order to be generically compatible with Visual Web Developer controls. However where the document structure is dictated by a specific control, such as an AdRotator, the required structure may be very different.

Create a new XML document that will contain data related to contents insurance quotes. Use the following data in your document:

- First quote
    - o no accidental cover, a cover amount of 10000, no policy excess and an insurance quote of 40
- Second quote
    - o no accidental cover, a cover amount of 20000, a policy excess of 500 and an insurance quote of 72
- Third quote
    - o no accidental cover, a cover amount of 30000, a policy excess of 1000 and an insurance quote of 96
- Fourth quote
    - o accidental cover, a cover amount of 50000, no policy excess and an insurance quote of 200
- Fifth quote
    - o accidental cover, a cover amount of 10000, a policy excess of 500 and an insurance quote of 36

Remember that to be generically compatible with Visual Web Developer controls, your document must have only one level of nested element beneath the root element, and all the data must be represented using attributes rather than elements. Make sure the file is well-formed (i.e. when the XML editor in Visual Web Developer does not indicate any problems with the file).

Create a new web form and add an XmlDataSource control to it. Configure the data source so that it uses the XML file you have created.

Add a GridView control to your web form. Associate it with your XmlDataSource to display the data from your XML document.

Add a DetailsView control to your web form. Like the GridView, you will find this control in the Data section of the Toolbox. Use its 'Tasks' menu to use the same XmlDataSource as your GridView. Check the 'Enable Paging' check box, so that you can see more than one element of the XML document in the view (by default the DetailsView will only display the first element). You can of course apply one of the AutoFormat options if you wish, and resize the control. View the web form in the browser so you can see the DetailsView in action.

8

8.5 Using XPath to select XML data

In the examples and exercises from the previous section that used the GridView control to display XML data, the GridViews showed all the elements from the XML source files. For XML files as small as the ones we have used so far this is not an issue. However in other cases we might want to filter the contents of an XML document so that only some of the elements are selected from it, depending on some criteria. The configuration dialog for the XmlDataSource enables you to do this by adding an XPath expression. As the label on the dialog explains; 'An XPath expression allows you to filter the data in the XML file and return only a subset of the file'.

XPath (XML Path) provides a language for accessing parts of an XML document. It is also used by eXtensible Stylesheet Language Transformations (XSLT), which we look at later in this chapter. The main role of XPath is to provide an expression syntax appropriate for selecting one or more nodes from an XML document.

8.5.1 XPath and XML nodes

To understand the way that the XPath data model works, we need to visualize an XML document as a tree of nodes. There are seven types of node, but the main node types that we process in XPath expressions are elements and attributes. Much of the syntax in XPath is based on the relationships between nodes, expressed as if the tree was in fact a family tree. Therefore we refer to 'parent', 'child', 'ancestor' and 'descendant' nodes. In the following document, for example, 'date' is a child node of 'dates'. From the other perspective, 'dates' is therefore the parent of 'date'. 'dates' is an ancestor of 'day', because the 'day' element is ultimately nested within, although it is not its direct child. Of course, this being the case, 'day' is a descendant of 'dates'.

```
<?xml version="1.0" encoding="utf-8"?>
<!-- File: Example8-4.xml -->
<dates>
    <date calendar="gregorian">
        <day name="Saturday" number="20" month="9" year="2008" />
    </date>
    <date calendar="gregorian">
        <day name="Sunday" number="21" month="9" year="2008" />
    </date>
</dates>
```

The nodes in an XML document appear in a *document order*. In the example above, the 'dates' element, which is at the document root, comes first in the document order. Then we come to the first 'date' node. Inside the 'date' node is a 'day', followed by the next 'date' node, and so on until we have traversed the whole document and got back to the root. XPath expressions take account of the document order. When several elements are returned by an XPath expression, they are returned in the same order as they are encountered in the document.

8.5.2 The context – the starting point of an XPath expression

In order to evaluate an expression, the XPath query has to start at a particular node. The starting node used for the query is known as the *context*. From there, the expression will use a *location path* to identify parts of an XML document. Location paths can be either relative to the current node or absolute (from the root node). A relative path begins with the name of a node. The path from a parent node to a child node is indicated by the '/' character. For example, the expression:

```
date/day
```

would be relative to the current context node, and would therefore only make sense if the current context was the 'dates' node. In contrast, an absolute path begins with the root node, which is the '/' character with no preceding parent node, as in this example:

```
/dates/date/day
```

Here, it does not matter what the current context is because we are not using an expression that is relative to it. An absolute path is the same regardless of the current context.

It is important to note that there is a distinction in XML between the document root and the root element. The root element is the first element after the document root. In the XPath expression above, the first '/' character means the document root, whereas 'dates' is the root element. This distinction is important when writing XPath expression and later when we create XSL transformations.

Elements in an XPath expression are identified simply by their names. Attributes, however, are preceded by the '@' symbol. For example the 'calendar' attribute in 'Example8-4.xml' would be identified as '@calendar' in an XPath expression.

8.5.3 Applying XPath expressions to an XmlDataSource

To explore how XPath works, we will use the 'policies.xml' XML document that we have already linked with an XmlDataSource in 'Example8-6.aspx' and see the results of applying different XPath queries to it. To access nodes that are nested, one approach is to use a series of 'child' operators to specify the full path through the document. Starting from the document root, the following XPath expression traverses through the nodes of the XML tree to the 'policy' elements, returning them in their original document order.

```
/policies/policy
```

The resulting nodes would therefore be all of the policy elements, i.e. the whole document for our example.

Instead of navigating through each sub-element to define the query context, we can use the // (descendant) operator to directly select an element without specifying the full path. e.g.:

```
//policy
```

8

Just specifying elements from our document is not very helpful, since there is only one level of nesting. This means that both of our examples so far will return the entire document. To select only some parts of the document, we can apply filter patterns (enclosed in square brackets) to the XPath expression. The filter pattern must evaluate to a Boolean value and is tested against each node that is selected by the main part of the expression, so that only nodes that pass the test are returned. For example, the following expression will return only those 'policy' elements where the value of the 'policy-type' attribute is 'contents' (three of the policy elements in our example document). This expression uses the equality operator ('=') in the filter:

```
/policies/policy[@policy-type = "contents"]
```

This particular example is comparing text values, so the string we are looking for (contents) must appear in either quote marks or apostrophes. To see this XPath expression in action, you can reopen the 'Configure Data Source' dialog from the XmlDataSource 'Tasks' menu and add the expression to the 'XPath expression:' text field (Figure 8.13).

FIGURE 8.13 Adding an XPath expression to the data source configuration dialog

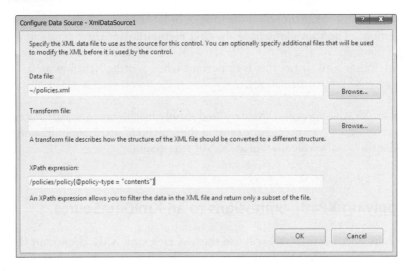

If changes have been made to the configuration, when you click the 'OK' button in the Configure Data Source dialog a notification similar to that in Figure 8.14 will appear for any view components that are linked to the data source that has been updated. In our example there is a single GridView that uses the XmlDataSource, which will be regenerated (have its data updated to reflect the XPath expression). Note the warning on the dialog that all existing column fields will be deleted. This will include any column headings that you have manually updated.

Figure 8.15 shows what the GridView looks like after the XPath expression has been added to the data source configuration. Now, only the elements that relate to 'contents' polices are shown in the table. Once the view has been regenerated, then any changes to the column headings will of course be lost, as can be seen from Figure 8.15 where the column headings are back to the attribute names again. Therefore it is best not to modify these headings until you are happy with the data source configuration.

FIGURE 8.14	The dialog that appears if view components are dependent on a data source that has been reconfigured

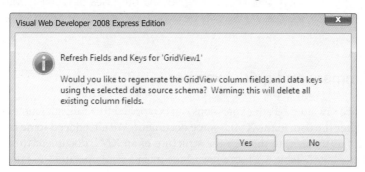

FIGURE 8.15	The resulting GridView after the XPath expression in Figure 8.13 has been applied to the related XmlDataSource

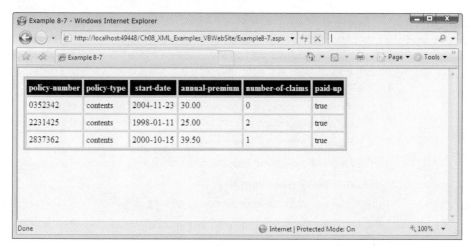

Our first XPath example used the equality operator ('=') with some text data. The inequality (not equal to) operator (the '!=' symbol) can also be used with text data. When working with numeric data, XPath expressions can also include the usual set of relational operators ('>', '<', '>=', '<='). Here, for example, we apply an expression that only returns policy elements where the annual premium is more than 50 (only two elements in our example). Note that numeric data in an XPath expression is not enclosed in quote marks or apostrophes:

```
/policies/policy[@annual-premium > 50]
```

It is also possible to combine multiple conditions together using 'and', as in this example where we select all paid up policies that have had no claims made against them. Note that one part of the expression uses text-based data and the other uses numeric data:

```
/policies/policy[@paid-up = "true" and @number-of-claims = 0]
```

Similarly, we can use 'or' in these expressions:

```
/policies/policy[@paid-up = "true" or @number-of-claims = 0]
```

NOTE XPath expressions can also do arithmetic and express quite complex query criteria. However, for the purposes of working with XmlData-Sources, we will only be using basic aspects of XPath syntax.

Section summary and quick exercises

In this section we saw how XPath expressions can be applied to XmlDataSources in Visual Web Developer to filter the data in the XML source document. We introduced some basic XPath syntax that enables us to navigate through the structure of an XML document to identify specific elements and attributes. Table 8.2 lists a few of the main XPath operators and their meanings.

TABLE 8.2   XPath operators

Operator	Meaning
/	Child operator. Selects children of whatever is to the left of it. If there is nothing to the left, it starts at the root element. In XPath a 'child' is an immediate child (e.g. grandchildren are not children)
//	Stands for any number of intermediate elements, to express ancestor–descendant relationships
.	The current context (the current node)
..	The parent of the current node
*	Wildcard. Matches all elements
@	Distinguishes attributes from elements (attribute prefix)

For the following exercises we will be applying XPath expressions to the 'policies.xml' document used for the examples in this section. To test an XPath expression, add it to the configuration dialog of an XmlDataSource control that uses the 'policies.xml' document as its data source. You will also need a view component (such as a GridView) on the web form, associated with this data source, to see the results of your XPath expressions.

EXERCISE 8.5

Write an XPath expression to select all buildings insurance policies.

EXERCISE 8.6

Write an XPath expression that would select only the element with policy number '2231425' from the XML document.

EXERCISE 8.7

Write an XPath expression to select all the policies where there has been at least one claim.

Write an XPath expression to select all policies that are paid up and have had more than one claim.

8.6 eXtensible Stylesheet Language Transformations (XSLT)

In previous examples we have seen that the XmlDataSource control in Visual Web Developer can only handle XML documents that have elements nested to one level below the root element, and represent that data using attributes rather than nested elements. However there may be occasions when we want to use data from an XML document in a web form that does not have this simple structure. One option that we have when configuring an XmlDataSource is to apply an eXtensible Stylesheet Language Transformation (XSLT). XSLT is part of the eXtensible Stylesheet Language family (XSL), which is a set of standards for XML document transformation and presentation. It consists of three parts; XSLT, XPath and XSL Formatting Objects (XSL-FO). XSL transformations can transform XML documents into various other types of document. These may be other XML documents, HTML / XHTML documents or any type of text document. For our purposes the main focus will be the transformation of XML documents to enable their data to be used in an XmlDataSource. As we saw in the previous section, XPath is an expression language that can select certain parts of an XML document. It is used by XSLT to help specify which parts of the source document are to be included in the output document.

8.6.1 Processing XSLT

An XSLT stylesheet, or transform, consists of a number of aspects. An important part of XSLT is XPath, because it is XPath that is used to identify content from the input document that will be included in the output document. XSLT uses *template matching* to process different parts of the input document in different ways. When an XML document is transformed using an XSLT stylesheet, a process of pattern matching takes place, where the XPath expressions used in the XSLT identify particular parts of the input document. Nodes that match the template's XPath expression are included in the output document. For the examples in this section we will be using the following 'policy-claims.xml' document. In its current state, we cannot use this document in an XmlDataSource, but we can apply an XSLT transformation to create a different XML document that contains the same data but has the structure that we require.

```
<?xml version="1.0" encoding="utf-8"?>
<!-- File: policy-claims.xml -->
<policy-claims>
 <policy type="contents">
  <policy-holder>A. Liu</policy-holder>
  <claim-history>
   <number-of-claims>1</number-of-claims>
   <total-claim-value>250</total-claim-value>
```

```
    </claim-history>
   </policy>
   <policy type="contents">
    <policy-holder>B. Singh</policy-holder>
   </policy>
   <policy type="buildings">
    <policy-holder>C. Jones</policy-holder>
     <claim-history>
      <number-of-claims>1</number-of-claims>
      <total-claim-value>7500</total-claim-value>
     </claim-history>
   </policy>
   <policy type="contents">
    <policy-holder>D. Umaga</policy-holder>
    <claim-history>
      <number-of-claims>2</number-of-claims>
      <total-claim-value>875</total-claim-value>
    </claim-history>
   </policy>
   <policy type="buildings">
    <policy-holder>E. Tolstoy</policy-holder>
   </policy>
  </policy-claims>
```

8.6.2 Creating a XSL transformation in Visual Web Developer

Visual Web Developer includes an 'XSLT file' option in its 'Add New Item' dialog (Figure 8.16).

FIGURE 8.16   Creating a new XSLT file in the Add New Item dialog

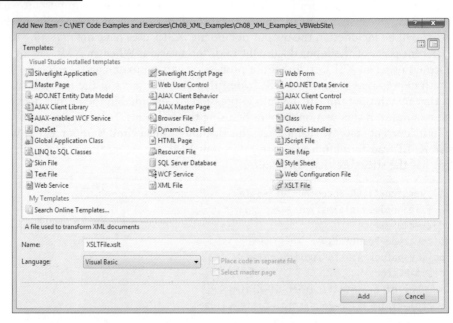

Rather bizarrely, Visual Web Developer by default adds an 'xslt' extension to an XSLT file, but when it looks for XSL transformation files to use with XmlDataSources it looks for files with an 'xsl' extension. Because of this, it is helpful if you edit the file extension from 'xslt' to 'xsl' before clicking the 'Add' button. For the remainder of this section we will assume that we have created an XSLT file called 'policy-claims.xsl'.

When you first create a new XSLT file, when it opens in the editor it will already contain a number of elements. You will see from this that an XSLT file is itself an XML document:

```
<?xml version="1.0" encoding="utf-8"?>
<xsl:stylesheet version="1.0"
  xmlns:xsl="http://www.w3.org/1999/XSL/Transform"
  xmlns:msxsl="urn:schemas-microsoft-com:xslt"
  exclude-result-prefixes="msxsl">
  <xsl:output method="xml" indent="yes"/>

  <xsl:template match="@* | node()">
    <xsl:copy>
      <xsl:apply-templates select="@* | node()"/>
    </xsl:copy>
  </xsl:template>
</xsl:stylesheet>
```

The first element of the XSL document ('xsl:stylesheet') includes attributes that specify the version number ('1.0' or '2.0') and a namespace reference. The usual prefix for the XSLT namespace is 'xsl', as specified by the 'xmlns:xsl' attribute. The value of namespace attribute ('http://www.w3.org/1999/XSL/Transform') is a good example of a URI, since it does not represent a downloadable resource. However if you put the URI into a browser the resulting page identifies it as being the XSLT namespace. The root element for an XSL transform can be either 'xsl:stylesheet', as it is in the file generated by Visual Web Developer, or 'xsl:transform', but both mean exactly the same thing. The other attributes in the root element need not concern us here as they are Microsoft-specific.

XSL Transformations can generate output using three different methods ('xml', 'html' or 'text'). The required method can be specified by using the 'xsl:output' element, which has a 'method' attribute. In the generated file you can see that the method is set to 'xml' (which is in fact the default for XSL transformations). The 'indent' attribute specifies if the generated output document will include indents:

```
<xsl:output method="xml" indent="yes"/>
```

8.6.3 Template matching

An XSL transformation contains one or more 'xsl:template' elements. These elements have a 'match' attribute, the value of which is an XPath expression:

```
<xsl:template match="XPath expression">
```

Visual Web Developer generates a default 'xsl:template' element, with some example syntax that we can safely ignore and replace with our own XPath expressions:

```
<xsl:template match="@* | node()">
```

In fact the asterisk is a wild card, so '@*' means any attribute, and 'node()' means any node (including both elements and text nodes). The vertical bar ('|') means 'or', so the default 'match' attribute matches any attribute or any node in the current context. Inside this template match there is a 'copy' element that copies any elements or attributes below the current context using a recursive 'apply-templates' element:

```
<xsl:copy>
 <xsl:apply-templates select="@* | node()"/>
</xsl:copy>
```

The effect of this default transformation file is that it simply makes a copy of the entire input document and writes it to the output document. Our match criteria will need to be a little more specific, so you should delete this default 'xsl:template' element to create your own transformations.

The expression used in the 'match' attribute must match something in the XML document being processed. The basic idea is that an XSL transformation includes one or more 'template' elements that match some part, or parts, of a source XML document, with the matching being done by XPath expressions. The body of the template element defines what is sent to the output document if that element is matched. An 'xsl:template' element therefore has this structure:

```
<xsl:template match="XPath expression">
...specify what goes to the output document here
</xsl:template>
```

The 'match' attribute of an 'xsl:template' start tag must contain a valid XPath expression, using the syntax we introduced earlier in this chapter. To apply a template to the document root, for example, the value of the 'match' attribute is the XPath expression for the root, which is '/':

```
<xsl:template match="/">
...define the transformation for the document root here
</xsl:template>
```

Another example from the 'policy-claims.xml' document might be to match the 'policy-claims' elements, again using standard XPath:

```
<xsl:template match="//policy-claims">
...define the transformation for the policy-claims elements here
</xsl:template>
```

8.6.4 Transformations using template matching

XSLT gives us two different ways of designing a transformation; output driven (pull) and input driven (push). In an output driven transformation, the required structure of the output document drives the transformation. This is appropriate when the structure of the output document is something like XHTML, where much of the generated mark-up will be specifically created for the output document but is not present in the input document. In the case of transforming one XML document into another for use in an XmlDataSource, an input driven approach is probably better because we will be converting the whole XML document into one with a related structure.

An input driven transformation applies *template rules* to particular elements wherever, and however, many times they may be found in the input document. In this type of transformation we define multiple template rules, with each 'xsl:template' element providing a rule for how one particular type of node should be processed when it is found, enabling us to transform the nodes of an XML document without having to anticipate their order or number. Instead of managing the flow of execution, as we would in an output driven transformation, we leave the XSL processor to apply the template rules to the input document, generating the output from the structure of the input.

The first thing to do when creating a transformation that matches template rules is to identify the nodes that we want to process in the document. There are two things that we need to do to our document in order to make it compatible with an XmlDataSource. First, we need to ensure that elements are not nested more than one level below the root element. Second, we need to convert element data to attribute data. If we look at the structure of the current document, there are two levels of nesting below the 'policy' element (highlighted in bold here). Our transformation will have to take the data contained in these nested elements and convert it into attributes of the 'policy' elements.

```
<?xml version="1.0" encoding="utf-8"?>
<!-- File:policy-claims.xml -->
<policy-claims>
 <policy type="contents">
  <policy-holder>A. Liu</policy-holder>
  <claim-history>
   <number-of-claims>1</number-of-claims>
   <total-claim-value>250</total-claim-value>
  </claim-history>
 </policy>
 <policy type="contents">
  <policy-holder>B. Singh</policy-holder>
 </policy>
 <policy type="buildings">
  <policy-holder>C. Jones</policy-holder>
  <claim-history>
   <number-of-claims>1</number-of-claims>
   <total-claim-value>7500</total-claim-value>
  </claim-history>
 </policy>
 <policy type="contents">
  <policy-holder>D. Umaga</policy-holder>
  <claim-history>
   <number-of-claims>2</number-of-claims>
   <total-claim-value>875</total-claim-value>
  </claim-history>
 </policy>
 <policy type="buildings">
  <policy-holder>E. Tolstoy</policy-holder>
 </policy>
</policy-claims>
```

We will need a template rule for the document root, since this is where our processing will start, a template for the 'policy-claims' element so that we can recreate it in the output document, a template rule for the 'policy' element so that we can convert the nested 'policy-holder' element into an attribute, and another template rule for the 'claim-history' element so that both of its sub-elements can also be converted into attributes:

```
<xsl:template match="/">

<xsl:template match="policy-claims">

<xsl:template match="policy">

<xsl:template match="claim-history">
```

To trigger the process of pattern matching that will apply all of the template rules, we need to use the 'xsl:apply-templates' element. This has the effect of applying all the template rules that match to descendants of the current node. The XSLT processor will then work through all the template matches beneath this level and apply the necessary templates, preserving the original document order.

By default, using the 'xsl:apply-templates' element will apply to all of its descendants. To stop all descendants of the current node having templates applied, we can specify individual nodes to be selected using the 'select' attribute, as here, where we apply a template to the 'policy-claims' node, but not to all its descendants:

```
<xsl:apply-templates select="policy-claims"/>
```

What then will we do in these template rules? For the transformation required to convert the existing input document into an output document suitable for use with an XmlDataSource, we will be using the following elements:

- xsl:element
  - o Creates a new element in the output document.
- xsl:attribute
  - o Creates a new attribute in the output document.
- xsl:copy-of
  - o Copies complete elements or attributes from the input document directly into the output document.
- xsl:value-of
  - o Takes the value from an element or attribute in the input document so it can be copied to the output document.

8.6.5 Writing elements and attributes to the output document

The 'xsl:element' and 'xsl:attribute' tags, used to write elements and attributes to the output document, both have a 'name' attribute that specifies the name of the element or attribute to be used in the output document. This does not have to be same as a name in the input document, though in this example we will be using the same element names in both the input and output documents. This, for example, will create an element called 'policy' in the output document:

```
<xsl:element name="policy">
   ...element body here
</xsl:element>
```

This example will create an attribute called 'policy-holder' and write it to the output document:

```
<xsl:attribute name="policy-holder">
  ...attribute body here
</xsl:attribute>
```

Of course you have to organize your XSL transformation in such as way that this attribute is being written as part of an enclosing element. Here, for example, we can see that the 'policy-holder' attribute is being added to the 'policy' element, by nesting 'xsl:attribute' inside 'xsl:element':

```
<xsl:element name="policy">
 <xsl:attribute name="policy-holder">
 ...attribute body here
 </xsl:attribute>
</xsl:element>
```

Sometimes, rather than creating new elements and attributes, we simply want to copy existing elements or attributes from the input document to the output. The 'xsl:copy-of' element can be used to do this. For example, in our policy claims document, the policy elements contain a 'type' attribute:

```
<policy type="contents">
```

We can use 'xsl:copy-of' to simply copy this attribute directly from the input to the output. The 'select' attribute contains an XPath expression that specifies the element or attribute to be copied:

```
<xsl:copy-of select="@type"/>
```

In our example, the primary purpose of the transformation is to convert a set of nested elements into attributes. Therefore there is not much that can be directly copied from the input document. What we need to do is select the values from inside the elements so they can be written to attributes in the output document. In XSLT the 'xsl:value-of' element is used to indicate that the transformation will select the value of an element or an attribute from the source document. Again, the 'select' attribute specifies the XPath expression that will be used to identify the required node.

```
<xsl:value-of select="XPath expression"/>
```

The value returned from the XPath expression is inserted into the output document. A single 'xsl:value-of' element will only match a single node from the source document, which will be the first one that it matches in the document order.

In this example we can see the newly created 'policy-holder' attribute is being given a value from the 'policy-holder' element. Simply put, this code takes a 'policy-holder' element and converts it into a 'policy-holder' attribute.

```
<xsl:attribute name="policy-holder">
  <xsl:value-of select="policy-holder"/>
</xsl:attribute>
```

Having introduced the parts of XSLT syntax that will be used in our transformation, we now work through a complete transformation that will convert our 'policy-claims.xml' document into another document that can be handled by an XmlDataSource. First, there is a template rule applied to the root node. This template simply specifies that the next template rule will only apply to 'policy-claims' elements.

```
<xsl:template match="/">
 <xsl:apply-templates select="policy-claims"/>
</xsl:template>
```

The next template rule shows how a template is applied within the 'policy-claims' node. Here, an element called 'policy-claims' is written to the output document. The next template rule is then applied to 'policy' elements:

```
<xsl:template match="policy-claims">
 <xsl:element name="policy-claims">
  <xsl:apply-templates select="policy"/>
 </xsl:element>
</xsl:template>
```

If we applied only these two template rules, the generated output document would consist only of an empty 'policy-claim' element (since we have not yet defined what happens to 'policy' elements):

```
<policy-claims>
</policy-claims>
```

The next template rule will process all of the 'policy' elements. The template rule for a 'policy' creates a new element in the output document using the 'xsl:element' tag. It then directly copies an existing attribute ('type') using the 'xsl:copy-of' tag. Next, it converts an element into another attribute by creating a new attribute (with the 'xsl:attribute' tag) and putting a value into it using the 'xsl:value-of' tag. Further template rules are then applied to 'claim-history' elements:

```
<xsl:template match="policy">
 <xsl:element name="policy">
  <xsl:copy-of select="@type"/>
  <xsl:attribute name="policy-holder">
   <xsl:value-of select="policy-holder"/>
  </xsl:attribute>
  <xsl:apply-templates select="claim-history"/>
 </xsl:element>
</xsl:template>
```

After this template rule has been applied, the generated output document would contain the 'policy-claims' and 'policy' elements. Each policy element would contain two attributes:

```
<policy-claims>
 <policy type="contents" policy-holder="A. Liu"></policy>
 <policy type="contents" policy-holder="B. Singh" /></policy>
 <policy type="buildings" policy-holder="C. Jones" /></policy>
 <policy type="contents" policy-holder="D. Umaga" /></policy>
```

```
<policy type="buildings" policy-holder="E. Tolstoy" /></policy>
</policy-claims>
```

Here is the final template rule, applied to 'claim-history' nodes. This rule simply converts the two sub-elements ('number-of-claims' and 'total-claim-value') into attributes. Note that no new element is created in this template rule. These attributes are simply added to the 'policy' element created by the previous template rule. Since there are no further nodes to process, there is no 'apply-templates' element:

```
<xsl:template match="claim-history">
 <xsl:attribute name="number-of-claims">
  <xsl:value-of select="number-of-claims"/>
 </xsl:attribute>
 <xsl:attribute name="total-claim-value">
  <xsl:value-of select="total-claim-value"/>
 </xsl:attribute>
</xsl:template>
```

The final result of the transformation, when it is applied to the XML input document, will look something like this, though you will only be able to see this output by using a suitable software tool:

```
<policy-claims>
 <policy type="contents" policy-holder="A. Liu" number-of-claims="1"
 total-claim-value="250">
 </policy>
 <policy type="contents" policy-holder="B. Singh">
 </policy>
 <policy type="buildings" policy-holder="C. Jones" number-of-claims="1"
 total-claim-value="7500">
 </policy>
 <policy type="contents" policy-holder="D. Umaga" number-of-claims="2"
 total-claim-value="875">
 </policy>
 <policy type="buildings" policy-holder="E. Tolstoy">
 </policy>
</policy-claims>
```

 NOTE Different XSLT processors may generate slightly different output documents from the same transformation. For example, elements with no text content may be represented as true empty elements rather than using start and end tags.

8.6.6 Linking an XSLT stylesheet to an XML document

Unfortunately, the Express edition of Visual Web Developer does not provide us with a tool to view the output of an XSL transformation. This can cause problems, since if we associate a view component with an XmlDataSource that uses a transformation, and there is some problem with the output document, then the view will simply not show our data. Therefore before we link the XSLT to the source XML document via the data source configuration dialog, it is useful to test our transformation using other tools. A simple way of testing an XSL transformation is to use a browser such as Internet Explorer.

The first step is to directly link an XSLT to an XML document, which will help us to test the transformation using a browser. This is not required when applying a transformation in Visual Web Developer, because the XmlDataSource will apply the transformation to the XML externally, but is useful for testing. It is done by adding an XML stylesheet processing instruction to the top of the document. You may recall that a processing instruction looks very much like the XML declaration, because it is also surrounded by the '<?' and '?>' characters. The processing instruction for an XSLT transformation is 'xml-stylesheet' with 'text/xsl' as the value of the 'type' attribute. For example, here we link our 'policy-claims.xml' document to an XSLT stylesheet called 'policy-claims.xsl' by adding the following processing instruction to the top of the XML document:

```
<?xml version="1.0" encoding="utf-8"?>
<?xml-stylesheet type="text/xsl" href="policy-claims.xsl"?>
```

This processing instruction can be used by, for example, an XSLT enabled browser to transform the XML into the specified output document.

8.6.7 Testing XSL transformations in Internet Explorer

An XSLT enabled browser, like Internet Explorer 7, can perform XSL Transformations without additional configuration. If an XML document has a link element to an XSL stylesheet, then loading that XML document into the browser will trigger the transformation. The document that results from this transformation will be shown in the browser. There are, however, major limitations to this. First, most browsers only display non-empty elements from the resulting XML document, not attributes. In our case, we only want attributes in the output document, so even if the transformation is successful the browser display will be blank. In addition, when you choose the 'view source' option from the pop-up menu in the Internet Explorer window, you will see the original XML input document, not the generated output from the XSLT. Fortunately, there is an additional Internet Explorer XML/XSL Viewer Tools application ('iexmltls.exe') that you can download from Microsoft and install into your browser. If you install this tool, then the Internet Explorer pop-up menu will include the additional menu option 'View XSL Output'. Selecting this menu option will open up another window that shows you the document that the browser generated from the transformation.

NOTE	The download page for 'iexmltls.exe' explains the installation procedure for the XSLT tool and also for the XML validation tool that is part of the same application.

Figure 8.17 shows the XML document that results from this transformation, as displayed by the XSLT viewer tool added to Internet Explorer. The spelling error in the window title comes from the tool itself!

FIGURE 8.17   The XML document generated from the XSL Transformation of the 'policy-claims.xml' input document

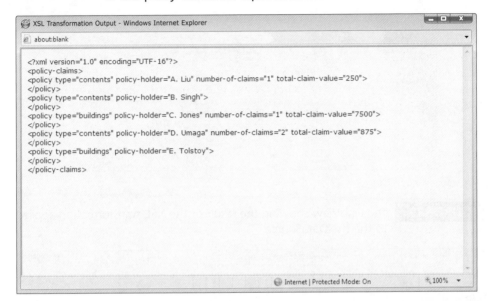

> **NOTE** The character encoding ('UTF-16') of the output document has been applied by the XSLT engine in Internet Explorer, and does not come from the original document which would use the default UTF-8 encoding.

8.6.8 Applying an XSL transformation to an XmlDataSource

Once we are happy that our XSL transformation is working as we want it to, by testing it in a browser, we can apply it to an XmlDataSource. This can be done in the Configure Data Source dialog, available from the 'XmlDataSource' Tasks menu. In this example, 'Example8-10.aspx', the XML file being used for the data source will be 'policy-claims.xml'. If you press the 'Browse' button next to the 'Transform file:' text box, you can select an XSLT file to apply to the XmlDataSource. Remember that this dialog will only look for a file with an 'xsl' extension, not an 'xslt' extension. In this example, the 'XPath expression' text field has been left empty, so we are only applying a transformation, not applying an XPath filter (Figure 8.18).

Figure 8.19 shows a Grid View in Design View connected to an XmlDataSource that uses the 'policy-claims.xsl' XSL transformation. Because the resulting data is semi-structured (not all policies have claims associated with them) parts of the grid are empty.

FIGURE 8.18 Applying an XSL Transform file to an XmlDataSource configuration

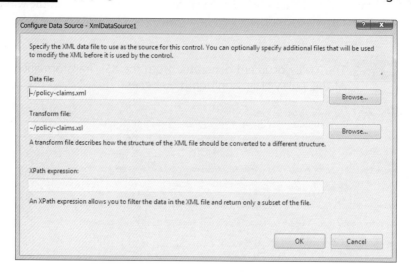

FIGURE 8.19 The GridView showing the result of the XSL transformation applied to the XmlDataSource

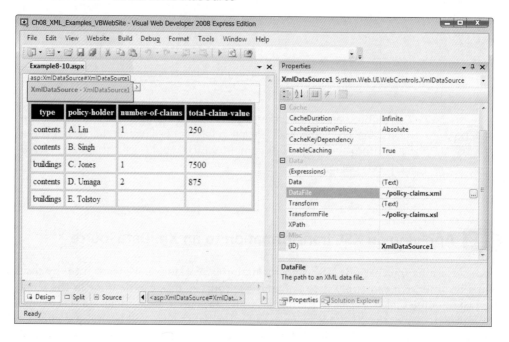

It is also possible to apply both an XSL transformation and an XPath expression to an Xml-DataSource. Here, we add an additional XPath filter so that only policies that have claims made against them are shown (see 'Example8-11.aspx'). In this case, the expression simply checks if a 'number-of-claims' attribute is present in the policy element. If it is not, the expression returns false and the element will not be included in the output (Figure 8.20). No operators are used in this XPath expression. Simply naming the attribute is enough for the XPath processor to check for its presence in a particular element.

FIGURE 8.20 Applying an XPath expression to the output document of an XSL transformation

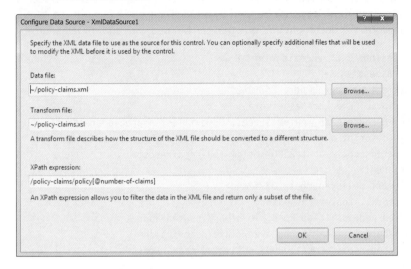

FIGURE 8.21 The resulting GridView after an XPath expression has been applied to the XSL transformation used by the XmlDataSource

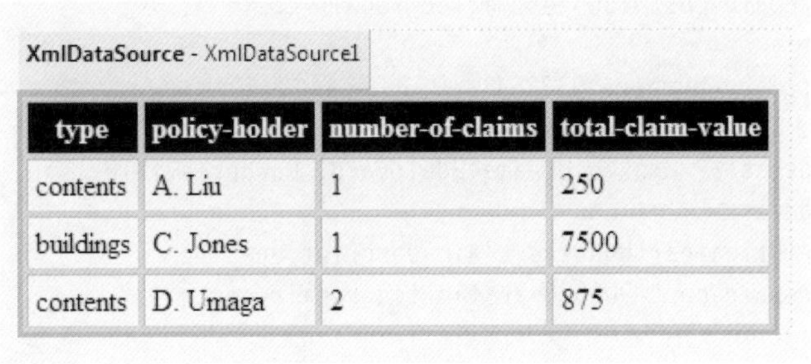

XmlDataSource - XmlDataSource1

type	policy-holder	number-of-claims	total-claim-value
contents	A. Liu	1	250
buildings	C. Jones	1	7500
contents	D. Umaga	2	875

Figure 8.21 shows the GridView after the XPath expression has been applied and the schema has been refreshed.

Section summary and quick exercises

In this section we applied an XSL transformation to an XML document in order to render its structure compatible with an XmlDataSource. The main job of the transformation in this context was to convert all nested elements into attribute data, and to remove any elements nested more than one level below the root element. We linked the XSL transformation to the XML document using the configuration dialog of the XmlDataSource. We also saw that it was possible to apply an XSL transformation directly to an XML document using a processing instruction, which is useful for testing XSLT using a browser, providing additional tools have been installed to view the resulting output document. Finally, we saw that the data source configuration dialog allows XPath expressions to be applied to the document that results from an XSL transformation.

EXERCISE 8.9

Here is an XML document ('assessments.xml') containing information about insurance claims assessments. In its current form, it cannot be used by an XmlDataSource component. Write an XSLT file that can transform this document into one that can be used with an XmlDataSource:

```xml
<?xml version="1.0" encoding="utf-8"?>
<claims-assessments>
 <assessment policy-number="2635142">
  <assessor>C. Checker</assessor>
  <insured-address>25 Medium Street, Homeville</insured-address>
  <claim-description>water leak</claim-description>
  <estimated-repair-cost>2500</estimated-repair-cost>
 </assessment>
 <assessment policy-number="0336254">
  <assessor>L. Looker</assessor>
  <insured-address>1 Top Road, Townton</insured-address>
  <claim-description>kitchen fire</claim-description>
  <estimated-repair-cost>10000</estimated-repair-cost>
 </assessment>
 <assessment policy-number="1162534">
  <assessor>T. Tester</assessor>
  <insured-address>118 Treelined Avenue, Suburbia</insured-address>
  <claim-description>meteorite strike</claim-description>
  <estimated-repair-cost>150</estimated-repair-cost>
 </assessment>
 <assessment policy-number="0322541">
  <assessor>I. Investigator</assessor>
  <insured-address>12 Broken Dreams Boulevard, Nowheresville
  </insured-address>
  <claim-description>earthquake</claim-description>
  <estimated-repair-cost>300000</estimated-repair-cost>
 </assessment>
</claims-assessments>
```

Create a web form containing an XmlDataSource, and configure this data source to use 'assessments.xml' and your XSLT file. Add a view component to the web form and configure it to use your XmlDataSource. Check that the view is able to display the data from the XML document. Figure 8.22 shows an XmlDataSource and a GridView in Design View, displaying the data that you should see if your transformation is successful.

EXERCISE 8.10

Modify your XSL Transformation so that it create attributes with different names from the elements in the input document, and puts them in a different order in the output document. Figure 8.23 shows an example.

EXERCISE 8.11

Add an XPath expression to the configuration of your XmlDataSource so that only those assessments with an estimated repair cost of over 5000 are shown in the associated view component.

8

FIGURE 8.22 A GridView using the input document and transformation for Exercise 8.9

policy-number	assessor	insured-address	claim-description	estimated-repair-cost
2635142	C. Checker	25 Medium Street, Homeville	water leak	2500
0336254	L. Looker	1 Top Road, Townton	kitchen fire	10000
1162534	T. Tester	118 Treelined Avenue, Suburbia	meteorite strike	150
0322541	I. Investigator	12 Broken Dreams Boulevard, Nowheresville	earthquake	300000

XmlDataSource - XmlDataSource1

FIGURE 8.23 A GridView showing data from an XmlDataSource that applies an XSL Transformation that reorders and renames the attributes in the output document

XmlDataSource - XmlDataSource1

description	cost	name	address	policy-number
water leak	2500	C. Checker	25 Medium Street, Homeville	2635142
kitchen fire	10000	L. Looker	1 Top Road, Townton	0336254
meteorite strike	150	T. Tester	118 Treelined Avenue, Suburbia	1162534
earthquake	300000	I. Investigator	12 Broken Dreams Boulevard, Nowheresville	0322541

8.7 Adding a site map

One of the page design patterns we introduced in Chapter 2 was the site map. The purpose of a site map is to provide a single-page overview of the whole website, enabling easy navigation to any page or webflow. Visual Web Developer provides a way of creating a site map based on an XML file called 'Web.sitemap'. To add one of these XML files to your web application, select 'Site Map' from the Add New Item dialog (Figure 8.24).

By default, the source of a site map file looks like this:

```
<?xml version="1.0" encoding="utf-8" ?>
<siteMap xmlns="http://schemas.microsoft.com/AspNet/SiteMap-File-1.0" >
 <siteMapNode url="" title="" description="">
  <siteMapNode url="" title="" description="" />
  <siteMapNode url="" title="" description="" />
 </siteMapNode>
</siteMap>
```

When a file like this is used by Visual Web Developer to display a site map, the nested elements are displayed using either a nested menu structure or a tree view, depending on which control you choose, as we will see in our examples. In either case there needs to be one node that acts as the root of the menu or tree view. The default file shows how the XML file needs to be structured in order to be valid. The root element is 'siteMap'. Within this element there must be a siteMapNode element that will act as the top level menu or tree view node. Within this element there can be many other siteMapNode elements,

FIGURE 8.24   Adding a site map XML file to the web application

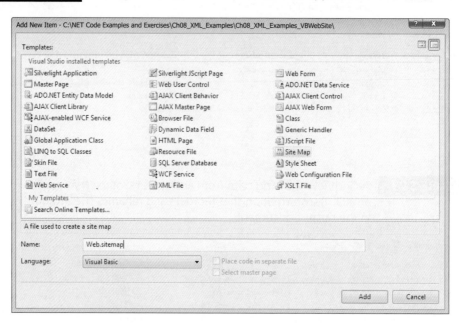

which in turn can be nested inside each other, or appear as empty elements without further nesting. Each siteMapNode element has a 'url' attribute (the URL of the page), a 'title' attribute (used in the displayed site maps) and a description (used as a tool tip). If you want to add a node to the tree or menu that simply acts as a heading for a group of items, but does not have its own associated page, then the 'url' attribute can be left as an empty string. First, we will populate the site map with some initial page references. In this example, there are links to the pages that were created in the examples and exercises in Chapter 7: 'Home.aspx', 'RegisterWizard.aspx', 'Services.aspx', 'AboutUs.aspx', 'ContactUs.aspx', 'Mail.aspx', 'Email.aspx' and 'Phone.aspx'. The home page ('Home.aspx') is acting as the root of the site map menu. Beneath this we have links to the 'About us' 'Register', 'Services' and 'Contact Us' page. The remaining pages show how the site map nodes can be nested inside each other to multiple levels, since they are nested inside the element for 'ContactUs.aspx'.

```xml
<?xml version="1.0" encoding="utf-8" ?>
<siteMap xmlns="http://schemas.microsoft.com/AspNet/SiteMap-File-1.0" >
    <siteMapNode url="Home.aspx" title="Home Page"
        description="WebHomeCover home page">
        <siteMapNode url="AboutUs.aspx" title="About Us"
            description="About our company" />
        <siteMapNode url="RegisterWizard.aspx" title="Register"
            description="Register yourself on our site" />
        <siteMapNode url="Services.aspx" title="Services"
            description="Find out about our insurance services" />
        <siteMapNode url="ContactUs.aspx" title="Contact Us"
            description="Different ways to contact WebHomeCover">
            <siteMapNode url="Mail.aspx" title="Mailing Addresses"
                description="Mailing addresses of our international offices" />
```

```
                <siteMapNode url="Email.aspx" title="Email Addresses"
                    description="Email addresses of our international offices" />
                <siteMapNode url="Phone.aspx" title="Phone and Fax numbers"
                    description=" phone and fax numbers of our international offices" />
            </siteMapNode>
        </siteMapNode>
    </siteMap>
```

8.7.1 Using a site map file in a web page

The XML site map we have created can be used as a data source to Visual Web Developer navigation controls. These can be found in the Toolbox in the 'Navigation' section (Figure 8.25). Both the Menu and TreeView controls can be used to display the site map data. As we will see later in this chapter, the SiteMapPath control can be used to implement the 'breadcrumbs' page design pattern that we introduced in Chapter 2. This, too, uses the data in the site map file.

For this example ('Example8-12.aspx') we will use a TreeView control to display the site map. Once we have added a TreeView control to the form we need to configure its data source. If you add a TreeView to a web form and try to view it in a browser before setting up the data source you will get a run time error. If you look at the form in Design view, you should see that the tree view is displayed as an outline of generic 'Root, 'Parent' and 'Leaf' entries. To make the TreeView display data from the site map file, you need to select the site map control in Design view and then click on the small arrow head at the top right of the control to get the 'TreeView Tasks' menu. In the TreeView Tasks dialog there is a 'Choose Data Source' select list. From the drop-down list, select <New data source...> (Figure 8.26).

FIGURE 8.25   The navigation controls in the Toolbox

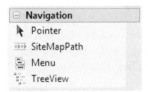

FIGURE 8.26   Selecting a new data source from the TreeView Tasks menu

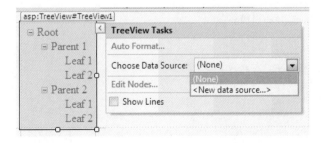

The Data Source Configuration Wizard that appears will give you the option of choosing from a 'Site Map' or an 'XML File'. Here, we will select the 'Site Map' icon (Figure 8.27). When you click 'OK', the site map file will be used as the data source for the tree view. You do not have to specify the name of the Site Map file, since the default name ('Web.sitemap') is the one that the Wizard expects to use. The default name used for the data source will be 'SiteMapDataSource1', though you can change this if you wish.

FIGURE 8.27 Selecting the Site Map icon in the Data Source Configuration Wizard

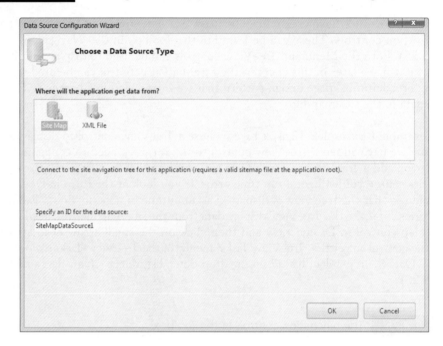

After adding the Site Map file as the data source, you should see that a SiteMapDataSource control has been added to Design view. In Source view, you will see that the TreeView has now been associated with the SiteMapDataSource.

```
<%@ Page Language="VB" AutoEventWireup="false" CodeFile="Example8-
12.aspx.vb" Inherits="Example8_12" %>
<!DOCTYPE html PUBLIC "-//W3C//DTD XHTML 1.0 Transitional//EN"
"http://www.w3.org/TR/xhtml1/DTD/xhtml1-transitional.dtd">
<html xmlns="http://www.w3.org/1999/xhtml">
 <head runat="server">
  <title>Example 8-12</title>
 </head>
 <body>
  <!-- File: Example8-12.aspx -->
  <form id="form1" runat="server">
   <div>
```

```
        <asp:TreeView ID="TreeView1" runat="server"
          DataSourceID="SiteMapDataSource1">
        </asp:TreeView>
        <asp:SiteMapDataSource ID="SiteMapDataSource1" runat="server" />
      </div>
    </form>
  </body>
</html>
```

Now the page can be successfully viewed in the browser, and you should be able to see all of the options we have added to the site map XML file. The tree view can also be collapsed or expanded (using the plus or minus signs next to the nodes) where the items are nested (Figure 8.28).

FIGURE 8.28   The site map page using a TreeView control

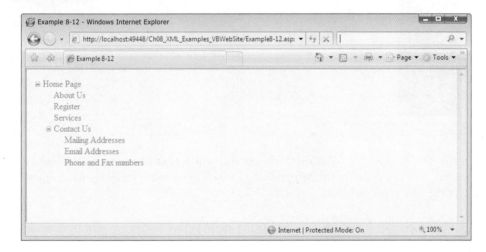

An obvious problem when we click on the links in the site map is that the page that it links to is using the master page, whereas our example web form is not. It would be useful to integrate the site map into the rest of our website by making it also use the master page.

To create a site map page that integrates with the rest of our pages, we will make a copy of 'Example8-12.aspx' and name it 'SiteMap.aspx'. Using the same approach that we introduced in Chapter 7, we can rearrange the content to use the master page and the main side navigation bar.

To make everything work together it would be useful to add a link to the site map page to the navigation bar of the master page, like this (added before the closing </div> tag of the 'navigationbar' div element):

```
<span class="topnavigationlink">
  <a href="SiteMap.aspx">Site Map</a>
</span>
```

8

Figure 8.29 shows the SiteMap.aspx page displayed in a browser. Note that the 'Site Map' link has also been added to the navigation bar of the master page.

FIGURE 8.29   The SiteMap.aspx page displayed in a browser

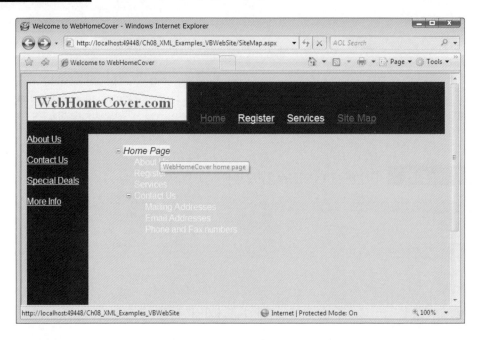

When the site map is displayed on the page, the white text of the unvisited links is not very visible. We can remedy this situation by cascading an extra stylesheet ('sitemap.css') that sets the link color to black:

```
a:link
{
 color: black
}
```

The 'SiteMap.aspx' file can then include a link to this stylesheet in its header, overriding the 'a:link' style in the master page stylesheet:

```
<asp:Content ID="Content1" ContentPlaceHolderID="head" Runat="Server">
<link href="sitemap.css" type="text/css" rel="Stylesheet" />
</asp:Content>
```

 NOTE   We could have created the 'SiteMap.aspx' directly from the master page. However if you try to do this you should add the TreeView to the form and set its data source before adding in the elements for the side navigation bar, otherwise you will probably find that Visual Web Developer adds the 'form' element around the side navigation bar Web User Control, instead of around the TreeView and its data source. In this situation, the 'form' element will have to be manually moved to its correct position.

8.7.2 Using the SiteMap file for menu controls

In the previous section we used the site map XML file as the data source for a TreeView control which we used in a web form. However an alternative way to display the site map file data is in a menu. In this example, we use the site map XML file as the data source for a menu that we use instead of the TreeView.

Like the TreeView, the menu control is in the 'Navigation' group in the Toolbox. In this example ('Example8-13.aspx') we add a menu control into the page. Just as when we used the TreeView control, we have to associate this menu with the site map file data source. Figure 8.30 shows the default appearance of the menu control in Design view, with the 'Choose Data Source' option in the 'Menu Tasks' menu.

As before, the data source we choose will be the site map file (see Figure 8.27). Once the data source has been applied, the top level option of the menu ('Home Page') will be visible in design view and in the browser when the page is displayed. Figure 8.31 shows the page with the different levels of the menu manually expanded, and a tool tip being

FIGURE 8.30 Choosing a data source for a menu control

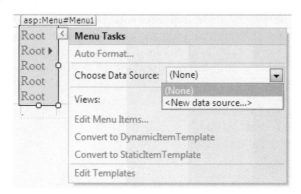

FIGURE 8.31 The menu control with all options expanded and a tool tip displayed

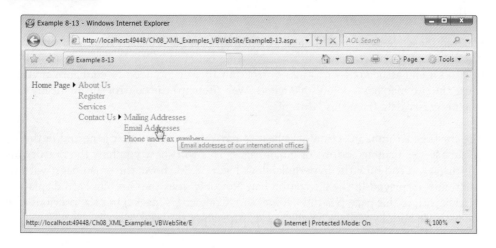

displayed. Although the menu by default will only display the top level option, you can override this in the properties window, by changing the 'StaticDisplayLevels' property. By default this will be set to '1', showing only one level of the menu, but you can use a higher value to show more levels by default.

8.8 Adding breadcrumbs with a SiteMapPath control

As well as providing the data for a site map displayed as a tree view or a menu, the site map XML file is also the data source for implementing the breadcrumbs pattern. The purpose of this design pattern is to provide the user with a trail that shows where they currently are within the navigation paths of the website. In addition, the pattern suggests that the elements of the breadcrumb trail should also be clickable hyperlinks. Visual Web Developer provides this functionality using the SiteMapPath control (from the 'Navigation' group of the Toolbox).

Since we would want to have a breadcrumb trail available at all times, it makes sense to add the SiteMapPath control to the navigation bar, which is indeed where the page design pattern specifies that it should appear. Therefore we need to add a SiteMapPath control to the master page, inside the 'navigationbar' div element. The breadcrumb trail normally appears on the line below the main hyperlinks in the navigation bar, so here we use a line break element after the SiteMap link, and add a span element beneath it. This does not need to have the same styles as the links in the main navigation bar so has not been assigned a css class in this example. The SiteMapPath control can then be added to the span from the Toolbox:

```
...previous span elements...
<span class="topnavigationlink">
 <a href="SiteMap.aspx">Site map</a>
</span>
<br />
<span>
 <asp:SiteMapPath ID="SiteMapPath1" runat="server">
 </asp:SiteMapPath>
</span>
</div>
```

If you add these elements and then view the master page in design view, you should see that a SiteMapPath now appears in the navigation bar (Figure 8.32). There is a SiteMap-Path Tasks menu associated with this control, but there is no need to configure anything. Because the site map has a default file name (Web.sitemap) the control automatically picks up the necessary data from this XML file.

To see the breadcrumbs in action, it is best to navigate to a page that is nested in the site map, such as the mailing address or email pages. This will show you how the breadcrumb trail is displayed and how the hyperlinks flow. Figure 8.33 shows the email page, with the breadcrumbs displayed in the navigation bar. Not only does the SiteMapPath display the navigation path to this page (via the 'Home' and 'Contact Us' pages) but the previous steps in the path are both hyperlinks, enabling easy navigation to those pages.

FIGURE 8.32 A SiteMapPath added to the navigation bar in Design view

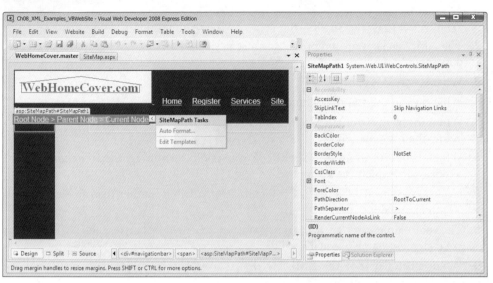

FIGURE 8.33 The breadcrumbs in the SiteMapPath control displayed in the navigation bar

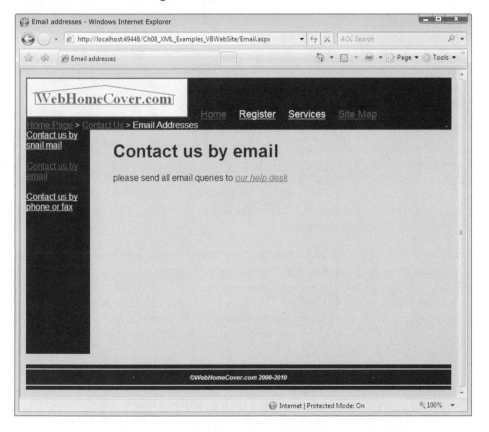

Self Study questions

1. What is the sequence of elements in an XML document known as?
2. The XML declaration and processing instructions are part of what section of an XML document?
3. What is utf-8?
4. What do you use to provide unique IDs for elements in an XML document?
5. When using an XmlDataSource control, how many levels of nesting can you have below the root element?
6. Which property of an AdRotator control specifies an integer that weights the frequency with which the ad appears?
7. How do we specify that we are referring to an attribute rather than an element in an XPath expression?
8. The root element for an XSL transform can be called 'xsl:stylesheet'. Which alternative element name is equally valid?
9. What is the name of the XML file that is used to create site maps in Visual Web Developer?
10. A site map file can be used with a TreeView control. What is the other control that we can use this file with?

Exercises

8.12 Add the 'Special Deals' and 'More Info' pages to the website (there are currently broken links to these on the main side navigation bar). Add any content you think appropriate to these pages, which will be simple information pages, like the contact pages. Modify the site map file so that links to these pages are included. Check that links to this page appear in both the site map page and the breadcrumbs.

8.13 You may have noticed that the XML files used with an XmlDataSource cannot have nested elements more than one level below the root, but the XML file used for the site map can have nested elements. You may also have noticed that the TreeView and Menu controls can be configured to use an XML file rather than a site map data file as their data source. One example of using this option is to create an XML file viewer that can navigate through XML files that have multiple levels of nested elements, which we will do in this exercise.

Create a new web form and add a site map control to it. Set the data source for this site map to be an XML file, and choose 'policy-claims.xml' from the list of available XML files. Using the 'Tree View Tasks' menu, select 'Auto Format' and choose the 'XP File Explorer' format option. If you view the resulting page in a browser, you will be able to expand and collapse the nodes in the document tree. Note, however, that this will only display the element structure of the document, it will not display the attributes or any content.

SUMMARY

We began this chapter by introducing semi-structured data, and saw how XML follows its principles. We looked at how XML is a metalanguage, able to be used to define any number of specific mark-up languages due to its extensible nature. We applied XML documents to an XmlDataSource to enable XML data to be viewed on a web form, and filtered this data using XPath expressions. We also looked at some aspects of XSLT in order to transform an XML document into suitable format for use with an XmlDataSource. Later in the chapter we made use of the navigation controls in Visual Web Developer to support two of the page design patterns introduced in Chapter 2, 'site map' and 'breadcrumbs'. All three of the navigation controls (SiteMapPath, Menu and TreeView) can be configured using XML data as a datasource. The XML file we used in with the navigation controls was a special file called Web.sitemap. We implemented a site map page using first a TreeView and then a Menu control, and implemented the breadcrumbs pattern using a SiteMapPath control, again using the site map XML data file.

References and further reading

BBC. 2005. *Radio Times*. http://xmltv.radiotimes.com/.

Bray, T., Paoli, J., Sperberg-McQueen, C., Maler, E. and Yergeau, F. 2005. *Extensible Mark-up Language (XML) 1.0 (Fourth Edition)*. W3C http://www.w3.org/TR/REC-xml/#sec-origin-goals.

Bray, T., Paoli, J., Sperberg-McQueen, C., Maler, E. and Yergeau, F. 2004. *Extensible Mark-up Language (XML) 1.1*. W3C. http://www.w3.org/TR/2004/REC-xml11-20040204/.

Eckstein, R. 2002. *Java Enterprise Best Practices*. Farnham: O'Reilly.

Eden, R. 2005. *XMLTV wiki*. http://xmltv.org/.

UniProt. 2008. *The Universal Protein Resource*. http://www.uniprot.org/uniref/UniRef100_P71715.xml.

8

CHAPTER 9

Layered Architecture and Multi-Page Webflows

LEARNING OBJECTIVES

- **To understand the model, view and controller layers of a web application**

- **To be able to manage the routing of a webflow**

- **To understand the role of the HTTP request and response in a web form**

- **To be able to maintain user sessions**

- **To be able to apply the data transfer object and façade design patterns within a webflow**

- **To be able to implement a complex webflow with variable routing**

INTRODUCTION

So far in this book we have seen how to use individual pages to provide web-based content to client browsers. We have also seen some aspects of how dynamic content can be provided by adding event handlers to form controls. In several of the examples in Chapters 6 and 7, the content of the current web form was updated by code written in an event handler method. Updating a single page can be a useful technique in web applications, but in order to provide a more complete web experience we have to look at how a series of forms can be integrated together to provide a *webflow* (a workflow through a web application) that implements a use case. In this chapter we will explore some aspects of the architectural design of web applications that use server-side components to represent an application domain model, interact with these components using dynamic web pages and manage user sessions over multiple request-response cycles.

9.1 Model View Controller (MVC) architecture

Model View Controller (MVC) is a well-known design pattern that was first formalized as part of the Smalltalk programming language. The original idea was that a single data model (let's say information about the state of a virtual aeroplane in a flight simulator) can be simultaneously viewed in different ways in different concurrent windows (e.g. a cockpit view, a view from above the plane and a radar view). In addition, the user's control of the system (for example using the flight controls in the cockpit) will update the underlying model, changes which should then be seen automatically in the other views. For example, if the flight controls in the cockpit view are used to turn the aircraft to the left, then not only will the cockpit view change but so will the other views (Figure 9.1).

The MVC architecture explicitly separates out the roles of the model (the underlying data) the view (what is presented to the user) and the controller (the handling component that manages user interaction and triggers appropriate updates to the model). In the context of a web application, we have a slightly different perspective on what is meant by multiple views, because instead of having these views on a single screen, the multiple views will be different clients with separate browsers looking at the same application in different ways. For example, if there are many people shopping on-line, each one may be looking at a different part of the catalog, but the underlying model (the catalog itself) is the same for all of these views. Updates to the model (e.g. a shopper buying an item) need to be reflected in all the views, so that what the users see in terms of product availability is always as up to date as possible. In the following section we look at how a web application architecture implemented using .NET relates to the MVC pattern.

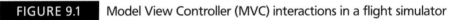

FIGURE 9.1   Model View Controller (MVC) interactions in a flight simulator

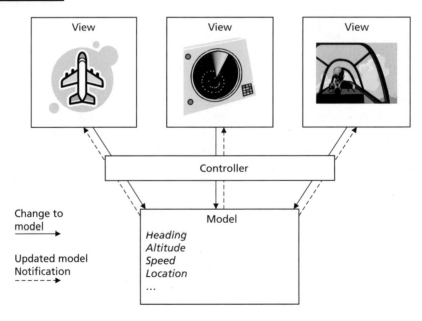

9.2 Web application architecture

In previous chapters we have seen how event handlers, written in either C# or VB.NET, can be used to generate dynamic content. In terms of the model view controller architecture, the web forms that trigger the event handler and present the results comprise the view, while the event handlers are part of the controller mechanism, though much of the actual controller layer (for example the way that an event is linked to an event handler) is part of the .NET framework itself. Behind the controller layer there needs to be some kind of model layer that represents the domain objects within the application. In this chapter we will see how the view and the controller layers can be linked to this model. Figure 9.2 shows a simple diagram of these layers in a .NET web application.

FIGURE 9.2   Model, view and controller layers in a .NET web application

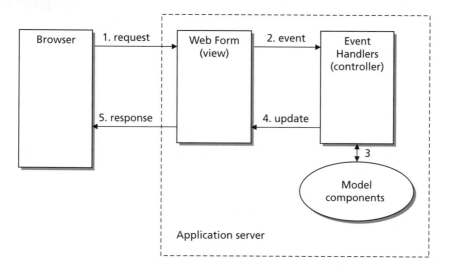

9.3 Building a simple webflow

In Chapter 6 we introduced event handlers and showed how they are able to post back to and update the current web form. However in many cases a web application needs to consist of a number of different forms that may have various paths between them, depending on the users' requirements. In such cases, using a single web form that posts back to itself is not the best solution.

Having introduced the concepts of model, view and controller, and suggested that a web application needs to incorporate multiple web pages that are integrated together, our next example introduces a very simple multi-page webflow that introduces some components from the model layer. A webflow is simply the flow of pages through a particular use case. In many web applications these will take the form of a 'Wizard', namely a series of pages that take the user through the various steps of a particular process.

NOTE	The Wizard control we introduced in Chapter 7 can be used for simple webflows, but is not flexible enough for complex webflows where the route through the webflow depends on user choice.

For this example we will create a simple multi-form webflow from one of our insurance system use cases, a customer lodging an insurance claim. We will need to gather some data from the user, namely their policy number, what type of policy they are making a claim against (either buildings or contents insurance), an approximate amount for the claim and a general description of what they are claiming for. We will break this data collection into two separate web forms, one that collects data about the policy number and the policy type, and another that asks for the claim amount and description. Separating that data into two pages makes the user interaction simpler, but more importantly, in a complete system it would enable us to identify the customer from the first form, and check that they have the appropriate type of policy, before asking for claim details in the second form. This would, of course, require us to have policy details stored somewhere in a database, which at this stage of our example we do not have, so for the moment we will assume that the policy number and claim type entered by the user are acceptable.

Here is the source of a web form ('ClaimForm1.aspx') for the first part of the webflow, containing a TextBox to allow the user to enter a policy number, a RadioButtonList to select the policy type, and a 'submit' button that will invoke an event handler. Note that the ID of the TextBox is 'PolicyNumber', the ID of the RadioButtonGroup is 'PolicyType' and the ID of the button is 'SubmitButton'. This is important, because these identifiers will be used later in the event handler. To keep things simple, we will not be using the master page in this example:

```
<%@ Page Language="VB" AutoEventWireup="false"
CodeFile="ClaimForm1.aspx.vb" Inherits="ClaimForm1" %>

<!DOCTYPE html PUBLIC "-//W3C//DTD XHTML 1.0 Transitional//EN"
"http://www.w3.org/TR/xhtml1/DTD/xhtml1-transitional.dtd">

<html xmlns="http://www.w3.org/1999/xhtml">
  <head runat="server">
   <title>Make a Claim</title>
  </head>
  <body>
  <h1>WebHomeCover insurance claim form</h1>
   <p>
     Please enter your policy number in the text box below,
     and also select the type of insurance claim you wish
     to make. Then press the 'Submit' button"
   </p>
   <form id="form1" runat="server">
    <div>
      <asp:Label ID="Label1" runat="server" Text="Policy Number: ">
      </asp:Label>
      <asp:TextBox ID="PolicyNumber" runat="server"></asp:TextBox>
      <br />
```

```
        <asp:RadioButtonList ID="PolicyType" runat="server">
          <asp:ListItem Value="contents">Contents Insurance Claim
          </asp:ListItem>
          <asp:ListItem Value="buildings">Buildings Insurance Claim
          </asp:ListItem>
        </asp:RadioButtonList>
        <br />
        <asp:Button ID="SubmitButton" runat="server" Text="Submit" />
      </div>
    </form>
  </body>
</html>
```

Figure 9.3 shows this web form displayed in a browser.

FIGURE 9.3 The first web form in the insurance claim webflow displayed in a browser

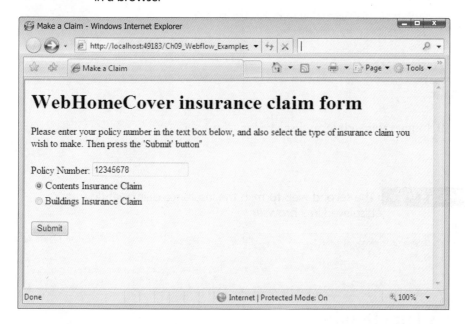

The second form contains a TextBox to gather the amount of the claim ('ClaimAmount'), and a multi line TextBox for the user to enter a description of the claim ('Description'). Once again there is a button that will have an event handler ('SubmitButton').

```
<%@ Page Language="VB" AutoEventWireup="false"
CodeFile="ClaimForm2.aspx.vb" Inherits="ClaimForm2" %>

<!DOCTYPE html PUBLIC "-//W3C//DTD XHTML 1.0 Transitional//EN"
"http://www.w3.org/TR/xhtml1/DTD/xhtml1-transitional.dtd">

<html xmlns="http://www.w3.org/1999/xhtml">
  <head runat="server">
    <title>Claim Details</title>
```

```
      </head>
      <body>
        <form id="form1" runat="server">
          <div>
            <h1>Claim Details</h1>
            <p>
              Please enter the approximate amount of your claim
              in the box below
            </p>
            <asp:TextBox ID="ClaimAmount" runat="server"></asp:TextBox>
            <p>
              Please enter a brief description of your claim in
              the box below
            </p>
            <asp:TextBox ID="Description" runat="server"
              TextMode="MultiLine">
            </asp:TextBox>
            <br />
            <asp:Button ID="SubmitButton" runat="server"
              Text="Submit My Claim" />
          </div>
        </form>
      </body>
    </html>
```

Figure 9.4 shows this web form displayed in a browser.

FIGURE 9.4 The second web form in the insurance claim webflow
displayed in a browser

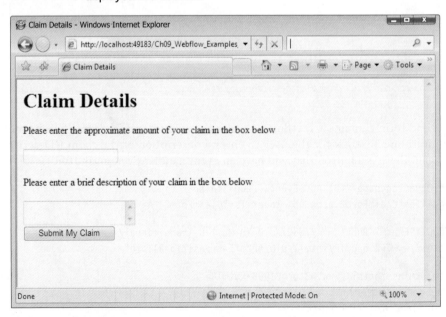

9.3.1 Linking pages in a webflow

So far we have two separate web forms. If you view either of these in a browser, and press the submit button, the page will redisplay. This is because, by default, a web form always submits the next request back to itself, as we saw in Chapter 6. You can see this in both of these pages by looking at the 'action' attribute of the form element in the generated XHTML, by viewing the page source in the browser. How, then, do we create a web application where we can move through a webflow consisting of multiple pages? The answer is to add some code to the event handler that specifies which web form should be displayed next. The essential piece of code here is the 'Transfer' method of the 'Server' class, which takes as a parameter the name of the next web form to be sent to the client (the same in both VB and C#, except that the line in C# ends with a semicolon):

```
Server.Transfer("webform.aspx")
```

Here is an event handler for the submit button control in 'ClaimForm1.aspx'. In this event handler, the 'Server.Transfer' method is used to route the webflow to the next web form, 'ClaimForm2.aspx'. The line in bold has been added.

VB code

```
Protected Sub SubmitButton_Click(ByVal sender As Object,
    ByVal e As System.EventArgs) Handles SubmitButton.Click
  Server.Transfer("ClaimForm2.aspx")
End Sub
```

C# code

```
protected void SubmitButton_Click(object sender, EventArgs e)
{
  Server.Transfer("ClaimForm2.aspx");
}
```

To complete our simple webflow, we will add a third page that acknowledges receipt of the claim. At this stage, it just contains a simple text message, using standard XHTML elements:

```
<%@ Page Language="VB" AutoEventWireup="false"
CodeFile="ClaimForm3.aspx.vb" Inherits="ClaimForm3" %>

<!DOCTYPE html PUBLIC "-//W3C//DTD XHTML 1.0 Transitional//EN"
"http://www.w3.org/TR/xhtml1/DTD/xhtml1-transitional.dtd">

<html xmlns="http://www.w3.org/1999/xhtml">
  <head runat="server">
   <title>Claim Acknowledgment</title>
  </head>
  <body>
   <form id="form1" runat="server">
    <div>
```

```
    <h1>Claim complete!</h1>
    <p>
      Thank you for submitting your insurance claim.
      You will hear from us within 7 days
    </p>
   </div>
  </form>
 </body>
</html>
```

To route to this final page, the event handler for the button on the second web form (ClaimForm2.aspx) also needs to include the 'Server.Transfer' method:

VB Code

```
Partial Class ClaimForm2 Inherits System.Web.UI.Page
 Protected Sub SubmitButton_Click(ByVal sender As Object,
    ByVal e As System.EventArgs) Handles SubmitButton.Click
   Server.Transfer("ClaimForm3.aspx")
 End Sub
End Class
```

C# code

```
protected void SubmitButton_Click(object sender, EventArgs e)
{
  Server.Transfer("ClaimForm3.aspx");
}
```

Figure 9.5 shows the third web form in the webflow displayed in a browser.

Now our brief webflow is complete in terms of page routing, and we can progress through the three web forms in sequence. However we are not yet gathering the data from the web forms in order to be able to process the insurance claim. In order to do this, we will need to add some additional processing to the event handlers and introduce the idea of HTTP request parameters and session management.

9.3.2 Handling request parameters

When data is entered into a web form and is submitted to the server as an HTTP request, the data entered into the controls is included as part of the request, as *request parameters*. This data can be retrieved from the request on the server-side in an event handler. Request parameters are only available while the current request still exists. Once the HTTP response has been returned to the client browser, any data in the request will be lost. If separate web forms are displayed by separate HTTP request-response cycles, this means that when the request is received for the second page, it is a different request to the one used for the previous page, so it is not normally possible to access request

FIGURE 9.5 The final web form in the three-page webflow displayed in a browser

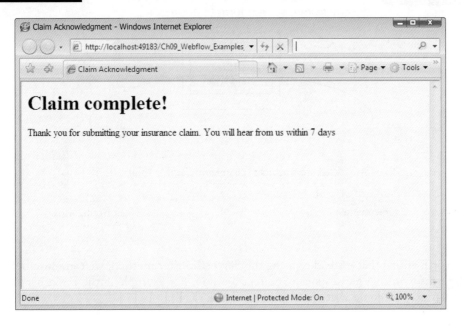

data from one web form in another. The 'Server.Transfer' method, however, does not send back the response directly to the client. Instead, it transfers control to another web form on the server, without redirecting via the client browser. This means that the request data can still be available. There is, however, an important point to note about this method which is that it can take a second parameter, which is a Boolean value. If it is set to *true*, the request data is maintained between pages. If it is set to *false*, then it is not. To be certain that the request data will be retained, therefore, we should add 'True' (VB) or 'true' (C#) as the second argument in the submit button event handler for ClaimForm1, if we still want to have access to the request parameters originally submitted with that web form:

VB code

```
Server.Transfer("ClaimForm2.aspx", True)
```

C# code

```
Server.Transfer("ClaimForm2.aspx", true);
```

Figure 9.6 shows how the request is transferred from 'ClaimForm1.aspx' to 'ClaimForm2 .aspx' on the server, without sending a response back to the client browser. This means that 'ClaimForm2.aspx' will have access to the PolicyNumber and ClaimType parameters from 'ClaimForm1.aspx'. In the next example, we will see how we can retrieve this data from the request using a page event handler.

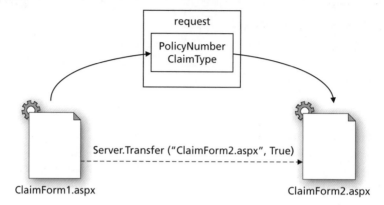

FIGURE 9.6 The Server.Transfer method enables the transfer of parameter data directly from one web form to another

It is worth noting that instead of using the Server.Transfer method, we can move between web forms by using the Response.Redirect method. For example in the event handler for ClaimForm1, we could write (with a semicolon for C#):

```
Response.Redirect("ClaimForm2.aspx")
```

However the effect of this method is to send a response to the client that triggers a new request to the next page. This means that any parameters from the first request will be lost by the time the second page is requested.

9.3.3 Page event handlers

The event handlers we have used so far in this example are triggered when a 'submit' button is pressed. This event occurs when a web form is submitted to the server as an HTTP request, but of course there are a number of other types of event handler, including those associated with the web-page itself. Perhaps the most useful of these is the 'Load' event, which occurs when the web page is first loaded. This event can be used to write dynamic content to the page when it is first displayed. For our next example, we will display the user's policy number and policy type, which they enter in ClaimForm1, at the top of the page when ClaimForm2 is displayed. The first thing we will do is to add two labels to ClaimForm2 that will display the data entered by the user in ClaimForm1. Note that the first label has the ID 'Policy' and the second has the ID 'Type'. These names will be used in the event handler:

```
<p>Your policy number: <strong>
<asp:Label ID="Policy" runat="server" Text=""></asp:Label>
</strong>
<br />
Your policy type: <strong>
<asp:Label ID="Type" runat="server" Text=""></asp:Label>
</strong>
</p>
```

To create an event handler for the page load event so we can put data into these two labels, we need a suitable method. When you work with C#, Visual Web Developer will automatically provide an empty 'Page_Load' event handler method for you, which looks like this.

```
protected void Page_Load(object sender, EventArgs e)
{

}
```

However if you are working with VB this empty method is not provided automatically. To add this method, you will need to open the 'Claimform2.aspx.vb' source file in Visual Web Developer, select '(Page Events)' from the drop-down list in the top left corner of the editor window, and then select the 'Load' event from the drop-down list in the top right corner of the window. A new event handler method called 'Page_Load' will then be added to your code (Figure 9.7).

Inside the page load handler method, we will retrieve the value of the PolicyNumber and PolicyType TextBoxes from 'ClaimForm1.aspx'. To do this we use a special object called 'Request', which represents the HTTP request and encapsulates all the parameter values posted from the web form. The code to retrieve the parameters is a little different between VB and C#. In VB the Request has an 'Item' method. This method takes a String parameter that is the value of an 'id' attribute of one of the form controls (sent as a parameter to the HTTP request). We can then assign that value to a variable or another control. For example, to get the value of the policy number from our web form and put it into a Label called 'Policy' using VB code, we would write something like:

```
Policy.Text = Request.Item("PolicyNumber")
```

FIGURE 9.7 Adding a page load event handler to VB code in Visual Web Developer

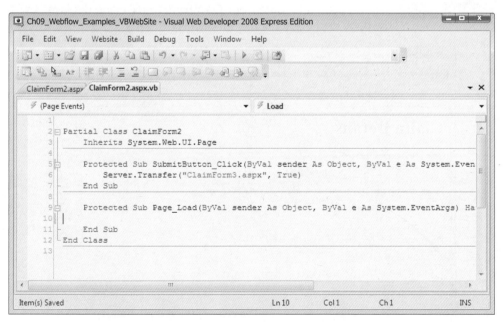

In C#, interaction with a Request object uses an array-like syntax. Square brackets are used around the name of the parameter, returning the value stored under that name.

```
Policy.Text = Request["PolicyNumber"];
```

Case is important here, since the name of the parameter must exactly match the ID used for the web form control. Here is the complete event handler, which sets the values of both of the labels we added to 'ClaimForm2.aspx'.

VB code

```
Protected Sub Page_Load(ByVal sender As Object, ByVal e As System.EventArgs)
Handles Me.Load
  Policy.Text = Request.Item("PolicyNumber")
  Type.Text = Request.Item("PolicyType")
End Sub
```

C# code

```
protected void Page_Load(object sender, EventArgs e)
{
  Policy.Text = Request["PolicyNumber"];
  Type.Text = Request["PolicyType"];
}
```

Figure 9.8 shows ClaimForm2.aspx after data has been added into ClaimForm1 and the submit button has been pressed. The policy number and the type of policy selected are shown on this page.

FIGURE 9.8   Request parameter data from 'ClaimForm1.aspx' being displayed by the page load event handler in 'ClaimForm2.aspx'

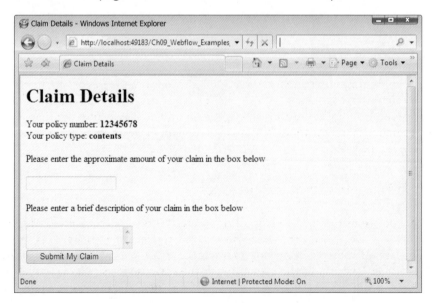

In this example, we have seen how data can be retrieved from the request, and that the request can be made available to a second web form by using the Server.Transfer method. However, once the second web form has been sent back to the browser, the previous request has been lost. Figure 9.9 shows how this works in our three-page webflow. The initial request comes from the client browser to load 'ClaimForm1.aspx'. Just loading the page does not invoke the event handler associated with the button, so the first response is simply the XHTML page generated by the web form. Since all web forms submit initially post back to themselves, the next request is also to 'ClaimForm1.aspx' but, when the submit button is clicked, the button event handler transfers control on to 'ClaimForm2.aspx', which provides the next response to the client. Then the client sends a new request back to the button event handler in 'ClaimForm2.aspx', which transfers to 'ClaimForm3.aspx' to generate the final response.

FIGURE 9.9 Multiple request-response cycles in the insurance claim webflow

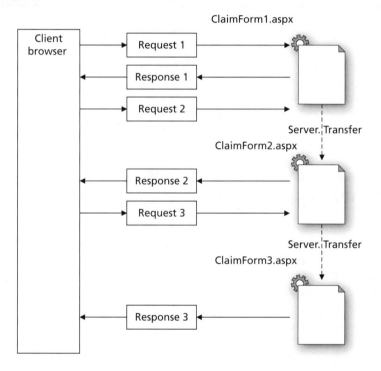

It can be seen from Figure 9.9 that the user's interaction with a series of web forms involves multiple request-response cycles, so we cannot store client data for a complete webflow by using the request. In order to maintain client data over webflows of more than two pages, we need to understand how to use session management in a web application, which we will cover in the next section.

Section summary and quick exercises

In this section we introduced web application architecture in the context of the Model View Controller design pattern, which divides the application into layers of responsibility. In the webflow example of making an insurance claim, we saw how the event handlers in the controller layer route the user through the various views (pages) available in the webflow. We used the Request object to access the values of HTTP parameters sent from the client browser using data from the controls in the web form, and used the Server. Transfer method to maintain the current request on the server, by routing directly from one web form to another without redirecting via the client.

EXERCISE 9.1

Create a simple web form containing a TextField and a Button. Create a second web form that contains an empty Label control. In the button event handler for the first form, use the Server .Transfer method to route directly to the second web form, and populate the Label in the second form with the text from the TextField in the first form. Check that the text you type into the Text-Field appears in the Label on the second form when you view the webflow in a browser. Now replace the Server.Transfer method with Response.Redirect. You should find that the text does not appear in the Label in the second form, as the previous request has been replaced by a new one and the original parameter values have been lost.

EXERCISE 9.2

In one of the exercises in Chapter 6 we created a web form with an event handler that worked out the user's age in days and displayed the result on the original web form. Rewrite this simple web application so that it uses two web forms. The age of the user should be displayed on the second web form using data from the request.

9.4 Session management: conversational state in a web application

Having looked at the syntax for transferring between the forms in a webflow, and seen how client form data is contained in the request, we now need to look at how we can maintain client information throughout a webflow as we move between multiple web forms. In the previous section we saw how an event handler has access to the data contained in the request, but as soon as the HTTP response is sent back, and the next page is displayed in the browser, that information is lost because the next HTTP request will contain different data. In web applications that gather client data, we need a solution that will be able to reliably store client data over several pages so that, for example, a client using an on-line store can start shopping, browse through a catalog, add items to their shopping cart (or remove them) and eventually purchase all the items in the cart, regardless of how many pages they have viewed in the meantime. For this to work, we need to maintain state on the server because HTTP is a *stateless protocol*, which is not designed to keep long-term connections open between the client and the server. This means that something other than the HTTP connection has to be used to keep information on behalf of the client. We cannot store state on the client if the client is a browser, so we must keep it on the server, along with some way of identifying the client so that everyone has access to their own shopping cart, claim details, bank account etc. (and no-one else's). In a .NET web application, we can maintain this type of information in the 'Session' object, a separate instance of which will be created for each client that is using the web application. This object represents a client session, which is effectively a conversation between a client and a server that includes multiple request / response cycles. A session could be a shopping process at an on-line store, a series of interactions with a share trading system, or any other application where the client needs to maintain some state (shopping cart, logon information etc.) over a series of different web pages (Figure 9.10).

FIGURE 9.10   A 'Session' can be used to maintain client form data over a series of
pages in a webflow

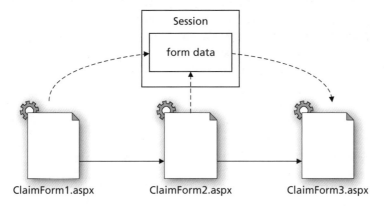

A 'Session' object is basically like a Hashtable in that it can contain a collection of key-value pairs, where the keys are Strings and the values are Objects. In fact this is very similar to the way that data is stored in the Request object. A session object will be created for a client automatically when it is accessed by an event handler.

In VB, we can get or set the items in a session using the 'Item' method. To set an item, we simply assign a value to a key (the key is a String provided as a parameter to the 'Item' method). In this example we will return to the event handler for ClaimForm1, and add the data from the two form controls to the session:

```
Partial Class ClaimForm1 Inherits System.Web.UI.Page

  Protected Sub SubmitButton_Click(ByVal sender As Object,
      ByVal e As System.EventArgs) Handles SubmitButton.Click
    Session.Item("PolicyNumber") = PolicyNumber.Text
    Session.Item("PolicyType") = PolicyType.Text
    Server.Transfer("ClaimForm2.aspx", True)
  End Sub
End Class
```

In C#, interaction with a session object uses the same array-like syntax that we have already seen used with the Request. Square brackets are used around the item key, and then we assign the value to that key.

```
protected void SubmitButton_Click(object sender, EventArgs e)
{
  Session["PolicyNumber"] = PolicyNumber.Text;
  Session["PolicyType"] = PolicyType.Text;
  Server.Transfer("ClaimForm2.aspx", true);
}
```

We can still retrieve this data from the request in the event handler for 'ClaimForm2 .aspx', but we also need to put the data from the controls in 'ClaimForm2.aspx' into the session. Here is a modified version of the button event handler for the second form, which adds the 'ClaimAmount' and 'Description' values to the session.

VB code

```vb
Protected Sub SubmitButton_Click(ByVal sender As Object,
    ByVal e As System.EventArgs) Handles SubmitButton.Click
  Session.Item("ClaimAmount") = ClaimAmount.Text
  Session.Item("Description") = Description.Text
  Server.Transfer("ClaimForm3.aspx", True)
End Sub
```

C# code

```csharp
protected void SubmitButton_Click(object sender, EventArgs e)
{
  Session["ClaimAmount"] = ClaimAmount.Text;
  Session["Description"] = Description.Text;
  Server.Transfer("ClaimForm3.aspx", true);
}
```

In the final part of our webflow, we will summarize all the client data on the final web form, rather than just displaying a static message, as we do at the moment. Here is a modified version of 'ClaimForm3.aspx'. Note that it now includes four empty labels, intended to display the data gathered from the webflow:

```aspx
<%@ Page Language="VB" AutoEventWireup="false"
CodeFile="ClaimForm3.aspx.vb" Inherits="ClaimForm3" %>

<!DOCTYPE html PUBLIC "-//W3C//DTD XHTML 1.0 Transitional//EN"
"http://www.w3.org/TR/xhtml1/DTD/xhtml1-transitional.dtd">

<html xmlns="http://www.w3.org/1999/xhtml">
 <head runat="server">
  <title>Claim Acknowledgment</title>
 </head>
 <body>
  <form id="form1" runat="server">
   <div>
    <h1>Claim complete!</h1>
    <p>Your policy number:
     <strong>
      <asp:Label ID="Policy" runat="server" Text=""></asp:Label>
     </strong>
     <br />
     Your policy type:
     <strong>
      <asp:Label ID="Type" runat="server" Text=""></asp:Label>
     </strong>
     <br />
     The amount of your claim:
     <strong>
      <asp:Label ID="Amount" runat="server" Text=""></asp:Label>
```

```
        </strong>
        <br />
        What happened:
        <strong>
          <asp:Label ID="Description" runat="server" Text=""></asp:Label>
        </strong>
      </p>
      <p>
        Thank you for submitting your insurance claim.
        You will hear from us within 7 days
      </p>
    </div>
  </form>
 </body>
</html>
```

To populate these labels with data, the page load event handler for 'ClaimForm3.aspx' needs to retrieve all the data from the session. To get an object from the session in VB we simply assign the result of calling the 'Item' method to a variable or control. Here, we assign the four values from the session to the appropriate label controls:

```
Policy.Text = Session.Item("PolicyNumber")
Type.Text = Session.Item("PolicyType")
Amount.Text = Session.Item("ClaimAmount")
Description.Text = Session.Item("Description")
```

In C#, we again the use the array-like syntax to access the items in the session. However we also need to do some casting, since the type of an item returned from a session is always 'Object'. In this example, we cast all four items to type String, so they can be put into text labels on the form, though note that the ClaimAmount represents a floating point number, so could have been cast to a suitable numeric type if we were not putting the value directly into a text-based label.

```
Policy.Text = (String)Session["PolicyNumber"];
Type.Text = (String)Session["PolicyType"];
Amount.Text = (String)Session["ClaimAmount"];
Description.Text = (String)Session["Description"];
```

Figure 9.11 shows ClaimForm3.aspx in a browser at the end of a webflow, displaying the data from the session.

9.4.1 Session management

Typically we would simply put data into a session in one event handler and retrieve it in another, as we have been doing in our example so far, but there are some other useful methods associated with sessions that can help us to successfully manage client state. One important aspect of session management is freeing up resources that are no longer required. When we purchase the items in a shopping cart, for example, then the shopping cart is no longer needed. If the cart is represented by a session object then we should dispose of the session at the end of the webflow, since as long as it exists it is taking up storage space and

FIGURE 9.11   Data from the session displayed in ClaimForm3.aspx

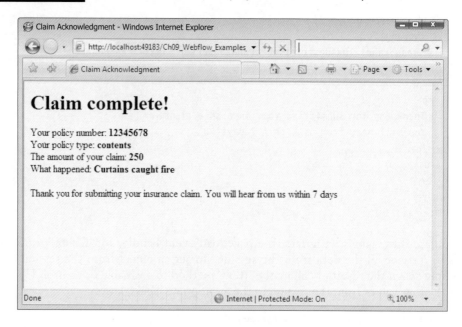

having to be managed by the server. To get rid of a session that has served its purpose we can use the 'Abandon' method to dispose of the session and any objects within it:

```
Session.Abandon()
```

At the beginning of a webflow we may want to check if the session that we are using is in fact a new one, or whether the client has restarted their activity with an existing session. To do this we can use 'IsNewSession' (a method in VB but a property in C#), which returns 'True' if the session has just been created and 'False' if it already existed. At this point we may choose to clear any remaining data from the existing session.

Similarly, we may find ourselves in an event handler where the session should already exist but for some reason it does not. If the session turns out to be new we can send the client back to start the webflow from the beginning. We could do this by transferring, or alternatively by redirecting. The following page load event handler for 'ClaimForm3.aspx' uses some of the techniques previously described, checking that the session exists when the page is loaded (if it does not then we are redirected to the first claim form) and abandoning the session at the end of the webflow.

VB code

```
System.EventArgs) Handles Me.Load
  If Session.IsNewSession() Then
     Response.Redirect("ClaimForm1.aspx")
  End If
  Policy.Text = Session.Item("PolicyNumber")
  Type.Text = Session.Item("PolicyType")
```

```
    Amount.Text = Session.Item("ClaimAmount")
    Description.Text = Session.Item("Description")
    Session.Abandon()
End Sub
```

C# code

```
protected void Page_Load(object sender, EventArgs e)
{
  if(Session.IsNewSession)
  {
    Response.Redirect("ClaimForm1.aspx");
  }
  Policy.Text = (String)Session["PolicyNumber"];
  Type.Text = (String)Session["PolicyType"];
  Amount.Text = (String)Session["ClaimAmount"];
  Description.Text = (String)Session["Description"];
  Session.Abandon();
}
```

Getting the value of a session item leaves the item in the session, while abandoning the session destroys it completely. However we sometimes we need to actually remove an individual item from the session. To do this (if a client chooses to remove something from a website shopping cart, for example) we would use the 'Remove' method, passing in the necessary key value:

```
Session.Remove("itemKey")
```

Similarly we can remove all of the keys and values from a session with the 'RemoveAll' or 'Clear' methods (which both have the same effect). These methods empty the session but do not abandon it (all of these session methods have the same names in both VB and C#).

NOTE	Abandoning the session can have side effects if the user navigates to a page that expects the session to still exist. For example a user may press the 'back' button in the browser after the session has been abandoned, leading to possible errors. This means that you should check for the existence of the session in all event handlers that require it, and redirect the request if necessary.

Section summary and quick exercises

This section introduced session management in a web application, and showed how a session object can be used to maintain client state over multiple request-response cycles in a webflow. We saw how data can be added to, or retrieved from, a session in event handlers, and how we can also check the state of a session (to see if it is newly created), remove its contents or abandon it.

EXERCISE 9.3

In the insurance claim form example that we modified in this section, we are still using the request to display data in the second web form. However this information has now also been stored in the session. Modify the page load event handler for 'ClaimForm2.aspx' to display the policy number and policy type using data from the session rather than from the request.

EXERCISE 9.4

Modify the two-page webflow that calculates the user's age in days (from exercise 9.2) so that it transfers data between the two pages using the session rather than the request. Instead of transferring between the two web forms on the server, modify the event handler to use the 'Response .Redirect' method. Because you are using a session, you should find that the webflow still works, even though you are redirecting via the browser between the two web forms.

9.5 Using Data Transfer Objects (DTOs) in a web application

In the event handlers we have developed so far, we have been writing all our code in the body of the event handler method. This is fine for the type of processing we have been working with, for simple examples of page routing and gathering form data, but continuing with only this approach is not going to give us a very good separation of concerns between different parts of the model, view and controller layers. In this section we introduce code components known as *Data Transfer Objects* (DTOs) that can be used to encapsulate related sets of data and act as intermediaries between the event handlers in the controller layer and the underlying model. A DTO often follows a simple component architecture based on *properties*, and it is this aspect that we will explore here. Property-related rules are:

- Objects have properties that are defined by methods
- A property may be configured as 'writeable', meaning that the value of the property in the object can be set
- A property may be configure as 'readable', meaning that the value of the property can be retrieved from the object
- A property may be both writeable and readable
- A property may be based on an internal attribute that maintains the value of the property

The way that object properties are expressed in .NET languages is quite simple. For this example, we will assume that an object has a 'description' property. Here, there is a private attribute in the class called 'attrDescription' that will maintain the state of the property:

VB code

```
Private attrDescription As String = ""
```

C# code

```
private String attrDescription = "";
```

In VB, the methods that enable the property to be written and read are defined using a 'Property' block containing both 'Get' and 'Set' blocks:

```
Property Description() As String
  Get
    Return attrDescription
  End Get
  Set(ByVal Value As String)
    attrDescription = Value
  End Set
End Property
```

The syntax in C# is even simpler. The name of the 'value' parameter in the set' block is predefined (i.e. this must be called 'value' in the code; 'value' is a reserved word in C#), so does not have to be specified:

```
public String Description
{
  get
  {
    return attrDescription;
  }
  set
  {
    attrDescription = value;
  }
}
```

In these cases, there is an attribute that contains the value of the property and the name of the attribute and the name of the property cannot be the same. However C# also provides us with the option of a very concise syntax that does away with the attribute name altogether, and focuses only on the property name, like this:

```
public String description {set; get;}
```

Some properties, in particular those that are 'read only' (i.e. have a 'get' method but no 'set' method) do not relate directly to attributes. Here, for example, is the definition in VB of a 'ReadOnly' property called 'Year' that returns the current year when called:

```
ReadOnly Property Year() As Integer
  Get
    Return DateTime.Now.Year
  End Get
End Property
```

In this method, the 'year' is not derived from an attribute of the class but is generated within the body of the method. Note that a ReadOnly property will only have a 'Get' block, there will be no 'Set' block.

In C# there are no explicit 'ReadOnly' properties. However the same effect is achieved simply by creating a property with a 'get' method but no 'set':

```
public int Year
{
  get
  {
    return DateTime.Now.Year;
  }
}
```

<table>
<tr><td> NOTE</td><td>When declaring and using properties in this book we will adopt the convention of using Pascal case (upper-case first letter, upper-case for the first letter of embedded words) for property names, in both C# and VB.</td></tr>
</table>

In the next example, we will introduce a complete class called 'ClaimFormDTO' that includes properties to match the data that is being submitted in our web forms; 'Policy-Number', 'PolicyType', 'ClaimAmount', and 'ClaimDescription'. Note that we use Pascal case for the names of the controls in the forms, an approach also used for the names of the properties in the DTO class. Figure 9.12 shows a UML diagram of the ClaimFormDTO class, showing its properties. Three of the properties are handled as Strings, but the Claim-Amount is a Decimal. By declaring the property to be of type Decimal, there will need to be a conversion process when we set the value of the property from an HTTP parameter value, because these parameters are passed to the server as Strings. However if a numeric value is not typed into the text box for the claim amount, the code will fail as the data conversion is not possible. Therefore some exception handling will need to be added to the event handler, though we might also add a validation control to the web form.

FIGURE 9.12   A UML class diagram of the 'ClaimFormDTO'

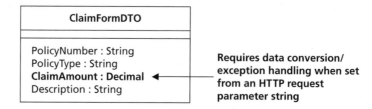

9.5.1 Creating a DTO class in Visual Web Developer

All of the code we have written so far has been in event handlers associated with controls on web forms. A DTO class, however will be a stand alone class. This type of class is created in Visual Web Developer by choosing 'Class' from the 'Add New Item' dialog. The icon in the dialog will be slightly different depending on whether you choose 'Visual C#' or 'Visual Basic' from the 'Language' drop-down at the bottom of the page. Figure 9.13 shows the creation of a new class with C# as the chosen language.

FIGURE 9.13   Creating a new class in the 'Add New Item' dialog

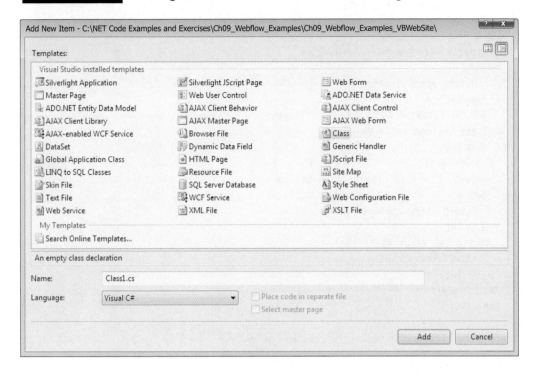

When a new class is created, it should be placed in the 'App_Code' folder of the website project, which contains stand alone classes that are not part of web form event handlers. Visual Web Developer should use this folder automatically for new classes.

Here is the source of the ClaimFormDTO in VB:

```vb
Imports Microsoft.VisualBasic

Public Class ClaimFormDTO
  Private attrPolicyNumber As String = ""
  Private attrPolicyType As String = ""
  Private attrClaimAmount As Double = 0.0
  Private attrClaimDescription As String = ""

  Property PolicyNumber() As String
    Get
      Return attrPolicyNumber
    End Get
    Set(ByVal Value As String)
      attrPolicyNumber = Value
    End Set
  End Property
  Property PolicyType() As String
    Get
      Return attrPolicyType
    End Get
```

```
      Set(ByVal Value As String)
        attrPolicyType = Value
      End Set
    End Property
    Property ClaimAmount() As Double
      Get
        Return attrClaimAmount
      End Get
      Set(ByVal Value As Double)
        attrClaimAmount = Value
      End Set
    End Property
    Property ClaimDescription() As String
      Get
        Return attrClaimDescription
      End Get
      Set(ByVal Value As String)
        attrClaimDescription = Value
      End Set
    End Property
  End Class
```

Here is the DTO in C#, using the concise syntax

```
public class ClaimFormDTO
{
  public String PolicyNumber { set; get; }
  public String PolicyType { set; get; }
  public Decimal ClaimAmount { set; get; }
  public String ClaimDescription { set; get; }
}
```

 NOTE When you are working with classes in the App_Code folder, rather than web forms, you check your code for errors by right clicking on the website folder in the Solution Explorer window and selecting 'Build WebSite'. This will compile all your code (including all your event handlers) and show any errors or warnings in the 'Error List' window.

This is the modified event handler code for 'ClaimForm1.aspx', this time creating an instance of the ClaimFormDTO to encapsulate the data from the web form. Once the form data has been added to the DTO, the DTO itself is added to the session.

VB code

```
Protected Sub SubmitButton_Click(ByVal sender As Object, ByVal e As
System.EventArgs) Handles SubmitButton.Click
  Session.Item("PolicyNumber") = PolicyNumber.Text
  Dim Policy As String = PolicyNumber.Text
```

```
    Dim Type As String = PolicyType.Text
    Dim Claim As ClaimFormDTO = New ClaimFormDTO()
    Claim.PolicyNumber = Policy
    Claim.PolicyType = Type
    Session.Item("ClaimFormDTO") = Claim
    Server.Transfer("ClaimForm2.aspx", True)
  End Sub
```

C# code

```
protected void SubmitButton_Click(object sender, EventArgs e)
{
  String Policy = PolicyNumber.Text;
  String Type = PolicyType.Text;
  ClaimFormDTO claim = new ClaimFormDTO();
  claim.PolicyNumber = Policy;
  claim.PolicyType = Type;
  Session["ClaimFormDTO"] = claim;
  Server.Transfer("ClaimForm2.aspx", true);
}
```

In the button event handler for 'ClaimForm2.aspx', the DTO is retrieved from the session, and then the amount and description are added to the DTO. Note that the DTO remains in the session while it is updated; we retrieve a reference to the DTO from the session and update it in-situ. It is in this event handler that there is a 'try...catch' block to catch any exceptions that may occur if the value entered into the text box cannot successfully be parsed into a Decimal value. If this occurs, we simply set the claim value to zero.

VB code

```
Protected Sub SubmitButton_Click(ByVal sender As Object,
    ByVal e As System.EventArgs) Handles SubmitButton.Click
  Dim ClaimForm As ClaimFormDTO = Session.Item("ClaimFormDTO")
  Try
    ClaimForm.ClaimAmount = ClaimAmount.Text
  Catch ex As Exception
    ClaimForm.ClaimAmount = 0.0
  End Try
  ClaimForm.ClaimDescription = Description.Text
  Server.Transfer("ClaimForm3.aspx", True)
End Sub
```

C# code

In C#, the conversion from the string in the text field that contains the claim amount and the double value needed by the DTO is not automatic, so we need to use the Parse method to do this conversion explicitly. In the 'catch' block, the literal zero also needs an 'M' suffix to make it compatible with the Decimal type:

```
protected void SubmitButton_Click(object sender, EventArgs e)
{
  ClaimFormDTO claimForm = (ClaimFormDTO)Session["ClaimFormDTO"];
  try
  {
    claimForm.ClaimAmount = Decimal.Parse(ClaimAmount.Text);
  }
  catch(Exception)
  {
    claimForm.ClaimAmount = 0.0M;
  }
  claimForm.ClaimDescription = Description.Text;
  Server.Transfer("ClaimForm3.aspx", true);
}
```

In the page load event handler for ClaimForm3.aspx the DTO is retrieved from the session and its properties are used to populate the various controls on the web form.

VB code

```
Protected Sub Page_Load(ByVal sender As Object, ByVal e As
System.EventArgs) Handles Me.Load
  If Session.IsNewSession() Then
    Response.Redirect("ClaimForm1.aspx")
  End If
  Dim ClaimForm As ClaimFormDTO = Session.Item("ClaimFormDTO")
  Policy.Text = ClaimForm.PolicyNumber
  Type.Text = ClaimForm.PolicyType
  Amount.Text = ClaimForm.ClaimAmount
  Description.Text = ClaimForm.ClaimDescription
  Session.Abandon()
End Sub
```

C# code

```
protected void Page_Load(object sender, EventArgs e)
{
  if(Session.IsNewSession)
  {
    Response.Redirect("ClaimForm1.aspx");
  }
  ClaimFormDTO claimForm = (ClaimFormDTO)Session["ClaimFormDTO"];
  Policy.Text = claimForm.PolicyNumber;
  Type.Text = claimForm.PolicyType;
  Amount.Text = claimForm.ClaimAmount.ToString();
  Description.Text = claimForm.ClaimDescription;
  Session.Abandon();
}
```

9.5.2 Refactoring

Of course with this particular change to our webflow, just adding a DTO into the mix, the actual behavior of the application is unchanged. We have improved the architecture but have not affected the way the application works. This is an example of *refactoring*; improving the design of existing code without changing its behavior (Fowler, 2000). The change we have made to the design in this step will make it easier to pass client data down into the model layer at the end of the webflow. Refactoring is important because it means we can replace a complex or confusing architecture with a better, simpler one that makes it easier to progress with subsequent enhancements and new requirements. When we refactor, although the behavior remains the same, we are making improvements to the software architecture of the application. Refactoring should normally be done in conjunction with a testing framework that makes sure that changes do not have any adverse effects on the functionality of the system. However for the tiny example we are working with here, it will be sufficient to manually test the code by just filling in the form and making sure everything still works each time we modify the application.

9.6 Model layer façades

We have added the necessary code to the event handlers to route the webflow, gather the data from the web forms and populate a DTO, but now we need to add some further processing to the event handlers to enable us to pass this data on from the controller layer to the underlying model for processing.

DTOs are simple sets of properties, but there will be other objects in the model layer of the application that will be more complex, representing processes or concepts from the business logic of the system. These objects might represent a user's shopping cart, or be responsible for a business process such as validation, which may of course require interacting with a database or other persistent data store. For example, if the request contained data sent from a form on a 'checkout' page, comprising the contents of the user's shopping cart, a program component would have to interact with the data store containing the part of the system that could process the contents of the shopping cart. Introducing these components to our interaction model enables us to separate the model from the web interaction layer, so the event handlers can delegate any business logic processes to these model layer components. A simple but useful design pattern to apply here is the 'façade' (Gamma *et al.*, 1995). A façade is a class that acts as a central point of contact with an underlying subsystem. We can use a façade in a web application to separate the view/controller layer components from the underlying model, and the façade object can take responsibility for converting between DTOs and the objects in the model layer, and vice versa. Figure 9.14 shows a façade object between a DTO and two model layer objects that both relate to insurance claims. The ClaimFormDTO is simply a way of grouping form data about an insurance claim together into a single object, but is no more than a set of properties, in a transient object that lasts the lifetime of the webflow. It also an amalgam of data relating to both claims and policies, so does not directly relate to a single business concept in the domain model. The Claim and Policy classes, on the other hand, represent an insurance claim and policy in the underlying domain model, and though they too may consist largely of properties, in a more fully developed system than our simple example it will be likely to have other methods relating to their roles in the business processes of the home insurance

FIGURE 9.14 A façade used to separate the view/controller layer from the model layer, and transform between DTOs and model objects

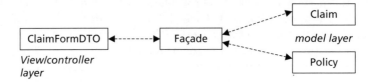

system, and will probably also be persistent (we will look at how business objects can be stored in the database in Chapter 11).

Classes that reside in the model, and have responsibilities related to the underlying processes of the application, may still need to be populated with data that originates from HTTP requests. Therefore in the controller layer we need to be able to translate between form data in DTOs and model layer objects. These transformations can take place within the façade.

9.6.1 Using a façade in a web application

In the next example we use the ClaimFormDTO from the view/controller layer and a new class called 'Claim' that will represent insurance claims in the model layer. The difference between the ClaimFormDTO and the Claim is that the DTO is only designed to contain the data gathered from the web forms that create the claim. Once it has been used to do this then it has served its purpose. It also contains data about both policies and claims, so does not relate to a single model layer object from the domain model we introduced in Chapter 2. The Claim class however represents more complex objects that will contain data not entered by the user, such as the date the claim was made, a generated claim reference and whether or not the claim has been approved. Objects of the Claim class will also need to represent data that is stored persistently in the database. You might also note that a claim needs to have a relationship with an associated insurance policy. Figure 9.15 shows the ClaimFormDTO, Claim and Policy classes. In this example the Policy is very simple, containing only a policy number and policy type (we will develop this class further in

FIGURE 9.15 The ClaimFormDTO is used to encapsulate data from the view/controller layer, while in the underlying model the Claim class represents an insurance claim, and the Policy represents the associated policy.

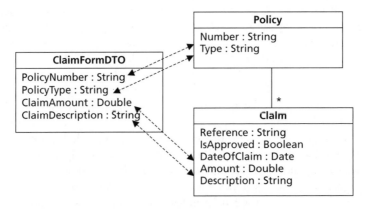

Chapter 11). For simplicity, we will only implement the one to one relationship between Claim and Policy in our code, though there is also a one to many relationship between Policy and Claim (one policy may have many claims made against it).

Here is the code for the Policy class used in this example. It consists only of the Number and Type properties:

VB code

```
Public Class Policy
  Private attrNumber As Integer
  Private attrType As String
  Property Number() As String
    Get
      Return attrNumber
    End Get
    Set(ByVal Value As String)
      attrNumber = Value
    End Set
  End Property
  Property Type() As String
    Get
      Return attrType
    End Get
    Set(ByVal Value As String)
      attrType = Value
    End Set
  End Property
End Class
```

C# code

```
public class Policy
{
  public int Number { set; get; }
  public String Type { set; get; }
}
```

Here is the code for the Claim class. Note in particular that there is a 'Policy' property that provides the link between the Claim object and a Policy object:

VB code

```
Public Class Claim
  Private attrPolicy As Policy
  Private attrAmount As Double = 0.0
  Private attrDescription As String = ""
  Private attrReference As String = ""
```

```
Private attrIsApproved As Boolean = False
Private attrDateOfClaim As DateTime
Property Policy() As Policy
  Get
    Return attrPolicy
  End Get
  Set(ByVal Value As Policy)
    attrPolicy = Value
  End Set
End Property
Property Amount() As Double
  Get
    Return attrAmount
  End Get
  Set(ByVal Value As Double)
    attrAmount = Value
  End Set
End Property
Property Description() As String
  Get
    Return attrDescription
  End Get
  Set(ByVal Value As String)
    attrDescription = Value
  End Set
End Property
Property Reference() As String
  Get
    Return attrReference
  End Get
  Set(ByVal Value As String)
    attrReference = Value
  End Set
End Property
Property IsApproved() As Boolean
  Get
    Return attrIsApproved
  End Get
  Set(ByVal Value As Boolean)
    attrIsApproved = Value
  End Set
End Property
Property DateOfClaim() As DateTime
Get
    Return attrDateOfClaim
  End Get
  Set(ByVal Value As DateTime)
    attrDateOfClaim = Value
  End Set
End Property
End Class
```

C# code

```csharp
public class Claim
{
  public Policy Policy { get; set; }
  public Decimal Amount { set; get; }
  public String Description { set; get; }
  public String Reference { set; get; }
  public Boolean IsApproved { set; get; }
  public DateTime DateOfClaim { set; get; }
}
```

Figure 9.16 shows the main relationships between components in this interaction. The modified page load event handler for 'ClaimForm3.aspx' uses an instance of the Claim-FormDTO class, which it passes to a façade class called 'ModelFacade' to create a Claim object and partially populate it from the DTO. In order to fully populate the Claim, we need some way of creating a reference number for it. We will pass this responsibility to a ReferenceGenerator class (described next). This is an example of a *process object*, a component that encapsulates one or more related business processes. The event handler then uses the Claim object to render the view by using its properties to populate labels on the web form.

| FIGURE 9.16 | Using a façade in the interaction between the view/controller and model layers of the web application |

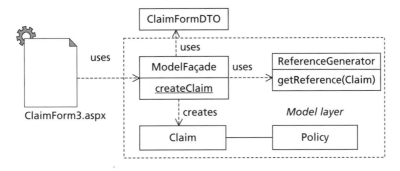

The first class we look at is the ReferenceGenerator. Each Claim will need a reference number so that it can be uniquely identified. For this example we will use reference numbers similar to this one:

```
C384475-20090509-751
```

The basic structure of these references is that they begin with the first letter of the type of claim ('B' for buildings or 'C' for contents), followed by the associated policy number. This is followed by the date of the claim in YYYYMMDD format, separated from the policy number by a hyphen. Finally, again separated by a hyphen, there is a randomly generated number. The following implementation takes a Claim object as a parameter, gets the type and number from its associated policy (retrieving the first letter of the policy type and converting it to upper-case) and then retrieves the date of the claim. It then generates the final number using the millisecond value from the time of the claim, formatted to three characters. The components of the reference are appended to a String, which is returned from the method when it is complete. This is not a totally robust implementation, since the same reference could potentially be generated more than once, if multiple claims were made on the same policy on the same day, and the truncated millisecond value also happened to be the same (unlikely, but not impossible). A more realistic approach would be to use a database to generate unique sequence numbers, but this implementation will serve for our examples:

C# code

```
public class ReferenceGenerator
{
public String getReference(Claim claim)
{
  String reference;
  String polType = claim.Policy.Type.Substring(0, 1).ToUpper();
  DateTime claimDate = claim.DateOfClaim;
  reference = polType + claim.Policy.Number.ToString() +
    "-" + claimDate.Year.ToString() + claimDate.Month.ToString("00") +
    claimDate.Day.ToString("00") +
    "-" + claimDate.Millisecond.ToString("000");
  return reference;
}
}
```

VB code

```
Public Class ReferenceGenerator
  Public Function getReference(ByVal claim As Claim) As String
    Dim reference As String
    Dim polType As String = claim.Policy.Type.Substring(0, 1).ToUpper()
    Dim claimDate = claim.DateOfClaim
    reference = polType + claim.Policy.Number.ToString() + "-" _
      + claimDate.Year.ToString() + claimDate.Month.ToString("00") + _
      claimDate.Day.ToString("00") + _
      "-" + claimDate.Millisecond.ToString("000")
    Return reference
  End Function
End Class
```

Next, we look at the ModelFacade and its static 'createClaim' method, which copies the properties of the ClaimFormDTO into a newly created Claim object. It also creates a new Policy object, though as we have noted before this is rather unrealistic. In a real system the policy would already exist and would need to be retrieved from the database. Once the relevant properties have been copied from the ClaimFormDTO into the Claim and Policy objects, the values of the 'ClaimDate' and 'IsApproved' properties are set manually for the

Claim, since these do not come from the ClaimFormDTO. We set the Claim's reference number using the ReferenceGenerator, but before this we must create the association between the Claim and the Policy, i.e.:

```
Claim.Policy = policy
```

At the end of the method we return the claim, which by this stage will be fully populated with data and have an association with a policy object.

VB code

```vb
Public Function createClaim(ByVal dto As ClaimFormDTO) As Claim
  Dim claim As Claim = New Claim()
  ' we only create a policy here because we do not yet
  ' use a database. more realistically, the Policy
  ' would already exist and need to be retrieved
  Dim policy As Policy = New Policy()
  ' we must set up the relationship between Claim and Policy
  ' before attempting to generate the reference, because the
  ' ReferenceGenerator uses properties from both classes
  claim.Policy = policy
  claim.Policy.Number = dto.PolicyNumber
  claim.Policy.Type = dto.PolicyType
  claim.Amount = dto.ClaimAmount
  claim.Description = dto.ClaimDescription
  claim.DateOfClaim = DateTime.Now
  claim.IsApproved = False
  Dim generator As ReferenceGenerator = New ReferenceGenerator()
  Dim reference As String = generator.getReference(claim)
  claim.Reference = reference
  Return claim
End Function
```

C# code

```csharp
public class ModelFacade
{
  public Claim createClaim(ClaimFormDTO dto)
  {
    Claim claim = new Claim();
    // we only create a policy here because we do not yet
    // use a database. More realistically, the Policy
    // would already exist and need to be retrieved
    Policy policy = new Policy();
    // we must set up the relationship between Claim and Policy
    // before attempting to generate the reference, because the
    // ReferenceGenerator uses properties from both classes
```

```
claim.Policy = policy;
claim.Policy.Number = Int32.Parse(dto.PolicyNumber);
claim.Policy.Type = dto.PolicyType;
claim.Amount = dto.ClaimAmount;
claim.Description = dto.ClaimDescription;
claim.DateOfClaim = DateTime.Now;
claim.IsApproved = false;
ReferenceGenerator generator = new ReferenceGenerator();
String reference = generator.getReference(claim);
claim.Reference = reference;
return claim;
  }
}
```

 NOTE This code assumes that the policy number has been entered as an integer. If it is not, an exception will be thrown. A validation control on the web form would resolve this potential issue.

To display all the details from the Claim object on the final web form, we will need to add to its controls. Here is a modified version of 'ClaimForm3.aspx'. We have added three more Label controls to display the Reference, Approved and ClaimDate properties. Another minor change is that we are now using an Image control to display an image representing the policy type, just to make the generated web page a little more interesting. Note that the Image control should include an 'alt' attribute to ensure that the generated XHTML is valid.

```
<%@ Page Language="VB" AutoEventWireup="false"
CodeFile="ClaimForm3.aspx.vb" Inherits="ClaimForm3" %>
<!DOCTYPE html PUBLIC "-//W3C//DTD XHTML 1.0 Transitional//EN"
"http://www.w3.org/TR/xhtml1/DTD/xhtml1-transitional.dtd">
<html xmlns="http://www.w3.org/1999/xhtml">
  <head id="Head1" runat="server">
    <title>Claim Acknowledgment</title>
  </head>
  <body>
    <form id="form1" runat="server">
      <div>
        <h1>Claim complete!</h1>
        <p>
        <asp:Image ID="PolicyTypeImage" alt="policy type"
          runat="server" />
        <br />
        Your claim reference: <strong>
        <asp:Label ID="Reference" runat="server" Text="">
        </asp:Label></strong>
        <br />
        Claim Approved? <strong>
```

```
<asp:Label ID="Approved" runat="server" Text="">
</asp:Label>
</strong>
<br />
The date you made your claim: <strong>
<asp:Label ID="ClaimDate" runat="server" Text="">
</asp:Label></strong>
<br />
Your policy number: <strong>
<asp:Label ID="Policy" runat="server" Text="">
</asp:Label></strong>
<br />
Your policy type: <strong>
<asp:Label ID="Type" runat="server" Text="">
</asp:Label></strong>
<br />
The amount of your claim: <strong>
<asp:Label ID="Amount" runat="server" Text="">
</asp:Label></strong>
<br />
What happened: <strong>
<asp:Label ID="Description" runat="server" Text="">
</asp:Label></strong>
  </p>
  <p>
    Thank you for submitting your insurance claim.
    You will hear from us within 7 days
  </p>
 </div>
</form>
</body>
</html>
```

The following modified page load event handler from 'ClaimForm3.aspx' handles the claim data by interacting with the model layer via the façade. It retrieves the ClaimFormDTO from the session and then invokes the ModelFacade's 'createClaim' method, which returns a Claim object. This object is then used to populate the label and image controls on the page so the complete claim details can be displayed. One point to note is that the policy properties (Number and Type) are retrieved from the Policy object associated with the Claim.

VB code

```
Protected Sub Page_Load(ByVal sender As Object,
   ByVal e As System.EventArgs) Handles Me.Load
  If Session.IsNewSession() Then
   Response.Redirect("ClaimForm1.aspx")
  End If
  Dim ClaimForm As ClaimFormDTO = Session.Item("ClaimFormDTO")
  Dim facade As ModelFacade = New ModelFacade()
```

```
Dim claim As Claim = facade.createClaim(ClaimForm)
If claim.Policy.Type = ("contents") Then
  PolicyTypeImage.ImageUrl = "contents.gif"
Else
  PolicyTypeImage.ImageUrl = "buildings.gif"
End If
Reference.Text = claim.Reference
ClaimDate.Text = claim.DateOfClaim
Approved.Text = claim.IsApproved
Policy.Text = claim.Policy.Number
Type.Text = claim.Policy.Type
Amount.Text = claim.Amount
Description.Text = claim.Description
Session.Abandon()
End Sub
```

C# code

```csharp
protected void Page_Load(object sender, EventArgs e)
{
  if(Session.IsNewSession)
  {
    Response.Redirect("ClaimForm1.aspx");
  }
  ClaimFormDTO claimForm = (ClaimFormDTO)Session["ClaimFormDTO"];
  ModelFacade facade = new ModelFacade();
  Claim claim = facade.createClaim(claimForm);
  if(claim.Policy.Type.Equals("contents"))
  {
    PolicyTypeImage.ImageUrl = "contents.gif";
  }
  else
  {
    PolicyTypeImage.ImageUrl = "buildings.gif";
  }
  Reference.Text = claim.Reference;
  ClaimDate.Text = claim.DateOfClaim.ToShortDateString();
  Approved.Text = claim.IsApproved.ToString();
  Policy.Text = claim.Policy.Number.ToString();
  Type.Text = claim.Policy.Type;
  Amount.Text = claim.Amount.ToString();
  Description.Text = claim.Description;
  Session.Abandon();
}
```

Figure 9.17 shows how 'ClaimForm3.aspx' looks when displayed in the browser at the end of the webflow, using data from the Claim and Policy objects from the model layer of the web application.

FIGURE 9.17 'ClaimForm3.aspx' populated with data from the model layer Claim and Policy objects

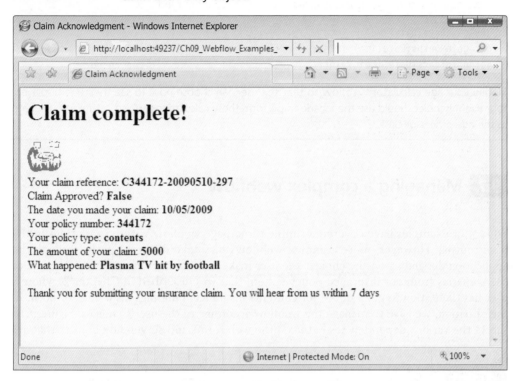

Section summary and quick exercises

This section introduced some objects that can be used in conjunction with web application event handlers. We began by introducing the Data Transfer Object as a way of encapsulating form data gathered from a webflow. We also introduced the façade pattern as a way of providing simplified access to the model layer of an application. In that model layer, we introduced two classes ('Claim' and 'Policy') that represented objects from the underlying application domain and a process object (ReferenceGenerator). We used a DTO in the insurance claim webflow to gather client data, and then used the DTO to create a domain level object via the facade. The domain objects were then used to populate the view of the final form in the webflow.

EXERCISE 9.5

Add a validation control to ClaimForm2.aspx so that the claim amount TextBox can be checked to make sure that the user has entered a string that can successfully be parsed into a Decimal number.

EXERCISE 9.6

Create a very simple DTO that encapsulates a DateTime property. Modify the webflow of your two-page age calculator so that it uses this DTO to maintain the client data in the session.

Create a façade and an age processor class that both have these methods:

```
getAgeInDays(DateTime) : int
getAgeInMonths(DateTime) : int
getAgeInYears(DateTime) : int
```

Modify your age calculator webflow so that the user can choose how to see their age displayed. Your event handler should use the façade to perform these calculations, which in turn will delegate to the age processor class.

9.7 Managing a complex webflow

So far our examples have covered a simple three-page webflow with no variations in the page routing. However, more complex webflows may take different paths through the application depending on the choices the user makes. In the next example we take one of the scenarios from our insurance policy system that was described in Chapter 2, where a user has the option to get a quote for contents insurance, buildings insurance, or both. In this situation, we have to manage the webflow according to the user's choices. Figure 9.18 shows the various dependencies between the web forms and server-side objects that are

FIGURE 9.18 The webflow design for the 'get insurance quote' use case.

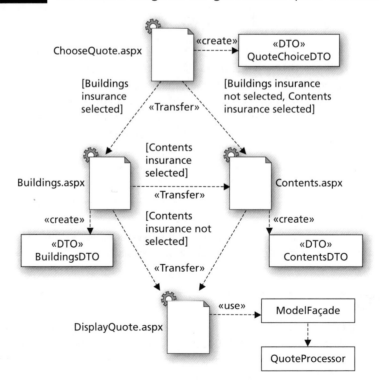

included in the webflow. To simplify the example a little, the first step in the use case (getting customer details) has been omitted, so we start at the point of asking the customer which type(s) of insurance they require. In this webflow, we need to make decisions about page routing at several points. These decisions will be made in event handlers depending on the state of the QuoteChoiceDTO.

9.7.1 Creating the web forms and classes for the webflow

We will now work our way through each stage of the webflow. First, there is a web form that asks the user which type(s) of insurance they would like a quote for. Here is the page ('ChooseQuote.aspx'). Initially, both the check boxes are 'checked', so the default selection is for both contents and buildings insurance:

```
<%@ Page Language="VB" AutoEventWireup="false"
CodeFile="ChooseQuote.aspx.vb" Inherits="ChooseQuote" %>

<!DOCTYPE html PUBLIC "-//W3C//DTD XHTML 1.0 Transitional//EN"
"http://www.w3.org/TR/xhtml1/DTD/xhtml1-transitional.dtd">
<html xmlns="http://www.w3.org/1999/xhtml">
  <head runat="server">
    <title>WebHomeCover - Insurance Quote Request</title>
  </head>
  <body>
    <h1>Choose your quote!</h1>
    <h2>
      Please choose buildings insurance, contents insurance,
      or both, by checking the boxes below
    </h2>
    <form id="form1" runat="server">
      <div>
        <p>What kind of quote do you require?</p>
        <p>Buildings insurance quote
        <asp:CheckBox ID="Buildings" runat="server" Checked="True" />
        </p>
        <p>Contents insurance quote
        <asp:CheckBox ID="Contents" runat="server" Checked="True" />
        </p>
        <asp:Button ID="SubmitButton" runat="server" Text="Submit"
          onclick="SubmitButton_Click" />
      </div>
    </form>
  </body>
</html>
```

Figure 9.19 shows what this page looks like in Internet Explorer 7.

From a programming point of view, the important aspects are the names of the two CheckBoxes; 'Contents' and 'Buildings'. These need to match properties in the DTO ('QuoteChoiceDTO') that will store this information on the server, inside the session

FIGURE 9.19 The 'ChooseQuote.aspx' page displayed in Internet Explorer 7

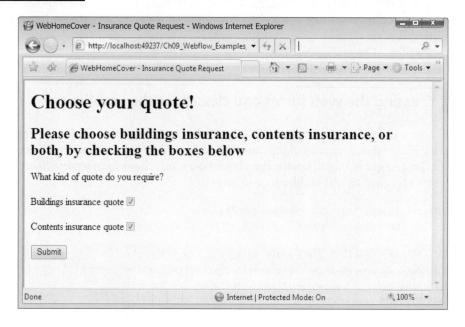

object. Here is the source code for the class, which only has two Boolean properties, 'Contents' and 'Buildings':

VB code

```
Public Class QuoteChoiceDTO
  Private attrBuildings As Boolean = True
  Private attrContents As Boolean = True

  Public Property Buildings() As Boolean
    Get
      Return attrBuildings
    End Get
    Set(ByVal Value As Boolean)
      attrBuildings = Value
    End Set
  End Property
  Public Property Contents() As Boolean
    Get
      Return attrContents
    End Gct
    Set(ByVal Value As Boolean)
      attrContents = Value
    End Set
  End Property
End Class
```

C# code

```
public class QuoteChoiceDTO
{
  public Boolean Buildings {get; set;}
  public Boolean Contents {get; set;}
}
```

The event handler for the submit button control has two responsibilities:

- To create and populate an instance of the 'QuoteChoiceDTO' class
- To direct the user to the next form page, depending on the choices they have made

The following code is the submit button event handler for 'ChooseQuote.aspx'. Note that the QuoteChoiceDTO object is added to the session to ensure that it is still available over multiple request/response cycles. 'If' statements are used to choose whether to forward to 'Buildings.aspx' or 'Contents.aspx' as the next form page. You will note that we have two sets of 'if' statements. This is necessary because we need to set both of the Boolean values in the DTO before we move to the next page.

VB code

```
Protected Sub SubmitButton_Click(ByVal sender As Object, ByVal e As
System.EventArgs) Handles SubmitButton.Click
  Dim QuoteChoice As New QuoteChoiceDTO()
  If Buildings.Checked Then
    QuoteChoice.Buildings() = True
  End If
  If Contents.Checked Then
    QuoteChoice.Contents() = True
  End If
  Session.Item("QuoteChoice") = QuoteChoice
  ' select which page to go to depending on the check box selected
  If (QuoteChoice.Buildings()) Then
    Server.Transfer("Buildings.aspx")
  ElseIf (QuoteChoice.Contents()) Then
    Server.Transfer("contents.aspx")
  End If
  End Sub
```

C# code

```
protected void SubmitButton_Click(object sender, EventArgs e)
{
  QuoteChoiceDTO QuoteChoice = new QuoteChoiceDTO();
  if(Buildings.Checked)
  {
    QuoteChoice.Buildings = true;
  }
```

```
    if(Contents.Checked)
    {
     QuoteChoice.Contents = true;
    }
    Session["QuoteChoice"] = QuoteChoice;
   // select which page to go to depending on the check box selected
    if (QuoteChoice.Buildings)
    {
     Server.Transfer("Buildings.aspx");
    }
    else
    {
     if (QuoteChoice.Contents)
     {
      Server.Transfer("Contents.aspx");
     }
    }
   }
  }
```

If the user has chosen to get a buildings insurance quote, then the application will forward them to the 'Buildings.aspx' web form, which looks like this:

```
<%@ Page Language="VB" AutoEventWireup="false"
CodeFile="Buildings.aspx.vb" Inherits="Buildings" %>

<!DOCTYPE html PUBLIC "-//W3C//DTD XHTML 1.0 Transitional//EN"
"http://www.w3.org/TR/xhtml1/DTD/xhtml1-transitional.dtd">
<html xmlns="http://www.w3.org/1999/xhtml">
 <head id="Head1" runat="server">
  <title>WebHomeCover - Building Details</title>
</head>
<body>
 <!-- File: Buildings.aspx -->
 <h1>Buildings Policy Details</h1>
 <h2>
    Please provide information about where you live
    in the form below, then click submit
 </h2>
  <form id="form1" runat="server">
   <div>
   <table>
    <tr>
     <td>Type of building:</td>
     <td>
      <asp:DropDownList ID="PropertyType" runat="server">
      <asp:ListItem Value="apartment">Flat / Apartment
      </asp:ListItem>
       <asp:ListItem Value="terraced">Terraced</asp:ListItem>
       <asp:ListItem Value="semi">Semi-detached</asp:ListItem>
       <asp:ListItem Value="detached">Detached</asp:ListItem>
      </asp:DropDownList>
     </td>
```

```
    </tr>
    <tr>
     <td>Number of bedrooms:</td>
     <td>
      <asp:DropDownList ID="BedroomCount" runat="server">
       <asp:ListItem>1</asp:ListItem>
       <asp:ListItem>2</asp:ListItem>
       <asp:ListItem>3</asp:ListItem>
       <asp:ListItem>4</asp:ListItem>
       <asp:ListItem>5</asp:ListItem>
       <asp:ListItem Value="6">More than 5</asp:ListItem>
      </asp:DropDownList>
     </td>
    </tr>
    <tr>
     <td>Date of construction:</td>
     <td>
      <asp:DropDownList ID="ConstructionDate" runat="server">
       <asp:ListItem Value="1900-01-01">pre 1900</asp:ListItem>
       <asp:ListItem Value="1901-01-01">1901 - 1950</asp:ListItem>
       <asp:ListItem Value="1951-01-01">1951 - 1970</asp:ListItem>
       <asp:ListItem Value="1971-10-01">1971 - 1990</asp:ListItem>
       <asp:ListItem Value="1991-01-01">after 1990</asp:ListItem>
      </asp:DropDownList>
     </td>
    </tr>
    <tr>
     <td>Type of construction</td>
     <td>
      <asp:RadioButtonList ID="ConstructionType" runat="server">
      <asp:ListItem Selected="True" Value="timber"> Timber
       </asp:ListItem>
       <asp:ListItem Value="masonry">Masonry</asp:ListItem>
      </asp:RadioButtonList>
     </td>
    </tr>
    <tr>
     <td>Estimated market value:</td>
     <td>
     <asp:DropDownList ID="MarketValue" runat="server">
      <asp:ListItem Value="30000">up to 30,000</asp:ListItem>
      <asp:ListItem Value="60000">30,000 - 60,000</asp:ListItem>
      <asp:ListItem Value="100000">60,000 - 100,000</asp:ListItem>
      <asp:ListItem Value="200000">100,000 - 200,000</asp:ListItem>
      <asp:ListItem Value="500000">200,000 - 500,000</asp:ListItem>
      <asp:ListItem Value="1000000">above 500,000</asp:ListItem>
      </asp:DropDownList>
     </td>
    </tr>
    <tr>
     <td> </td>
```

```
            <td>
              <asp:Button ID="SubmitButton" runat="server" Text="Submit"
              onclick="SubmitButton_Click" />
            </td>
          </tr>
        </table>
      </div>
    </form>
  </body>
</html>
```

Figure 9.20 shows what this page looks like in Internet Explorer 7, with the default data selected in the form components.

FIGURE 9.20   The 'Buildings.aspx' web form displayed in Internet Explorer 7

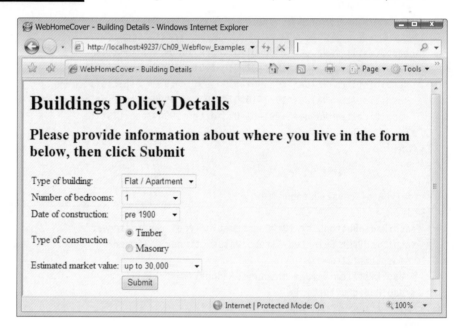

The information gathered from the user on this page includes the type of building ('PropertyType'), the number of bedrooms ('BedroomCount'), the approximate date of construction ('ConstructionDate'), the type of construction ('ConstructionType') and the approximate market value of the property ('MarketValue'). All of these form components are mirrored in the 'BuildingsDTO' object:

VB code

```
Public Class BuildingsDTO
  Private attrPropertyType As String = ""
  Private attrBedroomCount As Integer = 0
  Private attrConstructionDate As DateTime
```

```vb
    Private attrConstructionType As String = ""
    Private attrMarketValue As Integer = 0

    Property PropertyType() As String
      Get
        Return attrPropertyType
      End Get
      Set(ByVal Value As String)
        attrPropertyType = Value
      End Set
    End Property
    Property BedroomCount() As Integer
      Get
        Return attrBedroomCount
      End Get
      Set(ByVal Value As Integer)
        attrBedroomCount = Value
      End Set
    End Property
    Property ConstructionDate() As DateTime
      Get
        Return attrConstructionDate
      End Get
      Set(ByVal Value As DateTime)
        attrConstructionDate = Value
      End Set
    End Property
    Property ConstructionType() As String
      Get
        Return attrConstructionType
      End Get
      Set(ByVal Value As String)
        attrConstructionType = Value
      End Set
    End Property
    Property MarketValue() As Integer
      Get
        Return attrMarketValue
      End Get
      Set(ByVal Value As Integer)
        attrMarketValue = Value
      End Set
    End Property
  End Class
```

C# code

```csharp
public class BuildingsDTO
{
  public String PropertyType { get; set; }
```

```
public int BedroomCount { get; set; }
public DateTime ConstructionDate { get; set; }
public String ConstructionType { get; set; }
public int MarketValue { get; set; }
}
```

The event handler for the button on the 'Buildings.aspx' page creates a new 'BuildingsDTO' object and populates its properties from the components on the web form. It also needs to retrieve the 'QuoteChoiceDTO' object from the session to find out which web form to forward to next. If the user has also chosen a contents quote, the next page will be 'Contents.aspx'. If not, we need to transfer directly to the final page in the webflow, which will calculate the insurance quote.

VB code

```
Protected Sub SubmitButton_Click(ByVal sender As Object, ByVal e As
System.EventArgs) Handles SubmitButton.Click
  Dim bdto As BuildingsDTO = New BuildingsDTO()
  bdto.BedroomCount = BedroomCount.Text
  bdto.ConstructionDate = ConstructionDate.Text
  bdto.ConstructionType = ConstructionType.Text
  bdto.MarketValue = MarketValue.Text
  bdto.PropertyType = PropertyType.Text
  Session.Item("BuildingsDTO") = bdto
  Dim choose As QuoteChoiceDTO = Session.Item("QuoteChoice")
  If (choose.Contents) Then
    Server.Transfer("Contents.aspx")
  Else
    Server.Transfer("DisplayQuote.aspx")
  End If
End Sub
```

C# code

```
protected void SubmitButton_Click(object sender, EventArgs e)
{
  BuildingsDTO bdto = new BuildingsDTO();
  bdto.BedroomCount = Int32.Parse(BedroomCount.Text);
  bdto.ConstructionDate = DateTime.Parse(ConstructionDate.Text);
  bdto.ConstructionType = ConstructionType.Text;
  bdto.MarketValue = Int32.Parse(MarketValue.Text);
  bdto.PropertyType = PropertyType.Text;
  Session["BuildingsDTO"] = bdto;
  QuoteChoiceDTO choose = (QuoteChoiceDTO)Session["QuoteChoice"];
  if (choose.Contents)
  {
    Server.Transfer("Contents.aspx");
  }
  else
```

```
    {
    Server.Transfer("DisplayQuote.aspx");
    }
  }
```

Here is the 'Contents.aspx' web form that gathers information from the user about their contents insurance requirements, if they have chosen to ask for a contents insurance quote:

```
<%@ Page Language="VB" AutoEventWireup="false"
CodeFile="Contents.aspx.vb" Inherits="Contents" %>

<!DOCTYPE html PUBLIC "-//W3C//DTD XHTML 1.0 Transitional//EN"
"http://www.w3.org/TR/xhtml1/DTD/xhtml1-transitional.dtd">

<html xmlns="http://www.w3.org/1999/xhtml">
 <head runat="server">
  <title>WebHomeCover - Contents Details</title>
 </head>
 <body>
  <!-- File: Contents.aspx -->
  <h1>Contents Policy Details</h1>
  <h2>Please provide information about the contents cover you require
in the form below, then click submit</h2>
  <form id="form1" runat="server">
    <div>
    <table>
     <tr>
      <td>Accidental damage cover (tick box)</td>
      <td>
       <asp:CheckBox ID="AccidentalCover" runat="server" />
      </td>
     </tr>
     <tr>
      <td>Amount of cover required:</td>
      <td>
       <asp:DropDownList ID="CoverAmount" runat="server">
        <asp:ListItem Value="10000">10,000</asp:ListItem>
        <asp:ListItem Value="20000">20,000</asp:ListItem>
        <asp:ListItem Value="30000">30,000</asp:ListItem>
        <asp:ListItem Value="50000">50,000</asp:ListItem>
        <asp:ListItem Value="100000">100,000</asp:ListItem>
       </asp:DropDownList>
      </td>
     </tr>
     <tr>
      <td>Policy excess / deductible required</td>
      <td>
       <asp:RadioButtonList ID="DeductibleAmount" runat="server">
        <asp:ListItem Selected="True">0</asp:ListItem>
        <asp:ListItem>500</asp:ListItem>
        <asp:ListItem Value="1000">1,000</asp:ListItem>
```

```
        </asp:RadioButtonList>
      </td>
    </tr>
    <tr>
      <td></td>
      <td>
        <asp:Button ID="SubmitButton" runat="server" Text="Submit"
         onclick="SubmitButton_Click"/>
      </td>
    </tr>
  </table>
  </div>
  </form>
  </body>
</html>
```

Figure 9.21 shows what the 'Contents.aspx' page looks like when it is displayed in Internet Explorer 7.

FIGURE 9.21   The 'Contents.aspx' page displayed in Internet Explorer 7

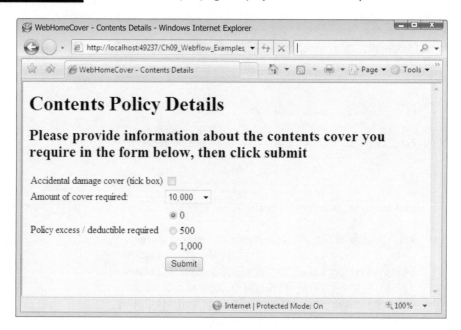

The event handler for 'Contents.aspx' is quite simple, since at this stage of the webflow it does not need to make any decisions about page routing. All it needs to do is to populate the 'ContentsDTO' object from the request before forwarding on to the final web form.

VB code

```
Protected Sub SubmitButton_Click(ByVal sender As Object, _
    ByVal e As System.EventArgs) Handles SubmitButton.Click
  Dim cdto As ContentsDTO = New ContentsDTO()
```

```
  If AccidentalCover.Checked Then
    cdto.AccidentalCover = True
  Else
    cdto.AccidentalCover = False
  End If
  cdto.CoverAmount = CoverAmount.Text()
  cdto.DeductibleAmount = DeductibleAmount.Text()
  Session.Item("ContentsDTO") = cdto
  Server.Transfer("DisplayQuote.aspx")
End Sub
```

C# code

```
protected void SubmitButton_Click(object sender, EventArgs e)
{
  ContentsDTO cdto = new ContentsDTO();
  if(AccidentalCover.Checked)
  {
    cdto.AccidentalCover = true;
  }
  else
  {
    cdto.AccidentalCover = false;
  }
  cdto.CoverAmount = Int32.Parse(CoverAmount.SelectedValue);
  cdto.DeductibleAmount = Int32.Parse(DeductibleAmount.SelectedValue);
  Session["ContentsDTO"] = cdto;
  Server.Transfer("DisplayQuote.aspx");
}
```

The 'ContentsDTO' object has much in common with the 'BuildingsDTO' object. It has properties that match the form submitted from the browser.

VB code

```
Imports Microsoft.VisualBasic

Public Class ContentsDTO
  Private attrAccidentalCover As Boolean = False
  Private attrCoverAmount As Integer = 0
  Private attrDeductibleAmount As Integer = 0

  Property AccidentalCover() As Boolean
    Get
      Return attrAccidentalCover
    End Get
    Set(ByVal Value As Boolean)
      attrAccidentalCover = Value
    End Set
  End Property
```

```
    Property CoverAmount() As Integer
      Get
        Return attrCoverAmount
      End Get
      Set(ByVal Value As Integer)
        attrCoverAmount = Value
      End Set
    End Property
    Property DeductibleAmount() As Integer
      Get
        Return attrDeductibleAmount
      End Get
      Set(ByVal Value As Integer)
        attrDeductibleAmount = Value
      End Set
    End Property
  End Class
```

C# code

```csharp
public class ContentsDTO
{
  public Boolean AccidentalCover { get; set; }
  public int CoverAmount { get; set; }
  public int DeductibleAmount { get; set; }
}
```

Finally, either the 'Buildings.aspx' or 'Contents.aspx' web form event handlers will forward to the last page in the webflow, 'DisplayQuote.aspx'. The page load event handler for this web form needs to retrieve the DTOs from the session and pass them to a suitable component in the model layer to calculate the insurance premium. For this step, we need an object that is able to process the necessary information about insurance premiums.

So far all the pages of our webflow just gather information from the user and store it in the session in objects. We do not yet invoke any business processes using this data, though of course this is in fact the key part of any web-based system. In this case, the main business process that we need is one that calculates an insurance quote based on the information that the user has provided. This task is performed by another server-side component, the 'QuoteProcessor'. In other words the event handler is responsible only for managing the page routing in the webflow. In contrast, the QuoteProcessor is an object from the model layer, able to manage the business process to get an insurance quote. It is an example of a *process object*, a component that encapsulates one or more related business processes. In our case, we need a process object that can calculate quotations for buildings and contents insurance. Its interface might look something like the UML diagram in Figure 9.22.

FIGURE 9.22 UML diagram of the QuoteProcessor class

9

QuoteProcessor
getBuildingsQuote(BuildingsDTO) : Double getContentsQuote(ContentsDTO) : Double

What then, is the implementation of the QuoteProcessor class and its methods? Since this is a fictional website, we can make up any algorithms we like to calculate the insurance, such as this one here for buildings insurance:

- Calculations begin with a base premium which is .2% of the market value.
- The base premium is then adjusted by property type. For a terraced building this is unchanged. However the premium for an apartment is 95% of the base, for a semi-detached building 105% and a detached building 110%.
- An additional 1% is then added to the premium for each bedroom.
- Depending on which of the four age ranges the building falls into, we add 1%, 2% 3% or 4% to the premium (the older the property the higher the premium).
- Finally, we add 10% for a timber building (more likely to burn down).

Here is a fictional formula for calculating contents insurance:

- The base premium is .4% of the required cover.
- If accidental damage cover is required, we add 25% to the premium.
- If the deductible amount on claims is more than 500, then we reduce the premium by 10%.
- If the deductible amount is more than 1,000, then we reduce the premium by 20%.

Here is the code for the 'QuoteProcessor' class that interacts with the various components in the application. It uses data from DTOs to generate the necessary insurance quotes.

VB code

```
Public Class QuoteProcessor
  Public Function getBuildingsQuote(ByVal buildingsDetails _
     As BuildingsDTO) As Double
   Dim premium As Double = 0.0
   Dim basicQuote As Double = buildingsDetails.MarketValue * 0.002
   Dim propertyType As String = buildingsDetails.PropertyType
   If (propertyType.Equals("apartment")) Then
     premium = basicQuote * 0.95
   End If
   If (propertyType.Equals("semi")) Then
     premium = basicQuote * 1.05
   End If
```

```
      If (propertyType.Equals("terraced")) Then
        premium = basicQuote
      End If
      If (propertyType.Equals("detached")) Then
        premium = basicQuote * 1.1
      End If
      premium = premium + (buildingsDetails.BedroomCount _
        * (premium / 100))
      Dim year As Integer = buildingsDetails.ConstructionDate.Year
      If (year = "00") Then
        premium += premium * 0.04
      End If
      If (year = "01") Then
        premium += premium * 0.03
      End If
      If (year = "51") Then
        premium += premium * 0.02
      End If
      If (year = "71") Then
        premium += premium * 0.01
      End If
      If (buildingsDetails.ConstructionType().Equals("timber")) Then
        premium += (premium * 0.1)
      End If
      Return premium
    End Function

    Public Function getContentsQuote _
        (ByVal contentsDetails As ContentsDTO) As Double
      Dim accidentalCover As Boolean = contentsDetails.AccidentalCover
      Dim cover As Integer = contentsDetails.CoverAmount
      Dim deductible As Integer = contentsDetails.DeductibleAmount
      Dim premium As Double = cover * 0.004
      If (accidentalCover) Then
        premium *= 1.25
      End If
      If (deductible >= 1000) Then
        premium -= (premium * 0.2)
      ElseIf (deductible >= 500) Then
        premium -= (premium * 0.1)
      End If
      Return premium
    End Function
  End Class
```

C# code

```
public class QuoteProcessor
{
  public double getBuildingsQuote(BuildingsDTO buildingsDetails)
```

```
{
 double premium = 0.0;
 double basicQuote = buildingsDetails.MarketValue * 0.002;
 String propertyType = buildingsDetails.PropertyType;
 if (propertyType.Equals("apartment"))
 {
  premium = basicQuote * 0.95;
 }
 if (propertyType.Equals("semi"))
 {
  premium = basicQuote * 1.05;
 }
 if (propertyType.Equals("terraced"))
 {
  premium = basicQuote;
 }
 if (propertyType.Equals("detached"))
 {
  premium = basicQuote * 1.1;
 }
 premium = premium +
   (buildingsDetails.BedroomCount * (premium / 100));
 String yearString = buildingsDetails.ConstructionDate.Year.
   ToString().Substring(2, 2);
 int year = int.Parse(yearString);
 switch (year)
 {
  case 00:
   premium += premium * .04;
   break;
  case 01:
   premium += premium * .03;
   break;
  case 51:
   premium += premium * .02;
   break;
  case 71:
   premium += premium * .01;
   break;
 }
 if (buildingsDetails.ConstructionType.Equals("timber"))
 {
  premium += (premium * 0.1);
 }
 return premium;
 }

public double getContentsQuote(ContentsDTO contentsDetails)
{
 Boolean accidentalCover = contentsDetails.AccidentalCover;
 int cover = contentsDetails.CoverAmount;
```

```
      int deductible = contentsDetails.DeductibleAmount;
      double premium = cover * 0.004;
      if (accidentalCover)
      {
        premium *= 1.25;
      }
      if (deductible >= 1000)
      {
        premium -= (premium * 0.2);
      }
      else
      {
        if (deductible >= 500)
        {
          premium -= (premium * 0.1);
        }
      }
      return premium;
    }
  }
```

To maintain our architectural layers, the QuoteProcessor should reside in the model layer of the application. This means it will be behind the façade, and should be accessed though it (Figure 9.23).

FIGURE 9.23 The QuoteProcessor is in the model layer, accessed from the view/controller layer via the Façade

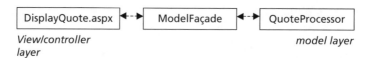

View/controller layer · · · model layer

Therefore we need to add the necessary methods to the ModelFacade class to enable a view layer component like the final web form to get insurance quotes from the Quote-Processor. These are quite simple, with the 'getQuote' method being overloaded by its parameter type. The code behind the web form will add the appropriate DTO (representing either buildings or contents insurance) to the matching method, which then in turn invokes the required method of the QuoteProcessor.

VB code

```
Public Function getQuote(ByVal dto As BuildingsDTO) As Double
  Dim quoter As QuoteProcessor = New QuoteProcessor()
  Return quoter.getBuildingsQuote(dto)
End Function

Public Function getQuote(ByVal dto As ContentsDTO) As Double
  Dim quoter As QuoteProcessor = New QuoteProcessor()
  Return quoter.getContentsQuote(dto)
End Function
```

C# code

```csharp
public double getQuote(BuildingsDTO dto)
{
  QuoteProcessor quoter = new QuoteProcessor();
  return quoter.getBuildingsQuote(dto);
}
public double getQuote(ContentsDTO dto)
{
  QuoteProcessor quoter = new QuoteProcessor();
  return quoter.getContentsQuote(dto);
}
```

The final page in the webflow, 'DisplayQuote.aspx', displays the result of the insurance quote process. To do this, its 'Page_Load' event handler needs to use the facilities of the ModelFacade. The QuoteChoiceDTO is used to decide which quotes are needed, and then the relevant DTOs are passed to the Façade in order to retrieve the required quote(s), which are then displayed in the page. To make the quote appear in a currency format, we can use the Format method of the String class. At its simplest, this takes two parameter arguments; first, a string that contains the required format, and second, the string to be formatted. The string containing the format is expressed using a special placeholder notation, which take this form:

```
{placeholderNumber:formatCharacter}
```

The 'placeholderNumber' relates to one of the arguments to the method. If there is only one, this would be '0'. The 'format character' relates to the type of formatting. For currency, this would be 'c'. In this event handler, we format both contents and buildings quotes. Here is the code that formats the buildings quote:

```
String.Format("{0:c}", facade.getQuote(buildingsDTO));
```

 NOTE Claudio Barba's blog has a good introduction to formatting in .NET, see http://www.cyberactiva.com/dettaglio.asp?id=367.

Here is the complete event handler.

VB code

```vb
Protected Sub Page_Load(ByVal sender As Object, _
   ByVal e As System.EventArgs) Handles Me.Load
 Dim choose As QuoteChoiceDTO = Session.Item("QuoteChoice")
 Dim facade As ModelFacade = New ModelFacade()
 If (choose.buildings) Then
   Dim buildingsDTO As BuildingsDTO = Session.Item("BuildingsDTO")
   BuildingsInsuranceLabel.Text = "Your Buildings Insurance Quote:"
   Dim BuildingsQuote As String = String.Format("{0:c}", _
      facade.getQuote(buildingsDTO))
```

```
      BuildingsInsurance.Text = BuildingsQuote
    End If
    If (choose.contents) Then
      Dim contentsDTO As ContentsDTO = Session.Item("ContentsDTO")
      ContentsInsuranceLabel.Text = "Your Contents Insurance Quote:"
      Dim ContentsQuote As String = String.Format("{0:c}", _
          facade.getQuote(contentsDTO))
      ContentsInsurance.Text = ContentsQuote
    End If
  End Sub
```

C# code

```
protected void Page_Load(object sender, EventArgs e)
{
  QuoteChoiceDTO choose = (QuoteChoiceDTO)Session["QuoteChoice"];
  ModelFacade facade = new ModelFacade();
  if (choose.Buildings)
  {
    BuildingsDTO buildingsDTO = (BuildingsDTO)Session["BuildingsDTO"];
    BuildingsInsuranceLabel.Text = "Your Buildings Insurance Quote:";
    String buildingsQuote = String.Format("{0:c}",
        facade.getQuote(buildingsDTO));
    BuildingsInsurance.Text = buildingsQuote;
  }
  if (choose.Contents)
  {
    ContentsDTO contentsDTO = (ContentsDTO)Session["ContentsDTO"];
    ContentsInsuranceLabel.Text = "Your Contents Insurance Quote:";
    String contentsQuote = String.Format("{0:c}",
        facade.getQuote(contentsDTO));
    ContentsInsurance.Text = contentsQuote;
  }
}
```

NOTE	In this handler we are creating the ModelFacade again, as we did in the insurance claim example. This is not a very scaleable or maintainable approach. A more realistic system would ensure that there was one ModelFacade creation point, with all other components accessing the same façade instance. The Singleton pattern (Gamma *et al.*, 1995) is often used for this type of object.

The source for the final web form (DisplayQuote.aspx) is shown on the next page. It is quite simple, consisting of a series of Label controls. Because the 'Page_Load' event handler populates the Label controls on the web form depending on the user's earlier selections, it may display a buildings insurance quote, a contents insurance quote, or both:

```
<%@ Page Language="VB" AutoEventWireup="false"
CodeFile="DisplayQuote.aspx.vb" Inherits="DisplayQuote" %>

<!DOCTYPE html PUBLIC "-//W3C//DTD XHTML 1.0 Transitional//EN"
"http://www.w3.org/TR/xhtml1/DTD/xhtml1-transitional.dtd">
<html xmlns="http://www.w3.org/1999/xhtml">
  <head id="Head1" runat="server">
    <title>WebHomeCover Insurance Quote</title>
  </head>
  <body>
    <h1>Here is your insurance quote from WebHomeCover</h1>
    <form id="form1" runat="server">
      <div>
        <h2>
          <asp:Label ID="BuildingsInsuranceLabel" runat="server" Text="">
          </asp:Label>
        </h2>
        <asp:Label ID="BuildingsInsurance" runat="server" Text="">
        </asp:Label>
        <h2>
          <asp:Label ID="ContentsInsuranceLabel" runat="server" Text="">
          </asp:Label>
        </h2>
        <asp:Label ID="ContentsInsurance" runat="server" Text="">
        </asp:Label>
      </div>
      <p>
    </form>
  </body>
</html>
```

Figure 9.24 shows what the final page looks like if the data shown in Figures 9.20 and 9.21 has been chosen, requesting both contents and buildings quotes.

9.7.2 Handing request parameters with master pages

So far in this chapter we have not applied a master page to any of our web forms. One reason for this is that applying a master page to a web form has one rather unfortunate side effect. It changes the way that request parameters are referred to in event handlers. You can see the problem if you apply the master page to the web forms in the insurance claim webflow. Here, for example, is the second claim form modified to use the master page from Chapter 7:

```
<%@ Page Language="VB" AutoEventWireup="false"
CodeFile="ClaimForm2Master.aspx.vb" Inherits="ClaimForm2Master"
MasterPageFile="WebHomeCover.master" %>

<%@ Register src="SideNavMain.ascx" tagname="SideNavMain"
tagprefix="uc1" %>
```

```
<asp:Content ID="Content1" ContentPlaceHolderID="head"
  Runat="Server">
 <title>Claim Details</title>
</asp:Content>
<asp:Content ID="Content2" ContentPlaceHolderID="SideNavigation"
  Runat="Server">
 <uc1:SideNavMain ID="SideNavMain1" runat="server" />
</asp:Content>
<asp:Content ID="Content3" ContentPlaceHolderID="Content"
  Runat="Server">
  <form id="form1" runat="server">
   <div>
    <h1>Claim Details</h1>
    <p>Your policy number:
     <strong>
      <asp:Label ID="Policy" runat="server" Text=""></asp:Label>
     </strong>
     <br />
     Your policy type:
     <strong>
      <asp:Label ID="Type" runat="server" Text=""></asp:Label>
     </strong>
     </p>
     <p>
      Please enter the approximate amount of your claim
      in the box below
    </p>
    <asp:TextBox ID="ClaimAmount" runat="server"></asp:TextBox>
    <p>
     Please enter a brief description of your claim in the box below
    </p>
    <asp:TextBox ID="Description" runat="server"
     TextMode="MultiLine">
    </asp:TextBox>
    <br />
    <asp:Button ID="SubmitButton" runat="server"
     Text="Submit My Claim" />
   </div>
  </form>
</asp:Content>
```

The second page in the flow, which previously displayed the policy number and the type of insurance, no longer does so when we integrate this web form into a master page. Why is this? In fact it is because the page load event handler refers to Request parameter names directly, in the following way:

```
Protected Sub Page_Load(ByVal sender As Object, ByVal e As System.EventArgs)
Handles Me.Load
  Policy.Text = Request.Item("PolicyNumber")
  Type.Text = Request.Item("PolicyType")
End Sub
```

FIGURE 9.24 The 'DisplayQuote.aspx' page displayed in Internet Explorer 7, showing one of the many possible results of the webflow that implements the 'get insurance quote' use case

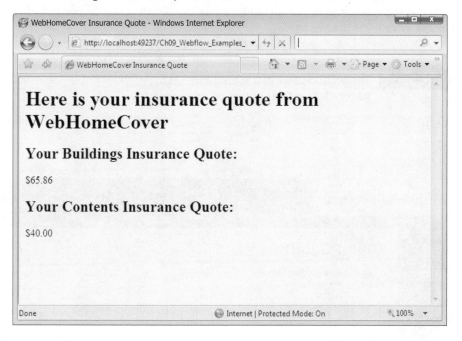

Unfortunately, the request parameter names 'PolicyNumber' and 'PolicyType' actually change when we are using a master page. We need to prefix these names with 'ctl00$Content$', in other words something that identifies the content place holder that the control appears in. To make our insurance claim webflow behave as it did before, we need to modify the event handler to look like this:

```
Protected Sub Page_Load(ByVal sender As Object, ByVal e As
        System.EventArgs) Handles Me.Load
  Policy.Text = Request.Item("ctl00$Content$PolicyNumber")
  Type.Text = Request.Item("ctl00$Content$PolicyType")
End Sub
```

If you want to make sense of these identifiers, set the 'Trace' attribute to 'true' in the ASP tag at the top of the web form and view the trace in the browser, as we demonstrated in Chapter 6. If you look at the 'Control Tree' section of the trace output, you should see that 'ctl00' is the top level control in the page, and has the value 'ASP .webhomecover_master' (i.e. the master page is the top level control). Further down the trace, you should see that 'ctl00$Content' is within the master page, and is of type 'System.Web.UI.WebControls.ContentPlaceHolder', i.e. this is the identifier of the content place holder that contains our other controls. However inside this section you will not find the request parameters. These can be found further down the trace under the 'Form Collection' heading. There, you should see both 'ctl00$Content$PolicyNumber' and 'ctl00$Content$PolicyType' listed, with their values, passed from the first web form via the Request.

With the parameter names updated, the webflow should behave as it did before, displaying the policy number and insurance type on the second web form (Figure 9.25). Since we rarely use request data directly in our examples, this problem does not impact very much on our code, but it is important to be aware of this effect on the names of request parameters when using master pages.

FIGURE 9.25 The second page in the insurance claim webflow displaying request parameters in the context of a master page

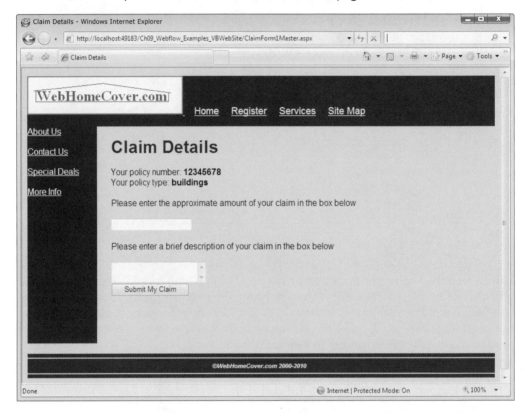

Self Study Questions

1. What are the three components of an MVC architecture?
2. What method do we use to move between web forms on the server using the same request? What method is used to go to another page via the client browser using a new request?
3. Why is a Wizard control not suitable for all types of webflow?
4. Why might we choose to put values from a client form in a session rather than the request?
5. How can we empty the contents from a session without actually destroying it?
6. How do we implement a read-only property?
7. What is the term given to improving the design of existing code without actually changing its functionality?
8. The 'Façade' and the 'Singleton' are examples of what?
9. Should process objects and model objects be in front of or behind the façade?
10. What happens to the names of request parameters in event handlers when a master page is used?

Exercises

9.8 Convert the pages in the insurance claim form webflow to use the WebHomeCover .master master page from the previous chapter. Modify the master page navigation bar to include a 'Make a Claim' anchor that links to 'ClaimForm1.aspx'. Don't forget that you have to change the names of the request parameters in event handlers when using master pages.

9.9 Convert the pages in the insurance quote webflow to use the master page. Modify the master page navigation bar again to include a 'Get a Quote' anchor that links to 'ChooseQuote.aspx'.

9.10 Create a web form containing a Label control called 'UserAgent'. In the event handler for the page load event, access the 'User-Agent' field of the HTTP header and display its value on the page by setting the text of the Label control. To get a specific header value from the HTTP request, use the 'Get' method of the request headers, passing the name of the required header as the parameter value:

```
Request.Headers.Get("header-name")
```

9.11 Another field of the HTTP header contains the client's language preferences, as set in their particular browser, represented by the 'Accept-Language' header. This contains a string comprising the language options in the browser's list.

Create a new web form that gets the user language preferences from the browser and displays these using the page load event handler. Try changing the language settings in your browser to make the web form display different content for different preferences ('Tools...Options...Content' tab in Firefox 3, 'Tools...Internet Options' in

Internet Explorer). You have to close and reopen the browser for changes in language preference to take effect. Be aware that if the browser has more than one preference then they are all sent as part of the same string, so if your browser lists English, French and German in that order as its preferred languages, then the string will contain the elements 'en', 'fr' and 'de'. Depending on your browser there may be other characters too.

We will be (indirectly) using the language information provided by the client browser when we look at building multi-language web applications in the on-line bonus Chapter 15.

9.12 Create a webflow for the questionnaire application that maintains a record of the user's responses in a DTO that is stored in the session. Display all the responses of the user in the final screen.

SUMMARY

We began this chapter by looking at how the commonly used Model View Controller architectural pattern may be applied to web applications. We built a simple webflow, using event handlers to route between the web forms in the application. To pass data between these web forms, we used both the request and the session to store data throughout the webflow. We refactored the webflow to include a DTO, which we stored in the session while it was being populated with form data. In the final version of the insurance claim webflow, we introduced the concept of the façade to the underlying model, and integrated Claim and Policy objects from the model layer into our webflow. We followed this by building a more complex webflow from the home insurance domain, using multiple request / response cycles and management of user sessions. An important aspect of this webflow was the possibility for the user's path through the webflow to vary depending on their choices.

References and further reading

Fowler, M. 2000. *Refactoring: Improving the Design of Existing Code*. Reading, Mass. Addison-Wesley.
Gamma, E., Helm, R., Johnson, R. and Vlissides, J. 1995. *Design Patterns: Elements of Reusable Object-Oriented Software*. Reading, Mass. Addison-Wesley.
Sussman, D. and Homer, A. 2006. *Wrox's ASP.NET 2.0 Visual Web Developer 2005 Express Edition Starter Kit*.

CHAPTER 10

Web Applications and the Database

LEARNING OBJECTIVES

- To be able to use ASP.NET data controls to connect to a database

- To be able to use Visual Web Developer's Database Explorer to create, configure and populate database tables

- To understand how to use stored procedures to create, configure and populate database tables

- To be able to use an SQLDataSource control to connect to a database in a web form

- To be able to use the DetailsView, FormView, and GridView to display database tables

- To be able to use format specifiers to control the display of data

- To be able to use Language INtegrated Query (LINQ), LinqDataSource and LINQ to SQL

INTRODUCTION

In this chapter we take a look at the ASP.NET data controls which are used to access and update dynamic content stored in a relational database. These controls are used to build dynamic, database-driven web pages, and also allow you to create web forms to update the database, typically using Design view with minimal coding required. We also cover a range of database programming topics including the use of the Structured Query Language (SQL), Microsoft's new Language INtegrated Query (LINQ) technology and the LINQ to SQL tool.

This chapter assumes you have a basic understanding of relational databases and the Structured Query Language (SQL). For those who are less familiar with these topics, the first section presents a review of relational databases, and explains why they are important in dynamic web application development.

The dynamic content in our web applications needs to come from somewhere. In most cases, business-critical data and other dynamic content comes from a database, possibly via some external web service. Therefore, we need to know how to get data in and out of a database so we can use it in our web applications. Although there are several kinds of databases, including hierarchical and object-oriented, the most commonly used ones are relational. The focus of this chapter is how to bridge between the table schemas of a relational database and web forms. In other web development frameworks this can be quite a complex operation. Fortunately, Microsoft has provided .NET controls such as the SqlDataSource and GridView, and also the LINQ to SQL tool. Together these mean that accessing and editing dynamic content stored in a database can be surprisingly simple with ASP.NET.

Following on from this chapter, further examples of database access can also be found in Chapters 11, 12 and 14 (on-line). Taken together, these chapters illustrate the ASP.NET data access techniques you are most likely to need to use in your web applications.

 NOTE

The examples presented in this chapter depend on an appropriate database management system being available. It is assumed you have SQL Server Express Edition installed along with Visual Web Developer. If you are using another edition of SQL Server you will find some minor differences, and similarly if you are using Visual Studio rather than Visual Web Developer. These differences are explained in the first section of Chapter 15 on-line. If you use another database management system altogether, it is likely that you will need to make significant changes to the examples as covered here. In particular, note that LINQ currently works only with SQL Server or SQL Server Express Edition.

Finally note that administrator privileges will be required to be able to create database tables, procedures and diagrams. The easiest way to ensure you have the required authority is to install Visual Web Developer and SQL Server Express Editions on your own PC, and use Run as administrator when you launch Visual Web Developer from the All Programs task menu. To use a database on another computer, you may have to ask its administrator to grant you the required access permissions.

10.1 Review of relational databases

A database is a collection of structured records stored on a computer that can be accessed and updated by application programs. According to this definition, any computer file containing structured data can be considered to be a database, for example an XML file. The word 'database' is, however, usually reserved for structured data storage which provides additional features such as:

- a logical, or application-independent, view of the data
- a language for searching, or querying, the data based on the logical view

- the facility to optimize the query, using for example, automatically generated indices
- a mechanism to enforce data integrity even when multiple applications are, or could be, updating the data simultaneously

These features indicate why dynamic web applications benefit from the use of a database or databases. It is important to remember when developing a web application that it should support multiple simultaneous users. If your website has only one user it is probably not going to be very useful or successful. Not only that, web applications typically have multiple pages that provide different ways to view and update their persistent data. Even though, as discussed below, databases date back to the very early days of computing, they remain popular even in modern, web-based computing. Indeed, according to some sources, SQL is still the most popular computing language of all.

NOTE	We are using the word *database* to describe the stored structured data. The phrase *database management system* describes the software which provides access to this data, and supports the features described above. The most commonly used relational database management systems today are Oracle (from Oracle Corporation), Microsoft's SQL Server, IBM's DB2, and the open source MySQL and PostgreSQL systems.

The need for databases, and database management systems, was recognized in the 1960s, when network and hierarchical databases were invented. These remained popular until the 1980s. It was found, however, that these data models made it difficult to re-organize databases without having to re-write the applications that accessed and updated them, so network and hierarchical databases were gradually replaced by databases organized according to the relational data model.

In a relational database, records are stored in a number of uniquely named database *tables* which are organized in rows and columns. Each row holds a *record*, and each column has a name and type which is declared when the table is created. All records in the same table must conform to the same structure, with each named column, or field, of each record containing a data value of the required type, or else NULL to indicate there is no data to record. Records may be, and usually are, uniquely identified by a *key* field. Relationships between records may be identified using *foreign* keys, whereby a field in one table holds a value which is used as a *primary* key in another table. Collectively, the declared structure and relationships of a database are known as its *schema*.

The relational data model uses concepts from set theory and logic to define the Structured Query Language used by database applications. This mathematical basis helps database query processors to ensure they do not change the meaning of the search terms as they are being optimized. The database tables can be re-organized without requiring the applications to be re-coded, provided of course that no information is lost in the new organization.

A popular way to visualize a database schema is using the Entity-Relationship Diagram popularized by Chen (1976). In these diagrams, each type of record, or *entity*, is shown using a square box, and relationships are shown as lines linking two boxes going via a diamond with the name of the relationship. Many variants on this notation exist, and indeed a database schema can be captured using the popular UML class diagram notation.

Relational databases have a long history. The roots of SQL, for example, go back to research at IBM in the 1970s, following the ideas proposed by Codd in his famous paper on the relational model (Codd, 1970). The SQL language itself was first standardized in 1986, and the standard has continued to be developed ever since, with new versions and updates to the standard being approved in 1989, 1992, 1999, 2003, 2006, and 2008 from the American National Standards Institute (ANSI) and the International Organization for Standardization (ISO).

There are now many mature textbooks which cover relational databases and SQL programming; two classics are by Date (2003) and Celko (2005). An accessible introduction to the theory and literature of relational databases can be found on-line in Wikipedia.

With the increase in popularity of object-oriented programming in the 1990s, the object-relational impedance mismatch began to cause concern. This term emphasizes the incompatibilities between the object-oriented and relational data models, which often require developers to write significant amounts of repetitive code to transfer data and convert it from database tables to objects and back again. For a while, it was believed that object databases would replace relational databases, thereby avoiding the mismatch. Currently, however, the most commonly adopted solution is to use object-relational mapping (ORM) tools which automatically generate this code, enhancing developer productivity and reducing errors. The LINQ to SQL tool is an example of an ORM tool, albeit a rather sophisticated one.

Although LINQ was only officially released in 2007, it has benefited from earlier research and development. Functional programming has been studied and taught in Computer Science departments since the 1960s, and a number of useful programming techniques developed from this, such as mapping a function over a list. Languages such as LISP, ML and Haskell, remained more popular among universities than in industry. Some functional programming experts, however, joined Microsoft Research in the 1990s. This led to a number of projects such as CΩ (Meijer *et al.*, 2003), which extended C# with ideas from functional programming, and influenced the design of LINQ, and indeed C# itself. It is fair to say that many of the language extensions in versions 2 and 3 of C# were introduced specifically to support the development of LINQ, which was first announced at the 2005 Professional Developer's Conference (PDC 2005).

Anders Hejlsberg, designer of C# and LINQ, speculates that within 5 to 10 years, all programming languages will have queries as a built-in concept (LINQ 2007).

10.2 Creating a database using the Database Explorer

Before you can create or access data in a database, you must first of all define and create the tables it contains. In this chapter we will work with a simple database that will represent three entities from the home insurance domain, 'claim', 'policy', and 'policyholder'. In our simplified model of this business, we will assume that each policy holder may have multiple policies, while each policy belongs to one policy holder. Each claim is made against a single policy, but one policy may have many claims made against it. This domain model is illustrated in Figure 10.1. This diagram shows an entity-relationship diagram (ERD) of these entities and their relationships using Chen's notation (Chen, 1976) where entities are rectangles and relationships are diamonds, with 'n' used to signify a 'many' relationship.

Figure 10.2 shows the three tables with their column names and foreign key relationships.

FIGURE 10.1   Entity relationship diagram of the entities in the example database

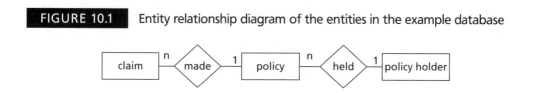

FIGURE 10.2   The three database tables and their relationships

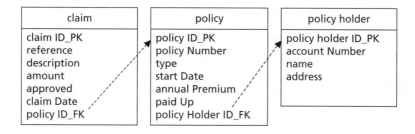

For this chapter, you are advised to create a new website using the 'File' → 'New WebSite...' menu command in the usual way.

Next, you should create a database file. To create a new database file, use the 'File' → 'New File...' menu command, and choose 'SQL Server Database' as the type of file or template to use. You will be asked to confirm that you wish to store this file in the App_Data directory, which is the recommended location.

When you are using Visual Web Developer the simplest way to create a new table is via the built-in Database Explorer Window. You can bring this window to the front using the 'View' → 'Database Explorer' menu command. In this window you should see a view of your new database file, similar to that shown in Figure 10.3. Note that this file may contain a number of different types of database objects such as diagrams, tables, views, and so on. As with other explorer windows, you can click on a plus sign such as the one attached to 'Tables' to expand any node, and you can then click on its minus sign to collapse it again.

If you right click over the word 'Tables' you are then presented with a context menu including the 'Add New Table' menu command. You use this to create a table in your database using the database editing window shown in Figure 10.4. Here you can type in the name of each column and provide its data type, for example 'int' or 'varchar', using the drop-down list as shown. Finally, you can select whether or not null values are allowed in this column using the check boxes to the right. You can also edit the column properties using the tabbed pane at the bottom of the database editor window. It is worth commenting here on the data types available in SQL Server (the available data types vary somewhat between

FIGURE 10.3 Using the Database Explorer to view a recently created SQL Server database file

FIGURE 10.4 Creating a new table using the Visual Web Developer database editor

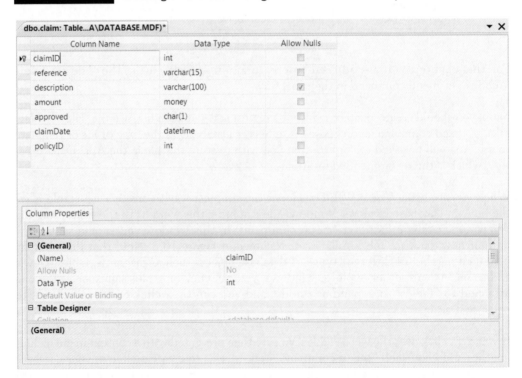

different database management systems). The integer type is called 'int' in SQL Server, for example, and the date type is called 'datetime'. Also note that SQL Server does not have a Boolean data type, which means you must choose another type; for example you could use char(1), with 'Y' for yes and 'N' for no (or 'T' for true and 'F' for false), or indeed the 'bit' type which allows you to use Boolean values instead. Finally note the 'money' type, which is handy for storing monetary values.

To create a new column, you simply click on the empty box below the most recently defined Column Name, and type in the name of the new column. Note that when working with the table definition, you can use the cursor and tab keys instead of the mouse to move around the editor window, if you prefer. When you have created all the columns in the table as required, use the 'File' → 'Save' menu command, or press Ctrl+S, to save the database file. You will be prompted to provide a name for the table. In Figure 10.4 the table has been saved as 'claim'.

When using the Visual Web Developer database editor two extra items appear in the top level menu bar; 'Data' and 'Table Designer'. The 'Data' menu allows you to add a new table, or any other database object, to create a query, to edit the definition of an existing table, and to view or edit its data. The 'Table Designer' menu allows you to add or delete columns, and to flag which column (if any) is the primary key of a table. It also has a number of more specialized commands which allow you to manage relationships, indices and constraints. There is also a Table Designer toolbar, which appears automatically when you open the database designer window. The toolbar buttons repeat the commands available through the top level Table Designer menu.

The simplest way to indicate which column is the primary key is to click on the name of the column to select it, and then click on the key symbol in the Table Designer toolbar, or use the 'Table Designer' → 'Set Primary Key' menu command. In Figure 10.4, 'claimID' has been set as the primary key (the key symbol appears in the left-hand column). Both the toolbar button and the menu option act like a toggle, allowing you to also remove the primary key setting if required.

10.2.1 Refining and illustrating a database schema

When a database contains more than one table, there are usually foreign key relationships between them. Suppose, for example, you have created the 'claim', 'policy' and 'policy-holder' tables as previously shown in Figure 10.2. It is intended that the policyID' field of the 'claim' table refers in each case to the 'policyID' field of a record in the 'policy' table, and similarly for policyHolderID.

To define the foreign key relationships, you should use the 'Table Designer' → 'Relation-ships...' menu command, or the equivalent icon on the Table Designer toolbar. This gives you a 'Foreign Key Relationships' dialog box in which you can click to Add or Delete relationships, as shown in Figure 10.5.

Within the 'Foreign Key Relationships' dialog you are able to provide properties for the relationship. Among these properties is the 'Tables and Columns Specification', which must be provided. You configure this by clicking on the ellipsis (or dots) to the right of this property, so that a second dialog box appears (Figure 10.6). In this dialog you select the table and column at the source and target of the relationship. In this case the foreign key

| FIGURE 10.5 | The 'Foreign Key Relationships' dialog box, including the 'Tables And Columns Specification' property |

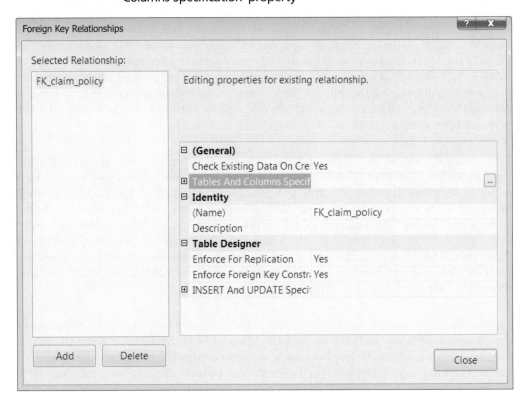

relationship is being set up between the 'policyID' field of the 'claim' table and the 'policyID' field in the 'policy' table (which is the primary key being referenced).

As well as declaring primary and foreign key relationships, it is also possible to use the column properties tab shown in Figure 10.4 to indicate fields, such as claimID in the claim table, whose value will be automatically generated by SQL Server. For example, you can set the 'Identity Specification' and 'Is Identity' properties of this column to Yes, and the 'Identity Increment' and 'Seed' properties to 1 (the default). This process is illustrated in Figure 10.7. Note that you must scroll down through the column properties to reach the Identity Specification. With the settings shown here, each new claim record you insert in the claim table will automatically be given the claimID 1, 2, 3, and so on in sequence. Allowing the database server to generate these numbers avoids the need for you to do the required book-keeping yourself, and also speeds up the process of allocating the next free ID.

Finally note that it is possible to draw database diagrams using the Database Explorer. These are basically entity relationship diagrams, but using somewhat different, Microsoft-specific, symbols. An example is given in Figure 10.8.

Note that in many real-world situations, our application may be only one of many that use the same database. In this case, it is most likely that we will need to extract data from tables organized according to a different schema, rather than one we define ourselves. In this case you

FIGURE 10.6 Using the tables and columns specification dialog box to declare a foreign key relationship between the 'claim; and 'policy' tables

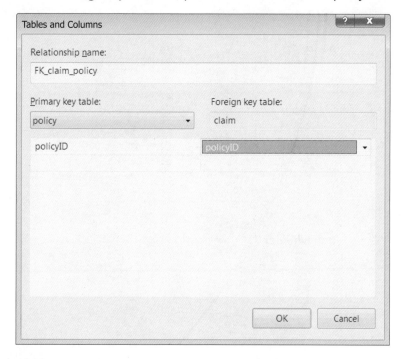

FIGURE 10.7 Using column properties tab to define a column as an identity field

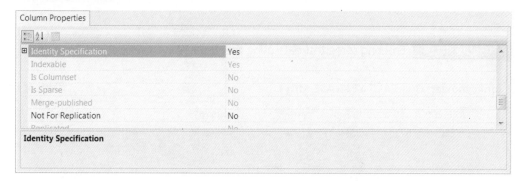

may find it useful to define a database *view* which automatically extracts the items of interest from the external database, rather than creating new tables and copying the data across.

10.2.2 Adding data to tables

You may also wish to populate your database tables with some initial data for testing purposes. This can be done using the 'Data' → 'Show Table Data' command, or right clicking your mouse over the table in the Database Explorer and selecting 'Show Table Data' from the pop-up menu. You are then presented with a grid where you can enter the required

FIGURE 10.8 An entity relationship diagram created using Visual Web Developer

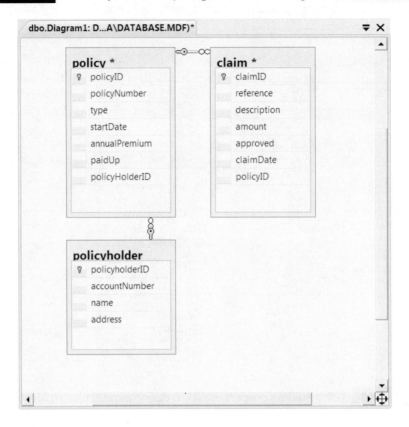

FIGURE 10.9 Entering some test data using the Visual Web Developer database editor

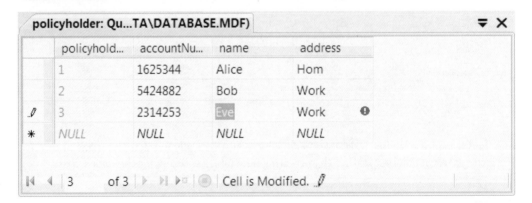

numbers and strings (Figure 10.9). Note that the data must conform to the types and constraints you have declared. This means, for example, that you cannot enter a policy without first creating a policyholder to link it to. If you enter invalid data, the Database Explorer will warn you that the insert failed and you will have to try again.

10.3 Creating and populating databases using stored procedures

A more professional way to initialize these tables is via a stored procedure or script. A stored procedure is a program written in a procedural version of SQL consisting of the familiar SELECT, INSERT, UPDATE and DELETE statements together with additional declarations or commands in a special syntax. This syntax is rather baroque, and varies between different database management systems, but the ability to write stored procedures is essential for specialist database developers and database administrators. Here we will only create a couple of simple scripts using Microsoft's Transact-SQL dialect.

 NOTE It is not necessary for you to write stored procedures very often, so you may skip this section if you are happy creating database tables and populating them manually as described in the previous pages. The benefit of writing a script, however, is that you can more easily return to a known state if testing your database updates leaves the system with erroneous or unwanted entries.

To create a stored procedure you can use the 'Data' → 'Add New' → 'Stored Procedure' menu command. Alternatively, you can right click over the word 'Stored Procedure' in the Data Explorer window and select 'Add New Stored Procedure' from the context menu which appears.

You can add the code for the procedure into the database editor window which appears. This window features syntax highlighting, but not Intellisense. Instead, the syntax of your code is checked when you try to save it. If an error is found you must correct it before you can successfully save. Finally, once you have saved your stored procedure you can execute it using its context menu in the Data Explorer window, which includes an 'Execute' command. The code for the stored procedure is shown below (and provided, as with all other code, in the on-line support materials for this book).

```
CREATE PROCEDURE ReInitializeDB
  /*
  Resets the database to a known initial state
  Use only for testing purposes
  */
AS
  /*
    Empty the current contents of the tables
  */
DELETE FROM claim
DELETE FROM policy
DELETE FROM policyholder
  /*
    Insert the standard test data
  */
```

```
INSERT INTO policyholder VALUES(1625344,'Mr. Charles Babbage',
   '55, Old Road, London, United Kingdom')
INSERT INTO policyholder VALUES(5424882,'Dr. Bjarne Stroustrup',
    '4, Wellington Road,Auckland, New Zealand')
INSERT INTO policyholder VALUES(2314253,'Ms. Grace Hopper',
   '1,Forest Heights, San Francisco, United States')

INSERT INTO policy VALUES(233142,'buildings','2007-02-12',45.60,'Y',1)
INSERT INTO policy VALUES(384475,'contents','2006-11-21',37.00,'Y',1)
INSERT INTO policy VALUES(332574,'buildings','2005-06-03',120.50,'N',2)
INSERT INTO policy VALUES(928376,'buildings','2008-12-30',120.50,'Y',3)
INSERT INTO policy VALUES(885746,'contents','2007-10-13',120.50,'Y',3)

INSERT INTO claim VALUES
  ('B233142-20101103-051','Broken window',150.00,'Y','2010-11-03',1);
INSERT INTO claim VALUES
  ('C384475-20100423-131','Stained carpet',1000.00,'N','2010-04-23',2);
INSERT INTO claim VALUES
  ('C885746-20100322-011','Stolen camera',650.00,'Y','2010-03-22',2);
INSERT INTO claim VALUES
  ('B928376-20100402-226','House burned down',350000.00,'Y',
   '2010-04-02',3);

RETURN
```

Note that when you save a stored procedure, the first line changes from CREATE PRO-CEDURE....to ALTER PROCEDURE..., in anticipation of any changes you may make in future.

Figure 10.10 shows the results of executing the ReInitializeDB procedure. The output window gives some tracing information about the commands executed, and a database table has been displayed using the 'Show Table Data' command.

You will note that the records have been numbered 1, 2, 3, in accordance with the IDENTITY column property which has been set. Alternatively, if you have not set this property, you would have to add an extra value to each of the INSERT statements, for example:

```
INSERT INTO policy VALUES(1,233142,'buildings','2007-02-12',45.60,'Y',1)
```

For completeness, we also need code which creates the database with the required tables, columns and constraints. This can be achieved by adding another stored procedure as follows:

```
CREATE PROCEDURE ResetDB
/*
 Recreate all tables
 Use only for testing purposes
*/
AS
 DROP TABLE claim
```

```
CREATE TABLE claim (
 claimID INT PRIMARY KEY IDENTITY(1,1) NOT NULL,
 reference VARCHAR(20),
 description VARCHAR(100),
 amount MONEY,
 approved CHAR(1),
 claimDate DATETIME,
 policyID INT
)

DROP TABLE policy
CREATE TABLE policy (
 policyID INT PRIMARY KEY IDENTITY(1,1) NOT NULL,
 policyNumber INT,
 type VARCHAR(20),
 startDate DATETIME,
 annualPremium MONEY,
 paidUp CHAR(1),
 policyHolderID INT,
)

DROP TABLE policyholder
CREATE TABLE policyholder (
 policyholderID INT PRIMARY KEY IDENTITY(1,1) NOT NULL,
 accountNumber INT,
 name VARCHAR(30),
 address VARCHAR(50)
)

ALTER TABLE claim
ADD CONSTRAINT claimFK
 FOREIGN KEY (policyID)
 REFERENCES policy(policyID)

ALTER TABLE policy
ADD CONSTRAINT policyFK
 FOREIGN KEY (policyHolderID)
 REFERENCES policyHolder(policyHolderID)


RETURN
```

In this procedure, all the primary and foreign key constraints and other column properties we entered manually are declared using SQL keywords and syntax. For example, the *xxx*ID field in each table is declared to be a PRIMARY KEY, and constrained to be a non-null integer value. In addition, the IDENTITY(1,1) declaration is used to require that the first record created has an ID of 1, and that subsequent records have an ID which is 1 larger than the previous one. If you are familiar with other database management systems, you may have seen the keyword AUTOINCREMENT used to give the same effect. SQL Server's syntax is more flexible, as in general any starting value can be used, and any increment, by declaring IDENTITY(start, increment).

FIGURE 10.10 The results of executing a stored procedure

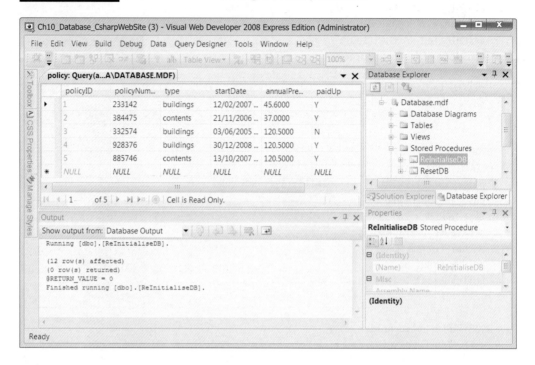

Note that the foreign key constraints are, by necessity, added after the relevant tables have all been created. The ALTER TABLE command is therefore used to make these additions to the original table definitions.

 NOTE You can create and edit databases using other tools, not just Visual Web Developer. The SQL Server Management Studio, for example, has a similar look and feel to the Database Explorer, but provides additional functionality to help database administrators monitor and manage their data. In many organizations the role of database administrator is a separate one from that of Web Developer.

Section summary and quick exercises

Up to this point in this chapter we have reviewed the basic concepts of the relational model, such as the database table with its named columns, key fields, and constraints such as foreign key relationships. We have showed how to create a SQL Server database file (typically called 'App_Data\Database.mdf'), and have covered the use of Visual Web Developer's Database Explorer window to create, configure and populate database tables in our database. In particular, we have considered how to declare key fields and how to specify that these can provide a unique IDENTITY generated automatically from a sequence such as 1, 2, 3 and so on. We also showed how to declare constraints such as a column being NOT NULL and foreign key relationships between two tables. In addition to being able to use the Database Explorer window, it is also useful to know how to automate this process using Transact-SQL stored procedures, so a couple of examples of stored procedures were given.

The exercises below give you the opportunity to learn more about Transact-SQL by editing the ResetDB stored procedure.

EXERCISE 10.1

You will notice that the ResetDB stored procedure constrains the *xxx*ID identity fields in the database tables to be NOT NULL. Consider carefully which of the other fields should also include this constraint, and modify the ResetDB procedure accordingly. Remember to execute it once you have saved your changes to test that they work.

EXERCISE 10.2

The ResetDB stored procedure can generate errors when first run, as it tries to DROP TABLEs which may not in fact exist. Change the procedure to avoid this problem. Hint: to find the solution you will need to find and read the on-line description of the Transact-SQL OBJECT_ID function.

EXERCISE 10.3

In the database schema described previously, it is intended that the fields 'paidUp' and 'approved' should contain only the values 'Y' or 'N', and the insurance type should contain only a value from a pre-defined list, for example 'buildings' or 'contents'. How, using your knowledge of SQL Server constraints, can you express these additional requirements in the ResetDB stored procedure?

EXERCISE 10.4

In a schema such as the one used in this chapter, it is desirable that no two customers have the same account number, and that no two claims have the same claim reference. Use the Visual Web Developer help system, or search on-line, to discover how to CREATE a TABLE with such a constraint, and add these as needed to the ResetDB stored procedure.

EXERCISE 10.5

Where you add constraints to your database, you should also execute ReInitialiseDB to confirm that the test data satisfies your new constraints. Rather than having to remember to do this, change ResetDB so that it executes ReInitialiseDB before it terminates.

10.4 Configuring a data source in Visual Web Developer

Now we have created the database, and entered some test data, you can create web pages which access and update it. In this section you will build a web form which displays the contents of one of your database tables.

Start by creating a blank web form, and add a SqlDataSource web control from the Data controls group in the Tool Box. Clicking on this control's smart tag's 'Configure Data Source...' menu command presents you with a Wizard, which you use to set up and define how your web page accesses the database.

The first dialog box this Wizard displays is shown in Figure 10.11 and allows you to choose your data connection. If you click on the drop-down arrow, you are able to select the database file created above, which by default was called 'Database.mdf'. Alternatively, if you wish to use some other source of data you can click the 'New Connection' button to the right, which pops up an additional dialog whereby you can specify details of the database server, authentication protocol and database file to use. In Figure 10.11 we have chosen to connect to 'Database.mdf'. You will note that a connection string is also shown. Visual Web Developer has generated this automatically based on the information provided, and will offer you the chance to include it in the site's web.config file so that the same connection can be re-used later in other data sources or code you write to access the database. You can hide or display this connection string by clicking on the button to the left which alternatively displays a plus or, as here, a minus sign.

FIGURE 10.11   Configuring the data source of a SQLDataSource web control

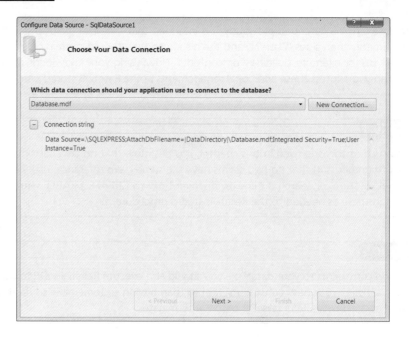

You can now click 'Next' to progress through the Wizard to its second dialog box. This asks if you would like to save the connection string in your web application's configuration file, which is the recommended action. The third dialog box then asks you to define the data you intend to retrieve from the database, and should look like the example given in Figure 10.12.

Here you should select a table such as claim, policy, or policyholder from the dropdown list. You can also select some of the columns to include in the results or, as shown here, simply check the box labeled '*' to retrieve all columns. For now, ignore the buttons labeled 'WHERE...',

FIGURE 10.12 Configuring the select statement associated with a SQLDataSource web control

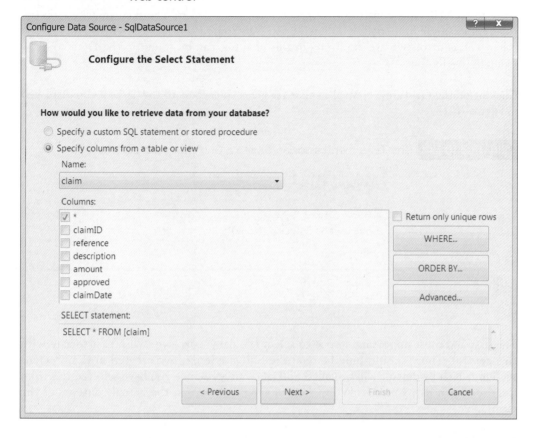

'ORDER BY...', and 'Advanced...' which we will cover later on in this chapter. At the bottom of this dialog box, you can see that an SQL SELECT statement is displayed: this is the one that will be used by the data source to retrieve the required data. You will notice this statement change if, for example, you select the 'Return only unique rows' check box.

The fourth and final dialog box displayed by the Wizard then gives you the opportunity to test your query (always a good idea!) and finish. When you have configured the data source, you will probably notice that its Tasks menu now includes another command: 'Refresh Schema'. You should use this to keep your data source up to date if for any reason the database schema is changed later on.

The SqlDataSource web control is an example of an invisible control. When you view the web page in your browser, this control does not appear at all. (As you know from Chapter 6, this means that its Render method did not generate any HTML output.) That is to say, we have created a control that connects to the database and queries its contents, but as yet there is no way to display the dynamic data which results. Fortunately, ASP.NET provides a number of other web controls which are used to display the data retrieved via a DataSource control, and in a variety of different formats. The most useful is perhaps the GridView control, which we previously used to render data from an XMLDataSource in Chapter 8.

10.4.1 Using a GridView control to display data from a SqlDataSource

Now add a GridView control to your web form. This control could go anywhere on the page, for example immediately following the DataSource control. The GridView, like the other web controls we are exploring in this chapter, can be found in the Data controls group in the ToolBox.

Clicking on the GridView control's smart tag gives you access to the Tasks menu displayed in Figure 10.13.

FIGURE 10.13   The Tasks menu associated with a GridView web control

The first and most important step is to select the data source you wish to associate with this control. There should only be one, the SqlDataSource we created in the previous section, which by default will be called SqlDataSource1. Once you have selected this from the dropdown list, your GridView control should show you the actual contents of the claim table.

If you think about it, this is quite a remarkable feature. The Visual Web Developer IDE is communicating with the SQL Server database to execute an SQL SELECT statement to access and display the data for you. In fact, SQL Server is executing this SELECT statement because, again under the covers, Visual Web Developer has called a method in your GridView control, which has then called another method in your SqlDataSource control, which actually generates the required SELECT statement. All of this happens without any perceptible delay. (Actually, the first time you require the database, there is sometimes a slight delay, while it is being loaded, but thereafter access is virtually instantaneous.)

There is some further configuration that you can add to your GridView if you wish. You will notice that some additional check boxes have been added to the GridView's task menu. You can use these to enable Paging, Sorting, and Selection. You can choose one of the Auto Format schemes available. Figure 10.14 shows the web form viewed in a browser after Paging, Sorting and Selection have been added and an Auto Format ('Apple Orchard') applied. Here you can see the contents of the 'claim' database table displayed in the internal web browser based the query configured in the SqlDataSource.

With 'Sorting' applied, each column heading in the table is a link. Clicking on one of these links will sort the rows according to data in that column, firstly in ascending order and then, if you click again, in descending order, and so on. With 'Selection' applied, you can use the 'Select' links to the left of the grid to select any given row; the second row has

	claimID	reference	description	amount	approved	claimDate	policyID
Select	1	B2007-11-051	Broken window	150.0000	Y	11/05/2007 00:00:00	1
Select	2	C2007-04-131	Stained carpet	1000.0000	N	13/04/2007 00:00:00	2
Select	3	C2007-22-011	Stolen camera	650.0000	Y	22/01/2007 00:00:00	2

1 2

been selected in Figure 10.14, though there is nothing we actually do at present with the selected row. The 'Paging' facility is not effective when there are only a few records, as the default is to display 10 records at a time. To see how paging works, you can set the GridView's 'PageSize' property to 3. The effect of this change can be seen in Figure 10.14: hyperlinks have been added that enable the user to view different pages.

If you wish, you can also use the properties window to control the appearance of the Grid-View. If you view your control's properties, you will see that these include several (in the appearance group) that control its appearance such as its BackColor, CssClass, and Font, which work in the usual way. In addition, there is also a group of styles such as Header-Style, FooterStyle and RowStyle which allow you to control the appearance of the header, footer and data rows. The style of individual data cells can also be controlled using the 'Edit Columns...' menu command and the Fields dialog box which is covered later in this chapter.

Finally note that, although in this section we created first a SqlDataSource control, then a GridView control, it is possible to combine both of these into a single step by adding a GridView control, and selecting the 'New Data Source...' command from its Tasks menu.

10.5 Editing data using the GridView and DetailsView web controls

The next step is to create a web-based interface which allows database administrators or your web application's users (or both) to edit the data in the database. This is usually a better approach than accessing the database directly, as it is then possible to provide more appropriate validation and error messages, as well as any additional logging or auditing the application or business logic may require.

As is often the case with ASP.NET, it is possible to provide a simple solution to this without writing any code. (It is also true, of course, that simple solutions are not always sufficient, so that later on in this chapter and in Chapter 11 we will look at alternative solutions which do require some coding.)

The first step is to re-configure our SqlDataSource. This can be done by clicking on the control's smart tag and selecting the 'Configure Data Source...' command from its Tasks menu. Visual Web Developer will now display the same Wizard we used to create the data source in the section before last. This time, page through to the dialog box (shown in Figure 10.12) with the 'Advanced...' button which we skipped over previously. Click on this button, and check the boxes marked 'Generate INSERT, UPDATE, and DELETE statements' and 'Use optimistic concurrency' which appear (for these buttons to be available, it is essential you have defined the table's primary key, and this column must be included in the query). Complete the Wizard and click the Finish button to save your changes. The data source can now be used for editing. As usual, however, we need to make use of another web control to provide the user interface for this task. The simplest way of doing this is to use the same GridView control as in the previous section. Go back to its smart tag menu and you will see that its Tasks menu now offers you the options to 'Enable Editing' and 'Enable Deleting', as shown in Figure 10.15. Click on the check box to select these.

FIGURE 10.15 The smart tag menu associated with a GridView web control once the data source has been configured to generate INSERT, UPDATE and DELETE commands

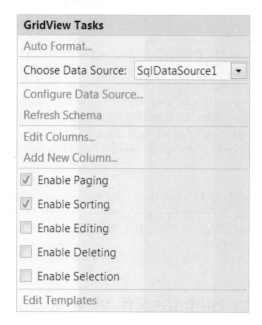

If you view your web page again, you will see that each row now has Edit and Delete links. Clicking on one of the Edit links will redisplay the page with all the data items now shown in a text box (Figure 10.16). You can overtype the data in any or all of these text boxes and press the Update link to change the data stored in the database. Note that the 'claimID' column cannot be edited in this way: it is usually not sensible to change the primary key associated with a record, so the GridView does not allow us to do this. In fact, database fields which are declared as IDENTITY columns are by default read-only.

The Delete link has the obvious effect of removing the row of data from the database. In each case you should note that the SQL Server, the database management system we are using here, will check the update or delete operations. If these violate any declared constraint, the change will fail. For example, if you try to enter a claim with an invalid date, the update will fail, displaying a server error page such as the one shown in Figure 10.17. Note that the error message here is not particularly user-friendly, so a more professional approach would be to code your own error handler and display a more meaningful message. Later in this chapter, to try to avoid such problems, we will apply some of the validation controls we first introduced in Chapter 7.

FIGURE 10.16 Using the GridView to edit a database record: note that the data items for record 2 are now editable text fields, except for the claimID which is still read-only

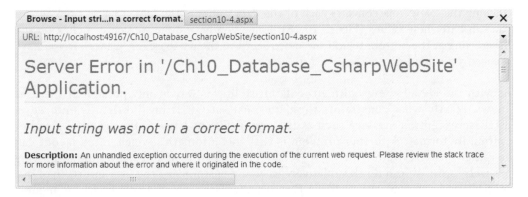

FIGURE 10.17 The default, rather unfriendly, Server Error message generated in response to the user clicking Update having entered the invalid amount 'loads!'

```
Browse - Input stri...n a correct format.  section10-4.aspx                    ▼ ✕

URL: http://localhost:49167/Ch10_Database_CsharpWebSite/section10-4.aspx           ▼

Server Error in '/Ch10_Database_CsharpWebSite'
Application.

Input string was not in a correct format.

Description: An unhandled exception occurred during the execution of the current web request. Please review the stack trace
for more information about the error and where it originated in the code.

◀           III                                                              ▶
```

10.5.1 Using a DetailsView to create new records

The GridView does not provide a facility to add a new record into the database. To do this you need to use a different data web control such as the DetailsView. To see how this works, add a third data control, this time a DetailsView, to your web form. Using the control's smart tag menu, configure it to use the same SqlDataSource that your GridView is also using. Once you have done so, you will notice that the DetailsView's smart tag menu now includes checkboxes which allow you to enable paging, inserting, editing, and deleting. Tick these and save the web form. If you now view the page in your browser, you will see that at the bottom of the page is a table showing a single record. At the bottom of this table are links which allow you to edit and delete the current record, to move to a numbered record and also to insert a new record (Figure 10.18).

FIGURE 10.18
Viewing the database using a DetailsView web control, with links to edit, delete and create records in the database. The effect of clicking the Edit link is shown in the screen second shot

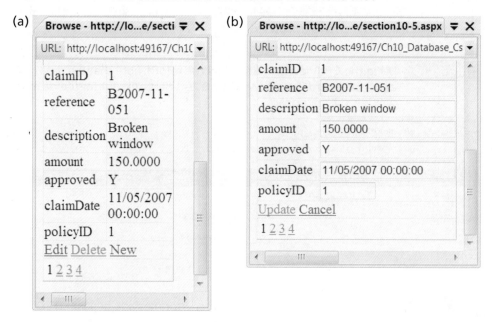

Clicking the 'New' link converts each of the data values in the table to a text box where you can enter new values (Figure 10.18). Once you have done so, you can click on the 'Insert' link at the bottom to add the new record to the database, or 'Cancel' if you have changed your mind.

As with the DetailsView, editing the database in this way is only possible if the user knows exactly what constraints the data must satisfy. If invalid data is entered, a database exception message such as the one in Figure 10.17 is displayed in a rather unfriendly format. A further problem is that the automatically generated layout can be rather unattractive for the user. We therefore need to spend some time improving our web form. We can do this relatively easily by customizing the user interface of our controls using the options available through the data web control's smart tag menus. In particular, we need to define the layout of the tables that are dynamically generated, the format of the data values the user can enter, and how to provide meaningful, user-friendly messages in case they enter incorrect or invalid data. These topics will be covered in the following section.

Section summary and quick exercises

In this section we created a new SQL Server Database component in our website, and used the database explorer, along with associated menu options and toolbars, to create and populate a database using SQL Server Express Edition. We used a SqlDataSource in a web form to make a connection to the database and apply a SQL query, and configured a GridView control to display the data that resulted from the query. We also looked at some of the configuration options of the GridView for sorting, selecting and paging the data retrieved from the database. We also saw how Data controls can be configured to enable the contents of the database to be edited, including creating new records using a Details-View control.

EXERCISE 10.6

SQL Server includes a bit datatype which can be used to store Boolean values. This gives us another way to represent Boolean or two-valued data. When displaying and editing bit fields, the GridView and DetailsView controls convert them to check boxes, a more user-friendly form of presentation than having to type 'False' or 'True'. As an exercise, create a database table with a bit field, and use a GridView to display and edit these values. Note that if you change the structure of an existing database, you should then refresh all data web controls which depend on that database, which can be problematic. For the purposes of this exercise, therefore, you are advised to create a dummy table rather than changing an existing one.

EXERCISE 10.7

You will have noticed that the DetailsView controls can appear in different 'modes'; sometimes the data is read-only, and sometimes it is editable. The mode can be set via the control's DefaultMode property. You can save the user the trouble of clicking the New link in Figure 10.16, for example, by setting this property to Insert rather than ReadOnly.

10.6 A database-driven project

The techniques we have looked at so far have allowed us to create simple web pages which allow users to perform simple operations on our database. The pages are not particularly sophisticated, nor are the operations being performed, and as we have seen above the error handing is unsatisfactory. The purpose of this section is to investigate some of the more advanced features of ASP.NET which allow us to build more professional database editing pages and forms, but still without needing to write any code (approaches using database programming will be discussed at the end of this chapter, and explored in Chapter 11).

Imagine you are asked to implement an intranet system which allows telephone call center operators to update the database according to instructions from policy holders who have called the center. These intranet pages will be similar to the ones you would develop for an on-line Internet-based insurance system, but there are a few differences. For one thing, there is no need for the policy holder to log in. Instead, their identity will be established by a sequence of telephone questions and answers. The user interface for an intranet system should be more oriented to functionality, as there is no need to establish or promote your brand.

The pages we will create in this section are by no means a complete system, but are sufficient to allow the completion of a few common use cases whereby the policy holder can:

1. confirm the status of their policies and claims
2. amend their details by reporting a new address for written communication
3. make a new claim on one of their policies
4. amend details of an existing claim

To begin with, the call center operator determines the caller's name. Entering this will take them to a page with details of all policy holders of that name. The operator can select one of these by eliciting further information from the caller such as their address and customer account number. (The details of such a dialogue are outside the scope of this book. In reality, there may be additional security checks based on items of personal information or security codes that are not included in our current database design.)

Once the policy holder's identity has been established, a page is displayed with details of their policies and claims. By clicking a link or button the call center operator can bring up further details and amend them according to the policy holder's instructions. Alternatively, the policy holder may provide details of a new claim they wish to make against one of their policies.

The requirements imply the need for certain web pages and interactions. A number of different interaction designs are possible, and there is a trade-off between the amount of information displayed on each page and the number of links or buttons which must be clicked to reach that information. An appropriate design is typically constructed as a result of detailed task analysis, and refined through prototyping and usability trials. These techniques again are beyond the scope of this text, but we suppose here it has been decided that two main pages are needed, the first to allow the operator to list the details of all policy holders with a certain name, or part of a name, and the second to list all policies of a specific policy holder. Selecting one of the policy holders listed on the first page brings up the second one, which also includes a link back to the first. Additional pages or dialog boxes are called up by clicking on the appropriate link or button to allow the operator to:

1. change the policy holder's address
2. make a new claim on a policy
3. amend an existing claim

Our goal is to implement web pages which conform to this rough design sketch, using ASP.NET's Data controls to reduce the amount of code which must be written. In general, a system with less code requires less effort and expense to maintain and extend in future, allowing us to benefit from our decision to commit to using the ASP.NET framework and controls. In our mini-project there will be two ASP.NET web forms:

1. FindPolicyHolder.aspx: to list policy holders matching a supplied name or part of name.
2. ShowPoliciesAndClaims.aspx: to list policies and claims from an identified policy holder.

The second of these will be a rich page with multiple tables to show all the required details. In addition, it will support the other operations of making and editing claims and policy holder details.

10.6.1 Creating the 'Find Policy Holder' page

The development starts, therefore, by creating the pages named as above, with just a heading to distinguish them, and no other contents. A suitable heading to use for the 'FindPolicy Holder.aspx' web form is 'Find Policy Holder' and so on. Having these skeleton pages makes it easier to add and test links between them. In fact, all the required content can be added and tested in stages.

The required content for 'FindPolicyHolder.aspx' consists of a TextBox for the operator to enter a name, or part of a name, and a GridView listing the policy holders that match. Below the heading, therefore, add from the Toolbox a Label, Textbox, SqlDataSource, and GridView web controls as shown in Figure 10.19. To start with, your GridView will look somewhat different to the one shown here, and the following paragraphs will explain how to set it up with the required appearance and behavior.

FIGURE 10.19 The 'FindPolicyHolder.aspx' web form should consist of a Heading, Label, Textbox, SqlDataSource and GridView, though the GridView control requires configuration to match the appearance shown here

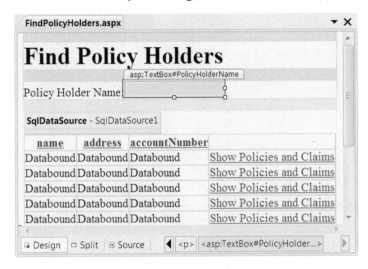

Configure the SQL data source in the usual way, selecting the same database (in fact you can re-use the connection string that was generated in the preliminary exercises in the preceding sections) and choosing to specify columns from the policyholder table (select all the available columns, as before). This time, however, rather than move directly on from configuring the SELECT statement, click on the 'WHERE...' button. This takes you to an additional dialog box which allows you to refine your SELECT statement. Here you should select the 'name' column from the policyholder table, the LIKE operator, and a web control as the source. Continue by selecting your textbox control's ID (this is PolicyHolderName in Figure 10.20, but yours may have another name). To complete the WHERE clause dialog, click the 'Add' button (which will make the generated SQL expression appear in the 'SQL Expression' window) and then click 'OK'. Back in the previous dialog, check that your SQL SELECT statement is now:

```
SELECT * FROM [policyholder] WHERE ([name] LIKE '%' + @name + "%")
```

and press 'Next >' as your SELECT statement is also now complete. The % symbol is an SQL wild card, so that the search will match any name in the database containing the supplied text as a substring.

FIGURE 10.20 Adding a WHERE clause to your SELECT statement when configuring the SQL data source

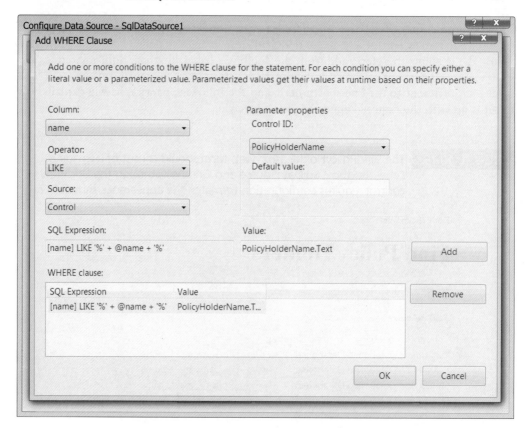

As usual, you can test the SQL statement before finishing the data source configuration. If you choose to do so, you are prompted for a customer name to use as a test value when running the query. You could enter 'Babbage' for example. Note that in Figure 10.20, the SQL statement includes a named parameter, @name. It is this parameter whose value you are supplying as a test value and, similarly, when the query executes for real as part of the web form, it is this parameter which is replaced by the current contents of the Policy Holder Name textbox. Remember that PolicyHolderName is the ID being used for the TextBox, whereas the database column is called 'name'.

The final web control on this page is the GridView, which will display the results of the data source we have just configured. Use the GridView's Tasks menu to choose this data source (which should not be difficult as there is only one on the page!). You can also use the Tasks menu to enable paging and sorting, which should help the operator to identify the correct policy holder more quickly. Finally, click on the 'Edit Columns…' command in the Tasks menu to bring up the 'Fields' dialog box, which allows you to add, remove and reorder the columns to be displayed by the GridView control, as shown in Figure 10.21.

To start with, ensure the 'Auto-generate fields' box is not checked. This prevents Visual Web Developer from automatically generating one column in the GridView for each database column. Next, use the red 'X' beside the second pane to remove the policyholderID which does not need to be displayed. Then select 'HyperLinkField' in

FIGURE 10.21 The 'Fields' dialog box allows you to add, remove, and re-order the columns which the GridView control displays

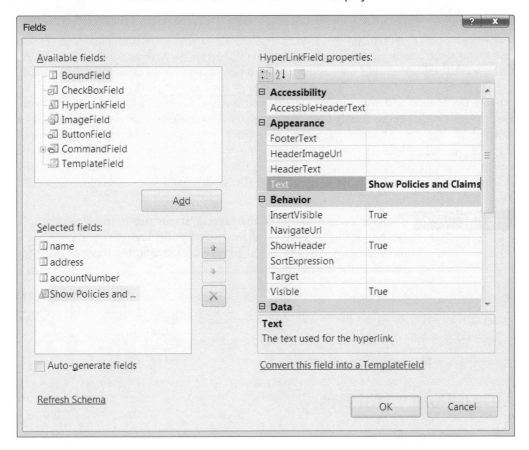

the top-left pane and click 'Add' to create a new field (or column, the two terms have identical meanings here). A HyperLinkField will display as a URL the user can click on to navigate to another page. Enter the anchor text 'Policies and Claims' as shown here in the right-hand 'HyperLinkField properties' pane. Finally, scroll down the properties pane until you reach the Data properties, and carefully enter the following values:

DataNavigateUrlFields	policyholderID
DataNavigateUrlFormatString	~/ShowPoliciesAndClaims.aspx?policyholderID={0}

These properties control the target of the hyperlink, which now depends on the policyholderID value in the current row (this still exists, even though we have chosen not to display it). The target consists of the 'ShowPoliciesAndClaims.aspx' web form, with a query string parameter called policyholderID. The value of this parameter is given in the format string as {0}, which is replaced at runtime by the actual value of the first field given in the property above, which is policyholderID. As an example, consider row 5 of the table, which might display a policy holder whose ID is 42. The value of the policyholderID field is therefore 42, and the hyperlink's target URL is '~/ShowPolicies AndClaims.aspx?policyholderID=42'. (The ~ here is replaced at run-time by the name of your website directory.) Finally, use the up and down arrows to the side of the second pane to order the selected fields as shown in Figure 10.18, and click on OK to complete the Fields dialog box.

You are now ready to save and test your web form. Press Ctrl+S, Alt+F and B, or use the File menu's 'Save' and 'Browse with...' commands to view your form using a browser. All being well, the form should now appear, and you can type in a name such as 'Stroustrup' in the textbox, press the enter key, and see a result such as that shown in Figure 10.22. By moving the mouse over the hyperlink field, you can see the target URL displayed. Note that in this case, as there is only one 'Stroustrup' in our database, only one policy holder is listed. To see more than this, you can enter (say) 'a' in the textbox, which matches all three of our policy holders, who each have names containing that letter. With only three policy holders, of course, the paging and sorting functions we have enabled are not actually needed, but they would be helpful in a more realistic situation.

FIGURE 10.22 The web page resulting from entering 'stroustrup' in the dialog box. Note that the target URL of the hyperlink field has policyholderID=2 as its query string (which you can see by allowing the mouse cursor to rest over the anchor text)

Finally note that in building this page you can create the SQL data source via the Grid-View's Tasks menu, rather than from the Toolbox, if you prefer.

10.6.2 Creating the 'Show Policies and Claims' page

The next page to construct is the one which shows policies and claims for a given policy holder. This page will be a complex one, with multiple web data controls providing a rich user interface. It is best to develop complex web forms in small steps, testing each control as you introduce it.

We start as usual by adding a SqlDataSource control. The data source should select those records from the policyholder table where the policyholderID is that given in the query string parameter called policyholderID, the one which we generated using the HyperLinkField just now. To select these records, click 'WHERE...' when configuring the SQL SELECT statement. This shows you a dialog box similar to Figure 10.20, where you can choose the policyholderID column, the '=' operator, and QueryString as the parameter source. Then enter policyholderID as the required QueryString field. Remember to click 'Add' before 'OK' to complete the WHERE clause. Finally, as this data source will be used for editing, use the 'Advanced...' command to generate INSERT, UPDATE and DELETE statements, and use optimistic concurrency.

Below the SqlDataSource control, add a table with two columns and one row. In the left-hand cell, add a DetailsView control, and select as its data source the SqlDataSource we just created. To meet the requirements, and to improve its appearance, some further customization and configuration is required, which we describe in the following paragraphs.

In the layout group of properties, set the DetailsView Width to 100% to ensure it fills the whole of the left half of the table, and in the FieldHeaderStyle group, set the Width to 20% to reduce the space taken by the field or column names, and to increase the amount of space for their values, and in particular long items such as the address.

Use the DetailsView smart tasks menu to Enable Editing (but not deletion nor insertion). Next, use its Edit Fields ... command to bring up the Fields dialog box. Use the red X in the Fields dialog box to remove the policyholderID from the list of fields to be displayed. Select the 'Edit, Update, Cancel' field, change its 'EditText' property to 'Change Policy Holder Details', and in its 'ItemStyle' group set its 'HorizontalAlign' property to 'Center'. Finally, select the address field, and click 'Convert this field to a TemplateField' to turn it into a template field. There is no obvious effect of this, but if you now OK the Fields dialog box, and select the Edit Templates command from the DetailsView smart menu, you will notice that the address field is now the first item in the Display drop down shown in Figure 10.23a.

Pane (a) in Figure 10.23 shows the DetailsView Tasks menu in template editing mode. Selecting the EditItemTemplate associated with the address field gives rise to pane (b) in which this template is displayed and can be edited. In the figure, the selected Text-Box somewhat obscures the name of the template. Each of the various templates controls how the address is displayed in various situations. The ItemTemplate is used when the DetailsView is in normal read-only mode, and the EditItemTemplate is used when it is in edit mode. When the database record is being edited, the address field will in appear in a textbox like that shown in the EditItemTemplate. We can use properties of this Text-Box, therefore, to control the appearance of the address field while it is being edited. In this case, use the properties window to set its Height to 35%, its Width to 100%, and its TextMode to MultiLine. This will increase the size of the address textbox when the policy holder details are being updated.

Note that you can also view the address field templates all at once by picking the first item (Field[1] – address) from the Display drop down, if are happy with a somewhat more cluttered user interface.

When you are done, remember to use the Details View tasks menu to End Template Editing. This returns the control's appearance to its normal Design view, and ensures that the changes you have made are saved and synchronized. You can see the effect of these changes in Figure 10.24. Note that the call center operator is permitted to change policy holder's details, but not delete or add them. Note also how the address is given additional vertical space when being edited.

(a)
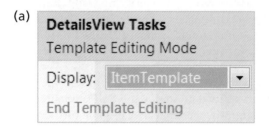

(b)

(c)

Finally, add a hyperlink control with 'Find Other Policy Holders' as its anchor text and '~/FindPolicyHolders.aspx' as its target URL. The call center operator can follow this link back to the initial web page when they have finished dealing with one policy holder's requests, or if they find they have selected the wrong policy holder in the first place. The effect of this can be seen in Figure 10.25.

The next section of the web form starts with a level 2 heading: 'Policies for this Policy Holder'. Under this heading, add an SqlDataSource and a GridView. Configure the data source to access our insurance database and select all fields from the policy table where the policyholderID matches the Query String parameter of the same name. Select this as your GridView's data source, and use the 'Edit Columns...' command on its smart tag menu to arrange the database fields in a sensible order, and to ensure that the policyID and policyholderID fields do not appear. Also Enable Selection. The desired effect is indicated in Figure 10.25.

By default, the display of datetime database fields includes the time as well as the date. That is inappropriate here, so the DataFormatString property of the startDate field has been set to {0:d} which causes just the date to appear. Similarly, the annualPremium field has a DataFormatString of {0:c} which shows the amount to two decimal places, rather than four. There are a variety of other format specifiers available, a list of which

FIGURE 10.24 Editing a policy holder's details

(a)

(b)

FIGURE 10.25 Testing the ShowPoliciesAndClaims.aspx web form

you can find using Visual Web Developer's help facility. Finally, to improve usability, use the properties pane of the GridView to set the BackColor of the SelectedRowStyle to Black, and the ForeColor to White. This will ensure the selected row stands out from the other rows.

The third section of our ShowPoliciesAndClaims.aspx web form, unsurprisingly, shows the claims. This starts with another level 2 heading: Claims for this Policy. Under this heading, add yet another SqlDataSource and GridView. Configure the data source to access our insurance database and select all fields from the claim table where the policyID matches the policy selected in the GridView on the previous page. To do this, use that GridView web control as the source for the comparison. Visual Web Developer automatically chooses to use the SelectedValue property of this control, which will contains the primary key of the selected row, if there is one. Configure the new GridView to use the new SqlDataSource, and then use the 'Edit Columns...' command from its smart tag menu to ensure the database fields are displayed in a sensible order, that the policyID and claimID fields do not appear, and to format the amount and claimDate fields using the currency and date format specifiers ({0:c} and {0:d}). Also Enable Selection, and set the SelectedRowStyle's BackColor and ForeColor to Black and White respectively. The resulting web form is shown in Figure 10.26.

FIGURE 10.26 The ShowPoliciesAndClaims.aspx web form now shows claims as well as policies, thanks to a third GridView control which has been added

We are reaching the end of our work with this web form, as there are just two more controls to add and configure. At the bottom of the form, below the previous GridView, add a SqlDataSource and FormView control. The FormView control is similar in functionality to the DetailsView, but somewhat more configurable, so it is also worth knowing about. Configure the data source to access our database as usual and select all fields from the claim table where the claimID matches the claim selected in the GridView. Then configure the FormView to use this new SqlDataSource. At this point you have a workable means of changing claims and adding new ones, but the appearance and functionality remain rather unpolished. In the following paragraphs, therefore, we show how to give the FormView control a more professional appearance and behavior.

First, use the FormView's smart tag menu and select the Edit Template command, as shown in Figure 10.27. Note that there are several templates, and in particular the ItemTemplate, which determines the appearance of this control's normal or read-only mode, the EditItemTemplate, which determines its appearance when its data is being edited, and the InsertItemTemplate, which determines how the control appears when it is being used to insert a new database record. Note that the default appearance includes a number of labels, showing the names of the database fields, such as 'claimID:'. Beside each of these

FIGURE 10.27 The FormView tasks menu allows you to edit its templates such as the ItemTemplate. Click the 'End Template Editing' command when you have finished editing

(a)

(b)

labels is a 'bound field' which determines how and where the actual database values appear (the bound fields are the ones shown inside square brackets). Finally, at the bottom of the template are the command fields such as Edit, Delete and New, displayed here as link buttons. In this case, we do not want the call center operator to be able to delete existing claims, so select the Delete link button, and press the delete key to remove it from your web form.

To give the ItemTemplate a more regular appearance, insert a table (using the 'Table' → 'Insert Table' command from the main menu) with 6 rows and 2 columns into the item template. Then cut and paste the various labels and fields from the default item template into the table, as shown in Figure 10.28. This also shows the InsertItemTemplate, where a 3 column table has been inserted, and the fields cut and paste as shown. The third column has been used to insert validation controls associated with each of the textboxes in the middle row, either a simple RequiredFieldValidator to ensure that, for example, a claim reference is entered, or a CompareValidator to check that the data entered in the amount field is compatible with a currency type.

To improve the appearance of the FormView still further, the format of the amount and claimDate in each template needs to be set to display the data more appropriately. This requires using the Edit Template command to access each of the templates being used (the ItemTemplate, InsertItemTemplate, and EditItemTemplate). Click on the field you wish to format, and you will see it has a smart tag giving access to a tasks menu, containing the 'Edit Databindings . . . ' task. If you click this, you will see the DataBindings dialog box. This can be used to change the data binding which determines how fields are retrieved from the database and substituted into the template. All we wish to do, however, is change the format used to display the field, for example as shown in Figure 10.29. One minor problem is that the currency format includes the currency symbol (in this case, a pound symbol, but in general this depends on your locale). Unfortunately, when editing or inserting, this is not required, as the database expects only a numeric value to be returned. For this reason, you should use a different format for the amountTextBox which appears in the

FIGURE 10.28 Using the EditItemTemplate to lay out the claim FormView control in tabular format

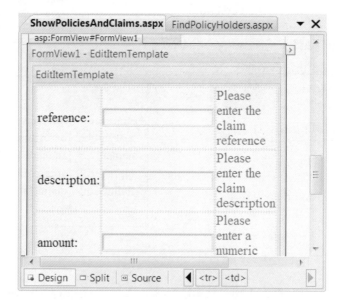

FIGURE 10.29 The DataBindings dialog box. Mostly, you will use this just to determine the format used to display a bound field, for example to select the currency format specifier {0:C}, as here.

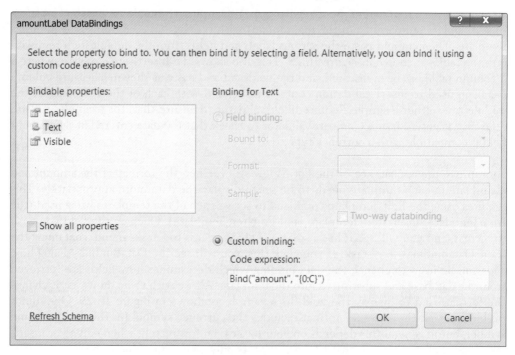

EditItemTemplate and InsertItemTemplate; instead of {0:C} use {0:0.00} which formats the value as a decimal with at least one digit before the point, and two after.

A useful organization for the FormView is as a six row three column table, allowing each field to have its name, a text box for data entry, and its own validation control, as shown in Figure 10.30. The ShowPoliciesAndClaims.aspx web form can now be used to edit and add claims. Note how the validation controls prevent data type errors such as a non-numeric amount being entered.

FIGURE 10.30 The FormView control being used to edit the selected claim and create a new claim, also showing one of the validation controls in action

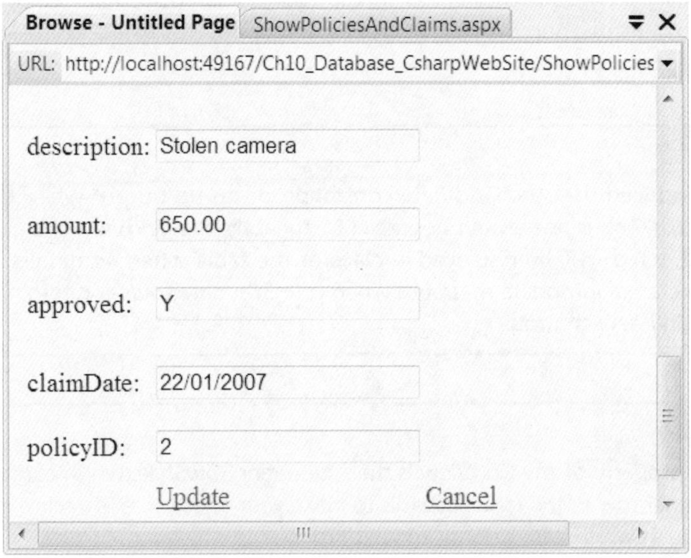

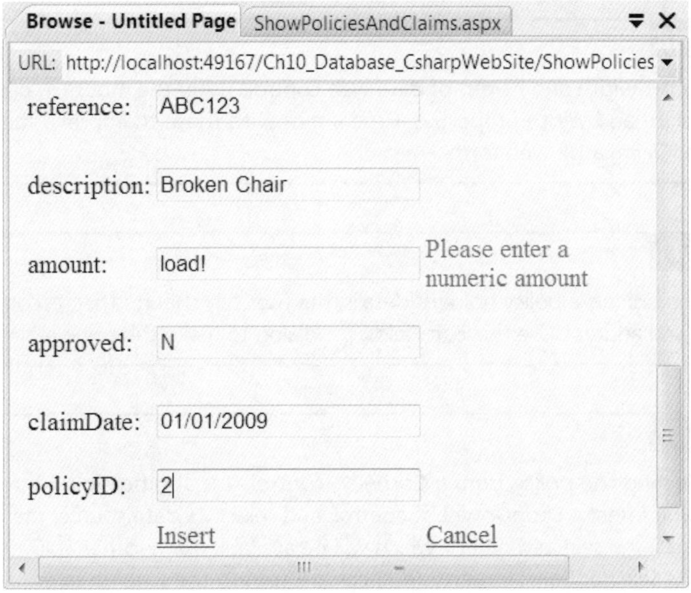

Section summary and quick exercises

This section has showed how to use the SqlDataSource, GridView, DetailsView and Form-View controls to create a web application satisfying the business requirements given at the start of the section. This involved adding a WHERE clause to the data source, including a query parameter connecting it to another data control. We also saw how to edit the columns in a GridView control, making use of bound, hyperlink, and template fields. It was shown how to change the appearance and format of Data controls using template editing and format specifiers. Finally we showed how to customize a FormView template and add validation controls to create a more professional web user interface for entering and updating claim details.

The following exercises suggest some improvements for you to make to the ShowPoliciesAndClaims.aspx web form. These introduce you to additional features of the ASP .NET data web controls, and provide additional experience of using Visual Web Developer to edit their appearance and behavior.

EXERCISE 10.8

You may have noticed that the GridView control produces no output when the data source returns no records. This is not always desirable. Fortunately, the GridView has a property called EmptyDataText, which will be displayed in place of the table when no data is found. Use this property to generate appropriate messages when your SQL data sources return no policies, or no claims, to your GridView controls.

EXERCISE 10.9

Another useful property of the GridView is the AlternatingRowStyle, which controls the appearance of every other row in the table. Use this to make your grids more attractive, and to help the operator distinguish which item belongs to which row.

EXERCISE 10.10

You can change the width and height of data web controls using the mouse in design view, or by setting their Height and Width properties. Experiment with these to improve the layout of your ShowPoliciesAndClaims.aspx web form.

EXERCISE 10.11

At present, when editing a policy holder's details, the user can change their account number, not just their name and address. Use the 'Edit Fields . . . ' dialog to make this value read-only.

EXERCISE 10.12

Rather than selecting the policy from a GridView control, it is also possible to use a drop down list. To do this, you insert a DropDownList control, and select its data source, the data to display, and the key values, the selected one of which will be available for another SqlDataSource control to query using its SelectedItem property. (If necessary, refresh the schema to ensure you have the

FIGURE 10.31 Configuring the data source of a database-driven DropDownList control

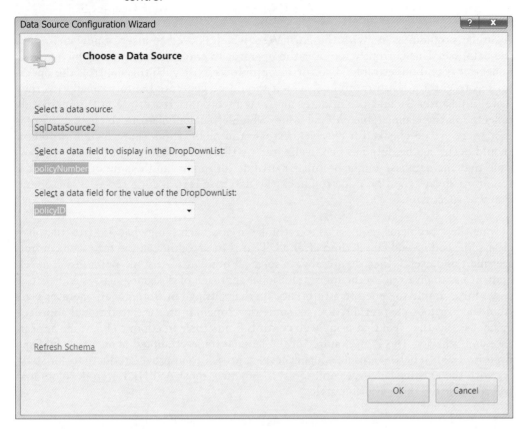

correct list of data fields to choose from.) Figure 10.31 shows the dialog for configuring the data source of a database-driven DropDownList control. The first data field selected here determines what is displayed in the drop down list, whereas the second one determines the value made available other data controls, via the DropDownList's SelectedItem property. Note that to ensure the page refreshes after the user selects another value in the DropDownList control, you need to set its AutoPostBack property.

10.6.3 Discussion

At this point, we have achieved a lot. Using a handful of web controls, we have created a usable web application which allows the call center operator to perform the use case tasks we identified at the start of the previous section. Our second web form, in particular, has a rich appearance and dynamic behavior and we have not written a line of code! Of course, the two pages we have not produced are not perfect, but it is a fact of life in web development that there is always room for improvement. Nonetheless it is worth considering their main deficiencies and how these can be addressed.

One obvious concern is the way that 'FindPolicyHolders.aspx' communicates the ID of the selected policy holder via a query string. This is not particularly professional because our goal should be to hide all *xxx*ID fields from the user. These are just the way the database links the tables together, and should not be visible, nor editable. A standard solution would be to pass the ID using the Session object, which was introduced in Chapter 9.

A similar problem exists with the FormView which is used to insert a new claim into the database. This currently requires the operator to enter the policyID, which is both unnecessary and undesirable. Two further problems exist with this control; the operator has to enter a claim reference, which should be generated automatically (as they were in Chapter 9), and the updates and new records it creates are not immediately reflected in the claims table. A final issue, which affects all changes to the database, is that there are no checks for database errors. You might think that no such problems should occur, as the data has been validated by the web controls, but it is always possible that the database might be full, or off-line, or might fail in some other way. It is therefore always good practice to check the database return code to see if the operation was successful.

Solving these problems requires us to rethink our approach somewhat. In particular, it is clear some coding will be required after all. That is to say, although the data web controls are smart and useful, they do not always solve all problems. At some point visual development has to give way to the more traditional approach of designing classes and writing code, for example to generate a reference, perhaps using our ReferenceGenerator class from the previous chapter. Of course, some developers prefer the traditional approach in any case, as they feel that using web controls limits their freedom to fine tune appearance and behavior. This is an example of the familiar trade-off, noted in an article by Dino Esposito (2008), between using a higher-level approach to improve productivity, or sticking with the existing languages and tools. In practice, most ASP.NET web development will combine the three available styles:

- Visual (using Design view, with its drag and drop visual editing)
- Declarative (setting properties and editing ASP.NET mark-up using source view)
- Programmatic (procedural and object-oriented coding and scripting)

10.7 Programmatic database access with LINQ

The most popular mechanisms used in Microsoft .NET to access data from a database are ADO.NET and LINQ. ADO.NET is the mechanism traditionally used by the ASP.NET data web controls to interface with the underlying database. LINQ (which stands for Language INtegrated Query) is the most expressive and advanced database access technology that Microsoft have developed so far, and in fact one of its benefits is that it can be used to access a variety of data sources, not just SQL but also XML-based information or any structured collection, so in this section we will focus on using LINQ.

To use LINQ to access your database, use the 'File' → 'New File...' menu command and select LINQ to SQL Classes from the list of available file templates. This will then bring up the LINQ to SQL designer, a visual editing tool which allows you to select from the available database tables and draw any required associations. It then generates code, stored by default in the App_Code directory, with declarations of classes which represent the underlying database, which you will use to write code access database in the LINQ style.

In Figure 10.32, the three tables from our database have all been added, by dragging them from the Database Explorer Window, to the database model, which can now be saved in the usual way. There will now be three files in the App_Code directory: the DataClasses.dbml database model, DataClasses.dbml.layout which represents the drawing layout, and DataClasses.designer.cs, which contains the LINQ code which has been generated from the model.

FIGURE 10.32 Using the LINQ to SQL tool to map database tables to .NET classes

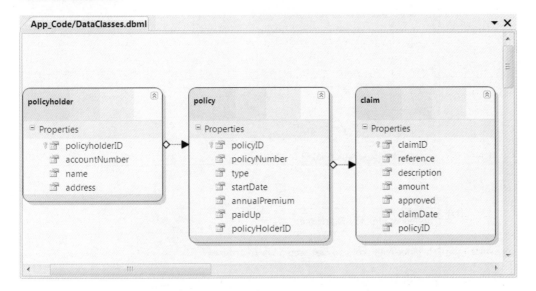

You can now access your database, if you choose, using a LinqDataSource rather than a SqlDataSource. To see this in action, create a new web form and add a LinqDataSource to it. Configuring this data source brings up a Wizard with a sequence of dialog boxes very similar to those displayed by the SqlDataSource Wizard. The main difference is that the first screen asks you to select a DataContext object rather than a data connection or connection string. Assuming you have only used the LINQ to SQL designer once, there will only be one DataContext object to choose from, after which you will be given the opportunity to filter and sort the data using the 'Where . . . ', 'OrderBy . . . ' and 'Advanced . . . ' dialog boxes. The second of these is rather different than we have seen before, and is shown in Figure 10.33b which, as you can see, is self-explanatory.

Once the LinqDataSource has been configured, it can be used by data web controls such as the GridView, DetailsView and FormView in the usual way. A web form making use of a LinqDataSource in this way, called 'UsingLinqDataSource.aspx', is provided with the on-line supporting materials.

Note that we have now seen XML, SQL, and LINQ data sources. It is worth noting that there are several other kinds of data source: the AccessDataSource, EntityDataSource, ObjectDataSource, and SiteMapDataSource. These all behave in similar ways, but allow your web pages direct access to data from a Microsoft Access database, entity data model, business object, or site map data file. Of the various kinds, the LINQ data source is the most flexible as it may be used to access databases, XML files, in memory collections, and most other kinds of structured data.

FIGURE 10.33

Configuring a LinqDataSource involves choosing a DataContext object and (optionally) determining the order to sort by

(a)
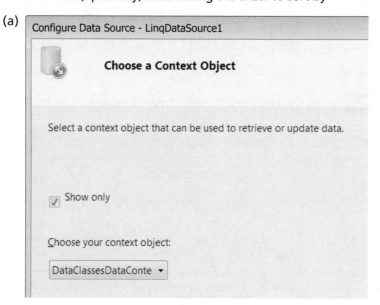

(b)
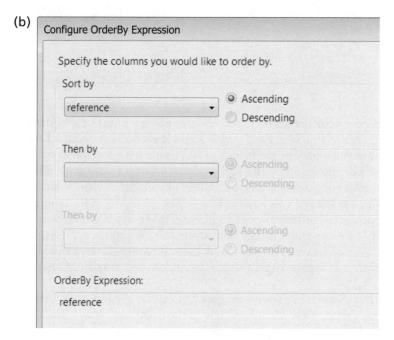

Our goal in this section, however, is to explain how to write database access code, rather than explore the visual style further, so we consider now the classes and methods provided by LINQ which enable us to query and update our database tables and records.

To make use of LINQ in your code, you need a collection to operate on. In the case of our database, the LINQ to SQL designer has generated a class definition for us which we can use to program database access code. This class is called DataClassesDataContext and can be used to query and update the database. The first step is to declare an instance of this class, as shown below:

```
DataClassesDataContext insuranceDB = new DataClassesDataContext();
```

We can now use this object to process a LINQ query. As with SQL, LINQ queries are written using operators such as 'from', 'where' and 'select'. An example of a LINQ query in C# is given below:

```
var selectedPolicies = from p in insuranceDB.policies where p.policyID == 1
select p;
```

The equivalent Visual Basic code is:

```
Dim insuranceDB DataClassesDataContext = new DataClassesDataContext()
Dim selectedPolicies = From p In insuranceDB.policies _
    Where p.policyID = 1 Select p
```

This statement makes use of some new language features introduced into Visual Basic and C# in order to support LINQ. Firstly the 'var' keyword introduces a variable whose type can be inferred from the context. In this case, the selectedPolicies object is an enumerable list of policy objects, of type IEnumerable<policy>. Secondly we see the new LINQ operators themselves. Here, the query is constructed by declaring a variable 'p' which is local to (or bound to) the query, and has the same type as the policy table in our database. Note that the LINQ to SQL tool has pluralized this name for us when generating the equivalent .NET class definition, so policy has become policies, claim has become claims, and so on. The policies 'p' with policyID equal to 1 are filtered by the where clause, and the result of this query is the policy object 'p' itself. It also worth noting that the original table name is used as the name of a class representing a single record. Thus, in the query above, the type given to the bound variable 'p' is policy.

This LINQ query is therefore equivalent to the following SQL, and has quite a similar syntax (albeit with the clauses in a different order):

```
SELECT * FROM policy WHERE policyID = 1
```

In fact, to execute the LINQ query above, LINQ to SQL will actually generate an SQL statement such as the above. Thus when using LINQ to query an SQL database, you have the convenience of writing your queries using C# or VB.NET code but can still be confident that, under the covers, efficient SQL queries are being sent to the database. It is possible to see the SQL queries as they are sent to the database, and the results returned, by directing the database log or trace output to the console using a statement such as:

```
db.log = console.out
```

While we are discussing technical issues, it may also be of interest to you that the LINQ operators are in fact just a prettier or 'sugared' syntax for calls to associated methods such as .Where(), and the parameters to these operators are lambda expressions representing delegates or higher order functions. For example, in the raw form, without the syntactic sugar, you would write:

```
Where(p => p.policyID == 1)
```

in order to select the required records. The 'sugared' syntax is, in this case, not only prettier, but also easier to read and understand.

In addition to the three most common operators, 'select', 'from', and 'where', there are also LINQ operators for aggregation (Average, Count, Min, Max, Sum), partitioning (Skip, SkipWhile, Take, TakeWhile), quantifiers (Any, All), selecting individual elements (First, FirstOrDefault, ElementAt, Single), sorting (OrderBy, ThenBy, Descending) and many others. These allow LINQ to express a range of queries equivalent to more complex and compound SQL queries. A quick summary of common usage patterns in both C# and VB.NET can be found via MSDN's 101 LINQ Samples article (101 LINQ Samples).

The LINQ query above has, we hope, generated a list with a single policy object; the unique database record with policyID equal to one. The list of objects can be turned into single object using the Single() operator. Note that this operator will throw an exception unless there is precisely one element in the list it is supplied:

```
var singlePolicy = selectedPolicies.Single();
```

Finally, a specific column such as the policy type can be selected in the usual way.

```
var policyType = singlePolicy.type;
```

Of course, it is possible to combine all these statements together:

```
var policyType = (from p in insuranceDB.policies where p.policyID == 1
select p).Single().type;
```

or, in Visual Basic:

```
Dim policyType = (From p In insuranceDB.policies _
  Where p.policyID = 1 Select p).Single().type
```

LINQ can also be used to update the database. For example, having selected a single policy object, this can be updated and the change applied to the database using code such as:

```
singlePolicy.paidUp = 'Y';
insuranceDB.SubmitChanges();
```

As the name indicates, the SubmitChanges method can be used after multiple changes have been made to a LINQ object, or indeed to multiple LINQ objects, each representing a record in the original database. To remove an object from the database, use the DeleteOnSubmit method, whereas to add a new one, construct it in the usual way, then call the InsertOnSubmit method on the appropriate table. For example, to add a new claim, you can use code such as:

```
claim newClaim = new claim();
newClaim.claimDate = System.DateTime.Now;
newClaim.description = description.Text;
newClaim.amount = Convert.ToDecimal(amount.Text);
/* and so on for the other database fields */
insuranceDB.claims.InsertOnSubmit(newClaim);
insuranceDB.SubmitChanges();
```

Note that the new claim is not visible to other users until it has been committed to the database using the SubmitChanges method. For this reason, it was decided that it would be wrong to call the insert and delete methods 'Add' and 'Remove' as originally proposed.

One way to learn more about LINQ is by experiment. Joseph Albahari's LINQpad tool allows you to type in and execute LINQ queries interactively. This tool is covered in the LINQ Pocket Reference (Albahari and Albahari, 2008). The first two examples in Figure 10.34 show LINQ queries which process an array of integers as their input. The first example shows the use of the three standard LINQ operators, and an anonymous type for the results. Example (b) shows the same query but using explicit calls to the .Where()

FIGURE 10.34   Using the LINQpad tool to execute C# LINQ queries interactively

(a)
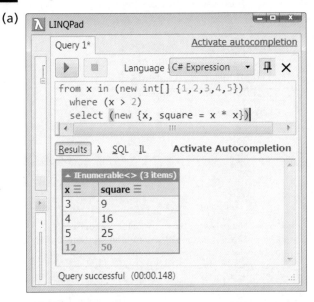

(b)
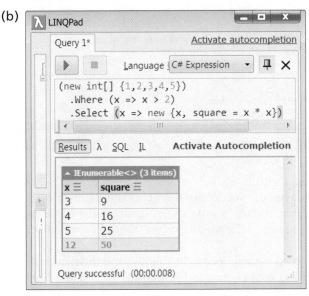

FIGURE 10.34 continued

(c)

(d)

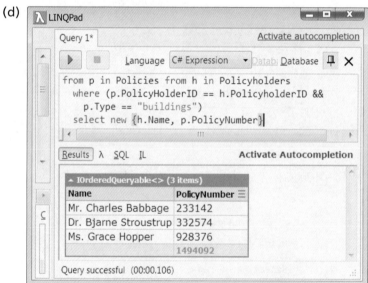

and .Select() methods, with lambda expressions as arguments. A lambda expression is a way of writing an anonymous function, or delegate. The argument(s) to the function occur before the => operator, and the results after. Note that the LINQpad tool automatically totals columns with numeric data, which explains the final row's contents.

The LINQ query is typed in the upper right window, and the right pointing arrow, or F5, or the 'Query' → 'Execute' menu command is used to run it. The results are then displayed as a table in the lower right window.

The second two examples in Figure 10.33 show the use of LINQ to query our insurance database. The first LINQ to SQL database query shows the use of the orderby clause to sort the results, in this case by policy type. The second LINQ to SQL database query shows how multiple tables can be used in a single query to select the names of customers with a buildings policy, and also the numbers of those policies, items of data which are extracted from two different tables. Note the use of double equals and double ampersand in the condition: this is a C# expression and not SQL!

Before these queries can be run, LINQ must first establish a connection to the database, using the Add Connection command, which pops up a dialog box as shown in Figure 10.35 below.

You can see that LINQpad has capitalized the names of our database tables and fields as well as pluralizing them. There are options (also shown in Figure 10.35) to control these behaviors, if you wish.

FIGURE 10.35 The LINQpad Connection dialog box

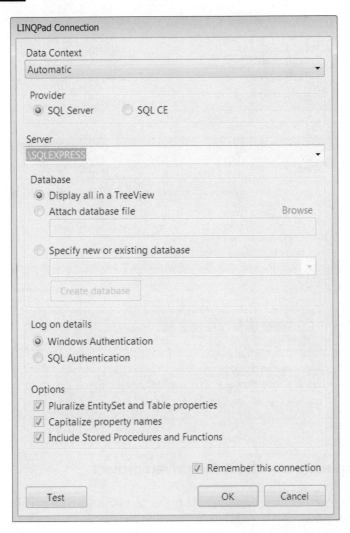

The Visual Basic syntax for the LINQ operators is similar to that used in C#, as can be seen from the two LINQ to SQL queries shown in Figure 10.36. The main difference is the use of continuation characters to allow the use of multi line expressions, which is often necessary for complex queries.

FIGURE 10.36 Using the LINQpad tool to execute Visual Basic LINQ queries interactively

(a)
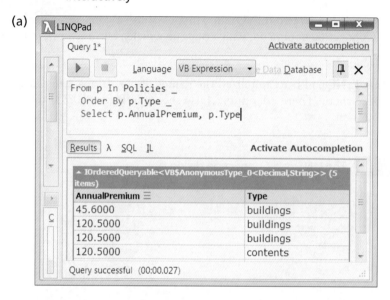

(b)
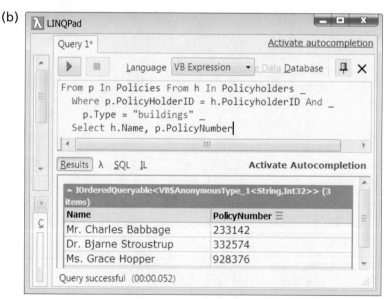

10.7.1 Completing our database-driven project

Putting all this together, it is now possible for us to revise our 'ShowPoliciesAndClaims. aspx' web form to address the deficiencies noted in the discussion above.

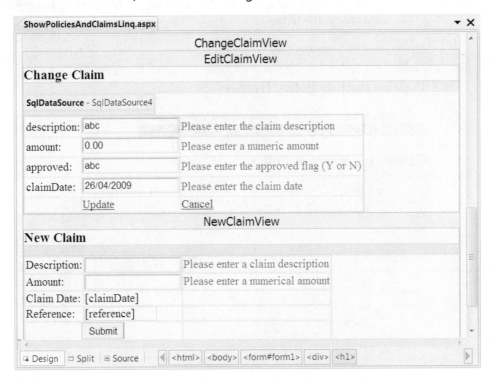

One issue concerns the need to construct the claim reference prior to the user completing a form for a new claim. The text for the reference, for example, is assigned using code such as the following:

```
int policyID = Int32.Parse(Request.QueryString["policyID"]);
var policyType = (from policy in insuranceDB.policies
    where policy.policyID == policyID select policy.type).Single();
reference.Text = polType.Substring(0, 1).ToUpper() +
  policyID.ToString() + "-" +
  System.DateTime.Today.Year.ToString() +
  System.DateTime.Today.Month.ToString() +
  System.DateTime.Today.Day.ToString() + "-" +
  System.DateTime.Now.Millisecond.ToString("000");
```

A more modular approach would be to encapsulate this code into a ReferenceGenerator class as introduced in Chapter 9.

In this design we will avoid the FormsView and instead build our own web form for creating a new claim, though we will continue using the same FormView for editing existing claims, as this is already working satisfactorily. Obviously it would confuse the user to see both of these forms on our web page at the same time. A solution to this problem is to use a MultiView control. As you may recall from Chapter 7, this control contains a number of views, each of which can itself contain any kind of web control. At most one view will be

FIGURE 10.38 The 'ShowPoliciesAndClaims.aspx' web form now has a MultiView control which switches between showing the New Claim and Change forms (or not showing anything) depending on the state of the other controls on the page

(a)

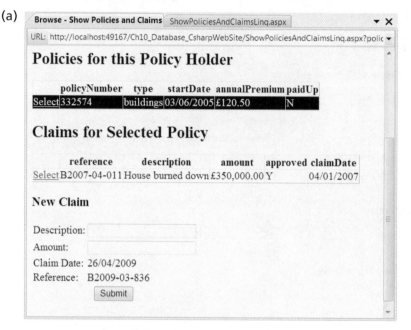

(b)

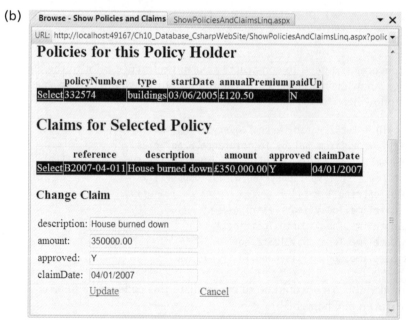

shown at one time. Switching between the MultiView involves setting its ActiveViewIndex property, which is initially set to -1, meaning none of the views are displayed.

You should therefore add a MultiView control with two view controls inside it. For ease of recognition, these can be called ChangeClaimView, EditClaimView, and NewClaimView.

The NewClaimView consists of a heading, a five by three table, six labels, two textboxes, two validation controls, and a button. The text properties of the last two labels are empty, so Visual Web Developer shows their IDs in brackets instead, hence [claimDate] and [reference]. The EditClaimView has the same SqlDataSource and FormsView controls as in our previous version.

You will note that the FormView, which is now inside the EditClaimView, no longer shows the claim reference and policy ID, as it is not intended for call center staff to change these. The data source only selects the fields which are actually required to be changed, and the primary key, which is mandatory when updates are required.

To determine which View is displayed, we need event handler code to test whether there is a selected claim, in which case the FormView should be displayed, or just a selected policy, in which case the New Claim form should be displayed. This code takes the form of conditional statements such as:

```
if (ClaimsView.SelectedRow == null) ChangeClaimView.ActiveViewIndex = -1;
else ChangeClaimView.ActiveViewIndex = 1;
```

Figure 10.38 shows an example of switching the view. To start with the New Claim form is displayed, but once the operator selects one of the claims for the selected policy, the Change Claim form is displayed instead. The code which controls this switch has been added to the handler for the ClaimsView_SelectedIndexChanged event. Note that some care is required to ensure the MultiView is always in the correct state depending on which events are triggered, and the state of the other controls on the .aspx web form. When a policy has been selected, but no claim, the view that allows a new claim to be added is shown. When a claim has been selected, the other view, which allows the operator to edit it, is shown instead.

The full code of the 'ShowPoliciesAndClaims.aspx.cs' event handling file is shown on the following pages, followed by the Visual Basic equivalent:

```
using System;
using System.Collections;
using System.Configuration;
using System.Data;
using System.Linq;
using System.Web;
using System.Web.Security;
using System.Web.UI;
using System.Web.UI.HtmlControls;
using System.Web.UI.WebControls;
using System.Web.UI.WebControls.WebParts;
using System.Xml.Linq;

public partial class ShowPolicies : System.Web.UI.Page
{
  /* we will be using the LINQ to SQL generated data context */
DataClassesDataContext insuranceDB = new DataClassesDataContext();

protected void Page_Load(object sender, EventArgs e)
  {
```

```
    /* No error message to display */
    DatabaseError.Enabled = false;
}
protected void PoliciesView_SelectedIndexChanged(object sender
    EventArgs e)
{
  if (PoliciesView.SelectedRow == null)
  /* Don't display any edit/new claim dialog */
    ChangeClaimView.ActiveViewIndex = -1;
  else
  /* a policy has been selected by the user */
  {
    ChangeClaimView.ActiveViewIndex = 1;
  /* get the policy ID of the selected policy */
    int polID = (int)PoliciesView.SelectedValue;
    var polType = (from policy in insuranceDB.policies
    where policy.policyID == polID
    select policy.type).Single();

    DateTime today = System.DateTime.Today;
    string newRef = polType.Substring(0, 1).ToUpper() +
today.Year.ToString()
  + "-" + polID.ToString("00") + "-"
    + System.DateTime.Now.Millisecond.ToString("000");

  /* initialise claim date and reference */
    reference.Text = newRef;
    claimDate.Text = today.ToShortDateString();
  }
}

protected void Button1_Click(object sender, EventArgs e)
{
  /* Only go ahead if validation has succeeded */
  if (Page.IsValid)
  {
    claim newClaim = new claim();
    newClaim.claimDate = System.DateTime.Parse(claimDate.Text);
    newClaim.reference = reference.Text;
    newClaim.description = description.Text;
    newClaim.amount = Convert.ToDecimal(amount.Text);
    newClaim.policyID = (int) PoliciesView.SelectedValue;
    newClaim.approved = 'N';

    try
    {
      DatabaseError.Text = "";
      insuranceDB.claims.InsertOnSubmit(newClaim);
      insuranceDB.SubmitChanges();
      /* refresh view of claims, and remove new claim dialog */
      ClaimsView.DataBind();
```

```
        ChangeClaimView.ActiveViewIndex = -1;
      }
      catch (Exception myEx)
      {
        DatabaseError.Enabled = true;
        DatabaseError.Text = "Database insertion failed.";
      }
    }
  }

  protected void ClaimsView_SelectedIndexChanged(object sender,
      EventArgs e)
  {
    if(ClaimsView.SelectedRow == null)
      ChangeClaimView.ActiveViewIndex = -1;
    else
    /* show edit claim dialog */
    ChangeClaimView.ActiveViewIndex = 0;
  }

  protected void FormView1_ItemUpdated(object sender,
    FormViewUpdatedEventArgs e)
  {
    if (e.Exception != null || e.AffectedRows != 1)
    {
      DatabaseError.Enabled = true;
      DatabaseError.Text = "Database update failed.";
    }
    ClaimsView.DataBind();
  }
}
```

The Visual Basic equivalent is as follows:

```
Imports System
Imports System.Collections
Imports System.Configuration
Imports System.Data
Imports System.Linq
Imports System.Web
Imports System.Web.Security
Imports System.Web.UI
Imports System.Web.UI.HtmlControls
Imports System.Web.UI.WebControls
Imports System.Web.UI.WebControls.WebParts
Imports System.Xml.Linq


Partial Class ShowPoliciesAndClaimsLinq Inherits System.Web.UI.Page
  ' we will be using the LINQ to SQL generated data context
  Private insuranceDB As DataClassesDataContext = _
    New DataClassesDataContext()
```

```vbnet
Protected Sub Page_Load(ByVal sender As Object, ByVal e As EventArgs)
' No error message to display
DatabaseError.Text = ""
End Sub


Protected Sub PoliciesView_SelectedIndexChanged(ByVal s As Object, _
    ByVal e As EventArgs)
 If PoliciesView.SelectedRow Is Nothing Then
' Don't display any edit/new claim dialog
  ChangeClaimView.ActiveViewIndex = -1
 Else
' a policy has been selected by the user
  ChangeClaimView.ActiveViewIndex = 1
' get the policy ID of the selected policy
  Dim polID As Integer = CInt(PoliciesView.SelectedValue)
  Dim polType As String = _
     (From policy In insuranceDB.policies _
     Where policy.policyID = polID _
     Select policy.type).Single()
  Dim today As DateTime = System.DateTime.Today
  Dim newRef As String = polType.Substring(0, 1).ToUpper() + _
    today.Year.ToString() + "-" + polID.ToString("00") + "-" _
    + System.DateTime.Now.Millisecond.ToString("000")

' initialise claim date and reference
  reference.Text = newRef
  claimDate.Text = today.ToShortDateString()
  End If
 End Sub


 Protected Sub Button1_Click(ByVal sender As Object, _
 ByVal e As System.EventArgs) Handles Button1.Click
' Only go ahead if validation has succeeded
 If Page.IsValid() = True Then
  Dim newClaim As claim = New claim()
  newClaim.claimDate = System.DateTime.Parse(claimDate.Text)
  newClaim.reference = reference.Text
  newClaim.description = description.Text
  newClaim.amount = Convert.ToDecimal(amount.Text)
  newClaim.policyID = CInt(PoliciesView.SelectedValue)
  newClaim.approved = "N"
 Try
  DatabaseError.Text = ""
  insuranceDB.claims.InsertOnSubmit(newClaim)
  insuranceDB.SubmitChanges()
' refresh view of claims, and remove new claim dialog
     ClaimsView.DataBind()
     ChangeClaimView.ActiveViewIndex = -1
   Catch myEx As Exception
     DatabaseError.Text = "Database insertion failed." + _
        myEx.Message
```

```
      End Try
    End If
  End Sub


  Protected Sub ClaimsView_SelectedIndexChanged(ByVal sender As Object, _
    ByVal e As EventArgs)
  If ClaimsView.SelectedRow Is Nothing Then
    ChangeClaimView.ActiveViewIndex = -1
  Else
' show edit claim dialog
    ChangeClaimView.ActiveViewIndex = 0
    End If
  End Sub


  Protected Sub FormView1_ItemUpdated(ByVal sender As Object, _
    ByVal e As FormViewUpdatedEventArgs)
  If e.Exception Is Nothing Then
    If e.AffectedRows = 1 Then
      DatabaseError.Text = ""
    Else
      DatabaseError.Text = "Rows affected: " + _
          e.AffectedRows.ToString()
    End If
  Else
    DatabaseError.Text = "Database update failed. " + _
        e.Exception.Message
  End If
  ClaimsView.DataBind()
  ChangeClaimView.ActiveViewIndex = -1
  End Sub
End Class
```

In addition to the logic already discussed, it is worth noting some lines of code here. The event handler which responds to the Submit button being clicked, tests to see whether Page.IsValid is true. This flag is set automatically by the validation controls, which have all been included in the InputValidation validation group, as has the Submit button itself. The database insertion code has an exception handler which sets the text of the DatabaseError label, and enables it. This displays the message at an appropriate point in the page, using an appropriate color and font.

An ItemUpdated handler has been added to the FormView which is used to edit an existing claim. This tests the second event argument to see whether there was a database exception, and whether the number of rows affected was 1. If not, a database error is reported as described in the previous paragraph.

Where the claim table has been updated, the event handlers call the DataBind method of the ClaimsView GridView control. This method causes this control to refresh its data, ensuring that the view on-screen is synchronized with the data in the database.

A final issue with this approach concerns the awkward way the page refreshes as the user selects different policies and claims. These refreshes are caused by the full page being

POSTed back in response to these interactions. A more modern style would be to use AJAX, which is covered in Chapter 14, in order to update only the parts of the page which have actually changed.

10.8 Final thoughts on database programming

This chapter has covered a lot of ground. There is still, of course, a lot more to say about database programming. The following sub-sections cover ODBC database programming, optimistic concurrency, transactions, web applications patterns and maintainability.

10.8.1 ADO.NET and ODBC database programming

Microsoft's Open DataBase Connectivity API is a well-established means of accessing relational database management systems. An ODBC driver is available for all the commonly used RDMS packages. This means it is worth considering as an alternative means of accessing data in your database. ODBC was first introduced by Microsoft in 1992, and is significant because it implements the SQL standard CLI (Call Level Interface).

In 2002, Microsoft introduced ADO.NET (Active Data Objects for .NET), which provides a somewhat higher level and more object-oriented API for database access. ADO.NET builds on and extends ODBC.

Compared to LINQ, however, both ODBC and ADO.NET are somewhat low level. SQL queries and commands must be constructed by concatenating strings together, or using parameter string substitution, and then passing the result to the database engine to execute. The result is returned as a table that is also rather awkward to unpack when accessing the desired field. For example, the two lines of LINQ below:

```
DataClassesDataContext insuranceDB = new DataClassesDataContext();
int policyID =
   (from p in insuranceDB.policies where p.policyID == 1
   select p.policyID).Single();
```

would require rather more lines to implement using ODBC or ADO.NET. Typical code in C# would look something like:

```
SqlConnection myConnection = newSqlConnection(connString);
myConnection.Open();
SqlCommand myCommand =
  new SqlCommand("SELECT * FROM policy WHERE policyID=" +
policyID.ToString(), myConnection);
SqlDataReader myReader;
myReader = myCommand.ExecuteReader();
int policyID = myReader.GetInt32(0);
```

and similarly in Visual Basic (but without the semicolons).

Note that executing the query returns an SqlDataReader object whose Read method can be used to iterate through an SQL result set, which also provides methods such as GetInt32 and GetString to access database fields in the current row. In this case, we are only interested in the first field of the first record.

Database updates also involve passing the SQL command as a string using code such as:

```
SqlCommand myCommand = newSqlCommand(myConnection);
myCommand.CommandText =
    "UPDATE policy SET amount=@amount WHERE policyID=@policyID";
myCommand.Parameters.Add("@amount", amount);
myCommand.Parameters.Add("@policyID", policyID);
rowsAffected = myCommand.ExecuteNonQuery()
```

Here the SQL command string is built up one parameter at a time. The ExecuteNonQuery method executes the command and returns the number of rows affect, which should be one in this case, if the update has been successful.

As you can see, using somewhat more code is required here than when using LINQ, and it is also harder to read. One disadvantage with LINQ to SQL, however, is that it is only supported at present by Microsoft's SQL Server and SQL Server Express Edition databases.

The following chapter gives working examples of ADO.NET code in both C# and Visual Basic.

10.8.2 Optimistic concurrency and transactions

Earlier in this chapter, we advised you to select optimistic concurrency in the Advanced… dialog box whenever you configured a data source to allow database updates. You are probably wondering what optimistic concurrency is, and why you should select it. If you look at the data source in design view after you have done so, you will note that this includes the SQL INSERT, UPDATE and DELETE statements which will be used for database changes. For example, in 'ShowPoliciesAndClaims.aspx' there are a number of definitions such as the one below:

```
<asp:SqlDataSource
  . . .
  UpdateCommand="UPDATE [policyholder]
    SET [name] = @name,
    [address] = @address, [accountNumber] = @accountNumber
    WHERE [policyholderID] = @original_policyholderID AND
    [name] = @original_name AND
    [address] = @original_address AND
    [accountNumber] = @original_accountNumber"
  . . .
/>
```

Here you will see that the SQL UPDATE statement is only executed if all the values currently associated with the particular policy holder are the same as they were when the record was originally read (as indicated by the parameters with names such as

@original_address). Why should these values have changed? It is important to bear in mind when programming a web application that there may be many users all accessing the website at the same time. These concurrent users may happen to generate web requests which attempt to update the same database records. Concurrent updates can lead to the classic parallel programming problem of interference. Suppose two operators are updating the customer details at the same time (an unlikely, but not impossible scenario); one of their updates will get lost (not such a big deal). A more serious problem occurs when recording transfers of money. Imagine, for example, two payments (worth $100 and $200) are being made into the same account concurrently. The database code typically works by reading the amount present in your account, adding the payment, and writing the new value back into the account. If two such updates occur simultaneously, your balance ($1,000, say) is read twice, and two new balances are computed ($1,100 and $1,200) are computed. If these two balances are used to update your database account record, the final balance (which might then be $1,100 or $1,200) will not increase by the full $300 total which was being transferred, which is not a good way to keep your customers happy. To guard against this 'lost update' problem, the UpdateCommand above checks carefully that no field in the selected record has been updated since it was last read before changing it.

The generated DeleteCommands have similar checks built in to them. The LINQ Submit-Changes() method also automatically uses its own version of this approach when sending the database a batch of updates. Note, however, that the InsertCommands do not follow this pattern, as they do not suffer from the same problem of interference by concurrent requests, as they create new records rather than updating existing ones.

The approach is called optimistic concurrency because it allows requests to go ahead on the assumption that there will be no problems with interference such as lost updates. This is a reasonable assumption as it is relatively rare for concurrent requests to update the same database record. Most of the time the checks in the UpdateCommand will successfully match the values originally read, and the update can go ahead without any problems.

This contrasts with traditional transaction programming in which a sequence of database updates is grouped together using a programming construct called a transaction, often involving a call to a transaction processing monitor at the start and end of the sequence to delimit the transaction. The transaction processing system then monitors all database updates to ensure that no two transactions interfere. Transaction processing systems can use a pessimistic approach, for example locking database records to avoid clashes, or an optimistic approach similar to that described above. Depending on the pattern of accesses, the pessimistic approach may out-perform the optimistic one, or vice versa. The optimistic concurrency implemented by ASP.NET and LINQ therefore provides similar benefits to that obtained by using traditional transaction programming, but with less coding.

Note however that optimistic concurrency can fail where fields contain NULL values. A feature of SQL is that the result of testing whether NULL = NULL is, somewhat surprisingly, false. The test as shown in the UpdateCommand above can never succeed if any of the old, or any of the new, values are NULL. You can guard against this, of course, by using the NOT NULL constraint noted above. It may also be wise to ensure that all your data entry fields have their ConvertEmptyStringToNull property set to false. Alternatively you can wrap up your LINQ queries and updates into a conventional transaction. To do this, use the ExecuteNonQuery method with the command text BEGIN TRANSACTION at the start, and COMMIT if the updates succeed, or ROLLBACK if there is an error.

Finally note that if you prefer you can arrange for your database updates to use stored procedures rather than simple SQL DELETE/INSERT/UPDATE statements. In some organizations stored procedures are used to implement a final layer of checks to ensure that all data stored in the database is valid. This is particularly important if a large number of applications all use and update the same database, in which case the web application patterns described below may not be sufficient to guarantee database consistency.

10.8.3 Web application patterns and maintainability

One criticism which can be made of our web application is that the web forms access and update the database directly. Indeed, ASP.NET makes it very easy for us to create web pages which work like this. In a fully object-oriented application, however, there should be objects which represent the important business entities such as policy holder, policy, and claim. Larger websites therefore typically include a layer of code between the user interface and the database. This layer of code consists of the *business objects* derived from our domain model, whose methods include the business logic which defines and controls how the insurance business operates. For example, there may be a limit to how much a customer can claim on their policy without requiring special investigation before a claim is approved. There may also be rules about how many different insurance policies an ordinary customer can have before they are recognized as a business customer, to whom different rules (and discounts) may apply. These situations are best implemented in well-defined and isolated classes so that they can easily be changed without affecting the rest of the application.

A popular pattern, particularly in the Java Enterprise world, is that of the *data access object*, which provides an abstract interface to encapsulate all database accesses. This ensures that changes to persistence logic do not affect the rest of the web application.

Note that in this chapter, we have been using a local database, one which is stored on the same computer you are using to run your web application. In most business environments, the database will be stored on a separate computer, called the database server. Fortunately, the protocol used to access the database is one which was designed for accessing the database remotely, which means it works the same when the database is remote or local. This means it is trivial to switch your web application from targeting a local database to a remote one, or vice versa. Only the database connection mark-up or code has to change, which is just a 'one-liner'. One approach is to edit the connection string which Visual Web Developer has added to your web.config configuration file.

A more serious change, however, would be to move to a different relational database management system (RDMS) altogether. The new RDMS might not support the newer .NET libraries such as ADO.NET or LINQ. It will, almost certainly, have a slightly different dialect of SQL. Changing RDMS therefore very often involves a considerable number of source code changes as well. To localize the effect of these, it certainly helps to have restricted database access using the patterns mentioned above.

The following chapter demonstrates the use of Data Access Objects, which help to address these concerns.

Self Study Questions

1. Name three different data source controls.
2. Name three data web controls which consume data from a data source.
3. When configuring a data source, which dialog box allows the database to be edited?
4. When configuring a data web control, which dialog box allows you to select and order the database fields being displayed?
5. If you wish to control the appearance of a data web control, how do you do this for the table, row and individual cell?
6. Which format specifiers should you use to display a database field as currency, or as a date?
7. What does LINQ stand for?
8. Give the names of four of the LINQ operators.
9. Give two .NET programming language features introduced specifically to support LINQ.
10. Why is the InsertOnSubmit() method so called?

Exercises

10.13 Research the Session object and use this instead of the QueryString to pass the policyholderID from 'FindPolicyHolders.aspx' to 'ShowPoliciesAndClaims.aspx'. Hint: one solution is replacing the HyperLink field of the GridView in the FindPolicy Holders with a Select Command button, then adding the code to set the session key Session["policyholderID"] to the GridView1.SelectedValue before redirecting to the 'ShowPoliciesAndClaims.aspx' form. You also need to change the SqlData-Source objects on the latter page to use session parameters rather than the query string parameters. Note that when you change a data source in this way, Visual Web Developer will prompt to see if you wish to automatically regenerate the Grid-View's columns. If you have manually edited, added or removed any columns, this is probably not desirable, as these changes will be lost, so you should select 'No' in response.

10.14 Change the SqlDataSource used by the GridView1 control in the 'FindPolicyHolders. aspx' web form to a LinqDataSource instead. Note that when you change a data source in this way, Visual Web Developer will prompt to see if you wish to automatically regenerate the GridView's columns. If you have manually edited, added or removed any columns, this is probably not desirable, as these changes will be lost, so you should select 'No' in response.

10.15 Design and implement a web form which allows the operator to create a new policy for a new policy holder. Note that to be able to insert the new policy, it must refer correctly to policy holder, to avoid violating the policyFK foreign key constraint.

10.16 The code so far presented constructs external identifiers such as the claim reference in an ad hoc fashion using the system clock. This approach could in theory generate the same reference more than once, leading to confusion. A better approach would be to use a database sequence to ensure each number used is unique. Change the code that generates claim references to create a new reference with an embedded number that is one more than any existing reference number. For this exercise, you may wish to implement and use a ReferenceGenerator class such as the one introduced in Chapter 9. You should familiarize yourself with .NET's Globally Unique IDentifiers, or GUIDs, which are 128 bits or 32 hexadecimal digits. These have a very high probability of being unique, but are not well suited for human communication. Another option would be to retrieve the automatically generated primary keys from the Claim table (the claimID field) and use these to provide a unique number to append to each reference.

SUMMARY

In this chapter we covered how to create, configure, and populate a database using the Data Explorer directly and through stored procedures.

We looked at a number of new ASP.NET controls, and explored some that were previously introduced in more detail:

- SqlDataSource, LinqDataSource
- DetailsView, FormView and GridView
- MasterView, View

We saw how to use the data sources to query and update our database. We also wrote some small event handlers to add extra functionality in order to develop a rich web database-driven web form. Microsoft's new Language INtegrated Query (LINQ) technology and the LINQ to SQL tool were covered. A number of other database topics were also considered, including ADO.NET, optimistic concurrency, transactions, and data access objects.

References and further reading

Albahari, J. and Albahari, B., 2008. *LINQ Pocket Reference.* O'Reilly. This introduces the LINQpad tool, which can be downloaded from http://www.linqpad.net/.

Celko, J., 2005. SQL for Smarties: *Advanced SQL Programming* (3rd edition). Morgan Kaufmann.

Codd, E.F., 1970. *A Relational Model of Data for Large Shared Data Banks.* Communications of the ACM 13 (6): 377–387.

Date, C.J., 2003. *An Introduction to Database Systems* (8th edition). Addison Wesley.

Esposito, D., 2008. *Are Server Controls Still Useful?* Dr Dobbs. http://www.ddj.com/windows/211100195.

Meijer, E., Schulte, W. and Bierman, G. 2003. *Unifying Tables, Objects and Documents.* Microsoft Research.

PDC 2005. *Language Integrated Query for Databases, Professional Developers Conference, LA.* http://www.microsoft.com/presspass/features/2005/sep05/09-13NETLanguage.mspx.

Schwartz J. and Desmond, M. 2007. *Looking to LINQ.* Redmond Developer. http://reddevnews.com/features/article.aspx?editorialsid=707.

101 LINQ Samples, MSDN, in VB.NET. http://msdn.microsoft.com/en-us/vbasic/bb688088.aspx.

101 LINQ Samples, MSDN, in C#. http://msdn.microsoft.com/en-us/vcsharp/aa336746.aspx.

CHAPTER 11

Building a Persistence Layer Using Data Access Objects

LEARNING OBJECTIVES

- **To understand the Data Access Object pattern**

- **To understand how data transfer objects can be used with Data Access Objects**

- **To be able to create a connection string to a database in the web.config file**

- **To be able to write Data Access Objects that can read and write objects to and from the database**

- **To understand the complexity of object-relational mapping**

INTRODUCTION

In Chapter 10 we saw how Visual Web Developer controls from the 'Data' group in the Toolbox can be used for directly interacting with the database from a web form. However, this approach on its own is not flexible enough for all types of data access required in a web application. For example, we may want to build a web interface that will work on a mobile device browser that cannot support the Visual Web Developer data controls, so if we want to be able to interact with the database from a mobile web application, we need a somewhat different strategy. There will also be other operations in a web application that require access to the data layer from the business model layer of the application, which again will not be using data controls. Therefore we sometimes need a way of accessing data stored in the database without using these controls. At the end of Chapter 10 we noted that as an alternative to using the data controls to access the database we could use Data Access Objects (DAOs). This is the approach that we will use in this chapter to enable parts of our application to interact with persistent data stored in the database or file system. We noted in Chapter 1 that applications have layers for different concerns. One of those layers is the data management, or *persistence* layer. There should ideally be a clear distinction between this layer and the business logic layer above. To some extent, data controls shortcut that separation, enabling data to move directly between the presentation layer and the persistence layer. However beyond the simple interactions possible with data controls, we should enforce the separation of layers to make the application flexible and easier to maintain. One way that we can do this is to apply the data access object pattern, which helps us to encapsulate the persistence layer behind a set of these objects. In this chapter, we create the beginnings of a persistence layer for our web application by creating DAOs for insurance claims and policies.

11.1 Data Access Objects

Once we have a layer of persistent data in a web application, we have to provide a way of mapping between the objects in our application and the database, using some kind of translation component as the link between them. Linking object-oriented code to a relational database is known as object relational (O/R) mapping, and is quite a challenging aspect of software development. The data controls we have seen so far do not really address this issue, since they simply present relational data in web forms. While this is a very useful and productive facility, it does not actually enable us to integrate the data layer of our web applications with the object model layer. Data controls do not provide a mapping between, for example, a table of claim data in a relational database and a claim object in a web application. To get true object persistence, we need to consider how we can store objects in relational tables, when the two approaches to modeling data are quite different. There are many different approaches this problem, but here we will be applying a simple design pattern known as the Data Access Object (Figure 11.1).

The basic idea of the Data Access Object is that it encapsulates the CRUD (create, read, update and delete) processes necessary for passing objects to and from the database. Data is passed to and from the DAO by a Data Transfer Object (DTO) which is a model layer component that does not contain any database access code, but contains the data that is going to or from the database. Business objects can pass DTOs to and from the DAO. The advantage of this pattern is that only the DAO needs to know about the persistence mechanism being used, so that the database layer could be changed without affecting any other objects. For example we could switch between ADO.NET and LINQ in a DAO without affecting any other part of the system.

FIGURE 11.1   The Data Access Object pattern (from Alur *et al.*, 2003)

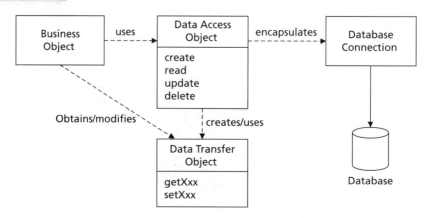

We have, of course, already used DTOs as a way of passing data between the view/controller layer and the model layer of a web application. Whether the same DTO can be used for both purposes will depend on the application. In many cases, we may find that a DTO that is needed to transfer data from a web form to the model layer of an application will not be the same as a DTO that is used to move data in and out of the database. In practice we will probably find that the data being entered into a web form will not match exactly with a specific data table in the database. Therefore we may well need different DTOs for these different contexts. For example in Chapter 9 we introduced the ClaimFormDTO, which related to the fields on a web form relating to insurance claims. The DTO was tailored to the contents of the form, not to the contents of a database table, and contained data that related to both claims and policies. In contrast, the DTO we introduce in this chapter as part of the DAO pattern will be designed so that it relates directly to the Claim table in the database. Another perspective on the DAO pattern is that instead of returning a lightweight DTO it may create an instance of a complete model layer object. Again, we have already seen these being introduced in Chapter 9, where we used a Claim object (and a Policy object) in our webflow examples. In this chapter, we are going to continue to use the classes 'Claim' and 'Policy' as the DTO classes used to read and write data to and from the database. In more complex systems, it would be necessary to have separate model layer objects and database DTOs. However to simplify our examples we will not use separate DTOs for interacting with the DAO, but use the model layer objects directly. The main reason for this is that our Policy and Claim objects are much simpler than they would be in a real world application, so if we added more DTOs to the mix the difference between these and their associated model objects would be minimal.

 NOTE The general distinction between a DTO and a model layer object is that a DTO is typically just a set of properties with their associated get and set operations, whereas a model layer object will have a complete set of relevant business operations (in addition to its properties). The information stored in a DTO can be used to initialize a model layer object, and vice versa.

As an example of implementing a DAO, we are going to create a 'ClaimDAO' object, which will use a 'Claim' object to encapsulate the data being moved to and from the database. This 'Claim' class will be the class we first introduced in Chapter 9, which contrasts with the 'ClaimFormDTO' class we also introduced in Chapter 9. That class was used as a DTO between the insurance claim web form and the controller layer of the web application, and contained some information about the claim (the amount and description) and some information about the related insurance policy (the policy number and type). In contrast, the Claim contains a complete set of properties for the claim that are stored in the associated database table, but not data that belongs in the policy table (though it does contain a reference to its associated Policy object, and the key of the related policy so that policy information could be retrieved if necessary). Figure 11.2 shows the methods of the ClaimDAO and the properties of the Claim, which relate directly to database columns. A typical DAO may have a number of 'read' methods, as well as methods to create, update and delete claims in the database (we will gradually implement the various methods of the DAO throughout this chapter).

FIGURE 11.2 The methods of the ClaimDAO and the properties of the Claim that relate to persistent data

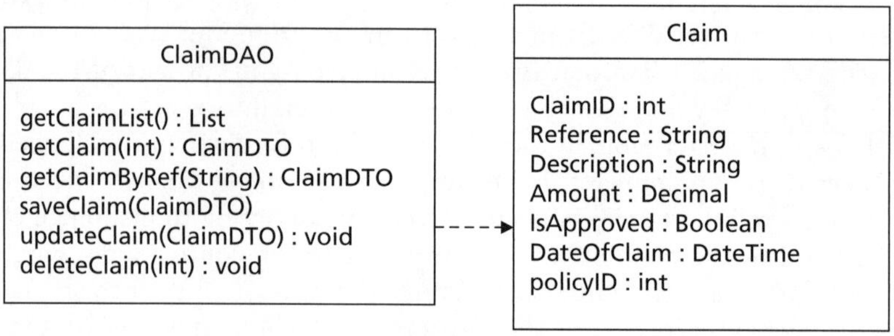

The Claim class is very much like the version that we introduced in Chapter 9. However you will note that it has two extra properties, 'ClaimID' and 'PolicyID'. At the end of this chapter we will discuss some issues related to the problems of object relational mapping. One of these is the mismatch between objects in memory, which do not need unique identifiers, and rows in a database table, which do need some kind of primary key. For some of the later examples in this chapter, we will need to be able to relate objects to database rows, and these identifier properties will help is to do that:

```
public class Claim
{
  public int ClaimID { get; set; }
  public String Reference { get; set; }
  public String Description { get; set; }
  public Decimal Amount { get; set; }
  public Boolean IsApproved { get; set; }
  public DateTime DateOfClaim { get; set; }
  public int PolicyID { get; set; }
  public Policy Policy { get; set; }
}
```

The equivalent Visual Basic class is as follows:

```
Public Class Claim
  Private attrPolicy As Policy
  Private attrAmount As Double = 0.0
  Private attrDescription As String = ""
  Private attrReference As String = ""
  Private attrIsApproved As Boolean = False
  Private attrDateOfClaim As DateTime
  Private attrClaimID As Integer
  Private attrPolicyID As Integer
  Property ClaimID() As Integer
    Get
      Return attrClaimID
    End Get
    Set(ByVal Value As Integer)
      attrClaimID = Value
```

```
   End Set
 End Property
 Property PolicyID() As Integer
  Get
    Return attrPolicyID
  End Get
  Set(ByVal Value As Integer)
    attrPolicyID = Value
  End Set
 End Property
 Property Policy() As Policy
  Get
    Return attrPolicy
  End Get
  Set(ByVal Value As Policy)
    attrPolicy = Value
  End Set
 End Property
 Property Amount() As Double
  Get
    Return attrAmount
  End Get
  Set(ByVal Value As Double)
    attrAmount = Value
  End Set
 End Property
 Property Description() As String
  Get
    Return attrDescription
  End Get
  Set(ByVal Value As String)
    attrDescription = Value
  End Set
 End Property
 Property Reference() As String
  Get
    Return attrReference
  End Get
  Set(ByVal Value As String)
    attrReference = Value
  End Set
 End Property
 Property IsApproved() As Boolean
  Get
    Return attrIsApproved
  End Get
  Set(ByVal Value As Boolean)
    attrIsApproved = Value
  End Set
 End Property
```

11

```
    Property DateOfClaim() As DateTime
      Get
        Return attrDateOfClaim
      End Get
      Set(ByVal Value As DateTime)
        attrDateOfClaim = Value
      End Set
    End Property
  End Class
```

11.2 Writing a DAO for database access

To implement the Data Access Object, we need to be able to connect to the database. This requires the connection information (the 'connection string') to be available to the DAO. A good place to put this information is in the web.config file, so that it can be reused by multiple DAOs. Back in Chapter 10, when we used a SQLDataSource, the connection string was generated automatically by the SQLDataSource Wizard, and added to the web .config file. If we do not have a SqlDataSource, then we will have to add this information manually. If you open the web.config file in an editor window, you should see the following 'connectionStrings' element quite near to the top of the file:

```
<connectionStrings/>
```

By default this will be an empty element with no attributes. This is where we can define the connection strings to enable objects to connect to the database. Replace the empty element with the following (*do not include the line feed in the 'connectionString' attribute, which appears here due to the page width*):

```
<connectionStrings>
  <add name="ConnectionString" connectionString=
  "DataSource=.\SQLEXPRESS;AttachDbFilename=|DataDirectory|\
    Database.mdf;Integrated Security=True;User Instance=True"
    providerName="System.Data.SqlClient"/>
</connectionStrings>
```

 NOTE If you look back at Figure 10.11 you will see that the value of the 'connectionString' attribute here is the same string that was generated by the SqlDataSource. It assumes that the database is in the 'App_Data' folder of the current web application. If the database is elsewhere, then the '|DataDirectory|' part of the connection string must be replaced with the actual path to the database.

For the purposes of this chapter, we will assume that you will recreate the database in a new website, using the stored procedure introduced in Chapter 10. However you may also connect to an existing database. If you right click on the 'DataConnections' entry in

the Database Explorer window, you can choose to browse for an existing database using the 'Add Connection' dialog (Figure 11.3). Remember to make sure that your connection string contains the correct path to the database if you choose to do this.

11.2.1 Viewing the data tables

In this chapter we will be interacting with the database via code, rather than through view components like the GridView. In order to be able to still see an up-to-date view of the contents of the database, we can use the services of the Database Explorer. You may recall that in Chapter 10 we used the Database Explorer to manually enter data into the tables. The same views can be used to monitor the current contents of the database. This will be particularly useful later in this chapter when we begin writing to, and updating, the database tables. To check that our inserts and updates have been successful we can use the table data windows to observe the changes to the database being made by our code. You should, however, be aware that these views are populated when they are opened by the automatic execution of a SQL query. This query is not automatically re-run when the database is updated. To update the view, right click on the window that shows the view of the table and select 'Execute SQL' from the pop-up menu. This will re-run the select query that populates the table, and update the view with the current contents of the database.

11.2.2 The methods of the DAO

The DAO has several methods, so we will look at each part of the class in turn (for out first implementation we will focus only on the 'read' methods). The first thing to note is that the DAO has a property called MyConnString.

C# code

```
public String MyConnString {set; get;}
```

VB code

```
Private attrMyConnString As String
Property MyConnString() As String
  Get
    Return attrMyConnString
  End Get
  Set(ByVal Value As String)
    attrMyConnString = Value
  End Set
End Property
```

This is used so that the connection for the DAO is not hard coded into the class, but can be provided at run time. This makes the DAO flexible if the connection string is changed. The connection string is set in the constructor (the 'New' method in VB), using the following code, where 'ConnectionString' is the name of the connection declared in web.config (the same in both C# and VB except that the C# code would end with a semicolon):

```
MyConnString = ConfigurationManager.
  ConnectionStrings("ConnectionString").ConnectionString
```

One of the methods of the DAO is 'getClaim', which enables client code to access an individual claim using a claim ID. The method first creates and opens a new SqlConnection using the 'MyConnString' property. Then an SQL statement is constructed to select a record from the table that matches the provided key value, and is passed as a parameter to an SqlCommand object that is also passed the SqlConnection object. This command is executed and the result returned to a SqlDataReader. If the read is successful, the private 'makeDTO' method is called to create a DTO from the relational data.

C# code

```
/* fetch a claim by ID (primary key) */
public Claim getClaim(int claimKey)
```

```
{
  SqlConnection myConn = new SqlConnection(MyConnString);
  myConn.Open();
  String mySelectStatement = "SELECT * FROM claim WHERE (claimID=";
  mySelectStatement += claimKey.ToString() + ")";
  SqlCommand myComm = new SqlCommand(mySelectStatement, myConn);
  SqlDataReader myDR;
  myDR = myComm.ExecuteReader();
  if (!myDR.Read()) return null;
  return makeDTO(myDR);
}
```

VB code

```
' fetch a claim by ID (primary key)
Public Function getClaim(ByVal claimKey As Integer) As Claim
  Dim myConn As SqlConnection = New SqlConnection(myConnString)
  myConn.Open()
  Dim mySelectStatement As String = _
     "SELECT * FROM claim WHERE (claimID=" _
     + claimKey.ToString() + ")"
  Dim myComm As SqlCommand = _
    New SqlCommand(mySelectStatement, myConn)
  Dim myDR As SqlDataReader
  myDR = myComm.ExecuteReader()
  If myDR.Read() = False Then
    Return Nothing
  End If
  Return makeDTO(myDR)
End Function
```

The private 'makeDTO' method is quite simple. It creates a new instance of the DTO class, then takes the values from the SqlDataReader and uses them to populate the attributes of the DTO, which is returned at the end of the method.

C# code

```
private Claim makeDTO(SqlDataReader myDR)
{
  Claim myClaim = new Claim();
  myClaim.ClaimID = myDR.GetInt32(0);
  myClaim.Reference = myDR.GetString(1);
  myClaim.Description = myDR.GetString(2);
  myClaim.Amount = myDR.GetDecimal(3);
  myClaim.IsApproved = (myDR.GetString(4).StartsWith("Y"));
  myClaim.DateOfClaim = myDR.GetDateTime(5);
  myClaim.PolicyID = myDR.GetInt32(6);
  return myClaim;
}
```

VB code

```
Private Function makeDTO(ByVal myDR As SqlDataReader) As Claim
  Dim myClaim As Claim = New Claim()
  myClaim.ClaimID = myDR.GetInt32(0)
  myClaim.Reference = myDR.GetString(1)
  myClaim.Description = myDR.GetString(2)
  myClaim.Amount = myDR.GetDecimal(3)
  myClaim.IsApproved = myDR.GetString(4).StartsWith("Y")
  myClaim.DateOfClaim = myDR.GetDateTime(5)
  myClaim.PolicyID = myDR.GetInt32(6)
  Return myClaim
End Function
```

There is a similar method to 'getClaim' called 'getClaimByRef'. This also returns a record from the database, but does so using a reference number rather than the primary key. This is an example of searching by a secondary key. Secondary keys are values that can be useful for searching, but are not the main primary key. Secondary keys are not necessarily guaranteed to be unique, though in this particular example they should be. As is common with searching by secondary keys, in this example the row with the first matching reference will be returned. This is very similar in its implementation to the 'getClaim' method, except that the reference is already a String so (unlike the integer claim key in the 'getClaim' method) does not need to be converted before being used in the SELECT statement.

C# code

```
/* fetch a claim by reference number (the first one to match) */
public Claim getClaimByRef(String claimRef)
{
  SqlConnection myConn = new SqlConnection(MyConnString);
  myConn.Open();
  String mySelectStatement = "SELECT * FROM claim WHERE (reference='";
  mySelectStatement += claimRef + "')";
  SqlCommand myComm = new SqlCommand(mySelectStatement, myConn);
  SqlDataReader myDR;
  myDR = myComm.ExecuteReader();
  if (!myDR.Read()) return null;
  Claim myClaim = makeDTO(myDR);
  return myClaim;
}
```

VB code

```
' fetch a claim by reference number (the first one to match)
Public Function getClaimByRef(ByVal claimRef As String) As Claim
  Dim myConn As SqlConnection = New SqlConnection(myConnString)
  myConn.Open()
```

```
   Dim mySelectStatement As String =
     "SELECT * FROM claim WHERE (reference='" _
     + claimRef + "')"
   Dim myComm As SqlCommand = New SqlCommand(mySelectStatement, myConn)
   Dim myDr As SqlDataReader = myComm.ExecuteReader()
   If myDr.Read() = False Then
     Return Nothing
   End If
   Dim myClaim As Claim = makeDTO(myDr)
   Return myClaim
 End Function
```

In an application, there may be a number of other secondary key related methods that will retrieve data using different criteria.

As well as being able to return a single row from the table using a key, another useful operation is to be able to read multiple rows from the table. To make this flexible, we may want to have the option to either read all rows from the table, or apply a 'where' clause to select only certain rows. To do this, we apply a little overloading to the methods of the DAO.

Here is one version of the method called 'getClaimList'. This version of the method takes a String parameter that represents a 'where' clause. If the parameter is null, an empty string is substituted. Then a select statement is created, using the 'where' clause. The rest of the code is similar to that used in the 'getClaim' method except that there is a while loop that iterates over all the rows read by the SqlDataReader, and creates multiple DTOs, adding them to a generic List collection.

C# code

```
   public List<Claim> getClaimList(String whereClause)
   {
     if (null == whereClause)
     {
       whereClause = "";
     }
     List<Claim> foundClaims = new List<Claim>();
     SqlConnection myConn = new SqlConnection(myConnString);
     myConn.Open();
     String mySelectStatement = "SELECT * FROM claim " + whereClause;
     SqlCommand myComm = new SqlCommand(mySelectStatement, myConn);
     SqlDataReader myDR;
     myDR = myComm.ExecuteReader();
     while (myDR.Read())
     {
/* create new DTO and add to list */
       foundClaims.Add(makeDTO(myDR));
     }
     return foundClaims;
   }
```

VB code

```vb
' fetch list of claims which have not yet been approved
Public Function getClaimList(ByVal whereClause As String) As List(Of Claim)
  If IsNothing(whereClause) Then
    whereClause = ""
  End If
  Dim foundClaims As List(Of Claim) = New List(Of Claim)
  Dim myConn As SqlConnection = New SqlConnection(myConnString)
  myConn.Open()
  Dim mySelectStatement As String =
    "SELECT * FROM claim " + whereClause
  Dim myComm As SqlCommand = New SqlCommand(mySelectStatement, myConn)
  Dim myDR As SqlDataReader
  myDR = myComm.ExecuteReader()
  While myDR.Read()
    foundClaims.Add(makeDTO(myDR))
' create new DTO and add to list
  End While
  Return foundClaims
End Function
```

The overloaded version of 'getClaimList' is very simple. It takes no parameters, but calls the parameterized version of the method by passing 'null'. The purpose of this method is to give client code the option of not needing to provide a 'where' clause parameter when none is required because DTOs for all records need to be returned.

C# code

```csharp
public List<Claim> getClaimList()
{
  return getClaimList(null);
}
```

VB code

```vb
Public Function getClaimList() As List(Of Claim)
  Return getClaimList(Nothing)
End Function
```

Here is the complete ClaimDAO class in terms of the methods we have described so far. These all relate to reading Claims from the database in various ways. Later in this chapter we will extend the DAO to enable other types of database operation.

C# code

```csharp
public class ClaimDAO
{
  public String MyConnString {set; get;}
```

```csharp
  public ClaimDAO()
  {
   MyConnString = ConfigurationManager.
   ConnectionStrings["ConnectionString"].ConnectionString;
  }
  public List<Claim> getClaimList()
  {
   return getClaimList(null);
  }
/* fetch list of claims which have not yet been approved */
  public List<Claim> getClaimList(String whereClause)
  {
   if (null == whereClause)
  {
   whereClause = "";
  }

   List<Claim> foundClaims = new List<Claim>();
   SqlConnection myConn = new SqlConnection(MyConnString);
   myConn.Open();
   String mySelectStatement = "SELECT * FROM claim " + whereClause;
   SqlCommand myComm = new SqlCommand(mySelectStatement, myConn);
   SqlDataReader myDR;
   myDR = myComm.ExecuteReader();
   while (myDR.Read())
   {
/* create new DTO and add to list */
     foundClaims.Add(makeDTO(myDR));
   }
   myConn.Close();
   return foundClaims;
  }
/* fetch a claim by ID or key */
  public Claim getClaim(int claimKey)
  {
   SqlConnection myConn = new SqlConnection(MyConnString);
   myConn.Open();
   String mySelectStatement = "SELECT * FROM claim WHERE (claimID=";
   mySelectStatement += claimKey.ToString() + ")";
   SqlCommand myComm = new SqlCommand(mySelectStatement, myConn);
   SqlDataReader myDR;
   myDR = myComm.ExecuteReader();
   if (!myDR.Read()) return null;
     return makeDTO(myDR);
  }
/* fetch a claim by reference number (the first one to match) */
  public Claim getClaimByRef(String claimRef)
  {
     SqlConnection myConn = new SqlConnection(MyConnString);
     myConn.Open();
     String mySelectStatement =
       "SELECT * FROM claim WHERE (reference='";
```

```
      mySelectStatement += claimRef + "')";
      SqlCommand myComm = new SqlCommand(mySelectStatement, myConn);
      SqlDataReader myDR;
      myDR = myComm.ExecuteReader();
      if (!myDR.Read()) return null;
        Claim myClaim = makeDTO(myDR);
      return myClaim;
    }
  /* helper method */
    private Claim makeDTO(SqlDataReader myDR)
    {
    Claim myClaim = new Claim();
    myClaim.ClaimID = myDR.GetInt32(0);
    myClaim.Reference = myDR.GetString(1);
    myClaim.Description = myDR.GetString(2);
    myClaim.Amount = myDR.GetDecimal(3);
    myClaim.IsApproved = (myDR.GetString(4).StartsWith("Y"));
    myClaim.DateOfClaim = myDR.GetDateTime(5);
    myClaim.PolicyID = myDR.GetInt32(6);
    return myClaim;
  }
}
```

VB code

```
Public Class ClaimDAO
  Private attrMyConnString As String
  Property MyConnString() As String
    Get
      Return attrMyConnString
    End Get
    Set(ByVal Value As String)
      attrMyConnString = Value
    End Set
  End Property

  Public Sub New()
    myConnString = ConfigurationManager. _
        ConnectionStrings("ConnectionString").ConnectionString
  End Sub

  Public Function getClaimList() As List(Of Claim)
    Return getClaimList(Nothing)
  End Function

  ' fetch list of claims which have not yet been approved
  Public Function getClaimList(ByVal whereClause As String) _
      As List(Of Claim)
    If IsNothing(whereClause) Then
      whereClause = ""
    End If
```

```
Dim foundClaims As List(Of Claim) = New List(Of Claim)
Dim myConn As SqlConnection = New SqlConnection(myConnString)
myConn.Open()
Dim mySelectStatement As String = _
  "SELECT * FROM claim " + whereClause
Dim myComm As SqlCommand = New SqlCommand(mySelectStatement, _
  myConn)
Dim myDR As SqlDataReader
myDR = myComm.ExecuteReader()
While myDR.Read()
    foundClaims.Add(makeDTO(myDR))
   ' create new DTO and add to list
  End While
  Return foundClaims
  End Function

  ' fetch a claim by ID or key
  Public Function getClaim(ByVal claimKey As Integer) As Claim
  Dim myConn As SqlConnection = New SqlConnection(myConnString)
  myConn.Open()
   Dim mySelectStatement As String = _
     "SELECT * FROM claim WHERE (claimID=" _
     + claimKey.ToString() + ")"
   Dim myComm As SqlCommand = New SqlCommand(mySelectStatement, _
     myConn)
   Dim myDR As SqlDataReader
   myDR = myComm.ExecuteReader()
   If myDR.Read() = False Then
    Return Nothing
   End If
   Return makeDTO(myDR)
End Function

' fetch a claim by reference number (the first one to match)
Public Function getClaimByRef(ByVal claimRef As String) As Claim
  Dim myConn As SqlConnection = New SqlConnection(myConnString)
  myConn.Open()
  Dim mySelectStatement As String = _
    "SELECT * FROM claim WHERE (reference='" + claimRef + "')"
  Dim myComm As SqlCommand = New SqlCommand(mySelectStatement, _
    myConn)
  Dim myDr As SqlDataReader = myComm.ExecuteReader()
  If myDr.Read() = False Then
   Return Nothing
  End If
  Dim myClaim As Claim = makeDTO(myDr)
  Return myClaim
End Function

' helper method
Private Function makeDTO(ByVal myDR As SqlDataReader) As Claim
  Dim myClaim As Claim = New Claim()
```

11

```
    myClaim.ClaimID = myDR.GetInt32(0)
    myClaim.Reference = myDR.GetString(1)
    myClaim.Description = myDR.GetString(2)
    myClaim.Amount = myDR.GetDecimal(3)
    myClaim.IsApproved = myDR.GetString(4).StartsWith("Y")
    myClaim.DateOfClaim = myDR.GetDateTime(5)
    myClaim.PolicyID = myDR.GetInt32(6)
    Return myClaim
  End Function
End Class
```

11.2.3 Accessing data via the façade

In Chapter 9 we introduced the ModelFacade class, to provide a common entry point to the model layer for components in the view/controller layer. In order to enable the web forms in the view/controller layer to access the components returned from the DAO, we need to add appropriate methods to the façade. The following 'getClaims' method, for example, uses the DAO to create a List of Claim objects that it returns to the caller, based on a 'where' clause being supplied as a parameter.

C# code

```csharp
public List<Claim> getClaims(String whereClause)
{
 ClaimDAO myDAO = getClaimDAO();
 List<Claim> claimCollection = myDAO.getClaimList(whereClause);
 return claimCollection;
}
private ClaimDAO getClaimDAO()
{
 ClaimDAO myDAO = new ClaimDAO();
 return myDAO;
}
```

VB code

```vb
Public Function getClaims(ByVal whereClause As String) _
    As List(Of Claim)
 Dim myDAO As ClaimDAO = getClaimDAO()
 Dim claimCollection As List(Of Claim) = _
    myDAO.getClaimList(whereClause)
 Return claimCollection
End Function

Private Function getClaimDAO() As ClaimDAO
 Dim myDAO As ClaimDAO = New ClaimDAO()
 Return myDAO
End Function
```

Here is another similar method that can be used if no 'where' clause is required, and all rows are to be returned from the database as Claim objects.

C# code

```csharp
public List<Claim> getClaims()
{
  ClaimDAO myDAO = getClaimDAO();
  List<Claim> claimCollection = myDAO.getClaimList();
  return claimCollection;
}
```

VB code

```vb
Public Function getClaims() As List(Of Claim)
  Dim myDAO As ClaimDAO = getClaimDAO()
  Dim claimCollection As List(Of Claim) = myDAO.getClaimList()
  Return claimCollection
End Function
```

We will add other methods to the façade as we need them.

11.3 Using the DAO with a web form

Having set up the DAO, DTO and ModelFacade methods to connect to a database without using a data control, our next example will be a web form that will test some of the functionality of our ClaimDAO. The web form will display data from the 'claim' table. We will use the ClaimDAO to connect to the database and create a List of Claim objects from it. Figure 11.4 shows the classes and methods that we will use in this process. The web form ('ReadClaims.aspx') will use the List of Claims, acquired from the ModelFacade, to display claim details on the page.

'ReadClaims.aspx' will be a simple web form that contains a Table control (from the 'Standard' group in the Toolbox). The control has been configured in Design view to have a single TableRow, which in turn contains three TableCells. This row will act as a header for the table, and the data will be added dynamically by the code behind. Figure 11.5 shows the table in design view after the row and cells have been added, and some formatting has been applied. In this example we have chosen just to use three of the properties of a claim in the table, but any or all of the claim's properties could be displayed.

| FIGURE 11.4 | The components used to read claims from the database and display them in a web form |

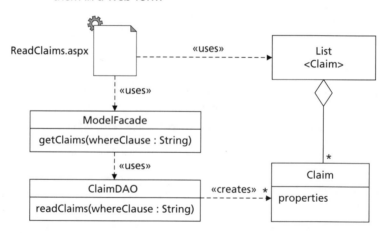

| FIGURE 11.5 | A Table control in Design view with a TableRow and TableCells added and formatted |

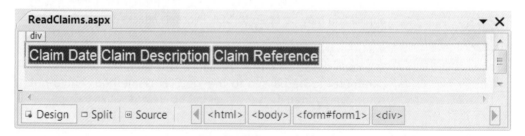

TableRows can be added to a Table control by clicking the button labeled '(Collection)' in the Rows property of the table. Similarly, in the dialog that appears for the TableRow, there is a Cells property that is also represented by a collection. Figure 11.6 shows the Table-Row Collection Editor that appears when you press the button associated with the Table's 'Rows' property. The 'Cells' property can be seen on the lower right of the 'TableRow' properties list.

FIGURE 11.6 The TableRow Collection Editor which enables you to add TableRows to a Table and also to add TableCells to a TableRow

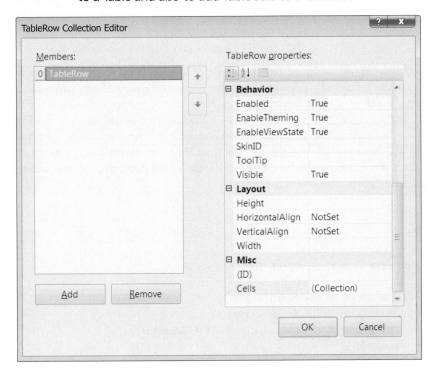

Here is the web form in Source view, after the table has been modified and formatted in Design view. Of course at this point the table has no data rows, only a row of headings. The rows of data will be added dynamically at run time.

```
<%@ Page Language="C#" AutoEventWireup="true"
CodeFile="ReadClaims.aspx.cs" Inherits="ReadClaims" %>
<!DOCTYPE html PUBLIC "-//W3C//DTD XHTML 1.0 Transitional//EN"
"http://www.w3.org/TR/xhtml1/DTD/xhtml1-transitional.dtd">
<html xmlns="http://www.w3.org/1999/xhtml">
  <head runat="server">
   <title>View Claims Table</title>
  </head>
  <body>
   <form id="form1" runat="server">
    <div>
```

```
<asp:Table ID="Table1" runat="server" Font-Names="Arial"
    GridLines="Both">
<asp:TableRow runat="server" BackColor="Black"
    ForeColor="White">
<asp:TableCell runat="server">Claim Date</asp:TableCell>
<asp:TableCell runat="server">Claim Description</asp:TableCell>
<asp:TableCell runat="server">Claim Reference</asp:TableCell>
</asp:TableRow>
</asp:Table>
</div>
</form>
</body>
</html>
```

In the code behind file, we need to read a List of Claims from the Model Façade and use these objects to dynamically populate the table. Therefore we will need to add some code to the 'Page_Load' event handler to do this. Here is a page load event handler that reads a List of Claims from the Façade, then uses an Enumerator to iterate over the List. In this example, we are calling the 'getClaims' method with no 'where' clause parameter, so all the claims will be returned into the List by the DAO. For each Claim, a new table row is created, with three table cells. Into these cells, the claim date, description and references are added, using properties of the Claim.

C# code

```
protected void Page_Load(object sender, EventArgs e)
{
  ModelFacade facade = new ModelFacade();
  List<Claim> claims = facade.getClaims();
  List<Claim>.Enumerator enumer = claims.GetEnumerator();
  enumer.MoveNext();
  while (enumer.Current != null)
  {
    Claim claim = enumer.Current;
    TableCell cell1 = new TableCell();
    cell1.Text = claim.DateOfClaim.ToString();
    TableCell cell2 = new TableCell();
    cell2.Text = claim.Description;
    TableCell cell3 = new TableCell();
    cell3.Text = claim.Reference;
    TableRow row = new TableRow();
    row.Cells.Add(cell1);
    row.Cells.Add(cell2);
    row.Cells.Add(cell3);
    Table1.Rows.Add(row);
    enumer.MoveNext();
  }
}
```

VB code

```vb
Protected Sub Page_Load(ByVal sender As Object, ByVal e As EventArgs)
  Dim facade As ModelFacade = New ModelFacade()
  Dim claims As List(Of Claim) = facade.getClaims()
  Dim enumer As List(Of Claim).Enumerator = claims.GetEnumerator()
  enumer.MoveNext()
  While IsNothing(enumer.Current) = False
    Dim claim As Claim = enumer.Current
    Dim cell1 As TableCell = New TableCell()
    cell1.Text = claim.DateOfClaim.ToString()
    Dim cell2 As TableCell = New TableCell()
    cell2.Text = claim.ClaimID
    Dim cell3 As TableCell = New TableCell()
    cell3.Text = claim.Reference
    Dim row As TableRow = New TableRow()
    row.Cells.Add(cell1)
    row.Cells.Add(cell2)
    row.Cells.Add(cell3)
    Table1.Rows.Add(row)
    enumer.MoveNext()
  End While
End Sub
```

Figure 11.7 shows what the web form looks like in Internet Explorer 7 when there are four records in the 'claim' table, read into Claim objects and dynamically added to a Table control in a web form.

FIGURE 11.7 Data from four 'Claim' objects read from a database and displayed by a web form in Internet Explorer 7

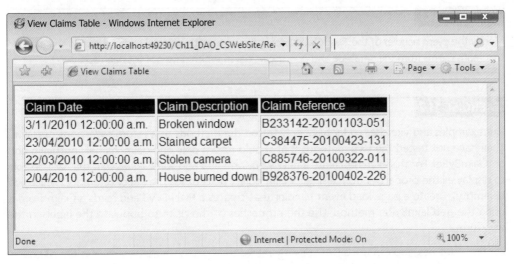

NOTE	There is an important limitation to the way that the DAO creates Claim objects, which is that it does not also create the associated Policy object. This means if you were to try to access the 'Policy' property of a Claim, you would get a run time exception because the Policy object would not exist. We could of course modify the DAO to also read the associated Policy, but it is important to note that this type of decision is not a simple one. If we load the Policy as well, should we then load its associated PolicyHolder? Should the Policy load any other claims that have been made against it? Before long, we may find ourselves trying to load the entire database into memory because of all the object associations. This is why only the Claim is created by the DAO. If we needed to also load the associated Policy, we would do so using the PolicyID property (which will have a value in the Claim object), via a separate DAO.

Section summary and quick exercises

This chapter has so far concerned itself with using the DAO pattern to enable objects to be created from rows in database tables. Specifically, we have focused on reading from the claim table to create one or more Claim objects. The DAO has been used to isolate the persistence layer of the application from the view/controller and model layers, encapsulating the database access code into the DAO so that the model layer objects are independent of the persistence layer. We have also discussed some potential issues with the DAO pattern, in particular the problem of objects being associated with each other in the model. In the context of the example, we looked at why we only read Claim objects into memory, and not the associated Policy objects. To enable us to read associated objects as and when we need them, we have included properties in the Claim class that would enable us to locate the related Policy in the database if required. This has meant some changes to the class from the first version introduced in Chapter 9, which was only concerned with the properties of the object model and not issues of key data. In this respect, it proves difficult to completely isolate our model layer objects from the persistence layer.

EXERCISE 11.1

Modify the event handler of the 'ReadClaims.aspx' page so that it applies a 'where' clause to the method that reads Claims from the database and only shows claims which have not yet been approved.

EXERCISE 11.2

Our examples and exercises so far have only tested the methods that return collections of claims. They have not tested the two methods that should return only one claim, namely getClaim and getClaimByRef. For this exercise, create a new web form and add some labels to it that will be able to display all the properties from a single Claim object (except for the Policy reference, which will be empty). Create a page load event handler that creates a ClaimDAO and reads a Claim from it using the getClaimByRef method. Use the properties of the claim to populate the labels in the web form.

For test purposes, you can use a DAO directly rather than going via the façade. You can of course also add the necessary methods to the façade and use those.

Create another web form and event handler similar to the ones in Exercise 11.2, but this time test the 'getClaim' method. The identifiers used as arguments to this method are not as predictable as the claim reference, because they are autogenerated by the database, but you should be able to see a valid claim ID in the web form in Exercise 11.2, when it is viewed in a browser. Alternatively you can, of course, look at all the data in the database using the Database Explorer window, as we described earlier in this chapter. Use one of the valid claim IDs in your test code.

11.4 Using a DAO to write to the database

In our previous example, we saw how data stored in the database can be read using a DAO, and the resulting objects used by a web form event handler. In this section we will see how to use DAOs to write objects to the database and ensure that foreign key relationships are maintained. We return in the next example to the insurance claim use case that we first implemented in Chapter 9. However this time, rather than simply echoing the input data back to the user when the claim form is submitted, we will write the claim to the database, link it with its matching policy (both in the database and in the model layer), and provide the user with suitable feedback. Since each claim in the database should be associated with a specific insurance policy, we will check that the policy number supplied by the user is valid. If the policy number exists in the policy table then we will write the claim to the database (setting up the foreign key relationship with the matching row in the policy table) and retrieve the related policy information by creating a Policy object. Then both the Claim and Policy objects can be used in the web application. If, however, the policy number does not exist then we will display an error page to the user and no changes will be made to the database. Figure 11.8 shows a simple flowchart that outlines the processes involved. There is a small change to the first web form in this version of the insurance claim use case. Previously, we asked the user to supply the type of insurance policy. Now that we can access policy information from the database, this is not necessary. Therefore the first form will only ask the user for their policy number. This is useful too, because it means the user does not have to enter any further information until the policy number has been checked.

To implement the steps of the process, the application needs to do several things:

- Get the policy number from the ClaimFormDTO.
- Look for a policy in the database that matches the policy number and, if one is found, create a Policy object from the data in the table. We will need a PolicyDAO to help us do this.
- If no matching policy is found, the user is directed to an error page.
- If it finds a matching policy it must create a Claim, copying the relevant properties from the ClaimFormDTO and also populate the remaining properties of the Claim ('IsApproved', 'DateOfClaim', 'Reference').
- The Property and Claim objects then need to be associated together and made available to the façade. Once the policy is associated with the claim, the claim will have access to the primary key of the policy, enabling the foreign key value to be set in the claim table.
- Finally we can write the claim to the database via the ClaimDAO.

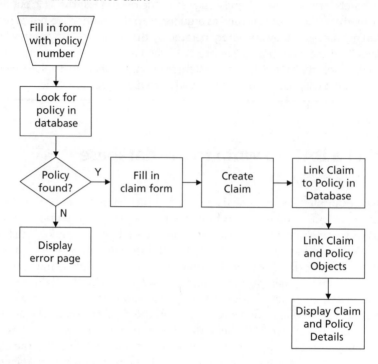

FIGURE 11.9   The Policy and PolicyDAO classes

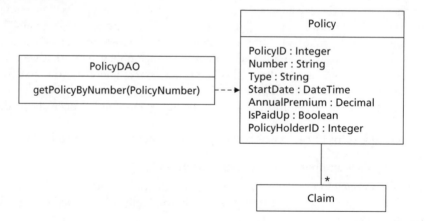

Since the process starts with being able to read the correct policy from the database, we will begin by looking at the Policy and PolicyDAO classes. Figure 11.9 shows the Policy class, (which we first introduced in Chapter 9, where it only had two properties) and its related DAO. Policy and Claim objects are associated together in a one-to-many relationship (i.e. a single Policy can have many Claims, but a Claim is made against a single Policy).

Here is the updated Policy class, with its additional properties to match the columns in the database table.

C# code

```
public class Policy
{
  public int PolicyID { get; set; }
  public int Number { get; set; }
  public String Type { get; set; }
  public DateTime StartDate {get; set;}
  public Decimal AnnualPremium { get; set; }
  public Boolean IsPaidUp { get; set;}
  public int PolicyHolderID { get; set; }
}
```

VB code

```
Public Class Policy
  Private attrPolicyID As Integer
  Private attrNumber As Integer
  Private attrType As String
  Private attrPolicyHolderID As Integer
  Private attrAnnualPremium As Decimal
  Private attrIsPaidUp As Boolean
  Private attrStartDate As DateTime
  Property PolicyID() As Integer
    Get
      Return attrPolicyID
    End Get
    Set(ByVal Value As Integer)
      attrPolicyID = Value
    End Set
  End Property
  Property Number() As Integer
    Get
      Return attrNumber
    End Get
    Set(ByVal Value As Integer)
      attrNumber = Value
    End Set
  End Property
  Property Type() As String
    Get
      Return attrType
    End Get
    Set(ByVal Value As String)
      attrType = Value
    End Set
  End Property
  Property PolicyHolderID() As Integer
    Get
```

```
      Return attrPolicyHolderID
    End Get
    Set(ByVal Value As Integer)
      attrPolicyHolderID = Value
    End Set
  End Property
  Property AnnualPremium() As Decimal
    Get
      Return attrAnnualPremium
    End Get
    Set(ByVal Value As Decimal)
      attrAnnualPremium = Value
    End Set
  End Property
  Property IsPaidUp() As Boolean
    Get
      Return attrIsPaidUp
    End Get
    Set(ByVal Value As Boolean)
      attrIsPaidUp = Value
    End Set
  End Property
  Property StartDate() As DateTime
    Get
      Return attrStartDate
    End Get
    Set(ByVal Value As DateTime)
      attrStartDate = Value
    End Set
  End Property
End Class
```

The PolicyDAO has a similar implementation to the ClaimDAO, except that of course it processes Policy objects. For the current example, the only method we require is one that will return a Policy given a policy number ('getPolicyByNumber'), along with the helper method that creates the DTO.

C# code

```
public class PolicyDAO
{
  public string connectionString { set; get; }

  public PolicyDAO()
  {
    connectionString = ConfigurationManager.
        ConnectionStrings["ConnectionString"].ConnectionString;
  }
```

```
/* fetch a policy by policyNumber */
public Policy getPolicyByNumber(int policyNumber)
{
 SqlConnection myConn = new SqlConnection(connectionString);
 myConn.Open();
 String mySelectStatement =
    "SELECT * FROM policy WHERE (policyNumber=";
 mySelectStatement += policyNumber.ToString() + ")";
 SqlCommand myComm = new SqlCommand(mySelectStatement, myConn);
 SqlDataReader myDR;
 myDR = myComm.ExecuteReader();
 if (!myDR.Read()) return null;
 Policy myPolicy = makeDTO(myDR);
 myConn.Close();
 return myPolicy;
}

/* helper method */
 private Policy makeDTO(SqlDataReader myDR)
 {
  Policy myPolicy = new Policy();
  myPolicy.PolicyID = myDR.GetInt32(0);
  myPolicy.Number = myDR.GetInt32(1);
  myPolicy.Type = myDR.GetString(2);
  myPolicy.StartDate = myDR.GetDateTime(3);
  myPolicy.AnnualPremium = myDR.GetDecimal(4);
  myPolicy.IsPaidUp = (myDR.GetString(5).StartsWith("Y"));
  myPolicy.PolicyHolderID = myDR.GetInt32(6);
  return myPolicy;
 }
}
```

VB code

```
Public Class PolicyDAO

 Private attrMyConnString As String

 Property MyConnString() As String
  Get
   Return attrMyConnString
   End Get
   Set(ByVal Value As String)
    attrMyConnString = Value
   End Set
 End Property

 Public Sub New()
 MyConnString = ConfigurationManager.
   ConnectionStrings("ConnectionString").ConnectionString
 End Sub
```

```vb
' fetch a policy by policyNumber
Public Function getPolicyByNumber(ByVal policyNumber As Integer) _
  As Policy
  Dim myConn As SqlConnection = New SqlConnection(MyConnString)
  myConn.Open()
  Dim mySelectStatement As String = _
    "SELECT * FROM policy WHERE (policyNumber=" _
      + policyNumber.ToString() + ")"
  Dim myComm As SqlCommand = New SqlCommand(mySelectStatement, _
    myConn)
  Dim myDR As SqlDataReader
  myDR = myComm.ExecuteReader()
  If myDR.Read() = False Then
    Return Nothing
  End If
  Return makeDTO(myDR)
End Function

' helper method
Private Function makeDTO(ByVal myDR As SqlDataReader) As Policy
  Dim myPolicy As Policy = New Policy()
  myPolicy.PolicyID = myDR.GetInt32(0)
  myPolicy.Number = myDR.GetInt32(1)
  myPolicy.Type = myDR.GetString(2)
  myPolicy.StartDate = myDR.GetDateTime(3)
  myPolicy.AnnualPremium = myDR.GetDecimal(4)
  myPolicy.IsPaidUp = (myDR.GetString(5).StartsWith("Y"))
  myPolicy.PolicyHolderID = myDR.GetInt32(6)
  Return myPolicy
End Function
End Class
```

The PolicyDAO will enable us to read a policy from the database, but we also need to be able to write a new claim to the database using the ClaimDAO. Unlike the methods we have looked at so far, the 'saveClaim' method writes a record to the database, rather than reading from it. The method takes a Claim object as a parameter, and simply copies the property values from it and uses them as the values for an INSERT statement, managed by an SqlCommand object. It uses the ID of the associated policy object to set the foreign key value to the matching primary key in the policy table. Note that there is a dependency here (i.e. a precondition) on the Claim already being associated with a Policy before this method is executed. Otherwise the foreign key property (PolicyID) will have no value and the database insertion will fail due to the foreign key constraint on the claim table.

C# code

```csharp
/* save a claim object to the database */
public void saveClaim(Claim myClaim)
{
  char isApproved = 'N';
```

```
  if (myClaim.IsApproved == true)
  {
    isApproved = 'Y';
  }
  String claimDate = myClaim.DateOfClaim.Day + "/" +
    myClaim.DateOfClaim.Month + "/" + myClaim.DateOfClaim.Year;
  SqlConnection myConn = new SqlConnection(MyConnString);
  myConn.Open();
  string insertString = "insert into claim (reference, description,
    amount, approved, claimDate, policyID) " +
    "values (@reference, @description, @amount, @approved, @claimDate,
    @policyID)";
  SqlCommand myComm = new SqlCommand(insertString, myConn);
  myComm.Parameters.Add("@reference", SqlDbType.NVarChar).
    Value = myClaim.Reference;
  myComm.Parameters.Add("@description", SqlDbType.NVarChar).
    Value = myClaim.Description;
  myComm.Parameters.Add("@amount", SqlDbType.Decimal).
    Value = myClaim.Amount;
  myComm.Parameters.Add("@approved", SqlDbType.NVarChar).
    Value = isApproved;
  myComm.Parameters.Add("@claimDate", SqlDbType.DateTime).
    Value = claimDate;
  myComm.Parameters.Add("@policyID", SqlDbType.Int).
    Value = myClaim.PolicyID;
  int rows = myComm.ExecuteNonQuery();
  myConn.Close();
  if (rows != 1) throw new Exception("Unexpected Result for Insert");
}
```

VB code

```
' save a claim object to the database
Public Sub saveClaim(ByVal myClaim As Claim)
  Dim isApproved As Char = "N"
  If myClaim.IsApproved Then
    isApproved = "Y"
  End If
  Dim claimDate As String = myClaim.DateOfClaim.Day.ToString() + _
    "/" + myClaim.DateOfClaim.Month.ToString() + "/" + _
    myClaim.DateOfClaim.Year.ToString()
  Dim myConn As SqlConnection = New SqlConnection(myConnString)
  myConn.Open()
  Dim insertString As String = "INSERT INTO claim (reference, _
    description, amount, approved, claimDate, policyID) " + _
    "VALUES(@reference, @description, @amount, @approved, _
    @claimDate, @policyID)"
  Dim myComm As SqlCommand = New SqlCommand(insertString, myConn)
  myComm.Parameters.AddWithValue("@reference", myClaim.Reference)
  myComm.Parameters.AddWithValue("@description", myClaim.Description)
```

```
myComm.Parameters.AddWithValue("@amount", myClaim.Amount)
myComm.Parameters.AddWithValue("@approved", isApproved)
myComm.Parameters.AddWithValue("@claimDate", myClaim.DateOfClaim)
myComm.Parameters.AddWithValue("@policyID", myClaim.PolicyID)
Dim rows As Integer = myComm.ExecuteNonQuery()
myConn.Close()
If rows <> 1 Then
  Throw New Exception("Unexpected Result for Insert")
End If
```

Now that we have suitable DAOs in place, we can update the ModelFacade to access the database through them. In Chapter 9, the ModelFacade simply copied the properties of a ClaimFormDTO object into those of a Claim, set a couple of other values of the Claim, and associated it with a new Policy object that had only two properties, but it needs to do more in this version of the application. This time, it must use the PolicyDAO to read the correct policy from the database using the policy number provided in the ClaimFormDTO. If the policy number is found, then Policy and Claim objects are created and associated together (if not, then the method terminates). Assuming the object creation has been successful, the claim data is written to the database, and the Claim object returned from the method. Here is the modified 'createClaim' method. Note the importance of the sequence of events in this method. The Policy and Claim objects must both have been created and associated together before the 'saveClaim' method is called in the ClaimDAO, because of the precondition of this method that the Claim must be associated with a Policy.

C# code

```
public Claim createClaim(ClaimFormDTO dto)
{
// get the policy number and look for a
// matching policy in the database
  int policyNumber = Int32.Parse(dto.PolicyNumber);
  PolicyDAO policyDAO = new PolicyDAO();
  Policy policy = policyDAO.getPolicyByNumber(policyNumber);
  if(policy == null)
    return null;
// if we find a match, create a Claim and link it to the policy
// we must set up the relationship between Claim and Policy
// before attempting to generate the reference, because the
// ReferenceGenerator and ClaimDAO use properties from both classes
  Claim claim = new Claim();
// link the two objects
  claim.Policy = policy;
  claim.PolicyID = policy.PolicyID;
  claim.Amount = dto.ClaimAmount;
  claim.Description = dto.ClaimDescription;
  claim.DateOfClaim = DateTime.Now;
  claim.IsApproved = false;
  ReferenceGenerator generator = new ReferenceGenerator();
```

```
    String reference = generator.getReference(claim);
    claim.Reference = reference;
  // write the claim to the database
    ClaimDAO claimDAO = new ClaimDAO();
    claimDAO.saveClaim(claim);
  // return the claim, associated with the policy
    return claim;
  }
```

VB code

```
Public Function createClaim(ByVal dto As ClaimFormDTO) As Claim
  ' get the policy number and look for a
  ' matching policy in the database
  Dim policyNumber As Integer = dto.policyNumber
  Dim policyDAO As PolicyDAO = New PolicyDAO()
  Dim policy As Policy = policyDAO.getPolicyByNumber(policyNumber)
  If IsNothing(policy) Then
    Return Nothing
  End If
  ' if we find a match, create a Claim and link it to the policy
  ' we must set up the relationship between Claim and Policy
  ' before attempting to generate the reference, because the
  ' ReferenceGenerator and ClaimDAO use properties from both classes
  Dim claim As Claim = New Claim()
  ' link the two objects
  claim.Policy = policy
  claim.PolicyID = policy.PolicyID
  claim.Amount = dto.ClaimAmount
  claim.Description = dto.ClaimDescription
  claim.DateOfClaim = DateTime.Now
  claim.IsApproved = False
  Dim generator As ReferenceGenerator = New ReferenceGenerator()
  Dim reference As String = generator.getReference(claim)
  claim.Reference = reference
  ' write the claim to the database
  Dim claimDAO As ClaimDAO = New ClaimDAO()
  claimDAO.saveClaim(claim)
  ' return the claim, associated with the policy
  Return claim
End Function
```

We will also add a convenience method to the façade to enable us to get a policy from the database, using the policy number as the search key. We will use this in the event handler of the first web form so that it can check the validity of the policy number. This method, 'getPolicy' uses the PolicyDAO to do this. As with the façade methods that read claims, there is a separate method that creates the DAO, which can potentially be reused.

C# code

```
public Policy getPolicy(int policyNumber)
{
  PolicyDAO myDAO = getPolicyDAO();
  Policy myDTO = myDAO.getPolicyByNumber(policyNumber);
  return myDTO;
}

private PolicyDAO getPolicyDAO()
{
  PolicyDAO myDAO = new PolicyDAO();
  return myDAO;
}
```

VB code

```
Public Function getPolicy(ByVal policyNumber As Integer) As Policy
  Dim myDAO As PolicyDAO = getPolicyDAO()
  Dim myDTO As Policy = myDAO.getPolicyByNumber(policyNumber)
  Return myDTO
End Function

Private Function getPolicyDAO() As PolicyDAO
  Dim myDAO As PolicyDAO = New PolicyDAO()
  Return myDAO
End Function
```

11.5 Using DAOs in the insurance claim webflow

Now we will turn our attention to the web forms and their event handlers. 'ClaimForm1.aspx' is simplified now that it does not have radio buttons to select the insurance policy type. Now there is just a TextBox for the policy number.

```
<!DOCTYPE html PUBLIC "-//W3C//DTD XHTML 1.0 Transitional//EN"
"http://www.w3.org/TR/xhtml1/DTD/xhtml1-transitional.dtd">

<html xmlns="http://www.w3.org/1999/xhtml">
 <head id="Head1" runat="server">
  <title>Make a Claim</title>
 </head>
 <body>
  <h1>WebHomeCover insurance claim form</h1>
  <p>
   Please enter your policy number in the text box below.
   Then press the 'Submit' button
  </p>
  <form id="form1" runat="server">
```

```
        <div>
          <asp:Label ID="Label1" runat="server" Text="Policy Number: ">
          </asp:Label>
          <asp:TextBox ID="PolicyNumber" runat="server"></asp:TextBox>
          <br />
          <asp:Button ID="SubmitButton" runat="server" Text="Submit" />
        </div>
      </form>
  </body>
</html>
```

Figure 11.10 shows the modified web form displayed in a browser.

The event handler for the 'ClaimForm1.aspx' page still interacts with the ModelFacade as it did in Chapter 9. However this time there are two possible results; the Policy that is returned from the façade's 'getPolicy' method may be a fully populated object, but it may also be a null/nothing reference (if the policy number was not found). Therefore we need some conditional code to route the webflow accordingly. Here is a modified version of the event handler. It checks if the 'dto' reference is null/nothing. If it is, then we forward to 'PolicyNotFound.aspx'. If the Policy exists, then the page adds the ClaimFormDTO to the session and forwards to 'ClaimForm2.aspx'.

FIGURE 11.10   The modified ClaimForm1.aspx page displayed in a browser

C# code

```
protected void SubmitButton_Click(object sender, EventArgs e)
{
  Int32 Policy = Int32.Parse(PolicyNumber.Text);
```

```
ClaimFormDTO ClaimData = new ClaimFormDTO();
ClaimData.policyNumber = Policy;
ModelFacade facade = new ModelFacade();
Policy policy = facade.getPolicy(Policy);
if (policy == null)
{
  Server.Transfer("PolicyNotFound.aspx");
}
Session["ClaimFormDTO"] = ClaimData;
Server.Transfer("ClaimForm2.aspx", true);
}
```

VB code

```
Protected Sub SubmitButton_Click(ByVal sender As Object, _
    ByVal e As System.EventArgs) Handles SubmitButton.Click
  Dim Policy As Int32 = PolicyNumber.Text
  Dim ClaimData As ClaimFormDTO = New ClaimFormDTO()
  ClaimData.policyNumber = Policy
  Dim facade As ModelFacade = New ModelFacade()
  Dim dto As Policy = facade.getPolicy(Policy)
  If dto Is Nothing Then
    Server.Transfer("PolicyNotFound.aspx")
  End If
  Session.Item("ClaimFormDTO") = ClaimData
  Server.Transfer("ClaimForm2.aspx", True)
End Sub
```

If the policy number is matched and we forward to 'ClaimForm2.aspx', this web form will ask for the details of the claim. 'ClaimForm2.aspx' is unchanged from previous versions, but there is a small change to the Page Load event handler, since there is no longer a policy type in the request to display on the form, just a policy number. Therefore only one Label gets populated on the form.

C# code

```
protected void Page_Load(object sender, EventArgs e)
{
  Policy.Text = Request["PolicyNumber"];
}
```

VB code

```
Protected Sub Page_Load(ByVal sender As Object, _
    ByVal e As System.EventArgs) Handles Me.Load
  Policy.Text = Request.Item("PolicyNumber")
End Sub
```

NOTE	With a different approach, we might have chosen to retain the Policy object created in the previous event handler by adding it to the request or to the session, and then it could be used to provide more policy details on the page. However in this example, to try to keep things simple, we have chosen not to make substantial changes to the session management from the earlier version of this webflow.

'ClaimForm2.aspx' transfers control to 'ClaimForm3.aspx'. The Page Load event handler for this web form uses the façade's 'createClaim' method to write the Claim to the database and load its associated Policy object. It then gathers data from both the Claim and its associated Policy to write information to the controls on the web form.

C# code

```csharp
protected void Page_Load(object sender, EventArgs e)
{
  if (Session.IsNewSession)
  {
    Response.Redirect("ClaimForm1.aspx");
  }
  ModelFacade facade = new ModelFacade();
  ClaimFormDTO claimFormDTO = (ClaimFormDTO) Session["ClaimFormDTO"];
  Claim claim = facade.createClaim(claimFormDTO);
  if (claim.Policy.Type == "contents")
  {
    PolicyTypeImage.ImageUrl = "contents.gif";
  }
  else
  {
    PolicyTypeImage.ImageUrl = "buildings.gif";
  }
  Reference.Text = claim.Reference;
  ClaimDate.Text = claim.DateOfClaim.ToString();
  Approved.Text = claim.IsApproved.ToString();
  Policy.Text = claim.Policy.Number.ToString();
  Type.Text = claim.Policy.Type;
  Amount.Text = claim.Amount.ToString();
  Description.Text = claim.Description;
  Session.Abandon();
}
```

VB code

```vb
Protected Sub Page_Load(ByVal sender As Object, _
    ByVal e As System.EventArgs) Handles Me.Load
  If Session.IsNewSession() Then
    Response.Redirect("ClaimForm1.aspx")
  End If
```

```
Dim facade As ModelFacade = New ModelFacade()
Dim claimFormDTO As ClaimFormDTO = Session.Item("ClaimFormDTO")
Dim claim As Claim = facade.createClaim(claimFormDTO)
If claim.Policy.Type = ("contents") Then
  PolicyTypeImage.ImageUrl = "contents.gif"
Else
  PolicyTypeImage.ImageUrl = "buildings.gif"
End If
Reference.Text = claim.Reference
ClaimDate.Text = claim.DateOfClaim
Approved.Text = claim.IsApproved
Policy.Text = claim.Policy.Number
Type.Text = claim.Policy.Type
Amount.Text = claim.Amount
Description.Text = claim.Description
Session.Abandon()
End Sub
```

Of course if the policy number entered into the first web form does not match a policy number in the database, control is transferred to 'PolicyNotFound.aspx'. Here is this web form, which displays an error message and includes a Label control that will contain the policy number from the claim form:

```
<!DOCTYPE html PUBLIC "-//W3C//DTD XHTML 1.0 Transitional//EN"
"http://www.w3.org/TR/xhtml1/DTD/xhtml1-transitional.dtd">
<html xmlns="http://www.w3.org/1999/xhtml">
  <head runat="server">
   <title>Policy Not Found</title>
  </head>
  <body>
    <form id="form1" runat="server">
      <div>
        <p>
          Policy number
         <asp:Label ID="PolicyNumberLabel" runat="server" Text="">
         </asp:Label>
          not found
        </p>
        <hr />
        <asp:HyperLink ID="HyperLink1" runat="server"
          NavigateUrl="~/ClaimForm1.aspx">
        Return to form page
        </asp:HyperLink> </div>
          </form>
          </div>
  </body>
</html>
```

Here is the Page Load event handler for this web form. It uses the original policy number entered by the user that will still be in the request object to populate the Label.

| FIGURE 11.11 | The web form showing details both of a claim and its related policy |

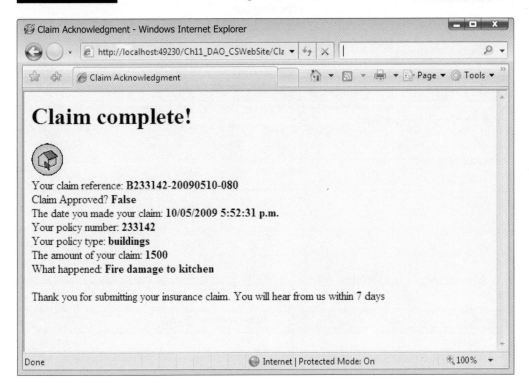

C# code

```
protected void Page_Load(object sender, EventArgs e)
{
  PolicyNumberLabel.Text = Request["PolicyNumber"].ToString();
}
```

VB code

```
Protected Sub page_load(ByVal sender As Object, ByVal e As EventArgs)
  PolicyNumberLabel.Text = Request.Item("PolicyNumber").ToString()
End Sub
```

Figure 11.11 shows an example of what the display page might look like if given a valid policy number, while Figure 11.12 shows the 'PolicyNotFound.aspx' page that appears if the policy number does not appear in the database.

11.6 Using DAOs for update

In this section we will show a simple example of using a DAO to update existing records. Here is an additional method from the ClaimDAO class that allows a claim record to be updated:

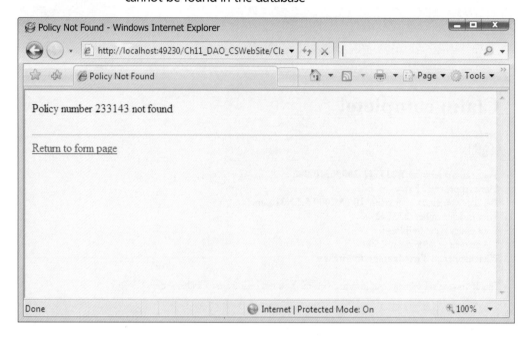

FIGURE 11.12 The error page that appears if the policy number entered for a claim cannot be found in the database

C# code

```
/* update claim object in the database */
public void updateClaim(Claim myClaim)
{
 SqlConnection myConn = new SqlConnection(MyConnString);
 myConn.Open();
 SqlCommand myComm = new SqlCommand("UPDATE claim SET reference =
  @reference, description = @description, amount = @amount, approved
  = @approved, claimDate = @claimDate, policyID = @policyID WHERE
  claimID = @claimID", myConn);
 myComm.Parameters.AddWithValue("@claimID", myClaim.ClaimID);
 myComm.Parameters.AddWithValue("@reference", myClaim.Reference);
 myComm.Parameters.AddWithValue("@description", myClaim.Description);
 myComm.Parameters.AddWithValue("@amount", myClaim.Amount);
 myComm.Parameters.AddWithValue
    ("@approved", (myClaim.IsApproved ? "Y" : "N"));
 myComm.Parameters.AddWithValue("@claimDate", myClaim.DateOfClaim);
 myComm.Parameters.AddWithValue("@policyID", myClaim.PolicyID);
 int rows = myComm.ExecuteNonQuery();
 myConn.Close();
 if (rows != 1) throw new Exception("Unexpected Result for Update");
}
```

VB code

```vb
' update claim object in the database
Public Sub updateClaim(ByVal myClaim As Claim)
 Dim myConn As SqlConnection = New SqlConnection(myConnString)
 myConn.Open()
 Dim myComm As SqlCommand = New SqlCommand( _
   "UPDATE claim SET reference = @reference, description = _
   @description, amount = @amount, approved = @approved, _
   claimDate = @claimDate, policyID = @policyID WHERE _
   claimID = @claimID", myConn)
 myComm.Parameters.AddWithValue("@claimID", myClaim.ClaimID)
 myComm.Parameters.AddWithValue("@reference", myClaim.Reference)
 myComm.Parameters.AddWithValue("@description", myClaim.Description)
 myComm.Parameters.AddWithValue("@amount", myClaim.Amount)
 If myClaim.IsApproved Then
  myComm.Parameters.AddWithValue("@approved", "Y")
 Else
  myComm.Parameters.AddWithValue("@approved", "N")
 End If
 myComm.Parameters.AddWithValue("@claimDate", myClaim.DateOfClaim)
 myComm.Parameters.AddWithValue("@policyID", myClaim.PolicyID)
 Dim rows As Integer = myComm.ExecuteNonQuery()
 myConn.Close()
 If rows <> 1 Then
  Throw New Exception("Unexpected Result for Update")
 End If
End Sub
```

To make this method available through the facade, we need to add a simple delegation method to the ModelFacade class.

C# code

```csharp
public void updateClaim(Claim claim)
{
 ClaimDAO myDAO = getClaimDAO();
 myDAO.updateClaim(claim);
}
```

VB code

```vb
Public Sub updateClaim(ByVal claim As Claim)
 Dim myDAO As ClaimDAO = getClaimDAO()
 myDAO.updateClaim(claim)
End Sub
```

We will also need access to the 'getClaimByRef' method of the DAO, so we will add this delegation method to the façade (you may already have done this in a previous exercise).

C# code

```
public Claim getClaimByRef(String reference)
{
 ClaimDAO myDAO = getClaimDAO();
 return myDAO.getClaimByRef(reference);
}
```

VB code

```
Public Function getClaimByRef(ByVal reference As String) As Claim
 Dim myDAO As ClaimDAO = getClaimDAO()
 Return myDAO.getClaimByRef(reference)
End Function
```

To use the update method, we will explore a simplified use case, where insurance assessors need to approve insurance claims. When a claim is created, it is always initially not approved. At some point, therefore, an assessor needs to approve the claim before it can be processed further. Here is a simple web form that enables an insurance assessor to see a list of unapproved claim references. The most important control is the DropDownList that will show unapproved claim references. In order for us to respond to the event of the user selecting something from the list, we set the AutoPostBack attribute to 'true' and specify the 'OnSelectedIndexChanged' event handling method. There is also a Label that will be used to display a message to the user when a claim is approved.

```
<!DOCTYPE html PUBLIC "-//W3C//DTD XHTML 1.0 Transitional//EN"
"http://www.w3.org/TR/xhtml1/DTD/xhtml1-transitional.dtd">

<html xmlns="http://www.w3.org/1999/xhtml">
 <head runat="server">
  <title>Claim Approval</title>
 </head>
 <body>
  <form id="form1" runat="server">
   <div>
     <asp:Label ID="Label1" runat="server" Text=
     "Select claims for approval from the following list">
     </asp:Label>
     <br />
     <asp:DropDownList ID="DropDownList1" runat="server"
      AutoPostBack="True"
      OnSelectedIndexChanged="DropDownList1_SelectedIndexChanged">
     </asp:DropDownList>
     <br />
```

```
        <asp:Label ID="ClaimRefLabel" runat="server" Text="">
        </asp:Label>
      </div>
    </form>
  </body>
</html>
```

In the code behind, we need to be able to initially populate the drop-down list, and update the database and the list when the user selects a claim reference. The class here uses the initial page load event to initially call the 'loadClaims' method, which uses the getClaims method of the façade (already introduced earlier in the chapter) to read all the unapproved claims from the database and add their references to the drop-down list.

The event handling method ('DropDownList1_SelectedIndexChanged') uses the methods of the façade that encapsulate the DAO to locate the selected claim and update it. Then the Label is updated with a message and the reference of the updated claim.

C# code

```csharp
protected void Page_Load(object sender, EventArgs e)
{
  DropDownList1.AutoPostBack = true;
  if (!IsPostBack) LoadClaims();
}


protected void DropDownList1_SelectedIndexChanged
    (object sender, EventArgs e)
{
  String claimRef = DropDownList1.SelectedValue;
  if (claimRef != "")
  {
    ModelFacade facade = new ModelFacade();
    Claim myClaim = facade.getClaimByRef(claimRef);
    myClaim.IsApproved = true;
    facade.updateClaim(myClaim);
    ClaimRefLabel.Text = "Claim reference " + myClaim.Reference +
      " has been approved";
    LoadClaims();
  }
}

private void LoadClaims()
{
  ModelFacade facade = new ModelFacade();
  var claimRefs = from d in facade.
    getClaims("where approved = 'N'") select d.Reference;
  DropDownList1.DataSource = (new String[] { "" }).Concat(claimRefs);
  DropDownList1.DataBind();
}
```

VB code

```
Protected Sub Page_Load(ByVal sender As Object, ByVal e As EventArgs)
  DropDownList1.AutoPostBack = True
  If IsPostBack = False Then
    LoadClaims()
  End If
End Sub

Protected Sub DropDownList1_SelectedIndexChanged
    (ByVal sender As Object, ByVal e As EventArgs)
  Dim claimRef As String = DropDownList1.SelectedValue
  If claimRef <> "" Then
    Dim facade As ModelFacade = New ModelFacade()
    Dim myClaim As Claim = facade.getClaimByRef(claimRef)
    myClaim.isApproved = True
    facade.updateClaim(myClaim)
    ClaimRefLabel.Text = "Claim reference " + myClaim.reference +
      " has been approved"
    LoadClaims()
  End If
End Sub

Private Sub LoadClaims()
  Dim facade As ModelFacade = New ModelFacade()
  Dim claimRefs = _
    From d In facade.getClaims("where approved = 'N'") Select
    d.reference
  DropDownList1.DataSource = (New String() {""}).Concat(claimRefs)
  DropDownList1.DataBind()
End Sub
```

Figure 11.13 shows the web form with the drop-down list showing two references for unapproved claims. Figure 11.14 shows the web form after the first of these claim references has been selected by the user.

11.7 The object-relational impedance mismatch

In this chapter, and the previous one, we have been looking at ways of accessing data stored in a database within a web application. We have seen that Visual Web Developer provides us with more than one way of accessing this data: Data Controls, ADO.NET, LINQ and Data Access Objects. However it is worth concluding this chapter by highlighting the complexity of object-relational mapping (i.e. mapping objects in a program to tables in a database). A number of the issues described below have not been addressed directly by the examples we have covered in this (and the previous) chapter. For example we have been working with DTOs rather than fully fledged business objects, and our persistence layer is rather simplistic. However if you are working with objects and persistent data, it is important to at least be aware of some of the more tricky aspects of mapping the two together.

FIGURE 11.13 Unapproved claims displayed in a drop-down list

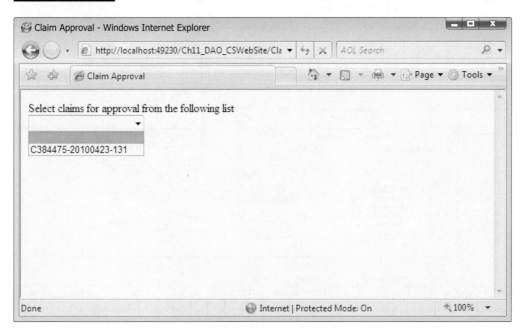

FIGURE 11.14 After a reference has been selected the claim record is updated in the database as approved

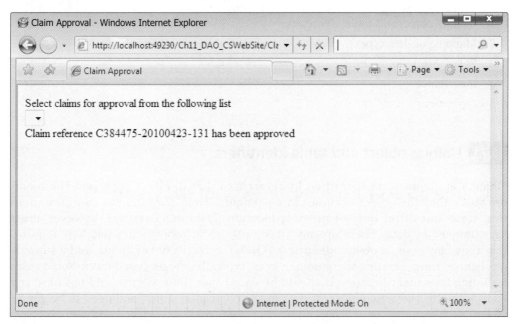

At first glance there seems to be a simple relationship between objects and rows in a database table, which we have taken advantage of in the relatively simple examples used in this chapter. An object is defined by a class, which defines (among other things) the structure of its internal data. Similarly, a database table has a schema that defines its columns. An

FIGURE 11.15   The relationship between classes and tables, objects and columns, fields and rows

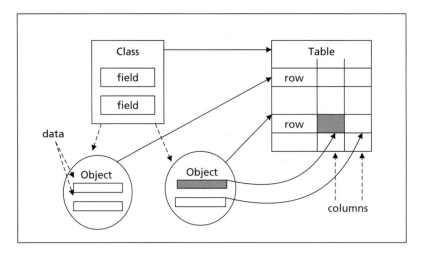

instance of a class (an object) contains data in the same way that a row (or tuple) contains data (Figure 11.15).

However, although there are some apparent similarities between an object-oriented model and a database schema, there are many areas where there is not a particularly good fit between the two technologies. This is often known as the *impedance mismatch*. This mismatch covers a number of problem areas:

1. Unique object and table identifiers
2. Mapping of data types
3. Relationships and normalization
4. Inheritance
5. Operations

11.7.1 Unique object and table identifiers

Objects in memory are identified by references that in effect represent the memory space that the object occupies at a particular time. Two objects can have identical state, but differ in their memory location. Data in a database, however, must have unique key data. Therefore any attempt to persist objects in a database requires that they have unique object identifiers (OIDs), effectively key fields, and a suitable mechanism for generating these unique keys, typically integer based but in some cases including type identification. It should be noted that these keys should not have any relationship to the actual business data in the objects or tables, and need to be generated in such way that an appropriate level of uniqueness is achieved without excessive locks on the database (Ambler, 2006). Using database features to generate keys is an effective solution, but is not standard across different database products. Therefore more portable strategies are sometimes needed that do not rely on a particular database (Reese, 2003).

11.7.2 Mapping of data types

Although simple data types have straightforward conversion mappings between .NET languages and SQL data types (e.g. String to VARCHAR and vice versa), more complex types do not have a natural mapping. For example, Boolean types are not supported in SQL Server and have to be mapped to character or number based fields, and serialized objects are frequently stored as BLOBS (binary large objects) or other binary representations, which means that the data in these objects cannot be accessed directly while they are in the database. It is also sometimes necessary to use finer grained components in the database than those in the object model, so that one field of an object may have to be mapped to more than one column of a database table.

11.7.3 Relationships and normalization

Objects that might be regarded as a single instance in an object model might be seen very differently in a normalized database schema. Whereas an object might maintain relationships using collections of objects, a database will need to use many tables and keys. What appears as a simple many-to-many relationship in an object model requires complex foreign key management in the database. There are different strategies to consider too, for example modeling one-to-many relationships can be done using either back pointers or a separate table. Alternatively a one-to-many relationship represented in an object model by a collection of references may simply be written to a single field as a serialized object. In all of these scenarios, the implementation of the object model must take account of the actual data representation in the database and handle type conversions and table navigation appropriately.

11.7.4 Inheritance

Relational databases do not directly support inheritance, so we have to find some workaround. There are a number of strategies to do this, each with their own advantages and disadvantages, but a common solution is to join multiple tables with common keys to represent the classes in the hierarchy. Although a reasonable design choice this can lead to poor performance, requiring other more pragmatic solutions (Brown and Whitenack, 1996).

11.7.5 Operations

Objects encapsulate both process and data, with operations (methods) that relate specifically to the data in the object. In contrast, database operations such as stored procedures are not tied to particular object representations, so only the data from an object can be directly stored in a database, not its other characteristics. This usually means that objects can be aware of their data representation in the database but not vice versa: the object-relational metadata is not in the database but implicitly in the code. This means that forward engineering a database schema from an object model is likely to be more successful than reverse engineering an object model from a database schema, since the reverse engineering provides no information about what operations objects should have.

Self Study Questions

1. What does DAO stand for?
2. What does CRUD stand for?
3. What is the default |DataDirectory| called?
4. What is 'injected' during an SQL injection attack?
5. Give an example of a one-to-many relationship.
6. Name three methods supported by the SqlDataReader class.
7. What property must be set to allow the code behind file to respond to the user selecting a new item in a drop-down list?
8. And what is the name of the event triggered by such a selection?
9. What is a delegation method?
10. Give three problems covered by the term 'object relational impedance mismatch'.

Exercises

11.4 Refactor the ClaimDAO and PolicyDAO classes so that they inherit from a common superclass. The superclass can contain a constructor that retrieves the connection string so that this does not have to be repeated in every DAO.

11.5 So far in this chapter we have used the ClaimDAO to create, read and update records. Create a variant of the 'ClaimApproval.aspx' web form which deletes the selected claim. This will require you to add new delete methods to the Model-Facade and ClaimDAO classes as well.

SUMMARY

In this chapter we saw how to use the data access object pattern to provide a persistence layer to our web application. We looked at using a DAO to read data from the database and create DTOs from the data, which could then be used by the web forms in the view layer. We also looked at the rather more complex issue of writing to the database using DAOs and maintaining foreign key relationships while doing so. We saw how to manually set up a connection string in the web.config file, and how to retrieve that connection string inside a DAO. Our final discussion included some coverage of further issues in object relational mapping.

References and further reading

Alur, D., Crupi, J. and Malks, D. 2003. *Core J2EE Patterns: Best Practices and Design Strategies*, 2nd edition, Upper Saddle River, NJ: Prentice Hall.

Ambler, S. 2006. *The Object-Relational Impedance Mismatch*, http://www.agiledata.org/essays/impedanceMismatch.html.

ASP.NET Data Access Overview: http://msdn.microsoft.com/en-us/library/ms178359.aspx.

Brown, K. and Whitenack, B. 1996. *Crossing Chasms: A Pattern Language for Object-RDBMS Integration in Vlissides*, J., Coplien, J. and Kerth, N. (Eds.): *Pattern Languages of Program Design* 2, Addison-Wesley.

Gamma, E., Helm, R., Johnson, R. and Vlissides, J. 1995. *Design Patterns: Elements of Reusable Object-Oriented Software*. Reading, Mass: Addison-Wesley.

MSDN. ASP.NET Data Access Overview. http://msdn.microsoft.com/en-us/library/ms178359.aspx.

Reese, G. 2003. *Java Database Best Practices*. Sebastopol, CA: O'Reilly.

Walther, S. 2007. *Data Access in the ASP.NET 2.0 Framework (Video Training)*, Sams Publishing.

11

Membership and Security

INTRODUCTION

This chapter covers the ASP.NET Login controls. It also explains how to use the ASP.NET WebSite Administration Tool to create users, roles, and access rules. You will also learn how to create and use an ASP.NET personalization profile. These ASP.NET features allow you to identify your website users, to personalize pages with a different appearance and contents, and to restrict access to certain parts of your site. Finally, you will see how to deploy your site to another server, and what is involved in configuring your site for production use.

Security and personalization are important considerations for any website, particularly a dynamic e-business one. In terms of security, web developers must ensure that data integrity cannot be compromised by accident, or a malicious user. Regular users need to be reassured that their data is safe, and that their privacy cannot be compromised. Regarding personalization, adding content or changing the appearance of a page to suit the current user can improve their opinion of your site, and encourage them to return more often.

The notion of using access control lists as a security mechanism became popular towards the end of the 1980s when, for example, it was proposed as part of the POSIX standard. Clear definitions of role-based access control were first published in 1992 by David E Ferraiolo and colleagues from the National Institute of Standards and Technology (Ferraiolo and Kuhn, 1992). Today, all major operating systems support this or a similar mechanism.

This chapter covers the facilities that ASP.NET provides to help you to secure and personalize your web applications. Note that these topics are related, as both of them rely on knowing who the current user is, which means we will start by looking at the ASP.NET Login controls. After that we will consider how you can add users, roles and access rules using the ASP.NET WebSite Administration Tool to set up a membership provider database. We will then create a few pages which illustrate the use of the Login controls and the membership database. Finally, you will see how to augment the membership database with user specific data collected into an ASP.NET personalization profile, and create additional pages which allow you to store and retrieve personalization data items.

We also revisit site maps, and look at site map trimming. Site map files are often used by the web crawlers that create indices for search engines. Google, for example, has published its XML format so that webmasters can ensure their sites are indexed promptly and accurately. This format differs from the one used by Microsoft in that it focuses on how often, or how recently, web pages have changed, rather than how users navigate between pages. ASP.NET, by contrast, uses site maps to automate the creation of navigation aids such as hierarchical menus and breadcrumbs (as we saw in Chapter 8). The notion of trimming site maps based on the role of the currently logged in user also appears to have been invented by Microsoft.

In the final part of this chapter we will review the mechanisms provided in Visual Web Developer for copying your website to a remote server, how multiple configuration files are managed, and issues you are likely to encounter when deploying your site to a production server administered by another person.

12.1 Login controls and the membership provider

As has already been mentioned, the Visual Web Developer Toolbox includes a 'Login' group of controls which allow you to add login access to your website. There are seven controls, described in Table 12.1.

These controls make use of a database of users called the *membership provider*. You can configure the location of this membership data, and the relational database management system (RDMS) used to access this database. Alternatively, you can implement the membership provider API and manage the user data yourself, so it does not actually need to be stored in a database at all. For simplicity, and for testing purposes, however, the easiest solution is to make use of the default membership provider which is included as part of ASP.NET.

12.1.1 Configuring the ASP.NET membership provider and authentication type

To select the default membership provider, you use the ASP.NET WebSite Administration Tool (AWSAT), which we saw in Chapter 6 when discussing debugging and tracing. For simplicity, it is assumed you will create a new website before following the instructions or trying the exercises in this chapter. When you are confident you have understood the

TABLE 12.1   The Visual Web Developer Login controls

Login Control	Description
Login	A compound control containing text boxes where users can enter their username and password, and a 'Log In' button
LoginName	Displays the username if the user is currently logged in, otherwise displays nothing
LoginView	A compound control with two templates, the LoggedInTemplate whose contents are displayed if the user has currently logged in, and the AnonymousTemplate, which is displayed otherwise
LoginStatus	Provides a LinkButton which allows the user to log in if they have not already done so, and to log out if they are currently logged in
CreateUserWizard	Provides a dialog box where the user can enter their details, including username and password, and a button to create their user identity and thereby register with your site
ChangePassword	A dialog that allows the user to change their password
PasswordRecovery	A dialog that allows the user to request their forgotten password by email, which is sent to the email address provided when they originally registered. This facility requires your web server to be configured and able to send email

Login controls and the other ASP.NET facilities described here, you can then include them in sites you design and develop in future.

Note that the login controls will not work until you have defined your membership provider. To start the WebSite Administration Tool, use the 'WebSite' → 'ASP.NET Configuration' menu command, and select the 'Provider' tab. Then click on the link that says 'Select a single provider for all site management data'. You should then see a screen similar to Figure 12.1. You can test the membership set-up by clicking the 'Test' link on this page.

Note that by default this provider uses SQL Server Express edition. With the standard installation of Visual Web Developer, therefore, AWSAT should be able to connect immediately to AspNetSqlProvider. If you are using the full version of SQL Server, however, some editing of configuration files is required before you will be able to connect successfully to your database. The following section provides some advice on how you can safely edit configuration files.

 NOTE   You will need to check that the Windows service called SQL Server Active Directory Helper is running before you can successfully make a connection to the database.

Note that if you do have to edit a configuration file, you should of course take a backup first. Also note that you may have to restart your web server before certain changes take effect. In addition to selecting your membership provider, you should also use AWSAT

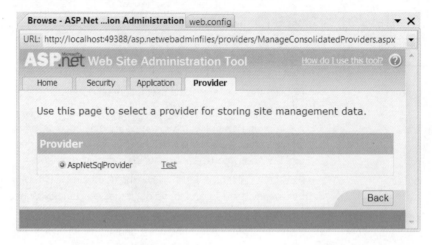

to configure the type of authentication you want your site to use. For an internet-based application you will certainly need to use *Forms Authentication*. For an intranet application running over a local network you may prefer the alternative authentication method, which is also known as *Windows Authentication*. In this case your users can log in using their standard Windows user names and passwords, which will be checked by the web server using Active Directory or a similar local directory. In our example we will use Forms Authentication. To do this, click on the Security tab, and then follow the link called 'Select authentication type', and then check the radio button next to 'From the internet', (i.e. Forms Authentication) as shown in Figure 12.2. The Wizard will then take you to the next step in the security management procedure.

Once you have configured security settings using the administration tool, your choice of authentication type will be stored in your website's web.config file, where you will now find the following element:

```
<authentication mode="Forms" />
```

12.2 Creating users and roles

While you are still running AWSAT, it is also convenient to create some users. You can do this by clicking on the Security tab and selecting 'Create User'. For each user you create, you will be asked to enter their user name and password (twice) as you can see in Figure 12.3. You must also provide other data such as their email address and a security question, which are used by the PasswordRecovery control. Note that in this dialog, the password must by default have at least 7 characters of which at least one must be non-alphanumeric; neither a letter nor number but, for example, a punctuation symbol. The email address must be of the form x@y.z to be accepted. Finally, the user name must not already exist, or you will be told to enter another user name. Acceptable data must be provided for all the fields in the form before the 'Create User' button can be clicked successfully.

FIGURE 12.2
Using the ASP.NET WebSite Administration Tool to select the authentication type. Here, we are selecting 'From the internet' for Forms Authentication

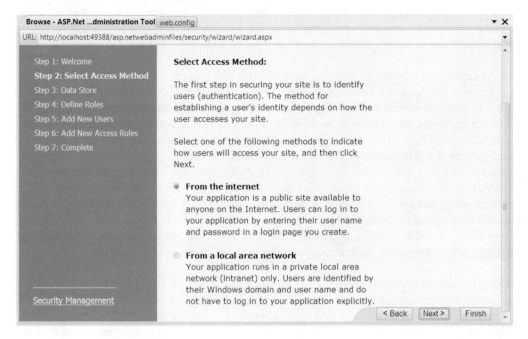

FIGURE 12.3
Using the ASP.NET WebSite Administration Tool to create a new user

The next step is to define some roles. Like most operating systems, ASP.NET allows you to control access to resources based on the user's name and roles or groups to which they belong. Websites often have thousands of users, so it is not particularly convenient or sensible to define privileges for each user separately. Instead, you should associate each user with a role or roles, and then define which roles are allowed to access which web pages. It is therefore worth spending a little time up front considering what roles are needed.

In the case of our insurance company, we have seen that this can have both an externally facing Internet site, and also an intranet site used by employees. The Internet site might distinguish between potential and existing policy holders, just two different groups of users. The intranet site might need rather more roles. For example, one class of employee may be authorized to create a new claim, but approving a claim might require a user with more authority and experience. There might also be managers who would be able to view additional information such as statistics on how each operator is performing. That is to say, it depends on the web application exactly which roles are required. These will usually be identified in the requirements workshops, where it is agreed which use cases are needed, and which actors should have access to them. From our discussion or roles, then, we seem to need at least the roles shown in Table 12.2 (in an iterative development cycle, new roles may be added, and existing roles changed, as further requirements become apparent over time).

ASP.NET automatically recognizes the special case of a user who has not logged in as a so-called anonymous user. In the case of our Internet site, we can identify and treat such users as potential customers, so it is only necessary to create one role, policyholder. However for the intranet site, it is unlikely the insurance company would allow a user who has not logged in access to any dynamic business data, so the anonymous user would be restricted to viewing a single page which asks them to login. It is therefore necessary to define all three intranet site roles shown in Table 12.2.

To define a role, click on the AWSAT Security tab and select the 'Create or Manage roles' link. This allows you to type in the roles you have recognized you need, as shown in Figure 12.4. You can also delete roles that are no longer needed, and manage roles.

Managing a role means choosing a user to add or remove from that role, as shown in Figure 12.5. This web page allows you to search for a user by entering their user name directly, or selecting the initial letter of their name. You can also search by their email address. Once you have located a specific user, you can check the box to include them in the selected role, or clear it to remove them. Unfortunately it is not possible with this tool to assign the user to multiple roles in one step, which means the tool is not particularly useful. Its main purpose, however, is to allow you to develop a website and

TABLE 12.2 User roles needed for WebHomeCover Internet and Intranet sites

	Internet Site	Intranet Site
Roles Needed	potential customer	operator
	policy holder	approver
		manager

FIGURE 12.4   Using the ASP.NET WebSite Administration Tool to create a new role

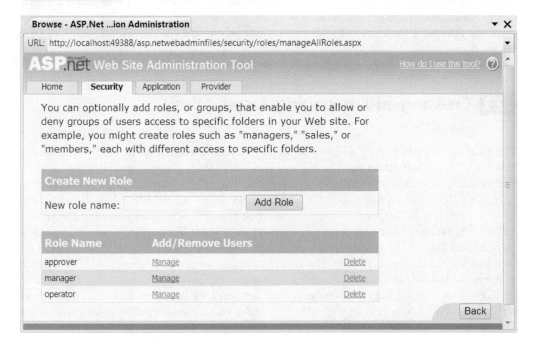

FIGURE 12.5   Using the ASP.NET WebSite Administration Tool to manage a role. This allows you to find users and add them to or remove them from the chosen role

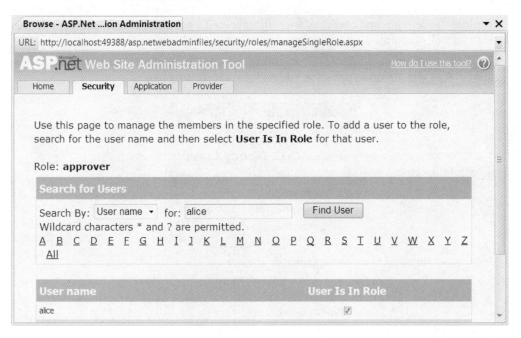

test out your pages as you create them. When the website is up and running, your pages will be served up by Microsoft's Internet Information Services (IIS) which has its own configuration and management tools. These are similar to, but rather more sophisticated than, the ASP.NET WebSite Administration Tool provided by Visual Web Developer that we are using here.

12.3 Creating and managing access rules

The final facility offered by AWSAT to help you secure your website is defining access rules. The approach taken by ASP.NET is similar to that of most operating systems in that access is defined either by user or role. One difference, however, is that rules apply only to a folder, not an individual file: if you allow access to a folder, that allows access to all files in the folder; and if you deny access, that prevents access to any file in the folder. This means that you must organize your ASP.NET files into folders in such a way that all files in the folder are accessible by the same group or groups of users. The simplest way to do this is to have one folder per role, where you keep all files accessible to users in that role, but more complex structures are possible. Obviously, if you have to move files around between folders, you may end up breaking links between your web pages. This is one reason why it is important to consider security roles early when designing your website.

Another difference compared to standard operating system security is that, in this context, access means read access. It would not make sense for users to be given write access to your web pages.

The first step therefore in creating access rules is to decide what folders or sub-directories you should create. In this chapter we will follow the simple approach of having one folder per role, sharing the same name as the role itself. Thus there will be folders named 'approver', 'manager', 'operator', and 'policyholder' (Figure 12.6). You do not need a special folder for anonymous users, as we will have just one web form in the root of our website, a welcome page inviting users to log in.

FIGURE 12.6   Creating separate folders for each security role

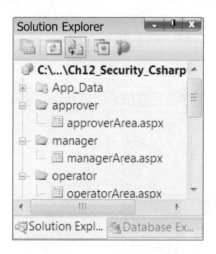

Figure 12.7 shows AWSAT being used to create and manage access rules. The first rule allows the operator role access to the operator folder, and the second rule denies all users access. Rules are processed in order, however, so that users in the operator role will match the first rule and be granted access regardless of the second one. The access rule manager allows you to re-order and delete rules after you have created them.

FIGURE 12.7 Using AWSAT to define access rules

(a)
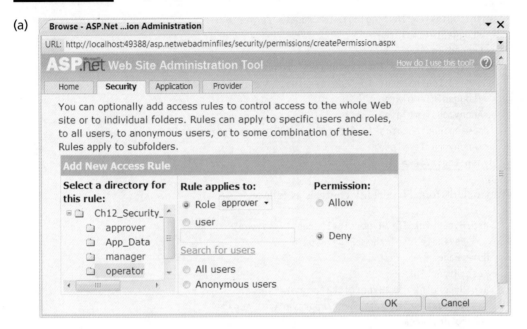

(b)
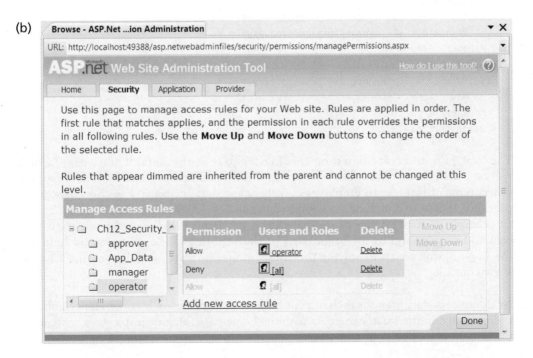

12.4 Using Login controls in web forms

In this section, we will work through an example that uses the Login controls and associated users and roles. For this example, each web form will be based on the same master page. This master page will have the company logo and standard links to different areas of the intranet site. You should save this in the root directory of the website. It should include a LoginStatus control including LoginName and LoginStatus controls as shown below:

```
<asp:LoginView ID="LoginView1" runat="server">
  <LoggedInTemplate>
  Logged In As:
    <asp:LoginName ID="LoginName1" runat="server" />
    <asp:LoginStatus ID="LoginStatus1" runat="server" />
  </LoggedInTemplate>
  <AnonymousTemplate>
    <asp:LoginStatus ID="LoginStatus2" runat="server" />
  </AnonymousTemplate>
</asp:LoginView>
```

Also include four HyperLink controls as follows:

```
<asp:HyperLink ID="HyperLink1" runat="server"
      NavigateUrl="~/HomePage.aspx">
  Home Page
</asp:HyperLink>
<asp:HyperLink ID="HyperLink2" runat="server"
      NavigateUrl="~/approver/approverArea.aspx">
  Approvers Area
</asp:HyperLink>
 <asp:HyperLink ID="HyperLink3" runat="server"
      NavigateUrl="~/manager/managerArea.aspx">
  Managers Area
</asp:HyperLink>
<asp:HyperLink ID="HyperLink4" runat="server"
      NavigateUrl="~/manager/managerArea.aspx">
  Managers Area
</asp:HyperLink>
```

The first page to create based on this master page is the default start page, which will be a web form called 'HomePage.aspx'. Most companies will include news and other items of interest to employees on this page, but for brevity in this chapter the pages we create will include no content beyond a short message. See Figure 12.8 for an example of such a page. Note that in the left-hand column of the table are links back to this page and to the other parts of the site. Below the content page holder is the LoginStatus control showing the AnonymousTemplate, which contains a LoginView control.

Next, create a start page for each of your folders, a target for each of the HyperLink controls included in the master page. As with the home page, include just a short sentence in the content place holder of each page.

FIGURE 12.8 The intranet home page in Design view

Before you can test the pages you have created, and the rules which control access to them, you must also create a page whereby users can login. By convention, this should be called 'Login. aspx', and should include a Login control. Locate this file in your website's home directory:

```
<asp:Content ID="Content1" ContentPlaceHolderID="ContentPlaceHolder1"
  Runat="Server">
<asp:Login ID="Login1" runat="server">
</asp:Login>
```

Now test the pages you have created and the links between them. As you navigate around, you will find that your 'Login.aspx' page is displayed whenever the user tries to view a page which they are not allowed to access. If, however, they login as a user belonging to a role with access rights to that folder they are then able to follow the link without interruption Figure 12.9). The screen shots show how, after clicking a link to one of the restricted area, the 'Login.aspx' page is displayed. When the user, in this case 'alice' or 'bjarne', has logged in, they can access any restricted page provided their user name is registered as belonging to the associated role.

It is important in this approach to ensure the 'Login.aspx' page includes a link back to the home page. If the user clicks by accident on a page to which they do have not access, they can always rescue themselves by returning to the home page.

An alternative is to hide links which the current user cannot follow. This can be achieved by including code such as the following in the Page_Load() event of the master page:

```
HyperLink2.Visible = Roles.IsUserInRole("approver");
HyperLink3.Visible = Roles.IsUserInRole("manager");
HyperLink4.Visible = Roles.IsUserInRole("operator");
```

Similarly, it is not particularly desirable to show a login ButtonLink from the 'Login.aspx' page. This can also be suppressed using code such as the following in the Page_Load event handler of the 'Login.aspx' page.

```
Page.Master.FindControl("LoginView1").Visible = false;
```

Note the indirection which is required to hide the LoginView control, which belongs to the master page, not the 'Login.aspx' page itself.

FIGURE 12.9 Navigating the intranet home pages

(a)

(b)

(c)

(d)

These Page_Load handlers have been implemented in the pages displayed in Figure 12.9 as you can see from the final screen shot, where the link to the manager area is not displayed, since user 'alice' is not defined to belong to the manager role. Similarly, the 'LoginView' has been suppressed in the second screen shot.

12.4.1 Other Login controls

Two of the three remaining Login controls, CreateUserWizard and ChangePassword, display dialogs that are self-explanatory. Figure 12.10 shows the CreateUserWizard which AWSAT itself makes use of to create a new user, as you can see if you compare this screen shot with Figure 12.3.

FIGURE 12.10   The NewUser control

Figure 12.11 shows the ChangePassword control. This control provides a similar dialog, illustrating the standard security checks whereby the user must enter their current password and their new password twice before any change can be allowed.

The final login control is the PasswordRecovery control. This also displays a dialog which is self-explanatory: the user just has to enter their user name and click Submit, which then emails their current or a new password to them. Sending their password, or a new password, to the user obviously requires your web server to communicate with a mail server. This requires that there is a mail server running, to which your web server has the appropriate access.

NOTE	If the SqlMemberShip provider is configured to stored passwords in hashed format, they cannot be recovered from the database, so a new password is sent instead.

FIGURE 12.11 The ChangePassword control

FIGURE 12.12 The properties associated with a PasswordRecovery control are shown here. They can be edited in the usual way in order to customize the dialog with the user

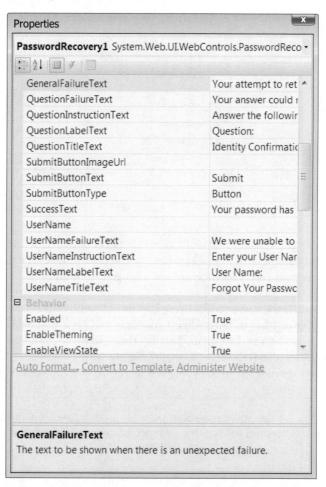

12.4.2 Configuring the Login controls

The Login controls are, of necessity, very configurable. Each organization has its own approach to security, so these controls would not be very useful if their appearance and behavior were fixed or inflexible. The PasswordRecovery control, for example, has properties which allow you to define the text used to contrast each sub-control contained in the dialog box, so you can easily change the wording and advice given. There is also a URL for a page providing additional help. The best way to find out about configuring these controls is to view their properties via their property window, as shown in Figure 12.12. Password recovery properties include InstructionText strings which are used to prompt the user to enter their security credentials, and FailureText strings which give the error messages to be shown to the user in case of security failures or other errors.

In addition, you can also configure certain aspects of the Login controls using the ASP.NET WebSite Administration Tool. To configure your email server, for example, you can use AWSAT's Application Settings tab, then click on the SMTP Settings link. You will be presented with a dialog similar to that shown in Figure 12.13. To complete this dialog you need details of your email server, and also your web server must have authority to generate and send emails. Hence the advice at the top of the web page to contact your network administrator.

FIGURE 12.13   Using AWSAT to configure SMTP settings so that password recover can function

12.5 Web application configuration management

So far we have been building web applications using many of the default settings in Visual Web Developer, and deploying applications onto the local test server. However, to deploy an application to a production server, we need to understand something of web application configuration management and deployment. In the remainder of this chapter, we look at a number of aspects related to these issues.

12.5.1 Configuring build and start options

Website property pages can be accessed by selecting the project root directory in the Solution Explorer window, right-clicking, then selecting Property Pages, or via the 'Website' → 'Start Options . . .' menu command. These pages allow you to define the website's references, build, and start options, as shown in Figure 12.14. Most of these options are self-explanatory. The 'References' listed show the external libraries which are included in each page by default as it is built. The 'Build' options allow you to select whether the whole site or just the current page is built, and the 'Target Framework', which will typically be the latest version, as shown here. The 'Start Options' allow you to control the behavior of your website when it is first launched, for example to select the default page to view. In addition, you can select an alternative web server such as IIS to be used to host the site's pages. This could be useful, for example, when testing parts of the site which require email functionality to work properly, such as the password recovery dialog.

Note that the website property pages allow you to add references to libraries you would like your pages to be able to use; to define options to be used when building the site; and to specify the default start page and action to take when starting the site.

12.5.2 Configuring websites with the ASP.NET WebSite Administration Tool

As you are aware, you can configure ASP.NET using the ASP.NET WebSite Administration Tool, which provides a user-friendly set of screens and dialogs you can interact with. You can also edit your website's web.config configuration file directly, either using Visual Web Developer's code editor, or an external editing tool. In addition, Microsoft provide various environments for systems management such as the Microsoft Management Console, which has plug-in support for re-configuring ASP.NET in a production setting.

NOTE	You should exercise care when changing configuration settings, as errors may cause your website to fail altogether. In general, you should read the documentation carefully, check on-line sources to assure yourself there are no traps for the unwary, and make sure you take a back-up of your configuration file or files before you change them.

In a large organization, it is standard to have separate servers for development, test, and production (real-life operation). Even in a smaller organization, it is good practice to have at least two separate servers, one for development and test, and the other for production use. This saves you the embarrassment of users seeing every mistake you make as you create new forms and pages. Potentially each of these servers may differ, and there may be good reasons, for example, for each to make use of

FIGURE 12.14 The WebSite Property Pages

(a)

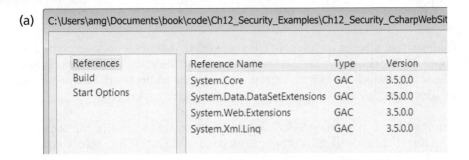

(b)

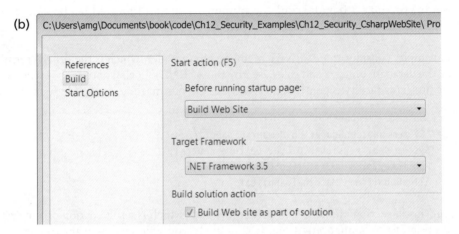

(c)

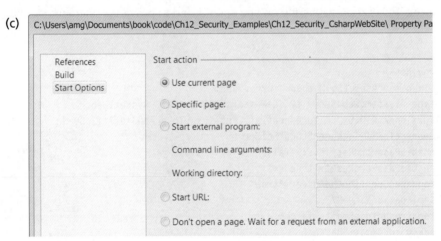

a different database. This implies that you should be prepared to manage multiple configuration files.

ASP.NET assists with this process in two ways. Firstly, the web.config configuration file is arranged in a number of sections. Each section holds the settings for some aspect of your website, and it is easy relatively to identify and edit one part of the configuration file without needing to understand the rest of it. Secondly, you can if you wish make use of multiple configuration files. There can be multiple web.config files in your directory hierarchy, and settings at a lower level override settings closer to the root, except where these are 'locked'.

The configuration schema for the .NET Framework is described on-line on the Microsoft Developer Network site.[1] This covers all aspects of Microsoft .NET and includes, for example, settings which configure compiler, cryptography and network behavior. In addition, further web pages describe the settings which are specific to ASP.NET.

The topmost level of settings is contained in the machine.config file located in the C:\WINDOWS\Microsoft.NET\Framework\vn.nnn\CONFIG directory (where n.nnn is the ASP.NET version number you are using). Somewhat curiously, the configuration settings for versions 3.0 and 3.5 of the framework are still located in the v2.0.50727\ CONFIG subdirectory of the Framework folder.

As an example, consider the ASP.NET membership provider, which is the official terminology for the database of users and roles used by the ASP.NET Login controls to restrict access to your site. This facility is controlled via settings in your machine.config file such as:

```
<section name="membership"
type="System.Web.Configuration.MembershipSection,
    System.Web, Version=2.0.0.0, Culture=neutral,
    PublicKeyToken=b03f5f7f12d50a3a"
    allowDefinition="MachineToApplication"/>
```

This declares a section element called 'membership' which is a sub-section of the system. web section of the configuration file. It is unlikely you will need or want to change this declaration. Further on in the file on you should find a 'providers' element similar to the following:

```
<membership>
 <providers>
  <add name="AspNetSqlMembershipProvider"
   type="System.Web.Security.SqlMembershipProvider, System.Web,
   Version=2.0.0.0, Culture=neutral, PublicKeyToken=b03f5f7f12d50a3a"
   connectionStringName="LocalSqlServer"
   enablePasswordRetrieval="false"
   enablePasswordReset="true"
   requiresQuestionAndAnswer="true"
   applicationName="/"
   requiresUniqueEmail="false"
   passwordFormat="Hashed"
   maxInvalidPasswordAttempts="5"
   minRequiredPasswordLength="7"
   minRequiredNonalphanumericCharacters="1"
   passwordAttemptWindow="10"
   passwordStrengthRegularExpression=""/>
 </providers>
 </membership>
```

---

[1] References to web pages have been collected and are all shown at the end of this chapter.

This defines various aspects of the membership provider that you may wish to alter, particularly the settings which relate to the usage and storage of passwords. The default settings require users to provide passwords at least 7 characters long, including at least one non-alphanumeric character. Users may reset their passwords, but not retrieve them via email. Passwords are hashed, which protects them even if database security if compromised, but means that the original password can never be recovered.

The AspNetSqlMembershipProvider is also defined and configured further on:

```
<profile>
 <providers>
  <add name="AspNetSqlProfileProvider"
   connectionStringName="LocalSqlServer"
   applicationName="/"
   type="System.Web.Profile.SqlProfileProvider, System.Web,
   Version=2.0.0.0, Culture=neutral, PublicKeyToken=b03f5f7f12d50a3a"/>
 </providers>
</profile>
```

The most important declaration here is that of the connection string which will be used to access the provider database. This is defined in a separate element:

```
<connectionStrings>
 <add name="LocalSqlServer" connectionString="data
 source=.\SQLEXPRESS;Integrated
 Security=SSPI;AttachDBFilename=|DataDirectory|aspnetdb.mdf;User
Instance=true"
 providerName="System.Data.SqlClient"/>
</connectionStrings>
```

As you can see, ASP.NET expects by default that the database is stored using SQL Server Express Edition, which runs using the process name SQLEXPRESS. To alter this you are recommended to use the aspnet_regsql tool rather than editing the connection string directly. Most other databases, and in particular, the full edition of SQL Server do not automatically create the required database tables; aspnet_regsql not only sets up the correct connection, but also defines the required tables. Note that the |DataDirectory| substring will be replaced at run-time with a path to your website's app_data directory.

In the same directory, you will also find a web.config file, with some additional settings. For example, we can see that ASP.NET personalization also makes use of the same SQL connection string – and hence by default also uses SQL Server Express Edition.

```
<personalization>
 <providers>
  <add connectionStringName="LocalSqlServer"
   name="AspNetSqlPersonalizationProvider"
   type="System.Web.UI.WebControls.WebParts.SqlPersonalizationProvider,
   System.Web, Version=2.0.0.0, Culture=neutral,
   PublicKeyToken=b03f5f7f12d50a3a"/>
```

It is also worth noting that there are a number of other configuration files the same such as web.config.default, web.hightrust.config and web.lowtrust.config which may also be useful in different configurations and as backup.

Remembering that there is a hierarchy of configuration files, you should consider which of these files to edit when making a specific change. If the change is specific to an individual website, the new settings should be incorporated in your website's web.config file. If the change applies across all sites, you will probably wish to edit the .config files in the root or framework directory as described above.

At the bottom of the hierarchy are the leaf directories of your website. For example, to illustrate the use of role-based security, you created some access rules for a variety of directories. If you examine these, you will find they each now contain their own web.config file – a rather small one with a single section containing an XML version of your access rules, such as the one shown below:

```
<?xml version="1.0" encoding="utf-8"?>
<configuration>
 <system.web>
  <authorization>
   <allow roles="employee" />
   <deny users="*" />
  </authorization>
 </system.web>
</configuration>
```

There are many other aspects which you can configure via .config file settings. These include compilation settings, device and browser capabilities, HTTP and custom error handlers, security (authentication, authorization, cryptography and identification), session handling, user profiles and roles, XHTML settings, and the web server and hosting environment. It is recommended you browse the web-based resources listed in the References for detailed information on these topics.

12.5.3 Site map trimming

A useful ASP.NET feature combines the XML site maps we covered in Chapter 8 and the roles we have just explored. Clearly, the idea of using roles is to restrict access, and the idea of a site map is to encourage access. There is little point, however, in showing users links to pages that they are not authorized to access. One solution might be to provide multiple site maps, one for each role, but this would increase the effort required to maintain the site when, for example, changing its directory or folder structure. A better solution therefore would be to produce a site map covering the whole site, and automatically remove, or trim, links from this which the current logged in user cannot follow. This is the idea behind site map trimming, which is also called security trimming.

To enable trimming you should add lines such as the following to your application's web.config file:

```
<siteMap defaultProvider="XmlSiteMapProvider" enabled="true">
 <providers>
```

```
  <add name="XmlSiteMapProvider"
    description="Default SiteMap provider."
    type="System.Web.XmlSiteMapProvider"
    siteMapFile="Web.sitemap"
    securityTrimmingEnabled="true" />
  </providers>
</siteMap>
```

Note that this is a root element, so do not include these lines inside any other element. Also, before adding these lines, check that this section is not already defined – if it is you will probably only need to add the securityTrimmingEnabled="true" attribute.

The effect of enabling this feature is two-fold: firstly folders which the currently logged user is not allowed to access will be removed from the navigation controls before they are displayed. This saves the user the frustration of clicking on a link they are not allowed to follow. Secondly, you can now add roles to the nodes in your site map file. For example:

```
<siteMapNode title="Performance Management Policies"
  description="Policies on monitoring and managing employee performance"
  roles="manager">
```

You can assign to the 'roles' attribute a comma separated list of roles who are allowed to see the associated node. What is more, users in one of these roles will be able to follow the link, overriding the usual file and URL authorization rules. This is a powerful feature, whose use requires some care and review to ensure that it adheres to corporate security policies.

File and URL authorization refer to the processes whereby ASP.NET decides whether to grant the current user access to a requested file in a particular directory. In addition to the configuration options described above, ASP.NET automatically denies direct access to certain types of file (such as .config and .sitemap files) and special directories (such as App_Code and App_Data). These restrictions obviously make sense from a security perspective, and it would be rare for you to want or need to override them.

12.6 Configuration APIs

As we have just seen, there is a significant amount of information in the ASP.NET configuration files. These settings affect the behavior of various components and sub-systems of ASP.NET. Occasionally it is useful for your code to be able to query these settings at run-time. To do this, you make use of the ASP.NET configuration classes and methods such as the ones described in this section.

You can, for example, use methods from the WebConfigurationManager class to access and if necessary set configuration settings directly from your application. This avoids the need for you to write code which locates and parses the desired section of whichever .config file applies to your application.

In addition, certain other APIs provide more specialized access to specific information in the configuration such as user membership roles and profiles. We have seen, for example, the Roles.IsUserInRole() method in the sample code above. Another useful method is GetRolesForUser(). The standard implementation of these methods accesses the membership database stored in the ASPNETDB.MDF file, whose contents are shown in Figure 12.15. These screen shots show the tables in this file, and the database definitions for two of them: aspnet_Membership and aspnet_User, which both have the same primary key: UserID.

Rather than accessing these tables directly, however, which only works if you are using the default membership provider, you should use the membership methods provided such as:

```
Membership.CreateUser("UserName@DomainName", "P@ssw0rd",
  "userName@emailAddress");
```

Other useful methods include UpdateUser(), DeleteUser(), FindUsersByName(), GetAllUsers(), and GetNumberOfUsersOnline().

It is also possible to write and use your own implementation of this membership API, which for example would make sense if your organization had already developed a user database of its own.

Finally, there are APIs which allow you to access the personalization and profile database, which is included in the membership tables as shown in Figure 12.14. To make use of this facility, you start by adding a 'profile' sub-element within the 'system.web' element of your application's web.config file. For example:

```
<profile enabled="true">
 <properties>
  <add name="PageStyle" type="string"/>
 </properties>
</profile>
```

This profile property can be set and used by a web form such as the following. For brevity, only the body of the web page is shown:

```
<p>Choose Your Favored Page Style</p>
<p>
  Currently selected:
  <asp:Label ID="Label1" runat="server" Text="Label"></asp:Label>
</p>
<p>
 <asp:DropDownList ID="DropDownList1" runat="server" AutoPostBack="True"
      onselectedindexchanged="DropDownList1_SelectedIndexChanged">
  <asp:ListItem Selected="True" Value="BlackOnWhite">
    Black Text On White Background
  </asp:ListItem>
  <asp:ListItem Value="WhiteOnBlack">
    White Text On Black Background
   </asp:ListItem>
 </asp:DropDownList>
</p>
```

(a)

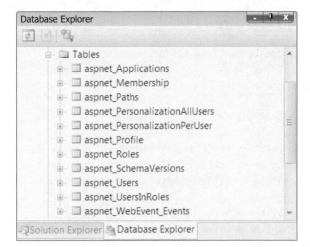

(b)

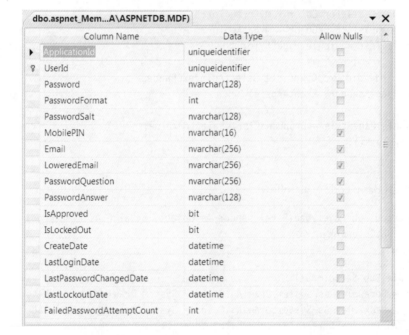

(c)

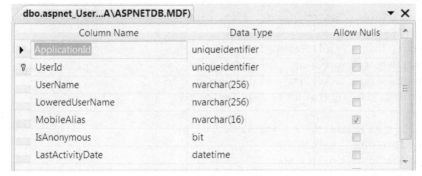

This page has some explanatory text followed by a label and a dropdown list, from which users can select either black or white text, in each case on a complementary background.

The code behind this page is shown below, first in C#, then in Visual Basic:

```csharp
protected void Page_Load(object sender, EventArgs e)
{
 SetColors();
}
private void SetColors()
{
 System.Drawing.Color myForeColor = System.Drawing.Color.White;
 System.Drawing.Color myBackColor = System.Drawing.Color.Black;
 if (Profile.PageStyle == "BlackOnWhite")
 {
  myForeColor = System.Drawing.Color.Black;
  myBackColor = System.Drawing.Color.White;
 }
 DropDownList1.ForeColor = myForeColor;
 DropDownList1.BackColor = myBackColor;
 Label1.Text = Profile.PageStyle;
}
protected void DropDownList1_SelectedIndexChanged
    (object sender, EventArgs e)
{
  Profile.PageStyle = DropDownList1.SelectedValue;
  SetColors();
}
```

The Visual Basic code is as follows:

```vbnet
Protected Sub Page_Load(ByVal sender As Object, ByVal e As EventArgs)
 Call SetColors()
End Sub

Private Sub SetColors()
 Dim myForeColor As System.Drawing.Color = System.Drawing.Color.White
 Dim myBackColor As System.Drawing.Color = System.Drawing.Color.Black
 If Profile.PageStyle = "BlackOnWhite" Then
  myForeColor = System.Drawing.Color.Black
  myBackColor = System.Drawing.Color.White
 End If
 Label1.Text = Profile.PageStyle
 DropDownList1.ForeColor = myForeColor
 DropDownList1.BackColor = myBackColor
 For Each c As Control In Me.Page.Controls
  Try
   Dim d As WebControl = CType(c, WebControl)
   d.ForeColor = myForeColor
   d.BackColor = myBackColor
  Catch myEx As Exception
  End Try
```

```
  Next
End Sub

Protected Sub DropDownList1_SelectedIndexChanged(ByVal sender As Object, _
  ByVal e As EventArgs)
  Profile.PageStyle = DropDownList1.SelectedValue
  Call SetColors()
End Sub
```

Here, the selected color scheme is recorded using the PageStyle profile property you just added to your site's web.config file. This selection persists from one session to the next. The selection is tested and put into effect by the SetColors() method. The effect of this is shown in Figure 12.16. The selected scheme is applied to the dropdown list, and also reported using the label control in the middle of the screen shot.

 NOTE If the user is not logged in, attempting to set a property will generate an exception (as properties cannot be set for anonymous users).

FIGURE 12.16 These two pages demonstrate the effect of the currently logged in user, alice, selecting from the two alternative color schemes

(a)

(a)

12.7 Website deployment

When creating a new website, you can choose a different location and protocol to use rather than the local file system which we have used so far. You can use the 'Browse' button to bring up the 'Choose Location' dialog, which allows sites to be accessed via FTP or HTTP (and the front page extensions) as well as via the local file system, as shown in Figure 12.17. These screen captures show the dialog boxes which you can use to select and configure the user of FTP or HTTP (with front page extensions) to access and manage your site.

12.7.1 Copying a website to a deployment server

In most cases you will be using Visual Web Developer to develop and test a website locally before deploying it, so it is not often you will wish to create an FTP or Remote site on which to initially develop your site. Instead, it is more likely you will develop and test locally, and then copy or deploy your working site afterwards.

FIGURE 12.17 Using the 'Choose Location' dialog to choose the location and protocol of a new website

(a)

(b)

To copy a website, you should use the 'Website' → 'Copy WebSite' menu command to bring up the 'Copy Web' dialog box. The 'Source WebSite' on the left of this dialog lists your current website. Use the 'Connect' button at the top to define the 'Remote WebSite', which can be accessed via FTP or can simply point elsewhere in your own file system. Use of FTP has security implications, and you are required to have appropriate authority to access and update the site you connect to. Once you have established the connection, the 'Copy Web' dialog lists files in both sites. You can navigate around and select files in the usual way (the button with the green up-pointing arrow allows you to go back up your directory hierarchy). If you select a file or files, the blue arrows offer you the chance to copy from one directory to the other (using the button with a single arrow), or to synchronize the files between directories (using the button with two arrows pointing in both directions). These elements of the dialog are shown in Figure 12.18.

Note that you can in fact copy files back from the remote website, as shown in Figure 12.18, or copy them to the remote website. You do this using the buttons with single arrows in the middle of the dialog box. You can also synchronize between sites using the button with arrows pointing in both directions. The fourth button is used to cancel a copy operation. When copying either way, you start by selecting the file or files you wish to copy. When copying, a newer version is not overwritten. If one of the files has been deleted since the last copy, you will be asked whether to delete the file on the target site. To ensure both sites are identical, you should synchronize rather than copy them. When you synchronize, new and changed files are copied from one site to the other. You will still be asked to decide how to deal with deleted files, or files which have been changed on both sites, as these are situations where automatic synchronization mechanisms may give poor results.

The 'Copy Web' dialog attempts to highlight in a visual fashion files which need copying. If the version on one site or other is clearly an older version, the files will be tagged with

FIGURE 12.18 The Copy WebSite dialog box allows you to copy from the 'Source' to the 'Remote' website, or vice versa

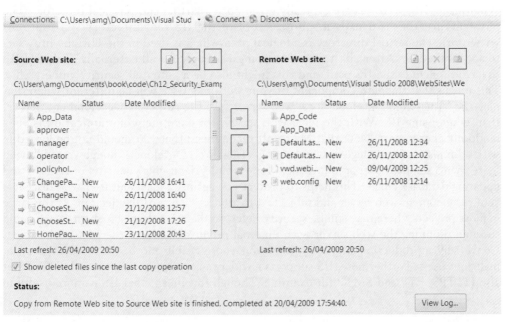

an arrow pointing in the direction required to synchronize the sites. If the files are simply different, but it is not clear which way to copy, then a question mark will be used instead, as can be seen in Figure 12.18.

Finally note that if the remote site is a production site, or an IIS installation, you should be beware of automatically copying .config files. It is likely in such cases that the remote site requires a different configuration and it is probably undesirable to copy across the settings used on your development machine. Similarly, you should think carefully before copying a database file, as shown here, from one site to another.

In addition to the ability to copy a website, Visual Studio has a command which allows you to 'publish' your site. This command compiles and builds all code and .aspx pages into a set of executable files, which you can then copy to the target computer. This reduces the risk of your intellectual property being compromised, for example if you are publishing to a third party website. It also avoids the need to compile each page as it is viewed, so that the very first person to access your site will see the same performance as later visitors.

To publish a website, you use Visual Studio's 'Building' → 'Publish WebSite' menu command, and specify the target location. This should be a directory used specifically for this purpose, as output from the build process will overwrite any existing file or files. If you are running IIS locally, you can then specify this directory as a virtual directory, as described below, from which to run your website. Alternatively, you can copy the files – by any means, including the Copy WebSite dialog described above – to your remote web server.

12.7.2 IIS virtual directories

Visual Web Developer supports websites located in the local file system or in a local or remote IIS installation, where remote sites can be accessed via FTP or the Microsoft specific front page extensions.

When using IIS, websites are typically given both a virtual and physical directory. The physical directory is usually a sub-directory of the IIS root directory (C:\Inetpub\wwwroot). The virtual directory is a logical path which is used in the URL by browsers to access the site. After all, it would be somewhat ugly for all externally visible URLs to have to include the IIS path, and this might also be a potential security vulnerability. This means that the path component of your website's URL will be different when running the Visual Web Developer local web server (aka the ASP.NET Development Server) than when using IIS. With the local web server, for example, communication is via a randomly chosen port. Note that Microsoft recommend that you should not be logged in with administrator privileges when running Visual Web Developer, though you will need more than a standard user account when, for example, debugging your site, or creating and updating database tables. This helps to protect you against a malicious user who discovers your development web server and subjects it to attacks such as SQL injection. At this stage in most projects, there may still be security holes, so there is a danger such an attack could succeed. Running the web server with minimal privileges reduces the potential impact. Conversely, a production site is, by definition, more visible and hence more exposed to malicious users. Furthermore, IIS supports a wider range of protocols, not only HTTP but also HTTPS, FTP and SMTP for example. Though this means that IIS is more useful in a production environment, it also implies that even more care is required to ensure it is configured in a secure fashion.

Finally, note that IIS makes use of the same or similar machine.config and web.config files which are used in your development machine. Typically, however, IIS administrators will use more specialized configuration tools such as the Microsoft Management Console or the IIS Manager, which are beyond the scope of this book.

12

Self Study Questions

1. Name five different login controls.

2. What three aspects of your site does the ASP.NET WebSite Administration Tool cover?

3. What three aspects of your site can be controlled using its property pages?

4. What are the default rules which apply to new user's passwords?

5. What role is, as a special case, associated with a user who has not logged in yet?

6. Name two properties of the PasswordRecovery control which contain prompts and error messages.

7. What method can you call to validate whether a user is assigned to a particular role?

8. Which file contains access rules defined by the ASP.NET WebSite Administration Tool?

9. Where on your PC would you look for the default .NET configuration settings?

10. Which configuration setting and attribute is used to enable site map trimming?

Exercises

12.1 Replace the HyperLinks on your master page with a TreeView navigation control which accesses a site map file using a site map data source.

12.2 Enable site map trimming in your web.config file, and make use of it in your site map files.

12.3 Use Visual Web Developer to edit your site's web.config file to change the minimum password length required by your site.

12.4 Rather than simply changing the color settings for one control, it would make more sense to offer the user a choice of themes. Change the ChooseStyle web form to allow the user to select from a list of themes, and change the code behind to apply the chosen theme. Note that the Page.Theme may only be set in the page's PreInit event handler.

12.5 Use the ASP.NET WebSite Administration Tool to select a specific starting page for your site, rather than the standard default.aspx web form.

12.6 Use the Copy WebSite dialog to copy your website to a backup device such as a memory stick. Use an ordinary text editor to change one of the files on your backup device, for example by adding a comment. Use the Copy WebSite facility again to copy the changed file back, noting how it is tagged by VWD as you do so.

SUMMARY

In this chapter, you looked at and learned how to use the ASP.NET login controls. You also used the ASP.NET WebSite Administration Tool to create users, roles, and access rules. You examined aspects of the web.config files which control the behavior of VWD's built in web server, and made minor changes to web.config. You saw and used the Copy WebSite facility which allows you to deploy your site by copying it elsewhere on the same computer, or to a remote computer using a protocol such as FTP or HTTP plus the front page extensions. The need for separate development, test and/or production sites and servers was discussed, and some reasons given why each might be configured differently. A number of security issues were also covered, and the ASP.NET facility to trim your site map automatically was explained.

References and further reading

ASP.NET Authorization. http://msdn.microsoft.com/en-us/library/wce3kxhd.aspx.

ASP.NET Configuration Settings. http://msdn.microsoft.com/en-us/library/b5ysx397.aspx.

ASP.NET Site-Map Security Trimming. http://msdn.microsoft.com/en-us/library/ms178428.aspx.

Configuration File Schema for the .NET Framework. http://msdn.microsoft.com/en-us/library/1fk1t1t0.aspx.

Ferraiolo, D.F. and Kuhn, D.R. 1992. *Role Based Access Controls.* 15th National Computer Security Conference, pages 554–563.

Google, *Webmaster Tools: Improve your site's visibility in Google Search,* https://www.google.com/webmasters/tools/docs/en/protocol.html.

Guthrie, S. 2005. *How to add a Login, Roles and Profile system to an ASP.NET 2.0 app in only 24 lines of code,* http://weblogs.asp.net/scottgu/archive/2005/10/18/427754.aspx.

How To Use Membership in ASP.NET 2.0. http://msdn.microsoft.com/en-us/library/ms998347.aspx.

Publishing WebSites. http://msdn.microsoft.com/en-us/library/377y0s6t(VS.80).aspx.

CHAPTER 13

AJAX and Web Services

LEARNING OBJECTIVES

- **To understand the basic principles of Asynchronous JavaScript and XML (AJAX)**

- **To be able to use the Visual Web Developer AJAX controls in a web form**

- **To understand the role of web services in web applications**

- **To be able to build a simple web service using Visual Web Developer**

- **To be able to use the various tools within Visual Web Developer to test web services**

- **To be able to develop a web service client within a .NET web application**

INTRODUCTION

This chapter focuses on two XML based features that go beyond the traditional website in ways that are becoming increasingly important in web application development; AJAX and web services. The first part of the chapter describes how Visual Web Developer can be used to build AJAX applications that are able to communicate behind the scenes with the server and update pages asynchronously, without the need to replace or refresh the whole of the current web page. In the second section we look at the role of web services in XML messaging between web applications. Web services are based on sending XML documents over an HTTP connection, regardless of the type of server, the type of client, or the programming languages that either the client or the server are written in. However, in the context of this book we will be looking at how to implement web services and clients within Visual Web Developer.

13.1 The emergence of AJAX

One of the big talking points around web application development in 2005 was the emergence of AJAX (Asynchronous JavaScript and XML) as a way of bringing some aspects of the desktop application experience into browser-based applications. AJAX is not a particularly new concept, following on as it does from a longer tradition of client-side processing that includes JavaScript and DHTML. However the significant difference between AJAX and previous approaches is the concept of the 'one page web application', whereby page content is updated asynchronously from the server without the whole page being rebuilt. An early example of this approach was Google Suggest, which was able to dynamically populate a search text box with suggestions for search terms as characters were typed into it, providing, of course, that the browser was able to support it. The most important component of an AJAX application is the 'XMLHttpRequest' component, which was first introduced by Microsoft into Outlook Web Access 2000 and later into Internet Explorer 5.0. Other browsers followed with their own implementations of the 'XMLHttp Request'. This component enables browser-hosted applications to send requests to the server and receive responses without replacing or fully refreshing the current web page. Instead, the response that is returned from the server, which may be an XML document or a simple stream of characters, can be handled by a client-side script and used to update parts of the page using the DOM. Figure 13.1 shows the general architecture of AJAX-based systems. The key to this architecture is that the AJAX engine mediates between the user interface and the server, processing on the client where possible (using DHTML) and, where necessary, sending asynchronous HTTP requests and receiving XML data (or indeed data in any other suitable format) that it renders in the browser via the DOM.

FIGURE 13.1 AJAX architecture (adapted from Garrett, 2005)

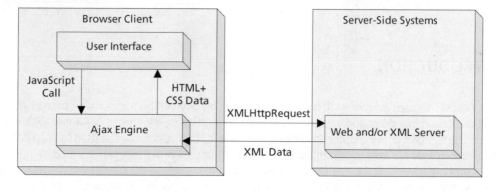

Equally importantly, this processing can take place asynchronously. This means that the user does not have to wait for the server to respond in order to continue interacting with the application. Instead, the application is able to continue serving the user while at the same time handling the server response as and when it arrives. Figure 13.2 shows the general idea. User activity in the browser continues even while the AJAX engine is submitting XMLHttpRequests to the server and waiting for responses. The AJAX engine is responsible for handling events associated with getting back the server response but the user does not have to wait for it. AJAX applications do not have to be asynchronous, however. In some cases it might be appropriate to wait for the server's response before continuing with the current process.

FIGURE 13.2 Using asynchronous communication in AJAX (adapted from Garrett, 2005)

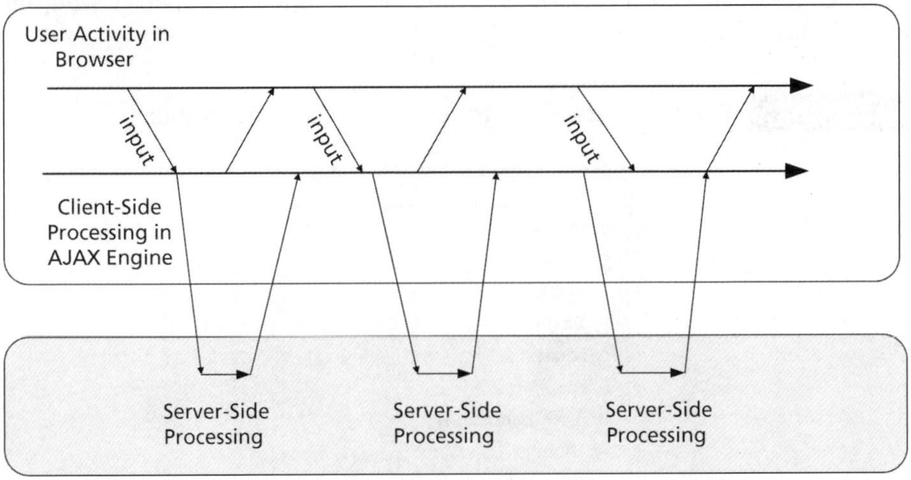

AJAX itself is not a technology but a label, applied by Garrett (2005), to a way of building web applications that uses the 'XMLHttpRequest' object within client-side scripts to seamlessly update web pages. Garret summarized AJAX as a combination of:

- Standards-based presentation using XHTML and CSS
- Dynamic display and interaction using the Document Object Model
- Data interchange and manipulation using XML and eXtensible Stylesheet Language Transformations (XSLT)
- Asynchronous data retrieval using the 'XMLHttpRequest'
- JavaScript binding everything together

Of course the technologies listed by Garrett are not the only way to provide one-page applications on the web, since alternative technologies like Silverlight or Flash can be used to similar effect.

NOTE	As we indicated in Chapter 1, Garrett used the term 'Ajax' rather than the upper-case acronym AJAX. However, since Visual Web Developer controls are listed in the Toolbox under the category of 'AJAX Extension' controls, we will use the upper-case version in this chapter.

13.2 AJAX Extension controls in Visual Web Developer

There are basically two approaches to writing an AJAX application. One is to hand build your own AJAX code using standard JavaScript, which can be complex and difficult to maintain. The other is to use some kind of API and/or development tool that encapsulates the underlying AJAX code. Fortunately, Visual Web Developer includes a set of AJAX Extension controls that can be used to quickly and efficiently incorporate AJAX into your web applications. These are included in a special group in the Toolbox (Figure 13.3).

FIGURE 13.3   The AJAX Extensions group of controls in the Toolbox

If we use these controls to build AJAX functionality into a web form, then we do not need to concern ourselves with the low level processes of the XMLHttpRequest, or the JavaScript event handling that is necessary to manage this object. Instead, we simply drag and drop the appropriate controls onto the page and configure them as necessary.

The key control for creating an AJAX-enabled web form is the ScriptManager. This component takes care of the underlying JavaScript that is used to implement the AJAX processing. Therefore to create an AJAX page, the first step is to add a ScriptManager from the Toolbox to the web form. We also need an area of the page that can be controlled by the ScriptManager. This is represented by an UpdatePanel component. Figure 13.4 shows a web form that has both a ScriptManager and an UpdatePanel added to it in Design view (the UpdatePanel has been selected here to show its identifying tab, otherwise it just appears as a rectangular area on the form).

 NOTE   The 'Add New Item' dialog also has the option to create an 'AJAX Web Form'. This option simply creates a web form that already contains a ScriptManager component.

Any control that you want to be managed by the script manager, so that it can have its events and state managed by AJAX, needs to be placed inside an UpdatePanel. As a simple initial example, we will revisit the 'age calculator' web form, but this time

FIGURE 13.4

FIGURE 13.4   A ScriptManager and an UpdatePanel added to a web form

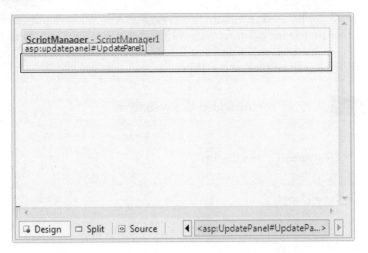

the components of the form will be added to the UpdatePanel. Figure 13.5 shows the web form with the age calculator components added to the body of the UpdatePanel. The implementation of the button click event is unchanged from the example in Chapter 6, so the only real change here is the addition of the ScriptManager and the UpdateManager.

If you view the AJAX web form in a browser, type in a date and press the button, you should find that the result label is updated immediately without a page refresh. One easy way of comparing the AJAX page with a traditional request response cycle is to set the 'EnableViewState' property of the ScriptManager to 'false'. This will effectively disable the AJAX processing so the page uses a normal postback. If you test the page in a browser with this setting, then you should see the difference between the two ways of updating the page.

FIGURE 13.5   Controls added to the UpdatePanel so they can be managed
by the ScriptManager

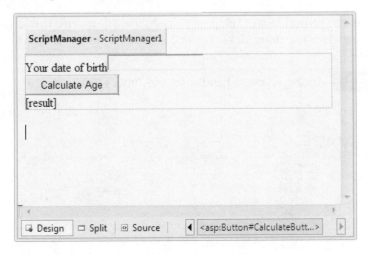

13.2.1 The AJAX Timer control

The Timer control can be used to initiate timed events. A simple example of this would be to add a clock to a page using a Timer. Figure 13.6 shows a simple web form that contains a ScriptManager, an UpdatePanel that has a Label inside it (the ID of the Label will be set to 'ClockLabel' for this example), and a Timer.

FIGURE 13.6 A Timer control added to a web form

To use the Timer we need to configure its 'Interval' property. By default this will be 60000 (milliseconds) so the Timer will be able to trigger an event approximately once every minute. For our example, we will create a clock that updates itself every second, so the 'Interval' property should be set to '1000'.

Although the Timer component is part of the AJAX set of controls, by default it will trigger Page Load events rather than AJAX page updates. You can see this behavior by viewing the web form in a browser. In its current state, the Timer fires an event every second, forcing the page to reload from the server. You should be able to see the default Label text flickering as it does so.

Before addressing the problem of the page refresh, we will specify the behavior that we want to happen when the timer ticks. Figure 13.7 shows the editor for the code behind

FIGURE 13.7 Adding an event handler for the Timer's 'Tick' event

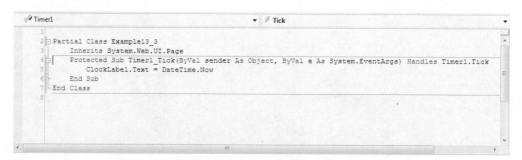

the web form. Note that 'Timer1' (the name of the timer) has been selected from the left-hand drop-down list, and the 'Tick' event has been selected from the right-hand drop-down. The code that has been added to this event simply sets the text in the label to the current timestamp. Now if you view the web form in a browser, you will see the time updating every second. However the whole page is still being refreshed each time.

To get the page to update using AJAX, we need to add a trigger property to the UpdatePanel. If you look at the Properties window when the UpdatePanel is selected, you should see a 'Triggers' property with a button next to it. If you press this button you will see the UpdatePanelTrigger Collection Editor (Figure 13.8). Here, you can add triggers to the update panel. In Figure 13.8 we have added one trigger. Using the drop-down list on the right we have selected 'Timer1' as the control associated with this trigger, and the 'Tick' event of this control as the event that will fire the trigger.

FIGURE 13.8 Linking the Timer's 'Tick' event to the UpdatePanel using the UpdatePanelTrigger Collection Editor

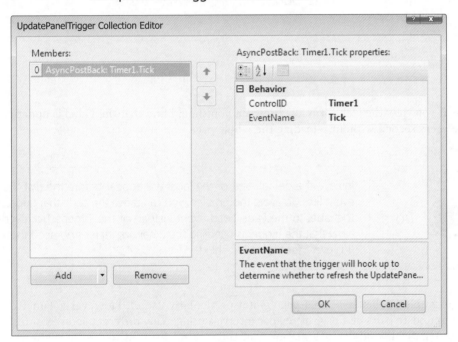

Once this trigger has been added, if you look at the source view of your web form, you should see something like the following (the Trigger element has been highlighted in bold):

```
<%@ Page Language="VB" AutoEventWireup="false"
CodeFile="Example13-3.aspx.vb" Inherits="Example13_3" %>

<!DOCTYPE html PUBLIC "-//W3C//DTD XHTML 1.0 Transitional//EN"
"http://www.w3.org/TR/xhtml1/DTD/xhtml1-transitional.dtd">

<html xmlns="http://www.w3.org/1999/xhtml">
 <head runat="server">
  <title>Example 13-3</title>
 </head>
```

```
<body>
  <!--File: Example13-3.aspx -->
  <form id="form1" runat="server">
    <div>
    <asp:ScriptManager ID="ScriptManager1" runat="server">
    </asp:ScriptManager>
    <asp:UpdatePanel ID="UpdatePanel1" runat="server">
      <ContentTemplate>
        <asp:Label ID="ClockLabel" runat="server" Text="Label">
        </asp:Label>
      </ContentTemplate>
      <Triggers>
        <asp:AsyncPostBackTrigger ControlID="Timer1"
          EventName="Tick" />
      </Triggers>
    </asp:UpdatePanel>
    <asp:Timer ID="Timer1" runat="server" Interval="1000">
    </asp:Timer>
    </div>
  </form>
</body>
</html>
```

Now if you view the web form in a browser, you should find that the Label is updating the time every second without reloading the whole page.

NOTE	Initially, the default text of the label will appear before the first 'Tick' event fires. To avoid this problem you can move the code that updates the label to the Page Load event instead of the Timer's Tick event. Now that the trigger is handling the timer tick there is no need to use this event for the code behind.

The example of the clock on a page is not particularly useful. However a Timer can be used to update parts of a page at regular intervals using many different sources of data. We could update all kinds of information that the user might want to ensure is always up to date without having to manually refresh the page. Examples might include current stock prices, road conditions, flight arrivals/departures, weather conditions, etc.

13.2.2 The UpdateProgress control

Another simple (but useful) control in the AJAX group is the UpdateProgress control. One of the potential problems with using AJAX is that there is no obvious sign to indicate what is happening if there is a delay in updating the page. Unlike a normal page refresh, where a delay in loading the page is made quite obvious by the browser (e.g. an hour glass cursor, indicators in the tabs, pages loading one piece at a time, etc.). signals to the user about delays in updating an AJAX page have to be added using some other mechanism. This is the purpose of the UpdateProgress control. It can be linked to a particular UpdatePanel on a web form and indicate to the user if there is a delay in updating that panel.

In this example we will add an UpdateProgress control to the AJAX version of the age calculator web form that we introduced earlier in this chapter. When you add one of these controls to a web form, it needs to be configured to be associated with a specific UpdatePanel. This can be done by selecting an UpdatePanel from the drop-down list contained in the 'AssociatedUpdatePanelID' property of the UpdateProgress control.

This is what the control will look like in Source view if it has been associated with the UpdatePanel on the web form ('UpdatePanel1'):

```
<asp:UpdateProgress ID="UpdateProgress2" runat="server"
  AssociatedUpdatePanelID="UpdatePanel1">
</asp:UpdateProgress>
```

This, however, is not enough to make the control useable. In fact if you attempt to view the web form in a browser after adding an UpdateProgress control, you will get a run time error message that states: 'A ProgressTemplate must be specified.' What this means is that you have to add a 'ProgressTemplate' element to the body of the control that specifies what message is displayed when the UpdateProgress is being used. Here is a simple example, where the ProgressTemplate simply contains the message 'Connecting to server – please wait...':

```
<asp:UpdateProgress ID="UpdateProgress1" runat="server"
    AssociatedUpdatePanelID="UpdatePanel1">
  <ProgressTemplate>
   Connecting to server – please wait...
  </ProgressTemplate>
</asp:UpdateProgress>
```

Figure 13.9 shows the UpdateProgress control added to the web form in Design view, after the ProgressTemplate has been added. The position of the control specifies where the message will appear if there is a delay in updating the panel.

So now we have an UpdateProgress control added to a web form, but how do we test it? When we view the page in the browser running within Visual Web Developer, we are unlikely to see any significant delay in the response, making it hard to see if our UpdateProgress is actually working. Simply as a test, we can add a delay to the event handler that calculates the age. Here, we have added a line that uses a Thread to pause for 5000 milliseconds.

VB Code

```
Protected Sub CalculateButton_Click(ByVal sender As Object, ByVal e
As System.EventArgs) Handles CalculateButton.Click
  ' the following line is only to test the UpdateProgrss control
  ' it should be removed before deployment
  Threading.Thread.Sleep(5000)
```

```
      Dim age As TimeSpan = Date.Now - Date.Parse(DoB.Text)
      result.Text = "You are " + (age.Days).ToString() + " days old"
   End Sub
```

FIGURE 13.9   An UpdateProgress control added to a web form with a
               ProgressTemplate message

ScriptManager - ScriptManager1

Your date of birth

    Calculate Age

[result]
Connecting to server – please wait...

| Design | Split | Source | ◄ | <html> | <body> | <form#form1> | <div> | ►

Figure 13.10 shows the effect of the UpdateProgress at run time. While the event handler
is sleeping, the UpdateProgress displays the message from the ProgressTemplate on the
screen.

FIGURE 13.10   The message for an UpdateProgress control being displayed
               in a browser while the UpdatePanel waits for the event handler
               on the server to respond

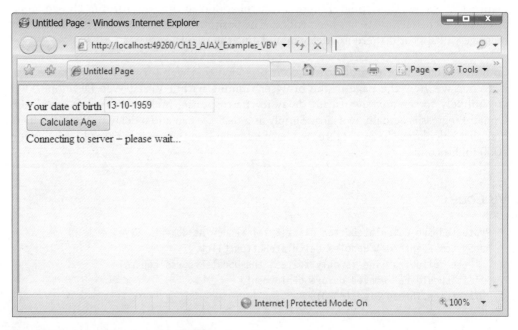

Untitled Page - Windows Internet Explorer

http://localhost:49260/Ch13_AJAX_Examples_VBW ▾

Untitled Page   ▾ ▾ ▾ ▾ Page ▾ Tools ▾

Your date of birth 13-10-1959
    Calculate Age
Connecting to server – please wait...

                              Internet | Protected Mode: On   100% ▾

	NOTE	The period of time before the UpdateProgress message appears on the screen is controlled by the 'DisplayAfter' property. By default this is set to 500 milliseconds (half a second) but you can change this value if a longer or shorter pause seems appropriate.

Section summary and quick exercises

In this section we introduced the basic concepts of AJAX and converted a simple web form to use controls from the AJAX Extensions group in the toolbox. The number of AJAX controls in the Toolbox is quite small. However the Microsoft ASP.NET website also provides an ASP.NET AJAX Control Toolkit that can be downloaded separately for Visual Web Developer. This contains a large number of additional AJAX controls that can be used in your web forms.

EXERCISE 13.1

Create a web form that uses AJAX to implement a contents insurance quote web page. Make sure the web form has a ScriptManager component and gather the necessary details using standard controls in an UpdatePanel. Display the insurance quote in a Label control on the same page.

EXERCISE 13.2

Convert the implementation of the insurance claim use case into a single web page that uses AJAX to make the claim, rather than the multiple web forms used in the current version.

13.3 Web services

There is no single concrete definition for what constitutes a *web service*, since the term is used to describe a range of XML message-based systems that work over the web. In essence a web service is a technology that enables distributed applications to provide data and services to other applications, based on common web protocols and data formats. Using these common protocols supports interoperability between different applications regardless of their platform, language or location. Web services are good for niche applications that do not require high levels of interaction, such as weather services, stock quotes, mortgage interest rates and credit card validation. They are not, however, limited to providing content for parts of a web application; they can also be used as a way for different organizations to communicate with one another in B2B (Business to Business) systems, or be used inside an organization to integrate internal systems that do not run on the same technology platform. Although the concept of a web service is generic, the set of technologies that are commonly used to implement web services are governed by standards published by the W3C, while the Web Services Interoperability Organization (WS-I), an industry consortium, provides a set of test tools that measure a given service against a set of *profiles* that mandate certain technologies and behaviors. Therefore the common use of the term 'web service' tends to refer to a specific technology stack that includes SOAP

(Simple Object Access Protocol), WSDL (Web Services Description Language) and UDDI (Universal Description, Discovery and Integration).

Technologies that enable distributed computer systems to communicate with one another have been around for a long time, but web services are easier to implement than many other approaches because they are based on commonly used existing standards, in particular HTTP and XML. The benefits of the common communication mechanism provided by sending XML documents over HTTP connections are that we can have loosely coupled systems, using different underlying implementations, running on different platforms, working together. A particular advantage of using HTTP connections is that the HTTP ports (80, and 443 for HTTPS) are generally enabled by Internet firewalls, while different ports that might be used by other communication channels may be blocked for security reasons.

13.3.1 Web service technologies

Web services provide a Service Oriented Architecture (SOA) on the web. In this type of architecture, different providers can make a range of XML services available to any clients that have an HTTP connection. For a service oriented architecture to work, there are three basic requirements. First, you need some way of finding out which web services are available for use. You then need to know where these services are located, and finally you need to know how to interact with a particular service in terms of how to invoke it and then how to interpret the reply. For this interaction to be successful there has to be an agreed messaging format and a standard way of publishing and looking up web services. Figure 13.11 shows the main standards that are used to support these requirements. A common messaging format for web services is the Simple Object Access Protocol (SOAP), which is used to send XML messages over an HTTP connection. Web service providers can publish their available services to potential clients using Universal Description, Discovery and Integration (UDDI). The details of an individual service are then described using the Web Services Description Language (WSDL). In addition, WS-Inspection can be used to provide a list of services that are available at a particular web service provider location.

FIGURE 13.11   The standards, components and relationships that may be used in a web service implementation

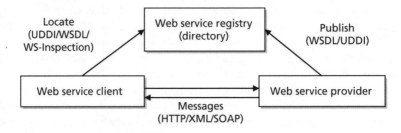

13.3.2 The Simple Object Access Protocol (SOAP)

The Simple Object Access Protocol (SOAP) is a web service message format using XML. It consists of an envelope that describes a message and how to process it, data encoding rules for describing data types (based on XML Schemas) and a set of rules for how to make remote calls and get responses. Those calls and responses can be either Remote Procedure Calls (RPC) or messages. The difference is that a remote procedure call is very much like making a standard HTTP request to a web application, where the client makes a call to the service and then waits for the response. In contrast, messaging is asynchronous. A message is sent but the client does not wait for the response (similar to the asynchronous XMLHttpRequest in AJAX systems).

SOAP is designed to be simple and independent of other protocols and languages, emphasizing interoperability between different systems. A SOAP 'envelope' contains two main parts, the message itself (the data) and a header (the metadata) that provides information about the message. The actual contents of the header are not specified by the SOAP standard, but the basic idea is that the header may be made available to *SOAP intermediaries* that may process the message as it goes from the sender to the receiver, as well as being available to the actual receiver. Both the header and the body will contain application-specific XML content. This is the basic element structure of a SOAP message:

```
<?xml version='1.0'?>
<env:Envelope xmlns:env="http://www.w3.org/2003/05/soap-envelope">
 <env:Header>
 ...
 </env:Header>
 <env:Body>
 ...
 </env:Body>
</env:Envelope>
```

SOAP messages can be carried within the body of an HTTP 'post' request. Figure 13.12 shows an HTTP request containing the HTTP header and also a SOAP envelope, which in turn contains a SOAP header and body.

FIGURE 13.12 A SOAP message in an HTTP request

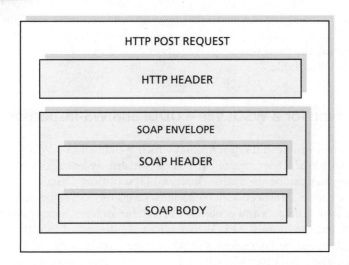

13.3.3 The Web Services Description Language (WSDL)

The Web Services Description Language (WSDL) uses XML to describe web services. A WSDL document describes the operations available from the web service, the input and output data for these operations and the mechanism for contacting the web service. Each of these operations exchanges messages; an incoming message and an outgoing message, which will either be the response from the successful operation or an error message. Each XML message structure is defined by an XML Schema. Figure 13.13 shows the main components described by the elements of a WSDL document. A WSDL 'portType' describes all the operations of a service, and the input and output 'message' components used for each operation. The 'binding' describes the supported protocol(s) of the service and the transport mechanism used, while the 'service' provides the URI of the service (the 'port').

FIGURE 13.13   WSDL components

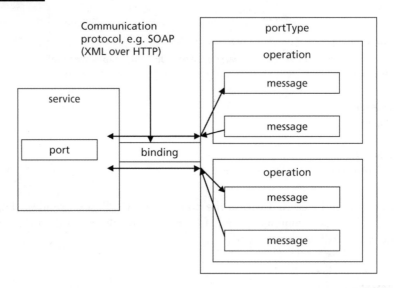

WSDL provides the XML-based contract for a web service, but we also need to provide the actual implementation of the service so that messages can be processed. This implementation can be easily generated using tools (coding web services by hand is rather complex and tedious). In general, the tools that help us to generate the web service implementation will also generate the WSDL file.

13.3.4 Searching for a WSDL file – UDDI and WS-Inspection

To invoke a service, you need its description, which is defined in a WSDL document, but how can you find a WSDL description? If you do not already know its URI, then there are two approaches that can be used; the Universal Description, Discovery and Integration (UDDI) service and WS-Inspection. UDDI allows web services to be published to clients on a web-wide basis, and acts as a general directory for web services. It has two APIs, the publishers API and the inquiry API. Web services are described in different ways using three types of directory, yellow, green and white pages. White pages directories are based on addresses, contacts and other identifiers. In the white pages directory, each element has attributes such as name, description, address, and a unique universal identifier (UUID) which is generated by the system. The yellow pages directory is based on service types, with elements classified by hierarchical categories such as the North American Industry Classification System (NAICS), the United Nations/Standard Products and Services Codes (UN/SPSC) and ISO 3166 geographical region codes. A single element can belong to more than one of these categories. Finally, the green pages directory contains technical information about services, such as the industry-specific XML specifications that they implement. Examples of these include RosettaNet (introduced briefly in Chapter 8) and ebXML (Electronic Business using eXtensible Mark-up Language). The main features of the UDDI API are the ability to manage the publication of services (creating, updating and deleting) and to search for published services. Using the search API, any type of element can be searched for and the search criteria may be based on all three directory types.

WS-Inspection is different from UDDI in that it is not used to provide a global directory space. Rather, it is used as a directory to a single service provider. WS-Inspection allows you to search a provider site for available web services. It provides a 'natural-language' description of the services and the URI of the WSDL service description. WS-Inspection provides an intermediate solution between the global approach of UDDI and a solution where you already know the service and WSDL. To locate WS-Inspection files an 'inspection.wsil' file is located at a common location. A single organization may provide numerous web services with a large number of associated descriptions. WS-Inspection can help manage this by referencing other files, so that a WS-Inspection document may reference other WS-Inspection documents.

13.4 Implementing web services

Although web services provide generic interoperability between different systems using common web protocols, a *provider* or *agent* is required to actually implement the underlying service on a specific technology platform. While XML web service standards that relate to how services are exposed to clients such as SOAP and WSDL are common across the web, the underlying implementations of different web services will vary widely. Whichever platform is chosen, it must provide support for publishing, consuming and locating web services, so there are a number of different aspects to each web service implementation platform. Depending on the technology you are using on your server, there are a range of possible things that can be exposed as a web service. These include enterprise components, objects, server pages, database stored procedures, or indeed any other process that a particular tool is able to expose as a web service. To get an idea of the range of things that can be made available as web services, it is interesting to have a look at http://www.xmethods.com, a website that gathers together a large number of example services. As well as the more usual types of services, such as weather and currency exchange rates, you will find examples like the Icelandic phone book, Urdu to English translations, German bank codes, verses from the Quran and a whole raft of other fascinating possibilities. In many cases the implementation platform of the service is given as well as the available clients that have been implemented for that service.

In our examples we will, of course, be using Visual Web Developer to build web services, and the components that implement these services will be web service files (with an 'asmx' extension). In the following section we will use a simple example to show how an ASP.NET web service can be implemented and integrated into a web application. Our example relates to a fictional pet insurance company, WebPetCover, which sells pet insurance on-line. One potential use of web services is for organizations with complementary products or services to provide these to each others' customers. In this context, WebHomeCover and WebPetCover might decide to partner on-line, to sell their respective insurance services through each others' websites. Figure 13.14 shows the web service interaction from the perspective of WebHomeCover using a web service from WebPetCover. Clients of WebHomeCover's web application will be able to access some pet insurance services that are made available via the WebHomeCover web pages but are supported by services provided by WebPetCover. Communication between WebHomeCover's web application and WebPetCover's web service is made using XML over HTTP so the message can pass between both companies' firewalls.

FIGURE 13.14 A web service example; using a pet insurance web service in a home insurance web application

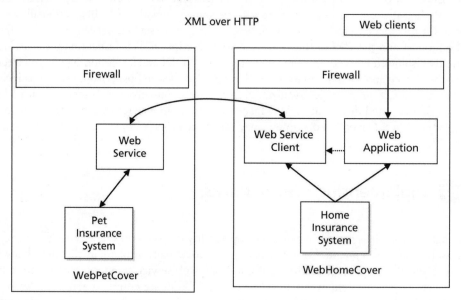

13.4.1 Creating a web service in Visual Web Developer

Creating a web service in Visual Web Developer is quite a simple process. First of all we need to create a new 'Web Service' file using the Add New Item dialog. This creates a file with an 'asmx' extension. In Figure 13.15 we are creating a new web service file called 'PetInsuranceWebService.aspx'.

 NOTE You can alternatively choose to create a new 'ASP.NET Web Service' site. This has the effect of creating a new site that already has a web service in it using a default name.

Assuming we are placing the code in a separate file (as we have done throughout the examples in this book), in the newly created Web Service file there is a single tag that defines the name of the web service and a reference to the 'CodeBehind' file that will actually implement the service.

FIGURE 13.15 Creating a new Web Service file in the Add New Item dialog

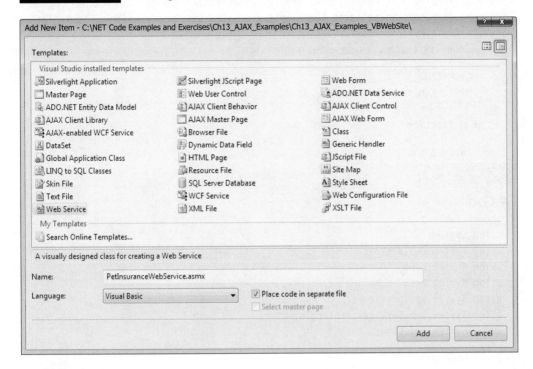

VB Code

```
<%@ WebService Language="VB"
CodeBehind="~/App_Code/PetInsuranceWebService.vb"
Class="PetInsuranceWebService" %>
```

C# Code

```
<%@ WebService Language="C#"
CodeBehind="~/App_Code/PetInsuranceWebService.cs"
Class="PetInsuranceWebService" %>
```

In the 'CodeBehind' file is the skeleton of a class that will provide the basic functionality of the web service. By default, it contains a simple 'Hello World' web service.

VB Code

```
Imports System.Web
Imports System.Web.Services
Imports System.Web.Services.Protocols
' To allow this Web Service to be called from script,
' using ASP.NET AJAX, uncomment the following line.
' <System.Web.Script.Services.ScriptService()> _
```

```vb
<WebService(Namespace:="http://tempuri.org/")> _
<WebServiceBinding(ConformsTo:=WsiProfiles.BasicProfile1_1)> _
<Global.Microsoft.VisualBasic.CompilerServices.DesignerGenerated()> _
Public Class PetInsuranceWebService
    Inherits System.Web.Services.WebService

    <WebMethod()> _
    Public Function HelloWorld() As String
        Return "Hello World"
    End Function

End Class
```

C# Code

```csharp
using System;
using System.Collections;
using System.Linq;
using System.Web;
using System.Web.Services;
using System.Web.Services.Protocols;
using System.Xml.Linq;

/// <summary>
/// Summary description for PetInsuranceWebService
/// </summary>
[WebService(Namespace = "http://tempuri.org/")]
[WebServiceBinding(ConformsTo = WsiProfiles.BasicProfile1_1)]
// To allow this Web Service to be called from script,
// using ASP.NET AJAX, uncomment the following line.
// [System.Web.Script.Services.ScriptService]
public class PetInsuranceWebService : System.Web.Services.WebService
{

    public PetInsuranceWebService () {

        //Uncomment the following line if using designed components
        //InitializeComponent();
    }

    [WebMethod]
    public string HelloWorld() {
        return "Hello World";
    }

}
```

There are a number of aspects to this class that are special to web service classes. Perhaps the most important is that the 'HelloWorld' function is marked by the annotation 'WebMethod', which means that it can be used as the implementation of a web service. This simple method can be tested by viewing the 'PetInsuranceWebService.asmx' file in a browser. This launches a generated web service test page (Figure 13.16) that shows the available web service methods (in this case just the 'HelloWorld' method).

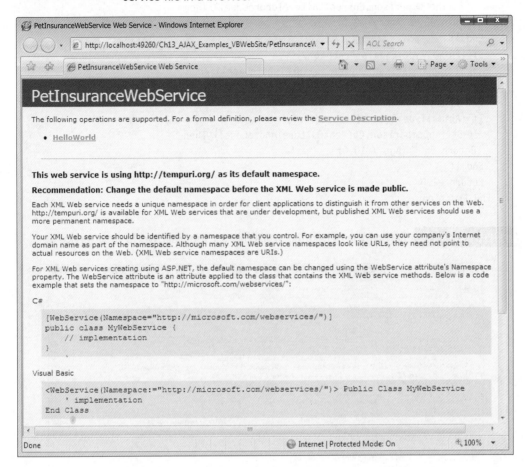

The web service test page contains some information about namespaces (there is a warning
about using the default namespace) and two hyperlinks. The first is the web method itself,
which links to a page that lets you test the method. The other is a 'Service Description'
hyperlink, which will show you the generated WSDL file (Figure 13.17).

The example web service just returns a string of text. However, for our example we will
replace the HelloWorld web method with a new one that can provide quotes for pet
insurance. The following code shows a new web service method ('GetPetInsuranceQuote')
added to the PetInsuranceWebService that takes an animal's type and age as parameters
and uses some trivial algorithms to generate quotes for different pets.

VB Code

```
<WebMethod()> _
 Public Function getPetInsuranceQuote(ByVal AnimalType As String,
     ByVal Age As Integer) As Double
   If (AnimalType.Equals("cat",
     StringComparison.CurrentCultureIgnoreCase)) Then
     Return 20 * (Age / 10.0)
```

```
      End If
      If (AnimalType.Equals("dog",
         StringComparison.CurrentCultureIgnoreCase)) Then
        Return 30 * (Age / 10.0)
      End If
      If (AnimalType.Equals("rabbit",
         StringComparison.CurrentCultureIgnoreCase)) Then
          Return 10 * (Age / 10.0)
      End If
      If (AnimalType.Equals("crocodile",
         StringComparison.CurrentCultureIgnoreCase)) Then
        Return 50 * (Age / 10.0)
      End If
      Return -1.0
    End Function
```

FIGURE 13.17   Part of the generated WSDL file for the HelloWorld web service

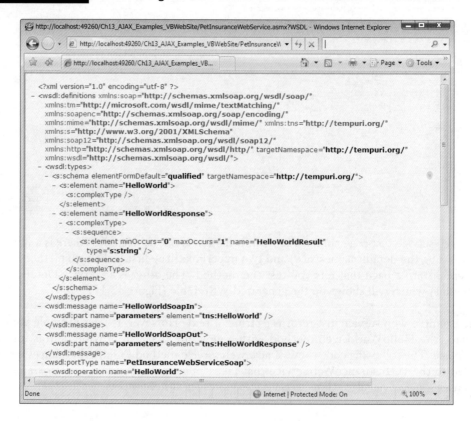

C# Code

```
[WebMethod]
public double GetPetInsuranceQuote(String AnimalType, int Age)
{
 if (AnimalType.Equals("cat",
    StringComparison.CurrentCultureIgnoreCase))
```

```
  {
    return 20 * (Age / 10.0);
  }
  if (AnimalType.Equals("dog",
      StringComparison.CurrentCultureIgnoreCase))
  {
    return 30 * (Age / 10.0);
  }
  if (AnimalType.Equals("rabbit",
      StringComparison.CurrentCultureIgnoreCase))
  {
    return 10 * (Age / 10.0);
  }
  if (AnimalType.Equals("crocodile",
      StringComparison.CurrentCultureIgnoreCase))
  {
    return 50 * (Age / 10.0);
  }
    return -1.0;
}
```

Another useful change is to modify the default namespace in the code file from 'tempuri.org' to something more appropriate, In this example, the URI has been changed to 'http://www .webpetcover.com/webservices/'.

VB Code

```
<WebService(Namespace:="http://www.webpetcover.com/webservices/")> _
```

C# Code

```
[WebService(Namespace = "http://www.webpetcover.com/webservices/")]
```

If you add the new method to the service, and then view the service in the browser, you will see a generated test page very similar to Figure 13.16, except that the name of the hyperlinked web method will be 'GetPetInsuranceQuote, and the warning about the namespace URI should no longer be displayed (Figure 13.18).

If you click on the link to the web method, a generated page that can be used to test the method's functionality will appear (Figure 13.19). This page enables you to enter test data into the text fields to exercise the web service, as well as providing generated examples of how to use SOAP messages with this particular web service. In Figure 13.19, 'Cat' has been entered for the 'AnimalType' parameter and '1' for the 'Age'.

If you enter the test data as shown in Figure 13.19 and press the 'Invoke' button, another page will appear that displays the XML document generated by the web service as a response to calling the web method with the chosen parameter values. Figure 13.20 shows that the generated pet insurance quote is '2'.

FIGURE 13.18 The generated test page for the 'PetInsuranceWebService'

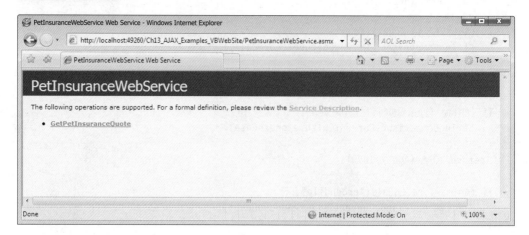

FIGURE 13.19 The generated test page for the GetPetInsuranceQuote web method

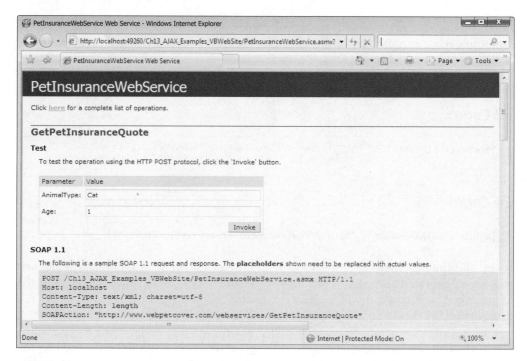

13.5 Developing a web service client

Of course creating and deploying a web service is only part of the story. We also need to have some way of creating a client application that can communicate with the service and integrating the service into a web application. Because web services provide interoperability between different types of system using XML messaging, a web service client may be

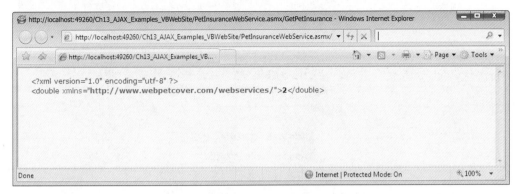

FIGURE 13.20 The generated pet insurance quote as an XML document created as the response from invoking a web service method

developed using any of a number of different technologies. However, for our particular example we need to create a web service client in Visual Web Developer. To keep our example simple, we will create the client in the same application as the service, though in practice we would expect separate web applications to connect to the service.

	NOTE	If you are using the built-in IIS test server in Visual Web Developer Express Edition, then you will only be able to test your web services from within the same web application. More realistic testing would require the web service to be deployed to an external server.

To create a web service client, simply right click on the website name in the Solution Explorer window. This will display the pop-up menu shown in Figure 13.21, which includes the option to 'Add Web Reference . . . '.

If you choose to add a new web reference using the pop-up menu in Figure 13.21, a dialog will appear similar to that shown in Figure 13.22. This dialog will enable us to connect to any available web services.

Since we are going to connect to the PetInsuranceWebService within the same website, the easiest option is to click the 'Web services in this solution' link, which should display a link to the web service we have created (Figure 13.23).

Clicking on the hyperlink to the web service shown in Figure 13.23 will take you to the dialog view shown in Figure 13.24. At this point we are able to add a reference to this service (by pressing the 'Add Reference' button.) This will enable us to code a web service client for this particular service using the web reference to make the connection. Note that by default the 'Web reference name' is 'localhost'. However in Figure 13.24 this has been edited to read 'webpetcover' instead.

Figure 13.25 shows a web form in Design view ('PetDetails.aspx') with two DropDown-List controls that enable the user to choose the animal type and age. There is no validation necessary here because in this simple example there is no possibility of invalid input. The select lists will always submit valid values to the web service. The first drop-down enables

FIGURE 13.21 The pop-up menu for the website in the Solution Explorer, with the 'Add Web Reference . . . ' option

	Build Web Site
	Add New Item...
	Add Existing Item...
	New Folder
	Add ASP.NET Folder ▶
	Add Reference...
	Add Web Reference...
	Add Service Reference...
	Copy Web Site...
	Start Options...
	View in Browser
	Browse With...
	Refresh Folder
	Cut
	Copy
	Paste
	Property Pages

FIGURE 13.22 The 'Add Web Reference' dialog that will search for available web services

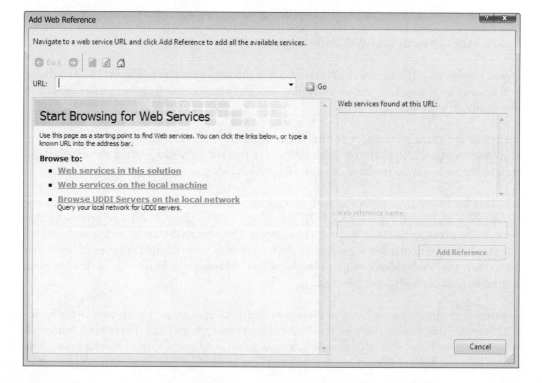

FIGURE 13.23   The PetInsuranceWebService available within the same website

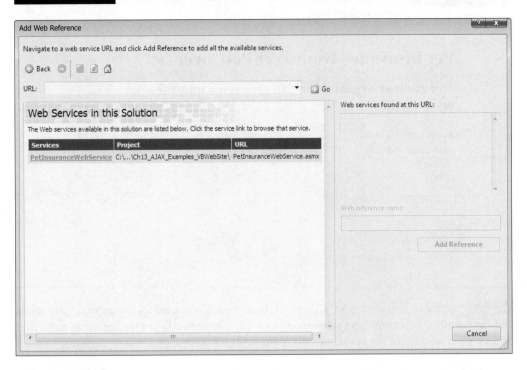

FIGURE 13.24   The dialog that enables us to add a reference to a web service

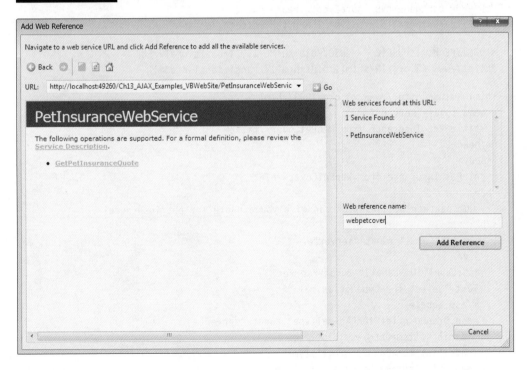

FIGURE 13.25 A simple web form using drop-down lists for the pet insurance web service client

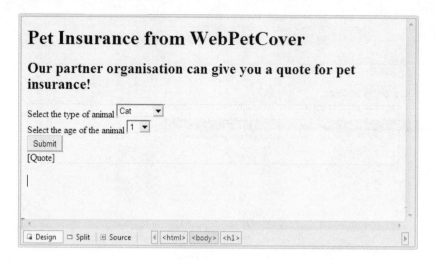

the user to choose between 'Cat', 'Dog', 'Rabbit' and 'Crocodile' as the animal type while the 'age' drop-down contains values from 1 to 12. There is a Label on the same page that will be used to display the result of calling the web service.

Here is the page source. Note that the two DropDownLists are given the IDs 'AnimalType' and 'AnimalAge' respectively, and that the Label's ID is 'Quote'.

```
<%@ Page Language="VB" AutoEventWireup="false"
CodeFile="PetDetails.aspx.vb" Inherits="PetDetails" %>

<!DOCTYPE html PUBLIC "-//W3C//DTD XHTML 1.0 Transitional//EN"
"http://www.w3.org/TR/xhtml1/DTD/xhtml1-transitional.dtd">

<html xmlns="http://www.w3.org/1999/xhtml">
 <head runat="server">
  <title>Pet Insurance from WebPetCover</title>
 </head>
 <body>
  <h1>Pet Insurance from WebPetCover</h1>
<h2>
    Our partner organisation can give you a quote for pet insurance!
</h2>
 <form id="form1" runat="server">
  <div>
  <asp:Label ID="Label1" runat="server"
   Text="Select the type of animal ">
   </asp:Label>
   <asp:DropDownList ID="AnimalType" runat="server">
    <asp:ListItem>Cat</asp:ListItem>
    <asp:ListItem>Dog</asp:ListItem>
    <asp:ListItem>Rabbit</asp:ListItem>
```

13

```
    <asp:ListItem>Crocodile</asp:ListItem>
   </asp:DropDownList>
   <br />
   <asp:Label ID="Label2" runat="server"
       Text="Select the age of the animal ">
  </asp:Label>
  <asp:DropDownList ID="AnimalAge" runat="server">
    <asp:ListItem>1</asp:ListItem>
    <asp:ListItem>2</asp:ListItem>
    <asp:ListItem>3</asp:ListItem>
    <asp:ListItem>4</asp:ListItem>
    <asp:ListItem>5</asp:ListItem>
    <asp:ListItem>6</asp:ListItem>
    <asp:ListItem>7</asp:ListItem>
    <asp:ListItem>8</asp:ListItem>
    <asp:ListItem>9</asp:ListItem>
    <asp:ListItem>10</asp:ListItem>
    <asp:ListItem>11</asp:ListItem>
    <asp:ListItem>12</asp:ListItem>
  </asp:DropDownList>
   <br />
   <asp:Button ID="SubmitButton" runat="server" Text="Submit" />
   <br />
   <asp:Label ID="Quote" runat="server"></asp:Label>
  </div>
 </form>
</body>
</html>
```

The event handler for the 'SubmitButton' is responsible for invoking the web service using parameter values from the drop-down lists on the web form. The connection to the web service itself is quite simple. We create a new 'webpetcover.PetInsuranceWebService' (i.e. the name of the web reference we created using the dialog in Visual Web Developer, and the name of the web service itself). Later in the method, we invoke the 'GetPetInsurance Quote' web method on this service.

VB Code

```
Partial Class PetDetails Inherits System.Web.UI.Page
 Protected Sub SubmitButton_Click(ByVal sender As Object, _
    ByVal e As System.EventArgs) Handles SubmitButton.Click
 Dim wsQuote As New webpetcover.PetInsuranceWebService
 Dim Type As String = AnimalType.Text
 Dim Age As Integer = Integer.Parse(AnimalAge.Text)
 Dim PetQuote As Double = wsQuote.GetPetInsuranceQuote(Type, Age)
 Quote.Text = "The insurance quote for a " + Age.ToString + _
    " year old " + Type + " is " + PetQuote.ToString
 End Sub
End Class
```

C# Code

```
public partial class PetDetails : System.Web.UI.Page
{
 protected void Page_Load(object sender, EventArgs e)
 {
 }
 protected void SubmitButton_Click(object sender, EventArgs e)
 {
  webpetcover.PetInsuranceWebService wsQuote =
    new webpetcover.PetInsuranceWebService();
  String Type = AnimalType.Text;
  int Age = Int32.Parse(AnimalAge.Text);
  double PetQuote = wsQuote.GetPetInsuranceQuote(Type, Age);
  Quote.Text = "The insurance quote for a " + Age +
    " year old " + Type + " is " + PetQuote;
 }
}
```

Figure 13.26 shows the result of calling the web service for a 10 year old crocodile.

FIGURE 13.26   The resulting web page when calling the web service for a pet insurance quote

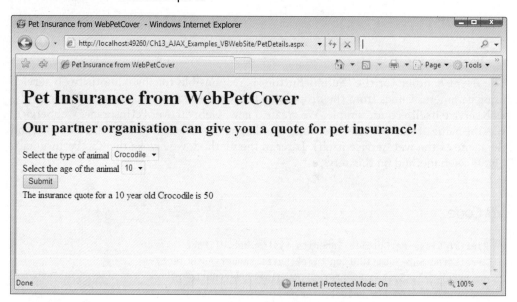

Self Study Questions

1. In which application was the XMLHttpRequest first used?

2. What type of document is usually returned to the browser from the server in an AJAX application?

3. Do all AJAX interactions with the server have to be asynchronous?

4. Which AJAX Extension control is an essential part of all web forms that use AJAX?

5. Why is an UpdateProgress control useful in an AJAX web form?

6. What is a common messaging format for web services?

7. What type of document described the operations available from a web service?

8. What type of UDDI directory might use United Nations/Standard Products and Services Codes (UN/SPSC)?

9. What is WS-Inspection for?

10. What is the annotation given to methods that are to be used in web services?

Exercises

In our earlier examples we created a web service for a pet insurance system. We also described how the pet insurance company might integrate home insurance quotes into their own web application. The following exercises are based on that concept.

13.3 Create a web service that provides contents insurance quotes. Use the same parameter values that are already used in WebHomeCover's web application, namely if accidental damage cover is required, the amount of the cover, and the deductible. You can use the existing 'getContentsQuote' method of the 'InsuranceQuoter' class as the basis for your implementation, though in this case there will not be a bean being passed as a parameter, but separate values. Once you have created your web service, check that you can access the generated WSDL using a browser.

13.4 Generate a web application client for your web service. Generate the client using the menus and dialogs described in the pet insurance example.

13.5 Create part of a web application for WebPetCover that includes a web form to submit data to the web service (you can simply adapt the 'Contents.aspx' page that we used in the 'WebHomeCover' application). Use AJAX controls to call the web service and display the result on the page.

SUMMARY

In this chapter we began by looking at the fundamental concepts of AJAX, which enables a web form to communicate with the server to update parts of the page without needing to reload it. We introduced the controls available in the AJAX Extensions group of the Toolbox and showed some simple examples of how these controls can be used in web forms. We also introduced web services, which enable XML messages over HTTP to be used as a common communication mechanism between different systems. We saw how common web service protocols such as WSDL and SOAP can be used with web applications to integrate third party services.

References and further reading

ASP.NET AJAX. http://www.asp.net/ajax/
ASP.NET AJAX Control Toolkit. http://www.asp.net/ajax/ajaxcontroltoolkit/
Garrett, J.J. 2005. *Ajax: A New Approach to Web Applications.* http://www.adaptivepath.com/publications/essays/archives/000385.php
MSDN Web Services. http://msdn.microsoft.com/en-us/library/ms950421.aspx

13

Answers to Self Study Questions

Chapter 1

1. **What is the term 'blog' short for?**
   Web log.

2. **What is a wiki?**
   A website that is open to editing by anyone.

3. **What is the format of an IPv4 IP address?**
   Four sets of dotted decimal numbers, each in the range 0–255, using the format nnn.nnn.nnn.nnn.

4. **Which of the following is not a top level domain? – org, int, ant, mil**
   ant.

5. **What type of HTTP request is normally used to send data to the server?**
   A POST request.

6. **What is the usual port number of non-secure HTTP connections?**
   Port 80 (443 is used for secure connections).

7. **What is the name given to web-based resources that are not public but only available behind an organization's firewall?**
   An Intranet.

8. **What are the window-based application links in a portal sometimes called?**
   Portlets.

9. **What is Wikipedia?**
   An on-line encyclopedia based in wiki pages.

10. **What is meant by an n-tier architecture?**
    An architecture that deploys its layers across multiple physical machines.

Chapter 2

1. **Is the Unified Process a waterfall or an iterative process?**
   An iterative process.

2. **What acronym is sometimes used to refer to the four levels of priority for requirements?**
   MoSCoW.

3. **What type of diagram shows the main concepts and relationships in a system?**
   A domain model.

4. **What name is given to a user in a particular role in a use case diagram?**
   An actor.

5. **What is a storyboard?**
   A representation of the webflow between the pages in a use case.

6. **In a sequence diagram, in which direction does the time axis usually go?**
   Vertically, though it can also be drawn horizontally.

7. **Is a server page used for static content or dynamic content?**
   Static content.

8. **Where is the site logo commonly found on web pages?**
   At the top left hand corner of the page.

9. **What is the purpose of breadcrumbs on a website?**
   To show you the sequence of pages that you have passed through to get to the current page.

10. **What is one way of reducing the size of HTML downloads?**
    Using text instead of images, or using cascading stylesheets.

Chapter 3

1. **What is the difference between a tag and an element?**
   An element consists of a start tag, an end tag, and the content in between. However an empty element consists of a single tag.

2. **What characters are used around an attribute name?**
   Either apostrophes or double quote marks.

3. **Is XHTML case sensitive?**
   Yes. All XHTML mark-up should be in lower case.

4. **What is the <hr /> element for?**
   It creates a horizontal rule when displayed in the browser.

5. **What do the terms 'strict', 'transitional' and 'frameset' refer to?**
   They are different versions of the XHTML DTD.

6. **What is the special character for the copyright symbol?**
   ©.

7. **What are the two required attributes for the image (img) element?**
   'src' (source file) and 'alt' (alternate text).

8. **What kind of XHTML list will display in the browser as a bullet list?**
   An unordered list (using the 'ul' element).

9. **What attributes are used to make part of a table spread over multiple rows or columns?**

   The 'rowspan' attribute is used to span rows, and the 'colspan' attribute is used to span columns.

10. **What is the name of the element that is used to create hyperlinks?**

    The anchor ('a') element.

Chapter 4

1. **What file extension is used for an external cascading stylesheet?**

   .css.

2. **When specifying styles, what character is used between the name of a style property and its value?**

   A colon (:).

3. **What browser foreground or background color does 'color:rgb(0, 255, 0)' refer to?**

   Green.

4. **How many color names are specified by the W3C HTML 4.0 standard?**

   Sixteen. The possible names are: aqua, black, blue, fuchsia, gray, green, lime, maroon, navy, olive, purple, red, silver, teal, white and yellow.

5. **Which element is used to apply a stylesheet to an XHTML page?**

   The link element. This must be nested inside the head element.

6. **What is the problem that may arise if we only use the generic font family names in a 'font-family' stylesheet entry?**

   The same text may appear differently in different browsers.

7. **When setting font sizes in a stylesheet, is it better to use absolute or relative measures?**

   In most cases it is better to use relative measures that will adapt to the browser window. However in some cases, where you know the type of device and browser that will use where the web page (e.g. in an intranet application), you may decide to use absolute measures.

8. **Why might we choose to add a 'class' attribute to a 'div' element?**

   This would enable us to apply styles to specific div elements without applying the same styles to every div in the document.

9. **How many styles can be applied to unordered list bullets?**

   Three; Disc, circle and square (though some browsers may support some other characters).

10. **What is the effect of applying the 'margin: auto;' style to a table?**

    The table will automatically center in the browser window.

Chapter 5

1. **What does it mean when we say that JavaScript is 'loosely typed'?**

   When we declare values, we do not specify a data type, only a name.

2. **In the JavaScript DOM, which object is the parent of the 'document'?**

   The 'window' object.

3. **If a script element is added to the body of an XHTML document, when is it executed?**

   When the page is loaded into a browser.

4. **What is the range of possible values that may be generated by the Math.random() method?**

   A number between zero and one, but not including one.

5. **What is the difference between the 'equal to' (==) and the 'identical to' (===) operators?**

   The 'equal to' operator allows some type conversions when it compares values, but the 'identical to' operator does not.

6. **What does DHTML refer to?**

   Dynamic HTML, a combination of JavaScript, CSS and the DOM.

7. **Which DOM method can be used to access an individual element with an 'id' attribute?**

   The getElementById(…) method.

8. **What does the 'innerHTML' property of XHTML element enable us to do?**

   It lets us directly access the text node within an XHTML element.

9. **What is the purpose of a JavaScript URL?**

   It enables us to create a hyperlink on a page that, instead of linking to another page or anchor, invokes a JavaScript function.

10. **Which properties of an element can be used to access or set the current CSS style?**

    style.display ('style' is an element property, and 'display' is a property of the style).

Chapter 6

1. **Which two languages are available to choose from when creating a new Web Form in Visual Web Developer?**

   C# or Visual Basic.

2. **Which property of a control can be used to set the class of that control so that styles may be applied?**

   The CSSClass property.

3. **What types of text input element can be created by setting the 'TextMode' property of a TextBox control?**

   A text box, a password box or a text area.

4. **How can we get multiple radio buttons to behave as a group, so that only one can be checked at any one time?**

   By using the RadioButtonGroup control.

5. **In an event handler, which property of a TextBox control can be used to set its current text value?**

   The 'Text' property.

6. **How can you add an existing file to an existing project?**

   Drag the file into the Solution Explorer window, or use the 'Website → Add Existing Item …' menu option.

7. **Where are the start options for a website stored?**

In the website.suo solution file in the website's main directory.

8. **Where are your ASP.NET website configuration options stored?**

In the web.config configuration file in the website's main directory.

9. **Which menu command can be used for setting and clearing a breakpoint? What is the alternative short-cut key to do the same thing?**

The Debug → Toggle Breakpoint command, or the F9 shortcut key.

10. **What is the name of the window which the debugger uses to display the values of variables?**

The Locals window.

Chapter 7

1. **What are the three types of HotSpot that can be added to an ImageMap?**

Circle, rectangle and polygon.

2. **What type of control can a View be added to?**

A MultiView.

3. **What are the four types of step in a Wizard control?**

'Start', 'Step', 'Finish' and 'Complete'.

4. **Where does validation always take place, and where can it additionally take place?**

It always takes place on the server, but it can additionally take place on the client.

5. **What kind of validation control would you use if you wanted to check if one date selected from a Calendar control occurred after another date selected from another Calendar?**

A CompareValidator.

6. **Is it possible to check that a credit card number is valid in a validation control?**

No. We can only check that the card number has the correct format. We cannot check if it is actually a valid card number.

7. **What kind of validator would you use if you wanted to check that a TextBox contained a valid U.S. Social Security Number?**

A RegularExpressionValidator. This is one of the built in validations in the Regular Expression Editor.

8. **Can the master page being used with a page be changed?**

Yes. You need to change the 'MasterPageFile' property of the page and also ensure that the number and ContentPlaceHolderIDs of the ContentPlaceHolders in your page match those in the new master page.

9. **How many content place holders can you specify in a master page?**

As many as you like. Visual Web Developer will ensure that they all have unique ID properties.

10. **What must you do to an empty ContentPlaceHolder before attempting to drag a Web User Control into it in Design View?**

You must provide some suitable mark-up that can contain the control, such as a paragraph element.

Chapter 8

1. **What is the sequence of elements in an XML document known as?**

   The document order.

2. **The XML declaration and processing instructions are part of what section of an XML document?**

   The prolog.

3. **What is utf-8?**

   A Unicode encoding scheme that is backward compatible with ASCII and uses from 1 to 4 bytes to represent each character.

4. **What do you use to provide unique IDs for elements in an XML document?**

   Attributes.

5. **When using an XmlDataSource control, how many levels of nesting can you have below the root element?**

   The document must only have elements nested to one level below the root element.

6. **Which property of an AdRotator control specifies an integer that weights the frequency with which the ad appears?**

   Impressions.

7. **How do we specify that we are referring to an attribute rather than an element in an XPath expression?**

   Attributes are preceded by the '@' character.

8. **The root element for an XSL transform can be called 'xsl:stylesheet'. Which alternative element name is equally valid?**

   xsl:transform.

9. **What is the name of the XML file that is used to create site maps in Visual Web Developer?**

   Web.sitemap.

10. **A site map file can be used with a TreeView control. What is the other control that we can use this file with?**

    A Menu control.

Chapter 9

1. **What are the three components of an MVC architecture?**

   Model, View and controller.

2. **What method do we use to move between web forms on the server using the same request? What method is used to go to another page via the client browser using a new request?**

   To use the same request, we use the `Server.Transfer` method. To send a new request from the browser we use the `Response.Redirect` method.

3. **Why is a Wizard control not suitable for all types of webflow?**

   Because the Wizard control does not allow for variations in the page routing.

4. **Why might we choose to put values from a client form in a session rather than the request?**

    Because we might want to retain access to those values over multiple pages, lasting beyond a single request-response cycle.

5. **How can we empty the contents from a session without actually destroying it?**

    We can use the `Clear` or the `RemoveAll` methods, which both achieve the same effect.

6. **How do we implement a read-only property?**

    By supplying only a 'get' method for that property. In VB we can additionally flag the property as being ReadOnly.

7. **What is the term given to improving the design of existing code without actually changing its functionality?**

    Refactoring.

8. **The 'Façade' and the 'Singleton' are examples of what?**

    Design patterns.

9. **Should process objects and model objects be in front of or behind the façade?**

    Behind the façade. Only web forms and their event handlers should be in front of the façade.

10. **What happens to the names of request parameters in event handlers when a master page is used?**

    Their names are changed to include the control identifiers that relate to parts of the master page.

Chapter 10

1. **Name three different data source controls.**

    LinqDataSource, SqlDataSource, and XmlDataSource.

2. **Name three data web controls which consume data from a data source.**

    GridView, DetailsView, and FormView.

3. **When configuring a data source, which dialog box allows the database to be edited?**

    The 'Advanced ...' dialog box includes an option to generate update statements.

4. **When configuring a data web control, which dialog box allows you to select and order the database fields being displayed?**

    The 'Edit Columns ...' dialog allows you to select, order and remove columns or database fields from the display. (Note that the dialog box is also called Edit Fields.)

5. **If you wish to control the appearance of a data web control, how do you do this for the table, row and individual cell?**

    The table's appearance can be set using the smart tasks , or using the properties window to set its visual properties. The row's appearance can be set using the properties belonging to styles such as the RowStyle. The individual cell is configured using the properties which appear in the Edit Columns/Fields dialog box.

6. **Which format specifiers should you use to display a database field as currency, or as a date?**

    The format specifier {0:c} or {0:C} is used for currency fields, and {0:d} for dates.

7. **What does LINQ stand for?**

LINQ stands for Language INtegrated Query.

8. **Give the names of four of the LINQ operators.**

From, select, where, and orderby are all LINQ operators (and there are many others).

9. **Give two .NET programming language features introduced specifically to support LINQ.**

Anonymous types and lambda expressions were introduced to support LINQ (as well as half a dozen other new language features).

10. **Why is the InsertOnSubmit() method so called?**

The new record does not appear in the database until the SubmitChanges() method is called.

Chapter 11

1. **What does DAO stand for?**

Data Access Object.

2. **What does CRUD stand for?**

Create, Read, Update, Delete.

3. **What is the default |DataDirectory| called?**

App_Data.

4. **What is 'injected' during an SQL injection attack?**

Malicious SQL commands.

5. **Give an example of a one-to-many relationship.**

One policy may have many associated claims.

6. **Name three methods supported by the SqlDataReader class.**

Read, GetInt32, GetString, ...

7. **What property must be set to allow the code behind file to respond to the user selecting a new item in a drop down list?**

AutoPostBack.

8. **And what is the name of the event triggered by such a selection?**

OnSelectedIndexChanged.

9. **What is a delegation method?**

One which simply calls another method to do the actual work.

10. **Give three problems covered by the term 'object relational impedance mismatch'.**

Unique object and table identifiers, mapping of data types, relationships and normalization, inheritance, and operations.

Chapter 12

1. **Name five different login controls.**

Login, LoginName, LoginView, LoginStatus, CreateUserWizard, ChangePassword, PasswordRecovery.

2. **What three aspects of your site does the ASP.NET WebSite Administration Tool cover?**
   Security, Application, and Provider settings.

3. **What three aspects of your site can be controlled using its property pages?**
   References, Build and Start options.

4. **What are the default rules which apply to new user's passwords?**
   Must be at least 7 characters, including one non-alphanumeric one.

5. **What role is, as a special case, associated with a user who has not logged in yet?**
   Anonymous.

6. **Name two properties of the PasswordRecovery control which contain prompts and error messages.**
   GeneralFailureText, QuestionInstructionText.

7. **What method can you call to validate whether a user is assigned to a particular role?**
   Roles.IsUserInRole(rolename).

8. **Which file contains access rules defined by the ASP.NET WebSite Administration Tool?**
   The folder's web.config file.

9. **Where on your PC would you look for the default .NET configuration settings?**
   C:\Windows\Microsoft.NET\Framework\vn.nnn\CONFIG machine.config (or web.config).

10. **Which configuration setting and attribute is used to enable site map trimming?**
    In the siteMap section, the securityTrimmingEnabled attribute is set to "true".

Chapter 13

1. **In which application was the XMLHttpRequest first used?**
   Microsoft Outlook Web Access 2000.

2. **What type of document is usually returned to the browser from the server in an AJAX application?**
   An XML document.

3. **Do all AJAX interactions with the server have to be asynchronous?**
   No. They can be synchronous if this is more appropriate to the application requirements.

4. **Which AJAX Extension control is an essential part of all web forms that use AJAX?**
   The ScriptManager control.

5. **Why is an UpdateProgress control useful in an AJAX web form?**
   Because one of the potential problems with using AJAX is that there is otherwise no obvious sign to indicate what is happening if there is a delay in updating the page.

6. **What is a common messaging format for web services?**
   SOAP (Simple Object Access Protocol).

7. **What type of document described the operations available from a web service?**
   WSDL (Web Services Description Language).

8. **What type of UDDI directory might use United Nations/Standard Products and Services Codes (UN/SPSC)?**

   A Yellow Pages directory.

9. **What is WS-Inspection for?**

   It allows you to search a single provider site for available web services.

10. **What is the annotation given to methods that are to be used in Web Services?**

    WebMethod.

INDEX